12.50

prophecy and protest:

SOCIAL MOVEMENTS
IN TWENTIETH-CENTURY CANADA

prophecy and protest:

SOCIAL MOVEMENTS IN TWENTIETH-CENTURY CANADA

Edited by

Samuel D. Clark, Ph.D.
Department of Sociology
University of Western Ontario

J. Paul Grayson, Ph.D.
Department of Sociology
York University

Linda M. Grayson, Ph.D.
Department of History
University of Waterloo

Gage Educational Publishing Limited • Toronto

ISBN 0-7715-5715-9 Hardcover
0-7715-5716-7 Paperback

1 2 3 4 5 6 7 8 9   AP   83 82 81 80 79 78 77 76 75

Contents

Chapter 6: Contemporary Developments

Editors' note: Aside from typography or spelling errors, we have followed the style and spelling preferences of the authors of these reprinted articles or of the journals and books in which they first appeared.

PREFACE

We began work on this reader with a number of purposes in mind. First and foremost was the desire to make available to university lecturers and students a set of readings on social movements in Canada. Our concern was not primarily to spare undergraduates the effort of searching for articles in their campus libraries, although we hope that we have provided some assistance in this regard. Our main objective was to bring to light a number of readings that we thought were not being used sufficiently in university courses. This cannot be said of all the readings we have included. Some articles, such as Guindon's on French-Canadian separatism, and Zakuta's on the CCF (Co-operative Commonwealth Federation), have not suffered from neglect. But others, such as Irving's on the Social Credit in Alberta, and Morton's on the Progressive Party, have, we felt, been overlooked at great cost to students, especially in view of the high standard of scholarship they attain. This volume was born from a certain measure of frustration with hearing some of our colleagues claim that no course material is available on Canadian social movements. In actual fact, there is.

The main difficulty, of course, is that to make use of this material one has to cross discipline boundaries. We have sought to help course instructors overcome this hurdle. To this end, we have tried to do a number of things. First, we have endeavoured to bring together readings on Canadian social movements that we believe are not only of high quality, but are also acceptable to more than one discipline. Second, we have endeavoured to combine the preference of some academic disciplines for general theory with the preference of other disciplines for emphasizing the singular characteristics of human events. On the one hand, we have declined to treat each social movement as completely unique, as some historians might have preferred. Instead, we have tried to show that similar concepts can be used to analyse a variety of social movements, even though the historical circumstances surrounding these movements may be quite different. On the other hand, except in the General Introduction, we have not ventured to use specific social movements to illustrate a theoretical model, as some sociologists might have preferred. Once we have presented our theoretical framework, we try to use it to aid the understanding of social movements in twentieth-century Canada, rather than using these social movements as evidence to support the theoretical framework. Throughout most of the book, we have been concerned primarily with investigating Canadian social movements for their own sake.

The book begins with a General Introduction in which a theoretical framework for the study of social movements is outlined. Those who wish to pursue available theories in great depth will require additional reading, since our statement is by no means a comprehensive review of the literature. Rather, it is an attempt to combine some of the current concepts and propositions about social movements into a theoretical perspective that sees social movements as a process of institutionalization, that is, a process in which new social arrangements are conceived, propagated, and, if possible, stabilized. In each chapter, articles are presented that examine some important Canadian social movements in this century. Each chapter begins with a brief introduction to the movement or movements in question. These introductions are intended to provide a linkage between the ideas expressed in the General Introduction and specific social movements. At the same time, they should enable those unfamiliar with relevant aspects of Canadian history to understand the historical context in which these movements emerged.

Needless to say, we have not been able to include readings on all social movements in twentieth-century Canada. In general, we have tried to focus on those we feel are the most important. Naturally, our selection was also influenced by the availability of good literature. Although we believe, as we have said, that much excellent research has been done on Canadian social movements, we would emphasize that there is a need for still more. Indeed, there are a number of movements on which very little research has been done at all. Several current movements, such as the contemporary struggle for women's liberation and the growing militancy among Canada's native peoples, fall into this latter category and are consequently not represented in our selection of readings. In certain instances, we have tried to overcome these omissions by including some discussion of the movements in question in the chapter introductions. But there is no escaping the fact that several very important social movements in twentieth-century Canada have not received anything like the attention they deserve.

In so far as there has been a division of labour, Samuel Clark has undertaken responsibility for the General Introduction, while J. Paul Grayson and Linda M. Grayson have undertaken responsibility for the chapter introductions, the Conclusion, and the selection of the readings. However, the work has been essentially collaborative. We would like to thank Conrad Wieczorek for helpful suggestions he has made with respect to both the organization of the book and the content of the introductions. Our greatest debt is, of course, to the authors of the selections. They are the ones who have done the painstaking research on which any real progress in the understanding of Canadian social movements depends.

General
Introduction

Although many of us would like to pretend otherwise, Canadians have not been a quiet people. Some have, at times, been swept by religious excitement; others have sought utopias in the name of political and social ideologies; still others have tried to dismantle Canada as a political union. There has been enough of this very noisy kind of behaviour that it deserves to be studied in its own right.

In this General Introduction, we hope to provide a set of basic theoretical tools that can be used to help understand these and other social movements. We can begin, as many writers do, by defining a social movement as a form of behaviour in which a large number of people try to bring about or resist social change.[1] This definition suggests that social movements have two important characteristics: first, they involve a large number of people; second, members of a social movement try to intervene in the process of social change. In most cases, the effort is quite conscious and deliberate, aimed either at producing new social arrangements or at restoring old ones. It is this conscious and deliberate attempt to intervene in social change that makes social movements exciting and popular topics for study.

In the following pages, we shall try to formulate a more precise definition of the term social movement by relating it to other concepts and concerns of social science. In doing so, we hope to provide students with a way in which to distinguish between social movements and other very similar kinds of human activity. We shall then try to identify some conditions that are necessary for the rise of a social movement. Finally, we shall briefly discuss what happens to social movements in the course of their typically short, yet significant, careers.

1. The Nature of Collective Behaviour[2]

Most social scientists study social movements under the more general rubric of *collective behaviour*. Here they are employing the term collective behaviour in an unusual way. In common parlance, what we mean by collective behaviour is any activity in which more than one person participates. Social scientists do use the term in this manner, but they also use it to refer specifically to such things as panics, crazes, fads, crowds, publics, and social movements. These are instances of behaviour involving more than one person, but instances of a very special kind. Regrettably, it is not always clear exactly what is special about them. What is it that panics, crazes, fads, crowds, publics, and social movements share in common?

An early attempt to answer this question claimed that the distinguishing feature was that they all resulted from an epidemic-like process called *social contagion*.[3] This theoretical approach began with the assumption that, under certain conditions, people may be influenced by the behaviour of others without subjecting this influence to critical analysis. The most common way in which this can happen is that people unthinkingly copy the behaviour of others. It is in this manner that fads often spread. A man grows a mustache because he sees other men wearing mustaches; a woman buys high-heeled shoes or a long skirt because she sees her friends in high-heeled shoes and long skirts. Social scientists who took this and other kinds of contagion seriously concentrated their research efforts on identifying the conditions under which such a process would likely occur. They generally concluded that situations of stress, crisis, or dislocation had the effect of reducing a person's critical capacities and so made him more vulnerable to social contagion. Similarly, one-way communication, particularly mass communication, could make people less critical because the receiver of information has no means of interrogating the sources. Finally, contagion theory held that any sort of group situation in which people are subject to pressures to conform can induce them to do things they would not otherwise do. Le Bon, the architect of the contagion approach, believed that the conditions for contagion would most likely be fulfilled by the milling of people in a public place, but even more organized gatherings, such as juries and parliaments, could, he argued, have similar properties.[4]

A more recent attempt to specify the nature of collective behaviour claims that it results from anti-social psychological drives.[5] These anti-social drives are usually controlled by social norms, but they may be released if a group of people with the same anti-social drives are brought together and are simultaneously triggered by a common stimulus. For instance, common instincts of flight might be stimulated by fear (producing a panic), or common instincts of aggression might be provoked by frustration (producing a crowd). Research in this school is, for the most part, devoted to identifying the common psychological characteristics of participants in collective behaviour. In addition to fear and aggression, the most noteworthy underlying characteristics that have been identified are alienation and authoritarianism. Authoritarianism, which is a psychological predisposition to be submissive to authority and to enforce submission onto others, has been identified by many writers as the basic cause of mass movements, in particular right-wing movements such as the Nazi movement in Germany.

There is a tendency in these approaches to assume a unanimity in the sentiments and actions of those who participate in panics, crowds, and other types of collective behaviour. At the same time, there is a tendency to assume that collective behaviour involves a breakdown in social norms, that is, a breakdown in the formal or informal rules that define what people should or should not do in any given situation. Hence, the central intellectual problem for scholars who adopt either of these approaches is to explain how unanimity can be achieved by a large number of people when the rules that usually govern their behaviour have broken down. They try to solve this problem either by arguing that social contagion radiates common sentiments, or by arguing that participants in collective behaviour possess a common psychological characteristic, such as authoritarianism. It would, however, be a serious mistake to over-emphasize the unanimity to be found in collective behaviour, or to over-emphasize the breakdown in social norms. By over-emphasizing unanimity, we can easily overlook the great variety of activities in which different participants can be seen to engage; for example, as we shall observe in the case of social movements, there often exist several factions pursuing different courses of action within the same movement. And by over-emphasizing the breakdown in social norms, we can readily fall into the trap of regarding collective behaviour itself as *normless*, in other words, as lacking in any kind of rules to govern what people do. From this it is an easy step to the erroneous, and yet very widespread, notion that collective behaviour is totally uncontrolled, irrational, and senseless.

An alternative approach suggests that it is not collective behaviour that is normless, but rather the situation in which collective behaviour emerges. This approach has become increasingly popular among social scientists and will be adopted by the editors of this reader. We shall consider collective behaviour to be one of a number of possible responses to normless situations. Actually, our conception of collective behaviour is more general than this. We shall argue that collective behaviour is a response to a wide variety of situations in which the common feature is that people are discontented because they do not believe that there exist satisfactory *institutional guides* (consisting of values, norms, and/or leaders)[6] to direct their behaviour.

Such a condition we shall call *perceived institutional deficiency*. The word *perceived* is an important part of the concept. It does not matter whether an institutional deficiency does or does not exist in some objective sense. What is crucial is whether or not people perceive a deficiency. This determines whether or not they are content. Perceptions of a deficiency often take the form of opposition to some aspect of the existing values, norms, or leaders under which people live. For one reason or another, people are unhappy with the way their society is operating and they blame it on the prevailing institutional guides or some portion of the prevailing institutional guides. Usually, they either disagree with some of the prohibitions stated by conventional rules or they object to some behaviours that conventional rules permit. The best-known forms of collective behaviour provoked by this sort of perception are groups of people protesting against social conditions. The contemporary protest among women, for example, has emerged because a sizable segment of the female population has become unhappy with the formal and informal rules that control women's lives, although these rules themselves have not undergone any significant change.

In addition, people can be discontented even though they are not actually opposed to existing institutional guides. They may simply find these guides inappropriate, confusing, or insufficient. This may happen because existing guides do not provide the excitement or "meaning" in life that people often seek. Experimenting with drugs is an obvious example of collective behaviour that originates in this way, but less dangerous crazes, such as "streaking", can be attributed to a similar desire to overcome the banality of conventional rules. It may also happen that people find themselves in a totally new situation for which established leaders seem unprepared, or for which there exist no precedents. Panics, in particular, result from a perceived absence of norms that tell people exactly what they should do under threatening conditions. People caught in a burning building would be much less likely to panic if they had been well drilled in the rules to be followed during such a crisis. It is when they perceive that they have no guides to follow and do not know what to do that they are most likely to panic.

Collective behaviour, then, is a response to a mixed category of situations to which we have applied the general concept, perceived institutional deficiency. In most cases, the response involves an attempt to discover new institutional guides to overcome the deficiency. New guides may not actually come into being. But usually an attempt is made to find them. Most often, when engaged in collective behaviour, people try to find new values, norms, or leaders to meet a situation in which the existing values, norms, or leaders are considered to be less than satisfactory. In this sense, collective behaviour itself is not normless. If anything, it is a struggle against normlessness. However, since collective behaviour does occur in a situation in which some aspect of existing institutions are perceived as unsatisfactory, the institutional guides of collective behaviour are spontaneous or what some social scientists call "emergent".[7] They are not the conventional guides; they are a creation of the collective behaviour itself. They are formulated as people seek direction for their behaviour, and as they, in turn, try to direct the behaviour of others. New institutional guides emerge as a large number of people begin to subscribe to a new set of values, conform to a new set of norms, or obey new leaders.

This does not necessarily mean that the new institutional guides are totally new. On the contrary, as we shall see, the availability of adaptable guides in the history or in contemporary subcultures of a society is a basic condition for the rise of at least one type of collective behaviour, namely, social movements. But it is through collective behaviour itself that institutional guides become activated to meet a specific situation. These guides are new in the sense that they are applied to a situation to which they were not directly applied before, and sometimes accepted by a population that did not accept them before.

Participants in collective behaviour do not always succeed in finding guides to their behaviour, nor in persuading others to adhere to the guides they accept. There is considerable variation on this score from one instance of collective behaviour to another. We can rank different types of collective behaviour according to the extent to which new institutional guides emerge. Ranked from low to high, they roughly fall into this order: panics, crowds, crazes and fads, publics, and social movements.

In most panics, the struggle to establish new institutional guides is almost a complete failure. Even if people look for direction, they are not given time to develop new guides, and their response to the crisis is largely individualistic. What occurs is usually little more than a collective decision to flee.

In crowds, there is almost always an attempt on the part of some members to direct activities, and to persuade themselves and others that these activities are appropriate and justified. In a crowd of looters, for example, participants may encourage one another with assurances that they are merely taking what society owes them — what they do not have because they have been oppressed. Similarly, members of a lynch mob will try to persuade one another that the nature of the crime or some other factor justifies drastic measures, and that otherwise justice would not be done. Yet these definitions of appropriate conduct are rarely spelled out clearly in a crowd; they are often confusing and self-contradictory; most participants only go along because they are excited by the crowd and not because they are really committed to the new standards; and the acceptance of the new standards only lasts so long as the crowd does. It is virtually impossible for the crowd itself to establish these standards as real social norms. The same is true if new values are expressed in a crowd or if new leaders are followed. Their influence on members of the crowd is both fragmentary and transitory.

In crazes and fads, we can clearly see the emergence of new norms: gold-fish swallowing, jogging, youth-hostelling, experimenting with drugs, bicycling, streaking, nude-bathing — each in its day became and, in some cases, has remained, a well articulated pattern of behaviour defined by a large collectivity as the "in" thing to do. On the other hand, leaders and values are usually far less developed. Although some crazes (e.g., experimenting with drugs) have had recognized leaders and have been associated with the emergence of a new set of values, in most crazes and fads there are no generally acknowledged leaders, and values appear to be either totally absent (e.g., streaking) or poorly defined (e.g., nude-bathing). Moreover, although less so than with crowds, the new institutional guides that emerge in crazes or fads, even their norms, are still highly transitory.

In contrast, in what we call publics, a common and relatively stable set of

values and norms generally appears. Large collectivities, although widely separated in space, can develop common opinions on matters such as killing baby
seals or polluting water and air. They may even adopt common solutions to these
problems. Especially in modern society, with advanced means of communication
and public-opinion polling, a remarkably large public can evolve with shared
ideas on a subject. To illustrate, in 1972 an immense public emerged in Canada
with a common viewpoint on expenditures by the Federal Unemployment Insurance Commission. Indeed, the near-defeat of the Trudeau government in that
year can be attributed, at least in part, to the widespread feeling among Canadians that the government was permitting a colossal rip-off by "UIC bums".
Through letters to newspapers, complaints to MP's, calls to talk-shows, and
replies to public-opinion polls, people expressed their indignation, and they
supported their views by reference to various general principles proclaiming the
work ethic. In this manner, a set of values and norms became articulated by a
public and was conveyed to the government in no uncertain terms.

Of all types of collective behaviour, social movements exhibit the most developed institutional structure. Relative to participants in panics, crowds, crazes,
fads, and even publics, members of social movements are more successful in
finding guides to their behaviour and in getting other people to conform to the
guides they accept. Through a common set of values, norms, and leaders, the
behaviour of members of a social movement is controlled to an extent that is not
matched in these other types of collective behaviour. Most social movements
possess one or more associations to which many members either belong or
acknowledge commitment. These associations may even possess a semi-formal
structure, with a division of labour and rules that regulate the conduct of members. In short, social movements develop more consistent and stable institutional
guides, or, to use a technical term, they become more *institutionalized*.

But the point can be over-emphasized. Although social movements develop
more of an institutional structure than do other types of collective behaviour,
they are always much less institutionalized than is ordinary, everyday behaviour
or what social scientists call *routine behaviour*. Especially in its early stages, the
values, norms, and leaders of a social movement are poorly defined, and acceptance of them is nothing like unanimous. True, a social movement may eventually become as institutionalized as routine behaviour, but then we no longer call
it a social movement. Actually, even routine behaviour is far from fully institutionalized, if by this we mean that there is complete consensus on values,
norms, and leaders. But it is nevertheless more institutionalized than are social
movements. We may have difficulty in determining exactly where to draw the
line in discriminating between social movements and routine behaviour, and how
to classify any particular empirical case. But, in theoretical terms, the one can be
distinguished from the other.

It is now possible to expand on our earlier definition of a social movement. In a social movement a large number of people are collectively responding to the perception of an institutional deficiency by endeavouring to establish new institutional guides or to adapt old ones to a new situation; and they have moved toward that goal, but have not yet reached it. A social movement is in the process of institutionalization, by which we mean that it is in the process of developing consistent and stable institutional guides. But the process is not necessarily a successful one. Quite the opposite: the emergence and maintenance of institutional guides are the most problematic aspects of a social movement; consequently, these need to be studied most carefully. How, and on what foundations, new institutional guides are created is the central question in the study of social movements.

2. The Rise of Social Movements

In order to understand when and why social movements emerge, it is necessary to investigate the social conditions under which they usually appear. Unfortunately, there has been a tendency, among some social scientists, to search for the one single factor that can explain all social movements. We would argue that the conditions that generate social movements are numerous and varied, and that at least two broad categories of conditions are necessary, in one form or another, for a social movement to develop.

Conditions: Category I. The Perception of Institutional Deficiency

The first category includes all those conditions that give rise to dissatisfaction with existing institutional guides. We have already proposed that a perception of institutional deficiency is most likely to take one of two forms: (1) people may be opposed to some aspect of the existing values, norms, or leaders in their society; or (2) they may perceive existing values, norms, or leaders as inappropriate, confusing, or insufficient. In either case, they are not content. They feel a sense of restlessness and an urge to do something to overcome the deficiency.

Why do perceptions of this kind arise? Why are people sometimes not content with existing institutional guides? Unfortunately these are not questions that can be answered by means of any single proposition or set of propositions. People find their institutional guides to be unsatisfactory for a great variety of reasons and it would be impossible for us to do justice to them all. We can put forward one general proposition that we believe covers most cases; but we want to caution the reader that further propositions would have to be included to arrive at a comprehensive theory. Our proposition says that people become discontented as a result of inconsistencies in the existing institutional structure. As a rule, we suggest, discontent is generated in a society when some institutional guides are inconsistent with other institutional guides, or with the way in which society actually operates.

Let us take an example. If people in a society begin to place a high value on personal liberty, they will not be content with established institutions in so far as these institutions seem to act in a way that restricts such liberty. The youth movement is a case in point. According to some writers,[8] discontent among young people increased in the sixties because values emphasizing the powerfulness and personal autonomy of man (taught to many middle-class members of the postwar youth generation through permissive child-rearing practices) were not fulfilled by most adult institutions, particularly universities. As children, they were taught to place a high value on their individual self-expression and on their personal creativity. Universities, however, were unable to handle all these *prima donnas*, largely because universities operated on the basis of a more traditional, authoritarian system of human relations. The inconsistency between the values that many young people had been taught in the home and the values that dominated the larger society motivated some of them to rebel against this society. It is important to note that, according to this explanation of the youth movement, the institutional deficiency itself was not new: universities had always been authoritarian. They only came to be perceived as deficient when a large collectivity acquired a set of values that were inconsistent with this authoritarian system.

Such a clash between personal liberty and the restrictions imposed by established social institutions is only one of the many kinds of inconsistencies that can generate discontent. Far more common is an inconsistency between what institutional guides define as a just distribution of rewards, and how people are, in fact, rewarded. It often happens that people acquire notions about how rewards should be distributed that are inconsistent with the rewards they are actually getting. People are most prone to becoming discontented when, to their disadvantage, what they receive does not conform to their conception of just rewards.[9]

We can use the term *expectations* to denote what people believe to be their just rewards and the term *achievements* to denote what they actually get.[10] Of course, in all societies, at all times, there are at least some differences between expectations and achievements, and, consequently, there is always some discontent with respect to existing institutional guides. But social movements can be expected to emerge only when there is a relatively high level of such discontent. What require analysis, therefore, are the factors leading to a wide gap between expectations and achievements.

Simple logic would tell us that this gap can widen for one of two reasons: either expectations are rising faster than achievements, or achievements are declining and falling below expectations. The first kind of situation is depicted in Figure 1, where the broken line represents the level of expectations over a period of time and the solid line represents the level of achievements over the same period. Exposure to mass media or to new cultures may, for example, raise expectations by introducing people to a standard of living that they previously thought unattainable, or at least attainable only by a chosen few. Ironically, an

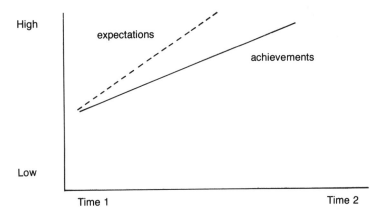

Figure 1: The gap between expectations and achievements widens because expectations are rising at a faster rate than achievements.

improvement in living standards can have the same effect. Even though it involves an increase in achievements, improved conditions may create expectations for even more improvements, and these expectations can easily outstrip any actual rise in achievements. More than a hundred years ago, Alexis de Tocqueville made this point in his famous study of the French Revolution. The Revolution occurred, he noted, precisely when the *ancien régime* was engaged in reforms and when conditions for the French masses were improving. Discontent rose, he argued, not in spite of, but rather because of the improved conditions. He wrote:

> It is a singular fact that this steadily increasing prosperity, far from tranquilizing the population, everywhere promoted a spirit of unrest. . . . It was precisely in those parts of France where there had been the most improvement that popular discontent ran highest. This may seem illogical — but history is full of such paradoxes. For it is not always when things are going from bad to worse that revolutions break out. On the contrary, it oftener happens that when a people put up with an oppressive rule over a long period without protest [and it] suddenly finds the government relaxing its pressure, it takes up arms against it. Thus the social order overthrown by a revolution is almost always better than the one immediately preceding it, and experience teaches us that, generally speaking, the most perilous moment for a bad government is one when it seeks to mend its ways.[11]

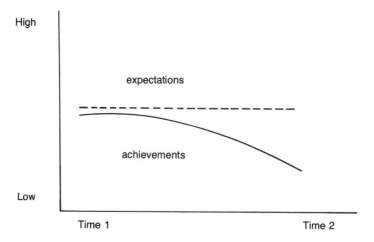

Figure 2: The gap between expectations and achievements widens because achievements decline while expectations remain stable.

On the other hand, the gap between expectations and achievements can widen because achievements are declining and falling below expectations. A situation of this kind is depicted in Figure 2. What people consider to be a just reward does not change, but the rewards they get decline as a result, for instance, of adverse economic conditions. Although de Tocqueville was undoubtedly correct in asserting that discontent does not increase only when things are getting worse, a deterioration in their standard of living certainly can make people angry. To illustrate, we shall cite the depression of the 1930's, which generated the discontent from which the Social Credit movement emerged in Alberta, and the recession of the late 1950's, which generated the discontent from which the Social Credit movement sprang in Quebec. In both cases, the standards of living that people enjoyed actually underwent a decline, resulting in a greater difference between their expectations and their achievements.[12]

The reader should not assume from our discussion that social movements occur only when there is a change in the level of expectations or achievements for everyone living in a given society. On the contrary, many movements arise when just some groups in a society experience a significant change. For example, specific occupational groups may be forced to endure a decline in achievements, which other occupational groups manage to avoid. This can happen even during periods of general economic prosperity. In a growing industrial society, a decline in achievement level often befalls small businessmen and artisans, whose social and economic positions can be adversely affected by the development of large business enterprises.

It is also possible for some members of a society to undergo what we can call a *relative* decline in achievements. In absolute terms their achievements may remain at a constant level or even increase, but other groups in their society may enjoy greater improvements, thus generating a sense of *relative deprivation* among those who do not share in the good fortune. This has happened to American blacks since World War II. Their achievement level has not declined; indeed, it has actually advanced. But it has not advanced nearly as much as that of whites, with the result that discontent among blacks has lately reached very high proportions, especially in the 1960's.[13] Recently, a sense of relative deprivation has become a source of discontent in Canadian labour. Terrence White argues that disaffection with international unions is a consequence of a feeling among some workers in Canada that their American counterparts are enjoying benefits at the expense of Canadian workers and that their own unions are contributing to this disparity. He asserts that this sense of relative deprivation has done more to promote opposition to international unions than have nationalist sentiments.[14]

Even people who are experiencing a relative rise in their achievement level can become discontented. As they move up the social ladder, they can acquire expectations of still further movement, which, if not fulfilled, may result in serious discontent. Discontent is especially likely if this upward mobility causes *status inconsistency*. The term refers to the presence of sharp differences between the expectations of two roles occupied by the same person. Inconsistency of this kind can be the source of considerable anxiety, since it is possible for the duties and rewards of one role to create unrealized expectations with respect to the other role. For example, as John H. Thompson argues, the First World War increased dissatisfaction among many women in Canada by placing them in positions that previously were almost exclusively held by men. The inconsistency of holding these positions, while not enjoying basic political rights, persuaded many women (and some men) of the justice of the women's suffrage cause.[15] In a similar vein, S.D. Clark suggests that movements of protest in the 1950's and 1960's resulted from the upward mobility of previously excluded social groups. Young people, whom he uses as his major example, have gained some of the status characteristics of adulthood (especially with respect to their range of knowledge and experience), but are still in the economically dependent position of children, and are still denied the political rights of adulthood. Clark implies that, as a result of upward mobility, there have developed in postwar Canada totally new social groups or "political publics", demanding status and recognition commensurate with their recently acquired importance.[16]

To sum up, the first category of conditions necessary for the rise of a social movement consists of all those factors that contribute to the perception, on the part of a large number of people, that there is a deficiency in existing institutional guides. We have not sought to provide a definitive statement of the causes of such perceptions. Instead we have focussed on those conditions that generate dissatisfaction by producing inconsistencies in the existing institutional structure, and, in particular, we have focussed on conditions that do so by producing a discrepancy between expectations and achievements. Although perceived institutional deficiency can arise and provoke social movements in a large variety of ways, the kind of perceived deficiency that most often provokes a social movement is that brought about by a discrepancy between the rewards people think they should be getting and the rewards they actually get.

Conditions: Category II. Mobilization

Yet by itself, a perception of institutional deficiency does not cause a social movement. People must not only recognize that something is wrong; they must be collectively activated to do something about it. The activation of human resources for collective participation in a social movement is called *mobilization*. It cannot be taken for granted. That a mass of individuals who perceive an institutional deficiency should respond to it collectively is hardly inevitable. A social movement tries to make the response collective by persuading people to accept a common definition of the institutional deficiency and a common set of new institutional guides to overcome it. However, as we have stressed once before, the new institutional guides are actually never entirely new. A careful examination of the process of mobilization reveals that its success depends, in large measure, on the extent to which people can find (both from within their own society and from without) suitable institutional guides on which they can build.

Initiating this process is extremely difficult. Once it is underway, mobilization itself will tend to assist further mobilization. Mobilization helps to convince people that the movement has some chance of succeeding; this will attract supporters who would otherwise dismiss the movement as hopeless, which, in turn, further raises its prospects for success, and so on. But mobilization has to be well advanced before this kind of circular reaction will set in. To reach this stage, certain pre-conditions must exist. In the following pages, we shall identify three elements that are necessary for the mobilization of a social movement.

(1) *An ideology on which potential members can be united*

Perhaps the major reason a collective response to an institutional deficiency is not inevitable is that, in most cases, the perceptions of potential members are confused and varied. Typically, people have only vague notions of what is wrong and what should be done to remedy it. What notions they have vary depending on the particular experiences they have undergone. They also vary because the mere act of rejecting some aspect of the existing social structure has opened the door to a wide range of alternatives.

In a social movement, people try to establish a common set of values and norms to overcome this confusion. To the degree that these values and norms are systematized and rationalized, they can be called an *ideology*. An ideology is usually formulated in the course of the social movement itself, but this process is made easier by the prior existence of values and norms appropriate to the dilemma faced by a discontented group. Social movements frequently revive or borrow portions of already developed ideologies, which they then apply to an immediate situation. Sometimes a set of values and norms are borrowed from other social contexts, as were Social Credit ideas first borrowed in the 1930's from abroad by Western farmers, and then later, in the 1950's and early 1960's, borrowed from the West by French Canadians. However, almost always, an important part of the ideology is indigenous. Most often an ideology evolves from a combination of imported and indigenous notions. As a matter of fact, this was even the case with the Social Credit movement in Alberta; the Social Credit programme fell on receptive ears in Alberta in the 1930's because the United Farmers of Alberta had promoted similar thinking in the previous decade.[17] As a rule, the availability in the indigenous culture of appropriate values and norms greatly increases the probability of mobilization.

An ideology does two concrete things. First, it provides a common perception of the institutional deficiency. It identifies what is wrong, who is responsible for it, and who are the victims. Again, to take the Social Credit movement in Alberta as an example, its ideology identified a permanent deficiency of purchasing power inherent in the capitalist system as the fundamental problem. It also identified Eastern capitalist interests as the agents responsible for this deficiency, and Western farmers as the principal victims. Second, an ideology provides a remedy for the deficiency. It tells people what they have to do and what changes must take place in society as a whole, if the deficiency is to be overcome. The ideology of Social Credit proposed state control of the monetary system, a National Dividend, and price controls, as remedies for the depression.·

By performing these two functions, an ideology increases commitment to the movement and promotes co-ordinated action. Indeed, more than occasionally, an ideology will contain internal norms to govern relationships among members of the movement, and perhaps a special language and dress for members. But even norms whose main function is to interpret and remedy the institutional deficiency also serve to promote commitment. Although every movement attracts at least some opportunists, and although people are susceptible to a wide variety of ideologies,[18] it is nevertheless the case that their conversion to the ideology of the movement is of crucial importance to their level of commitment. Consequently, the degree to which people believe in its ideology is the best single predictor of the amount of support they will give a social movement.[19]

It is, therefore, not surprising that social movements are generally more successful if their values and norms encompass sentiments that are already known to be strongly held in a society. The prohibitionists went to great trouble to identify their cause with patriotism during the First World War in order to attract the support of the considerably large number of people who were taking patriotism very seriously at that point in time.[20] On the other hand, values and norms in an ideology that could alienate potential support are often hushed up. For example, at various points in time, Communists in Canada have downplayed connections they might have had with Moscow. Yet it is frequently difficult to avoid alienating certain segments of the population without sacrificing important parts of an ideology, or at least parts that are important to a critical group of supporters. The prohibition movement was unable to avoid the loss of French-Canadian support in the West because it could not conceal its goal of unilingual education without losing key supporters.[21]

(2) *Willing and able leadership*
If people are to respond collectively to an institutional deficiency, they must have leaders with the motivation and skills needed to organize their activities and to articulate values and norms. However, social movements generally face two serious problems in developing effective leadership.

First, most people who become discontented do not possess the education, experience, and economic security necessary to perform this function. When those who are discontented do get leadership, it normally comes from a limited supply of politically experienced persons within their social group. S.M. Lipset has shown, for example, that local leaders of the Co-operative Commonwealth Federation (CCF) in Saskatchewan were, in most cases, relatively well-off farmers with experience in politics or in community organizations.[22] Occasionally, leadership actually comes from strata outside, or at least marginal to, the strata from which the main support for the movement is drawn. The mass support for the Social Credit movement in Quebec came from small businessmen, farmers, and workers, but the leadership was drawn primarily from the middle or lower-middle class.[23] But just as common as any of the above is the situation in which a movement fails to get off the ground because there exist no groups with leadership capabilities who are willing to provide the necessary leadership. Even if willing leadership is available, when it comes from outside the discontented group, there is usually great difficulty in establishing contact and a relationship of trust between would-be leaders and those who are discontented. Che Guevara and his comrades, to cite but one instance, were all too willing to lead a mass movement of Bolivian peasants, but they were unable to do so primarily because they were outsiders and were regarded with suspicion by the peasants.

The second leadership problem social movements face is that the structure on which leaders base their authority is weak. Since behaviour in social movements is relatively less institutionalized than routine behaviour, positions of authority are less clearly defined and there are fewer agreed upon norms for obedience to this or that individual. And since leaders play a crucial role in the development of a movement's norms, most social movements are frustrated by a chicken-and-egg problem: leaders are needed to develop an authority structure, but leaders will not be obeyed until an authority structure evolves. There are, however, some conditions under which this problem is comparatively less serious.

First, a social movement may borrow authority structures from existing institutions, using leaders who have already established a base for their authority. We shall say more about this later. Second, a social movement may develop a special kind of leadership that does not depend on institutionalized norms of obedience. This kind of leadership is called *charismatic*. The term was first employed by Max Weber to describe a type of leadership that people obeyed, not because they were conforming to traditional customs, nor because the leader held a legally defined position that gave him the right to give orders, but rather because the leader seemed to possess certain qualities that set him apart from ordinary men and endowed him with exceptional powers.[24] The chances of mobilization are greatly increased if a charismatic leader is available. The most successful social movements in this century all had leaders with outstanding charismatic appeal: Lenin, Gandhi, Hitler, and Mao Tse-tung, to name only a few. The best example of the importance of charisma in Canada is provided by William Aberhart, the leader of the Social Credit movement in Alberta. According to John Irving, Aberhart must be ranked "among the charismatic leaders of mankind".[25] The success of the Social Credit movement was, in large measure, due to Aberhart's charismatic qualities: "his imposing physical presence, his performance as an orator and organizer, his resolute and inflexible will, his infinite resourcefulness, his ability to hypnotize people by his voice [and] his contagious belief in himself."[26]

It is evident from this discussion that leaders of social movements are likely to be unusual people. In some cases, they must be able to identify with a social group to which they do not belong. In most cases, they must possess special qualities that stimulate enthusiasm in a following. They must also be sufficiently divorced from established institutions to be willing to challenge them, and they must have the uniqueness of character and experience to imagine unconventional solutions to problems. If all this were not enough to make it likely that leaders will be unusual people, there are, as well, the effects on these leaders produced by their very participation in the movement. Few individuals can survive the vicissitudes of leading a social movement without developing personality idiosyncrasies, even abnormalities, especially if the movement encounters heavy opposition from established institutions.

Thus, what is most important to understand is that the often peculiar character of leaders is generally a direct function of the exigencies of non-institutionalized behaviour. From an outside point of view, leaders may appear maladapted, but to the needs of the social movement they are, as a rule, supremely adapted. Certainly there is no truth to the generalization that they are typically deranged or bereft of reason. The skill and intelligence required to lead large numbers of people, without the benefit of institutional supports, precludes any such possibility.

(3) Channels for communication and a network of co-operative relationships

The potential supporters of a social movement are frequently dispersed throughout a society, living in different areas and occupying different roles. The likelihood that they will unite in a collective effort is much greater if there exist channels for communication and a network of co-operative relationships among them.

Channels for communication permit the dissemination of values and norms. In fact, it is through a back-and-forth flow of communications among supporters, and between supporters and the leadership, that values and norms get formulated. In addition, channels for communication facilitate what could be called the *mechanics* of mobilization. Even if people were of like mind about what should be done, they could not get together to do it unless they were able to communicate their intentions to one another and unless leaders were able to transmit directives. Too often researchers ignore the obvious fact that collective activity cannot take place without effective channels of communication among participants. In order, for example, to attend a demonstration, join in a boycott, or engage in co-ordinated violence, people have to receive communications. Otherwise, they have no way of knowing when, where, and how to act.

For all of these reasons, other things being equal, the probability that a social movement will emerge within any given social group is higher if pre-existing channels of communication are available for the social movement to utilize. If prospective supporters of a movement have been in the habit of engaging in frequent social interaction with one another, either directly or through intermediaries, or if they have had access to modern means of communication such as newspapers or radios, then the likelihood of their getting together in a social movement is much greater. For instance, among the many factors that should be considered in trying to explain the rapid rise of the Social Credit movement in Alberta, certainly one of the most important was the use that the movement could make of Aberhart's radio programme. In the 1920's Aberhart built up a personal following for his religious broadcasts that numbered between two and three hundred thousand persons. In 1932, he was able to use these broadcasts to propagate Social Credit ideas.[27] In a similar manner, Réal Caouette effectively used quarter-hour television programmes to promote Social Credit ideas in Quebec in the late 1950's. The broadcasts began in some rural areas on a bi-monthly basis in 1958, and then were gradually extended to cover other regions in the province.[28] According to Maurice Pinard, these broadcasts overcame the early skepticism of many individuals about Social Credit ideas. Pinard demonstrates that a comparatively high percentage of those who had been exposed to the broadcasts supported the Social Credit Party in Quebec during the 1962 federal election.[29]

What we mean by a co-operative relationship is a normal social relationship in which people engage in economic, political, or some other kind of co-operative activity. A series of co-operative relationships might form a co-operative network through which values, norms, and directives can be transmitted. Thus co-operative relationships can serve as channels for communication. In addition, they provide inducements to persuade people to accept these values, norms, and directives. Where co-operative relationships exist, people learn to understand, and perhaps trust, one another. They also reward one another for confromity and punish one another for nonconformity.

Consequently, again other things being equal, the probability that a social movement will emerge within any given social group is higher if a pre-existing network of co-operative relationships is available for the social movement to utilize. If prospective supporters of a social movement have been in the habit of co-operating with one another in day-to-day activities, then the likelihood of their also co-operating in a social movement is greater. Karl Marx believed that one of the factors that gave the modern proletariat the potential for revolution was that the capitalist system was bringing workers together in large economic enterprises. In contrast, he argued, peasants were incapable of representing their own interests because they did not engage in meaningful co-operative activity. In an often quoted passage, he described the political impotence of the French peasantry:

> The small-holding peasants form a vast mass, the members of which live in similar conditions but without entering into manifold relations with one another. Their mode of production isolates them from one another instead of bringing them into mutual intercourse. The isolation is increased by France's bad means of communication and the poverty of the peasants. Their field of production, the small holding, admits no division of labour in its cultivation, no application of science and, therefore, no diversity of development, no variety of talent, no wealth of social relationships. Each individual peasant family is almost self-sufficient; it itself directly produces the major part of its consumption and thus acquires its means of life more through exchange with nature than in intercourse with society. A small holding, a peasant and his family; alongside them another small holding, another peasant and another family. A few score of these make up a village, and a few score of villagers make up a Department. In this way, the great mass of the French nation is formed by simple addition of homologous magnitudes, much as

potatoes in a sack form a sack of potatoes. . . . They are consequently incapable of enforcing their class interest in their own name,
whether through parliament or through a convention. They cannot
represent themselves, they must be represented.[30]

In the light of the great revolutionary movements that have erupted among
peasants in the past three decades, particularly in Asia, Marx's views on the
peasantry have to be qualified. Actually, were one to study these peasant movements carefully, one would find that there is still considerable truth to Marx's
claim that peasants "cannot represent themselves"; most of these movements are
led by non-peasants. Furthermore, his emphasis on the importance of co-
operative relationships remains justified. Recent studies of peasant movements
still place considerable stress on the need for strong co-operative relationships.[31]
Peasant rebellions, it has been found, are most likely to occur in one of two types
of peasant societies: first, those in which social changes have weakened the
loyalties felt by peasants toward their landlords, but at the same time have not
destroyed the traditional bonds that hold the peasants themselves together; or,
alternatively, those in which peasants have, for one reason or another, acquired
some of the modern kinds of co-operative relationships that Marx claimed were
lacking among the French peasantry of the nineteenth century. Generally, the
most effective social movements appear in the latter type. Indeed, it seems to be
the case that the greatest political potential is to be found in rural populations
actually composed, not of peasants, but rather of commercialized farmers. This
is true, at least, if commercialization gives rise to co-operative relationships
among these farmers. The ability of western Canadian farmers to organize themselves in movements such as the CCF has often been attributed, at least in part, to
the variety of co-operative enterprises that developed among these farmers in the
early decades of the twentieth century. Western farmers themselves, usually
without the help of townspeople, were forced to establish their own local governments, hospitals, schools, telephone systems, and most important of all,
economic co-operatives, such as creameries, egg-grading plants, poultry markets, grain elevators, and even hardware, grocery, and gasoline co-operatives.
These organizations were both a consequence and a cause of strong social bonds
among Western farmers, which facilitated the growth of political associations
and movements to represent agrarian interests.[32]

We have discussed three basic elements that we consider necessary for the
mobilization of a social movement: (1) an ideology on which potential members
can be united; (2) willing and able leadership; and (3) channels for communication and a network of co-operative relationships. These elements must either be
adapted from existing institutions or be newly created. Whether or not they can
be adapted from existing institutions will depend on a variety of factors. Clearly

the most important is the extent to which the discontented have access to institutional guides that are strong, and yet are not tied to or identified with the institutional guides with which they are dissatisfied. Relatively autonomous institutional guides that can be adapted to the needs of a social movement are what we call the movement's *organizational base*. An organizational base is usually derived from existing institutional structures. Within such structures there will already be present values, norms, and leaders toward which people may still have some loyalties. There will also be channels for communication and networks of co-operative relationships through which these, or new values and norms (as well as the directives of leaders), can be transmitted.

Social scientists like to distinguish between two types of organizational structures.[33] First, there are *communal* structures to which people are bound by traditional linkages based on kinship, community, ethnic, or tribal attachments. Second, there are *associational* structures, consisting of social groups organized for specifically stated purposes — occupational, religious, political, civic, or economic special-interest groups. The principal building blocks for social movements in western Canada have been of the second type. As we have already noted, the success of the CCF in Saskatchewan can be understood, in part, as a consequence of the high level of participation among Saskatchewan farmers in economic co-operatives and civic associations. Often the associational structures used by a social movement are the creation of earlier social movements. As a matter of fact, this was the case with the CCF in Saskatchewan, where the high level of prior associational participation among farmers was closely related to earlier agrarian movements. It was also the case with the Social Credit movement in Alberta, which was built on the organizational base provided by the Calgary Prophetic Bible Institute as well as the organizational base provided by locals of the United Farmers of Alberta.[34] Still another possibility is for contemporaneous social movements to utilize the organizations established by one another. This was characteristic of reform movements of the early part of the century, which overlapped in personnel and organization.

It is important to understand that if existing organizational structures are going to provide an organizational base for a social movement they must not only be strong and well integrated, they must also be appropriate channels for the expression of the discontent that lies behind the movement. Membership in organizational structures may have either mobilizing or restraining effects.[35] What makes the difference is whether or not the organizational structure in question is tied to the institutional guides with which people are dissatisfied. It is quite possible for an organization to include both people who are discontented and some who are not discontented.

To illustrate, one of the weaknesses of the student body as an organizational base for the youth movement has been the great variety of attitudes within the Canadian student population; the discontent that generated the youth movement was shared by only a minority of students, who could not count on their fellow students to support demonstrations, sit-ins, or strikes against the university administration. Even less useful for a social movement is the organizational structure provided by traditional political parties (in Canada, the Liberals and the Progressive Conservatives). The discontented within these parties have always constituted a minority with the result that it has been difficult (though not impossible) for dissidents to use the organizations established by these parties as the basis on which to build a social movement. Indeed, the traditional parties in Canada have normally been controlled by their least disaffected members. This is a common situation in any organization. Most obviously, in associations in which people are gainfully employed, the greatest amount of power usually lies in the hands of those who are closely identified with the established social order. Rather than providing an organizational base for the mobilization of a social movement, these structures will, for the most part, exert restraining effects, since they will reward people for accepting established institutions, and punish them for not doing so. Unless it has undergone considerable transformation, the extensive organizational structure that binds an employee of General Motors to the General Motors Corporation, or an employee of a government department to that department, cannot serve as an organizational base for a social movement, or at least a movement that threatens those who manage these institutions. Only indirectly, and only through the formation of opposition organizations such as employee associations, can these organizational structures serve to facilitate the rise of a social movement that challenges established institutions.

It would, therefore, be incorrect to argue that strong organizational structures always facilitate mobilization. But it would be just as incorrect to argue that strong organizational structures always inhibit mobilization. Unfortunately the latter conclusion is implied by the well known theory of mass society.[36] This theory holds that social movements are most prevalent in societies that are characterized by a relative absence of organizational structures. The theory also holds that the people most likely to participate in a social movement are those who are least integrated into such structures. While the theory of mass society has the merit of calling attention to the manner in which organizational structures can discourage unconventional behaviour, it overlooks the fact that an organizational base of some kind is a prerequisite for large-scale mobilization. A social movement must have some sort of foundation on which to build a new set of values, norms, and leaders, and from which to derive channels of communication and a network of co-operative relationships. So it can hardly be true, as a general rule, that social movements are more likely in societies where organizational structures are weak. Nor can it be true, as a general rule, that people who participate in social movements are those who are socially isolated. On the contrary, most members of a social movement, especially in its early stages, are well integrated into existing organizational structures.

Social Segmentation

We have reviewed two broad categories of conditions that we consider necessary for the rise of a social movement: (1) conditions that contribute to a perception of institutional deficiency, and (2) conditions for mobilization. We are now going to suggest that the probability that these conditions will be found in any society depends primarily on the level of *social segmentation*. Other societal characteristics are certainly important, and social segmentation is not the only variable that should be considered. But it ranks sufficiently high in importance that it warrants special attention.

The term social segmentation refers to the presence of social cleavages in a society, dividing it into two or more groups among whom there is little effective communication, few co-operative relationships, and, in many cases, overt hostility.[37] The segments in a segmented society often have cultural characteristics of their own, and almost always have a "we-group" feeling that social scientists call *group consciousness*. People are aware of belonging to a certain group, and they believe that their personal goals or interests depend on the attainments of that group as a whole.

Social segmentation increases the probability of a high level of discontent. The more segmented a society is, the greater the probability of inconsistencies in the prevailing institutional structure. Some groups are bound to hold or acquire values or norms that other groups do not share. Accordingly, it becomes more difficult for institutions to operate in a way that is consistent with everyone's idea of how they should operate.

Social segmentation also affects the probability of mobilization. In a highly segmented society, discontent will most likely take the form of dissatisfaction with institutions linked to an opposing segment. As a result, there will be, relatively speaking, few organizations composed of both discontented and non-discontented individuals, and so people will face relatively less pressure to remain loyal to established institutions. Instead, they will likely belong to organizations composed almost entirely of people from their own social segment, who could potentially share their discontents. They will be able to utilize the values and norms of such organizations to arrive at common definitions of the institutional deficiency, and to begin the formulation of new values and norms. The elites who hold leadership positions in these organizations will more likely identify with the discontented, rather than with other elites. Finally, channels for communication and networks of co-operative relationships will more likely be available because alternative channels and alternative networks will be blocked by social cleavage. In short, the discontented will stand a better chance of finding an appropriate organizational base on which to build new institutional guides.

We can derive two tentative hypotheses from these observations. First, other things being equal, the more segmented a society, the more likely it will experience social movements. Second, if a society is segmented, this segmentation will likely determine the social base of most movements that emerge. In Canada, ethnic, regional, and rural-urban cleavages have been much more pronounced than class cleavages. These ethnic, regional, and rural-urban cleavages have seriously divided the working class and have rendered difficult the formation of significant working-class movements. In contrast, Canada has witnessed a number of social movements based on ethnic cleavages, most notably in Quebec, and a number of movements based on regional and rural-urban cleavages, most notably in Western Canada.

In later chapters of this book emphasis will be placed by the editors and by the authors of selected readings on the importance of social segmentation for understanding social movements in twentieth-century Canada. To be sure, there have been several movements that cross-cut social cleavages, and these too deserve our attention. But the most outstanding feature of social movements in this country is the relationship they have generally borne to the major lines of segmentation that divide our society. As we focus on specific cases, we shall be able to see how this segmentation has generated discontent and how it has provided the organizational bases on which a variety of movements have arisen.

3. The Careers of Social Movements

We have argued that the mobilization of a social movement cannot be taken for granted. Inasmuch as a social movement begins in a relatively non-institutionalized situation, mobilization is always in doubt until it actually happens. For the same reason, the particular course that a social movement will follow during its career will also be in doubt. Social movements are very unpredictable: their course is determined by a constant interaction among various forces both within and outside the movement. There is, first of all, *internal* interaction among different leaders, among different groups of followers, and between leaders and followers. Second, there is *external* interaction between the social movement and those who do not directly support it.

Internal Interaction

Under this heading, we could explore a number of different topics. We could discuss the ways in which the activities of supporters of a social movement are controlled, how and to what extent their behaviour is directed through rewards and punishments to conform to the emerging values and norms of the movement. Alternatively, we could examine how commitment to the movement is fostered, how rituals, symbols, dress, language, gatherings, *et cetera* can be used to generate and maintain enthusiasm. Or we could investigate what it is that supporters of the movement find personally satisfying, whether they derive most of their enjoyment from interaction with other supporters or whether their participation is mainly utilitarian and contingent upon the success of the movement in progressing toward its goals.

Since we are limited in the space we have available, we shall focus exclusively on still another topic that comes under the heading of internal interaction, namely factionalism. Virtually all social movements are prone to some measure of factionalism if for no other reason than because the conditions for mobilization that we discussed above never exist in ideal form. Almost all social movements face the problem of mobilizing people who hold diverse values and norms, and/or belong to diverse organizations. Rarely does a social movement draw its support from neat homogeneous populations with ample channels for communication and networks of co-operative relationships among them. Even a social movement that emerges in a highly segmented society, and draws its support entirely from one social segment, will not enjoy completely homogeneous support. If the movement persists over a long period of time, there will, at the very minimum, be different generations, which will be inclined to pursue the goals of the movement in different ways. Moreover, as mentioned once before, the mere fact that social movements reject some aspect of the existing social structure opens the door to a wide range of alternatives. To put it colloquially, once the system is rejected, anything goes. By what authority does one decide that a certain non-institutionalized remedy is better than some other non-institutionalized remedy? This is a problem faced by all social movements, but especially by those that reject a large part of the existing institutional structure. Finally, we can suggest that factionalism develops in social movements as a result of rivalries among leaders. Leaders of social movements are often unwilling to compromise, even with their own comrades, and yet, at the same time, they are usually unable to establish exclusive control over the movement. This kind of rivalry can often divide a social movement into competing camps.

Whatever the reason, there is no doubt that many social movements are characterized by some form of factionalism. They frequently consist of two or more fragments, with distinct leaders, associations, and supporters. Sometimes these different fragments try to work together and pursue common goals; in other cases, they are in conflict with one another as much as they are in conflict with established institutions. A few writers have argued that this fragmentary structure actually contributes to the success of social movements. For example, it has been asserted that, if a social movement has a fragmentary structure, different groups are able to find their own niche in the movement, something that would not be possible if one dominant approach prevailed. It has also been argued that different factions compete with one another and are, therefore, motivated to pursue the goals of the movement more energetically. And, still further, it has been suggested that a fragmentary structure makes a movement less predictable and, hence, more difficult for opponents to combat.[38]

There is certainly some truth to these claims. There is especially good evidence to support the argument that factionalism can assist the growth of a social movement. Some movements expand through the multiplication of factions. The

Indian movement in Canada has grown in this manner. Both the early development of the movement in the 1930's, 1940's, and 1950's, and its more recent development in the late 1960's and early 1970's, have been characterized by a proliferation of different associations — different associations for each province and even different associations within the same province. Every effort to unite these groups has seen the emergence of new groups outside the central body. For example, the Saskatchewan Indian Association was founded in 1944; a year later, the Protective Association for Indians and their Treaties was established in the same province. By 1946, disagreements between these two bodies had been overcome and they merged to form the Union of Saskatchewan Indians; but still another association, the Queen Victoria Protective Association emerged in opposition to the Union, and it was more than ten years before these two groups amalgamated to form the Federation of Saskatchewan Indians.[39] More recently, the National Indian Brotherhood has tried to form a federation of provincial associations, but a variety of rival Indian associations have sprung up at the same time to take a leading role in the current Indian movement. In this way, through the multiplication of associations, the movement has expanded to include Indians in most parts of the country.

However, the multiplication of associations has also been one of the major weaknesses of the Indian movement. The presence of a large number of different groups within the movement has made it difficult for Indian leaders to present a unified programme. Whether or not there are great differences among these groups in the goals they envisage, the impression given to the government and to the public is that the Indians themselves are uncertain about what they want. Any one association can only claim, at best, to represent a portion of the Indian population. Government officials can, and frequently have, rejected their demands on this basis. Time and again they have been able to avoid making any real concessions by playing one faction off against the other.

Moreover, for any individual member of a social movement, factionalism is frustrating. While the movement may grow through factionalism, growth of this kind does not give members a feeling of getting closer to their ultimate objective. Indeed, even social scientists who argue that a fragmentary structure is functional admit that members of social movements see it differently: members almost invariably regard fragmentation as evidence of failure.[40] This is not surprising in view of the fact that people who join a social movement are trying to establish new ways in which human beings should relate to one another, and are trying to persuade others to accept these new ways. So long as they cannot even convince other followers of the movement to accept their version of the new life, they are far removed from this goal. The failure of factions to win over other factions has often been a source of discouragement to members of social movements, and has often meant that social movements work at cross-purposes.

Factionalism is a common cause of the decline of social movements — all too common for us to accept, without serious qualification, the contention that the fragmentary structure of social movements is always functional to their success. The Social Gospel movement, for example, was unable to resolve serious differences between its conservative and its radical wings, with the result that the movement disintegrated during the labour unrest that followed the First World War.[41] The Progressive movement was unable to overcome a disagreement among its supporters over whether the movement ought to reform the Liberal Party or establish a new party representing agrarian interests. Inevitably, the movement was in no position to use its impressive showing in the federal election of 1921 to achieve either goal, and, consequently, it fell apart.[42] In contrast, although the Social Credit movement in Alberta was also seriously plagued by factionalism, one faction was able, at least temporarily, to emerge as dominant and to carry the movement to the provincial seat of power.[43]

External Interaction

Interestingly enough, it is possible to study societal response to social movements in much the same way that we study social movements themselves — indeed, in the way that we study any kind of collective behaviour. People who do not directly support a social movement are, nevertheless, faced with a perceived institutional deficiency as represented by the social movement itself. The very existence of a social movement signifies that something is wrong in the society; and people will often follow some of the typical patterns of collective behaviour in responding to this deficiency. What remedy they select will depend on how they view the social movement. There will emerge in the society various interpretations of what has caused the movement, various definitions of what it is, and various policies as to how it should be handled.

At the least institutionalized level, response to a social movement may take the form of a panic. The rise of a social movement may, to cite one possibility, cause migrations of people afraid of the consequences the movement might have for their own well-being. Even before the Nazi movement in Germany began systematically to persecute Jews and intellectuals, many of them had seen the writing on the wall and had fled the country. Most recently, and closest to home, the rise of the separatist movement in Quebec has brought about a small-scale, but nevertheless noticeable, migration of English-speaking Canadians out of Montreal. In both cases, people were or are responding to a social movement in a manner that conforms to the social scientist's definition of a panic.

It is also possible for the response to a social movement to take the form of a crowd. Angry crowds may attack members of a social movement engaged in demonstrations or in some other sort of activity. The American anti-war movement in the late sixties, for example, was frequently subjected to attacks by "hard-hats" and occasionally these attacks reached violent proportions. Conflict between religious groups in Northern Ireland intensified in 1968 and 1969 as a result of attacks by Protestant mobs on marches organized by the Catholic Civil Rights movement. And, on numerous occasions in 1973 and 1974, left-wing rallies in Italy have been set upon by neo-fascists. In these, and in many other instances of this kind, the response of at least some people to a social movement can be placed in the category of crowd behaviour.

In modern society, societal response to a social movement almost invariably entails the formation of one or more publics, which will debate and articulate opinions about the movement. The movement will be discussed in letters to newspapers and on talk-shows, and views on the movement will be expressed through public opinion polls. Sometimes, there will emerge what could be called a *derived* movement, that is, another social movement that seeks to persuade people to accept a certain interpretation of the original movement. We can distinguish between two types of derived movements. First, there may emerge a *sympathy-movement*, which will endeavour to promote a positive interpretation of the original movement and will try to assist it in achieving its goals. Usually sympathy-movements will try to spread concern for a social movement in places removed from the original conflict. The "Boycott Grapes" movement, for example, tried to spread support for the struggle to unionize grape-pickers in California. The anti-war movement in Canada tried to persuade Canadians that their own country was implicated in the Vietnam War and that it was not an exclusively American problem. And various groups have sought to promote sympathy in Europe and North America for native guerilla movements in Africa.

On the other hand, a social movement may provoke a *counter-movement*, which endeavours to promote a negative interpretation of the original movement and to interfere with its goals. A very effective counter-movement was launched during the Second World War against the CCF in Ontario.[44] The Protestant crowds that attacked Catholic marchers in Northern Ireland in 1968 and 1969 have been superseded by a formidable and violent Protestant terrorist movement, which is challenging, not only the Catholic movement, but even British rule itself in Northern Ireland. And the anti-abortion movement has arisen in opposition to the relaxation of laws on abortions advocated by the women's liberation movement. Although derived movements are relatively rare, they nevertheless indicate the lengths to which people sometimes go in reacting to a social movement.

Even the response of the government will be less than fully institutionalized. Ordinarily, governments are not prepared to cope with social movements. In fact, it is not unknown for some representatives of the state to respond to social movements with panic or crowd behaviour. Here we are referring, in particular, to so-called "police riots" — when police or military forces assigned to control a demonstration provoke a clash and engage in unrestrained attacks on demonstrators. The police riot that broke out during the 1968 Democratic National Convention in Chicago is the most publicized case in point in recent years, but a large number of instances of this kind have been documented.[45] Still more common is for various government officials to perceive a social movement differently, to respond differently, and, thereby, to make the overall response of the state inconsistent. Considerable time is required to develop an institutionalized response, and so it is only when a government has had to face a social movement over a long period of time that it can be expected to respond in a highly institutionalized manner.

Since, in modern society, interaction with the state is the most important external interaction in which a social movement engages, we shall try to classify the possible responses that government officials can adopt toward a social movement. We shall suggest three: (1) indifference, (2) accommodation, and (3) obstruction. Which response government officials adopt will depend on the way they view the social movement. We cannot, at this time, enter into a detailed discussion of how these views are arrived at. But let it be said that they are a result, not just of the characteristics of the social movement itself, but of a variety of influences that prevail on government officials.

If government officials respond to a social movement with indifference it is because they do not see it as a threat to the existing social or at least political order. Now and then there appears a social movement with which government officials actually sympathize, and they can be found expressing approval of its demands. But, more commonly, government officials simply ignore non-threatening social movements, often labelling them as "deviant" and justifying this label by claiming that support for the movement is very small. In our society, this is a standard government response to religious movements. True, the government has found it impossible to ignore some religious movements that clearly infringe on the concerns of the state, such as the Sons of Freedom sect of the Doukhobors. Occasionally, representatives of the state have also been concerned with the close relationship that religious movements can have with political unrest, as was the case in Alberta in the 1930's.[46] But most religious movements themselves, so long as they maintain an essentially religious orientation, have not seemed threatening to the guardians of established political institutions, although they certainly have seemed threatening to the guardians of established religious institutions. Most recently, the state has chosen to ignore several religious movements that have emerged in the early 1970's and have attracted support primarily among young people, movements such as the Hare Krishna movement, the "Jesus freaks" (e.g., the Children of God) and the followers of Guru Maharaj Ji.

When we say that a government adopts an accommodation response, we mean that it indicates a willingness to negotiate with the social movement. If government officials choose this course of action it is because they believe that the movement has some valid demands that could be accepted without threatening the social order. At the same time, they believe that the movement has mobilized sufficient support that they can no longer ignore it without risking the possibility of its ultimately *becoming* a threat to the social order. Whereas movements that are ignored are usually labelled as deviant, movements that are accommodated are usually labelled as "protest movements".[47] The important point is that a social movement will be accommodated only when government officials feel that negotiating with it constitutes less of a threat than not negotiating. This was how Mackenzie King's government responded to the rise of the Progressive Party in the early 1920's. It also seems to be the way in which the federal government is now coping with Indian land claims. On the one hand, government officials are conscious of the threat that failing to negotiate over land claims would contribute to the danger of eventual destructive unrest among Indians. At the same time, some government officials are influenced by a feeling that these demands are not unjustified, and that the state can afford to accept a limited number of them without stimulating similar demands from other groups, since Indian demands are based on claims to special rights.

Precisely the opposite kind of perception prompts a government to respond with obstruction. Government officials will obstruct a social movement if they are convinced that its success would threaten the social order. Often they believe that a social movement, and the demands it is making, constitute an immediate threat. In other cases, they will acknowledge that some of its demands could safely be met in the short run, but they will insist that the long-run outcome would be disastrous. For instance, the refusal of the government to accept the demands of workers for recognition of the Metal Trades Council during the Winnipeg General Strike was not motivated by opposition to the proposed council as such. Similar councils existed at that time in eight other Canadian cities.[48] However, government officials viewed the strike as part of a much larger campaign to organize workers in the One Big Union (OBU), and this they believed would threaten the social order.

Similarly, fears of long-run consequences motivated the government to reject the demands of the kidnappers of James Cross and Pierre Laporte, and to invoke the War Measures Act in October 1970. Undoubtedly, government officials were outraged by the demands themselves. But, more than that, they were concerned about the possibility that giving in to these demands, and failure to adopt repressive measures, would result in rioting and further kidnapping. The government's response was later defended by Gérard Pelletier, Secretary of State, in this manner:

> It is hard to see the basis for even a relative degree of confidence, on the part of those who advocated the release of the imprisoned terrorists, that a similar situation would not recur and that acceptance of the terrorists' conditions would not encourage further blackmail. In fact, no one can be sure that, even after the refusal to release the

prisoners, we might not have to face the same sort of crime in the future.

As soon as one establishes the precedent of yielding to blackmail involving threats of murder, one comes up against an implacable logic, whose inevitable conclusion is that sooner or later the authorities will have to say *no*. For it is obvious that if the weapon had proved effective, other FLQ cells would certainly have used it again on their own account, as would members of the underworld or other clandestine movements.[49]

Although we have made a point of contrasting three possible responses that governments can adopt toward social movements, we do not mean to imply that they are mutually exclusive. On the contrary, in empirical cases, it is common to find all three combined. In particular, it is common to find governments engaging in both accommodation and obstruction. Even when government officials perceive that a movement has valid grievances, they will usually want to limit its relatively threatening activities, such as demonstrations, pickets, and sit-ins. A case in point was the response of the government to the occupation of Anicinabe Park in Kenora by armed members of the Ojibway Warrior Society during the summer of 1974. On the one hand, government officials had good reason to be accommodating: the deplorable conditions under which Indians in the Kenora district live were well known and could evoke considerable public sympathy; the conflict was being watched carefully by other Indian groups in the country with whom the government was engaged in delicate negotiations on a variety of issues; and, most critical of all, a refusal to negotiate, or, even worse, any attempt to remove the Indians by force, ran a high risk of violence. On the other hand, there were aspects to the occupation that clearly called for a hard-line response: the government was very much afraid of the precedent that would be set by yielding to the demands of an armed group, or in the words of the newly appointed Minister of Indian Affairs, Judd Buchanan, negotiating "through the barrel of a gun"; government officials were also afraid of the precedent that would be set by granting the Indians their demand for ownership of the park since, in their view, this land was not, in any realistic sense, Indian land. Inevitably, the government's response included both accommodation and obstruction. Officials repeatedly expressed their willingness to negotiate on any of the issues, but refused to do so until the Indians had laid down their arms. They placed obstacles in the way of the occupiers (most notably, they closed off access to the park on 13 August), but they accepted, indeed themselves brought in, Dennis Banks of the American Indian Movement to assist in the negotiations. Through this combination of carrots and sticks government officials controlled the situation and brought it to, what was for them, a reasonably satisfactory conclusion.

Whatever the government's response, whether it tends toward indifference, accommodation, obstruction, or a combination of these, it will have significant consequences. We shall suggest a few. If an ignored social movement is not able to mobilize support, it will either disappear or persist as a deviant subculture. If it is able to mobilize support, the government's indifference will likely encourage it to seek attention by inflating its demands, demonstrating its power, and perhaps even engaging in threatening activities. A movement that a government is willing to accommodate benefits from the prestige of official recognition and also achieves some of its goals. This success may attract support, but it also creates difficulties for leaders of the movement. Some supporters will break with the movement because it appears to have abandoned those demands that the government would not accept; other supporters will fall away because the movement appears to have achieved its objectives, and, therefore, has lost its *raison d'être*. Hence, an accommodated social movement will typically start making new demands, or else it will decline.

To the extent that a movement faces obstruction, it will likely fail to achieve its goals and supporters will become discouraged. Obstruction may even make support for the movement personally costly. If, despite obstruction, a social movement survives, the obstruction usually induces members to reject more of the prevailing social structure, since, in addition to their original grievances, they now have the obstruction itself to complain about.

To sum up, each of the possible positions a government can take involves dangers. Some movements can be successfully ignored, while ignoring others will only induce them to become more threatening. The same is true with accommodation and obstruction. Given this dilemma, and given also the lack of institutionalized procedures for coping with social movements, it is not surprising that governments so often appear more confused and irrational than the movements they are trying to control.

Decline and Routinization

Most social movements do not last very long. They sometimes decline because the unrest that generated them is reduced owing to a change in social conditions (for example, improved economic conditions), or owing to the success of the movement in achieving its goals. Although only temporary, the labour movement in Canada suffered a decline in the 1920's because the prevailing prosperity and the very successes of the movement in earlier years gave most workers a measure of economic security that they could live with. And, among the many reasons that can be given for the decline of the CCF in the 1950's, certainly one factor was the tranquilizing effect of postwar economic prosperity.

Social movements may also decline, as we noted above, as a result of factionalism. Or they may decline because supporters come to realize that they were drawn into the movement under false pretences and that it never did offer them what they wanted. David Bercuson employs this kind of explanation to account for the rapid collapse of the OBU in 1922; he argues that workers who supported the OBU did so under the false assumption that it would provide a framework for industrial unionism.[50] Most often, of course, social movements decline because they fail to make satisfactory progress toward achieving their goals, and members get discouraged. The circular process of mobilization, mentioned briefly above, may reverse itself and become a vicious circle of demobilization. The failure to attain goals causes some members to fall away; this in turn adversely affects the movement's prospects, which in turn further reduces its support, and so on. Leo Zakuta illustrates this process when he describes the fortunes of the CCF in the 1950's. Along with postwar economic prosperity, the inefficacy of the CCF also contributed to its decline. Following its crushing defeat in the election of 1949, CCF prospects did not justify the personal costs of active participation. Not only did the party find it increasingly difficult to keep its supporters, it even experienced difficulty in retaining leaders, many of whom were tempted by more rewarding career alternatives or by more promising political avenues. As Zakuta says, "nothing fails like failure".[51]

Whatever the cause, the decline of a social movement almost invariably begins with the withdrawal of its least committed followers. Again we can take the CCF as an example. Its decline was swiftest in those areas, such as Ontario, where the number of active members was small relative to the number of inactive supporters.[52] Those who support the movement for very specific reasons are also among the first to withdraw. As a number of observers have pointed out, one reason the campaign for direct legislation declined so rapidly was that many of its supporters had specific items of legislation they wanted to see enacted, such as women's suffrage and prohibition. As the campaign for direct legislation encountered serious obstacles (while at the same time some of these specific items of legislation themselves met with success), support for the movement dropped off rapidly.[53] The point is that much of the support for any social movement, the support that makes it a *mass* movement, is very unstable and can evaporate quickly for a variety of reasons. The movement will then be left with little more than a hard core of leaders and supporters.

Another reason why the careers of social movements tend to be short is that many movements become *routinized*. Routinization often accompanies a decline in support for a movement, but it may even befall a movement that continues to hold onto its supporters. The term routinization refers to the establishment of consistent and stable institutional guides. A social movement becomes routinized when values, norms, and leaders are not so much being created, as they are simply being accepted and followed. Routinization is thus the end product of the whole process of institutionalization that all social movements follow. Indeed, many social scientists reserve the term institutionalization for this final stage, using it in a manner that is synonymous with the term routinization.[54] We prefer to describe the entire history of a social movement as a process of institutionalization, although we would be the first to admit that not all social movements actually reach the end point and become fully institutionalized.

Routinizations vary greatly. On the one hand, institutional guides that the movement has been developing may become part of the dominant institutional structure of a society. Now and then, a social movement actually overthrows the existing order, and succeeds in establishing its own guides as dominant. More often, some portion of the institutional guides sought by a social movement are absorbed by existing institutions, often in the form of government legislation. In contrast, at the other end of the spectrum, there are social movements that build stable institutional guides operating, in large measure, independently of dominant institutions; here we are referring to social movements that set up their own communities, such as communes, in which they seek to put their ideals into practice. The most prevalent kind of routinization falls somewhere in between these two extremes. Often a movement has some of its goals accepted by the established social structure, while the movement itself evolves into a specialized association, such as a church, a union, or a political party. An association of this kind is clearly distinguishable as the product of a social movement, but it has relatively stable relationships with established structures. It will typically have a formalized leadership and administrative staff, holding clearly defined positions of authority and operating under explicit rules and regulations. Supporters of the association will usually be less enthusiastic than were supporters of the movement, but often more reliable because their participation will follow certain stable norms that obligate them to give a specific amount of time and money to the association.[55]

It is almost impossible for a social movement to routinize in precisely the form prescribed by its ideology, and the vast majority of movements do not even approximate the ideal. Almost all are forced to accept a watered-down version of the institutional guides they sought to establish. Nevertheless, most members of social movements ultimately accept routinization. Although some may resist,[56] most give in to, indeed, in some cases, actively pursue, the establishment of stable institutional guides that are less than what the movement promised it would achieve. They do so for two reasons.

First, routinization provides guides to behaviour that will more likely be accepted by other people. Participants in a social movement gradually reach the conclusion that (in the near future, at any rate) their ideal institutional guides are impractical. In general, this revelation comes not from a realization that these institutional guides are unsatisfactory in themselves, but rather from a realization that they will not receive the support necessary to be put into practice. Consequently, members of the movement turn to alternative institutional guides that may be more acceptable to potential supporters. They do not necessarily lose sight of the fact that these values and norms are less than the ideal, but they feel they must sacrifice the ideal to the more important goal of seeing at least some of their values and norms institutionalized.

Secondly, routinization is tolerated because it provides members themselves with rewarding guides for their behaviour. Though not the ideal, the routinized institutional guides tell them how to behave in ways that will likely bring rewards. In the case of social movements that become specialized associations, the association itself is often converted into a source of power, prestige, and even monetary rewards, especially for its leaders and the administrative staff. It becomes an end in itself, its maintenance sometimes so important that the original goals of the movement may be reversed to save it. For movements that set up their own communities, routinization establishes stable human relationships that enable members to count on one another to provide certain gratifications and to help achieve certain goals. Even the hippies, who struggled as hard as the members of any movement to avoid social regulation, eventually sacrificed many of their ideals in order to organize themselves into communes in which they could provide for their wants and needs. Satisfaction of some basic necessities was required for the very survival of those humans who made up the hippie movement, and it forced them into routinization. "Communes", write Constas and Westhues, "signify the routinization of hippiedom." And they describe this routinization in these words:

> If one maintains the unstructured purity and predictable freedom of charisma over a long period of time, he simply starves to death. Survival requires at least sufficient discipline to eat somewhat regularly and to apply oneself somewhat systematically to procuring food, shelter, and other necessities of life. In rural communes, survival requires the planning of production of food products, from tilling the soil in early spring to picking the last vegetables in the fall. Group survival requires some system of conscious co-ordination of the behaviour of the group members. . . .
>
> Rural communes today display such organization. Any successful commune, no matter how innocent, well-intentioned, or altruistic are its members, has to impose a normative structure upon their behavior if the commune is to survive. For this reason, few communes with which we are familiar permit the use of any hard drugs, and in many communes even marijuana use is prohibited. Similarly, the casual attitude toward sexual behavior and sporadic orgiastic celebrations cannot survive in communal life. The maintenance of normative control over sexual and affective relationships among commune members is indeed one of the most difficult problems communes have to face. How can the commune be kept together while at the same time members be free to follow personal attractions? This question is answered differently in different communes, but always with some kind of normative structure that prohibits the utter spontaneity that surrounded sex in the charismatic stage of the movement.[57]

In order to understand routinization it is essential to recognize that it is not a completely new phase into which a social movement enters. As we have already said, it is the culmination of the process of institutionalization that has been going on throughout the whole career of the movement. We are not arguing that there are magical forces constantly operating to return society to a stable state whenever it experiences unrest. On the contrary, the pervasiveness of social movements and other forms of collective behaviour strongly suggests that instability is a more natural state for society than stability. People often, not just on rare occasions, find something wrong with the institutional guides under which they live. What we do assert, however, is that the response that people adopt toward deficiencies in these institutional guides is usually not chaotic or random, and is usually not a rejection of institutional guides as such. Throughout the course of a social movement, members seek to establish institutional guides as well as oppose them. The way in which they sometimes finally accept a watered-down version of their ideology is analagous to the way in which they explore and try to win support for new institutional guides in the early stages of the movement. In both the earlier and later stages, people try to find guides to their behaviour that they can persuade others to accept. In the early stages they are inclined to be idealistic, while in the later stages they are inclined to be more pragmatic, but what they are doing is essentially the same.

It is not surprising, therefore, that the point at which a social movement becomes routinized and ceases to be a social movement is never clear-cut. Indeed, it is not uncommon to find a newly formed social movement compromising its ideology in an effort to attract support. Peter R. Sinclair has documented this sort of manoeuvring on the part of the CCF in Saskatchewan.[58] He shows that, in order to win votes, the CCF abandoned much of its socialist programme (especially with respect to land nationalization) as early as 1936. On the basis of this evidence, Sinclair concludes that the CCF in Saskatchewan was more a political party than a social movement even in the 1930's. But it would be more useful to call it *both* a political party *and* a social movement; this description would recognize the possibility that social movements can, very early in their careers, behave in ways that we would associate with a fully institutionalized political party. To repeat, institutionalization is not just a final stage in the life of a social movement; it is an evolving characteristic of social movements from their very beginnings.

It is clear from what has been said that most social movements leave something behind them. They may or may not achieve any of their specific objectives. But in either case, they are often survived by institutionalized remnants of the organizations they created. As we know, at a later point in time, such organizations may be adapted for still another struggle. Even social movements that impart no concrete organizational remnants (that is, decline without becoming routinized) leave something. They leave a memory of an institutional deficiency that people perceived, defined, and tried to remedy, and a memory of values and norms that people were in the process of institutionalizing, although they never completed the process, perhaps hardly started it. Later, others may revive these perceptions and reformulate these values and norms. Social movements themselves are one of the major sources of inspiration for new social movements. In this sense, at least, they never die.

Notes

1. See, for example, George A. Theodorson and Achilles G. Theodorson, *A Modern Dictionary of Sociology.* New York: Crowell, 1969, p. 390; James B. McKee, *Introduction to Sociology.* New York: Holt, Rinehart and Winston, 1969, p. 580.
2. In the General Introduction as a whole, we have drawn from a number of theoretical approaches to social movements. But our discussion of the nature of collective behaviour has been influenced primarily by the work of Turner and Killian, and to a lesser extent by the writings of Robert Park, Herbert Blumer, Orrin Klapp, and other members of the so-called "Chicago school." See, in particular, Ralph Turner and Lewis M. Killian, *Collective Behavior.* Second edition. Englewood Cliffs, N.J.: Prentice-Hall, 1972.
3. For a description of this approach, see Turner and Killian, 1972, pp. 12-18.
4. See Gustave Le Bon, *The Crowd: A Study of the Popular Mind.* New York: Viking Press, 1895/1960.
5. Turner and Killian refer to these theories as *convergence theories.* See their *Collective Behavior,* 1972, pp. 18-21.
6. For readers unfamiliar with the use of these terms in social science, values are conceptions of what is good, beneficial, desirable, and worthwhile; they may be highly abstract and general or they may be quite specific. Norms, as we have already stated, are formal or informal rules that define what people should or should not do in any given situation. Leaders are persons who occupy central positions of dominance or influence in a group; if their dominance is accepted by members of the group, they have legitimized power, or what we call authority. Values, norms, and leaders are all components of the institutional structure that guide behaviour, and so we have referred to them as institutional guides.
7. The thesis that the institutional guides of collective behaviour are emergent was stated explicitly by Turner and Killian in the first edition of their *Collective Behavior.* Englewood Cliffs, N.J.: Prentice-Hall, 1957. For their statement of this approach as it appears in the second edition, see Turner and Killian, *Collective Behavior,* 1972, especially pp. 21-24. We have already called attention to the influence of Turner and Killian on our discussion of collective behaviour. The reader should be advised that this is not the only available sociological perspective on collective behaviour. Another significant approach is represented by Neil J. Smelser, *Theory of Collective Behavior.* New York: Free Press, 1962. In certain respects, Smelser's approach is similar to the one we have adopted. Smelser accepts the argument of the Chicago school that collective behaviour is a response to unstructured situations. (See Smelser, pp. 8-9.) There also exist some parallels between Smelser's "components" and our "institutional guides". (See Smelser, especially chapter II.) Nevertheless, the most important and influential features of Smelser's theoretical model are not reflected in the framework we present.
8. Richard Flacks, "The Liberated Generation: An Exploration of the Roots of Student Protest," *The Journal of Social Issues,* XXIII (July, 1967); and Kenneth Westhues, "Inter-Generational Conflict in the Sixties," below, Chapter 6.

9. This is Homans' fifth proposition of elementary social behaviour. For a thorough discussion of how one arrives at this proposition, see George Homans, *Social Behavior: Its Elementary Forms*. New York: Harcourt, Brace and World, 1961, pp. 72-78 and 232-264.

10. Obviously we are using the term expectations in the sense of what one expects as one's due. In English usage, expectations can also mean what one actually anticipates getting, which is, if anything, closer to what we are calling achievements. To confuse the two meanings would render pointless the whole distinction between expectations and achievements. Some writers get around this problem by using the word aspirations where we use expectations, but aspirations can mean far more than just rewards. One can aspire to be a Mozart, but not as a just reward.

11. Alexis de Tocqueville, *The Old Regime and the French Revolution*. Translated by Stuart Gilbert. New York: Doubleday, 1856/1955, pp. 174-177.

12. For an extensive treatment of the logically possible relationships between expectations and achievements, see T.R. Gurr, *Why Men Rebel*. Princeton, N.J.: Princeton University Press, 1970, pp. 46-55. Our Figures 1 and 2 are adapted from similar figures provided by Gurr. A third possibility is described by James Davies' J-curve. Davies has argued that revolutions are most likely to occur when a prolonged period of objective social and economic development is followed by a period of sharp reversal. This reversal, even if it does not bring people to their former low levels, can create intense dissatisfaction because expectations acquired during the prosperity are disappointed. Thus, the situation described by Davies' J-curve is actually a combination of rising expectations and falling achievements. See Davies, "Toward a Theory of Revolution," *American Sociological Review*, XXVII, No. 1 (February, 1962); and Davies, "The J-Curve of Rising and Declining Satisfactions as a Cause of Some Great Revolutions and a Contained Rebellion." In H.D. Graham and T.R. Gurr (eds.), *The History of Violence in America*. New York: Bantam, 1969.

13. See James A. Geschwender, "The Negro Revolt: An Examination of Some Hypotheses," *Social Forces*, XLIII (December, 1964).

14. T.H. White, "Canadian Labour and International Unions in the Seventies," below, Chapter 4.

15. J.H. Thompson, "The Beginning of Our Regeneration: The Great War and Western Canadian Reform Movements," below, Chapter 1.

16. S.D. Clark, "Movements of Protest in Post-War Canadian Society," below, Chapter 6.

17. John A. Irving, "The Evolution of the Social Credit Movement," below, Chapter 2.

18. For an argument to this effect, see Maurice Pinard, *The Rise of a Third Party: A Study in Crisis Politics*. Englewood Cliffs, N.J.: Prentice-Hall, 1971, pp. 94-98.

19. For some evidence to support this proposition, see Jane Jensen and Peter Regenstreif, "Some Dimensions of Partisan Choice in Quebec, 1969," *Canadian Journal of Political Science*, III, No. 2 (June, 1970).

20. Thompson, "The Beginning of Our Regeneration," below, Chapter 1.

21. *Ibid*.

22. S.M. Lipset, *Agrarian Socialism*. Second edition. Berkeley: University of California Press, 1950/1971, pp. 221-243.

23. Pinard, *The Rise of a Third Party*, pp. 92 and 124-132.

24. Max Weber, *The Theory of Social and Economic Organization*. Translated by A.M. Henderson and Talcott Parsons. Glencoe: The Free Press, 1947, pp. 358-359.

25. John A. Irving, "Psychological Aspects of the Social Credit Movement in Alberta: Part I: The Development of the Movement," *Canadian Journal of Psychology*, I, No. 1 (1947), p. 27.

26. John A. Irving, "Psychological Aspects of the Social Credit Movement in Alberta: Part III: An Interpretation of the Movement," *Canadian Journal of Psychology*, I, No. 3 (1947), p. 136.

27. See Irving, "Psychological Aspects . . . Part I," pp. 21-23; and Irving, "Psychological Aspects of the Social Credit Movement in Alberta. Part II: The Response of the People," *Canadian Journal of Psychology*, I, No. 2 (1947), p. 85.

28. Pinard, *The Rise of a Third Party*, pp. 121-122.

29. *Ibid*.

30. Karl Marx, *The 18th Brumaire of Louis Bonaparte*. New York: International Publishers, 1963, pp. 123-124.

31. See Barrington Moore, Jr., *Social Origins of Dictatorship and Democracy: Lord and Peasant in the Making of the Modern World*. Boston: Beacon, 1966, pp. 453-483; Eric R. Wolf, *Peasant Wars of the Twentieth Century*. New York: Harper and Row, 1969; and Paul Friedrich, *Agrarian Revolt in*

a Mexican Village. Englewood Cliffs, N.J.: Prentice-Hall, 1970.
32. A large number of sources could be consulted on this subject. One of the best is Jean Burnet, "Town-Country Relations and the Problem of Leadership," *Canadian Journal of Economics and Political Science*, XIII, No. 3 (August, 1947); see also, Lipset, *Agrarian Socialism*, pp. 244-246.
33. For applications of this distinction to the understanding of mobilization, see Charles Tilly, "Collective Violence in European Perspective," in Graham and Gurr, *The History of Violence in America*, pp. 38-41; and A. Oberschall, *Social Conflict and Social Movements*. Englewood Cliffs, N.J.: Prentice-Hall, 1973, pp. 118-124.
34. Irving, "Psychological Aspects . . . Part II," p. 84.
35. Maurice Pinard, "Mass Society and Political Movements: A New Formulation," *American Journal of Sociology*, LXXIII, No. 6 (May, 1968). This article also appears as Chapter 10 in Pinard, *The Rise of a Third Party*.
36. The definitive statement of the theory of mass society, as applied to social movements, is Kornhauser, *The Politics of Mass Society*. New York: Free Press, 1959. Other writings that fall into this school are Hannah Arendt, *The Origins of Totalitarianism*. New York: World Publishing Co., 1958; and Eric Hoffer, *The True Believer: Thoughts on the Nature of Mass Movements*. New York: Harper and Row, 1951.
37. The basis for the development of a theory of social segmentation was provided by Karl W. Deutsch, *Nationalism and Social Communication*. Cambridge, Mass.: M.I.T. Press, 1966. Deutsch was concerned primarily with the rise of nationalism, but his discussion of ethnic cleavages is still the best statement of how social cleavages evolve. More recently, Lipset and Rokkan have tried to specify the kinds of cleavages that are most prevalent in modern Western societies. See S.M. Lipset and S. Rokkan, "Introduction" to *Party Systems and Voter Alignments*. New York: Free Press, 1967. For an example of the application of the concept of social segmentation to social movements, see Oberschall, *Social Conflict and Social Movements*, pp. 118-124.
38. Luther P. Gerlach, "Movements of Revolutionary Change: Some Structural Characteristics," *American Behavioral Scientist*, XIV, No. 6 (July-August, 1971).
39. J.S. Frideres, *Canada's Indians: Contemporary Conflicts*. Scarborough: Prentice-Hall, 1974, p. 112.
40. Gerlach, "Movements of Revolutionary Change," pp. 812-816.
41. Richard Allen, "The Social Gospel and the Reform Tradition in Canada, 1890-1928," below, Chapter 1.
42. W.L. Morton, "The Western Progressive Movement, 1919-1921," below, Chapter 2.
43. Irving, "The Evolution of the Social Credit Movement," below, Chapter 2.
44. G.L. Caplan, "The Failure of Canadian Socialism: The Ontario Experience," below, Chapter 3.
45. Gary T. Marx, "Civil Disorder and the Agents of Social Control," *Journal of Social Issues*, XXVI, No. 1 (Winter, 1970).
46. See W.E. Mann, *Sect, Cult and Church in Alberta*. Toronto: University of Toronto Press, 1955.
47. Ralph Turner, "The Public Perception of Protest," *American Sociological Review*, XXXIV, No. 6 (December, 1969).
48. D.J. Bercuson, "The Winnipeg General Strike: Collective Bargaining and the One Big Union Issue," *Canadian Historical Review*, LI, No. 2 (June, 1970).
49. Gérard Pelletier, *The October Crisis*. Translated by Joyce Marshall. Toronto: McClelland and Stewart, 1971, pp. 95-99.
50. David J. Bercuson, "Western Labour Radicalism and the One Big Union: Myths and Realities," below, Chapter 4.
51. Leo Zakuta, "Membership in a Becalmed Protest Movement," below, Chapter 3.
52. Caplan, "The Failure of Canadian Socialism," below, Chapter 3.
53. Lionel Orlikow, "The Reform Movement in Manitoba, 1910-1915," *Papers Read Before the Historical and Scientific Society of Manitoba*, Series III, No. 16 (1961), pp. 60-61. See also Morton, "The Western Progressive Movement," below, Chapter 2.
54. Irving, for example, adopts this usage. See Irving, "The Evolution of the Social Credit Movement," below, Chapter 2.
55. Zakuta specifically makes this argument with respect to the CCF. See Zakuta, "Membership in a Becalmed Protest Movement," below, Chapter 3.
56. See, for example, Irving's discussion of such resistance by a faction within the Alberta Social

Credit movement. Irving, "The Evolution of the Social Credit Movement," below, Chapter 2.

57. Helen Constas and Kenneth Westhues, "Communes: the Routinization of Hippiedom," in Kenneth Westhues (ed.), *Society's Shadow: Studies in the Sociology of Countercultures*. Toronto: McGraw-Hill Ryerson, 1972, pp. 194-195.

58. Peter R. Sinclair, "The Saskatchewan CCF: Ascent to Power and the Decline of Socialism," below, Chapter 3.

CHAPTER 1

The Social Gospel and Early Reform

Introduction

It was suggested in the General Introduction that social discontent arises when people perceive a deficiency in the existing institutional structure of a society. Often, it was argued, established social institutions do not seem to operate in a way that is consistent with a particular set of values or norms that are held by some members of a society. The Social Gospel and reform movements of the early part of this century constitute good examples of movements that can be understood in these terms. The values and norms they espoused were (with the partial exception of those of the women's suffrage movement) firmly grounded in traditional and, more specifically, Christian values. As a result, compared to some of the movements examined in later chapters, all possessed a distinctly conservative character.

The general dissatisfaction of some Canadians with certain social institutions was rooted, at the turn of the century, in large-scale changes in the nature of society. Between 1890 and 1910 the total population of the nation increased an impressive 32 per cent.[1] A great part of this increase was due to the hundreds of thousands of immigrants from Europe, the United States, and the United Kingdom who came to till the soil of the recently opened "last best west" or to work in the factories of Canada's growing industrial enterprises. If one were to have taken seriously the words of businessmen and politicians it would have been impossible to deny that prosperity was the order of the day. So euphoric was the mood that Sir Wilfrid Laurier, then Prime Minister of Canada, declared: The nineteenth century was the century of the United States, the twentieth will be the century of Canada.[2]

Superficially, at least, Laurier's optimism was well founded. The success of Clifford Sifton's immigration policy was evident in the settlement of the Canadian West and in the agricultural bounty that poured into the grain elevators of numerous terminals along the Canadian Pacific Railway. Prosperity was also evident in the production of pulp and paper, non-ferrous metals, and a number of other staple products.[3] Likewise, largely as a result of the increased exploitation of these primary products, secondary manufacturing was on the upswing.[4] In more concrete terms, there were 36 per cent more people working in manufacturing in 1911 than in 1891.[5]

To a large extent this occupational change reflected the shifting population base of Canadian society during these years. Although Canada was still predominantly a rural society, urbanization was increasing at an accelerating pace. In the first decade of the century the urban population increased by 62 per cent. Montreal and Toronto doubled their populations while the population of Winnipeg quadrupled. New cities like Calgary and Regina increased their number of residents tenfold.[6]

It was inevitable that such growth was accompanied by a degree of misery that made a mockery of the prophecy of optimism trumpeted by many businessmen and politicians. Contemporary reformers, like J.S. Woodsworth, eloquently attested to the indifference of those who profited from the labour of the farmer or workingman in the mine or factory. In *My Neighbour*, Woodsworth severely criticized the "man of affairs".

> On the wild, lonely road between Jerusalem and Jericho the desperate plight of the stranger would arouse some sense of duty in the most primitive man. But when at breakfast this same modern man reads that, through the negligence of someone, ten workmen were maimed for life or hurled into eternity — well, what is that to him? He hardly pauses as he sips his coffee. His eyes and his attention pass to the next news item — the rise in the price of wheat or the account of the great race. Even if he should own stock in the corporation in whose factories the unfortunate workmen had been employed, it would hardly occur to him that he was even remotely responsible for their injury or death.[7]

That Woodsworth wrote with a bias is obvious. But too many other social commentators were making similar observations for us to dismiss his emotionally charged words. In speaking of Montreal as it was at the turn of the century, Herbert Ames commented on the deplorable conditions of the working-class area of the city. "The sanitary accommodation of 'the city below the hill'," he wrote, "is a disgrace to any nineteenth-century city on this or any other continent. I presume there is hardly a house in all the upper city without modern plumbing. . . . In 'Griffintown' only one home in four is suitably equipped, beyond the canal it is but little better."[8] If, as Sir Wilfrid Laurier claimed, the twentieth century belonged to Canada, he forgot to specify "upper class Canada".

The general indifference of prosperous Canadians to the plight of the workingman and immigrant is explained by the prevailing business ideology of the time — economic individualism. The consequences of such an ethic, when coupled with the demographic changes in Canadian society noted above, are succinctly analysed by S.D. Clark. "The background of the population," Clark argues, together with "the dominance of individualistic pecuniary motives, and the overpowering effects of a new physical environment, evident, for instance, with respect to housing, tended to a deterioration of cultural values and to the growth of an attitude of cultural indifference."[9] In the new urban working class the breakdown of traditional culture was most obvious. As a consequence, the saloon, not the family or the church, became the focus of a great deal of social activity. It was in the saloon that the worker could temporarily escape his misery. In such a situation, Clark points out, the "higher values of life lost meaning."[10]

Although social dislocation was by no means confined to the urban centres of Canada, it was in the city that the worst abuses could be found. After all, it was in the urban centres that three historical and economic forces were meeting head on — industrialization, immigration from foreign lands,[11] and migration from the countryside. Since the institutions found in these centres, and the elites in positions of authority in these institutions, were not entirely suited to an emerging industrial order, it is hardly surprising that certain sectors of the population should come to perceive deficiencies in the existing institutional structure. That Canadian institutions were inadequate to meet social needs generated by the emergent industrial order is explicitly stated by E.R. Forbes. "In Canada," he argues, "the rapid industrialization and urbanization of the Laurier era created or threw into sharp relief a host of social ills. Red light districts abounded in the towns and cities, alcoholism increased sharply, the exploitation of workers became blatant, and the failure of traditional institutions to provide security for the less fortunate was increasingly manifest. Rural residents," he adds, "were alarmed not only by the moral and social problems of the cities and towns but also by the depopulation of their own communities."[12]

By the turn of the century a number of social groups were becoming increasingly concerned with circumstances such as these. The most important, though by no means the oldest of these groups, consisted of the lay members and clergy of some Protestant churches, many of whom were struck with an apparent contradiction between Christianity and "cut-throat competition". In the early years of the twentieth century, the "social gospel", as the new philosophy was called, grew into a full-fledged social movement.[13] It emerged from within existing religious institutions with the result that it was essentially revivalistic. The intent was not necessarily to destroy the established churches, but to redirect them in pursuit of social goals that were embodied in Christian teaching. To this end, inter-denominational committees were established to facilitate communication and the actual implementation of specific reforms. The Social Gospel movement not only sought to influence the legislatures of the various provinces and the Dominion, but also established "settlement houses" and provided educational and welfare services to meet the immediate needs of the disadvantaged. To this extent, the Social Gospel movement, by and large, worked *within* the traditional structure of Canadian society while at the same time forming new institutions.

Closely connected with the Social Gospel movement were the temperance and women's suffrage movements. Although, in some provinces, the temperance movement dated from the middle of the last century, it did not really gain momentum until it became connected with the general reform zeal of the Social Gospel movement in the early nineteen hundreds. Indeed, in some provinces, leaders of the Social Gospel movement were also leaders of the temperance and suffrage movements.

Since many reformers made a connection between the emerging industrial order and alcoholism, it is not surprising that there was a close association between the Social Gospel movement and the forces favouring temperance. Less clear, perhaps, is the link between these two movements and the suffrage movement. But many supporters of the Social Gospel movement were convinced of the regenerative effect that female participation would have in an otherwise corrupt political system. Moreover, some practical concerns helped form a strong organizational link between these movements and a fusion of ideology. The women's cause could easily be seen as related to the struggle for decent wages. As C.L. Cleverdon pointed out, "women have emerged from their homes into the industrial and commercial worlds, either voluntarily or through pressure of economic necessity. Flooding the labour market, they forced down not only their own wages, but also the general wage level."[14] Many people reasoned that if women became enfranchised, they would assist more forcefully in the general fight against wage inequities for their own sex, as well as for the working class in general.

Although the fight for women's suffrage was less sensational in Canada than in either Great Britain or the United States, votes for women were eventually won. To this extent the suffrage movement achieved its objectives. Despite some remarkable concessions, success is perhaps less evident for the Social Gospel and temperance movements. Adherents to the Social Gospel, through persistence and hard work, managed to influence some very important welfare legislation. However, internal factionalism, disagreement regarding the stance to take on the Winnipeg General Strike, and labour unrest in church publishing houses, spelled disaster for the movement as a whole. In addition, although the temperance movement was able to achieve, for varying periods of time in different provinces, either partial or full prohibition of the sale of liquor, it became increasingly evident in the twenties that enforcement of such legislation was virtually impossible. This realization, together with other factors, led to a gradual abandoning of prohibitionist legislation and to the eventual dissolution of the movement that had advocated it. The suffrage movement alone fully realized its objectives.

From the discussion thus far, it is clear that an understanding of the social movements that blossomed during the early years of the twentiety century is dependent upon an appreciation of the historical context in which they developed. This period in Canadian history was marked by a great deal of immigration and urbanization. At the same time, although traditional staples such as timber and wheat retained places of prominence in the Canadian economy, the urban manufacturing sector was rapidly expanding. Since many Canadian institutions were unable to handle the consequences of these processes, and since the elite remained, for the most part, unconcerned with the increasing misery of great numbers of Canadians, a sense of ambiguity and discontent developed among some groups of Canadians, especially within the already established churches. Out of a concern with contemporary abuses arose three distinct yet highly inter-related social movements, with social reform as their primary objective. In none of these movements was there any significant attempt to go beyond already accepted ways of doing things. Within this framework the suffrage movement attained its goal, the Social Gospel movement influenced the enactment of a great number of legislative reforms, while the success of the temperance movement was fleeting to say the least. None became routinized or remained a permanent feature of the Canadian scene. It will be evident from later chapters, however, that the consequences of these movements went beyond the attainment of immediate goals.

The articles that follow have been arranged to facilitate an understanding of these social movements. In the first two, the Social Gospel movement and the prohibition movement are analyzed in some depth. The remaining article examines the relationship among several movements in the West, where they enjoyed their greatest success.

Notes

1. M.C. Urquhart and K. Buckley, (eds.), *Historical Statistics of Canada*, Toronto: Macmillan, 1965, p. 14. For an excellent analysis of this period see R.C. Brown and R. Cook, *Canada 1896-1921: A Nation Transformed*, Toronto: McClelland and Stewart, 1974.

2. Brown and Cook, *Canada 1896-1921*, p. 49.

3. G.W. Bertram, "Economic Growth in Canadian Industry, 1870-1915," in W.T. Easterbrook and M.H. Watkins, (eds.), *Approaches to Canadian Economic History*, Toronto: McClelland and Stewart, 1967, p. 89.

4. *Ibid.*

5. Urquhart and Buckley, *Historical Statistics of Canada*, p. 59.

6. R. Allen, Introduction to J.S. Woodsworth, *My Neighbour*, Toronto: University of Toronto Press, 1911/1972, p. ix.

7. Woodsworth, *My Neighbour*, p. 10.

8. Herbert Ames, *The City Below the Hill*, Toronto: University of Toronto Press, 1897/1972, p. 105. Also see T. Copp, *The Anatomy of Poverty: The Condition of the Working Class in Montreal, 1897-1929*, Toronto: McClelland and Stewart, 1974.

9. S.D. Clark, *Church and Sect in Canada*, Toronto: University of Toronto Press, 1948/1965, p. 389.

10. *Ibid.*, p. 390.

11. For a contemporary discussion of these processes see J.S. Woodsworth, *Strangers Within Our Gates*, Toronto: University of Toronto Press, 1909/1972.

12. E.R. Forbes, "Prohibition and the Social Gospel in Nova Scotia," *Acadiensis*, below. See also W.R. Young, "Conscription, Rural Depopulation and the Farmers of Ontario, 1917-1919," *Canadian Historical Review*, LIII, no. 3, (September, 1972). For further discussion of social problems see James Gray, *Red Lights on the Prairies*, Toronto: Macmillan, 1971; and James Gray, *Booze*, Toronto: Macmillan, 1972.

13. For a full discussion of the Social Gospel movement see R. Allen, *The Social Passion*, Toronto: University of Toronto Press, 1971. Also see S. Crysdale, *The Industrial Struggle and Protestant Ethics in Canada*, Toronto: Ryerson, 1961.

14. C.L. Cleverdon, *The Woman Suffrage Movement in Canada*, Toronto: University of Toronto Press, 1950, p. 10.

The Social Gospel
and the Reform Tradition
in Canada, 1890-1928

Richard Allen

The literature of social reform has not been extensive in Canada even though a sizable movement of reform was abroad in the land from the 1890s through the 1930s, a movement that was found in church and in secular society, and at municipal, provincial, and, progressively, federal levels. In the last chapter of his *Progressive Party in Canada*, Morton sees the decline of that party as a result in part of the waning of the impulse towards reform in society as a whole. Underlying and accompanying the movement towards reform through the political system had been the social gospel, a movement of which the most important function was to forge links between proposed reforms and the religious heritage of the nation, thus endowing reform with an authority it could not otherwise command. At the same time it attempted to create the religious and social attitudes thought necessary for life in a world reformed. But the world proved too intractable for the realization of the movement's high socio-religious hopes, and in the wake of the frustrating experiences of the early 1920s, supporters of the social gospel, and other reform movements, took different paths; some withdrew from politics, some retreated to pragmatic politics, some transferred their enthusiasm to other causes (notably peace movements and personal religion), and others moved towards a new radicalism. The reform movement may be viewed from many standpoints, but only when it is looked at as a religious manifestation, a striving to embed ultimate human goals in the social, economic and political order, is its success and failure fully appreciated. The history of the social gospel in Canada is an account of that process.

The social gospel rested on the premise that Christianity was a social religion, concerned, when the misunderstanding of the ages was stripped away, with the quality of human relations on this earth. More dramatically, it was a call for men to find the meaning of their lives in seeking to realize the kingdom of God in the

Reprinted from the *Canadian Historical Review*, Vol. 49, No. 4, 1968, pp. 381-389, by permission of the author and University of Toronto Press.

very fabric of society. It was a measure of the radicalism implicit in the Social Gospel that the Methodist church in 1918 called for complete social reconstruction by a transfer of the basis of society from competition to co-operation. It was a measure of the conservatism inevitably associated with such a call that even some of the most radical supporters of the social gospel believed that in the family as they knew it, and in the political democracy of their time, two essential elements of the society toward which Jesus pointed men were already in existence, or virtually so. Such a reduction was necessary to apply a pan-historical and transcendent concept to immediate needs. And without such reduction the reform movement would have enjoyed considerably less power.

The Protestant background out of which the Canadian social gospel had to emerge was one dominated overwhelmingly by the Anglican, Methodist, and Presbyterian churches. The similarities and disparities in the social outlook of these churches prior to the onset of depression in the late nineteenth century may be suggested by their reactions to a strike of the Toronto Printers' Union in 1872. The Anglican *Church Herald* condemned the labourers for usurping the role of the employer and blamed the strike upon "the insidious whimperings of a foreign-born league." The *Presbyterian Witness* argued that labour's campaign "strikes at the very root of . . . personal independence and perpetuates their social demoralisation. . . . No man ever rose above a lowly condition who thought more of his class than of his individuality." The Methodist *Christian Guardian* declared a profound sympathy with all honest workingmen and a sincere desire for their betterment, but went on to say: "we seriously question the wisdom and advantage of this movement — especially the strikes to which it is likely to lead."[1] When news of Henry George's Anti-Poverty Society reached Toronto in 1887, the other two churches would probably have echoed the response of the *Christian Guardian* on 29 June: "We have no faith in the abolition of poverty by any laws that can be made in legislatures. . . . The best anti-poverty society is an association of men who would adopt as their governing principles in life, industry, sobriety, economy and intelligence." Such an individualistic ethic was unable, however, to withstand the combined onslaught of extended depression, the rapid growth of industrial urban centres, and the spread of new social conceptions.

It has been argued that the social gospel in Canada was an indigenous development.[2] Although it is possible that a Canadian social gospel might have developed simply in response to domestic urban and industrial problems, it did not in fact happen that way. To be sure, the earliest expressions of the social gospel in Canada may still lie in sources untouched by historians' hands. And in those sources, the rise of the social gospel may be obscured by the gradual nature of its separation from older forms of Christian social expression characterized by a concern for church-state relations, education, political corruption, and personal and social vice. But almost all evidence regarding the emergence of the social gospel from this tradition points to currents of thought and action which were sweeping the western world, none of which originated in Canada. To trace this "North Atlantic triangle" of culture and religion underlying the social gospel at large and its transmission to and development within Canada is a worthy but massive project. In this paper, only a description of some of its salient features can be attempted.

The inspiration of the pioneers of the social gospel in Canada and the origin of some of its prominent institutions reveal the extent of its indebtedness. W.A. Douglass in the 1880s expressed his disagreement with individualistic methods of social regeneration by tirelessly campaigning for Henry George's panacea of the single tax.[3] Salem Bland, later to become the philosopher and mentor of the movement, was an omnivorous reader, and in the decade of the 1890s when he seems to have first formulated a social gospel outlook, was especially influenced by Carlyle, Tennyson, Emerson, Channing and Thoreau, by the historical critics of scripture, and by Albert Ritsehl, the great German theologian whose optimistic theology played a great role in the emergence of a social gospel theology. At least as significant for Bland was the literature of evolution.[4] The notes for his first socialist lecture, "Four Steps and a Vision," acknowledge various works of Darwin, Drummond's *Ascent of Man*, and Kidd's *Social Evolution*, as well as *Fabian Essays*, Arnold Toynbee, Edward Bellamy, and Henry George.[5] Canadians had attended the three great interdenominational conferences in the United States on social problems in 1887, 1889, and 1893, and one follow-up conference had been held in Montreal in the latter year.[6] Institutional vehicles and expressions of the social gospel such as the Brotherhoods, institutional churches, settlements and labour churches derived ultimately from British models, although American mediation and modification took place in some instances. This pattern of influence continued throughout the life of the social gospel in Canada.

The optimism of the social gospel drew on more than a generalized sense of progress, and even on more than the influence of evolutionary concepts. One of the more significant religious developments of the nineteenth century was the expansion of evangelicalism — expressed variously in German pietism, the Methodism of the English-speaking world, the missionary movement, and American revivalism. As against the reformed tradition of Calvinism, evangelicalism stressed free will, an immanent God, religious emotion, and a restrictive personal and social morality which made its followers formidably austere. Among its doctrines was a belief in the possibility of personal perfection beyond the temptation of sin. In the course of the nineteenth century it made an immense impact on all Christian traditions, especially in North America. As evangelicalism became more diffused in the latter half of the century and awareness of the social problem arose, the individualism of the evangelical way seemed to many to be less and less appropriate.[7] The demand "save this man, now" became "save this society, now," and the slogan "the evangelization of the world in our generation" became "the Christianization of the world in our generation."[8] The sense of an immanent God working in the movement of revival and awakening was easily transferred to social movements, and hence to the whole evolution of society. Thus Josiah Strong in the United States could speak of the "great social awakening," and many could come to view secular social action as a religious rite.

Such combinations of ideas and impulses were apparent in a sermon given to the first Brotherhood group in Canada on 14 April 1895. Speaking on "Social Resurrection," J.B. Silcox argued that Jesus' "resurrection means that humanity shall rise . . . into higher, nobler, diviner conditions of life." He joined several British thinkers, preachers, and writers, he said, in predicting a worldwide revolution for the people in the twentieth century. "This uprising of the people is divine in its source. . . . God is in the midst of it. . . . To the ecclesiastical and industrial Pharaohs of today, God is saying, 'Let my people go.' " He concluded by calling for "a political faith in Jesus" based on the charter of the Sermon on the Mount.[9] C.S. Eby in *The World Problem and the Divine Solution* (1914) was somewhat more philosophical in expression. Jesus Christ was the "type of coming man on this planet." The ultimate reality of which Christ was the revelation was in and through all things: "the universal spirit of Christ would reconstruct man and mankind." Trade unionism, socialism, and business organization were a work of this spirit developing a new social order.[10] On this basis Eby built his Socialist church in Toronto in 1909.[11] Many influences from the world of letters, science, religion, and reform were held in solution in the social gospel in various proportions. Few distilled the solution as did Douglass, Bland, Silcox, and Eby, and while they might be more radical than most, their thought represented the tendency of the movement as a whole.

The pressures of the last years of depression in the early 1890s precipitated a quickening interest in new forms of social thought and action among a growing group of Christian ministers and laymen. One of the most important centres of this interest was the Queen's Theological Alumni Conference, instituted by Principal G.M. Grant in 1893. At its annual meetings, the conference discussed papers on such topics as biblical criticism, economic development, the problems of poverty, socialistic schemes, the single tax, social evolution, interpretations of modern life by modern poets, studies of the prophets, Tolstoi, the relation of legislation and morality, and Christianity in its relation to human progress. As a Methodist minority among Presbyterians, Salem Bland was probably the most radical of the regular members.[12] At the beginning of the decade a pirated edition of General William Booth's *In Darkest England and the Way Out* was selling vigorously.[13] Booth's scheme, involving the establishment of labour exchanges, farm colonies and industrial towns, model suburban villages, paid holidays, and an intelligence service for processing useful social data, was branded by some as socialistic, but encouraged others to view social action as an essential part of true religion.[14] Two Canadian ministers, S.S. Craig and Herbert Casson, taking their cue from John Trevor in Manchester, attempted to found labour churches. Nothing more is known of Craig's venture in Toronto,[15] but Casson's attempt at Lynn, Massachusetts, lasted from 1893 to 1898, after which he became a well-known socialist lecturer in Canada as well as the United States.[16] The Congregationalist layman, T.B. Macaulay, in 1894 brought the Brotherhood movement from England to Montreal, whence its "brief, bright and brotherly" meetings, which mixed gospel songs with social reform, spread across the nation.[17]

Among social problems, those of slums and immigration prompted the larger part of the institutional response of the social gospel within the churches. Again, it was in the last decade of the nineteenth century that the more ambitious innovations were undertaken with the establishment of St. Andrew's Institute in 1890 by the Presbyterian, D.J. Macdonnell, and the Fred Victor Mission in 1894 by a Methodist group under the impetus of the Massey family. Together providing facilities for night school, library, savings bank, nursery, clubrooms, gymnasium, medical centre, and restaurant, they reflected ventures pioneered in England, Scotland, and the United States in the previous decade.[18] Further institutional response to urban problems came after 1902 with the development of settlement houses by Miss Sara Libby Carson, working under the Presbyterian church. By 1920 there were at least thirteen settlements in Canada, probably all of them formed under the impulse of the social gospel.[19] Where Miss Carson was not involved directly as organizer, she was often associated as consultant, as in the cases of the Toronto and McGill University settlements (1907 and 1909 respectively), which grew out of social concern in the student YMCAs. When the University of Toronto opened its Department of Social Service in 1914, the University Settlement provided the framework for practical work, and Miss Carson and the Rev. F.N. Stapleford of the Neighbourhood Workers' Association, among others, were recruited as lecturers.[20] Under J.S. Woodsworth, the settlement approach to the problems of north Winnipeg became a more potent spearhead of social reform, and the beginning, for Woodsworth, of an ever more radical formulation of the social gospel.[21]

In the 1890s, the churches were deeply involved in a mounting campaign against "drink." This was rationalized by leading figures such as F.S. Spence as part of the great gospel of liberty.[22] Significantly, however, a rude sort of environmentalism was creeping into the "ideology" of prohibition, placing it in the context of a reform programme based on the strategy of reform Darwinism: that the way to reform the individual was through alterations in his environment. As a wider array of social problems began to engage the minds of clergy and laymen alike, new committees and church structures were required. The Methodist Committee on Sociological Questions from 1894 to 1918 presented to general conference ever more progressive and comprehensive reports for church guidance. By 1914 committees or departments of temperance and moral reform had become full boards of social service and evangelism. The social task had been placed alongside that of evangelism in the official hierarchy of concerns of the Methodist and Presbyterian churches, and committees of social service were common in the other denominations. In 1913, when Methodists and Presbyterians combined in a programme of social surveys of major Canadian cities (and some rural areas), a systematic attack, chiefly upon the complex environment of the cities, was in the making.[23]

In the background of this escalation of social gospel enterprise was an ambitious effort at institutional consolidation. The Church Union movement, initiated in 1902, was making headway, and in 1907, an alliance of church and labour groups, having won the Lord's Day Act, blossomed into the Moral and Social Reform Council of Canada, jointly headed by J.G. Shearer and T.A. Moore, social service secretaries of the Presbyterian and Methodist churches respectively. Although until the middle of the second decade the provincial units of the council were largely engrossed in temperance campaigns, for several years thereafter they promoted a broad programme of social reform and community action that won the praise of young radicals like William Ivens and William Irvine.[24] In 1913 the national organization changed its name to the Social Service Council of Canada and further broadened its perspectives.[25]

These years were exciting ones for progressive churchmen. Not only were they advancing their campaign to win the churches to what they called sociological concepts, but they were also making significant progress in liberalizing the restrictive personal disciplines of their denominations and gaining ground for historical criticism and a reformation of theological curricula.[26] During and after 1908 a lively discussion on the relation of Christianity to socialism developed. The subject had been kept alive by a small group among whom were Bland, the Rev. Ben Spence, the socialist-prohibitionist who in 1904 managed A.W. Puttee's campaign to win a second term as a labour MP,[27] A.E. Smith, who endorsed labour candidates in successive pastorates at Nelson, B.C., and Winnipeg and Brandon, Manitoba,[28] and the Rev. W.E.S. James, who was general secretary from about 1905 of the Christian Socialist Fellowship in Ontario and organizer in 1914 of the Church of the Social Revolution in Toronto.[29] A wave of millennial socialism in Britain after the election of 1906, the controversy surrounding R.J. Campbell's *New Theology*,[30] and touring lecturers such as Keir Hardie (1908 and 1912) and the Rev. J. Stitt Wilson (1909 and 1910), who preached the message of socialism as applied to Christianity, undoubtedly spurred discussion in Canada.[31]

Both socialists and clerics picked up the theme. In 1909 W.A. Cotton, editor of the Canadian socialist journal, *Cotton's Weekly*, developed the notion that Jesus had been the original labour leader.[32] In 1910 a large meeting in Montreal heard an exposition of socialism based on the Bible, and the prominent socialist from British Columbia, E.T. Kingsley of the Socialist Party of Canada, declared

Christianity and socialism to be identical. The current did not run all one way, of course. A group of Toronto socialists in November 1910 devoted at least one evening to the subject, "Why a Socialist Can Not Be a Christian."[33]

After 1908 professed socialists in the churches seem not to have been so isolated or so peripheral. In that year the Rev. Dr. D.M. Ramsey in Ottawa described socialism as "carrying into economic regions the Christian doctrine of human brotherhood."[34] The Rev. Elliott S. Rowe organized socialist leagues in Sandon and Victoria, B.C.[35] Bryce M. Stewart in his survey of Fort William in 1913 found a considerable number of Christians sympathetic to socialism, and observed: "It is beyond question that in purity of purpose, ethics, and scientific reasoning the socialist position is far beyond any other political organization, and should appeal especially to the Christian."[36] In the same year, the Rev. Thomas Voaden of Hamilton, in a series of lectures later published, presented the thesis that socialism was the effect of Christianity forced outside the churches.[37] But that socialism was not entirely outside the churches was becoming more and more apparent. In a survey of London, Ontario, in 1913 by the Brotherhoods of that city, it was found to be common opinion in the churches that neither unions nor socialist groups threatened or interfered with the church's work, and further, men of both organizations were found among the church's workers.[38]

Given the groundswell that seemed to be building up for the social gospel as the twentieth century entered its second decade, it was not surprising that when the Social Service Council called a national congress on social problems for March 1914, the response was overwhelming. For three days over two hundred regular delegates from across the nation, representing welfare organizations, churches, farm and labour groups, municipalities, provinces, and the federal government, were subjected to a barrage of social statistics, social conditions, social challenges, and social exhortations.[39] Most of the forty Canadian speakers were from central Canada, and although the rural problem was considered, speakers overwhelmingly represented urban areas: social workers, city judges and politicians, city doctors, labour leaders, college professors, city clergy. Although city oriented, the world of business management and ownership was conspicuous by its absence.

This was primarily a professional man's conference. Its social sources lay outside and below the centres of power which were forging the new Canada. The lines of sympathy were clear in the enthusiastic response to the claim of a visiting speaker that "there is so much religion in the labor movement and so much social spirit in the Church, that someday it will become a question whether the Church will capture the labor movement or the labor movement will capture the Church."[40] Not all the speakers gave evidence of the social gospel, but when their concerns were related to other information about them, the inferences seemed clear: Dr. Charles Hastings, Toronto's medical health officer, was a Presbyterian elder, a past chairman of the Progressive Club, and a member of the

Public Ownership League;[41] J.O. McCarthy, Toronto city controller, was a leading figure in the Canadian Brotherhood Federation and a member of the Methodist Board of Social Service and Evangelism;[42] James Simpson, vice-president of the Trades and Labor Congress, was a Methodist local preacher, a lecturer for the Dominion Prohibition Alliance, a vice-president of the Toronto branch of the Lord's Day Alliance, and a perennially successful socialist candidate for offices of city government in Toronto who was consistently supported in his campaigns by the Epworth League, the Methodist young people's organization.[43] In short, it seemed that to scratch a reformer at the congress was to find a social gospeller.

So popular were the evening open meetings that the *Ottawa Citizen* could not recall any recent visiting theatrical production to rival them and, when the tumult had subsided, concluded on 6 March that the congress had been "one of the greatest assemblages ever held in Canada to grapple with . . . social and economical problems." The congress represented the social gospel entering a crest of influence. C.W. Gordon (Ralph Connor), writing the introduction to the report, was excited by the challenge thrown down to the "economic and social conditions on which the fabric of our state is erected." He may not have been aware of the hint of incongruity in his conclusion that "there is in our nation so deep a sense of righteousness and brotherhood that it needs only that the light fall clear and white on the evil to have it finally removed."[44] Was reform to be won so cheaply? An unevangelicalized Calvinist might have been pardoned his doubts.

During the generation of its ascent, from 1890 to 1914, the social gospel front had remained remarkably united. One could now discern three emphases or wings beginning to crystallize, however. The conservatives were closest to traditional evangelicalism, emphasizing personal ethical issues, tending to identify sin with individual acts, and taking as their social strategy legislative reform of the environment. The radicals viewed society in more organic terms. Evil was so endemic and pervasive in the social order that they concluded there could be no personal salvation without social salvation — or at least without bearing the cross of social struggle. Without belief in an immanent God working in the social process to bring his kingdom to birth, the plight of the radicals would surely have been desperate. Between conservatives and radicals was a broad "centre party" of progressives holding the tension between the two extremes, endorsing in considerable measure programmes of the other two, but transmuting them somewhat into a broad ameliorative programme of reform. The harmony of these wings was not to last. Between 1914 and 1928 the social gospel enjoyed and endured at one and the same time a period of crest and of crisis. Its growing differentiation in church, interdenominational, and secular organizations multiplied its impact on Canadian society, and at the same time initiated interaction between the various modes of its expression. These were the conditions of its potency. They were also the conditions of its crisis, for the encounter with social reality was the true test of social gospel concepts, and the very complexity of that reality and the conflict inherent within it inevitably set one wing of the social gospel in conflict with another. This involved process culminated in the years 1926-8, and the movement generally entered a period of weariness, reaction, and reconsideration.

The war of 1914-18 was the occasion, and in considerable measure the cause, of a crisis in relations between the radicals and the church. In the course of the war four radicals, then or later of some prominence, lost their professional posts: William Irvine, J.S. Woodsworth, Salem Bland, and William Ivens. The situation of each man was complex, but while they all believed their fate to be the result of increasing commercialism in the church and growing reaction in the state, and while Professor McNaught adopts the radicals' arguments as to what happened to them, the thesis is hardly acceptable.[45] It can only be maintained by slighting a number of facts: the acceptance of their radicalism, either prior to their appointment or without protest during a considerable period before severance of employment; the obvious support all had in the courts of the church; the complicating factor of pacifism in two cases; a host of evidence that Bland was more likely a victim of retrenchment in Wesley Theological College; and most important, the growing progressivism of the churches throughout the war period.

The evidence of church progressivism, 1914 to 1918, is more than substantial. All churches were dismayed by the outbreak of war, and the Methodists and Presbyterians at least condemned the profiteering that accompanied it. The Methodist general conference in the fall adopted the strongest reform programme to date and promised a further instalment in four years.[46] The Presbyterian Department of Social Service in 1916 regarded with hope the increase of nationalization and social control of industry in allied countries, and took heart at new Canadian legislation on prohibition, female suffrage, workmen's compensation, and protective legislation, the beginnings of provincial departments of labour, government encouragement of fishermen's co-operative societies in Nova Scotia, and the establishment of a bureau of social research under Woodsworth by the prairie provinces.[47] The Social Service Council sponsored regional congresses carrying on the spirit of its Ottawa success, added several more secular affiliates to its roster, and just prior to the war's end established the first national social welfare publication.[48] The church declarations of social policy in 1918 were further left than the manifestos of any major Canadian party, and approximated the British Labour party's programme for national minimum standards.[49] The Methodist call for a complete social reconstruction received international circulation, and, stated the *New Republic*, placed that church in the vanguard of reform forces.[50]

Radical social gospellers like Ernest Thomas of Vancouver, Bland, and A.E. Smith,[51] had played an important role in the formation of these church resolutions, but for the radicals the most important consequence of their mid-war crisis with church and state was the impact of their association, and hence of the social gospel, on agrarian and labour movements. J.S. Woodsworth was to be found addressing meetings of the Federated Labour party in Vancouver, and writing in the *B.C. Federationist*. William Irvine had become a leading figure in the Non-Partisan League in Alberta, editor of its journal the *Alberta Non-Partisan*, and a key person in the Dominion Labour party in Calgary. William Ivens in 1918 undertook an organizing tour in the prairie region for the Dominion Labour party,[52] stepped into the high priesthood, as the *Voice* put it, of labour forces at Winnipeg by founding a thriving labour church, and became editor of the *Western Labour News*.[53] From 1917 to 1919, Salem Bland contributed a regular column to the *Grain Growers' Guide*, and during the summer of 1918 addressed tens of thousands of westerners (with Henry Wise Wood) from the Chautauqua platform. Adding their voices to the journalism of reform were two more radicals of the social gospel, A.E. Smith as editor of the *Confederate* in Brandon,[54] and James Simpson as editor of the *Industrial Banner* in Toronto.

Despite the wartime crisis, the progressive and radical social gospellers had by 1918-19 reached a position of considerable power and consequence in the Canadian reform movement. And in the conservative wing, the progress of prohibition was startling. The war economy aided the cause, and in 1918 a government order-in-council prohibited further manufacture and sale of liquor until a year after the war's end. But it must be admitted that the temperance forces had won a national consensus on the subject. By 1919 only Quebec held out as a province, and it was at least two-thirds dry by local option. The farm organizations for some time had officially endorsed the reform, and now labour was finding near prohibition a stimulus to union membership.[55] Anglican publications joined other church journals in declaring that if prohibition was good in wartime, it was good in peace as well.[56]

There can be no doubt that the unrest, and especially the great Winnipeg strike of 1919, dealt the social gospel a rude jolt — and yet the impact can be easily exaggerated. The radicals, of course, were in the midst of it, sometimes carried to enthusiastic excesses of rhetoric which could easily be misunderstood. Their social millennialism undoubtedly contributed to the élan and discipline of the strike, but also to an element of unreality in which it was shrouded.[57] The Labour church provided its focus and strove as eight continuing churches in Winnipeg to maintain the essential unity of the left and the religious sense of labour's purpose which had been generated.[58]

The critical question, however, was how the progressive social gospel at large reacted to the events of 1919. The problem was complicated not simply by the growth of conservative reaction inside and outside the churches, but by the complex of attitudes in progressive minds to employers, unions, and social conflict. Generally sympathetic to labour, and persuaded that the spirit of Jesus was in social unrest calling the church to her true function as a defender of the oppressed,[59] they nevertheless believed that the "day of club and bludgeon is gone by," as Creighton described it in the *Christian Guardian*.[60] Misreading the face of power in industry, they were often, as was H. Michel in the *Canadian Churchman*, as pleased with the ending of a strike with improved conditions and shop committees as with recognition of a union and bargaining rights.[61] Nevertheless, the social gospel position held remarkably firm. Of the church press inclined toward the social gospel only the *Presbyterian and Westminster* attacked the Winnipeg strike outright.[62] The *Western Methodist Recorder* sympathized with labour and strike action but attacked the most radical element of strike leadership.[63] The *Churchman* reluctantly conceded the case in the face of government charges of sedition.[64] But the *Christian Guardian* and *Social Welfare* supported the strike throughout.[65] Clergy in and out of Winnipeg frequently spoke out on behalf of the strikers and questioned the government's interpretation and intervention. While the strike was on, numerous church conferences were in progress across the land, and it is difficult to find a case where social policies were modified in the face of unrest — quite the reverse.[66] S.D. Chown, superintendent of the Methodist church, in many addresses urged members to continue to cry out against injustice and to consider the social gospel the voice of prophecy in their time.[67] He has been charged with pronouncing a "ban" on the strikers.[68] He did not, but he was concerned that there was an indiscriminate injustice in the general strike weapon which he could not sanction, and believed that if labour continued such tactics the church might have to be more reserved in its support.[69]

Three events taken together served to heighten that reservation, however, to stalemate the progressives' programme for industrial peace and to perplex the social gospel. Even radicals of the social gospel had long argued that the very collective organization of industry bore out their arguments about the nature of society and hence the nature of the ethic required of modern man.[70] The businessman and industrial owner would surely come to recognize this. However, when in September 1919 the government gathered a national industrial conference with representatives from management, labour and the public, it was almost a total failure.[71] But when the churches conducted an immense Inter-Church Forward Campaign in the winter and spring to equip them for their enlarged social role in the new era, it was an immense success.[72] Some, like Chown, saw in the success a new alliance for progress — the socially minded clergyman and the "new businessman."[73] For some months, the Methodist social service officers had been aware of a small flood of enquiries from businessmen asking guidance as to how to apply the church's policies to their business operations.[74] J.G. Shearer in *Social Welfare* was astonished at the number of plants that had instituted joint industrial councils, although he was suspicious that some at least were intended to forestall unionization.[75]

The dilution of progressivism such developments entailed was completed for many by the printers' strike of 1921, in the course of which the church publishing houses, the Methodist in particular, experienced at first hand the hideous complexities of industrial conflict. The Methodist house encouraged union membership. Depressed business conditions of 1921 precluded meeting all union demands. Nevertheless, with most other printing establishments in Toronto, it was struck on 1 June. Its manager allowed himself to be drafted as chairman of the employers anti-strike committee and soon found himself in the midst of an outright open shop campaign. The union on the other hand not only rejected reasonable offers, but turned on the Methodists with special fury because they seemed not to be living up to their progressive declarations of 1918. Despite an outcry from Methodist summer schools, and frantic negotiations by Ernest Thomas of the Social Service Department, there was little that could be done. Neither the church nor any other business could live now on the terms of the envisaged economic order of social gospel prophecy.[76] Creighton concluded that strikes were simply stupid, and had no constructive word for labour in the great British Empire Steel and Coal Company conflicts of the mid-decade.[77] The Social Service Council drifted from its celebration of the significance of labour in its Labour Day issues to its calm notices of the day at the decade's end.[78] The United church's pronouncement on industry in 1926 simply launched the new church on a sea of ambiguities, which many recognized, but which none could chart more accurately.[79] The bright vision of the social gospel seemed to be going into eclipse.[80]

For a time the upward course of the agrarian revolt and the Progressive party offered new opportunities. From the earlier days of E.A. Partridge, the social gospel had had an intimate role in the theory and practice of the agrarian movements.[81] The churches had attempted to foster social life and community ideals through institutes, conferences, and summer schools.[82] The *Guide* promoted the notion of the church as a community centre.[83] Farm leaders like Drury, Good, Moyle, and Henders were prominent members of social service councils.[84] Band and the Congregationalist, D.S. Hamilton, worked closely with S.J. Farmer and Fred Dixon in Winnipeg on behalf of the single tax and direct legislation.[85] Henry Wise Wood counselled his farmers to look to the church for a social saviour, for it was just now beginning to recognize Jesus as a social leader as well as a personal saviour.[86] Wood's whole programme of civilizational reform was built on the theological assumptions of the social gospel.[87] Since 1903, from Wesley College, Winnipeg, Salem Bland had been sending out young ministers of the social gospel who frequently became members of local units of the Grain Growers' Associations.[88] By 1919 the social gospel had become, in effect, the religion of the agrarian revolt,[89] and its continued involvement in the process of party and policy formation was such that Norman Lambert, secretary of the Canadian Council of Agriculture, observed that religion and social work were inextricably linked with the farmers.[90]

The victories of the Progressive party can, then, be viewed in part as victories of the social gospel. But equally, the failure of the Progressives in 1926 must be weighed on the social gospel scales. In brief, it must be conceded that the social gospel belief that in the rise of such movements true religion and genuine democracy were triumphing together in the modern world contributed to the Progressive party's sense of being something other than a traditional party, and of fulfilling something more than a political role. This non-politics of hope inevitably was ground to pieces in a parliamentary world where alliances were necessary, but compromising, where decisions were mandatory, but the better alternative seldom clear.

At mid-decade, although the great accomplishment of Church Union brightened the horizon, that victory had been won at some cost. The drive to consolidate social service in the new church had worked to the disadvantage of other expressions of the social gospel. Support was withdrawn from the Brotherhood Federation, and the Social Service Council ran afoul of church financing and personal animosities. The former collapsed completely, and the latter, also hit by depression conditions, the counterattacks against prohibition, and the death of its secretary, G.J. Shearer, lived on in a maimed condition.[91] The campaign for a national church made church social service leaders more hostile than they would otherwise have been to the labour churches which had spread to at least ten other cities before collapsing in 1924-5.[92] T.A. Moore of the Methodist Social Service Department had for three critical years of their life played a dubious role with the RCMP in its investigation of the churches.[93] The labour churches, however, died chiefly of their own inadequacy as a religious institution. After 1924 they followed their logical course, with a transfer of religious commitment and zeal to the creation of a more radical reform party via Woodsworth's Ginger Group, and in A.E. Smith's case, one might observe, to the Communist party.[94] Not only did Church Union further drain progressive social gospel energies in the task of institutional reconstruction, but on the morrow of Union, the critical battle in defence of prohibition had to be fought. One by one after 1920 the provincial temperance acts had gone down to defeat. In 1926 the last main stronghold, Ontario, was under attack. The church which was to rally the forces of social righteousness was already fighting a rearguard battle.

At stake was the survival of the conservative social gospel. In the aftermath of defeat the temperance forces were shattered beyond repair.[95] "Old Ontario" has died, declared Ernest Thomas as he launched a careful critique of temperance strategy.[96] The consensus, carefully built up over the years, had disappeared, just as the association of social work and religion so long nurtured under the social service formula was now giving way to secular organizations quite outside, and often severely critical of, the churches.[97]

It was no coincidence that the crisis in the social gospel coincided so nearly with the crisis in Progressive politics and in the reform movement at large. The categories in which they all worked, and the divinities which moved them all, lay shattered. Nevertheless, the lessons of the encounter with reality were not easily absorbed, in part owing to the ease with which the social gospel could transfer its passion from one cause to another. Partly as a positive expression of the social gospel, but also, one suspects, as a sublimation of frustration, much progressive zeal in 1923 transferred itself to a resurgence of pacifism, and after 1926 to a more broadly conceived peace movement.[98] Only among a few individuals like Ernest Thomas and leaders in the Student Christian Movement were penetrating questions being asked about the adequacy of social gospel concepts.[99] Prosperous church expansion in the later 1920s was accompanied by an introversion religiously and by small fellowship groups.[100] But out of the latter, the reconsiderations of the more critically minded, the struggles of the survivors of the political wreck of Progressivism, and a growing dialectic with more radical forms of socialist thought, was to come a new thrust of a reconstructed social gospel in the 1930s.

Notes

1. These reactions of the church press are cited in Stewart Crysdale, *The Industrial Struggle and Protestant Ethics in Canada* (Toronto, 1961), pp. 18-19. It is not unlikely that among the strikers and those who rallied to their support were some who were not prepared to accept the editors' opinions as to their Christian duty (See Doris French, *Faith, Sweat and Politics*, Toronto, 1962). For a fuller account of the social stance of Methodism and Presbyterianism in these years, see Marion Royce, "The Contribution of the Methodist Church to Social Welfare in Canada" (unpublished M.A. thesis, University of Toronto, 1940), and E.A. Christie, "The Presbyterian Church in Canada and Its Official Attitude Towards Public Affairs and Social Problems, 1875-1925" (unpublished M.A. thesis, University of Toronto, 1955).
2. Crysdale, *The Industrial Struggle and Protestant Ethics in Canada*, p. 22.
3. C.D.W. Goodwin, *Canadian Economic Thought* (Durham, N.C., 1961), pp. 32-8; *Toronto World*, 7 Feb. 1898; *Grain Growers' Guide*, 21 Nov. 1917, pp. 32-3.
4. United Church Archives, Toronto (UCA), reading lists in the Bland Papers.
5. Bland Papers.
6. C.H. Hopkins, *The Rise of the Social Gospel in American Protestantism, 1865-1915* (New Haven, 1940), pp. 110-15.
7. For an expression of this transition, see the introduction to General William Booth, *In Darkest England and the Way Out* (London: International Headquarters of the Salvation Army, 1890).
8. The distinction was between bringing the message and creating the social reality. For an illuminating discussion of this process, see Donald B. Meyer, *The Protestant Search for Political Realism, 1919-1941* (Los Angeles and Berkeley, 1960), chap. 1.
9. UCA, J.B. Silcox, *Social Resurrection*.
10. C.S. Eby, *The World Problem and the Divine Solution* (Toronto: William Briggs, 1914).
11. W.S. Ryder, in a paper presented to the Pacific Coast Theology Conference, 1920; *Western Methodist Recorder*, Sept. 1920, pp. 4-5. See also David Summers, "The Labour Church" (unpublished Ph.D. thesis, University of Edinburgh, 1958).

12. Kingston *Daily News*, 14 Feb. 1894; 13 Feb. 1896; 20 Feb. 1896; 11 Feb. 1897; *Queen's Quarterly*, V (April 1898), 316-18; VI (April 1899), 314-16; VII (April 1900), 332; VIII (April 1901), 388.

13. Robert Sandall, *The History of the Salvation Army* (3 vols; London, 1955), III, *Social Reform and Welfare Work*, 80.

14. Alexander Sutherland, *The Kingdom of God and Problems of Today* (Toronto: William Briggs, 1898), p. xiii.

15. Bland Papers, Salem Bland, Sermon at St. James Bond United Church, 31 Oct. 1937.

16. Summers, "The Labour Church," pp. 427ff; Hopkins, *The Rise of the Social Gospel in American Protestantism, 1865-1915*, pp. 85-7; French, *Faith, Sweat and Politics*, pp. 129-30.

17. *Social Welfare*, Oct. 1923, pp. 14-15; W. Ward, *The Brotherhood in Canada* (London: The Brotherhood Publishing House, [1912]). See also F.D. Leete, *Christian Brotherhoods* (Cincinnati: Jennings and Graham, 1912).

18. J.F. McCurdy, *The Life and Work of D.J. Macdonnell* (Toronto: William Briggs, 1897), pp. 23-4, 289-309; Minutes of the Toronto City Missionary Society of the Methodist Church, 29 Dec. 1894, 10 Dec. 1895. For the less well-known Scottish side of the story, see Stewart Mechie, *The Church and Scottish Social Developments, 1780-1870* (London, 1960).

19. *Social Welfare*, Feb. 1929, p. 113. *The Social Service Congress of Canada, 1914* (Toronto: Social Service Council of Canada, 1914), pp. 134-6.

20. *Canadian Student*, Oct. 1919, pp. 16-20; *Social Welfare*, Feb. 1929, p. 113; Murray G. Ross, *The YMCA in Canada* (Toronto, 1951), pp. 215-32.

21. Kenneth McNaught, *A Prophet in Politics* (Toronto, 1959), chap. IV.

22. *Social Service Congress of Canada*, p. 307.

23. UCA, Methodist Church of Canada and Presbyterian Church in Canada, *Reports of Investigations of Social Conditions and Social Surveys*, 1913-14: Vancouver, Regina, Fort William, Port Arthur, London, Hamilton, Sydney.

24. *Voice*, 8 Dec. 1916, p. 8; *The Nutcracker*, 17 Nov. 1916, p. 8.

25. UCA, Moral and Social Reform Council, *Minutes of the Annual Meeting*, 5 Sept. 1913.

26. See H.H. Walsh, *The Christian Church in Canada* (Toronto, 1956).

27. A.E. Smith, *All My Life* (Toronto: Progress Publishing Co., 1949), p. 33.

28. *Ibid.*

29. W.E.S. James, "Notes on a Socialist Church," in Summers, "The Labour Church," pp. 690-6.

30. For an able discussion of these factors in their British context, see Stanley Pierson, "Socialism and Religion: A Study of their Interaction in Great Britain, 1889-1911" (unpublished Ph.D. thesis, Harvard University, 1957).

31. *Canadian Annual Review (CAR)*, 1908, p. 101; 1909, p. 307; 1910, p. 315; 1912, p. 277.

32. *Ibid.*, 1909, p. 306.

33. *Ibid.*, 1910, pp. 315-16.

34. *Ibid.*, 1908, p. 99.

35. Paul Fox, "Early Socialism in Canada," in J.H. Aitcheson, *The Political Process in Canada* (Toronto, 1963), p. 89.

36. Methodist and Presbyterian Churches, *Report of a Social Survey of Port Arthur* (n.p., 1913), p. 10.

37. Thomas Voaden, *Christianity and Socialism* (Toronto: Methodist Book Room, 1913).

38. Methodist and Presbyterian Churches, *Report of a Limited Survey of Educational, Social and Industrial Life in London, Ontario* (n.p., 1913), p. 43.

39. *Ottawa Free Press*, 2 Mar. 1914; *Ottawa Evening Journal*, 3 Mar. 1914; and the record of the conference proceedings cited above, *Social Service Congress of Canada, 1914*.

40. Charles Stelzle, "Capturing the Labour Movement," *Social Service Congress of Canada*, pp. 35-8.

41. *Canadian Men and Women of the Time*, 1912.

42. UCA, Canadian Brotherhood Federation, *Constitution* [and list of officers and General Council], c. 1916.

43. *Canadian Men and Women of the Time*, 1912; *Canadian Forum*, Nov. 1938, p. 229; Summers, "The Labour Church," pp. 690-6.

44. *Social Service Congress of Canada, 1914.*
45. McNaught, *A Prophet in Politics*, pp. 79-85. For a detailed discussion from another point of view, see A.R. Allen, "The Crest and Crisis of the Social Gospel in Canada, 1916-1927" (unpublished Ph.D. thesis, Duke University, 1967), chap. II.
46. See for instance the early reactions of the Methodist Church, *Journal of Proceedings of the General Conference*, 1914, pp. 404-6; 1918, pp. 290-3.
47. Presbyterian Church in Canada, *Acts and Proceedings of the General Assembly*, 1916, Appendix, pp. 13-14.
48. *CAR*, 1918, p. 598. Social Service Council of Canada, *Minutes*, Annual Meeting, January 1918.
49. See the first issues of *Social Welfare*, beginning Oct., 1918; Methodist *Journal of Proceedings*, 1918, pp. 290-3; Statement of the Presbyterian Board of Home Missions and Social Service, *Presbyterian and Westminister*, 10 April 1919, p. 351.
50. *New Republic*, 8 Feb. 1919.
51. *Hamilton Spectator*, 12 Oct. 1918; *Western Methodist Recorder*, March 1919, pp. 5-6.
52. *Voice* (Winnipeg), 19 Apr. 1918.
53. *Ibid.*, 21 June 1918; 5 and 12 July 1918.
54. Summers, "The Labour Church," pp. 379-80.
55. *Edmonton Free Press*, 10 May 1919; *Industrial Banner*, 10 Oct. 1919; *Youth and Service*, Aug., 1919, pp. 114-15; *Western Methodist Recorder*, Oct., 1920, p. 3; *Alberta Labor News*, 25 Sept. 1920; *Christian Guardian*, 30 July 1919, p. 2, quoting John Queen of the Winnipeg strike committee.
56. *Canadian Churchman*, 28 Nov. 1918, p. 763.
57. See William Ivens' euphoric mixture of prophecy, platform rhetoric, and industrial tactics in *Western Labour News*, Special Strike Editions, e.g., No. 3, 19 May 1919.
58. For more extensive discussion of the Labour Churches in Canada, see McNaught, *A Prophet in Politics,* Allen, "The Crest and Crisis of the Social Gospel," Summers, "The Labour Church," and D.F. Pratt, "William Ivens and the Winnipeg Labour Church" (unpublished B.D. thesis, St. Andrew's College, Saskatoon, 1962).
59. Editorial, "I Was Hungry," *Christian Guardian*, 27 Nov. 1918, p. 6.
60. *Ibid.*, 5 Mar. 1919, p. 5.
61. *Canadian Churchman*, 27 Feb. 1919, p. 133; 10 Apr. 1919, pp. 234-5.
62. *Ibid.*, 29 May 1919, p. 344; 10 July 1919, p. 441.
63. *Western Methodist Recorder*, June 1919, p. 8.
64. *Presbyterian and Westminster*, 22 May 1919, p. 497; 29 May 1919, pp. 518-19; 5 June 1919, pp. 549-50.
65. *Social Welfare*, 1 Aug. 1919, pp. 266-70; *Christian Guardian*, 28 May 1919, p. 5; 4 June 1919, pp. 4-5; 11 June 1919, p. 3; 18 June 1919, p. 4; 25 June 1919, p. 4.
66. For a detailed discussion of the more general church reaction, see Allen, "The Crest and Crisis of the Social Gospel," chaps. VI, VII.
67. *Western Methodist Recorder*, June 1919.
68. McNaught, *A Prophet in Politics*, p. 118.
69. *Christian Guardian*, 25 June 1919, p. 2; *Toronto Daily Star*, 12 June 1919, pp. 1, 8.
70. See for instance UCA, Bland Papers, Salem Bland, "Four Steps and a Vision."
71. *Social Welfare*, 1 Nov. 1919, p. 39; 1 Dec. 1919, p. 75; *Christian Guardian*, 1 Oct. 1919, p. 6.
72. *Canadian Baptist*, 1 May 1919, p. 4; 31 July 1919, p. 3; *Presbyterian and Westminister*, 19 June 1919, p. 603; 25 Dec. 1919, p. 594; *Christian Guardian*, 15 Oct. 1919, p. 22.
73. *Christian Guardian*, 30 June 1920, pp. 18-19.
74. *Western Methodist Recorder*, Oct. 1921, p. 4.
75. *Social Welfare*, 1 Sept. 1919, p. 287; 1 Aug. 1920, pp. 316-17; 1 Aug. 1922, p. 235.
76. See A.R. Allen, "The Crest and Crisis of the Social Gospel," chap. XI.
77. *Christian Guardian*, 25 Mar. 1925.
78. *Social Welfare*, Aug. 1927, p. 483; Aug. 1929, p. 242.
79. "The Christianization of Industry," *Social Welfare*, 1 Aug. 1927, pp. 488-9; see also, United Church, Department of Evangelism and Social Service, *Annual Report*, 1924-5, p. 10.
80. See Creighton's reflections on this possibility, *New Outlook*, 12 Jan. 1927, p. 19.
81. *Grain Growers' Guide*, 14 and 28 Aug. 1909; 30 Sept., 6 Oct. 1919.

82. McNaught, *A Prophet in Politics*, pp. 74, 74n.
83. *Grain Growers' Guide*, 7 June 1916; 20 Dec. 1916.
84. Moral and Social Reform Council, *Minutes*, 10 Sept. 1909; Social Service Council of Canada, *Minutes*, 5 Sept. 1913; Manitoba Conference of the United Church, *Minutes*, 1932, p. 42.
85. *CAR*, 1913, p. 578; Manitoba Conference, *Minutes*, 1929, p. 6o; *The Single Taxer and Direct Legislation Bulletin* (Winnipeg), III, 8 (1916).
86. See his Circulars Nos. 9 and 10 for United Farmers of Alberta, Sunday, 27 May 1917, Bland Papers, UCA.
87. *Grain Growers' Guide*, 29 Jan. 1917; 4 Dec. 1918.
88. *Christian Guardian*, 17 Mar. 1920, p. 25; 15 Dec. 1920, p. 14.
89. For further elaboration of this suggestion, see A.R. Allen, "Salem Bland and the Social Gospel in Canada" (unpublished M.A. thesis, University of Saskatchewan, 1961), chaps. V and VI.
90. *Presbyterian Witness*, 23 June 1921, pp. 10-11.
91. The documentation for this is too diffuse to be suggested through a few citations, but may be found in A.R. Allen, "The Crest and Crisis of the Social Gospel," chaps. XIV, XV, XVI.
92. *Ibid.*, chap. X.
93. See correspondence between Moore and Hamilton from 25 May 1920, to 25 April 1922, Papers on Methodist Industrial Relations, 1920-2, UCA.
94. A.E. Smith, *All My Life*, pp. 76-7.
95. United Church, Department of Evangelism and Social Service, *Annual Report*, 1927, pp. 24-5, 27-9; *New Outlook*, 21 Mar. 1928, p. 2; 8 Jan. 1930, p. 46; Dobson Papers, Union College Library, B.C., Hugh Dobson to L.C. McKinney, 30 April 1929.
96. *New Outlook*, 22 Dec. 1926, p. 5; 8 Jan. 1930, pp. 31, 44.
97. In 1926 the Canadian Association of Social Workers was formed, and in 1928 the Canadian Conference of Social Work held its first national meeting. The immediate shrinkage in size of the Social Service Council's annual meetings indicated the impact of these developments on the stature of the council. For an expression of the rationale upon which the council was founded, see *New Outlook*, 10 June 1925, p. 23. For expressions of the new social worker's outlook see J.D. Ketchum, "Judge and be Judged," *Canadian Student*, Nov. 1925; *Social Welfare*, June—July 1926, pp. 189-90; and for a warning about the dangers of a social work that had lost its sense of God, see United Church, Department of Evangelism and Social Service, *Annual Report*, 1927, p. 25. The social gospel stress upon the immanence of God of course abetted the very secularism about which some of them were now concerned.
98. See for instance, *Canadian Student*, Jan. 1924, p. 99; *Christian Guardian*, 20 Feb. 1924, and issues of subsequent months for discussion of the subject; *Social Welfare*, April 1923, pp. 137-9; *New Outlook*, issues of July through December 1925; *Canadian Churchman*, 21 Jan. 1926, p. 36.
99. *New Outlook*, 12 Aug. 1925, pp. 5-6; 12 Feb. 1930, p. 153; *Canadian Student*, March 1925, p. 163; March 1926, pp. 165-6. Student Christian Movement Archives, Minutes of the General Committee, 24-26 Sept. 1926.
100. [Ernest Thomas] *Fellowship Studies* (Toronto: United Church Department of Evangelism and Social Service [1927 or 1928]); *Canadian Student*, March 1926, p. 168; Dobson Papers, Dobson to Armstrong, 14 May 1928.

Prohibition and the Social Gospel in Nova Scotia

E.R. Forbes

The success of the Prohibition movement in Nova Scotia in 1921 was a result of the transformation of a narrow nineteenth century temperance crusade, based upon rural values and ideas of personal salvation, into a broad campaign for progressive reform. Armed with a new idealism, leadership and greatly expanded institutional support, prohibition became politically irresistable. The change was brought about largely through the churches, in which development of a collectivist reform theology accompanied the rise of progressive ideology in secular thought. As influential elements among the clergy became committed to the social gospel, as the new theology was called, they provided both an agency for the propagation of reform ideas and the leadership for their implementation.[1]

Viewed in this context, the popular image of the prohibitionists as frustrated puritanical zealots bent on suppressing the pleasures of others rapidly breaks down. A detailed examination of the prohibition movement in Nova Scotia suggests that the prohibitionists were motivated primarily by a desire to eliminate the roots of human unhappiness. They wanted to create a new society in which crime, disease and social injustice would be virtually eliminated. Their success in committing society to these goals would be reflected both in the victory of prohibition in Nova Scotia and in its ultimate defeat.

The Nova Scotia crusade for prohibition rested upon a strong temperance tradition. In 1827, the community of West River, Pictou County, established what was later claimed to be the first organized temperance group in North America.[2] The extension of an American fraternal order, Sons of Temperance, to Nova Scotia in 1847 gained immediate acceptance and the colony served as a point of export for this item of North American culture to Great Britain.[3] A similar group, the Order of Good Templars, entered the province in the early fifties. By 1900 other "total abstinence" groups included the Women's Christian

Reprinted from *Acadiensis*, Vol. 1, No. 1, Autumn 1971, pp. 11-36.

Temperance Union, the Church of England Temperance Association and the Roman Catholic League of the Cross.

The agitation for prohibition dated from the mid-nineteenth century. It seems to have been spearheaded by the fraternal groups and actively supported by the evangelical churches. By the end of the century the movement had made some progress towards regulating and restricting the sale of alcoholic beverages. The *Report of the Dominion Royal Commission on the Liquor Traffic* in 1895 described Nova Scotia as "a strong temperance province."[4] It noted that liquor could be legally sold only in Halifax City and the two counties of Halifax and Richmond. Of the remaining sixteen "dry" counties, sales were prohibited in twelve under the Canada Temperance Act (Scott Act) of 1878 and in the other four by a stringent provincial act which required an annual petition by two-thirds of the local electorate to permit the renewal of liquor licences. Strong popular support for prohibition appeared to be indicated by the plebiscites of 1894 and 1898 which yielded majorities of more than three to one in favour.[5]

Yet one could easily exaggerate both the extent of prohibition and the sentiment supporting it in Nova Scotia before 1900. Certainly the people had never experienced nor, perhaps, did many of them yet envision, the "bone dry" legislation which would later be attempted. While it is true that the saloon had largely disappeared from rural Nova Scotia, there was nothing in the existing legislation to prevent an individual from ordering liquor from legal outlets. Shipments were regularly sent out by mail coach or train, frequently under the guise of groceries and other merchandise. To facilitate matters, the Halifax merchants deployed agents to take orders and make deliveries. In several towns, sales persisted as local councils, which were responsible for enforcing the Scott and License Acts, arranged "deals" with retailers by which certain periodic fines served to replace the inconvenience of the licencing system.

It is clear that the prohibitionists of the nineteenth century had, to some degree, persuaded governments to regulate and remove the more blatant features of the liquor traffic. By the end of the century, however, it became evident that the politicians were unwilling to go farther. Both federal parties, after stalling by means of royal commissions and plebiscites, made it clear that action could not be expected from them. The Liberal government of Nova Scotia, under the leadership of George Murray, not only rejected any further extension of prohibition but in 1905 appeared to move in the other direction. In that year the government legalized the on-the-premises consumption of liquor in Halifax hotels and extended the hours of sale for that city. It is doubtful if the prohibition movement would have had any greater impact on Nova Scotia had there not been in motion at this time a fundamental change in the social theology of the churches which directly affected their attitude towards prohibition.

In broad terms this change might be seen as part of the growth of a collectivist trend in social thought. In' the 1870's, Herbert Spencer's widely publicized portrayal of society as an evolutionary organism governed by the law of the "survival of the fittest" was initially employed as a doctrine justifying poverty and laissez-faire capitalism. But it soon produced a strong progressive response. Henry George in *Progress and Poverty* and Edward Bellamy in *Looking Backwards*, for example, both accepted organic and evolutionary concepts, but made them the basis for an optimistic projection of social progress and reform.[6]

Collectivism in secular thought was closely paralleled in theology by a similar movement which became known as the social gospel. In the United States, Washington Gladden, Richard Ely and Walter Rauchenbush developed theories of an organic and dynamic society.[7] It was a society which might ultimately be perfected on the principles of the fatherhood of God and the brotherhood of man as expressed by Jesus in the "Sermon on the Mount" and elsewhere. Such a belief transformed the social attitude of many churches. No longer could the primary emphasis be placed on individual salvation. If "Christ . . . came to save society" as the Nova Scotia Methodist Conference claimed in 1907,[8] the churches were obligated to follow his example.

Both the secular and religious movements for reform owed much of their popular appeal to the serious social problems which confronted the people. In Canada the rapid industrialization and urbanization of the Laurier era created or threw into sharp relief a host of social ills. Red light districts abounded in the towns and cities, alcoholism increased sharply, the exploitation of workers became blatant and the failure of traditional institutions to provide security for the less fortunate was increasingly manifest.[9] Rural residents were alarmed not only by the moral and social problems of the cities and towns but also by the depopulation of their own communities. Nova Scotians, who were noted for their strong church allegiance,[10] tended to look to the clergy for leadership in solving their problems. The latter proposed as a general solution implementation of the social gospel — a fundamental reform of society on the basis of Christian principles.

In the latter half of the nineteenth century, the official attitude of most of the Nova Scotia churches towards intemperance was one of personal sin. This provided the basis for their limited support of prohibition. In replies to the survey by the Royal Commission of 1892-4, a spokesman for the Methodist Church based his advocacy of prohibition upon the Church *Discipline* which contained a "footnote" including intemperance among such "sins" as dancing and playing cards. The Presbyterians, although admittedly divided on the question of prohibition, denounced intemperance as "sinful". The Anglicans and Roman Catholics commended personal abstinence, but showed no sympathy for prohibition directly on humanitarian grounds.[11]

The acceptance of the new theology by the churches had profound implications for the prohibition movement. Firstly, the social gospel tended to justify or even compel a church's interference in politics. If society were capable of regeneration along Christian lines, a heavy responsibility rested with the churches to employ every means in bringing this about. To those firmly imbued with the reforming vision, traditional methods of teaching and preaching appeared too slow. Legislation and government activity represented the obvious method of implementing large scale reform. Secondly, the social gospel changed the emphasis and strengthened the motivation in the churches' advocacy of prohibition. It was understandable that progressive churchmen, as they surveyed the ills of their society, should emphasize the problem of intemperance. Not only was alcoholism a serious social problem in itself, but it was thought to be an important contributory cause to a host of other ills, including poverty, disease, the disintegration of the family, and traffic and industrial accidents. Prohibition thus became an integral part of a sweeping programme for social reform. In this form it exerted a much wider appeal particularly among the young and idealistic than under its previous image of a mere crusade against sin. Finally, in accepting the principle of an organic society, the church was subtly undermining the primary grounds for opposition to prohibition — that of the infringement of personal liberty. If Christ died to save society, individual whims and wishes would have to be sacrificed for the same goal. The reformer only need prove that society was being harmed by a certain abuse and it was the duty of the Christian to support its removal, individual "rights" notwithstanding.

If the social gospel contributed to prohibition, the question of prohibition played a key role in the transition of the churches to the social gospel. This was one issue on which religious conservatives and progressives could readily unite. It was thus no accident that the social gospel made its initial appearance in the churches by way of the temperance committees. These in fact served as useful agencies through which the social gospel ethic might be spread in each church.

The Methodists appear to have been among the first in Canada to accept formally the implications of the new ideas. A move in that direction was indicated by the change in name of the Committee on Temperance to that of Temperance, Prohibition and Moral Reform at the Canadian Conference of 1898. This committee became a permanent board in 1902 and Dr. S.D. Chown was appointed its full time secretary. In the Nova Scotia Conference, the change in name of the committee was accompanied in 1903 by what appeared to be a general acceptance of the social gospel. The report of the committee which was adopted by the 1903 Conference declared in its opening sentence that it was the "intention of the Lord that . . . through his faithful ones the principles of the gospel of Christ are to be made supreme in all departments of human activity."[12] The report went on to discuss tactics for the defeat of intemperance, cigarette smoking by the young, commercial dishonesty, social vice and political corruption. In the next three years, other abuses singled out for attack included the opium traffic, race track gambling, prize fighting and in 1906 the committee expressed its wish to investigate "any forms of commercial or industrial oppression affecting our people."[13] As part of their programme for social reform, the members of the Conference in 1905 endorsed the policy of provincial prohibition and pledged themselves to vote only for men who would support this measure in the Legislature. Ministers were urged to promote the cause of "temperance" in the pulpit and the church appointed delegates to attend a Temperance Convention in Truro called to organize a province wide campaign.[14]

More dramatic was the simultaneous adoption of the cause of prohibition and the social gospel by the Maritime Synod of the Presbyterian Church. The convener of the Temperance Committee which proposed the acceptance of the social gospel was H.R. Grant, the man who would dominate the prohibition movement in Nova Scotia for the next thirty years. A native of Pictou County, Grant had undertaken his theological studies at Queen's University where the new theological trends appear to have received full consideration under the principalship of George Monro Grant.[15] After further study at Edinburgh and experience in mission work in Manitoba and New Brunswick, H.R. Grant returned to take charge of the congregation of Trenton in his home county. Keenly interested in temperance and social reform, he served as convener of the Temperance Committee of the Maritime Synod from 1902 to 1907. In 1904 he resigned his charge in Trenton to undertake full time the task of temperance organization in Pictou County. In 1906 Grant participated in the formation of the Nova Scotia Temperance Alliance of which he became general secretary in 1907. He held his post until 1917 when he assumed a similar position in the Social Service Council of Nova Scotia.

In delivering the report of the Temperance Committee to the Maritime Synod in 1907, Grant rejoiced at the "advanced ground" which the General Assembly had taken in creating a committee to investigate such questions as the relation of the church to labour, political and commercial corruption, gambling and the liquor traffic. He then went on to present a clear statement of the principles of the social gospel.

> Public affairs, the social and political business of the country must be brought under the ten commandments and the sermon on the mount . . . the pulpit must have an outlook on the every day life of men . . . the state as well as the individual has a character and the social and political life of the state must obey the . . . teaching of Christ . . . temperance [is] but one of the social, we might say national, questions which the church must consider. . . . Abuses must not only be discovered but reformed as well.[16]

In the following year, the new committee on moral and social reform submitted a series of resolutions calling for the formation of moral and social reform councils and a direct commitment by the Synod to prohibition and other social measures. The resolutions went much further than those hitherto entertained by the General Assembly. One called for the Synod to express its "cordial sympathies with the workingman in all their just and worthy efforts to improve the conditions under which they live and labour" and denounced child labour, "undue long hours of labour" among adults and "conditions associated with the sweating system". Another demanded the adoption of a penal system designed to reform rather than punish.[17] The resolutions appear to have implied too sharp a transition for some members of the Synod and were referred to the presbyteries for further discussion. The next year they were introduced again in the same form, and after an amendment favouring local option had been defeated by "a large majority", passed *in toto*.[18]

The Baptists seem to have pursued a similar course in the direction of the social gospel. In 1903 the Temperance Committee of the Maritime Baptist Convention under the chairmanship of W.H. Jenkins submitted a report which clearly viewed the temperance problem in terms of the social gospel. Christ's "mission", it stated, was both "to save souls" and "to save society". Christ was "the greatest social reformer that the world has ever seen". "Loyal hearts" were needed "to battle boldly with that monster iniquity, the liquor traffic which . . . gathering under its banner all the supreme ills that afflict the people . . . stalks forth to challenge Christianity to mortal combat".[19] In 1908, a resolution of the Convention urged Baptists to "rise above party in voting on questions of temperance and moral reform" and denounced the idea of government control as "complicitly with the drink traffic."[20]

The Church of England, lacking a strong temperance tradition and proud of its conservative stance, responded more slowly to the new ideas. Yet respond it did. Some Anglicans seemed prepared to accept them on the grounds that if members did not find them being implemented in their own church, they might go elsewhere. This was the argument used by the Temperance Committee of 1902 in urging the need for a temperance organization in every parish.[21] Others such as Rev. D.V. Warner of Shelburne, advocated the acceptance of a new social ethic on theoretical grounds and pointed to a social gospel tradition within the Church of England itself. Warner in 1909 published a pamphlet entitled *The Church and Modern Socialism* in which he referred specifically to the tradition of "Christian Socialism" set forth in the writings of the nineteenth century English cleric, Charles Kingsley. By analyzing Christ's teachings as illustrated in the "Sermon on the Mount", the "Lord's Prayer" and other selections from the New Testament, he sought to prove that socialism was closer to "practical Christianity" than was the practice of the Church.[22]

The Anglican debate on the social gospel appeared to reach a climax in the Nova Scotia Synod of 1912. The conservative position was strongly stated in the opening address of Bishop C.L. Worrell. Worrell expressed his alarm that "some of the clergy . . . have endeavored to take up the socialistic tendency of the time" and cautioned against "undue playing with this dynamic force". While it might be proper for individual churchmen to take the lead in movements which tended to the "purity, sobriety and thrift" of the people, it was not the Church's duty to devote its attention to the social problems of the day "except through the general instruction of Christian principles." In conclusion he quoted the dictum of Dean Inge that "political agitation is not the business of the clergy".[23] The Synod disagreed. Its "Report of the Bishops Charge" opened with a reference to the "Sermon on the Mount" and argued that "The Church of God exists for his glory and the true happiness and well being of his children, the sons of men, and therefore anything which emphasizes this aspect of his kingdom is to be fostered and strengthened".[24] By 1914 this creed had been translated into practical action with the formation of a Diocesan Commission of Social Service. A year later the Synod passed a resolution calling for the "fullest possible measures" by Dominion and Provincial legislatures to prevent the sale and use of intoxicating beverages in Nova Scotia.[25]

The Roman Catholic Church in Nova Scotia also reacted favourably to the new ideas. The papal encyclical, *Rerum Novarum* of 1891, had paved the way by its rejection of economic liberalism and condemnation of the exploitation of workers by employers. The Antigonish *Casket*, a spokesman for Celtic Roman Catholicism in the eastern half of the province, displayed an increasing interest in the problems of labour, particularly in the mining areas. In 1909, the Rev. Dr. Thompson of St. Francis Xavier University represented the reform wing of the church in calling for the creation of a strong public opinion, which would empower governments to interfere in the "liberties" of persons and corporations and "put an end to the strikes and lockouts in the most effective way . . . i.e. by removing the causes which produce them."[26]

The Roman Catholic view of prohibition seemed ambiguous. The Antigonish *Casket* conceded that the liquor traffic should be suppressed, but argued that public opinion was opposed and advocated a generous licensing law providing for "drinking on the premises" but limiting licenses to 1 per 750 of population.[27] The *Casket* also suggested that the activities of the League of the Cross, the Roman Catholic temperance organization, should be limited to converting people to temperance through teaching. Yet as early as 1903 the League was reported to be nominating candidates in the municipal elections and in 1907 was campaigning for the repeal of the Scott Act so that the more stringent License Act might apply in Cape Breton County. In that year its president reported a membership of 2108 in 29 branches.[28] While the motivation of the League is unclear, from its actions it would appear that at least some of its leaders were fired by the reform spirit of the age.

Against this background of changing opinion and demand for reform by the churches, a political agitation was building up which would make the passage of prohibition almost unavoidable. But the Liberal administration of Premier George Murray did everything it could to keep from having to act on the question. In fact the story of the struggle for prohibition between 1904 and 1916 is largely the story of a political duel between the temperance forces led by H.R. Grant and the provincial government led by George Murray. On one side were the churches, leading moulders of public opinion in the province, on the other the Liberal Party, holding every seat but two in the Assembly and having as its leader one of the wiliest politicians in the country.

The object of the struggle soon became clear. The Liberals wanted to avoid taking a definite stand on the controversial issue of prohibition. The prohibitionists were determined to manoeuvre the government into a position where it would be compelled to act or publicly demonstrate its disdain for the stated wishes of a large element of the population.

Each year between 1902 and 1905, a bill was introduced to prohibit or render more difficult the sale and shipment of liquor into the dry areas of the province.[29] For the first three years, these were debated briefly and unceremoniously rejected. In 1905, when R.M. McGregor, Liberal MLA for Pictou County, introduced a bill prepared by H.R. Grant and the Pictou County Temperance Association, the members showed greater discretion. The bill, which provided for both the prohibition of the shipment of liquor into the "dry" areas and provincial enforcement of existing legislation, appeared to receive sympathetic consideration from the House. Government members vied with the opposition in expressing their admiration of temperance and "Temperance people". Premier Murray's enthusiasm, however, was tempered somewhat by statements to the effect that his government was not united on the issue and that such a law might be unconstitutional.[30] The bill was approved in principle and then disappeared into committee where it was effectively chopped to pieces.

The churches voiced their anger in unmistakeable terms. In the Presbyterian Synod, the Temperance Committee condemned the legislature for its encouragement of the liquor traffic and called for "more definite, united and aggressive action".[31] The report adopted by the Methodist Conference pledged its members to secure "by voice, influence, and vote the defeat of that portion of the Legislature that stood for the liquor traffic against the moral and material welfare of our people". It concluded:

> If we are to do permanent work we must enter the field of politics as our opponents the liquor interests have done and fight this battle for God and our homes. . . . [We] express the hope . . . [that] the curse of blind partisanship may be done away with and all our people . . . may rise in the strength of God and by the exercise of that God given privilege — the Ballot — smite the liquor traffic to the death.[32]

With an election planned for June of 1906 and the Conservatives committed to a promise of provincial prohibition,[33] Murray decided that an appropriate gesture to the churches would be in order. In the 1906 session, the government introduced a bill prohibiting the shipment of liquor from "wet" to "dry" areas of the province. In general, the bill was similar to those advocated by prohibitionists in previous years. But a large "joker" had been added by the phrase restricting the application of the bill to liquor "to be paid for on delivery".[34] The effect of the bill was merely to require people in rural areas to order their liquor prepaid rather than COD. The Conservatives strove valiantly to make this fact clear, while demonstrating their own championship of prohibition with an amendment designed to restore the restrictive intent of the legislation. Government members replied by strongly denouncing those who would make the "sacred" cause of prohibition a party issue. Only two Liberals broke party lines on the amendment which was defeated eighteen to four.[35]

In the election campaign which immediately followed, prohibition played a prominent role. The Conservatives included in their platform a promise of provincial prohibition within a year of a successful plebiscite on the question. At Pictou, Conservative Leader Charles Tanner issued a reform manifesto which called for prohibition, purity in elections, public interest as opposed to corporate power and betterment of the working classes.[36] In most counties, temperance groups attempted to pledge their members to support prohibitory legislation. The Methodist Conference even went so far as to endorse formally two independents in Kings County.[37] But the Government's last minute "prohibition" bill had helped to blur party divisions on the question and in the constituencies candidates adopted positions which were locally popular. In rural areas where temperance sentiment was strong, such as Yarmouth County for example, all candidates pledged themselves to support prohibition.[38] In Halifax, with its military and seafaring traditions, opposition to prohibition was predominant. Here local Conservative newspapers left the prohibition plank out of the party platform, while Liberal Premier Murray promised the inhabitants that his government would not impose prohibition upon the city without their consent.[39] Thirty-two Liberals, five Conservatives and one "Methodist" Independent were elected.

The Liberals had apparently suffered little on the issue, but the prohibitionists had gained in the election a solid corps of MLA's pledged to support their demands. Meanwhile, the temperance groups of the province co-ordinated their efforts in the formation of the Nova Scotia Temperance Alliance. As secretary of the new organization, Grant stationed himself in the gallery of the Legislature to direct the strategy of the temperance forces.[40] The first step was the introduction of a prohibition bill by E.H. Armstrong of Yarmouth, a young Liberal MLA pledged to the cause in the election. Armstrong made clear that he was serving as the mouthpiece of the Alliance and that he himself had nothing to do with the drafting of the measure.[41] The bill called for the prohibition of the sale of liquor throughout the province and enforcement by provincial inspectors.

The bill was immediately rejected as unconstitutional by the Premier on the grounds that only the government could introduce bills which encroached upon the revenue of the crown. Armstrong was prepared for this development and at once gave notice of a resolution requiring the introduction of the bill by the government.[42] Obviously Grant had manoeuvered the Government into the position he wanted. The resolution could only be debated on the open floor of the House. Members would have to take a definite stand which could be identified by their constituents. Meanwhile, as the debate proceeded, the Legislature was bombarded with over thirty petitions in favour of the legislation and resolutions of support from the Synods and Conferences of the Presbyterian, Methodist and Baptist churches, the Sons of Temperance, the Order of Good Templars and the Grand Orange Lodge.[43]

Armstrong's speech in introducing his resolution clearly reflected the characteristic social gospel approach to prohibition. The measure was necessary as a basic social reform. Problems of poverty, neglect of wives and children, disease, and accidents could be traced in large measure to intemperance. Its influence was both direct, as people on "sprees" caught pneumonia or were injured, and indirect, since in spending their money on "drink", men failed to provide the care and nourishment for themselves and their families necessary to ward off diseases such as typhoid fever or tuberculosis. Armstrong quoted a Dr. Reid who estimated that "90% of the cases in our hospitals are directly or indirectly due to the evil effects of intemperance" and suggested that prohibition might even put the hospitals out of business.[44]

In anticipating possible objections from the critics of the Bill, Armstrong's arguments reflected the growing collectivism of the period. Opponents of prohibition frequently argued that "prohibition was a curtailment of personal liberty". According to Armstrong this view might have some relevance in the "classic past" but not in the twentieth century. "The organic unity of society", he stated, "is a principle political science recognizes at the present time".[45] It was only a question of whether the social weakness at issue was great enough to require a stringent measure of reform.

Armstrong went on to deal with the constitutional argument, which had hitherto been one of the government's favourite means of escape. Reviewing the ancient controversy over whether Dominion or provincial governments had the power to impose prohibition, he cited various decisions of the Judicial Committee of the Privy Council to establish the limits of each level's authority. While it was true that only the federal government had the power to prohibit the shipment of liquor from outside of a province, provincial governments, as had been clearly determined in 1901 in the case of Manitoba, could legally prohibit the sale or shipment of liquor within the province. It was this and no more that the Alliance's Bill proposed to do.

But once again, the members of the Legislature were saved from having to declare themselves unequivocally on the issue. Liberal MLA, C.F. Cooper, Baptist clergyman from Queens County, proposed an amendment calling for an address to the Dominion Parliament to request legislation banning the importation of liquor into "dry" counties from other provinces. When this was achieved, provincial legislation could then be secured to prevent its importation from areas of the province where liquor was legally sold. This, according to Cooper, was a much greater step towards prohibition than the measure proposed by the Alliance.[46]

Certainly Premier Murray was much happier with the latter proposal. The imposition of prohibition in Halifax would be in Murray's words "a dangerous experiment." Nova Scotia was already far in advance of other provinces in temperance legislation and "fully up [to], if not in advance of what public opinion demands".[47] Nevertheless, Murray quite agreed with Cooper's idea of an address to the federal parliament. To Murray the ideal solution was Dominion legislation enforced by municipal authorities.

After a long and tedious debate which filled nearly one hundred pages in the official record, the amendment was carried twenty-two to twelve. The Liberal strategy had worked; the members of the party who wished could still pose as champions of prohibition. Nevertheless, the vote did reveal the friends of the Alliance, as in addition to the Conservative opposition, five Liberals and the independent member opposed the amendment.[48]

At its annual meeting of 1908, the Alliance outlined more clearly the goals which genuine prohibitionists would be expected to support. It wanted to replace the existing jungle of temperance legislation with a federal measure outlawing the importation and manufacture of alcoholic beverages, and a provincial law prohibiting their sale. Both would be enforced by provincial officers. These proposals were presented to an unsympathetic Premier Murray by a delegation from the Alliance led by H.R. Grant. Murray explained that it was government policy to seek an amendment to the Scott Act which would prevent the importation of liquor into the province. Grant refused to be associated with any such legislation, which would apply only to areas where the Scott Act was in effect and merely serve to increase the confusion.[49] In the legislature in 1909 Premier Murray described as "incomprehensible" the Alliance's repudiation of the Government's proposal and suggested that this could only arouse "suspicions" as to the motives of the organization. In a remarkable reversal E.H. Armstrong opposed the prohibition measure introduced by Independent MLA, C.A. Campbell, and suggested that the Alliance was plotting with the Tories.[50]

The Liberal concern was understandable. Far from keeping the "sacred" cause of temperance out of politics, prohibitionists appeared to be using every opportunity to embarrass the government politically and force them to adopt the Alliance programme. Speakers imported from other regions added their testimony to the failure of the government. For example, Dr. J.G. Shearer, secretary of the Committee on Temperance and Moral and Social Reform of the General Assembly of the Presbyterian Church, denounced the lack of law enforcement in Halifax claiming that "sixty-four bar-rooms, with shop licenses which expressly forbid selling for consumption on the premises, are doing business in direct violation of section 63 of the Licence Act".[51]

The prohibition forces were operating from an ever-expanding base. In January of 1909, H.R. Grant represented the Alliance in the creation of the Social Service Council of Nova Scotia, which included representatives of all the major churches, the farmers' associations, organized labour and boards of trade. The provincial organization was to be supplemented by similar councils in the municipalities. Intemperance was listed as one of the primary social problems with which the council proposed to deal and the solution advocated was education and prohibitory legislation.[52]

In 1909 and 1910, by-elections were fought in five counties. In two, Queens and Hants, Conservatives were elected on platforms including provincial probibition.[53] With a general election approaching, the worried Liberals introduced a bill in the session of 1910 providing for provincial prohibition. The bill forbade the sale of intoxicating beverages (those containing more than 3% alcohol) in the province outside the city of Halifax. The only exception was for medicinal, sacramental, art trade and manufacturing purposes. "Spirits" for these uses would be supplied by specially authorized vendors. Liquor might not be shipped from Halifax to any other part of the province unless actually purchased in the city for personal or family use. In the capital city, the number of licenses was reduced from 90 to 70 with further reductions promised. The act was to be enforced by municipal officers under the supervision of a provincial inspector-in-chief. Early in 1911, with an election still pending, the Act was tightened to include all beverages containing alcohol, to prevent societies and clubs from keeping such beverages on their premises and to provide mandatory sentences of three month imprisonment for second offenders. At the same time the Legislature passed a resolution urging the federal government to prohibit the transportation of liquor into the province.[54]

The Alliance had attained a large portion of its demands. The obvious reason for its success was political. The Liberal Government was acting to satisfy an aroused public opinion before the election — a public opinion which had been largely moulded by the influence of the churches under the impact of the social gospel. The weight of this opinion was responsible not only for prohibition. In fact the latter was only one item in a broad slate of reform legislation passed by the Murray Government in 1909 and 1910. Other measures included workmen's compensation, factory legislation, stricter limitations on child labour and a system of contributory old age pensions. In a relatively prosperous economy the vision of a transformed society was yielding practical results. The churches expressed their appreciation to the Government,[55] and in the election of 1911, the Liberals were returned by a comfortable majority of sixteen seats.

The Alliance's pressure on the government was not eased for long. H.R. Grant soon declared that prohibition must be extended to Halifax, both to save the young men of that city from destruction and to cut off a major source of supplies for illicit sale in the rest of the province.[56] In 1912 the Liberals sought to divert attention from this issue by "packing" the annual meeting of the Alliance with government supporters. E.R. Armstrong, by this time a member of the Cabinet, requested several MLA's to have their friends attend the meeting of the Alliance to block "unsound" proposals and the efforts of those who would "complicate the situation as far as the local government is concerned".[57] This attempt was a failure. The following year, Conservative leader C.E. Tanner openly championed the Alliance's cause by introducing an amendment to the Nova Scotia Temperance Act to extend the application of its prohibitory clauses to Halifax. This was defeated eighteen to thirteen. In May of 1914 a similar proposal was lost fourteen to thirteen and in 1915 the measure was defeated only by the vote of the speaker. Early in 1916, with another election just months away, a similar amendment by Conservative H.W. Corning passed with only the three members from Halifax in opposition.[58]

The War was an obvious factor in overcoming resistance. In the final debate, several of the members mentioned the endorsement of prohibition by the Nova Scotia Synod of the Church of England as influencing their decision on the question.[59] Although a prohibition resolution had been submitted to the Synod before the outbreak of war, the matter had been referred to the Social Service Commission for further study. Canon C.W. Vernon, who moved the resolution of 1915, was quoted as saying that he himself had been converted to prohibition by the needs of the war effort and that without the War his motion would never have passed.[60] The need for conservation created by the War was mentioned by some speakers and the need for sacrifice by others. Premier Murray, still very sceptical of the measure, called it "experimental legislation" which the province might afford in "days of strain and stress . . . as we perhaps could not do under more normal conditions".[61] The emotional climate in which the bill was passed was further illustrated in Corning's concluding speech in which he appealed for a moral regeneration of the Empire and quoted Admiral Beatty on the need for a religious revival as a necessary prelude to victory.[62] Amid this climate of idealism and sacrifice the standard objections to prohibition as an infringement of personal liberty appeared to carry little weight.

Yet one should not exaggerate the influence of the war on the prohibition movement in Nova Scotia. The major break-through had taken place in 1910 when the government, protesting that the Alliance's policy of pledging members was "unfair and indecent",[63] had nevertheless enacted a major part of the prohibitionists' demands. In 1914, before the outbreak of the War, prohibition for Halifax had been defeated by only one vote. With the Conservative party becoming clearly identified as the champions of prohibition, it is difficult to see how Murray could have avoided making this concession to the temperance interests before another election. He had acted to disarm his opponents on the issue before each of the previous elections and it is doubtful if he would have acted differently on this occasion. As it was, the Conservatives tried to make Murray's alleged fondness for the liquor interests a major issue in their campaign.[64]

Where the influence of the war did prove decisive, however, was in convincing the federal government to adopt prohibition. In 1916 the Dominion Temperance Alliance called for prohibition for the duration of the war and a three year reconstruction period thereafter. In January, H.R. Grant was a member of a delegation that called upon Robert Borden to press for Dominion prohibitory legislation. In March, the so-called Doherty Bill banned the importation of intoxicating beverages into provinces where provincial legislation was in effect. Since they still might be imported for personal use, this had little effect in Nova Scotia. In December, 1917, as a part of the war effort, the importation of intoxicating beverages was prohibited for the whole country. This still left the door open for Nova Scotians to order, legally, in unlimited quantities, liquor for personal use from Quebec.[65] Finally in March of 1918, by an Order-in-Council under the War Measures Act, the manufacture and sale of intoxicating beverages was prohibited throughout the whole country. Thus "bone-dry" prohibition came to Nova Scotia for the first time.

Thereafter attention shifted to the problem of enforcement. In 1917 the temperance forces of Sydney organized a citizen's league which campaigned in the Municipal elections and overturned a council which it claimed had failed to enforce the Act.[66] Inspector-in-chief J.A. Knight stated that "on the whole" prohibition in Halifax had been a success.[67] On this occasion Knight's opinion appeared to be supported by statistics, as the number of arrests for drunkenness in the province, which had reached 3614 in 1916, dropped to 2546 in 1917.[68] Evidence of improvement in restricting consumption of alcoholic beverages came from other sources as well. Sixty-nine per cent of the Anglican clergy of Nova Scotia who responded to a poll by the Council for Social Service of the Church of England in 1919, testified to the success of prohibition in their province.[69] Perhaps even more indicative of the drying up of traditional sources of supply was the Inspector-in-chief's report of 1919, which for the first time mentioned smuggling and moonshining.[70] It was apparent that prohibition was beginning to make a significant impact upon the province.

On December 31, 1919, the Orders-in-Council prohibiting the importation of liquor were repealed in favour of an amendment to the Canada Temperance Act, providing for provincial plebiscites on the question. A simple majority vote in favour of prohibition would result in the extension of the necessary federal legislation to the province concerned. In Nova Scotia the plebiscite was scheduled for October 25, 1920, after the provincial election of that year. Meanwhile, the people quenched their thirst and stocked up for the dry years to come.

By the time of the plebiscite, prohibition had acquired new enemies and friends. Organized labour made unsuccessful representations to the legislature to plead for the exemption of beer from prohibitory legislation and thereafter became increasingly hostile.[71] Organized farmers took the opposite view and in 1920 the newly-formed United Farmers' Party campaigned on a platform advocating "bone-dry" liquor legislation.[72] Nevertheless, with the plebiscite already scheduled, it is doubtful if prohibition played a major role in the election of 1920. Challenged by the new farmer and labour parties, but taking full advantage of the division among its opponents, the Murray Government remained in power on a minority of the popular vote and lost only one seat from its majority in the House.[73]

The most important accession to the temperance forces was the direct support of the Roman Catholic Church, the largest denomination in the province. During the campaign for the plebiscite, the Antigonish *Casket* came out strongly for prohibition claiming it "has done wonders but it has not yet had time to do its best". This was supported by a letter from Bishop James Morrison of Antigonish which concluded ". . . let me say once more than (sic) the adoption of the prohibitory law has my strongest word of approval, and let us all hope it will be given a fair trial in this province."[74] In the plebiscite, Nova Scotians declared for prohibition 82,573 to 23,953, the largest support for prohibition ever recorded in the province.[75] Every county yielded a majority except Halifax, whose people still appeared to resent the fiat imposed upon them in 1916.

The overwhelming victory of prohibition in the plebiscite again reflected the strength of the social gospel sentiment which seemed to reach its climax in Nova Scotia after the War. As in the rest of the country, however, other reform measures associated with the movement did not enjoy similar success. All provinces faced the problem of lack of revenue which most reforms required. The aging Murray Administration was prepared neither to incur the odium of increased taxes nor to offend corporations with fundamental changes in labour legislation. Its sole gesture to the mounting demands for reform immediately prior to the election of 1920 was the appointment of a Royal Commission to consider "mother's allowances".[76] That this was much less than the people demanded is indicated both by the appearance in the election of the new farmer and labour parties and the support of 55 percent of the voters for the hastily-assembled and divided opposition.

The prohibition movement had reached its zenith by 1921 and thereafter began a gradual decline. The social gospel ideology on which it was based was approaching a crisis which would undermine its position of influence within the churches. Already it had been compromised to some extent by the Russian Revolution. In urging a fundamental reconstruction of society most social gospel reformers were forced to distinguish after 1917 between the right and wrong kinds of revolution. Many clergymen apparently judged from the newspaper reports available in Nova Scotia that the Winnipeg General Strike of 1919 was a dangerous experiment of the wrong kind. The focus of Communist activity in Cape Breton in the early 1920's — especially the activities of J.B. McLachlan, leader of the largest union in the province (District 26 United Mine Workers), in promoting "Bolshevist" doctrines and attempting to affiliate his union with the Red International[77] — tended to confirm their fears and strengthened the conservative element in the churches. The dilemma of the social gospel wing was reflected in the churches' initial failure to support labour in its critical struggle with the British Empire Steel Corporation. Not until International President John L. Lewis dismissed McLachlan and his radical executive in 1923 did the assistance materialize which one might expect from a socially committed clergy.[78]

The re-imposition of Federal prohibitory legislation on Nova Scotia in February of 1921 did mark the beginning of a "new era" in the province, but it turned out to be the era of the "rum-runner". In January 1920, the Volstead Act prohibited the importation of liquor into the United States. An elaborate system of smuggling quickly evolved in which the Nova Scotian fisherman and ship owners came to play a prominent role. With the return of prohibition to Nova Scotia the new techniques were applied at home.

Attempts to enforce the legislation led to co-operation between Custom officers attempting to prevent smuggling, the Department of Revenue officers hunting for stills and the Temperance inspectors trying to suppress bootlegging. Assisting all three were the prohibitionists, operating on their own initiative in an attempt to make effective the legislation for which they had worked so hard. Thus in 1921, these groups began a game of "cops and robbers" with the smugglers, bootleggers and moonshiners which would continue until the end of the decade.

It was a game which before long the ill-equipped, untrained and quite inadequate municipal and provincial officers were obviously losing. In 1925, a discouraged Inspector-in-chief, J.A. Knight, gave the following assessment:

> So much liquor is now smuggled and distributed throughout the Province in motor cars and by bootleggers that the closing of bars and blind pigs does not have much effect on the total consumption. It is beyond the power of local inspectors to control smuggling or even check it to any appreciable extent. Dominion Officers, whose duty it is to deal with smuggling, are few in number and quite unable to keep an effective watch on all parts of the coast where liquor may be landed . . . Owing to the prevalence of home manufacture, the consumption of intoxicating beer in some country districts, probably, has been greater in recent years than it was under the old licence law.[79]

He might have added that in the three years between 1922 and 1924, the government had received over a million dollars in revenue from the sale of liquor for "medicinal, sacramental and scientific purposes".[80]

Despite the manifest difficulties of enforcing the law, which received such prominence in the daily press, there was some evidence that prohibition was fulfilling its main objective. Liquor was expensive, not always easily obtained and, by the time it had passed through the hands of several bootleggers, not very strong. This was reflected in the arrests for drunkenness which had risen steadily in Nova Scotia from 1,255 in 1900 to a high of 3,999 in 1914. With the resumption of federal prohibition they declined from 3,140 in 1920 to a low of 1,392 in 1923. In 1925 they were still only 1,466.[81]

In July of 1925 a Conservative government came to power in Nova Scotia. Murray had retired from politics in 1923 leaving the reins of government to the one-time prohibition advocate E.H. Armstrong. The luckless Armstrong was left to face a critical depression, disastrous strikes in the major coal and steel industries, mounting costs of government and dwindling revenues. The result of the election of June 25, 1925 was almost a foregone conclusion as the Conservatives under the leadership of E.N. Rhodes won 40 of the 43 seats in the Assembly.[82]

Rhodes appeared to have viewed the termination of prohibition as a potential solution to the critical problem of government deficits. By 1925 the four Western Provinces and Quebec had abandoned prohibition for a system of so called "government control," that is, government sale of liquor. It was proving an extremely lucrative business for the provinces involved. British Columbia for example in 1923 realized a net profit from liquor sales of over three million dollars,[83] an amount equal to three-fifths of the entire Nova Scotia budget. In 1926, Rhodes reported to Sir Robert Borden that he detected: "a marked swing towards Government control of liquor. This will probably be accelerated by our financial position as we are faced during the current year with a deficit of $1,050,000."[84]

Nevertheless, Rhodes was in no position to abandon prohibition. Temperance sentiment was still strong and well organized. Rhodes was also cognizant that a large element of his party's support in the election of 1925 had come from the reform element in the province. His personal manifesto and the party platform had contained promises of "mothers' allowances", a less partisan government, and full scale investigations of labour problems and rural depopulation — all of which had been urged by the churches and the Social Service Council. Although prohibition had not been mentioned in the platform, party candidates in rural areas had been strong in their denunciation of Liberal deficiencies in enforcement.[85] Within the first six months of coming to office his government was presented with petitions supporting prohibition from nearly five hundred organizations in the province — temperance societies, church groups, women's institutes and agricultural clubs. In September, 1925, the Maritime Conference of the newly created United Church endorsed prohibition by an "unanimous standing vote".[86] Early in 1926, Rhodes adopted a policy intended to reassure reform elements of his sincerity in enforcing prohibition while leaving the door open for its subsequent abandonment. He pledged his government to a determined effort to enforce the prohibition laws, but if, after a reasonable time, this proved impossible he would introduce a program for government control. Lest any should doubt his sincerity in enforcing prohibition he appointed as his inspector-in-chief Rev. D.K. Grant, a lawyer, clergyman and prohibitionist. It was an appointment which won the immediate and grateful approval of the United Church.[87]

D.K. Grant promised no miracles in enforcement. In his first report, after six months in office, he stressed the difficulties of reforming a situation which had become entrenched after "years of administrative neglect and indifference on the part both of the Federal and Provincial authority". The problem was also aggravated by "the fact of a sharply divided public opinion, a large element of society, including the magistry *(sic)* itself being either openly antagonistic or passively resistant to the present law".[88]

Nevertheless, Grant set to work in a burst of energy to increase the size of the provincial force, raise the wages of the municipal inspectors and propose fresh amendments to the Nova Scotia Temperance Act. Assisted by the newly created Dominion Preventive Force of the Department of Customs and Excise, Grant and his inspectors launched a determined assault upon illicit liquor traffic. During his first year in office, arrests, seizures and convictions by provincial inspectors more than doubled, while successful prosecutions by both provincial and municipal inspectors increased from 716 for 1926 to 938 for 1927.[89] This increased activity was far from appreciated by influential elements in both political parties. The Conservative Halifax *Herald* began a campaign against Grant for his "arbitrary" methods of prosecuting offenders.[90] Some Liberals indicated their displeasure by securing the dismissal of the federal Preventive Officer at Glace Bay for being "too active in his duties."[91]

In fact, despite Grant's best efforts at enforcement there was evidence of a gradual decline in support for prohibition and an increase in the consumption of alcohol. In 1926 there were 1,898 arrests for drunkenness, 2,053 in 1927 and 2,176 in 1928.[92] There also appeared to be an increased reluctance on the part of juries to convict bootleggers, especially in the case of second offenders for whom jail terms were mandatory.[93]

The resistance to prohibition as usual was strongest in Halifax. The Conservative MLA's from the city found it expedient to show their opposition by resolutions in the House. These Rhodes deflated with amendments to the effect that the law would not be changed without a referendum. Such signs of growing hostility stimulated a flexing of muscles by the prohibitionists. On January 1, 1928, H.R. Grant announced that the Social Service Council, the Women's Christian Temperance Union and the Sons of Temperance were joining forces to prevent any changes in the Temperance Act.[94]

The pressure upon the provincial administration to resort to government control was substantially increased in 1926 by the federal government's announcement of an old age pension scheme, the costs of which were to be shared equally by the provinces and the Dominion. While such a plan might be within the reach of the western provinces and their relatively young population, it was totally beyond the resources of the Nova Scotia government with its much larger percentage of potentially eligible recipients.[95] In 1928, Rhodes appointed a Royal Commission to explore methods of financing old age pensions and called an election before the Commission was due to report. During the campaign he reiterated his promise not to abandon prohibition without a plebiscite but gave no indication when such a referendum would be held.[96]

The election nearly proved disastrous for the Conservatives as their majority shrank from 37 to 3. Both prohibition and old age pensions were issues in the campaign. Discontent over the former was probably a factor in Halifax where Conservative majorities of over 7,000 in 1925 melted away and three of the five Conservative candidates were defeated.

After the election the Royal Commission presented its report. To the surprise of no one, it recommended government control of liquor sales as a possible source of revenue for old age pensions.[97] Shortly thereafter, Rhodes scheduled a plebiscite on the question of prohibition versus government control for October, 1929. Armed with the ammunition supplied by the Commission and with the tacit encouragement of the provincial government, a new Temperance Reform Association was organized in Halifax in September, 1929. Its President, J.A. Winfield, attacked the Nova Scotia Temperance Act for its adverse effect on youth and claimed that his Association was seeking through "moral suasion" and education the most effective means of encouraging temperance in Nova Scotia. This claim was scouted by the editor of the *United Churchman*, who pointed to the rapid disappearance of similar groups in other provinces once the prohibitory system had been destroyed.[98]

As the campaign increased in intensity, it became evident that the prohibitionists had lost many of their allies of 1920. The Anglican *Church Work* was conspicuously silent before the plebiscite and expressed its "relief" when it was over. The *Casket* went to considerable pains to explain that the Roman Catholic Church had never endorsed more than personal abstinence and that membership in the League of the Cross did not convey any obligation to vote for prohibition.[99]

The Rhodes administration apparently did everything possible to aid the campaign for government control. Rhodes, particularly, seems to have seen the future of the government riding on the question. His jaundiced explanation of the opposition to government control is perhaps more revealing of his own commitment than of the forces described. According to Rhodes, three elements were fighting for retention of prohibition: the Liberals, on the principle that "if government control carries, Rhodes is in power for twenty years", the towns, "because of the revenue from fines", and the bootleggers "who were practically solid against us and the rum-runner as well".[100]

Government control won a decisive victory in the plebiscite, 87,647 to 58,082. It received a majority in every county but six. Only the rural counties of Shelburne, Queens, Kings, Hants, Colchester and Annapolis — counties in which the Baptist and United Churches were predominant — did prohibition retain a majority.[101]

The government lost no time in implementing the wishes of the people. The old Act was quickly repealed and a Liquor Commission was set up with a complete monopoly of liquor outlets in the province. Sale by the glass was to be limited by local option; otherwise Commission sales would be unrestricted. Within less than a year the Commission had established a store in every town and city in the province plus a special mail-order agency in Halifax for the convenience of rural customers.

The prohibitionists were bloodied but unbowed; the Social Service Council and its indomitable secretary, H.R. Grant, denounced the Government for its "complicity" in the socially demoralizing liquor traffic, a position endorsed by the United Church.[102] Within a year Grant and other temperance workers were to be found hard at work in a vain effort to pledge members of the Legislature to support a measure for local option on a county basis.[103]

A number of obvious factors might be mentioned in explaining the defeat of prohibition in Nova Scotia. The *United Churchman* claimed that the lack of enforcement discredited the movement among its friends and led to the desire to experiment with government control.[104] This raises the question of whether enforcement was possible, given the opposition to the law by such a determined minority. The answer would appear to hinge on the goal desired. Even with the relatively lax enforcement of the early 1920's, the arrests for drunkenness had been halved throughout the period from 1922 to 1926. Still it is doubtful if even the most rigorous enforcement would have ended the accounts of smuggling, illegal manufacture and related crimes which filled the press of the period. And it was these which made many Nova Scotians wonder if the prohibition cure were not worse than the disease. Such doubts must have become more acute as the prohibitionists saw their cause abandoned by every other province but Prince Edward Island. Then came a positive factor in the Province's need for additional revenue, which the demand for other reforms made crucial. This was certainly the main consideration for the Rhodes' Government, and after the report of the Royal Commission on old age pensions, the issue apparently achieved a similar clarity for the people of Nova Scotia. They were given a choice between prohibition and old age pensions and opted decisively for the latter.

There were more fundamental reasons for the rejection of prohibition in 1929. In the early twentieth century, the movement had rapidly increased in strength, rising upon the tide of optimistic, idealistic reform which accompanied the churches' conversion to the social gospel. As the tide began to ebb, prohibition suffered accordingly. The reform movement of the social gospel reached a climax in Nova Scotia immediately following the World War. People had confidently prepared to create the new and better society which they expected would be within their reach. But conditions in Nova Scotia in the 1920's were conducive neither to optimism or reforms. Instead of the anticipated triumph of humanitarian justice, there came a critical and lingering depression, bankruptcy, wage-cuts, strikes, violence and emigration. In the industrial sphere, proposals for social reform were blocked by the financial difficulties of the corporations on one side, and compromised by the strident voice of radical Marxism on the other. Little could be expected in the realm of legislation from a Government whose economic difficulties precluded the social welfare legislation which seemed to be required as never before.

It is not surprising under such circumstances, that some churchmen apparently re-examined their consciences and concluded that the church was more useful in consoling suffering mortals, than in shattering lances against an unrepentant society. Disillusionment, however, was avoided by many, who apparently saw as the impediment to the attainment of their goals, nothing more invulnerable than an inept provincial administration, and a federal government whose policies accentuated regional injustices under which their province suffered. Their reform enthusiasm, retaining some of the rhetoric of the social gospel, became channeled into a broadly based movement to rehabilitate the region economically from within, while securing economic "justice" from without. Yet for those who looked with exaggerated hopes to the success of "Maritime Rights" candidates in provincial and federal elections, disillusionment was perhaps but the more severe for being deferred.

The decline of prohibition to some extent paralleled that of the general reform movement. As partially a utopian reform, it had suffered on implementation from the inevitable reaction. It did not yield the results predicted by its proponents. There was apparently no spectacular decline in disease, mental illness, poverty or crime in the province. On the contrary, prohibition was blamed by its opponents for much of the crime which did occur. For a time, many of its supporters maintained faith in their programme by attributing its deficiencies to the obvious lack of enforcement by the Murray-Armstrong administration. Then came the expected transition in government and with it the ultimate disillusionment of the prohibitionists, as one of their own number was no more successful in securing the desired results from prohibition than his predecessors.

Still another factor contributed to the decline in popular enthusiasm for prohibition. In the long battle for enforcement, the goals of reform appeared to receive less and less discussion. Harassed clergymen in their pre-occupation with the struggle began to denounce rum-running and bootlegging as "sins". Unconsciously, the prohibitionists were reverting to the language of the nineteenth century movement. Prohibition was becoming divorced in the mind of the public from the main stream of social reform. Gradually it was acquiring the image of censorious fanaticism, which, exaggerated by its opponents, it has retained to the present day.

There was a note of irony in the defeat of prohibition in 1929. Prohibition had acted as mid-wife at the birth of the social gospel in Canadian Churches. The two had been closely linked in the flowering of the reform movement. But the latter, in creating the public demand for social welfare legislation, contributed significantly to the economic pressure providing the immediate cause for the defeat of the former. It was a measure of the success of the social gospel that as one dream was being destroyed, others, perhaps more realistic, were gaining a hold on public opinion. J.S. Woodsworth's victory in forcing the Mackenzie King government to adopt old age pensions had contributed to the fall of prohibition in Nova Scotia. Yet it also symbolized a future victory of the social gospel ideals in secular society, the ultimate goal of the leaders of the prohibition movement in Nova Scotia.

Notes

1. Richard Allen's pioneering study of the social gospel provides the key to an understanding of the prohibition movement in Canada. Although more concerned with the impact of the social gospel in moulding attitudes towards labour, Allen devotes a chapter to prohibition and indicates the leading role played by the social reformers in the temperance movement. The Maritime Provinces, however, are largely neglected in this general study. A. Richard Allen, "The Crest and Crisis of the Social Gospel in Canada, 1916-1927" (unpublished Ph.D. thesis, Duke University, 1967). Also valuable are his "Salem Bland and the Social Gospel in Canada" (unpublished M.A. thesis, University of Saskatchewan, 1961); "The Social Gospel and the Reform Tradition in Canada, 1890-1928", *C.H.R.*, XLIX (1968), pp. 381-399; and "The Triumph and Decline of Prohibition" in J.M. Bumsted, *Documentary Problems in Canadian History* (Georgetown, Ontario, 1969).
2. *Report of the Royal Commission on Liquor Traffic* (Ottawa, Queen's Printer, 1895), p. 770. See also R. Elizabeth Spence, *Prohibition in Canada* (Toronto, The Ontario Branch of the Dominion Alliance, 1919), p. 38. Spence mentions similar claims by Montreal and Beaver River, N.S.
3. *Centennial Book of the Order of the Sons of Temperance of Nova Scotia. 1847-1947* (n.p., 1947), p. 22 and the *Sons of Temperance of North America Centennial* (n.p., 1942), p. 169.
4. *Report*, p. 661.
5. *Debates and Proceedings of House of Assembly of Nova Scotia*. 1907, pp. 308-309, and E. Spence, *op. cit.*, p. 218. In 1894 the vote was 42,756 to 12,355 in favour; in 1898, it was 34,678 to 5,370.
6. See Richard Hofstadter, *Social Darwinism in American Thought* (rev. ed., New York, 1959), pp. 42, 108 and 112-113, and Daniel Aaron, *Men of Good Hope* (New York, 1961), pp. 72, 103.
7. For a discussion of the origin and nature of the social gospel in the United States see Charles H. Hopkins, *The Rise of the Social Gospel in American Protestantism, 1865-1915* (New Haven, 1940) and P.A. Carter, *The Decline and Revival of the Social Gospel* (Ithaca, 1956).

8. *Minutes of the Nova Scotia Conference of the Methodist Church* (hereafter cited as *Minutes, Methodist*), 1907, p. 78; from the Report of the Committee on Temperance and Moral Reform as adopted by the Conference.

9. For a brief description of conditions in one Nova Scotian city see *Sydney, Nova Scotia: The Report of a Brief Investigation of Social Conditions by the Board of Temperance and Moral Reform of the Methodist Church and the Board of Social Service and Evangelism of the Presbyterian Church* (n.p., 1913).

10. W.S. Learned and K.C.M. Sills, *Education in the Maritime Provinces of Canada* (New York, 1922), p. 14.

11. *Report of the Royal Commission on Liquor Traffic*. 1895, pp. 81-82, 684. This is not to say that social concern was not behind the church's pronouncements on intemperance. But the language used in condemning intemperance appeared to be primarily that of personal censorship on moral grounds. Perhaps the most striking example of the change was the removal in 1911 of the list of "sins" which had been included in a footnote to the Methodist Discipline in 1886. See Marion V. Royce, "The Contribution of the Methodist Church to Social Welfare in Canada" (unpublished M.A. thesis, University of Toronto, 1940), pp. 263-265.

12. *Minutes, Methodist*, 1903, pp. 80-81.

13. *Ibid.*, 1906, p. 83.

14. *Ibid.*, 1905, pp. 76-77.

15. H.H. Walsh, *The Christian Church in Canada* (Toronto, 1956), p. 330. See also A. Richard Allen, "Salem Bland and the Social Gospel in Canada," pp. 30-32.

16. *Presbyterian Witness*, 19 October 1907, p. 34.

17. *Minutes of the Maritime Synod of the Presbyterian Church of Canada*, thereafter cited as *Minutes, Presbyterian*, 1908, p. 25: from the Report of Committee on Moral and Social Reform. Compare with the Report of Committee on Temperance and Moral Reform in *The Acts Proceedings of the General Assembly of the Presbyterian Church of Canada*, 1908, pp. 248-252.

18. *Minutes, Presbyterian*, 1909, pp. 28-29.

19. *Year Book Maritime Baptist Convention*, 1903, p. 22. Jenkins later became a staunch supporter of J.S. Woodsworth's Labour Party.

20. *Wesleyan* (Methodist), Halifax, 23 September 1908, p. 1. Taken from the *Maritime Baptist*.

21. *Journals of Nova Scotia Synod, Church of England*, Appendix N, printed in the *Year Book* (hereafter cited as *Year Book, Church of England*), 1901-1902, p. xxxi.

22. D.V. Warner, *The Church and Modern Socialism* (Truro, N.S., 1909).

23. *Year Book, Church of England*, 1911-1912, pp. 111-113.

24. *Ibid.*, Appendix Q, pp. xxvi-xxvii.

25. *Ibid.*, 1914-1915, pp. 149 and 320. The Nova Scotia Conference seems to have been acting in advance of the rest of the Church in urging prohibition as the National Synod remained uncommitted. See *The General Synod of the Church of England in the Dominion of Canada*, 1915, p. 268.

26. *Casket*, 12 August 1909. Students of the social gospel including A.R. Allen, C. Hopkins and P. Carter, have ignored the impact of its ideas on the Roman Catholic Church. That their influence was important is suggested most spectacularly by the leading role played by such reform minded priests as Fathers "Jimmy" Tompkins and M.M. Coady in the development of the co-operative movement in Nova Scotia in the latter part of the 1920's. Coady's later justification of the Church's role in this movement would appear to differ little from some Protestant versions of the social gospel. See M.M. Coady, *Masters of their own Destiny* (New York, 1939), pp. 144-148.

27. *Casket*, 29 August 1907, p. 4.

28. *Ibid.*, 31 January 1907, p. 6; 15 January 1903, p. 4; 8 August 1907, p. 2; and 12 September 1907, p. 2.

29. For a brief sketch of these early attempts see E. Spence, *op. cit.*, pp. 330-333.

30. *Debates*, 1905, pp. 311, 85-86.

31. *Minutes, Presbyterian*, 1905, p. 31.

32. *Minutes, Methodist*, 1905, p. 78.

33. See below n. 35.

34. *Debates*, 1906, p. 309.

35. *Ibid.*, pp. 312, 330-331.

36. J. Castell Hopkins, *The Canadian Annual Review*, 1905, p. 331 and 1906, p. 393 (hereafter cited as *C.A.R.*).
37. *Minutes, Methodist*, 1906, p. 81.
38. *Debates*, 1907, pp. 313 and 372.
39. *Ibid.*, pp. 313 and 400.
40. Speakers frequently gave H.R. Grant credit for supplying the information with which they "corrected" statements of the opponents of prohibition. See for example, *Debates*, 1916. p. 180.
41. *Debates*, 1907, p. 301.
42. *Ibid.*, pp. 224, 227.
43. Nova Scotia, *Journals of the House of Assembly* (hereafter cited as *J.H.A.*), 1907, various references pp. 45-154 and *Debates*, 1907, p. 310.
44. *Debates*, 1907, p. 304. This was probably Dr. J.W. Reid, M.D. of Windsor, N.S., who was elected to the House in 1911 and thereafter gave strong speeches in support of prohibition which were crammed with similar statistics. See for example, *Debates*, 1916, p. 170.
45. *Debates*, 1907, p. 306.
46. *Ibid.*, p. 317.
47. *Ibid.*, p. 385.
48. *Ibid.*, p. 400.
49. *C.A.R.*, 1908, pp. 426-427, 108.
50. *Debates*, 1908, pp. 334, 374.
51. *C.A.R.*, 1908, p. 427.
52. Halifax *Herald*, 22 January 1909, p. 6.
53. E. Spence, *op. cit.*, p. 339; *C.A.R.*, 1909, p. 432, and 1910, p. 459. In the latter constituency this was reputed to be the first election of a Conservative in thirty years.
54. *C.A.R.*, 1911, p. 551.
55. *Minutes, Presbyterian*, 1910, p. 29. *Minutes, Methodist*, 1910, p. 89.
56. E. Spence, *op. cit.*, pp. 341-342.
57. Armstrong to Dr. J.W. Reid, 15 February 1912 and Armstrong to W.M. Kelly, 15 February 1912, E.R. Armstrong Papers, P.A.N.S.
58. *Presbyterian Witness*, 4 March 1916, p. 5 and *Debates*, 1916, p. 225.
59. *Debates*, 1916, p. 176.
60. *Ibid.*, p. 143.
61. *Ibid.*, p. 206.
62. *Ibid.*, p. 258.
63. E. Spence, *op. cit.*, p. 341.
64. See Halifax *Herald*, 10 June 1916, p. 6.
65. See Report of the Inspector-in-chief for 1919, *J.H.A.*, 1920, Appendix 26, p. 1.
66. *Year Book, Church of England*, 1916-1917, p. 146.
67. Report of Inspector-in-chief, 1917, *J.H.A.*, 1918, Appendix 26, p. 1.
68. *The Control and Sale of Liquor in Canada* (Ottawa, Dominion Bureau of Statistics, 1933), p. 9, Table 5.
69. Compared with only 48.3% who were of a similar opinion in 1917. See *Prohibition II* (Kingston, 1919), p. 9, and *Prohibition I* (Kingston, 1917), p. 6. (Bulletins of the Council for Social Service of the Church of England).
70. Report of Inspector-in-chief, 1919, *J.H.A.*, 1920, Appendix 26, p. 9.
71. *C.A.R.*, 1919, p. 703; Halifax *Citizen*, 30 May and 22 August 1923.
72. *C.A.R.*, 1920, p. 678.
73. See J.M. Beck, *The Government of Nova Scotia* (Toronto, 1957), p. 162 and Anthony MacKenzie, "The Rise and Fall of the Farmer Labour Party in Nova Scotia" (unpublished M.A. thesis, Dalhousie University, 1969), p. 77.
74. *Casket*, 14 October 1920, pp. 1 and 6.
75. *Presbyterian Witness*, 20 November 1920.
76. *C.A.R.*, 1920, p. 673.
77. See William Rodney, *Soldiers of the International* (Toronto, 1968), p. 111. Rodney portrays a variety of Communists in this period optimistically channelling their energies into work in the industrial areas of Cape Breton.

78. The *Casket*, while bitterly denouncing agitators such as McLachlan, was equally critical of Besco (British Empire Steel and Coal Corporation) and suggested the problem might be solved by nationalization of the coal fields. *Casket*, 21 October 1920, p. 1. The Methodist *Wesleyan* in 1923 denounced the "nest of anarchists" in Cape Breton and suggested that the "firebrands" be eliminated from the country. *Wesleyan*, 4 July 1923, p. 1. By 1925 although still critical of labour's resort to violence, it was directing its fire against the Corporation and demanding relief "for the labourer who grinds his face to produce dividends for stocks for which no single dollar has been paid." *Wesleyan*, 1 April 1925, p. 4. In that year the clergy played an important role in providing relief for the families of the striking miners and in 1928 the Ministerial Association of Sydney petitioned the Tariff Advisory Board that the Corporation should not be given tariff or other subsidy until it had substantially improved the labouring conditions of the steelworkers. Papers of the Advisory Board on Tariffs and Taxation, Vol. 9, P.A.C.
79. Report of Inspector-in-chief, 1925, *J.H.A.*, 1926, Appendix 18, pp. 5-8.
80. *The Control and Sale of Liquor in Canada*, p. 8, Table 4.
81. *Ibid.*, p. 9.
82. See E.R. Forbes, "The Rise and Fall of the Conservative Party in the Provincial Politics of Nova Scotia, 1922-1933" (unpublished M.A. thesis, Dalhousie University, 1967), chapter 2.
83. *The Control and Sale of Liquor in Canada*, p. 8.
84. Rhodes to Borden, 1926, Rhodes Papers, P.A.N.S.
85. In Shelburne a Conservative convention even went as far as to nominate an "independent" candidate to run on a prohibitionist platform. Halifax *Herald*, 10 June 1925.
86. Rhodes Papers, P.A.N.S., vol. 81 and *Minutes of the Maritime Conference of the United Church of Canada*, 1925, p. 23.
87. *Minutes, United Church*, 1927, p. 27.
88. Report of Inspector-in-chief for 1926, *J.H.A.*, 1927, pp. 5, 12.
89. *Ibid.*, 1927; *J.H.A.*, 1928, pp. 6, 15.
90. Halifax *Herald*, 1 March 1928.
91. "Memorandum Re: N.S. Affairs," 1927, vol. 7, Col. J.L. Ralston Papers, P.A.C.
92. *Control and Sale of Liquor in Canada*, p. 9, Table 5.
93. Report of Inspector-in-chief for 1927, *J.H.A.*, 1928, Appendix 8, p. 10.
94. Halifax *Herald*, 1 January 1928.
95. 4.7% of Nova Scotia's population was over 70 years of age compared with 1.2% to 1.8% for the four Western provinces. Report of the Royal Commission on Old Age Pensions, *J.H.A.*, appendix No. 29, p. 43.
96. Copy of speech delivered at Windsor, 8 September 1928, Rhodes Papers, P.A.N.S.
97. *Report of the Royal Commission on Old Age Pensions*, p. 41.
98. *United Churchman*, 25 September 1929, p. 4.
99. *Church Work*, December 1929, p. 3 and *Casket*, 16 May 1929.
100. Rhodes to J. Philip Bell, 4 November 1929, Rhodes Papers, P.A.N.S.
101. *J.H.A.*, 1929, Appendix 27, p. 38.
102. *United Churchman*, 1 January 1930.
103. Halifax, *Chronicle*, 14 November 1929.
104. *United Churchman*, 6 November 1929.

"The Beginning of Our Regeneration":

The Great War and Western Canadian Reform Movements

John H. Thompson

> I know nothing about Germany. But I do know something about our own people. I know how selfish and individualistic and sordid and money-grabbing we have been; how slothful and incompetent and self-satisfied we have been, and I fear it will take a long war and sacrifices and tragedies altogether beyond our present imagination to make us unselfish and public-spirited and clean and generous; it will take the strain and emergency of war to make us vigourous and efficient; it will take the sting of many defeats to impose that humility which will be *the beginning of our regeneration*.
>
> Edith Duncan to Dave Elden, R.J.C. Stead, *The Cow Puncher*, 1918.

The Western Canadian reform movement was not created by the enthusiasm released by the Great War. Associations advocating prohibition, woman's suffrage, and economic reform had existed in Manitoba and the North West Territories before the turn of the century. After 1900, the problems of immigration, rapid urban growth, and an expanding wheat economy gave the political, social, and economic dimensions of reformism increasing relevance. In the decade before the war, reform causes won new supporters, and became an important theme in Western Canadian life. The "reform movement" which espoused this theme was not a monolith. It was composed of a variety of pressure groups, dedicated to such diverse objectives as tariff reform, the single tax, direct legislation, prohibition, and woman's suffrage. The movement's members belonged to no particular political party, and only in Manitoba did they find it necessary to capture a party to gain their ends. The movement's common philosophical denominator was the social gospel, which swept North American protestantism at the close of the nineteenth century.[1]

Reprinted from *Canadian Historical Papers*, 1972, pp. 227-245, by permission of the author and The Canadian Historical Association.

By 1914, Western reformers felt that they had made considerable progress toward their goals. Each Prairie Province had an active Social Service Council, committed to the eradication of the liquor traffic and prostitution, and to the amelioration of social conditions in Western cities. The Woman's Christian Temperance Union also spoke for prohibition, and was the leading force in demands for woman's suffrage. Direct Legislation Leagues promised to purify political life by using the initiative, referendum, and recall to make governments more responsive to their electorates. Grain Growers' Associations used their voice, *The Grain Growers' Guide*, to support these reforms and to promote tariff and tax reform as well.

But as of August 1914, none of these causes had enjoyed significant success. No Western province had enfranchised its women or introduced prohibition.[2] Direct legislation had been partially implemented in Saskatchewan in 1912 and Alberta in 1913, but Saskatchewan's electorate had failed to endorse the Direct Legislation Act in a referendum.[3] In January, 1914, the *bête noire* of Western reformers, Premier R.P. Roblin of Manitoba, observed sanctimoniously to his Attorney General that "seemingly crime does not decrease, seemingly the world is getting no better, seemingly the efforts of social and moral reformers is [sic] not as effective as we would like."[4]

It was on Premier Roblin that reform eyes were fixed in July 1914. The Manitoba Liberal Party, in the grip of the provincial reform movement, was challenging Roblin's fifteen-year-old Conservative government. The Liberal Platform was a reformer's banquet, with direct legislation as an appetizer, woman's suffrage as the *entrée*, and a promised referendum on prohibition to conclude the meal. Roblin opposed each of these items, and, for the first time, reform and the *status quo* were presented to a Western electorate as clear-cut alternatives. C.W. Gordon of the Social Service Council described the significance of the confrontation for Western reformers:

> On the one side are the Christian Churches, various [reform] organizations, social workers, and all the decent citizens, on the other the Roblin Government, the Liquor traffic, and every form of organized vice and crime.[5]

But "decent citizens" were apparently not a majority in Manitoba, for the Roblin Government was returned for a fifth consecutive term.

The defeat in Manitoba did not mean that reformers throughout the West faced a hopeless situation. The Liberals made significant gains in terms of seats and in their percentage of the popular vote. But the defeat did suggest that in a head to head confrontation with "the forces of reaction" (as Nellie McClung described those who opposed reform) reform ideas did not enjoy the support of a clear majority of the electorate. Although the reform movement had increased both in size and vigour, it had not succeeded in winning the enthusiastic endorsement of the general public. This endorsement was necessary if such reform objectives as prohibition and woman's suffrage were to be effectively implemented. It was in their quest for this broad public support that reformers were aided by the Great War.

A modern democracy with a literate population cannot engage in a major war without soliciting an enthusiastic mandate from its citizens. For this reason, the Great War was interpreted and described in terms very different from those applied to wars of the past. The Canadian Expeditionary Force was not fighting for territorial gain, but "in maintenance of those ideals of Liberty and Justice which are the common and sacred cause of the Allies" and for "the freedom of the world".[6] Although "there may have been wars in the history of the British Empire that have not been justifiable", "there never was a juster cause" than the war against German autocracy.[7]

But if Canadian soldiers were giving their lives for "Liberty and Justice" in Flanders, was it not the duty of those who remained behind to see to it that these same things existed in Canada? Reformers argued that the Great War was an opportunity to accomplish this very thing, a sign given to Canada in order that "the national sins which are responsible for this awful carnage may be eradicated so righteousness and peace may be established".[8] As Mrs. Nellie McClung told her many readers, the war was necessary for national regeneration, for "without the shedding of blood, there is no remission of sin".[9] If the sacrifice was not to be wasted, the reform programme had to be implemented. Even Clifford Sifton, hardly an ardent reformer, recognized that the Great War made it necessary for both Eastern and Western Canada to "cast out everything that threatens its moral health". The war produced a transformation in public attitudes to reformism, changing them to the point that "men [who] scoffed a few years ago are the foremost now to demand reform".[10] The transformation was particularly pronounced in Western Canada. As Mrs. Irene Parlby told the Saskatchewan Grain Growers, "before the war the real spirit of the West had been smothered in materialism," and public action had been difficult. Because of the common goal of victory, "the big broad free spirit is beginning to emerge again."[11]

In addition to changing public attitudes to the idea of reform, the wartime experience changed attitudes to the role of the state as the enforcer of reform measures. Many reform objectives, most notably prohibition and changes in the system of taxation, called for a previously unacceptable degree of state intervention into the lives of its citizens. The expansion of governmental power necessary to meet the wartime emergency gave government intervention a sanction which it had not had before 1914. The state became "more than a mere tax-collector or polling clerk," it became an organization capable of vigourous, positive activities.[12] An Alberta prohibitionist noted that "the European War has taught us that the State has a right to take such action as will best conserve its forces for the national good.''[13] Because of the demands of war, no truly patriotic citizen could react to such action with "resentment or resistance"; the correct course was "a new and affectionate loyalty."[14] This new willingness to grant a more active role to government combined with the wartime ideal of redeeming Canadian society to produce a climate of opinion favourable to reform. It was this climate that the reform movement exploited to gain its ends, in some facets of the movement more successfully than in others.

The reform objective which received the greatest impetus from the wartime atmosphere was the prohibition of alcoholic liquors. Despite the social problems which liquor created in the rapidly expanding West, prohibitionists had been unable to convince the Western public or their provincial governments that prohibition was the necessary cure. The events of August, 1914, introduced a new factor into the equation. The Great War provided the necessary catalyst in the public reaction which brought about prohibitory liquor legislation, not only in Western Canada, but throughout North America. More than any other reform group, prohibitionists were able to use the exigencies of the wartime situation to lend new credence to their arguments and to exploit the desire to purify society which emerged as part of the domestic side of the war effort.

Prohibitionists had long been fond of military metaphors to describe their struggle. The cause itself was *"warfare* waged against ignorance, selfishness, darkness, prejudice, and cruelty,'' while a successful referendum campaign might be compared to Wellington's victory at Waterloo.[15] Sara Rowell Wright of the WCTU liked to speak of her years as "a private in the rear ranks of the movement", and a book of temperance poems and songs was called *The Gatling*, in reference to the way its contents were to be deployed against the liquor traffic.[16] The war made these rhetorical flourishes a mainstay of temperance propaganda. The liquor traffic was clearly identified with the Kaiser and his brutal hordes as a force blocking the way to a more perfect society. Since a Westerner would "despise the Kaiser for dropping bombs on defenseless people, and shooting down innocent people", he should also despise the liquor traffic, since it had "waged war on women and children all down the centuries".[17] The techniques to be employed in the eradication of both the Kaiser and the liquor traffic were made to seem exactly the same. Rev. J.E. Hughson of Winnipeg urged Westerners to "use ballots for bullets and shoot straight and strong in order that the demon of drink might be driven from the haunts of men."[18] A cartoon in the *Grain Growers' Guide* carried on the analogy pictorially, depicting a 'war' on the entrenched liquor interests, with 'votes' being loaded into a field piece by the forces under the banner of "Temperance and Righteousness".[19]

It was not only the tone of prohibitionist rhetoric that was adapted to suit the Great War, its content was modified as well. The war provided the temperance movement with two important new arguments, with which to influence public opinion. The first concerned the moral and physical health of the thousands of young Westerners who had entered the army, many of whom were leaving home for the first time. What would happen to the decent boys from prairie farms when, befuddled by unfamiliar liquor, they fell victim to the prostitutes who haunted military camps in Canada and overseas? Blighted by horrible unnamed diseases, "thousands of clean-minded innocent young boys who would otherwise have been decent upright citizens will now be nothing but a scourge to their country when they return."[20]

One way to avoid such a result was to keep liquor out of the hands of soldiers. As the Medical Officer of Ralph Connor's *Sky Pilot in No Man's Land* pointed out, "Cut out the damned beer. Cut out the beer and ninety *per cent* of the venereal disease goes . . . (Soldier's) mothers have given them up, to death, if need be, but not to this rotten damnable disease."[21] To "cut out the beer," women's groups and WCT Unions bombarded legislators and commanding officers with resolutions demanding that bars and 'wet' canteens be closed "for the sake of our soldiers".[22] It was not enough to restrict such protection to the period when they were in uniform, only to allow them to become victims of the liquor traffic once they were civilians again. It was the responsibility of every Westerner to see that the veterans found "a clean pure Province for them when they return to us, in which they may rest their shattered nerves and poor wounded bodies."[23] This could only be guaranteed if prohibition became a reality.

No one thought to ask the "clean-minded innocent young boys" if they wanted to be rescued from the clutches of temptation. Evidence about the soldiers' opinion on the prohibition question is contradictory. During referenda on prohibition in Manitoba, Saskatchewan, and Alberta polls in military camps returned 'dry' majorities, and one Saskatchewan officer wrote Premier Scott to praise the provincial government's decision to make the liquor trade a public monopoly.[24] After prohibition was in force, however, a Calgary private wrote A.E. Cross of the Calgary Brewing and Malting Company that his comrades "would be solid for to have it back to the good old days again" on their return.[25] Soldier poets poked rude fun at both 'dry' canteens and prohibitionists. One particularly piquant rhyme entitled "From the Trenches", derided

> Preachers over in Canada
> Who rave about Kingdom Come
> Ain't pleased with our ability
> And wanted to stop our rum.
>
> Water they say would be better.
> Water! Great Scott! Out here
> We're up to our knees in water
> Do they think we're standing in beer?[26]

Thus it would seem that soldiers were as divided in their opinions of prohibition as most Westerners had been before 1914. But among the public as a whole, the prohibitionist movement was rapidly making converts, and producing a consensus in favour of prohibition.

An important factor in producing this consensus was a second new temperance argument, again one peculiar to the wartime situation. Canadians were told constantly by their governments that efficiency was a prerequisite for victory over Germany. Prohibitionists quickly capitalized on this theme, pointing to the production and consumption of liquor as a drain on Canada's ability to wage war. Not only did drunkenness squander the nation's human resources, it wasted its physical resources as well. A drunken soldier was unfit to fight, an alcoholic worker was unable to produce, and grain distilled into whiskey could not be used to feed starving Allies. Newspapers sympathetic to the war effort put this argument forcefully before the public, demanding that

> the bar must be closed (because) the national existence is at stake. The ship must be stripped for action. All dead weight must go by the boards if we are to win.[27]

As well as providing prohibitionists with two new important arguments, the situation created by the Great War gave them new answers to two of the most effective defences of the liquor traffic. With thousands of Westerners dying in France to serve their country, criticism of prohibition as a violation of individual liberty lost most of its impact. *Manitoba Free Press* editor John W. Dafoe reflected the popular mood when he pointed out that "the propriety of subordinating individual desires to the general good need not be elaborated at this moment, when millions of men, representing the cream of British citizenship have put aside all their individual inclinations and ambitions."[28] Nellie McClung was even more blunt. "We have before us," she wrote, "a perfect example of a man who is exercising personal liberty to the full. . . . a man by the name of William Hohenzollern."[29] The second anti-prohibitionist argument routed by the Great War was the claim that prohibition would produce widespread unemployment by wiping out the liquor industry and its associated outlets. The wartime demand for manpower created a labour shortage that made this contention ridiculous.

With their own rhetoric refurbished to suit the wartime situation, and with their opponents' most effective weapons temporarily silent, prohibitionist organizations intensified their efforts to put their case to the public and to the provincial governments. The traditional mainstays of the movement, the WCTU and the Social Service Councils, were joined in their campaign by groups which had not formerly been associated with prohibition. The Orange Lodge, the IODE, the Anglican Church, the Winnipeg Canadian Club; all came to the conclusion that prohibition was "the best way of dealing with the liquor traffic *at the present time*", and became war converts to the cause.[30] These new allies meant that prohibitionists could apply increased pressure on Western governments, and the movement began to gain concessions rapidly.

In Manitoba, for example, the anti-prohibitionist Roblin government raised the legal drinking age from sixteen to eighteen and suspended the licenses of seventy-two establishments found to be flouting the liquor laws.[31] The Liberal government of Saskatchewan engaged in the same sort of short-term measures, but Premier Scott and his colleagues began to realize that the public was demanding more and that "the time [was] high ripe for action." The step on which they decided fell short of prohibition. In March 1915, the government announced that the liquor trade in Saskatchewan was to become a state monopoly. Liquor was to be available only in provincially operated dispensaries, and all bars, saloons, and stores were to be closed. Scott viewed the decision as a frank concession to wartime public opinion, and confided to Senator James H. Ross that this opinion was so strong that "to stand still any longer meant suicide for this government."[32] Scott and his cabinet regarded their dispensary system as a radical step in the direction of prohibition. J.A. Calder considered introducing the dispensaries as "having decided to go the limit", and expressed "very grave doubts" as to whether a referendum on prohibition could ever be successful in Saskatchewan.[33] The events of the next two years were to show how rapidly the war could change public attitudes to prohibition, and make a mockery of the prediction of as astute a politician as Calder.

In July 1915, with the Saskatchewan dispensary system scarcely in operation, the voters of Alberta gave a solid endorsement to a prohibition referendum. All but sixteen of the fifty-eight provincial constitutencies returned prohibitionist majorities, with 'wet' victories coming only in "primarily mining or remote northern areas", beyond reach of prohibitionist propaganda.[34] Manitobans followed suit seven months later, with an even larger majority. Only three constituencies remained 'wet' in a prohibitionist landslide.

Saskatchewan, which had been so proud of its system of government control, suddenly found itself to the rear of temperance sentiment on the Prairies. One prohibitionist warned W.R. Motherwell that the situation had changed, and that the public was

> not satisfied with the working out of the Liquor Dispencery (sic) System. It is true that we are tremendously better off . . . this however does not alter the fact that more is needed. This is a matter which is receiving a good deal of unfavourable comment at this time. The people are ready for a total prohibition measure at this very time, let us have it.[35]

The Saskatchewan Liberal government responded once again to public demands, and Saskatchewan became the third Western Province to endorse prohibition by referendum, in December, 1916. The Saskatchewan majority was the largest of the three, demonstrating again that as the war against Germany became longer and more bitter, the war against booze enlisted more and more recruits.

There are several revealing similarities among the three referenda, in addition to the fact that all were resounding prohibitionist victories. In each campaign the Great War played an important rhetorical role, and temperance workers succeeded completely in convincing the Western public that prohibition and patriotism were synonymous. The referenda themselves were treated as an opportunity for those truly behind the war effort to stand up and be counted. As the Cypress River *Western Prairie* warned on the eve of the Manitoba balloting, "anyone who will vote in favour of liquor might as well enlist under the Kaiser as far as patriotism goes."[36]

This identification helped prohibitionists overcome opposition among a traditionally hostile group, the Catholic immigrants from Central and Eastern Europe. It had been "this very heavy foreign population" which J.A. Calder had thought would prevent a 'dry' Saskatchewan, and much of the opposition faced by prohibitionists during the war did come from this quarter.[37] But many of these people saw the prohibition referendum as a kind of loyalty test, through which they could prove that they were good Canadian citizens, even during this time of crisis. Prohibitionists encouraged this belief, and actively sought non-Anglo-Saxon votes. For the first time, their efforts were rewarded. In Manitoba, the Ruthenian Catholic Political Club and the Slavonic Independent Society "spoke fervently in favour of temperance," while *The Canadian Farmer*, a Western Ukrainian weekly, urged its Saskatchewan readers to "get organized and vote against the [Liquor] stores!"[38] Not all non-Anglo-Saxons were converted, but enough voted for prohibition in each of the three provinces to largely neutralize the ballots of their 'wet' countrymen. After the Alberta referendum, the WCTU's Superintendent of Work Among Foreigners "knelt in thanksgiving to our Heavenly Father that not all foreign-speaking people voted wet, but that right prevailed and carried the day, even in several of their own district communities."[39] North Winnipeg, perhaps the most aggressively 'foreign' community in the West, rejected prohibition by only sixty-five votes. The *Manitoba Free Press* made an observation which applied throughout the West when it noted with satisfaction that "the greatest disappointment of all to the wets was the foreign vote."[40]

The only group completely untouched by wartime arguments on behalf of prohibition was Western Canada's French Canadians. French Canadians and prohibitionists had never enjoyed cordial relations, partly because of the movement's Protestant character, and partly because of its wholehearted support for unilingual education. Since most French Canadians had centuries of North American ancestry, the idea that they needed to prove their loyalty by accepting prohibition did not occur to them. As the French language *Le Manitoba* was careful to point out, this did not mean that French Canadians were "plus intemperant que les autres", simply that they resented the totalitarian techniques of prohibition and prohibitionists. In each Western Province, Francophones rejected prohibition in the referenda of 1915-16.[41]

The second important similarity between the referenda campaigns in Manitoba, Saskatchewan, and Alberta was the demoralization of the traditional opponents of prohibition. The Great War not only defused the arguments used by the defenders of liquor, it sapped the strength of the defenders themselves. In Alberta, liquor dealers had "very little success" in raising funds to oppose prohibition during wartime.[42] In both Manitoba and Alberta, the licensed Victuallers' Association had to turn to the United States for anti-prohibitionist speakers. The Manitoba Association co-operated with the Bartenders Union to obtain Clarence Darrow, who received an enthusiastic reception from 'wet' faithful, but an icy one from the general public. The Alberta Victuallers did no better with A.C. Windle, an anti-war editor from Chicago. Windle's outspoken opposition to the Great War allowed prohibitionists to re-emphasize their argument that 'wet' sympathy meant a lack of patriotism, and that booze and Kaiserism were inextricably intertwined.[43] In Saskatchewan's referendum campaign of 1916, there simply was no opposition to the prohibitionists. The Government Dispensary system, in effect for more than a year, had decimated the ranks of hotel keepers, who generally provided the 'anti' leadership.

Because of a combination of new factors, all of them attributable to the Great War, the Prairie Provinces adopted prohibitory liquor legislation during the first two full years of the war. Provincial prohibition was not total prohibition, however. The right to restrict interprovincial trade belonged to the Dominion Government, and for this reason provincial Temperance Acts could not prevent individuals from importing liquor from another province for home consumption. A thriving interprovincial export business rapidly developed. Liquor dealers like William Ferguson of Brandon informed customers in the neighbouring province that "having decided to remain in business, and having still a large stock of draught Brandies, Scotch and Irish Whiskies, Rum, Holland Gin, Port and Sherries, [I] will continue to fill orders for *Saskatchewan.*"[44] So much liquor came into Alberta cross the British Columbia border that Bob Edwards' *Calgary Eye Opener* included the satirical "Society Note" that

> Percy M. Winslow, one of our most popular and dissipated young men, left Monday morning for Field, B.C., where he has accepted a lucrative position as shipping clerk in one of the wholesale liquor houses. We predict a bright future for Percy.[45]

Western prohibitionists were determined not to stop short of the ultimate goal. To plug the loopholes in provincial legislation, they turned to Ottawa. Petitions, letters, and resolutions reminded Members of Parliament of the gravity of the situation, and urged them to introduce measures to "abolish the sale and manufacture of alcoholic liquors during wartime."[46] Prohibitionists gave enthusiastic support to Unionist candidates throughout the West during the election of 1917. Dominion prohibition was one of the many reforms which they expected to emanate from Unionism, and the Union Government's bipartisan character and crusading style appealed to the prohibitionist mind. Many influential prohibitionists campaigned on behalf of Union Government, among them Dr. Salem Bland, Rev. C.W. Gordon, and Mrs. Nellie McClung. Their work was rewarded, for shortly after they took office the Unionists introduced federal prohibition as an Order-in-Council under the War Measures Act, to come into effect April 1, 1918.

This made the prohibitionist victory in theory complete. All that remained was the task of making certain that the hard-won legislation was enforced. The war aided prohibitionists in this respect as well, and 1917-18 became the most effective years of the prohibition experiment. Even before the Dominion Government put an end to importation, Manitoba could report that "drunkenness had been reduced 87% for the first seven months of the operation of the (Prohibition) Act . . . all other crime has been reduced by 32%" and that "the support accorded the Act has surpassed the most sanguine expectations of its friends."[47] A jubilant Saskatchewan farm wife wrote to Premier Martin that "our little town, which was formerly a drunkard's paradise, since the banishment of the bars and dispensaries has assumed an air of thrift and sobriety."[48] Alberta's Chief Inspector under the Temperance Act claimed that under prohibition arrests of drunks were reduced by ninety *per cent*, and drinking, crime, and drunkenness decreased in each Prairie Province during the last two years of the War.[49] Once the war ended, however, the prohibitionist solution to society's problems became increasingly less effective.[50] The assault on prohibition began almost as soon as the war ended, and prohibitionists no longer had the wartime situation to interest the public in their programme. By 1924 all three Western Provinces had replaced prohibition with government-operated liquor stores.

How much of the prohibitionists' fleeting success can be attributed to the Great War? To describe the imposition of prohibition as a purely wartime phenomenon would do an injustice to the work done before 1914 to convince Westerners of the need for liquor restriction. The foundations laid before the war began were a vital factor in the eventual success. But it was the emotional atmosphere of wartime which completed the prohibitionists' work, and which allowed prohibition to operate reasonably effectively for two short years. It was the Great War's accompanying national reappraisal which made once indifferent citizens listen to temperance arguments for the first time. Once this was accomplished, the majoritarian zeal which marked the domestic war effort ensured the right "psychological moment to strike the blow."[51] The *Saskatoon Phoenix* understood this process completely. "The temperance party," said an editorial, "has the war to thank for bringing public opinion *to a focus* on the matter of temperance reform."[52]

The second reformist group aided significantly by the Great War was the movement for woman's suffrage. The prohibition and suffrage movements were so closely intertwined in both programme and personnel that what advanced one cause almoşt automatically had the same effect on the other. In the three Western Provinces, the WCTU played a leading role in both movements and an ardent prohibitionist was usually an ardent suffragette as well. In many parts of the Prairies, the pre-war suffrage movement was the Equal Franchise Department of the local WCTU.[53]

The war's favourable effect on the achievement of woman's suffrage is paradoxical, for prior to 1914, the woman's movement had thought of itself as pacifistic, and regarded war as one of woman's greatest enemies. War was part of the scheme of masculine domination which denied women an effective voice in society. "History, romance, legend, and tradition," wrote Nellie McClung, "have shown the masculine aspect of war and have surrounded it with a false glory and have sought to throw the veil of glamour over its hideous face." It was for the "false glory" that men went to war, abandoning women to face the true responsibilities of life alone.[54]

The Great War challenged these pacifistic assumptions. The wars which women had so roundly condemned had been the wars with which they themselves were familiar; the South African War, the Spanish-American War, and colonial wars in Africa or the Far East. This new war was something very different. Germany was not the tiny Transvaal Republic, but an aggressive modern industrial power. Canada was not fighting for colonial conquest, but for 'liberty', 'justice', her very survival. Had it not been "the Kaiser and his brutal warlords" who had decided to "plunge all Europe into bloodshed?" And what about Belgium, gallant little Belgium where "the German soldiers made a shield of Belgium women and children in front of their Army; no child was too young, no woman too old, to escape their cruelty; no mother's prayers, no child's appeal could stay their fury!"[55] Surely such inhumanity had to be checked lest it dominate first Europe, then the world.

As with the prohibitionist movement, the Great War's first effect on the suffrage movement was on its rhetoric. As Aileen S. Kraditor has pointed out, pre-war suffrage arguments can be divided into two categories, those based on justice and those based on expediency. The older, justice-oriented theme contended that women had a natural right to vote, as did all citizens. Arguments which emphasized expediency stressed instead the good effects that women's vote could accomplish in society.[56] Both types of argument were suitable to adaptation to the wartime atmosphere.

The new significance which the Great War gave to arguments based on justice is obvious. If the war were really "the greatest fight for liberty since the Dutch and English broke the power of Spain in the 16th Century", why, women asked, could they not enjoy in Canada the same liberty for which their sons were fighting and dying? Since the war was to be the "vindication of democracy", should not the democratic rights of millions of Canadian women be vindicated at the same time? Men who indulged in such descriptions of the war found themselves caught on the hook of their own eloquence.[57] As W.L. Morton has succinctly pointed out, "those who would carry democracy abroad must see that it is without reproach at home."[58]

Arguments based on expediency gained more power in wartime as well. The public came to accept the idea that the war could be used to redeem Western Canada from her pre-war materialism. This might be accomplished without women's votes, but what would happen when the war ended, and reforming zeal dissipated? Women's votes were necessary to prevent backsliding, and a return to evil in the post-war era. If this should happen, all the sacrifice, all the bloodshed, would be in vain. As a "war widow" told R.J.G. Stead,

> We women, we women of the war — we have nothing left to be selfish for. But we have the whole world to be unselfish for. It's all different, and it can never go back. *We won't let it go back. We've paid too much to let it go back.*[59]

To prevent this "going back", women demanded the vote.

Not only the rhetoric, but the organization of the woman's movement was profoundly changed by the war. Initially, suffragists thought that the war would postpone the achievement of their goal, since it would force them to devote less time to suffrage activities. In reality, however, women's war work proved to be the greatest organizational aid the movement had ever been blessed with. The motivation provided by patriotic work increased the membership of existing women's groups, such as the United Farm Women of Alberta and Manitoba, and the IODE. Groups not formerly concerned with suffrage were brought into contact with their more activistic sisters in associations like the WCTU. As these women gathered to produce incredible quantities of towels and toques, socks and shirts, balaclavas and bandages, they did not sit mute. Quiet housewives conversed with ardent advocates of equal suffrage, and while

> the nimble fingers of the knitting women are transforming balls of wool into socks and comforters, even a greater change is being wrought in their own hearts. Into their gentle souls have come bitter thoughts of rebellion. . . . They realize now something of what is back of all the opposition to the woman's advancement into all lines of activity and a share in government.[60]

In their Annual Report of 1918, the United Farm Women of Manitoba credited "war relief and patriotic work" with the formative role in the development of "a spirit of national sisterhood".[61]

It was not knitting for the Red Cross alone which produced this new frame of mind. The Census of 1911 had already revealed a tendency for increasing numbers of women to seek employment outside their homes, a tendency accentuated by the wartime shortage of manpower. More important, Western women were entering fields which had formerly tended to employ men. The number of women engaged in professional occupations, mainly teaching,· increased 130% between 1911 and 1921. Alberta employed 630 more female teachers in 1916 than in 1914. Wartime vacancies also gave women an opportunity in Government Service, and Western governments employed four times as many in 1921 as they had ten years earlier.[62] New opportunities for women did not stop with employment. Women began to infiltrate other areas regarded once as *de facto* male preserves. At the University of Manitoba, for example, the "two major honours", student presidency and newspaper editorship, went to women in 1917.[63]

In addition to this role as men's replacements, women pointed to the fact that they bore much of the war's real suffering. They were the ones who struggled to keep farms working and families together in their husband's absence. They were also the ones who had to carry on after husbands and sons were killed or maimed in France. Wilson Macdonald caught this sense of sacrifice in verse:

Ah! the battlefield is wider than the cannon's sullen roar;
And the women weep o'er battles lost or won.
For the man a cross of honour; but the crepe upon the door
for the girl behind the man behind the gun.[64]

Suffragists enjoyed this image of the noble woman, quietly continuing with her duty and bearing her grief in silence. In reality, however, everything done for the war effort by woman was given the widest possible publicity and described in the most heroic terms possible. Women's pages of western dailies were filled with stories on patriotic service done by women. The caption accompanying a series of pictures featured in the *Winnipeg Tribune* provides an example:

It is the men warriors who reap all the material rewards of war; it is the men who have medals pinned upon their breasts; it is the men whom the world lauds as heroes. What of the women who labor and suffer at home in the cause of justice and freedom? In Winnipeg there are thousands of women who are doing as much to win battles as their soldier fathers, brothers, husbands and sons. There are women who are devoting every waking hour to the provision of comforts for boys at the front, and to planning for their care when they return.[65]

Magazine articles publicized the female side of the war effort, making it clear that women "count it an honour to engage in an occupation that strengthens the hands of our Empire."[66] Politicians especially were not allowed to forget women's contributions to the struggle with Germany. Letters reminded them how "truly and nobly our women have shown themselves equal to any emergency'', and urged that women be given still greater responsibilities.[67]

Because of this surge of publicity, and partly by direct contact with the new woman, the image men held of women began to change. Some resented the fact that the Red Cross and other activities fell largely into female hands. F.W. Rolt, secretary of the Edmonton Red Cross, found woman's new assertiveness so alarming that he resigned his position, claiming that although "I don't wish to control the ladies, still less do I wish to be controlled by them."[68] But most men, even if they shared Rolt's fears about female domination, were grudgingly forced to concede that women were proving that they deserved equal citizenship. When the Dominion Parliament debated the question in 1917, for example, R.B. Bennett reversed his former opposition to woman's suffrage. Since women during the war were "discharging their full duties with respect to service", he felt that they must be admitted, "side by side with the male population . . . to exercise the highest rights and highest functions of citizenship." Two Western members from the other side of the House voiced enthusiasm for Bennett's conversion. W.A. Buchanan stated simply that he was "in favour of women [sic] suffrage . . . because I believe the women have earned the right to that franchise since the war commenced." Michael Clark added that Bennett's opinion would be well received in the West, since it was "in accordance with the opinions of the vast majority of the people of Western Canada."[69]

It was the provincial governments, however, which acted first on the suffrage question. During the opening months of 1916, each Western Province granted its women the provincial franchise. Manitoba came first in January, and in March Alberta and Saskatchewan followed suit. Only one vote was cast against woman's suffrage in all three provinces, that by a French-Canadian member of the Alberta House. Albertans made up for this by returning Mrs. Louise McKinney to the Legislature in the provincial election of the following year, and by naming Mrs. Emily Murphy as the first woman magistrate in the British Empire.[70]

The federal franchise was not to come as suddenly or as completely. The Dominion Government's grant of woman's suffrage came in stages. It was established in principle by the Military Voters Act, which gave the vote to women serving in the Armed Forces, or as nurses. The controversial Wartime Elections Act, enfranchising close female relatives of men serving overseas, established it further, but still not completely. Those women who gained the ballot, especially those in Western Canada, used it to vote for the government which had given it to them. Complete woman's suffrage, like prohibition, was one of the many things reformers hoped for from the newly elected Unionists. Suffragists were not disappointed. Prime Minister Borden personally introduced a franchise bill in April, 1918, and parliamentary assent followed rapidly. On January 1, 1919, less than two months after the war ended, the crusade for woman's suffrage was over, as far as the Prairie Provinces were concerned.

Woman's suffrage would have come without the Great War. There can be little doubt that the women of the Western Provinces would have gained the provincial franchise before too many years had passed, and the federal franchise would have followed eventually, although probably after a much longer struggle. But the Great War, with its impact on the suffragists' rationale, organization, and public image, speeded the victory at both levels. Perhaps, however, the war's real importance to the woman's movement extends beyond the primary question of the right to vote. The dislocations of war won for women a foothold in fields of endeavour formerly reserved for men, and the traditional pattern of domestic service as the working woman's principal occupation. With these new opportunities came a new self-respect. By changing the average woman's image of herself and her position in a world dominated by men, the war advanced the cause of women in ways not simply political.

No other reform group was able to exploit the wartime situation as successfully as were the advocates of woman's suffrage and prohibition. The direct legislation movement enjoyed a brief moment of elation in 1916, when Manitoba's Norris government introduced an Initiative and Referendum Act. The Act was not accompanied by any large-scale campaign based on the mid-war enthusiasm for democracy, but was the fulfilment of a commitment Norris had made while Leader of the Opposition. The Saskatchewan Conservative Party attempted to ressurect the direct democracy issue during the 1917 Provincial Election, but were unable to use it to gain any political advantage.[71] This was in part because of the fact that a substantial number of those who had originally supported the initiative and referendum had done so as a means to obtain prohibition, not because of a strong belief in direct legislation for its own sake. By 1917 these people were satisfied, and saw no need to campaign for a tool they no longer needed to use.

The economic reforms sought by Western reformers proved even more difficult to obtain. Unlike prohibition, woman's suffrage, and direct legislation, most of these had to come from the Dominion Parliament, a body not as easily influenced as a provincial government. The war did pave the way for some specific objectives. During 1917 the first Canadian tax on incomes was imposed, and the principle of railway nationalization as exemplified by the case of the Canadian Northern was also well received in the West. Western support for Union Government was based on the assumption that more such action would be forthcoming, most particularly a reduction in the tariff. In this respect, and on the question of economic reform in general, Westerners were to be sadly disillusioned during the final year of war.

Notes

1. A. Richard Allen, *The Social Passion* (Toronto, 1971) Chapter 1, *passim*.

2. In Saskatchewan, for example, only six of the twenty-six local option referenda conducted in December, 1913, resulted in prohibitionist victories. Erhard Pinno, "Temperance and Prohibition in Saskatchewan" (unpub. M.A. Thesis, University of Saskatchewan, 1971), p. 29.

3. E.J. Chambers, "The Plebiscite and Referendum in Saskatchewan" (unpub. M.A. Thesis, University of Saskatchewan, 1965), Chapter 1.

4. Provincial Archives of Manitoba (P.A.M.), Colin H. Campbell Papers, R.P. Roblin to Colin H. Campbell, 9.1.14.

5. *Canadian Annual Review (C.A.R.)*, 1914, p. 598.

6. The first phrase is from a resolution passed by the Manitoba Legislature on the third anniversary of the War's declaration, while the second is included in a circular written by W.R. Motherwell on behalf of the 1918 Victory Loan. P.A.M., Norris Papers, Box 2. Archives of Saskatchewan (A.S.), Motherwell Papers, p. 26267.

7. Rev. Canon Murray, "Canada's Place in the War", in Canadian Club of Winnipeg, *Annual Report 1913-14*, p. 71.

8. Mrs. Louise McKinney, "President's Address", in Alberta WCTU *Report of the Annual Convention 1915*.

9. Nellie L. McClung, *In Times Like These* (New York, 1915), p. 161.

10. Clifford Sifton, "Foundations of the New Era", in J.O. Miller, *The New Era in Canada* (Toronto, 1918), pp. 37-38.

11. A.S., Saskatchewan Grain Growers' Association, *Convention Report*, 12.2.17.

12. Mrs. H.V. Plumptre, "Some Thoughts on the Suffrage", in Miller, *New Era*, pp. 328-9.

13. Archives of the Glenbow Foundation (Glenbow) Alberta WCTU Collection #1, f. 35, *Report of the Annual Convention, 1915*, p. 30.

14. Plumptre, *op. cit.*, p. 329.

15. McClung, *In Times Like These*, p. 5, R.E. Spence, *Prohibition in Canada* (Toronto, 1919), p. 71.

16. Sara Rowell Wright, "The WCTU Program" in *The Social Service Congress of Canada* (Ottawa, 1914), p. 322.

17. McClung, *In Times Like These*, p. 165.

18. *Manitoba Free Press*, 6.3.16.

19. *Grain Growers' Guide*, 16.6.15.

20. Frances M. Beynon in *Ibid.*, 30.5.17.

21. Ralph Connor, *The Sky Pilot in No Man's Land* (New York, 1917) pp. 149-50.

22. A.S., Martin Papers, Ladies of North Battleford Methodist Church to W.M. Martin, 7.11.16, p. 31654. See also Alberta WCTU Minute Book, 2.1.15; and P.A.M., Manitoba WCTU Collection, Winnipeg District Minute Book, 9.12.14.

23. Motherwell Papers, Mrs. W.R. Motherwell, Address at Lemberg, Sask., 5.12.16, f. 123.

24. A.S., Walter Scott Papers, Capt. J.L.R. Parsons to Scott, 25.3.15, p. 59695. See also Pinno, *op. cit.*, p. 121; John H. Thompson "The Prohibition Question in Manitoba, 1892-1928" (unpub. M.A. Thesis University of Manitoba, 1969), p. 2; and R.I. McLean, "Temperance and Prohibition in Alberta, 1875-1915" (unpub. M.A. Thesis, University of Calgary, 1970); p. 134.

25. Glenbow, Calgary Brewing and Malting Collection, W. Towers to A.E. Cross, 1.1.18, f. 577.

26. *Manitoba Free Press*, 7.3.16.

27. *Edmonton Bulletin*, 20.7.15. See also *Regina Leader*, 24.2.15.

28. *Manitoba Free Press*, 7.3.16.

29. McClung, *In Times Like These*, p. 170.

30. This quotation is from a resolution of the Manitoba Rural Deanery of the Church of England, *Manitoba Free Press*, 1.3.16. The Anglican conversion to prohibition is discussed in McLean, *op. cit.*, pp. 111-112. For the Orange Order's opinion see *C.A.R.*, 1915, p. 665 and P.A.M., R.P. Roblin Papers, J.J. Stitt to R.P. Roblin, 3.3.15. For an IODE attitude see Provincial Archives of Alberta (P.A.A.), Beaverhouse IODE Minute Book, 1.10.14. The Winnipeg Canadian Club's views are expressed in its *Annual Report*, 1913-14, pp. 6-7.

31. Lionel Orlikow, "A Survey of the Reform Movement in Manitoba, 1910-1920" (unpub. M.A. Thesis, U. of Manitoba, 1955), p. 150.

32. Scott Papers, Scott to Willoughby, 1.12.14, p. 48455; Levi Thomson to Scott, 8.4.15, p. 48503; Motherwell to Scott, 18.12.14, p. 12889; Scott to S.G. Hill, 1.7.15, p. 13300; Scott to J.H. Ross, 12.4.15, p. 13650.

33. A.S., J.A. Calder Papers, Calder to G.H.V. Bulyea, 23.3.15, G4, p. 11.

34. R.I. McLean, *op. cit.*, p. 135.

35. Motherwell Papers, T.A. Mitchell to Motherwell, 22.1.16, f. 71(2).

36. *The Western Prairie* (Cypress River, Manitoba), 2.3.16.

37. Calder to Bulyea, 23.3.15, Calder Papers, G. 4, p. 11. Opposition to prohibition during wartime was notable among those of German birth or descent. The German language *Der Courier, Der Nordwesten*, and *St. Peters Bote* all editorialized against prohibition, and the German Canadian Alliance of Saskatchewan publicly denounced the "aggressive and unscrupulous agitation" of the prohibitionists. See Erhard Pinno, *op. cit.*, pp. 121-3, Thompson, *op. cit.*, pp. 28-9, and *C.A.R.*, 1914, p. 630.

38. *Manitoba Free Press*, 6.3.16; *Canadian Farmer*, November, 1916, translation in Martin Papers, pp. 31616-8.

39. Alberta WCTU, *Annual Report*, 1915, p. 60.

40. *Manitoba Free Press*, 14.3.16.

41. Pinno, *op. cit.*, p. 122; *Le Courrier de l'Ouest* (Edmonton), 1.7.16; *Le Manitoba*, 13.4.16. The comparative effectiveness of patriotic arguments for prohibition on French Canadians and non-Anglo-Saxon immigrants can be demonstrated by an examination of referendum results in the Alberta constituencies of Victoria, Whitford, St. Albert, and Beaver River. All four rejected prohibition, but Victoria and Whitford, with heavy Ukrainian pupulations, did so by the relatively narrow margin of 1392 to 1022. St. Albert and Beaver River, with largely French-Canadian electorates, recorded a combined majority of 889 against prohibition, 1484 to 595.

42. Calgary Brewing and Malting Collection, A.E. Cross to D.R. Ker, 24.3.15, f. 550.

43. *Edmonton Bulletin*, 6.7.15.

44. Advertisement in Motherwell Papers, f. 71(2).

45. *Calgary Eye Opener*, 8.7.16.

46. Manitoba WCTU Collection, Recording Secretary's Book, 15.2.16.

47. Province of Manitoba, *Annual Report on the Temperance Act*, Sessional Paper #13, 1917.

48. Martin Papers, Mrs. G.V. Jewett to Martin, 23.4.17, p. 31759.

49. R.E. Popham and W. Schmit, *Statistics of Alcohol Use and Alcoholism in Canada* (Toronto, 1958), pp. 48-53. See also James H. Gray, *The Boy From Winnipeg* (Toronto, 1970), p. 126 and *Red Lights on the Prairies* (Toronto, 1971), pp. 149-151.

50. Alberta WCTU Collection #1, Social Service Council Convention Minutes, 18.2.19, f. 7.

51. Scott Papers, Levi Thomson to Scott, 8.4.15, p. 48503.

52. *Saskatoon Phoenix*, 19.3.15. Richard Allen has suggested that prohibition was "almost predictable" in Manitoba and Saskatchewan before the war began in 1914, (*Social Passion*, p. 22). This judgment seems exaggerated, given the lack of success of local option ballots, the defeat of the Norris Liberals in Manitoba, and comments such as those of Calder and Scott cited above, p. 93. '/

53. See June Menzies, "Votes For Saskatchewan's Women", in N. Ward ed., *Politics in Saskatchewan* (Don Mills, 1968), p. 90, Thompson, *op. cit.*, pp. 59-60, and C.L. Cleverdon, *The Woman's Suffrage Movement in Canada* (Toronto, 1950), pp. 49-64.

54. McClung, *In Times Like These*, p. 14. See also Carol Lee Bacchi Ferraro, "The Ideas of the Canadian Suffragists, 1890-1920" (unpub. M.A. Thesis, McGill University, 1970), pp. 109-111.

55. McClung, *op. cit.*, p. 27.

56. Aileen S. Kraditor, *The Ideas of the Woman Suffrage Movement* (New York, 1965), p. 38-63.

57. The first phrase is from P.A.C., Dafoe Papers, Clifford Sifton to J.W. Dafoe, 21.9.14. The second is from Stephen Leacock, "Democracy and Social Progress", in J.O. Miller, *New Era*, p. 13.

58. W.L. Morton, "The Extension of the Franchise in Canada: A Study in Democratic Nationalism", *Canadian Historical Association Report*, 1943, p. 79.

59. R.J.C. Stead, *The Cow Puncher* (Toronto, 1918), p. 342.

60. McClung, *In Times Like These*, pp. 28-29. For some examples of the effects of the war in

increasing the membership of women's organizations, see Glenbow, United Farmers of Alberta Collection, f. 35; Scott Papers, Eva Sherrock to Scott, 14.2.16, p. 59505; *Manitoba Free Press*, 27.2.15. For a good example of the co-operation among organizations promoted by the war, see Alberta WCTU Collection #2, North West Calgary Union, Minutes, 4.11.15, f. 5.

61. P.A.M., United Farmers of Manitoba Collection, United Farm Women Report, 1918.

62. The Census of 1921 revealed a sixty-three *per cent* increase in the number of women in the western provinces employed outside their homes. For comparative figures see Canada, *Fifth Census*, 1911, vol. VI, p. 10, passim, and *Sixth Census*, 1921, vol. IV, p. 10, passim. The statistics on women teachers in Alberta are taken from Alberta, Department of Education, *Annual Report*, 1916, pp. 16-17.

63. *Manitoba Free Press*, 4.10.17.

64. Wilson Macdonald, "The Girl Behind the Man Behind the Gun", in *Song of the Prairie Land* (Toronto, 1918), pp. 124-6.

65. *Winnipeg Tribune*, 9.10.15.

66. P.A.A., Miriam Elston Scrapbooks, "The Home Shall be an Honoured Place", *Everywoman's World*, November 1916.

67. Scott Papers, Ella B. Carroll to Scott, 1.2.16, p. 59492; Norris Papers, W.R. Wood to T.C. Norris, 26.1.18, Box 2. In his work on the domestic impact of the war on Great Britain, Arthur Marwick describes British women as "a gigantic mutual-admiration circle" during wartime. Marwick, *The Deluge* (London, 1965), p. 96. Marwick's comment can be applied to their Canadian counterparts as well.

68. University of Alberta Archives, Henry Marshall Tory Papers, F.W. Rolt to H.M. Tory, 15.5.15, f. 14082A.

69. Canada, House of Commons, *Debates*, 1917, vol. II, pp. 1515-19.

70. L.G. Thomas, *The Liberal Party in Alberta* (Toronto, 1959), p. 165. For a detailed description of the passage of each suffrage act see Cleverdon, *op. cit.*, pp. 46-83.

71. Chambers, "Plebiscite and Referendum", p. 63.

CHAPTER 2

Western Protest Between the Wars

Introduction

It was argued in the General Introduction that the segmentation of a society into distinct and self-conscious social groups increases the probability that people will find existing institutions unsatisfactory. On the other hand, it was also stated that, even in a highly segmented society, it is unlikely that there will be widespread agreement among the dissatisfied as to exactly what should be done to remedy social wrongs.

The number and variety of social movements arising in Western Canada during the inter-war years become easier to understand if we keep these two general propositions in mind. It is certainly clear that social cleavages in Canada between town and country, and between East and West, were the principal causes of the rejection of certain institutions on the part of the western farmer. It is equally clear that the segmentation of Canadian society gave to western farmers a feeling that they had common interests (were peas in the same pod, if you will). This "we" feeling made it easier for them to join together in concerted efforts to change the world in which they lived. At the same time, however, a careful analysis of these movements indicates that, a high level of social segmentation notwithstanding, there is no guarantee that people will arrive at a consensus regarding action to overcome the failings of existing institutions. During the period under consideration in this chapter, western farmers tried a variety of solutions including political action at the federal level, the establishment of provincial third parties, and, finally, other-worldly solutions of a religious nature. Even within specific social movements, there were often sharp divisions on what institutional forms should be sought to remedy inadequacies in the structure of society.

A convenient starting point for a study of these western social movements is Prime Minister Wilfrid Laurier's budget speech of 1903. "The best way you can help the manufacturers of Eastern Canada," he argued, "is to fill up the Prairie regions of Manitoba and the North West with a prosperous and contented people, who will be consumers of the manufactured goods of the East."[1] Clearly, Westerners were to provide a market for Eastern manufactured goods and thereby ensure Eastern prosperity. In articulating this sentiment, however, Laurier was expressing nothing new. Similar ideas had been advocated by Sir John A. Macdonald in support of his National Policy during the nineteenth century.

With the federal election of 1896, the Liberals had become heirs to this policy. Earlier Conservative attempts to promote prosperity through western settlement, by increasing manufacturing through the imposition of a protective tariff, and by completing the Canadian Pacific Railway, had been only partially successful. Coincident with the Liberal victory, however, there occurred a number of events that propelled Canada into the twentieth century and ushered in a period of unprecedented prosperity. These developments are concisely examined by W.L. Morton.

> The great depression was lifting in Europe and America. New supplies of South African gold were easing the shortages of money. The London investment market was seeking such opportunities as a booming Canada would afford. The price of wheat — and this was of special significance to Canada — though not high, was becoming profitable in terms of the goods and services the grain grower purchased. Not less significant for Canada was the fact that the frontier of free land had ended in the United States, and American farmers and European immigrants were turning to the wide wheat lands and free homesteads of the Canadian West. There a new frontier was being prepared, as dry farming techniques were introduced and early maturing strains of wheat developed. The West, after years of frustration, was in 1896 on the eve of a great advance.[2]

The ramifications of this advance were to be felt far and wide. First, the development of a wheat economy in the Canadian West stimulated changes in other sectors of the economy. "In view of its growth, linkages, and income effects," economist G.W. Bertram argues, "the propulsive sector in the period 1896-1914 appears to have been wheat. . . ."[3] Second, as a concomitant of development, the social composition of the West acquired a more heterogeneous character. Although, by 1926, those of British origin still formed the largest single ethnic group in the rural areas of the prairie provinces, they did not form a majority: only 46.5% of the population was British. The next largest group consisted of Germans with 9.79%, followed by Ukrainians with 9.22% and Scandinavians with 8.26%.[4]

The clustered settlement of a number of farmers of similar origins — like the

Mennonites — may have offset some of the disadvantages of early life in the West. But only a small proportion of the settlers enjoyed the advantages of "community" offered by this kind of group settlement. The words of a woman in the Peace River District illustrate the social isolation from which many suffered.

> My nearest neighbour was 60 miles away. The Bensons of Kleskun Lake had come in 1906, but they remained only a few months. Our oldest daughter was born in December, 1907. The nearest doctor was 250 miles distant at Lesser Slave Lake, and the only person one could dignify by the name of a nurse was at Spirit River. This woman was married to a half-breed minister (Anglican) and she agreed to care for me. However, she arrived when the baby was a day old and did the best she could.[5]

It should be emphasized that not all settlers faced the extremely lonely life of this particular woman on the fringes of settlement. For one thing, wide variations existed between regions. The nature of the economic activity carried out, however, automatically entailed certain privations, as is evident in the words of a south-western Albertan.

> We lived at the Oxley for about ten years and, on the whole, I was happy and contented. But it was a very lonely life, as far as human companionship went. For weeks at a time we saw no one outside our own circle, but there was always plenty to do about the house and garden, and we had a good supply of books sent to us regularly from the Times Book Club.[6]

The limited social activity of the prairie farmer during the early period of settlement was not the only factor that made his life a precarious one. There were also droughts, crop failures, pestilence, and fluctuations in demand for agricultural produce. These uncertainties, coupled with an apparently uncaring federal government, led to the eventual alienation of great numbers of Westerners from the two-party system.

As long as wheat prices remained high and the aspirations of farmers did not outstrip what they were able to produce on the land, they remained fairly quiet. Although the trend was often irregular, between 1896 and 1918, the price of No. 1 Northern gradually increased.[7] In the latter year, the price reached an unprecedented $2.24 a bushel.[8] While cost of living statistics are not available for the entire period under discussion, between the years 1913 and 1916, despite an astronomical rise in the price of wheat, the cost of living remained relatively stable. Between 1917 and 1919 it rose somewhat, but the effects of this rise were offset by the high price of wheat.[9] After 1919, however, while the cost of living remained relatively stable, the price of wheat declined in an irregular fashion.[10]

These developments alone might have been sufficient to generate prairie discontent.

Corresponding to these developments was a long-term suspicion held by the western farmer that the tariff, one of the planks of the National Policy, operated to his disadvantage. The tariff meant artificially high prices for products manufactured in the East, while the price of wheat was determined by the world market. As long as the price of wheat remained high, this discrepancy led to no serious manifestations of discontent on the part of farmers. However, "with the increase of agricultural indebtedness, and the disappearance of the advantageous price differential between agricultural prices and those of manufactured goods, on which the wheat boom had taken its rise, the discontent," W.L. Morton argues, "deepended."[11] There was a growing feeling among farmers that existing political and economic institutions held them in subordinate relationships to Eastern business interests. This belief was only re-affirmed when, time after time, both the Liberals and Conservatives refused to alter the tariff significantly or to implement reciprocity with the United States.

The first sign of agrarian discontent was the formation, throughout the Prairie Provinces, of farmers' associations. "The primary purpose of the new organizations", Morton has argued, "was to educate their members in collective action, a knowledge of their legal and political rights, and an appreciation of the dignity of their calling. The organized farmers began with a deep conviction that the root of the farmer's plight was his individualism, his isolation, and his ignorance of matters outside his narrow practical experience."[12] In essence, the farmers' associations began to formulate an ideology that put the farmers' plight into a larger perspective; they provided leadership; and through their meetings and publications (like the *Grain Growers' Guide*) they provided avenues for the dissemination of information. In this manner, they afforded an organizational base around which support for various issues could be mobilized.

The mobilization of prairie farmers to bring about institutional reforms was facilitated by two factors. First, by definition, all farmers were engaged in similar occupations. Consequently, the effects of economic hardship were experienced by all. Second, the source of their troubles was easily identified: the segmentation of Canadian society made it easy for Western farmers to choose a villain on whom they could legitimately place the blame.

To begin with, those who occupied advantageous positions in Canadian economic institutions (the executives of the CPR, the manufacturers, bankers, and so on) were resident in Eastern urban centres like Toronto and Montreal.[13] Furthermore, in some areas, serious divisions existed between the town and rural sectors of the province. This type of situation is examined by Jean Burnet.

> In the province of Alberta the United Farmers of Alberta and the related co-operative movement followed closely the pattern of farm rebellion against the small town. The UFA was established in 1909

through the amalgamation of the Alberta Farmers' Association and the Canadian Society of Equity and the locals of this association became the most active associations in the rural communities. In them the farmers discussed their difficulties and grew confident of their ability to secure a remedy by united effort. In the discussions, it appeared that the small town merchants and professional men were the obstacles to agricultural progress. Politically, as stalwarts of the Liberal Party, they dominated the rural communities; economically, as creditors in a situation where capital was in very short supply, they were again dominant.[14]

Despite the legitimate grievance of farmers vis-à-vis Eastern business interests and urban merchants, they were initially reluctant to introduce change by other than generally accepted means. Their first tactic was an attempt to make the old parties, especially the Liberals, respond to their plight. By 1919, however, it seemed obvious, even to the most optimistic of farmers, that both of the old parties were concerned primarily with the interests of Eastern business. And so, in the federal election of 1921, a group of western farmers, in the form of the Progressive Party, took their first reluctant step into the federal electoral arena.

The result was staggering! Sixty-four Progressives, mainly from the West, were elected to the House of Commons. No one, not even the Progressives themselves, had envisaged such an overwhelming success. Indeed, once elected to Parliament, large numbers of the Progressives were uncertain as to what to do. This uncertainty was aggravated by the fact that, despite some common grievances, the Progressives included supporters of different political persuasions. Perhaps the most important distinction is that between the Alberta and Manitoba wings. The former rejected the traditional parties and stressed "group government": according to this notion, representation in Parliament should be on the basis of occupational groups. The Manitoba faction, on the other hand, never really abandoned the Liberal Party; it saw Progressive action merely as one way to achieve reform.

Needless to say, factionalism of this kind made the Progressives a less effective force in Parliament than they otherwise would have been. Indeed, by the time of the 1925 federal election, Mackenzie King had managed to *co-opt* a great number of Progressives back into the Liberal fold. Some ran again as Progressive candidates in the 1925 election, but by the election of 1926 the movement had declined drastically.

The extent to which the Progressives attained their goals is difficult to assess. Because the King minority government required Progressive parliamentary support, certain reforms beneficial to the farmers were introduced between 1921 and 1925. But whether it was these reforms or an increase in the price of wheat in the late twenties that led to a decline in the movement is a moot point. Whatever the case, the problems of the Western farmers were not over.

While considerable effort was expended by farmers in the federal realm during the twenties, less third-party activity was evident at the provincial level. In Manitoba and Saskatchewan the traditional parties tried to incorporate farmer demands into their platforms. On some occasions, provincial party organizations even went to the extreme of downplaying their connections with their federal counterparts. Thus at the provincial level, especially in Saskatchewan, established institutions were more responsive to the demands of farmers and no new political movements of any consequence came into existence until later.

In Alberta the situation was different. Scandal and inaction on the part of the incumbent Liberals, and the ineffectiveness of the Conservatives, left no apparent alternative but for farmers to enter politics at the provincial level. An agrarian third party, known as the United Farmers of Alberta, won office in 1921 and held it until 1935. It is important to emphasize that, while both Manitoba and Saskatchewan had farmers' organizations that could have served as an organizational base for lasting political movements, large-scale mobilization of farmers in Saskatchewan did not occur until the early thirties with the founding of the CCF. In Manitoba, the degree of mobilization was minimal with the exception of the 1922 election. The point being made is that, in all three provinces, farmers' organizations could have provided an organizational base on which to mobilize support for a new and lasting political movement at the provincial level. That this occurred only in the case of Alberta illustrates that where existing institutions respond to the demands of certain groups in society, political mobilization is less likely than where resistance is encountered.

In Alberta, then, the farmers' associations that mobilized support for the Progressives also provided an organizational base for the UFA. The ideology guiding this movement found its ultimate expression in the writings of Henry Wise Wood and the theory of group government.[15] Since the political wing of the UFA was thought to represent the group interests of farmers, the party did not even seek support in urban centres until 1932 when it became obvious that they could "never attain federal power on the basis of an appeal to the electorate of their own class".[16]

By 1932, however, it was already too late for the UFA. A new movement, the Social Credit movement, would displace it in the forthcoming elections. Over the years the UFA had become routinized and largely unresponsive to the needs of Albertans during the Depression years. The economic consequences of the depression, coupled with drought and pestilence, made Albertans receptive to new appeals — appeals that would not only provide economic recovery but spiritual relief as well. Indeed, Albertans had always been unhappy with established churches and thus receptive to new religious movements. As W.E. Mann writes of the established churches in Alberta of the thirties, the "adjustments of these denominations to the outlook of the middle classes . . . implied an incapacity to meet the social needs of the urban working class and the poorer farmers. The services of the churches thus inevitably differed from those of the sects because they spoke to different social 'worlds'."[17]

The situation in Alberta in the thirties, then, was this. On the political level, discontent on the part of the electorate developed in partial response to the UFA's routinization and inability to cope with problems generated by the Depression. That these problems were grave is easy to substantiate. Perhaps some of the trials faced by rural Albertans are best illustrated not by harsh statistics on unemployment, but in letters such as the following sent to Prime Minister R.B. Bennett in 1934.

> I had my crop completely hailed out, I applied to the municipality for relief. I am on the sick list, & the Counciler got a certificate from the Docter that I was not to do any work I have a bad alcerated stomach, so that I could not go on the road to work. The Counciler told me that I would get $6.00 per month for myself and $8.00 for my Wife & daughter between them. They held me up for two months longer than all the rest then a week ago sent us $8.00 order for groacery. I am the only one here treated like this. If it had not been for our Storekeeper we would have starved I have been here nearly 22 years and have never asked for anything before. If I was a <u>foreinger</u> or <u>red</u> I would get the best of treatment, has it happens I am a <u>Loyal Englishman.</u> There is a lot of unjust work going on with this relief. There is lot getting it that should not get it. An Englishman could die here nobody trouble's about him.
>
> Will you please give this your consideration as we need fair play at once. I had to return the Docters medicine that he sent through the mail, Has I had not the money to pay for it.[18]

Dissatisfaction with the established political structure as a result of the very real problems of the Depression was compounded in Alberta by a major sex scandal involving John Brownlee, Premier of the province. On the social and psychological levels, Albertans were not only dissatisfied, they were also bewildered by the fate that had befallen them and did not know what measures could be taken to solve the Depression. Into this situation stepped the charismatic William Aberhart, who offered a program of religious as well as economic salvation.

Through the years of broadcasting a fundamentalist message from the Prophetic Bible Institute in Calgary, Aberhart had built up a substantial personal following. During the early thirties he became convinced that the only salvation for the ills of the Depression lay in the adoption of social credit monetary reform. Since certain members of the UFA had been considering similar ideas for a number of years, his appeals fell on receptive ears. Indeed, in many cases, study groups established by Aberhart throughout the province, virtually "took over" UFA locals. At the "grass roots" level, then, there was considerable organizational continuity between the UFA and the Social Credit movement. This continuity, coupled with a proliferation of social credit papers and pamphlets, mass meetings, and speaking tours, provided the movement with the means of communication needed to disseminate the social credit ideology. Leadership for the movement was effectively provided by Aberhart and his lieutenants, all of whom were articulate and forceful speakers.

It is important, at this point, to distinguish between the social credit movement *per se* and the political wing of the social credit movement. For one thing, Aberhart himself was reluctant to enter politics. Only when he was convinced that the existing political parties would not adopt his ideas did he consent to run for office. As running mates, he would accept only individuals he considered to be of morally upright character, for such men, he believed, would be needed to break the grip of Eastern business interests over the Albertan economy. In the federal and provincial elections of 1935, the Social Credit victories were overwhelming. At the provincial level, the Social Credit Party would not be displaced for 35 years.

Once electoral victory was achieved, the Social Credit rapidly lost the characteristics of a social movement. Despite the impressive electoral record of the Social Credit, however, there was a great deal of factionalism in both the movement and, later, in the party. Even before the elections, some social crediters were doubting the orthodoxy of Aberhart's brand of social credit. Later, after a government had been formed, a number of social credit supporters became dissatisfied on more than one occasion with Social Credit legislation. In each instance, however, Aberhart was able to put the blame for non-implementation on others; consequently, he was able to maintain control of the party. If Social Crediters were not able to achieve their goals, he claimed, it was not because of inherent weakness in their ideology, but because of evil forces in the world actively seeking to destroy the credibility of social credit. Most frequently, these forces were supposedly Jewish or socialist. Luckily for the Social Crediters, the trials of the Depression were drawing to an end before they were required to test their electoral strength a second time.

William Aberhart was not the only fundamentalist leader who met with success. Indeed, as previously suggested, the inability of established churches to accommodate themselves to the needs, especially, of working-class or rural Albertans led to the proliferation of a number of religious sects. With the exception of Aberhart's movement, though, these movements did not usually attempt to enter the political arena. Nor, for that matter, did they challenge the fundamental order of society. In a word, they were conservative. The institutional deficiencies with which they were concerned were largely confined to the established Christian churches, which they believed had strayed from the true path. Among the proponents of this type of religious ideology were many forceful and tireless leaders who spread the gospel through mass camp meetings, by travelling, sometimes on horseback, from one settlement or farm to the next, or through more modern means like papers, pamphlets, and radio. It is hard to assess the extent to which movements such as these realized their goals. Presumably one would have to count the members of the faithful who attain the kingdom of heaven.

In the province of Saskatchewan religion and politics were, on one notable occasion, as intertwined as they were in the social credit movement in Alberta. In the late twenties the Ku Klux Klan, an American-based organization, made great gains in the province. Large numbers of Saskatchewan residents, including prominent members of the Protestant clergy, Conservative and Progressive politicians, found the essentially revivalist, fundamentalist, and racist message of the Klan appealing.

The Klan's attraction is easy to account for. As a result of federal immigration policies, Saskatchewan had relatively large numbers of Catholic non-Anglo-Saxons in its population. Some groups in the province regarded these policies "as a conspiracy between the federal government and the Roman Catholic church".[19] At the level of provincial politics, some Saskatchewan Anglo-Saxon Protestants feared the determination of a French-origin minority to retain their language and culture. The Ku Klux Klan, which espoused doctrines of racial purity and fundamentalist protestantism, under circumstances such as these, was able to generate a great deal of support: it drew attention to perceived inadequacies in both federal and provincial policies regarding what were considered important matters to large numbers of people.

In disseminating its message, the Klan, to a large degree, relied on some existing Protestant churches and, in a less obvious fashion, the Conservative and Progressive parties. It was successful in spreading its message to the extent that the 1929 provincial Conservative-Progressive minority government was in part made possible by the overlapping membership on the part of Klansmen, Conservatives, and Progressives, who accepted the Klan's beliefs. The campaign itself was one in which ethnic and religious differences were consistently exploited by certain members of both the Conservative and Progressive parties.

Despite its initial impact, support for the Klan rapidly declined. Perhaps the Depression diverted attention to matters other than ethnicity and religion. Whatever the case, the career of the Klan, as the return of the provincial Liberals — who represented a cross-section of the Saskatchewan population — to office in 1934 indicates, was a short one. During its brief period of ascendancy it generated enough attention, however, to warrant inclusion in a discussion of Western protest between the wars.

In the following selection of articles, some of the processes described above are analysed in more detail. The article by Morton, although written almost thirty years ago, deserves distinction as a classic in Canadian social science. Likewise, Irving's analysis of the social credit movement is an excellent piece of Canadian scholarship. All too frequently, social scientists working on the Canadian scene ignore these and other milestones in the study of Canadian society.

Notes

1. *Report of the Royal Commission on Dominion-Provincial Relations*, Ottawa: King's Printer, 1940, p. 73.
2. W.L. Morton, *The Progressive Party in Canada*, Toronto: University of Toronto Press, 1950/1967, p. 4.
3. G.W. Bertram, "Economic Growth in Canadian Industry, 1870-1915," in W.T. Easterbrook and M. Watkins, (eds.), *Approaches to Canadian Economic History*, Toronto: McClelland and Stewart, 1967, p. 92.
4. C.A. Dawson, et al., *Pioneering in the Prairie Provinces: the Social Side of the Settlement Process*, Toronto: Macmillan, 1940, p. 34.
5. Quoted in C.A. Dawson, et al., *The Settlement of the Peace River Country*, Toronto: Macmillan, 1934, p. 33.
6. Quoted in Dawson, et al., *Pioneering in the Prairie Provinces*, p. 21.
7. M.C. Urquhart and K. Buckley, (eds.), *Historical Statistics of Canada*, Toronto: Macmillan, 1965, p. 359.
8. *Ibid.*
9. *Ibid.*, p. 304.
10. *Ibid.*, p. 359.
11. W.L. Morton, "The Western Progressive Movement, 1919-1921," below.
12. W.L. Morton, *The Progressive Party in Canada*, p. 11. See also W. Irvine, *The Farmers in Politics*, Toronto: 1920; P. Sharp, *The Agrarian Revolt in Western Canada*, Minneapolis: University of Minnesota Press, 1948; L.A. Wood, *A History of Farmers Movements in Canada*, Toronto: Ryerson, 1924.
13. See D.V. Smiley, (ed.), *The Rowell-Sirois Report Book 1*, Toronto: McClelland and Stewart, 1963. Also see A.K. Davis, "Canadian Society and History as Hinterland versus Metropolis," in R.J. Ossenberg, (ed.), *Canadian Society: Pluralism, Change and Conflict*, Toronto: Prentice-Hall, 1971.
14. Jean Burnet, "Town-Country Relations and the Problem of Rural Leadership," *Canadian Journal of Economics and Political Science*, XIII, no. 3, (August 1947), p. 396.
15. See C.B. Macpherson, *Democracy in Alberta*, Toronto: University of Toronto Press, 1953/1970; and W.K. Rolph, *Henry Wise Wood of Alberta*, Toronto: University of Toronto Press, 1950.
16. J. Irving, *The Social Credit Movement in Alberta*, Toronto: University of Toronto Press, 1959/1968, p. 232.
17. W.E. Mann, *Sect, Cult and Church in Alberta*, Toronto: University of Toronto Press, 1955/1972, p. 52.
18. L.M. Grayson and J.M. Bliss, (eds.), *The Wretched of Canada*, Toronto: University of Toronto Press, 1971, p. 97.
19, W. Calderwood, "Pulpit, Press and Political Reactions to the Ku Klux Klan," below.

The Western Progressive Movement, 1919-1921

W.L. Morton

The Progressive Movement in the West was dual in origin and nature. In one aspect it was an economic protest; in another it was a political revolt. A phase of agrarian resistance to the National Policy of 1878, it was also, and equally, an attempt to destroy the old national parties. The two aspects unite in the belief of all Progressives, both moderate and extreme, that the old parties were equally committed to maintaining the National Policy and indifferent to the ways in which the "big interests" of protection and monopoly used government for their own ends.

At the root of the sectional conflict, from which the Progressive Movement in part sprang, was the National Policy of 1878. Such conflict is partly the result of the hardships and imperfect adaptations of the frontier, but it also arises from the incidence of national policies.[1] The sectional corn develops where the national shoe pinches. The National Policy, that brilliant improvisation of Sir John A. Macdonald, had grown under the master politician's hand, under the stimulus of depression and under the promptings of political appetite, until it had become a veritable Canadian System Henry Clay might have envied. Explicit in it was the promise that everybody should have something from its operation; implicit in it — its inarticulate major premise indeed — was the promise that when the infant industries it fostered had reached maturity, protection would be needed no more.

This, however, was but a graceful tribute to the laissez-faire doctrine of the day. This same doctrine it was which prevented the western wheat grower from demanding that he, too, should benefit directly from the operation of the National Policy. That he did benefit from the system as a whole, a complex of land settlement, railway construction, and moderate tariff protection, is not to be denied. But the wheat grower, building the wheat economy from homestead to terminal elevator in a few swift years, was caught in a complex of production and marketing costs, land values, railway rates, elevator charges, and interest rates.

Reprinted from the *Canadian Historical Association Annual Report*, 1946, pp. 41-55, by permission of the author and The Canadian Historical Association.

He fought to lower all these costs by economic organization and by political pressure. He saw them all as parts of a system which exploited him. He was prevented, by his direct experience of it, and by the prevailing doctrine of laissez-faire, from perceiving that the system might confer reciprocal benefits on him. Accordingly, he hated and fought it as a whole. Of the National Policy, however, the tariff was politically the most conspicuous element. Hence, the political battle was fought around the tariff; it became the symbol of the wheat growers' exploitation and frustration, alleged and actual. Like all symbols, it over-simplified the complexities it symbolized.

This clash of interest had, of course, to be taken into account by the national political parties. The Liberal-Conservatives, as creators of the National Policy, had little choice but to extol its merits even in regions where they seemed somewhat dim. They could stress its promise that a good time was coming for all, they could add that meanwhile the Yankees must be held at bay. When the Liberals quietly appropriated the National Policy after attaining national power in 1896, the task of the Conservatives became much easier. Not only could the Liberals be accused of having abandoned their principles; they could even be accused of unduly prolonging the adolescence of infant industries. A western Conservative, Mr. Arthur Meighen, could indict the Laurier administration on the charge of being maintained in power "behind ramparts of gold"[2] erected by the "interests." This echo of the "cross of gold" was not ineffective in the West, where the charge that there was no real difference between the parties on the tariff not only promoted the growth of third party sentiment, but also prolonged the life of western conservatism.

The Liberals, for their part, had not only abandoned "continentalism" in the Convention of 1893, but with the possession of power had developed that moderation without which a nation-wide majority may not be won or kept in a country of sectional interests.[3] Liberal speakers might proclaim that the party was the low tariff party; Fielding might make the master stroke of the British preferential tariff; certain items might be put on the free list here, the rates might be lowered on certain others there; but the Liberal party had become a national party, with all the powers and responsibilities of government, among them the maintenance and elaboration of the now historic National Policy. In consequence each national party began to appear more and more in the eyes of the wheat grower as an "organized hypocrisy dedicated to getting and holding office,"[4] and the conditions were created for a third party movement in the West.

The tariff, then, was a major predisposing cause of a third party movement in the West. Down to 1906 the British preference and other concessions of the Fielding tariff, together with reiterated promises of further reductions, kept the western Liberals within the fold. The completion in that year, however, of the three-decker tariff marked the beginning of more serious discontent. It grew with the offer of reciprocity in the Payne-Aldrich tariff of 1909. With the increase of agricultural indebtedness, concomitant with the settlement of the West, and the disappearance of the advantageous price differential between agricultural prices and those of manufactured goods, on which the wheat boom had taken its rise, the discontent deepened. It found expression through the grain growers' organizations, those "impressive foci of progressive ideas."[5] In 1909 came the organization of the Canadian Council of Agriculture, in 1910 Laurier's tour of the West,[6] and the Siege of Ottawa by the organized farmers. Plainly, the West was demanding its due at last. The Liberal party, which had lost support in Ontario in every election since 1896, which saw its hold in Quebec threatened by the Nationalists under Bourassa, could not afford to lose the support of a new and rapidly growing section. In 1911 the helm was put hard over for reciprocity, and Liberal prospects brightened in the West.[7] But this partial return to continentalism in economic policy was too severe a strain for a party which had become committed as deeply as its rival to the National Policy. The "Eighteen Liberals" of Toronto, among them Sir Clifford Sifton, broke with the party, and it went down to defeat under a Nationalist and a National Policy cross-fire. At the same time the Conservative party in the West, particularly in Saskatchewan and Alberta, suffered strains and defections which were to show in a lowered vitality in succeeding elections. But the offer of reciprocity remained on the statute books of the United States for another decade, and year by year the grain growers in convention demanded that the offer be taken up.

The demand of the western agrarians for the lowering of the tariff, however, was by no means an only factor in the rise of the third party. Into the West after 1896 poured immigrants from the United States and Great Britain. Most of the Americans came from the Middle West and the trans-Mississippi region. Many brought with them the experience and the political philosophy of the farmers' organizations and the third parties of those regions. Perhaps the clearest manifestation of their influence on the political development of the West was the demand for direct legislation which found expression in those forums of agrarian opinions, the grain growers' conventions, and which also found its way to the statute books of the three Western Provinces. From the British Isles came labour and socialist influences, felt rather in labour and urban circles, but not without effect among the farmers. These populist and socialist influences were mild; their exponents were in a minority. Nonetheless, they did much to give western discontent a vocabulary of grievance. Above all, they combined to repudiate the politics of expediency practised by the national parties, to denounce those parties as indifferently the tools of the "big interests," and to demand that the farmer free himself from the toils of the old parties and set up a third party, democratic, doctrinaire, and occupational.[8]

In the Canadian West this teaching fell on a soil made favourable not only by a growing disbelief in the likelihood of either of the national parties lowering the tariff, but also by a political temper different from that of Eastern Canada. (One exception must be made to this statement, namely, the old Canadian West in peninsular Ontario, from which, indeed, the original settlement of the West had been largely drawn.) This difference may be broadly expressed by saying that the political temper of the eastern provinces, both French and English, is whiggish. Government there rests on compact, the vested and legal rights of provinces, of minorities, of corporations.[9] The political temper of the West, on the other hand, is democratic; government there rests on the will of the sovereign people, a will direct, simple, and no respector of rights except those demonstrably and momentarily popular. Of this Jacksonian, Clear Grit democracy, reinforced by American populism and English radicalism, the Progressive Movement was an authentic expression.

No better example of this difference of temper exists, of course, than the Manitoba school question. Manitoba was founded on a balance of French and English elements; this balance was expressed in the compact of the original Manitoba Act, the essential point in which was the guarantee of the educational privileges of the two language and religious groups. The balance was destroyed by the Ontario immigration of the eighteen-seventies and eighties; in 1890 Manitoba liberalism swept away the educational privileges of the French minority and introduced the "national" school, the chief agency of equalitarian democracy. This set in train a series of repercussions which, through the struggle over the Autonomy Bills in 1905, the introduction of compulsory education by the Liberal party in Manitoba in 1916, and the friction caused by Regulation 17 in Ontario, led up to the split in the Liberal party between the western and the Quebec Liberals on the Lapointe resolution in the federal Parliament in 1916. This split not only foreshadowed and prepared the way for that on conscription; it also contributed to the break-up of the old parties which opened the way to the rise of the Progressive party after 1919.[10] The western Liberals, that is to say, were turning against Laurier because they feared Nationalist domination of the party.

Thus it was that the ground was prepared for the West to throw its weight behind Union Government, first suggested as a war measure, then persisted in to prevent a Liberal victory under Laurier. Western Liberals and radicals did so with much reluctance and many misgivings. An independent movement was already taking root.[11] For the Liberal party, an electoral victory was in sight, following a succession of provincial victories and the discontent with the Borden Government's conduct of the war.[12]

This probable Liberal victory, to be based on anti-conscription sentiment in Quebec and low tariff sentiment in the West, was averted by the formation of the Union Government. The issue in that political transformation was whether the three western Liberal governments could be detached from the federal party. But the attempt made at the Winnipeg convention in August, 1917, to prepare the way for this change was defeated by the official Liberals.[13] The insurgents refused to accept the verdict of the convention; and by negotiations, the course of which is by no means clear, the support of the three western administrations and of the farmers' organizations was won for Union Government. Thus the leadership of the West was captured, and assurance was made doubly sure by the Wartime Elections Act. At the same time, the nascent third party movement was absorbed by the Union Government, and the Liberal party in the West was wrecked by the issue of conscription, as the Conservative party had been mortally wounded by reciprocity.

Though the Union Government was constituted as a "win the war" administration, which should still partisan and sectional strife, other hopes had gone to its making. It was thought that a non-partisan administration might also be an opportunity to carry certain reforms, such as that of civil service recruitment, that it would be difficult, if not impossible, for a partisan government to carry. There was also, and inevitably, the tariff. The Union Government was not publicly pledged to tariff reform, but there can be no doubt that western sentiment had forced Unionist candidates to declare themselves on the tariff; indeed many western Unionists were low tariff Liberals, or even outright independents. The eastern industrialists, on the other hand, were alert to see that the weighty western wing of the Cabinet should not induce the government to make concessions to the West. Thus there was an uneasy truce on the tariff question during the remainder of the war, the issue lying dormant but menacing the unity of the Government and its majority once the pressure of war should be removed. The test was to come with the first peace budget, that of 1919.

These, then, were the underlying causes of the rise of the western Progressive Movement. In 1919 they came to the surface, unchanged in themselves but now operating in a heated and surcharged atmosphere. That there would have been a Progressive Movement in any event is not to be doubted; the war and the events of the post-war years served to give it explosive force.

Certain elements in this surcharged atmosphere were general, others peculiar to the farmer, in effect. Chief of the general elements was the fact that the War of 1914-18 had been fought without economic controls of any significance. The result was inflation with all the stresses and strains inflation sets up in the body economic and social. The high cost of living, as it was called, was an invariable theme of speakers of the day, particularly of spokesmen of labour and the farmer. The farmer was quite prepared to believe that he, as usual, was especially the victim of these circumstances, and would point to the "pork profiteers," to clinch his contention. Inflation was at the root of the general unrest of the day, and the influence of the Russian Revolution, the radical tone of many organizations and individuals, the Winnipeg strike, and the growth of the labour movement are to be ascribed to inflation rather than to any native predisposition to radical courses.

Among the farmers' special grievances was the conscription of farmers' sons in 1918. The farming population of English Canada, on the whole had supported conscription, but with two qualifications. One was that there should also be "conscription of wealth," by which a progressive income tax was meant. The other was that the farms should not be stripped of their supply of labour, a not unreasonable condition in view of the urgent need of producing food. But the military situation in the spring of 1918 led to the revocation of the order-in-council exempting farmers' sons from military service. The result was a bitter outcry from the farmers, the great delegation to Ottawa in May, 1918, and an abiding resentment against the Union Government and all its works, especially in Ontario.

In the West itself, drouth, especially in southern Alberta, had come to harass a farm population already sorely tried. Suffice it to indicate that in the Lethbridge area of southern Alberta, the average yield of wheat between 1908 and 1921 ranged from sixty-three bushels to the acre in 1915 to two in 1918, and eight in 1921.[14] This was the extreme, but the whole West in varying degrees suffered a similar fluctuation in yield. It was a rehearsal of the disaster of the nineteen-thirties.

To the hazards of nature were to be added the hazards of the market. In 1917 the government had fixed the price of wheat to keep it from going higher, and had established a Wheat Board to market the crops of the war years. Now that peace had come, was wheat once more to be sold on the open market, or would the government fix the price and continue to market the crops through the Wheat Board, at least until the transition from war to peace was accomplished? Here was a chance to make the National Policy a matter of immediate benefit and concern to the western farmer, a chance not undiscerned by shrewd defenders of the National Policy.[15] Here also, under the stimulus of war, was the beginning of the transition from the old Jeffersonian and laissez-faire tradition of the frontier West, to the new West of wheat pools, floor prices, and the Cooperative Commonwealth Federation. The point of principle was clearly grasped by the farmers, but their response was confused. The Manitoba Grain Growers and the United Farmers of Alberta declined in annual convention to ask the government to continue the Wheat Board, but this decision was severely criticized, one might almost say, was repudiated, by the rank and file of the membership. The Saskatchewan Grain Growers, who met later, emphatically demanded that the Wheat Board be continued. In the upshot it was, but only for the crop yield of 1919, and in 1920 it was liquidated. From this action came much of the drive, indeed the final impetus, of the Progressive Movement.[16] Thereafter the western farmer was caught between fixed debt charges and high costs on one hand and falling prices on the other; his position seemed to him desperate. From his despair came first, the Progressive electoral sweep in the West, and then the economic action which created the wheat pools.

Finally, there was the question of tariff revision. It was, however, no longer the simple clash of sectional interests it had been. The customs tariff had been increased to help finance the war. Any revision now would affect governmental financing of the war debt, and also the financial resources of private individuals and corporations in the post-war period. In short, the question had now become, what place should tariff revision have in reconstruction?

It was to this question that the Union Government had to address itself, while preparing the budget of 1919 under the vigilant eyes of the farmers' organizations on the one side and of the Canadian Manufacturers' Association on the other. The decision was, in effect, to postpone the issue, on the ground that 1919 was, to all intents and purposes, a war year and that only a very moderate revision should be attempted. The decision was not unreasonable, and was clearly intended to be a compromise between eastern and western views on the tariff.[17] But western supporters of the Union Government were in a very vulnerable position, as the McMaster amendment to the motion to go into Committee of Supply was to show.[18] The pressure from the West for a major lowering of the tariff was mounting and becoming intense. In the outcome, the Honourable Thomas A. Crerar, Minister of Agriculture, resigned on the ground that the revision undertaken in the budget was insufficient. In the vote on the budget he was joined by nine western Unionists. This was the beginning of the parliamentary Progressive party.

The position of the remaining western Unionists became increasingly difficult, though also their pressure contributed to the moderate revision of 1919.[19] The fate of R.C. Henders is very much in point. Henders had been, as President of the Manitoba Grain Growers, an ardent and outspoken agrarian. In 1916 he had been nominated as an independent candidate for Macdonald. In 1917 he accepted nomination as Unionist candidate and was elected. In 1919 he voted with the Government on the budget on the ground that this was in effect a war budget, and the time premature for a revision of the tariff. In 1920 the United Farmers of Manitoba, following the action of their executive, "repudiated his stand, accepted his resignation, and reaffirmed [their] confidence in the principles of the Farmers' Platform."[20] In 1921 he vanished from political ken. An honest man had taken a politically mistaken line and was mercilessly held to account. Such was the fate of western Unionists who did not cross the floor or find refuge in the Senate. Western low tariff sentiment would admit of no equivocation.

The third party movement, stirring in the West before 1917 but absorbed and over-ridden by the Unionist Government, was now free to resume its course with a favourable wind fanned by inflation, short crops, and post-war discontent. A chart had already been provided. The Canadian Council of Agriculture had in 1916 taken cognizance of the mounting demand that political action be taken by the farmers. Without committing the Council itself, it prepared the Farmers' Platform as a programme which the farmers' organizations might endorse and which they might press upon the government. The events of 1917 diverted attention from it, but in 1918 it was revised and enlarged, and in 1919 was adopted by the farmers' organizations. In substance, the platform called for a League of Nations, dominion autonomy, free trade with Great Britain, reciprocity with the United States, a lowering of the general tariff, graduated income, inheritance, and corporation taxes, public ownership of a wide range of utilities, and certain reforms designed to bring about a greater measure of democracy, such as reform of the senate, abolition of titles, and the institution of direct legislation and proportional representation.[21] The platform gave the incoherent western discontent a rallying point and a programme, and was the occasion for the organized farmers entering federal politics. Its title, "The New National Policy," was a gage of battle thrown down before the defenders of the old National Policy, a challenge, direct and explicit, to make that policy national indeed.

This decision to enter federal politics was opportune beyond the dream of seasoned politicians. The prairie was afire in a rising wind, and soon the flames were flaring from one end of the country to the other. In October, 1919, the United Farmers of Ontario carried forty-six seats in a house of 111, and formed an administration. Later in the same month O.R. Gould, farmers' candidate in the federal seat of Assiniboia, defeated W.R. Motherwell, Liberal stalwart and a founder of the Grain Growers' Association, by a majority of 5,224.[22] A few days later Alex Moore carried Cochrane in a provincial by-election for the United Farmers of Alberta. In 1920 the organized farmers carried nine seats in Manitoba, seven in Nova Scotia, and ten in New Brunswick.[23] By-election after by-election went against the Government, usually to farmer candidates, until the smashing climax of the Medicine Hat by-election of June, 1921, when Robert Gardiner of the UFA defeated a popular Unionist candidate by a majority of 9,764.[24] Even the Liberals' tariff plank of 1919 did little to check the sweep of the flames. The political prophets were estimating that of the forty-three seats west of the lakes, the Progressives would carry from thirty-five to forty.[25]

All was propitious, then, for the entry of the Progressives into federal politics. There they might hope to hold the balance of power, or even emerge as the largest group. The work of organization was pushed steadily. In December, 1920, the Canadian Council of Agriculture recognized the third party in the House of Commons as the exponent of the new national policy and endorsed the members' choice of the Honourable T.A. Crerar as leader.[26] During 1920 and 1921 Progressive candidates were nominated by local conventions in all federal constituencies in the West.

Two major difficulties, however, were arising to embarrass the Progressives in their bid for national power. The first was the charge that they were a class party. The second was the demand that political action be taken in the provincial as well as the federal field.[27] These embarrassments were eventually to split the Movement, defeat its bid for national power, and reduce it to the status of a sectional party.

The origin of these divisions in the Movement may best be examined by turning to provincial politics in the West. That the entrance into federal politics could not be kept separate from a demand that political action be taken in the provinces, arose in part from the federal composition of national parties. Any federal political movement is driven to attempt the capture of provincial governments, in order to acquire the means, that is to say, the patronage, whereby to build an effective political organization. It is not to be supposed that this political maxim was unknown to the leaders of the Progressive Movement. They hoped, however, that national success would be followed by a voluntary adherence of the western governments, which would render capture by storm unnecessary.

The Progressive Movement, at the same time, was a genuine attempt to destroy machine politics, and there was in its leadership a sincere reluctance to accept the facts of political life. They hoped to lead a popular movement, to which the farmers' economic organizations would furnish whatever direction was necessary. It was the zeal of their followers, eager to destroy the old parties wherever they existed, that carried the Progressive Movement into provincial politics.

Province by province, the leaders were compelled to bow to the pressure of the rank and file, and allow the organized farmers to enter the provincial arenas. The methods and the results, however, were by no means identical, for they were conditioned by the different political histories of the three provinces.

In Manitoba the dominating fact was that from 1899 until 1915 the province had been governed by the Conservative Roblin administration. The sheer power and efficiency of the Roblin-Rogers organization, perhaps the classic example of the political machine in Canadian history, accounts in great part for the victory of the anti-reciprocity campaign in Manitoba in 1911. Its spectacular demise in the odour of scandal in 1915 left the provincial Conservative party badly shattered. Henceforth there were many loose Conservative votes in the most conservative of the Prairie Provinces, a province a whole generation older than the other two, and during that generation the very image and transcript of Ontario. But the succeeding Liberal Government, that of the Honourable T.C. Norris, was reformist and progressive. There was little the Grain Growers could ask of the provincial administration that it was not prepared to grant. Why then should the organized farmers oppose the Norris Government? The answer was that the Progressive Movement was, for many Progressives, a revolt against the old party system, and the provincial Liberal organization had been affiliated with the federal Liberals. It might, indeed, become a major buttress of Liberalism as the breach between the Laurier and the Unionist Liberal closed. If the old parties were to be defeated at Ottawa, they must be rooted out at the source of their strength in the provinces. Out of this conflict, largely one between leaders and rank and file, came the decision of the new United Farmers of Manitoba in 1920 that the organization as such should not enter provincial politics, but that in the constituencies the locals might hold conventions, nominate candidates, and organize. If a majority of constituencies should prove to be in favour of political action, then the executive of the United Farmers would call a provincial convention to draft a platform.[28] As a result, political action was taken locally, and nine farmer representatives were elected to the Manitoba legislature in 1920.[29] As a result of this success, the UFM placed the resources of the organization behind the farmers' political action,[30] and in the election of 1922 the farmers won a plurality of seats in the legislature. The suspected *rapprochement* of the Norris Government with the federal Liberals may have contributed to its defeat.[31]

In Saskatchewan and Alberta the dominating factor was that at the creation of the two provinces in 1905 the federal Liberal government used its influence to establish Liberal administrations. In Canada the possession of power is all but decisive. Governments fall not so much by the assaults of their enemies as through their own internal decay. From 1905 until 1921 the Liberals ruled in Alberta; from 1905 until 1929 they were in power in Saskatchewan. Moreover, in both, the Conservative party was cut off from patronage and unnaturally compelled to be a party of provincial rights. Both provincial Conservative parties declined from 1911 on, and rapidly after the provincial elections of 1917. In these provinces too, the administrations were careful to govern in harmony with the wishes of the organized farmers. Why then should the farmers enter provincial politics against the Liberal government? Again the answer is that the provincial Liberal parties were affiliated with the federal party, and were examples of the machine politics which Progressives hoped to destroy, politics rendered noisome by the corruption arising from the scramble for the resources of the West, and the political ruthlessness of the professional politicians of the day.

Down to 1917 the political developments of the two provinces were alike, but a remarkable diversion occurs thereafter. In Saskatchewan the Liberal party enjoyed shrewd leadership, considerable administrative ability, and a fine political organization. Threatened by scandal in 1917, it made a remarkable recovery under Premier William Martin. In that almost wholly rural province, the Liberal government was a government of the grain growers. Leadership, as in the instance of the Honourable Charles A. Dunning, graduated from the Association to the government. The slightest wish of the Saskatchewan Grain Growers became law with as much dispatch as the conventions of government allow.[32] When the demand for provincial political action arose, Premier Martin met it, in the Preeceville speech of May, 1920, by dissociating the provincial from the federal party. At the same time the weight of the executive of the Grain Growers was thrown against intervention as a separate party in provincial politics. As in Manitoba, when the demand, partly under pressure from the Non-Partisan League, became irresistible, it was referred to the locals.[33] The locals gave little response during 1920-1, and an attempt of third party men in 1921 to commit the central organization to political action was foiled.[34] As a result, the provincial

Progressive Movement in Saskatchewan became largely an attempt at organization by independents, under the leadership of Harris Turner of Saskatoon.[35] Before organization could be well begun, Premier Martin dissolved the legislature and headed off the movement by a snap election. This was decisive. Only thirteen independents were returned, to a great extent, it would seem, by Conservative votes, for the provincial Conservative party simply did not contest the election. Thus the Liberal administration in Saskatchewan survived the Progressive rising, but at the price of severing temporarily its ties with the federal party.

In Alberta the same story was to have a very different outcome. Not only was the Liberal party of that province less fortunate in its leadership, though no less realistic in its tactics, not only did it suffer division by the quarrel over the Alberta Great Waterways Railway scandal, which created a weakness in the party that the division into Laurier and Unionist Liberals did nothing to mend;[36] but the farmer organization of that province was separate in its leadership from the government, and that leadership was from 1915 the leadership of Henry Wise Wood. In Alberta, the forceful personalities were outside the government; in Saskatchewan, they were, on the whole, in the government or close to it. Alberta lost the brilliant A.L. Sifton to the Union Government in 1917, and Alberta alone possessed a Henry Wise Wood. Wood and the executive of the United Farmers of Alberta were no more anxious than other leaders of the farm organizations to go into provincial politics. He, indeed, was on principle opposed to going into politics at all. The drive for a third, independent, farmer party, however, developed much greater force in Alberta than elsewhere. This was partly because the decline of the Conservative party was even more pronounced in Alberta than in Saskatchewan. It was also because the Non-Partisan League became more powerful in that province than in Saskatchewan. American populism and British radicalism had freer play in frontier Alberta than in older Saskatchewan. The Non-Partisan League, for example, captured two provincial seats in Alberta in 1917, whereas it had captured only one in Saskatchewan in the same year, and that by a fluke. The League went on to threaten to capture the locals of the UFA by conversion and infiltration. This was a threat that could not be ignored, because it was in and through the locals that the farmers' organizations lived. Wood and the UFA leaderships were therefore caught on the horns of a dilemma. They knew that political action had invariably ruined farm organizations in the past, as the Farmers' Alliance in the United States had gone to wreck in the Populist party. They knew also that they might lose control of the UFA if the Non-Partisan League obtained control of a majority of locals and assumed leadership of the drive for political action. Wood solved the dilemma by his concept of "group government", and in doing so crystallized the strong tendency of the Progressive Movement, a tendency which owed much to the Non-Partisan League, to become a class movement, deeply averse to lawyers, bankers, and politicans. The UFA would take political action, but it would take it as an organization. It would admit only farmers to its ranks; it would nominate only farmers for election; its representation in the legislature would constitute a separate group, co-operating with other groups but not combining with any to constitute a political party. Guided by this concept, the UFA in 1919 entered politics, both federal and provincial.[37] In 1921 it won a majority of the seats in the Alberta legislature.

These varying fortunes of the Progressive Movement in the three provinces were significant for the character of the federal Progressive party. Broadly speaking, two concepts of the character and future of the party prevailed among its members. One, which may be termed the Manitoba view, was that the Progressive Movement was one of insurgent liberalism, which might have the happy result of recapturing the federal Liberal party from the control of the conservative and protectionist Liberals of the East. This was the view, for example, of J.W. Dafoe, a mentor of Progressivism. It aimed at building up a national, popular movement by "broadening out," by "opening the door" to all sympathizers. The Saskatchewan federal Progressives also accepted this view, the more so as the provincial movement had been headed off for a decade. The other concept may be called the Alberta concept. It was that the Progressive Movement was an occupational or class movement, capable of extension by group organization to other economic classes, but not itself concerned with bringing about such extension. Farmer must represent farmer, the group must act as a group.

It may be noted in passing that neither view of the Progressive Movement demands an explicit farmer-labour alliance. Why Progressivism did not develop this characteristic of the earlier Populist party and the later Cooperative Commonwealth Federation cannot be explained here, but it may be said that the leadership of both wings of the Movement was averse to an open alliance with labour.

Here again is the two-fold character of the Progressive Movement postulated in the opening paragraph. Progressivism which was an economic protest, seeking a natural remedy by political action little more unconventional than a revolt from caucus rule, is here termed Manitoban. Progressivism which was doctrinaire, class conscious, and heterodox, is here called Albertan. The former assumed that exploitation would cease in a society made competitive by the abolition of protection; the latter proposed to produce a harmony of interests by putting an end to competition by means of the co-operation of organized groups. Both tendencies, of course, existed all across the Movement. Each was personified and had as respective protagonists the Honourable T.A. Crerar and Henry Wise Wood.

The extremes, however, were fundamental and irreconcilable. Manitoban Progressivism sought economic ends through conventional political means and admitted of compromise with the old parties. Albertan Progressivism sought much the same economic ends, but also sought to transform the conditions of politics. In this it was closer to the essential nature of Progressivism, with its innate distrust of elected representatives and of party organization.[38] Its pledging of candidates, its frequent use of the signed recall, its levy on members for campaign funds, its predilection for direct legislation and for proportional representation, establish its fundamental character. That in so conducting itself it was to give rise to forms of political organization which old line politicians were to envy, is one of those little ironies which delight the sardonic observer.

An examination of the course of the general election of 1921 adds little to the exposition of the theme. As revealed in the campaign literature, it turned on the issues of protection and of the class doctrines of Henry Wise Wood. Prime Minister Meighen, first of those western men with eastern principles to be called to head the Conservative party, put on the full armour of protection, and fought the western revolt in defence of the National Policy. It was courageous, it was magnificent, but it was not successful. His party attacked the Progressives as free traders seeking to destroy the National Policy for selfish class advantage. Mr. W.L. Mackenzie King stood firmly on the Liberal platform of 1919, which, marvelously contrived, faced squarely all points of the political compass at once. Liberal strategy was to avoid a sharp stand, to pose as the farmers' friend — "There never was a Farmers' Party while the Liberals were in power"[39] — and to denounce the class character of Progressivism. Mr. Crerar was in the embarrassing position of a leader whose followers persist in treading on his heels, but he fought the good fight with dignity and moderation, protesting that his was not a class movement.

In the upshot, the Progressives carried sixty-five seats, and emerged as the second largest group in the House. Coalition with the Liberals was seriously considered and was rejected only at the last moment, presumably because Messrs. Crerar and Drury could not obtain from Mr. King those pledges which would have ensured the identity of the group and the curbing of the protectionist elements in the Liberal Cabinet. This decision marked the beginning of the disintegration of the Movement, for the Progressives neither imposed their policies on the Liberals nor definitely became a parliamentary party seeking office. With that fatal tendency of third parties to avoid responsibility, of which George Langley had warned a decade before,[40] they declined to become even the official opposition.

Thereafter Manitoban Progressivism lost its bright speed amid the sands and shallows of official Liberalism. Albertan Progressivism, represented by the Ginger Group, the federal UFA members and a few others, alone survived the decay of Progressive zeal, and remained for fourteen years to lend distinction to the national councils, and to bear in its organization the seeds at once of Social Credit and the Cooperative Commonwealth Federation.

Notes

1. *Cf.* Frederick Jackson Turner, *The Significance of Sections in American History* (New York, 1932), 314.

2. *Hansard*, 1910-11, I, 1918.

3. Wilfred E. Binkley, *American Political Parties* (New York, 1944) — ". . . Madison's principle that a nation wide majority can agree only on a moderate program," 87; also 17-18.

4. Dafoe Library of the *Winnipeg Free Press*, Dafoe Papers, Dafoe to Sir Clifford Sifton, July 21, 1919; on the prospects of re-organizing the Liberal party.

5. *Manitoba Free Press*, April 10, 1917, 9.

6. *Grain Growers' Guide*, September 14, 1910, 13. Fred Kirkham, advocate of a third party, wrote to the editor from Saltcoats, Saskatchewan: "If the memorials presented to Sir Wilfrid Laurier have failed to imbue him with the determination to battle with the vested interests of the East to grant our just requests, we have no alternative but to become democratic insurgents, and form a new party and find a new general to fight under. We must be courageous in politics before Laurier will treat with us as a big community of votes to be reckoned with."

7. Public Archives of Canada, Laurier Papers, 3089, J.W. Dafoe to Laurier, April 28, 1911. "In my judgment reciprocity has changed the whole political situation in the West. Until it was announced the drift out West was undoubtedly against the government; but now it is just other way about."

8. *United Farmers of Alberta, Annual Report*, 1910, 43. "Moved by the Vermilion Union: Resolved, that ten farmers, as members of Parliament with votes would have more weight in shaping the laws and influencing government than one thousand delegates as petitioners:

Therefore be it further resolved that the farmers, to secure this end, should vote for farmers only to represent them in Parliament and vote as a unit and cease dividing their voting power. Carried."

9. I am indebted to Professor J.R. Mallory of Brandon College, now of McGill, for a discussion clarifying this point.

10. *Manitoba Free Press*, May 13, 1916. Editorial, "Consequences." "Whatever may be the political consequences of this blunder to Liberalism in Canada at large, Western Liberalism will not suffer if it adheres to the independence which its representatives have displayed at Ottawa this week. These developments at the capital must tend to strengthen the feeling which has been growing steadily for years that Western Liberals need not look to the East, at present, for effective and progressive leadership. . . . Canadian public life will thus be given what it sorely needs, . . . a group of convinced radicals. . . . To your tents, O Israel!'"

11. *Ibid.*, June 28, 1917, 9. "The Saskatchewan Victory." "The Canadian West is in the mood to break away from past affiliations and traditions and inaugurate a new political era of sturdy support for an advanced and radical programme. The break-up of parties has given the West its opportunity; and there is no doubt it will take advantage of it." At least four independent candidates had been nominated in the West before June, 1917, in provincial and federal seats. In December, 1916, the Canadian Council of Agriculture had issued the first Farmers' Platform.

12. Henry Borden (ed.), *Robert Laird Borden: His Memoirs* (Toronto, 1938) II, 749-50, J.W. Dafoe to Borden, September 29, 1917.

13. Dafoe Papers, Dafoe to Augustus Bridle, June 14, 1921. "The Western Liberal Convention was a bomb which went off in the hands of its makers. It was decided upon at Ottawa by a group of conscription Liberals; the intention was to bring into existence a Western Liberal group free from Laurier's control who would be prepared to consider coalition with Borden on its merits, but the Liberal machine in the West went out and captured the delegates with the result that the convention was strongly pro-Laurier."

14. *Report of the Survey Board for Southern Alberta*, January, 1922.

15. *Hansard*, 1919, I, 558. Colonel J.A. Currie (Simcoe) "I am quite in agreement with the hon. member for Maple Creek (J.A. Maharg) when he says we should fix a price for the wheat of the West. That is in line with the National Policy." See also the Right Honourable Arthur Meighen's proposal for a modified Wheat Board in his speech at Portage la Prairie during the campaign of 1921. *Canadian Annual Review*, 1921, 449-50.

16. *Cf.* Vernon C. Fowke, *Canadian Agricultural Policy* (Toronto, 1946), 268.

17. The changes were as follows: the 7½ per cent increase for war purposes was removed from agricultural implements and certain necessities of life; the 5 per cent war duty was modified; an income tax was levied.

18. Fourteen western Unionists voted for the amendment. *Hansard*, 1919, IV, 3678.

19. *Hansard*, 1919, IV, 3475. W.D. Cowan, Unionist (Regina). "I believe that the changes which have been made in the tariff have been made entirely because of the agitation which has been carried on by the West. We have had, for the first time, I fancy, in the history of Parliament, a western caucus and in that we have been united. Old time Liberals united with old time Conservatives. On the one point that they should try to get substantial reductions in the tariffs. . . ."

20. *Canadian Annual Review*, 1920, 741.

21. See *ibid.*, 1919, for text. 365-8.

22. *Parliamentary Companion*, 1921, 196.

23. *Manitoba Free Press*, February 25, 1921; *Grain Growers' Guide*, August 4, 1920, 4, and October 27, 1920, 5.

24. *Parliamentary Companion*, 1922, 247.

25. Dafoe Papers, Dafoe to Sir Clifford Sifton, January 20, 1920.

26. *Grain Growers' Guide*, December 15, 1920, 3. Resolution of executive of the Canadian Council of Agriculture in meeting of December 7-9, 1920.

27. Dafoe Papers, Dafoe to Sir Clifford Sifton, January 26, 1921. "Crerar's only troubles out here arise from the ardor with which certain elements in his following insist upon organizing a purely class movement against the three local governments, thereby tending to antagonize the very elements which Crerar is trying, by broadening its basis, to add to his party."

28. *United Farmers of Manitoba Year Book*, 1920, 67.

29. *Grain Growers' Guide*, July 7, 1920, 6. Editorial, "The Manitoba Election." "The United Farmers of Manitoba, as an organization, took no part in the election, and each constituency where farmer candidates were nominated and elected acted entirely on its own initiative."

30. *Ibid.*, January 19, 1921, 3.

31. *Manitoba Free Press*, April 28, 1922. Dafoe Papers, Dafoe to Sir Clifford Sifton, July 7, 1922.

32. *Minutes of the Annual Convention of the Saskatchewan Grain Growers' Association*, February 18-21, 1919, 4. Report of Premier Wm. Martin's address. "There are questions now coming before you affecting the welfare of the whole community of the Province. It is the policy of the present government and will continue to be the policy of the present government to carry out these suggestions."

33. *Ibid.*, February 9-13, 1920, 114-19.

34. *Ibid.*, January 31-February 4, 1921. The debate on provincial political action was involved; a motion to enter provincial politics as an organization was defeated (118) and a motion to support action by constituencies was, it would seem, shelved (93).

35. *Saskatoon Daily Star*, June 1, 1921. Report of the convention of independents at Saskatoon, May 31, 1921.

36. John Blue, *Alberta Past and Present* (Chicago, 1924), 125. "The session of 1910 witnessed a perturbation and upheaval that split the Liberal party into two factions, which more than a decade afterwards regarded each other with some jealousy and distrust."

37. *United Farmers of Alberta, Annual Report*, 1919, 52-3.

38. *Grain Growers' Guide*, March 5, 1919, 26. Article by Roderick McKenzie on "Political Action." "The purpose of the movement inaugurated by the farmers is that whenever the time comes to make a choice of representation to parliament, the electors get together to make their selection."

39. P.A.C., Pamphlet no. 5081, *Group Government Compared with Responsible Government*.

40. *Grain Growers' Guide*, September 21, 1910, 13-14. "It may be urged that a separate farmers' party might influence the government even if it did not become strong enough to take on itself the actual work of governing. The answer to that is this. The legitimate objective of a political party is to control the legislative and administrative functions. Without [that] objective it cannot exist for any length of time. . . ."

The Evolution of the Social Credit Movement

John A. Irving

Although the doctrines of Social Credit have been systematically and extensively promoted throughout many parts of the British Commonwealth and the United States for nearly thirty years, it is only in Alberta that there has emerged a Social Credit movement sufficiently strong to win and maintain political power. It is proposed, in the present paper, to trace the historical development of this movement with specific reference to those data that are essential for its interpretation as a phenomenon of mass psychology. Such an approach must be restrictive and selective: data of primary importance to the economist, the political scientist, and even the sociologist must necessarily be omitted.

The Social Credit upsurge in Alberta was essentially a people's movement which sought to reform, but not to revolutionize, the existing social order by changing the pattern of certain existing institutions. It has passed through the four stages which constitute the natural history of a social movement — social unrest, popular excitement, formalization, and institutionalization; and it has exhibited, in the course of its evolution, the five mechanisms of reform movements — agitation, *esprit de corps*, morale, ideology, and operating tactics. From the perspective of social psychology, the movement may best be understood if, taking its more general sociological aspects for granted, we consider its appeal to the people of Alberta in terms of its leadership, its philosophy, and its techniques of organization and promotion. In analysing this particular social movement, the social psychologist is faced with two serious methodological difficulties: he must be careful not to confuse the evolution of the movement with the political history of Alberta, especially after 1935; and he must, as far as possible, present the movement as a dynamic rather than a static social phenomenon.

Social movements tend to appear during periods of widespread social unrest, when profound dissatisfaction with the existing social order arises. No conditions

Reprinted from the *Canadian Journal of Economics and Political Science*, Vol. 14, 1948, pp. 321-341, by permission of Mrs. Clayton Baxter and the Canadian Political Science Association.

could have been more favourable for the development of such unrest than those which existed in Alberta in the autumn of 1932. The farmers of the province had experienced every possible agricultural ordeal; they had been made the play-things of the high tariff manipulators; they had built up markets in the United States only to have them ruthlessly cut off; they had suffered drought and every agricultural pestilence from root-rot to grasshoppers; they had seen prices drop to such incredibly low levels that sometimes it did not pay to haul their produce to market. Under such circumstances, it is not surprising that a large percentage of the farms of Alberta had been heavily mortgaged. The utterly discouraged far-mers, looking for some tangible cause for all their miseries, focussed their resentment and hate upon the banks and loan companies. In the cities, towns, and villages the masses of the people were no better off. Unemployment was general; thousands were living on relief; still other thousands lacked the elementary provision of food, clothing, and shelter. Psychologically, hundreds of thousands of people were experiencing a profound personality disintegration: they were caught in a steel web from which there seemed no escape; their social environ-ment, their feeling for the process of life, their hope for the future, all became meaningless. Amid such desperate social and economic conditions, William Aberhart appeared as the prophet of a new social order.

Born at Egmondville, Ontario, in 1878, he was educated at the Seaforth Collegiate Institute, the Hamilton Normal School, the Chatham Business Col-lege, and Queen's University, from which he obtained extra-murally the degree of BA. After teaching in Ontario for several years, he settled in Calgary in 1910. Five years later he became principal of the Calgary Crescent Heights High School, one of the largest and best organized institutions in Western Canada. In addition to his heavy administrative duties, Aberhart was an efficient and suc-cessful teacher of arithmetic, transplanting to the West the nineteenth-century techniques of instruction he had acquired in Ontario. He first became prominent in Alberta, outside educational circles, as a religious leader. In his youth he had fallen under the influence of a great Bible teacher, and had hoped to enter the Presbyterian ministry. Almost as soon as he arrived in Calgary he organized a large Bible Class, which met in a succession of Presbyterian and Methodist churches, later in a Baptist church. By the early nineteen-twenties his following had become so large that he organized the Calgary Prophetic Bible Conference which assembled on Sunday afternoons in the largest theatre of the city to hear him give two-hour interpretations of Christian fundamentalism and Bible Prophecy to audiences that numbered 2,200. Owing to the enthusiasm of his followers he was persuaded, in 1925, to broadcast his Sunday services over CFCN, known as "The Voice of the Prairies" and, until recent years, the most powerful radio station in Canada. In addition to his Bible Conference, he or-ganized a Radio Sunday School which continued to function throughout the worst years of the depression. By his use of radio, he built up a personal following that, according to certain estimates, numbered between two and three hundred thousand persons. In 1927 his organization was put on a more permanent basis when he and his followers constructed in the heart of Calgary, at a cost of $65,000, the large Prophetic Bible Institute, which thenceforth became the centre of all his religious activities.

Until 1932, although Aberhart personally favoured the Conservative party, he had never taken part in civic or political activities at any level, nor had he engaged in public discussion of economic questions. But like most people, as the depression wore on, he gradually became acutely aware of the plight of unemployed youth, and more especially of the plight of the graduates of his own school. There is evidence that, in the autumn of 1931, certain young men who knew him well, both as high-school teacher and as religious leader, urged him to tackle the problem of the depression, but they elicited no apparent response. In the summer of 1932, when he was living in an Edmonton college during the period of marking matriculation examination papers, he was introduced by another teacher to the highly popularized version of the doctrines of Social Credit contained in Maurice Colbourne's *Unemployment or War*. After reading the book, Aberhart decided that Social Credit offered the hope of redeeming his province from the depths into which the politicians and bankers had plunged it. Without that fateful decision it is doubtful if there could have been a successful Social Credit movement in Alberta.

In its most developed and complex form, the philosophy of Social Credit includes a monetary theory which both "explains" the inner workings of the capitalistic financial system and offers a remedy for its unsatisfactory functioning in periods of depression and inflation, a political theory which re-interprets the role of the individual in the democratic state and an interpretation of history in terms of a long-existing Judaic plot or conspiracy to secure control of and dominate the world. Underlying these three basic doctrines of Social Credit is a moral-religious theory of the fundamental rights of man, which has been variously expressed in terms of elusive conceptions such as Cultural Heritage, Political Liberty with Economic Security, and the Struggle of the Powers of Light against the occult Powers of Darkness in the world. At no time has Social Credit advocated the overthrow of the capitalistic system or of private enterprise.

Social Credit owes its origin to a Scottish engineer, Major C.H. Douglas, who was impressed by the fact that many developments, *physically* possible from the engineer's point of view, are *financially* impossible. As assistant director in England of the Royal Aircraft Works during the First World War, he made comprehensive studies of cost accounting which led him to the conclusion that, in over 100 industrial establishments, the weekly sum total of wages and salaries was continually less than the weekly collective price of the goods produced. It was upon this conclusion that he formulated his now famous "A + B Theorem." In this theorem, A = the flow of purchasing power to the masses (as represented by wages, salaries, and dividends), and B = bank charges, overhead costs, taxes, and the cost of raw materials. If A + B represents the cost of production under the financial system, the rate of flow of purchasing power to the masses will be less than the rate of flow of prices in the same period of time. There will thus be a discrepancy, which Douglas maintains must be permanent, between A (the purchasing power of consumers) and A + B (the total cost of production). The "A + B Theorem" became the key conception of Douglas's economic theories, and provided him and his followers with one of their principal slogans, "Poverty in the Midst of Plenty," a paradox which clearly has very great propaganda value in a period of widespread social unrest fostered by an economic depression.

On its negative or critical side Social Credit maintains that a permanent deficiency of purchasing power is inherent in the capitalistic financial system in the Machine Age; on its positive or constructive side it seeks to solve the problem of distributing the abundance of goods produced, as well as to increase production. It is maintained that other proposals for social reconstruction suffer from three fallacies: that there is a limit to production; that work is the only just prior condition of individual income; and that there is magic in state ownership. Further, other reformers have not realized the significance of the distinction between financial credit, which is based upon gold, and real credit, which is based upon such factors as raw materials, power, and labour. Under the existing system, financial credit has fallen into the control of bankers who, through its manipulation, exploit the community for purposes of private profit. A functional financial system should be concerned with the issue of credit to the consumer up to the limit of the productive capacity of the producer, so that both the consumer's real demands may be satisfied, and the productive capacity of the industrial system may be utilized and developed to the fullest extent.

The present political system of democracy has led to the development of economic slaves: money has become the master rather than the servant of man. The people, as the sovereign authority, have lost their control over the monetary system; their sovereign authority has been usurped by bankers who have set up a financial dictatorship, and who use their control of credit to render ineffectual the voting power of the people. The economic system no longer fulfils a moral purpose: instead of economic security and freedom from want, the individual is faced with "poverty in the midst of plenty," misery, and unhappiness.

If the economic system is to function successfully, the state must make at least three fundamental changes: it must recover its control over the monetary system; it must issue social credit in the form of a *national dividend* (based upon a survey of the real wealth of the nation) to every person; and, to prevent the possibility of inflation, it must establish a *just price* for all goods. The evils in the existing economic system can be remedied by supplying the people with credit based upon the potential goods and services of society. This is the people's right, their *cultural heritage*. Only in this way will the individual be freed from wage slavery, be able to choose the work he likes best, be in a position to claim those goods which are rightfully his so that he can enjoy more leisure time. There was, from the beginning, a moral foundation for the changes in the monetary system proposed by Social Credit — the financial system must be reformed to enable the individual to achieve the fullest measure of self-realization.

As a political theory, Social Credit is presented as a "Way of Life": human nature is essentially good, and the individual, as the most important fact of society, is an end in himself, not a means to an end. Personal freedom is the most precious possession of life, and every individual should therefore have political freedom, at the same time that he enjoys economic security. The state exists solely to promote the individual's welfare, freedom, and security. The Social Credit Way of Life is compatible with both Chrisitianity and democracy, but its philosophers are extremely critical of the existing form of political democracy as well as being opposed to socialism and communism. It is asserted that there exists today only constitutional democracy, not functioning democracy. Parliament should be under the direct and continuous control of the electors; in actual practice, the people's representatives are controlled by the party machine. In place of the present system of limited state dictatorship, it is proposed to restore sovereign authority to the people: they must be organized in a "Union of Electors" through which the individual can directly express his aims and desires to his representatives in parliament.

It is as an interpretation of history that the theories of Social Credit are curiously familiar and at the same time most elusive. As the constant criticism of "Finance" wore somewhat threadbare, there gradually evolved the colourful doctrine that national and international events can only be understood in terms of the machinations of a select group of bankers (most of whom bear Jewish names) who are indissolubly linked with a long-standing Judaic conspiracy to dominate the world, working through the Masonic Order, and both international capitalism and international communism. The wars, depressions, and revolutions of our time can only be understood if one realizes that they are one and all the result of the activities of world conspirators or world plotters who will stop at nothing in their efforts to destroy both democracy and the system of free enterprise, and who are especially malicious in their attempts to ruin the British Empire. The emphasis that has been given in Alberta to each of these aspects of the philosophy of Social Credit has varied with the time, the occasion, and the person; but there can be no doubt that, for Aberhart, Social Credit was essentially a theory of monetary reform which had its moral foundation in the conception of the cultural heritage and its religious foundation in his own interpretation of Christian fundamentalism and Bible prophecy.

For a variety of reasons, monetary reform had long been advocated in Alberta as a solution of the shortage of money or "purchasing power" from which the province, like most frontier rural economies, has chronically suffered. As far as can be discovered, Social Credit literature was introduced into Western Canada by a magazine editor who, through his writings and personal friendships, brought the doctrines of Major Douglas to the attention of certain leaders of the United Farmers of Alberta in the House of Commons. Major Douglas himself came to Ottawa in 1923, at the suggestion of a UFA member, and testified before the Standing Committee of the House on Banking and Commerce. During the next ten years, the Social Credit theories, along with other proposals for monetary reform, were much discussed in the UFA locals. Monetary reform took on the psychological characteristic of a "preferred group tendency" in Alberta, and there can be no doubt that the long period of preparatory work by the UFA was one of the most powerful psychological factors in the rapid development of the Social Credit movement in the middle thirties. In addition, certain intellectual leaders in Calgary, who had formed the Open Mind Club, were vigorously engaged in discussing the theories of Social Credit at the very time that Aberhart became a convert; and the Edmonton teacher who introduced Aberhart to the doctrine was himself a member of a group of Social Crediters who had long been looking for a likely leader.

In the autumn of 1932, Aberhart gradually, and with cautious reservations, began to introduce Social Credit ideas into his Sunday afternoon religious broad-casts. In January, 1933, he prepared a series of mimeographed lessons, which in the main were incisive summaries of Douglas's earlier books, for use as the basis of discussion in a study group he organized in the Bible Institute. In the spring he held a number of meetings in various halls and schools in the suburbs of Calgary; and he published and sold extensively a pamphlet, *The Douglas System of Economics*. Leaving the study group in the Bible Institute during the summer months in the hands of several ardent followers whom he had instructed during the winter, Aberhart and the secretary of the Bible Institute, Mr. Ernest C. Manning, made a speaking tour of southern Alberta. Almost 95 per cent of their audiences during that summer consisted of persons who had long been listening to Aberhart's religious broadcasts, but enthusiasm rapidly began to spread beyond the religious following.

By September, 1933, hundreds of people were coming to the Institute to discuss Social Credit, and new techniques of organization had to be developed. Aberhart and his followers now began a systematic propagation of Social Credit theories throughout the city of Calgary and adjoining rural areas. As these early efforts were entirely educational, and in no sense political, he received many invitations to lecture to various Calgary groups and organizations and to many UFA locals in rural districts surrounding the city. The natural outcome of all this activity was the formation of local study groups in Calgary, in the towns and cities nearby, and ultimately throughout the whole of Alberta.

Public enthusiasm for Social Credit was apparent at the annual convention of the UFA held at Edmonton in January, 1934, and the delegates engaged in a hot debate on the advisability of forcing their government in Edmonton to introduce Social Credit legislation immediately. But there was grave dissension within the UFA organization owing to the presence in its ranks of many supporters of the Cooperative Commonwealth Federation which had been founded at Calgary in 1932. During the winter of 1934, Aberhart and his followers held so many meetings, and the movement developed such strength, that the UFA government very reluctantly invited him, along with others, to give evidence before the Agricultural Committee of the Legislature on the feasibility of introducing Social Credit legislation in Alberta. A petition signed by 12,000 people was offered as testimony of the wide appeal of Social Credit; many UFA locals, Social Credit groups, and various clubs forwarded resolutions to members of the legislature.[1] At the height of the investigation, Major Douglas himself came to Alberta, addressed a vast and memorable meeting in Calgary, and expounded Social Credit at length before the Agricultural Committee.

In the midst of the popular excitement over the Social Credit theories of monetary reform, there occurred the first of three serious schisms within the movement. Many of the members of the New Age Club, the most intellectual of all the Social Credit study groups, had contended for several months that Aberhart was not a strict disciple of Douglas, and that the Social Credit monetary theories could not be applied in the provincial sphere under the British North America Act. The Social Credit Secretariat in London seems to have shared in this view, and in February, 1934, Aberhart relinquished to his chief critic in the New Age Club, Gilbert McGregor, the presidency of the Central Council, the executive group which at that time controlled the movement. This schism, although it had many of the marks of a struggle for power, was nevertheless of very great importance, for its outcome determined that Aberhart, and not Douglas, was to be the chief inspiration of the Alberta movement. Within two months, the new president realized that he could accomplish little without the remarkable propaganda facilities of the Bible Institute and Aberhart's large, enthusiastic personal following. In April, public demand forced Aberhart's return as president of the Central Council and leader of the Social Credit movement. McGregor and most of the New Age Club members then formed an opposing organization known as the Douglas Social Credit League, which established its own newspaper, the *Douglas Social Credit Advocate*. In referring to this controversy, Aberhart's followers always insist that they merely "brushed aside" an insignificant minority group within the movement; but the idea of "Douglas Social Credit" as distinguished from "Aberhart Social Credit" could not, as we shall see, be so easily dismissed.

The bitter controversy within the inner circle of the movement, and the expected favourable report of the legislative investigation produced a temporary lull in the mounting popular excitement during the spring of 1934. Early in the summer of 1934 two important moves were made by the hard-pressed UFA administration in Edmonton: the report of the legislative investigation, which was definitely hostile to the Social Credit proposals, was published and widely circulated; and, upon a reorganization of the Cabinet, the premier and his minister of public works (both of whom had been involved in law-suits touching their personal conduct) resigned. Amid the public outcry over the moral *débâcle* within the UFA Cabinet, and the public disapproval of the negative results of the legislative enquiry, Aberhart returned to the leadership of the Social Credit movement with redoubled vigour. He and Manning spent the whole summer of 1934 on a second speaking tour which took them into almost every inhabited part of the province south of Edmonton; disciples who were prepared to engage in equally strenuous speaking tours appeared on all sides. The movement was consolidated further by the founding of a weekly newspaper, the *Social Credit Chronicle*, and by the development in the autumn of the famous "Man from Mars" series of week-night radio discussions of economic problems. Throughout all this intense educational activity there was still no hint of the formation of a political organization, and Aberhart constantly stated that he had no personal political ambitions. But during the autumn of 1934 there was an increasingly urgent demand from the masses of the people that a Social Credit political party should be organized to contest the provincial election which had to be held by the following August at the latest. In spite of pressure from his followers, Aberhart was so reluctant to take the extreme step of forming a new political party that he urged the leaders of the three existing political parties to include the Social Credit monetary theories in their platforms. The Conservatives were unequivocal in their opposition to Social Credit; the Liberals promised to give the theories careful study but would make no further commitments; at their annual convention in January, 1935, the UFA leaders debated with Aberhart for hours, and finally voted almost unanimously against the Social Credit proposals. The pressure from the people to transform the Social Credit movement into a political party now became so great that Aberhart realized it could not much longer be resisted. But he still hesitated to take the final step. To meet what he considered to be the moral needs of the hour he sent out clarion calls over the radio for "One Hundred Honest Men"; to determine more accurately the extent of Social Credit support he organized a straw vote. The results were beyond his most optimistic expectations: honest men, who were prepared to fight to the utmost for Social Credit, were named by the score; the results of the straw vote indicated that in many communities 93 per cent of the people were prepared to vote for the adoption of the Social Credit monetary theories. Aberhart was now convinced that a Social Credit party would be victorious in the forthcoming provincial election and in April, 1935, the Southern and Northern Alberta Social Credit Leagues met in Calgary and Edmonton. These enthusiastic conventions, which were made up largely of delegates from Social Credit study groups, voted to go into politics and gave almost supreme power to Aberhart to develop the tactics for the election. What had been a social movement now became a political party, but behind the party there remained always the inspiration of the social movement.

The decision to take the movement into politics produced a surging response from the people, and within a few weeks scarcely anyone in Alberta remained unaffected by the Social Credit propaganda. The number of secondary leaders who came forward to spread the doctrine was one of the most astonishing features of the movement. Between three and four hundred "Honest Men," who had been carefully selected from the names sent in earlier to Aberhart, now emerged as the principal organizers of the provincial constitutency conventions, and many of them were subsequently nominated as candidates. But the secondary leaders were by no means confined to Aberhart's religious following: they were drawn from town and country alike, and included farmers, small business men, teachers, clergy, and a few physicians, dentists, and lawyers. Their critics asserted that the average local leader in the movement was a man who had previously taken no part in politics and who was "sub-standard" in his thinking about economics. Aberhart had realized that the entrance of the movement into politics would attract the type of opportunist who is always waiting to climb on a new bandwagon, and he made a rule that no one who had been associated as a leader with any of the other political parties could be a Social Credit candidate in the election. The rigid application of this principle naturally brought to the front a new group of men, most of whom were entirely inexperienced in politics.

One of Aberhart's most successful devices, which was calculated to keep everybody working enthusiastically for the movement until at least official nomination day, was his method of selecting candidates. Douglas has always maintained that the people should be primarily concerned with *results* rather than with the *method* of attaining results. Aberhart argued that the people in a constituency were not electing a man but voting for a set of principles. In accordance with this doctrine, each constituency convention was asked to nominate four or five possible candidates, each of whom was subsequently interviewed by an advisory committee composed of representatives from the constituency and the province at large. Critics of the movement claimed that Aberhart personally made the final choice in a dictatorial manner, but his eager followers considered that such an accusation was merely comic. In spite of violent criticism from the opposition parties, this method of selecting candidates persisted until after Aberhart's death, but it was dropped by Manning in the election of 1944.

Faced with an overwhelming social movement, the opponents of Social Credit were guilty of serious tactical blunders. The Liberals, who were making their greatest effort to return to power since the disastrous collapse of 1921, remained evasive: their leaders, hoping for support if group government should be necessary, hesitated to alienate the Social Crediters, and in general directed their attack almost entirely against the greatly weakened UFA; in fact, the Liberals finally went so far in their efforts to win support from the new movement that, in their appeal to the people, they pledged themselves, when returned to power, to employ three expert Social Credit advocates to carry out a complete investigation of the schemes proposed by Aberhart, and to evolve and submit a plan to the new legislature for the application of Social Credit to Alberta.

Coerced by the people's enthusiasm for Social Credit, the UFA government summoned the Agricultural Committee of the Legislature, for the second year in succession, to hear the evidence of experts in law and economics on the constitutionality and economic aspects of Social Credit. But the subsequent publication of another legislative report hostile to Social Credit merely seemed to increase the momentum of the movement. The desperate UFA leaders, in spite of the negative vote of their annual convention only a few months previously, now proceeded to bring back Douglas himself under contract as their technical adviser. By this manoeuvre they hoped to secure from Douglas a repudiation of Aberhart's interpretation of Social Credit and a definite statement that his monetary theories could not be applied in the provincial sphere. Coincident with Douglas's arrival in Edmonton, both the constitutional issue and Aberhart's understanding — or lack of understanding — of Social Credit were being hotly debated by all sides over the radio and on public platforms. If the UFA believed that Douglas would resolve this great debate in their favour, they were greatly mistaken. Far from denouncing Aberhart's position, the shrewd Douglas merely dramatized anew for an ever-increasing following the basic theories of Social Credit; and before leaving for England in June he published in the *Social Credit Chronicle* an unequivocal statement that there were no essential differences between Aberhart and himself.

Realizing, unlike the Liberals, that the Social Crediters were the real challengers in the election, the UFA campaigners, in spite of Douglas's announcement, continued to insist, tediously and tirelessly, that Aberhart had no genuine understanding of the principles of Social Credit and that, in any event, the attempt to apply Douglas's monetary theories in Alberta would immediately be invalidated by the courts under the existing Canadian constitution. Their position was considerably weakened in the eyes of the people by the known adherence of certain of the UFA federal members to Social Credit principles, and by the failure of most of their speakers to condemn Aberhart's proposals outright. When challenged by the UFA to state precisely how he would apply Social Credit in Alberta, Aberhart invariably argued that the people wanted Social Credit as a "result"; the method of its application would be left to experts. But in spite of his evasive attitude regarding methods, tens of thousands of people came to believe, as a result of his speeches and their reading of the *Social Credit Manual*, which he issued shortly before the election, that each adult would receive as his share of the national dividend at least $25.00 monthly for the rest of his life. A month before the election, his followers had become so convinced of the essential rightness of their beliefs that they developed closed minds, and further discussion of the merits or otherwise of Social Credit was no longer possible. At this point a group of business and financial leaders realizing, for the first time, the possibility of a Social Credit victory, formed the Economic Safety League and threw its weight against the movement. Aberhart immediately dubbed it the Comic Safety League, and characterized it as the last desperate act of the financiers, the "Fifty Big Shots," to save themselves from the wrath of a people's movement.

The new party did not need to depend upon the weaknesses of its opponents for victory in the tumultuous election campaign of 1935. With charismatic leadership, a positive philosophy, and superb techniques of organization and promotion, the Social Credit movement developed into an avalanche that swept everything before it. The massive strength of the movement, apart from Aberhart and the Douglas theories, was based upon the study groups. When public enthusiasm for Social Credit was approaching the stage of mass hysteria a few weeks before the election, there were sixty-three groups in Calgary alone, and some 1,600 in the whole province. In addition to their functions as dynamic nuclei of propaganda in almost every city block or rural district, they were the principal media through which funds were raised for the movement. Aberhart often said in later years that the groups won the election of 1935.

The struggle of the Social Credit movement for political power was successful beyond reasonable expectations: the UFA was permanently eliminated as a political force in the province; the Liberal party was so crushed that it remained disorganized for the next twelve years; the Conservatives remained, as usual, a negligible factor. Of the 163,700 people who had voted for Social Credit, thousands now confidently expected that, with fifty-six supporters in a legislature of sixty-three, Aberhart would immediately introduce the necessary legislation to create in Alberta an economic paradise. It is said that the morning after the great victory several persons of central and eastern European origin were already "lined-up" at the city hall in Calgary to collect their basic dividend. Thousands of others, not quite so optimistic, interpreted Aberhart's statements to mean that the $25.00 a month would be forthcoming within at least a year and a half.

For several years after the election there was little diminution of the popular enthusiasm which the movement had evoked. The members of the legislature were in such demand as speakers that many of them found it impossible to resume their normal occupations, so insatiable was the public desire for further information concerning Social Credit. Aberhart himself, although now premier and minister of education, was constantly addressing such tremendous crowds throughout the province that no buildings large enough could be found to accommodate the people who wanted to hear him: in the smaller towns and villages he frequently had to force his way to his hotel or the place of meeting through crowd-jammed streets. To the year of his death he continued to ask his vast audiences for approval or disapproval of his government's actions and the thunderous roar of favourable applause would often shake the building. As time went on, he deliberately encouraged great mass meetings by the celebration of anniversaries, by bitter and dramatic attacks on his political opponents, and by the development of such devices as the registration for dividends and the dated stamp money experiment which were calculated to keep the people agitated and working for the movement. Events like the great insurgency of 1937 within the ranks of the movement, the disallowance of the Social Credit legislation some months afterwards, the establishment of treasury branches, the fierce controversy over the "Accurate News and Information Act," and the "bankers' toadies" incident, were all grist for Aberhart's mill: he was invariably "big" news, and until the outbreak of the Second World War his ingenious tactics kept Alberta in an almost constant state of tension if not of actual tumult. In the legislative press gallery, which had had representatives from only two Edmonton daily newspapers during the last years of the UFA régime, there were, during the hectic years from 1935-9, twenty regular and several special reporters sitting in every day. Aberhart himself was frequently interviewed by newspaper representatives of international reputation, including John MacCormac of the *New York Times*. Telegraph companies were kept working overtime to clear copy, and, on one day in 1937, 35,000 words were sent out over the wires.

During nearly eight years as premier, Aberhart carried on most of his former religious activities in the Calgary Prophetic Bible Institute and continued, in a manner that infuriated his political opponents, to link the philosophy of Social Credit with the basic principles of Christianity. In addition to the familiar expositions of Bible prophecy and pre-millenial fundamentalism, his Sunday afternoon radio addresses now contained announcements and defences of government policy, as well as mocking, satirical attacks on all who in any way opposed Social Credit. His use of divine sanctions coupled with his new prestige as premier of the province assisted immeasurably in the transition of the Social Credit movement from the stage of popular excitement to the stage of formalization and still later to the stage of institutionalization.

In 1936 the Southern and Northern Conventions of the movement were formally consolidated into the Alberta Social Credit League which thereafter met annually, usually in the late autumn, as the people's arm of the political party. The League's constitution indicates the continued importance of the Social Credit study groups: throughout the years they have remained as the nucleus of the movement, and to them its leaders still direct appeals for support in time of need. Propaganda facilities were strengthened in 1936, by the transformation of the *Social Credit Chronicle* into a new paper, *Today and Tomorrow*, which somewhat later, as *The Canadian Social Crediter*, became the organ of the national movement. Imitating the pattern of the old UFA organization, the Social Credit

Women's Auxiliary was organized in 1938 and has remained among the most active agencies in the propagation of Social Credit theories.

One of the most important factors in the institutionalization of the movement was the violent opposition that developed with the passage of the Social Credit legislation of 1937 and the Mortgage and Debt legislation of the following years. Although thirteen acts passed by the Alberta legislature were declared *ultra vires* by the courts or disallowed by the Dominion government, the business and financial leaders of the province now became thoroughly convinced that the Social Credit movement represented a dangerous threat to their interests, and it was not long before they began to organize a united front to defeat the Aberhart Government at the next election. The most scornful opponent of the movement was unquestionably the *Calgary Herald* which, in a series of incredibly brilliant cartoons, applied the whip-lash to Aberhart almost daily and more than once drove him to the breaking point. He retaliated by calling on his loyal supporters to boycott the paper, a strategy which seriously affected its circulation and even threatened it for a time with loss of advertising. The tactics of both Aberhart and the *Herald* in this great battle are indicative of the state of mind which developed in Alberta at the height of the movement. Lesser and more ephemeral publications, of which *The Rebel* may be selected as an example, did not hesitate to sink to the lower depths in their vilification of Aberhart personally and of the movement in general.

The most serious threat to the future of the movement, however, came not from the turbulent, external opposition but from within the ranks of the Social Crediters themselves. Shortly after the election Aberhart had attempted, in a somewhat perfunctory manner, to persuade Douglas to return and fulfil the two-year contract he had made with the UFA as reconstruction adviser to the government. For months the two men, as Douglas has revealed in *The Alberta Experiment*, carried on an equivocal correspondence, alternating cablegrams of miraculous compression with letters of miraculous length. The gap between Aberhart's conception of Social Credit and that of its originator now proved wider than expected; and, in any case, *Premier* Aberhart did not relish the idea of *Major* Douglas as an active collaborator. Far from engaging an expert on Social Credit as his adviser on financial policy and business administration, the premier shocked many of his supporters by bringing to Alberta an entirely orthodox financier, R.J. Magor, who had previously put Newfoundland's government on a better financial and administrative basis.

Faced with an empty treasury on their accession to power, the Social Credit members of the legislature readily accepted an orthodox budget during the session of 1936. They were encouraged regarding Aberhart's ultimate intentions when he defied the Money Power by defaulting on a large bond issue and when, several months later, he reduced by 50 per cent the coupon-rate of interest on all Alberta's bonds and debentures, including the bonds in default. The introduction of the so-called "prosperity certificates" later in the summer, although in no sense a part of Douglas's Social Credit plan, also appealed to thousands of people as evidence that drastic action was imminent. During the early winter, however, criticism of the Government for its delay in introducing Social Credit legislation increased among the less fanatical followers of Aberhart: the mounting tension was not eased by the arrival and sudden departure of John Hargrave, a colourful leader of the London Greenshirts, a group affiliated with the Douglas movement in England.

Criticism reached the boiling point only after eighteen months had passed and Social Credit was yet non-existent in Alberta. The province was still in the midst of the depression; although thousands of hungry people continued to exhibit a blind loyalty to Aberhart they began urging their representatives to insist on immediate Social Credit legislation. During the debate on the speech from the throne on the opening of the legislature in 1937, about twenty Social Credit members began holding closed meetings nearly every night in Edmonton hotel rooms. When the budget was presented by the Honourable Solon E. Low, the new provincial treasurer, the subject of the secret meetings was revealed. An insurgency had broken out. The insurgent Social Crediters charged that the Government had brought down merely a second orthodox budget, rather than one based on the credit of the province that would provide for the payment of the basic monthly dividend of $25.00. One after another of the insurgents arose in the House and demanded that Aberhart implement his promise to put Social Credit into effect within eighteen months after his election. The Government was narrowly sustained in several recorded votes, but the insurgency was strong enough to prevent the passage of the budget and to force an adjournment of the legislature until June.

Aberhart's attempts to pacify the insurgents by insisting that he was giving good administration were unsuccessful: they were in deadly earnest and demanded that qualified economic assistants be obtained at once so that Social Credit reforms could be instituted. Although a resolute, determined leader, Aberhart was forced, after considerable personal bitterness had developed on both sides, to agree to the appointment of a Social Credit Board, composed of five members of the legislature, the object of which would be the achievement of Social Credit in Alberta. The Chairman of the Board, Glen L. MacLachlan, then made a pilgrimage to England to try to induce Douglas to come to Alberta and assist in working out a plan for the institution of Social Credit. Douglas declined, but recommended two of his associates, G.F. Powell and L.D. Byrne, both of whom arrived in Edmonton for the re-convening of the legislature in June.

When the Social Credit Board was set up, both the insurgents and loyalists agreed to a truce until its chairman should return from England. But it was not long before both sides had taken their case to the people: the insurgents have always claimed that Aberhart was the first to break the truce by denouncing them in one of his Sunday afternoon religious broadcasts. Great mass meetings were held once again throughout the province: loyalist speakers frequently sought to state their position immediately after the insurgents had spoken, or if that privilege was refused they would hold another meeting in the same town the following night. The insurgents tried to put Aberhart at a disadvantage by outdoing him at his own techniques of mass appeal, but his position as prophet of the movement generally gave him the better of the bitter controversy. The loyalists charged that the insurgents were merely ambitious men, who were either seeking Cabinet posts if Aberhart's administration should fall or had been bribed by the Money Power to destroy the movement. The insurgents retaliated by questioning Aberhart's understanding of Douglas's theories and suggesting that he had truckled to the Money Power in taking advice from Magor, the Money Power's nominee.

The people, on the whole, were shocked and mystified by the disloyal attitude (as they supposed) of the members who challenged Aberhart's leadership: they refused to believe that he was merely marking time, and on at least one occasion resorted to stoning the insurgent speakers as an indication of their disapproval. As the months went by both insurgents and loyalists, having grown tired of endless stormy meetings, found the necessary pretext for healing the schism in MacLachlan's return from England with Powell (followed shortly thereafter by the arrival of Byrne), as well as in Aberhart's solemn promise that a special session of the legislature would be held in August to implement the recommendations of the Social Credit experts. As a formal indication to the people that the family quarrel was over Powell arranged for the Social Credit members of the legislature to sign a pledge that they would uphold the Social Credit Board and its technicians, and would work thereafter in harmony for the attainment of their common objectives. Magor and two cabinet ministers, who had never really been disciples of Aberhart, proved to be convenient scapegoats, and the public uproar created by the insurgency slowly subsided, although the essential differences between the followers of Douglas and the followers of Aberhart remained unresolved. The insurgency was the driving force behind the celebrated Social Credit legislation of 1937, the disallowance of which has formed the subject of so much controversy.

If the Social Credit, and Mortgage and Debt, legislation pacified the insurgents, it terrified the financial and business interests of Alberta whose representatives, infuriated by what they considered was a thoroughly high-handed attitude in Aberhart's dealings with them, now proceeded to give wide currency to the view that he was the leader of a Canadian form of fascism. His attempt to change the status of the Royal Canadian Mounted Police in the province, coupled with the "press gag" legislation, lent further strong support to this accusation, and also caused the newspapers to redouble their attacks on him. Organized opposition to the Social Credit movement crystallized around the People's

League, which developed into the Unity movement and finally emerged as the Independent party. Within the Independent party, as the bitter election of March, 1940, drew near, were included Liberals, Conservatives, and all others who were opposed to the Social Credit movement except the supporters of the Cooperative Commonwealth Federation, which was slowly and painfully developing from an alliance of labour groups with the socialistically minded members of the UFA.

During his second election campaign, Aberhart attributed his failure to introduce Social Credit to the Dominion government: under the influence of the Money Power it had sabotaged his constructive legislation. As the depression had not yet lifted, he was able to use again the shop-worn slogans of 1935 and make an issue of debt: he promised that, with more time, he could yet effectively destroy the power of the embattled Money Barons and pay the long over-due basic dividend. The Independents had no constructive programme to offer the people. Their one cry was, *"Throw out Aberhart!"* The very violence of the *Calgary Herald's* personal attacks on the premier caused many wavering Social Crediters to rally behind their old leader, and thousands of members of the League gave him the same unquestioning loyalty and enthusiastic support as in 1935. Apart from their lack of any positive policy, the greatest weakness of the Independents consisted in their association with the more prosperous classes of Edmonton and Calgary: although this connexion gave them a fairly large following in most of the urban centres, it proved an insuperable handicap in the rural, and especially the dried out, areas. Yet for all the weaknesses of the Independents, the Social Credit party almost lost the election. The issue was so close that a shift of only 1,000 votes, properly distributed in ten constituencies, would have led to Aberhart's fall. As it was, the Social Crediters won thirty-six of the fifty-seven seats in the new legislature.

Shortly after the election, the German Army began its great *blitzkrieg* in Western Europe. Aberhart, severely shaken by the insurgency, as well as by his near electoral defeat, realized that the people had become weary of the long years of political turmoil. He shrewdly suggested that the energies of all should now be devoted to Canada's war effort; and it would appear that some sort of agreement was reached that no further controversial Social Credit legislation would be attempted until the war was over.

Certain tendencies that were developing in the Social Credit movement had been clearly revealed as a result of the campaign of 1940. Many people who were interested only in the economic theories of Social Credit were beginning to object strongly to Aberhart's constant mixture of religion and politics, especially in his Sunday afternoon broadcasts. The halo that had formerly surrounded the leader had been somewhat dimmed by his fierce quarrel with the insurgents and his failure to cope successfully with the Money Power. Many of the Social Credit study groups had begun to lose their enthusiasm: people were growing tired of constantly attending meetings merely to hear the same doctrines expounded over and over again. The formalization of the media of propaganda served to enchannel the earlier popular enthusiasm into more determinate patterns of response. The rise of the CCF movement was slowly draining away from Social Credit its genuine left-wing supporters: immediately after the election of 1940, a defeated Social Credit candidate who had been one of Aberhart's most tireless supporters joined the CCF and began to work enthusiastically for socialism; still others deserted Social Credit through disillusionment with its doctrines or because of personal disappointment in not receiving satisfactory governmental appointments for long years of loyal effort. Finally, political power was tending more and more to turn a popular movement into a highly institutionalized political party: it was not only the Independents and socialists who asserted, at the height of the campaign of 1940, that the Social Credit movement had become "just another political party." The process of institutionalizing a remarkable social movement was completed, for all practical purposes, when Aberhart's death, in May, 1943, led to the selection, not by a representative convention but by the Social Credit members of the legislature, of his chief lieutenant, the Honourable Ernest C. Manning, as leader of the party and the movement. In his initial address, the new premier gave a pledge to his followers that the fight for Social Credit would never be given up and that the effective control of the monetary system would eventually be taken from private, monopolistic interests and restored to the people's democratically elected representatives. He also promised, while carrying on the fight for permanent social justice and economic security, to give the best possible administration in every department of government.

Aberhart's death gave the waning Social Credit movement a new impetus in that it attracted supporters from unexpected quarters. The more prosperous classes of the province, headed by the business and financial interests, had developed over the years such embittered attitudes toward the late leader that they could never had joined hands with him to oppose the rising CCF movement. But they entertained no such personal hostility to Mr. Manning, although they knew full well that he had long been Aberhart's ardent disciple in both religion and politics. The invalidation of Social Credit legislation by the courts and the attitude of the Dominion government had convinced them also that they no longer had anything to fear from Manning's Government, whereas the accession of the CCF to power might become a real threat to the continuance of the present economic system. The new premier was enthusiastically received by service clubs and other business men's organizations: his friendly manner and his persuasive defence of Social Credit against socialism led to an entirely new alignment in the provincial election of 1944.

No sooner had the election been called than Mr. Manning, taking his cue from certain large city newspapers, announced that the only significant issue was socialism. In the campaign that followed, the philosophy of Social Credit was thoroughly unmasked for the first time in Alberta: Douglas, its originator, turned out to be in reality no radical at all but the most rugged individualist, an arch conservative; for him, capitalism was the ideal form of economic organization, provided only that its monetary system could be changed. Accepting literally Mr. Manning's rightist interpretation of Social Credit and his frequently repeated statement that he sincerely wanted "to make Capitalism work," and convinced also that they could depend on him to give good government, thousands of people who feared socialism deserted the Independents and voted for the party which they had opposed so energetically only four years before. When the election was over the Independent party had been well-nigh destroyed, and the Social Crediters were returned to power with an even more overwhelming majority than that of 1935.

Three important trends in the Social Credit movement were revealed by the third election: its philosophy, which had hitherto been masked by seemingly radical monetary theories, no longer appealed to a considerable number of leftists who now turned to socialism; the support which it had drawn from the propertied classes more than made up for defections to the CCF; the undimmed enthusiasm of thousands of its original members, although the movement had become strongly conservative, seemed to indicate that Social Credit would long remain a powerful factor in Alberta politics. During the campaign, the CCF had suffered from poor organization and inadequate funds, but it had become the second strongest party in Alberta and was recognized as the only effective opposition to the Social Credit movement. Mr. Manning and his associates realized clearly that, if their movement was to survive, they must in the future shatter the Socialists as they had previously shattered the United Farmers and the Independents. Confronted with the challenge of another people's movement, the propaganda for Social Credit has, since 1944, taken on almost entirely the character of a crusade against socialism.

In the struggle with socialism during the campaign of 1944, Social Credit leaders had said little about basic dividends and the just price, partly because of the general understanding that such controversial issues would remain dormant for the duration of the war, partly because these doctrines would have disturbed those whom they hoped to attract from the Independent party. But over the years many of the original members of the movement had cherished the hope of basic dividends and, as soon as possible after the war ended, they revived at the annual meeting of the Social Credit League in December, 1945, the whole question of the legislative implementation of Douglas's monetary theories. There is reason to believe that the lively, almost revolutionary, statements made at the convention were inspired by certain cabinet ministers as a technique for retaining control of the discussion. At the same time, there can be no doubt whatever that the demand for the Government to keep Aberhart's promises of 1935, by paying the basic dividend, had a genuine source in the growing unrest and agitation among the people themselves. The League, in no uncertain terms, gave the Government instructions to carry out its long promised programme and also made clear that its members wanted most especially the basic dividend, now ten years overdue. Responding immediately to the popular demand, the Government presented the people with the Bill of Rights.

The new Charter of Freedom gave both a statutory declaration of the just rights and responsibilities of the citizens of Alberta and outlined the methods by which those rights could be realized in actual experience: it promised social and economic security with individual freedom to everybody. Its most spectacular feature was the offer of a social security pension and medical benefits to everyone between the age of nineteen and sixty who was unable to obtain employment or who was disabled; at the age of sixty every citizen would be entitled to retire and receive similar benefits. By an adequate "Social Security Pension" was meant, in terms of the price level of 1945, a payment to the individual concerned of an annual income of not less than $600 a year, or a minimum income of $1,200 for a married couple. The second part of the Bill contained an elaborate description of the Social Credit techniques by means of which money would be made available to the government to pay the pensions and medical benefits. An unusual feature of the Bill, which created considerable cynicism among non-Social Crediters concerning the good faith of the Government, was the provision that before being proclaimed it should be tested by the courts.

Printed copies of the Bill of Rights were widely distributed by members of the legislature and by the Social Credit Board. Its contents were thoroughly discussed at meetings of groups and constituency organizations but, unlike the earlier Social Credit legislation, it aroused neither great enthusiasm from within the movement nor violent antagonism from without. An informal straw vote conducted by the members of the legislature indicated that over 95 per cent of the people interviewed favoured the Bill, although to a certain number of pure Douglasites it seemed to bear the taint of socialism. The Bill was presented to the annual meeting of the Social Credit League in 1946 as evidence of the strong intentions of the government to overthrow the "Financiers," but the delegates exhibited little excitement. There was a widespread feeling that the Bill would be declared *ultra vires*, and when the expected adverse judgment of the Supreme Court of Alberta was confirmed by the Privy Council in mid-summer, 1947, the decision was received apathetically by most Social Crediters. Certain of them felt that the post-war prosperity had, in any case, made basic dividends unnecessary: Social Credit was not primarily a monetary theory but a way of life. The majority still felt, however, that there must surely be some way by which Douglas's monetary theories could be implemented, and much speculation arose concerning the future course of the movement.

As they faced the future in the late summer of 1947, the Social Credit leaders could no longer ignore, as they had tried to do for several years, the fact that deep within the structure of the movement there had developed another dangerous schism. The serious internal dissension with which they were confronted can best be understood in terms of an analysis of the media and the content of Social Credit propaganda which existed at that time.

In addition to the provincial and national leaders and members of the Alberta legislature and the House of Commons, the principal media of propaganda were the Social Credit League, the *Canadian Social Crediter*, and the Social Credit Board. The leaders of the movement, as well as the MLA's and MP's, were tireless in their efforts to promote Social Credit ideas, missing no opportunity of addressing any available group either in Alberta or elsewhere in Canada. The Social Credit League, on the other hand, appeared moribund: although it still met annually and passed resolutions for governmental consideration, its deliberations and actions (apart from the upsurge in 1945) had not for years inspired much enthusiasm among its membership, which had decreased considerably since 1940. In the early years of the movement the study groups had been its dynamic foundation, but they had also declined both in numbers and importance. For many Social Crediters the old group life had been replaced by the more institutionalized constituency organization which was taking on more and more the appearance of an old line party machine. The weekly newspaper, the *Canadian Social Crediter*, now had a national circulation, and was in the hands of John Patrick Gillese, a young and energetic editor who lost no opportunity of presenting to his readers the latest developments in Douglas's theories and their significance for the interpretation of provincial, national, and especially international events. Among its organs of propaganda, a unique feature of the movement was the Social Credit Board which had been set up by legislative action after the great insurgency of 1937.

Technically a committee of the whole legislature, financed by public funds, and theoretically non-partisan, the Board had become in actual practice the philosophical arm of the Social Credit movement. It was the principal and, apart from the newspaper, the only agency through which Douglas's developing ideas were systematically filtered through to the people. The four or five members of the Board, who were members of the legislature, gave numerous public addresses and exhibited pictures and films illustrating the basic principles of Social Credit; they also wrote occasional pamphlets and served as a centre for giving wide distribution to Douglas's books and articles. The activities of the Board, so obviously associated with the interests of one political party only, inevitably gave rise to the criticism that such an identification of the party with the state was fascism in its purest form. Douglas had originally sent out two associates to serve as technical advisers of the Board: after a stormy career ending with a term in prison for his part in the "bankers' toadies" incident, Powell returned to England. Byrne, a strict disciple of Douglas, then became and remained for ten years the principal intellectual force behind the Board's activities, a hidden hand, but a *recognized* hidden hand. Probably his most important task was to give some genuine understanding of Social Credit to the MLA's and MP's and subsequently to the people in general. He inspired, if he did not actually write, the reports which were presented annually to the legislature by the Social Credit Board. It was the submission of the tenth report in the spring of 1947 that precipitated the most recent crisis within the movement.

As we have already pointed out, there are three aspects to Douglas's philosophy: a monetary theory, a political theory, and an interpretation of history. During the middle and late thirties the second and third aspects began to appear more prominently in Douglas's writings than the monetary theories. He had apparently concluded, even before Aberhart came into power, that the grip of international finance was so unshakable that nothing short of a transformation of democracy and of the organization of the world in general would make it possible to put his monetary theories into practice. The changed emphasis in Douglas's position had already begun to appear in *Today and Tomorrow* as early as 1939, and it was reflected in the report of the Social Credit Board for the following year. Although the Board's reports were supposed to give a review of the progress made in the realization of the Social Credit monetary theories in Alberta and to explore possibilities for the future, from 1941 on more and more space was devoted to criticism of the functioning of the democratic process and to an analysis of the international situation. It is noteworthy that the Board viewed every proposed form of international co-operation, including Dumbarton Oaks, Bretton Woods, the United Nations, UNRRA, and UNESCO as indisputable evidence of the existence of the international Masonic-Judaic conspiracy, in league with high finance and communism, to secure control of the world by destroying nationalism, private enterprise, capitalism, and Christianity.

Inspired by Douglas's latest writings, the Board's analysis of problems in these terms reached a climax in its sensational report of 1947. After calling attention once again to the existence of the conspiracy, the report reviewed and analysed the various techniques by which the World Plotters had developed and extended their monopolistic control in both the financial and political spheres with world dictatorship as their ultimate goal. Realizing that freedom of the individual was their greatest obstacle, the Plotters had launched a planned attack against such freedom by encouraging socialism, communism, atheism, materialism, totalitarianism, and the weakening of the British Empire. The report asserted that any "programme for action" must begin with a criticism of democracy *as it functions at present*: majority rule, the secret ballot, and the political party system must all be abolished for they have become instruments, not of genuine democracy, but of the World Plotters. Political parties should be replaced by a union of electors with three objectives: "to state the results wanted from the management of the affairs of the country in all spheres affecting the lives of the People; to control the elected representatives of the people *at all times* [not merely on the day of an election] and through them, all of the People's governing bodies, — local, provincial, and national; to insist on and enforce obedience to the will of the People on all matters of Policy [results].'' Only in this way, the report concluded, could a genuine Christian democracy be established and security with freedom be enjoyed by everyone.

The report produced an uproar in the Social Credit caucus which had been given no knowledge of its contents prior to its submission to the legislature; and it caused a critical re-evaluation of Douglas's theories throughout the movement and the country at large. Immediately after the close of the session, the party caucus issued a statement in which it reaffirmed its unswerving allegiance to the principles of Social Credit as enunciated by Aberhart, while at the same time it dissociated both itself and the movement in Alberta ''from any statements or publications which were incompatible with the established British ideals of democratic freedom or which endorsed, excused, or incited anti-Semitism or racial or religious intolerance in any form.'' In the repudiation and condemnation of the world conspiracy theory of Douglas, the lead was given by Premier Manning.

But the storm would not blow over so easily, and it soon became evident that two sharply opposed factions, known as the realists and the Douglasites, had been developing within the movement during the past few years. The realists thought of Social Credit essentially in terms of Douglas's earlier monetary theories as propounded by Aberhart, and considered it suicidal to attack majority rule, the secret ballot, and the party system. The Douglasites, on the other hand, thought of Social Credit primarily in terms of the Jewish world conspiracy and insisted that it was essential to establish a union of electors without delay — for many of them, the monetary theories were no longer of immediate importance. Wherever one looked at the movement the conflict between the two factions was unmistakably evident — within the Cabinet, among the members of the legislature and the House of Commons, among the members of the Social Credit Board, among the staff of the official newspaper, and finally, among the members of the Social Credit League.

During the summer of 1947 the leaders of both groups, while they glared at each other across an ideological chasm, still entertained the hope that they might continue to work together in harmony for the movement in its crusade against socialism. But the differences in their interpretation of Social Credit ultimately proved irreconcilable. In the early autumn the premier and his associates skilfully began a carefully planned purge which has resulted in the removal from power or office of most of the Douglasites and their replacement in the cabinet, on the staff of the newspaper, and elsewhere by realists. The Social Credit Board itself was liquidated in March of this year [1948]; and even Byrne, whom many Social Crediters thought of as Douglas's personal representative, was dropped both as technical adviser and as deputy minister of economic affairs. The dismissal of Byrne and the "resignation" of the editor of the *Canadian Social Crediter* broke the last links (which had been growing steadily weaker since Aberhart's death) of the official Alberta movement with Douglas. The author of the Social Credit theories now proceeded to belabour the realists in his Liverpool weekly, the *Social Crediter*; and his strict disciples in Alberta, although deprived of their official positions, continued the propagation of their doctrines by organizing the Edmonton Council of the Douglas Social Credit Movement of Canada. In their new journal, the *Social Credit Challenge*, the Douglasites leave one with the impression that they believe the World Plotters are directly responsible for separating the premier of Alberta from Douglas as well as for dividing the movement.

It is too early to assess the impact of the third schism within the movement upon its future. But it is safe to say that Douglas's proposals for monetary reform mark the limits to which his teachings can hope to obtain general acceptance in Alberta. Such a limitation is not surprising if one remembers that monetary reform had become a preferred group tendency in the province long before the rise of the Social Credit movement; and, apart from obvious considerations such as the economic and political situation in Alberta and the remarkable leadership of Aberhart, this has been the determining tendency both in the origin and the evolution of the movement, when one examines it in historical and social psychological perspective.

Notes

1. For an analysis of the response of the people during the period from 1932 to April, 1935, see John A. Irving, "Psychological Aspects of the Social Credit Movement in Alberta" (*Canadian Journal of Psychology*, vol. I, 1947, pp. 17-27, 75-86, 127-40). Acknowledgment is made to the editor of the above journal, Dr. John A. Long, for permission to incorporate into the preceding pages certain material describing the early phases of the movement.

Pulpit, Press, and Political Reactions to the Ku Klux Klan in Saskatchewan

William Calderwood

The average person has difficulty in dissociating the Ku Klux Klan from the United States of America; the thought of it in a Canadian context appears to be somewhat incongruous. Yet the Klan did flourish, although briefly, in Canada. Here, as in the United States, the Ku Klux Klan was able to find and feed upon racial prejudice and religious bigotry of long standing. Before it faded into oblivion in the depression of the 1930's, the Klan had organized locals from British Columbia to the Maritimes.[1]

As in Canada at large, the province of Saskatchewan had not been free of racial and religious controversy. From its inception in 1905, Saskatchewan had to face the problems inherent in a heterogeneous society, one of which was the friction between the Anglo-Saxon and other segments of the population. Out of this situation problems arose which became chronic political issues.

One such issue was the teaching of languages other than English in the public schools. The determination of the French to preserve their language probably was the greatest bone of contention between them and the other racial groups, particularly the British. But it was obvious from the earliest settlement of the French in Saskatchewan that their culture would not be founded upon racial uniqueness alone, but upon the twin pillars of the French language and the Roman Catholic religion. Just as the struggle for the survival of their culture demanded the use of their mother tongue in educating their children, so too it demanded the practice of their religion in school. This led to yet another political grievance between the two opposing cultures in Saskatchewan: the charge of sectarian influence in the public schools of the province.

Another political issue which helped to prepare the way for the Ku Klux Klan was the immigration policy of the federal government. At the turn of the century, most Canadians agreed that Canada needed immigrants and concurred with the government's efforts to meet this need. But in the face of the great flood of

Reprinted from S. Trofimenkoff (ed.), *The Twenties in Western Canada;* Ottawa: National Museum of Man, 1972, pp. 191-229. Source: The National Museum of Man of the National Museums of Canada. Reproduction authorized by Information Canada.

immigrants in the first two decades of the century public sentiment had made an about-turn. In Saskatchewan the great influx of immigrants, many of them Catholic, was interpreted by some as a conspiracy between the federal government and the Roman Catholic Church.[2]

An issue with political implications as serious as the immigration question developed out of the natural resources controversy. This constitutional issue was even interpreted in the light of the religious question! For example, the viewpoint of a large segment of Protestantism was expressed on this problem at a meeting of the Anglican clergy of the Diocese of North Saskatchewan on November 18, 1926. In a resolution demanding that the natural resources of Manitoba, Saskatchewan, and Alberta be "unconditionally consigned" to the respective provincial governments, the clerics accused the federal government of exceeding the provisions of the BNA Act in retaining control of the natural resources of Saskatchewan and Alberta in the Act of Autonomy in 1905. Furthermore, the clerics contended, the federal government had bowed to pressure from the Roman Catholic clergy of Quebec and a "Papal legate from Rome": maintaining control of the natural resources was really a subtle attempt to force separate schools upon the provinces.[3] As with the language question, the sectarian issue, and the immigration problem, the clamour for the transfer of the province's natural resources increased in vituperation and verbosity throughout the late 1920's, and the subject became attached in turn to the issues of language, religion, and race.[4]

With these issues already troubling the political waters in Saskatchewan, it was not surprising that the Klan with its ultra-Protestant and pro-British pronouncements gained a foothold in 1927; what was surprising, however, was the degree of success the order attained in the province in the subsequent years.

For the immediate origins of the Ku Klux Klan in Saskatchewan, one must look to Ontario and Indiana. When the organization was formed in Toronto, C.L. Fowler and J.H. Hawkins, experienced Klan organizers, were placed in charge of the "Propagation of the Order" across the country.[5] In this capacity, Fowler contacted an organizer named Scott from Boston and offered him the Realm of New Brunswick.[6] It is most probable that this was Lewis A. Scott, later King Kleagle (Chief recruiter) of Saskatchewan. Whether Scott became King Kleagle of New Brunswick is not clear. About 15 November, 1926, however, he told Hugh Finley Emmons, alias Pat Emory, alias Pat Emerson, that Fowler had given him papers making him the King Kleagle of Saskatchewan. Scott invited Emmons, a former colleague who had been deeply involved with him in the infamous Indiana Klan,[7] to accompany him and his son as a Klan lecturer to Saskatchewan. Emmons accepted, and the three men arrived in Regina late in 1926.

No time was wasted. In the last week of 1926, Klan propaganda was being distributed in Regina. A pamphlet entitled *Why I Intend to Become a Klan Member* was slipped under doors and deposited in mail boxes. It outlined the objectives and principles of the KKK and invited the reader to send for further information to Post Office Box 363, Regina.[8] By this means and by public meetings and the sale of Klan propaganda, the Scotts and Emmons soon established a local Klan in Regina.

Having had experience as Klan organizers in Indiana, they knew how to build the organization. Their strategy was to conjure up situations which would appear to threaten the British nationality and Protestantism of Saskatchewan residents, and then present the Klan as the great defender and vociferously demand remedial action by the government. At a time when the province was being settled by many non-British immigrants and a sizeable French-Canadian minority was clamouring for language rights in the public schools, the Klan's exaggerations and falsehoods were readily accepted by many. Consequently, and ludicrous as it may seem for such an uniquely American organization as the Klan, a circular letter was sent to every home in Regina proposing that the government should place the Union Jack in every home and public school, and that only Protestants should be hired as civil servants and teachers in all public offices and schools in Canada.[9] These methods brought results, and within one year strong local Klans flourished in Regina and Moose Jaw, and numerous points in rural Saskatchewan.

All went well for the Saskatchewan Klan until September, 1927, when the local Klansmen discovered their leaders had disappeared. Not only were they gone, but "Evangelist" Emmons, as he liked to call himself, who "always . . . was reading his Bible", and Lewis A. Scott, once described as "a man of real worth, a real man of dependable character and sterling worth", had absconded with the funds of the Saskatchewan Klan, an amount estimated by Premier Gardiner as running in excess of $100,000.[10] The money was not recovered and Scott was never apprehended; Emmons stood trial on a charge of embezzlement in May, 1928, and was acquitted.[11]

The Emmons and Scott affair might well have been the end of the Klan. But enough real interest had been aroused that the Klansmen closed ranks at a private meeting in Moose Jaw on October 25th; they elected officers and appointed committees for a re-organized Ku Klux Klan of Saskatchewan. From then on, the leaders of the organization maintained that the Ku Klux Klan in Saskatchewan was a separate and independent body from other Canadian and American Klans. In great part this enabled the order to survive, and to thrive, after the humiliating spectacle of its leaders absconding with its funds. And thrive it did. By 1929, the geographical distribution of local Klans extended from the United States border in the south to Prince Albert in the north, and there were at least one hundred and twenty-five locals throughout the province.[12] The crowds in attendance at Klan rallies, the number of local Klans organized, and the numbers recruited, all bear witness to the enthusiastic response of Saskatchewan residents to the Ku Klux Klan.

I

Foremost in any explanation of the Klan's success in Saskatchewan must be the emphasis it placed on religion. The Klan had always claimed to be above all else a religious institution. Had the issues raised by the order not been connected with religious convictions and institutions its progress in most areas probably would have been curtailed. Its secret rites and ceremonies contained numerous references to biblical passages and had religious connotations.[13] Its public gatherings were opened and closed with prayer, and many times with hymns, while most of the speeches of the Klan organizers could be better described as sermons. Texts of scripture were often used and biblical quotations flowed freely. Throughout the Klan's colourful ceremonies and public utterances ran the thread of ultra-Protestantism. And with many Saskatchewan residents of the 1920's this struck a responsive chord, especially with those who were already members of popular Protestant fraternities and orders, such as the Orange Lodge.

While the ultra-Protestantism of the Klan appealed to many Saskatchewan residents, it was made even more palatable by the order's strong emphasis on fundamental Protestantism. This aspect of Klan propaganda appealed to that segment of Protestantism which was vaguely uneasy about the growth of more flexible liberal attitudes to the Bible and basic doctrine and which was reacting to an age of change in religion and elsewhere. In addition to anti-Catholicism — the negative aspect of its propaganda — this emphasis on popular Protestantism formed a positive part of the order's appeal in Saskatchewan.

In the period of the Klan's ascendance in Saskatchewan, all of the major Protestant churches were influenced by the tradition of ultra-Protestantism and affected by the new issue of fundamentalism. The Klan's position on these issues would obviously lead to its acceptance or rejection by the membership of the Protestant denominations. Although it is impossible to document with accuracy the response of these memberships at large, perhaps a good indication of that response was given in the ministerial reaction to the Klan.

Ministers of several Protestant denominations were members of the Klan. Saskatchewan was overwhelmingly dominated by the United, Presbyterian, Anglican, Methodist, Lutheran, and Baptist Churches.[14] With such an overwhelming majority belonging to historic Protestantism with its deeply ingrained distrust of the Roman Catholic Church and its hierarchy, Saskatchewan provided eager listeners to the preachings of ultra-Protestantism by the Ku Klux Klan.[15]

The United Church provided the Saskatchewan Klan with the most ministerial support. At least ten United Church ministers were Klansmen and three others expressed sympathy with the order.[16] However, since the United Church was by far the largest Protestant denomination with over one hundred thousand more members in 1927 than its nearest rival, the Anglican Church, it was not surprising that it had the largest ministerial representation in the ranks of the Klan.[17]

Rev. S.F. Rondeau, minister of the Woodrow United Church and former Moderator of the Saskatchewan Synod of the Presbyterian Church, openly associated with the Klan leaders and frequently spoke for the order.[18] At a memorable Klan rally at Regina on 16 February, 1928, the Reverend Rondeau declared:

> I lived in the United States nearly twenty years and I want to say that about 30,000 ministers belonged to the Klan. I want to say that some of the most notable professors, some of the wealthiest men by the thousands belonged to the Klan in the United States. . . . shall we judge the Klan in Canada which has not committed one immoral deed, so far as I know, shall we judge the Klan which came here with principles that are practically unassailable? I am a Klansman. . . .[19]

Reverend L.B. Henn, of Macrorie, declared that the primary aim of the Klan was to render service to one and all, "believing that through a greater service to humanity men and women are brought nearer to Christ the Criterion of Character."[20] Reverend W. Titley, of Imperial, asserted that the Klan was an old organization that had been revived to defend Protestant rights and truths and urged "every true Protestant" to support it.[21] And the Reverend Dr. W.S. Reid, while disclaiming membership in the Klan, was reported to have said that "there were certain problems facing the people of Canada today . . . and if the Protestant churches were not taking the same attitude as the Klan towards those problems he would like to know what attitude they were taking. . . . It was in the trend of events that one must look for the explanation of the Klan's present activity in the west." He then outlined some of the alleged problems which justified the Klan's existence: the spread of a "sense of suspicion and distrust of all political parties", the attitude of the Roman Catholic Church towards civil matters as revealed in a "veiled threat" in a recent edition of the *Roman Catholic Record*, and the Department of Education's refusal to remove a textbook from the curriculum which was "objectionable" to Protestants.[22]

The United Church, however, was only one of several Protestant denominations represented in the ranks of the Klansmen. Of the ministers that can be identified, the Baptists appear to be next in strength of numbers with at least four being involved with the Klan.[23] Reverend Hind, of the First Baptist Church in Moose Jaw, was one of the original members in Moose Jaw and soon became a prominent Klan spokesman. At the first great Klan rally at Moose Jaw, Emmons uttered those memorable words about the bootleggers and shady characters of Moose Jaw's seamy side: "I know the River Street gang is out to get me. . . . if they do I want you to use my hide as the skin of a drum and beat it loud and long as you march along carrying the crusade down that sinful street of depravity"; Reverend Hind immediately declared that he would gladly forfeit his own life, for his colleague was performing a more noble work.[24] Reverend Hind was actively engaged in Klan promotional work lecturing on Klan topics throughout the province.[25]

Reverend William Surman, minister of Cameron Memorial Baptist Church, Regina, chaired the widely advertised meeting of the Klan in Regina on February 16, 1928. He made his attitude toward the Klan clear in his opening remarks:

> I am proud to be Chairman of this meeting tonight because I am a Minister of the Gospel and, as a Minister of the Gospel, I see nothing contradictory in the principles which I teach and the principles of the Klan to which I belong. . . . I happen to be the man at the wheel of this Regina local organization.[26]

As Exalted Cyclops of the Regina Klan, Reverend Surman usually organized the order's rallies in Regina. In this capacity, he contacted M.J. Coldwell prior to the provincial election of 1929 and asked him if he would like to place his views "before a meeting of influential people to be held in the city of Regina". At first, Mr. Coldwell agreed but later refused on learning that the meeting was to be sponsored by the Klan.[27] Lecturing outside of Regina was another service Reverend Surman performed for the organization; on 14 March, 1929, the *Indian Head News* advertised him as one of the guest speakers at a local Ku Klux Klan gathering.[28]

Reverends Hind and Surman were the outstanding Baptist spokesmen for the Klansmen. Their involvement with the order was no secret as most of the city newspapers reported their participation in the first public Klan rally at Moose Jaw and the gathering at Regina on 16 February, 1928. Their relationships with the Ku Klux Klan, however, did not detract from the confidence placed in them by their fellow ministers — in 1930 they were elected President and Secretary, respectively, of the Baptist Convention of Saskatchewan.[29]

There were other indications that the Baptists were inclined to approve of the Klan. In 1927, the Baptist Convention at Saskatoon declared that Ottawa was biased towards Roman Catholic settlers and referred to the "Catholic Menace", expressing fear that the franchise in Western Canada would be controlled by a Catholic majority in a few years.[30] Baptist pulpits were open to ministerial Klansmen: a well-known Klan organizer lectured in the Moose Jaw First Baptist church in the fall of 1927;[31] the Reverend David Nygren, a United States Klansman who greeted the crowd at the spectacular Moose Jaw gathering, held special meetings at the Estevan Baptist church.[32] And J.J. Maloney, a prominent Klan spokesman in Saskatchewan, thought an article in *The Western Baptist* to be sufficiently anti-Catholic to reprint it in his paper, *The Western Freedman*.[33]

It appears that the Anglican Church ministry did not produce as many prominent Klansmen as did the United and Baptist Churches. However, at least four, and perhaps five, names of Anglican clergymen were listed in Klan memberships in their respective localities: at Limerick, Delisle, Rosetown, and Kinistino.[34] In addition, Reverend J. Harrison Hill gave the invocation at Hawkins' farewell meeting in Regina.[35] One of the ministers, Reverend W.R. Dent, who later became a successful author, offered his services to Mackenzie King in the federal election of 1930, stating in his qualification, "I know the troubles out there intimately, and I think I could safely say I could throw a monkey wrench in some Conservative machinery having been a member of the Klan."[36]

Such clergy were hardly supported by the national publication of their church, *The Canadian Churchman*. In commenting editorially on the Klan in Oklahoma, the paper described it as "such shocking folly and such loathsome tyranny".[37] Some important organizations within the Church did however lend the Klan incidental support. For instance, in the 1920's the Anglican Council of Social Service increasingly turned its energies to a British Empire colonization program in order to keep Canada British. Many Anglicans were disturbed when it appeared that Canada or any part of it would be flooded with non-British immigrants.[38] Premier Gardiner pinpointed this in a letter to King on 7 June, 1928, when he remarked that the Ku Klux Klan, working in conjunction with the Conservative party, had begun to capitalize on the activities of the Anglican Church and others in opposing the policy of the Federal Government.[39]

On immigration the pronouncements of the Right Reverend Dr. G.E. Lloyd, for example, could hardly be differentiated from Klan propaganda. The comment, "these dirty, ignorant, garlic-smelling, non-preferred continentals", was not the vituperation of a Klan Kleagle but of Dr. Lloyd, Anglican Bishop of Saskatchewan.[40] Again, on giving his reasons for urging the voters to oust the Government, the Bishop said that he would vote against the Gardiner government because Mr. Gardiner's policy on immigration was "non-British, if not anti-British" and that he had "deliberately thrown dust into the eyes of the public on this question". In addition, stated the Bishop,

> I shall vote against the Gardiner government because of its miserable conduct in connection with the objectionable French text book. If Mr. Gardiner cannot see the objections to such a book being used in any state aided school in this province, then he is not fit to be premier of the province and I shall do my best to unseat him and put someone else in his place.[41]

It was not surprising that Klan lecturers referred to the Anglican position in substantiating their condemnation of the Government's immigration policy.[42] Nor was it unexpected that someone should make the comment, regarding the ascendance of the Klan in Saskatchewan, that "a gentleman like Bishop Lloyd, of Saskatoon, is not helping the situation any in his province, but perhaps he is a member of the Klan himself."[43]

Other denominations were also represented in the ranks of the Klan. Reverends John Kovach, Kipling, and E.A. McLaren, Kinistino, of the Pres-

byterian Church, were involved in their respective local Klans, and Rev.
Walker, a chaplain in the Orange Lodge, closed with prayer the Klan organizational meeting in Kerrobert;[44] Reverend W. Kupfer, a Lutheran minister, was a
member of the Moose Jaw Klan,[45] and Reverend Thomas Bunting, a Klan
organizer, belonged to a Pentecostal denomination.[46]

Although the silence, and apparent acquiescence, of the majority of Saskatchewan clergymen was notable, not all Protestant clergy remained silent on the
issue. At least six ministers openly denounced the Ku Klux Klan — all of them
within the United Church.[47] One was Reverend H.D. Ranns, of Biggar, who had
been a devoted student of Salem Bland in Winnipeg and was an advocate of the
social gospel.[48] Ranns bluntly condemned the Knights from the pulpit and in the
press. "If we want our province to become like Indiana," he wrote in *The New
Outlook*, the national publication of the United Church of Canada, "terrorized
and dominated by a set of bigots and ignorant law breakers, then we ought to
welcome the Klan."[49] Closer to home, in the *Manitoba Free Press*, he informed
the editor that

> in Saskatchewan the net result of the coming of the infamous Klan
> has been to divide hitherto unified towns and cities, to breed an
> amount of bitterness and hate among neighbours that the writer has
> never before experienced in twenty years of western residence, and
> to embroil the politics of Saskatchewan in a hopeless tangle of re-
> criminations that are no manner of use to the public good.[50]

Dr. Charles Endicott, of Saskatoon, another minister of the social gospel
persuasion, stated clearly to a United Church conference, that he was absolutely
opposed to the Klan.[51] Reverend E.F. Church, minister of Zion United Church
in Moose Jaw, the hotbed of Saskatchewan Klanism, denounced the order as a
"shallow organization" and stated that "if he wanted to fight Catholics he would
do it as a gentleman, and not shrouded in a white hood."[52] Reverend W.A.
Davis of Birch Hills pointed to the unchristian activities of the American organization in a sermon on "Christianity and the Klan". The Klan was dying in the
United States, he declared, but was being "exploited" in Canada, especially in
Saskatchewan. "Men come along, claiming to be Protestant, the people know
little or nothing about them, but bow to them, hailing them as the Saviours of the
age."[53] And Reverend E.R.M. Brecken of Young, a former missionary in West
China for fifteen years, expressed in the columns of the local press the opinion
that the Klan was "unpatriotic, unchristian, mischievous in its methods, and can
prove to be only disastrous in its results."[54]

There might seem to be an incongruity in the fact that the United Church
should have harboured such diverse reactions to the Klan. The explanation seems
to lie not so much with the Klan itself as with the contrary currents sweeping
Protestantism. Fundamentalism was arising to contest the gains of liberal theol-

ogy; social conservativism was engaging in a counter-attack upon the social gospel. In Saskatchewan, as Richard Hofstadter observed for the United States,[55] the churches harbouring the leading advocates of the social gospel were also the churches giving the strongest support to the prohibition movement.[56] Furthermore, in Saskatchewan these same churches seemed to provide both a substantial part of the Klan membership and its opposition. On prohibition, the social gospel and fundamentalism could co-operate because, for the former, it would eradicate a social evil, and, for the latter, it would remove an obstacle of temptation impeding the christian pilgrim's progress on the road to salvation. When it came to the Klan, however, there was a distinct parting of the ways; the social gospellers either ignored or denounced it,[57] while many of the conservatives either joined and tacitly endorsed the organization or became ardent proponents of it.[58] Perhaps this dichotomy of response within the same Church is explained by the fact that the Klan offered the conservatives an opportunity to participate in a superficial way in the movement for social reform without compromising their fundamentalist theological viewpoint. Therefore, as a conservative appropriation of an element of social response and progressivism, the Ku Klux Klan became an outlet for the genuine concern of some social conservatives about current social conditions, for example, the effects of large-scale immigration and the language problem in the Public Schools.[59]

II

Whether the press represented public reaction to the Klan as accurately as the Churches and political parties may be open to question. It was, however, more influential in the formation of public opinion. Only a few newspapers in Saskatchewan expressed editorial approval of the Ku Klux Klan, but many reported its numerous gatherings sympathetically, a development which probably had a greater effect on the populace than candid editorial comment. The *Kerrobert Citizen*, however, made its policy plain:

> As we indicate in our report of the Ku Klux Klan meeting, we were 'agreeably disappointed' at the entire absence of any very radical utterances such as we had been led to expect from previous information or misinformation regarding this organization, and we quite frankly state it is our belief that the Klan has been grossly misrepresented. We found that the major principles propounded were, in the main, such as we had always held . . . and to this extent we approve of the order.[60]

Other weeklies voiced their approval of the organization indirectly. The *Esterhazy Observer*, for example, reminded its readers that in the election campaign of 1921 Premier Gardiner had "warned the voters of the grave danger of voting for Progressive candidates who were communistic if not 'Red' and quite unconstitutional if not treasonable.'' Therefore, his views on the Klan ought to be taken ''with a quantity of salt''.[61] Similarly, the *North Battleford Optimist* reported that Gardiner was out to ''dam the Klan with the most merciless criticism of which he is capable'', but that his arguments ought not to be accepted ''in toto'' as he was trying to link the Klan with the Conservative party.[62]

Although they did not express editorial approval of the Klan, the newspapers carrying sympathetic reports of its activities rendered the order invaluable service. Their reports approached the subject in several ways. One approach was to praise the speaker and his delivery while not quite openly endorsing the Klan. For example, the *Kinistino Representative* carried a report of a Klan speech liberally sprinkled with superlatives: Mr. Snelgrove, the Klan organizer, ''excelled in oratory'', ''his convincing and winning way has won for him a place in the hearts of his audience never to be forgotten'', his reference to the open Bible was ''magnificent'', and everyone should hear him for ''his lecture is a marvel.''[63] The *Qu'Appelle Progress* observed that Dr. Hawkins, the chief organizer in Saskatchewan, is a ''large man, physically and mentally, easy on eyes and ears, and gives one an immediate impression of earnestness and sincerity.''[64] Again, the *Nokomis Times* reported that Puckering ''gave a very fine speech, which was not accompanied by the usual 'mud-slinging' so much indulged in of late by other speakers on similar topics'' (Premier Gardiner had just begun his speaking tour of the province denouncing the Klan). The paper hoped that Puckering ''may be assured of a crowded house should he again speak at Nokomis''.[65]

Another approach was to reserve praise for the audience and organization of the meeting. ''It was a most orderly crowd'', commented one local newspaper, ''and many remarked that instead of being in an open air demonstration one almost realized they were in a church for everything was carried on reverently.'' The report continued: R.C. Snelgrove gave an ''interesting address receiving many applauses but no interruptions''; Dr. Hawkins was listened to with ''rapt'' attention; the audience with ''heads uncovered rose . . . and sang feelingly 'When I Survey the Wondrous Cross' ''; and, finally, ''the demonstration gave evidence that the KKK was of great strength in the north part of Saskatchewan.''[66] Again, in a report by the *Melfort Journal*, a Klan rally was described as ''one of the most spectacular and interesting affairs ever held in Melfort, or even in the Carrot River Valley'', ''the whole arrangement was very efficiently organized'', and ''at least 80 per cent of the audience were in sympathy with the movement and even those who do not favour this organization did not have a great deal to take objection to.''[67]

There was yet another type of report which concentrated its approval on the Klan's political goals. Some weeklies, for example, took advantage of the Klan's anti-Liberal bias. The *Broadview Express* commented on the order's introduction to Broadview:

The political soil in town is ripe for seeding. A number of grits are 'fed-up' with the brand of menu being put out from Regina. An organization like the KKK will no doubt receive a large following in Broadview. The hall was well filled and the speaker applauded many times. The government of Saskatchewan should take heed to 'the handwriting on the wall.'[68]

The *Rocanville Record* joined with the Klan in attacking the Liberal government by insinuating that Emmons' testimony regarding the Klan and the Conservatives was part of a Liberal scheme to embarrass the Conservative party:

The recent trial of . . . Emmons at Regina on a charge of misappropriating funds of the Ku Klux Klan, was the biggest farce as far as a court case was concerned we ever heard of, and the magistrate who sat on the case should be fired P.D.Q. But he won't be, of course, he was apparently following instructions.[69]

On the other hand, most of the province's large daily newspapers were clearly Liberally biased and, consequently, anti-Klan. The Regina *Standard* and *Star* were possibly the only exceptions. One method of combating the Klan used by all the large papers was to give comprehensive coverage to reports of criminal acts committed by the United States' Klan.[70] Some editors, however, made their opposition to the Klan explicit:

Canada has no place or need of any paid soap box orators from any organization in the USA to tell us how to run this country, Canada has no place for any organization that endeavors to stir up either racial or religious strife; nor do we think it desirable that any Imperial Wizard or Lizard should have a dominating influence on the politics of this country.[71]

Other newspapers maintained a neutral attitude in the controversy, some neither criticizing nor praising the Klan and others criticizing both the order and its chief antagonist, the Liberal government. Many an editor has traditionally taken the position of the *Rosetown Eagle* on controversial issues: "No matter what the editor's personal views are they have never been forced upon the public in these columns. . . . These columns are neutral and it is our purpose to keep them so."[72] Similar expressions can be found in the *Western Producer*,[73] the *Swift Current Herald*,[74] the *Swift Current Sun*,[75] the *Wadona Herald*,[76] and the *Wilkie Press*.[77]

No single reason seems to explain editorial attitudes adopted to the Klan. The larger city papers and rural weeklies that leaned towards the Liberal party seemed to be anti-Klan; the smaller city dailies, for example, the Swift Current papers, and the larger newspapers partial to the Progressive movement, for instance, the *Western Producer*, endeavoured to be neutral. Conservative papers, such as the

Regina Star and *Kerrobert Citizen*, openly approved of the order, and many of the rural weeklies were most sympathetic. In short, it seems that the attitudes the press adopted towards the Ku Klux Klan were, by and large, determined by political bias.

III

If many of the Saskatchewan clergy and newspaper editors emerged from the Klan episode with their image tarnished, the politicians fared just as badly and possibly worse. Although claiming to be primarily a religious organization the Ku Klux Klan in Saskatchewan had given every indication by 1928 that it was politically motivated. By that date it had shown itself to be an outright opponent of the Liberal governments at Ottawa and Regina and its new leaders were well-known Conservatives. To say that, however, is not to suggest that the Klan drew most of its support from a single party. On the contrary, if there is one thing clear about Klan involvement in Saskatchewan politics, it is that no one party had a monopoly on Klan memberships. The message preached by the Klansmen appealed so strongly to the latent prejudices of a large sector of the Saskatchewan electorate that it overcame the barriers erected by party politics. This fact turned out to be the key to the Klan's important influence on the political scene between 1928 and 1930. Even Liberal supporters succumbed to the emotional onslaught competently carried out by professional organizers.

Socially conglomerate, relatively non-ideological, and broadly provincial, the Liberal party and government were vulnerable to the intrusion of an ideology which stressed an identity of racial, religious, and provincial interest.[78] The Klan was such an intrusion. It would be too much to expect opposition parties not to exploit at least some of the unrest created. However, an unpredictable portion of the Anglo-Saxon Protestant segment of Saskatchewan Liberalism would be attracted by Klan arguments. The tradition of Canadian Liberalism carried within it enough of George Brown and Thomas Greenway for such Liberals to feel no disloyalty in associating with an ultra-Protestant and pro-British organization. In any case, they were doing so. As a Liberal party worker complained to Premier Gardiner after a Klan meeting in Kerrobert: "I am trying to keep out of things here on account of my position. It would do no good, but it is difficult. And about all I can do is to keep Liberals from wavering and we may as well admit there are quite a number."[79] Again, in a Moose Jaw newspaper editorial, after the Premier had attacked the Klan in the Legislature: "Worse than all he combines in his castigation all those who do not think as he does. He does not seem to realize that many of his own followers are members of the Klan."[80]

Rumours were circulating in the province to the effect that the Klan executive in Saskatchewan consisted primarily of Liberals and that members of the Cabinet were involved. In a debate between Gardiner and Hawkins, the Klan spokesman claimed that eight of the ten Klan executives and sixty-five per cent of the membership belonged to the Liberal party.[81] Records of Klan membership, however, do not substantiate so large a claim; but they do contain the names of some prominent Liberals.

It would be a mistake, however, to believe that more than a minority of Protestant Anglo-Saxon Liberals joined the Klan; the majority supported the Premier in his outright denunciation of the order. Some of them even tried to use their opposition and hostility to the Klan as a lever to pry favours from the provincial Government. The secretary of the Meyronne Board of Trade, for instance, brought the following to the Government's attention:

> Considering the support given the Government by the voters of Meyronne district heretofore; and the activity of the many Government supporters here at present in offsetting the Ku Klux Klan (which organization is undeniably strong in Woodrow), we believe that our petitions in regard to the Meyronne-Woodrow section of Highway No. 13 should receive your attention.[82]

The most outspoken opponent of the Klan in Saskatchewan was Premier J.G. Gardiner. M.J. Coldwell recalled that although he had "often tangled with him and criticized him", he greatly respected the Premier's courage for "the manner in which he stood firmly against the Klan".[83] Gardiner had begun his attack on the Klan in the Legislature in January, 1928. Armed with information gathered by detectives and willing informants from at least four localities in Saskatchewan, he spent the month of June denouncing the Klan in speeches throughout the province.[84] He squarely faced the order's charges against his Government in every speech, quoting statistics to prove that not more than six of 4,776 school districts were experiencing any racial or religious difficulties, that the census returns of 1921 and 1926 revealed that the alien population was not increasing, and that "the percentage of Catholics in the whole Civil Service is 12.88 per cent whereas . . . the percentage of our population which is Catholic is 19.44."[85]

Gardiner regarded the results of his meetings rather optimistically. He reported to one correspondent that the campaign had been a "very successful one" and that the Klan could "accomplish very little more in this Province".[86] And in a letter to Mackenzie King on 7 June, he stated rather boastfully, "As a result of the experience which I had in those meetings I would say that, when we have covered the whole province as we intend to do this month, Liberalism will be stronger in Saskatchewan than it has been previously."[87] It is probably true that the Premier's anti-Klan campaign did consolidate Liberal support, but within a few weeks, however, his optimism was shaken by the near defeat of his party in the Arm River by-election.

The majority of anti-Klan sentiment in Saskatchewan thus came from Liberals; the major part of Klan support was derived from Conservatives. This development, it appears, was not peculiar to Saskatchewan as the Conservative party in other provinces also looked favourably upon Klan support.[88] The secretary of the Vancouver Klan summed up the relationship quite succinctly:

> Klancraft as practised in this country since its inception . . . has been primarily a Conservative Political Organization, and as such was instituted in Canada about 1922.

He added that the Conservative leaders "were all ready and willing to receive our co-operation and indirectly supply funds during the campaign to the end of electing a conservative administration" but spurned the order after being elected.[89]

That Conservative leaders in Saskatchewan were involved with the Klan became apparent. Affidavits were sworn by two Klan organizers (Emmons and Puckering) that Dr. Anderson, the Conservative leader, had sought Klan assistance in his campaign against the Liberals. J.F. Bryant, a Conservative lawyer and later a Minister in Anderson's cabinet, represented Klansmen in court on several occasions. And, furthermore, Dr. W.D. Cowan, a former Conservative MP, was the treasurer of the Saskatchewan Ku Klux Klan. This was not the sum total of such evidence. Premier Gardiner wrote to the secretary of the Wapella Liberal Association and informed him that Dr. Anderson had met with Klan organizers in the towns of Simpson and Imperial on the same day that the Klan was organized in both towns.[90] "One of the reasons that I knew that there was an intimate connection between the Klan and [Conservatives]," recalled M.J. Coldwell, "was that one evening I was in the Kitchener Hotel and I saw Dr. Anderson and he introduced me to a man called Hawkins. . . ."[91] The very fact that the Klan membership records contain the names of prominent Conservatives suggests though does not prove conclusively, a direct link with the Conservative party.[92]

Other evidence, however, does strongly suggest such a connection. In early 1928, about the time Gardiner was launching his attack on the Klan, Dr. W.D. Cowan, the prominent Regina Conservative who was Klan treasurer, informed R.B. Bennett:

> The Liberal machine used to control all societies here and made them auxiliaries to their party. For the past two years we have been undermining them. We now have a good three years control of quite a number. We shoved the Grits out at the top and pushed Conservatives in at the bottom and then promoted. The one (initials scribbled on the back) is the most complete political organization ever known in the west. Every organizer in it is a Tory. It costs over a thousand dollars a week to pay them. I know it for I pay them. And I never pay a Grit. Smile when you hear anything about this organization. And keep silent.[93]

The letter is almost certainly a reference to the Ku Klux Klan.

Another interesting and significant letter was written to Bennett on March 12 by P.R. MacMillan, President of the Provincial Conservative Association. The letter had been written in explanation of a wire sent to Bennett cancelling a request for guest speakers from the Commons for the Saskatchewan convention; the reason given was that a "deal" was pending with the provincial Progressives and outside guests might not understand the circumstances.[94] Since Bennett, however, had informed MacMillan a few days earlier that Mr. Quinn, a Roman Catholic MP from Halifax, would address the Convention, it is more plausible to think that another "deal" was in the air — not with the Progressives, but with the KKK and hence particularly obnoxious to Quinn.[95]

That the leaders of the Conservative party and the Ku Klux Klan consulted on the planks to be included in the party platform, and that the great majority of delegates acquiesced in these negotiations, is the burden of personal reports of the convention to R.B. Bennett. J.F. Bryant, with obvious satisfaction, reported to Bennett:

> We were extremely careful in connection with our handling of the Church problem and handling of the language question. The KKK were very active indeed at the convention as were also the Orangemen. The head officers of both organizations were present and the organizers of the Klan being very evident throughout the hall. We had some difficulty in keeping them in the background but succeeded in doing so without any incident whatever. . . . The resolution however which was passed in connection with the school question met with the entire approval of the Protestant organizations.[96]

Mr. J.H. Hearn, a Roman Catholic Conservative, observed that Klan literature was distributed at the convention and suggested that a deliberate attempt had been made in the organization of the convention to have as many accredited delegates as possible members of the Klan. Further, out of fifty-seven candidates for office, the Nominating Committee named only two Catholics, Leddy of Saskatoon and MacKinnon of Regina. What was worse, Mr. Leddy was asked by the chairman of the committee to withdraw as "it was considered inexpedient that any Catholic should hold office in this organization." Leddy refused but was defeated in the election of the Advisory Council. MacKinnon met a similar, though more mysterious, fate. When the official list of nominees was read to the convention, MacKinnon's name was omitted and Dr. Guest's, from Regina, substituted.[97] J.F. Bryant, of Regina, wrote to Bennett about the incident on 11 April, 1928:

> MacKinnon stated that the person who did this was Fred Somerville as he dictated the list of officers from a pencil memorandum to Diefenbaker of Prince Albert who was running the typewriter and

> making the copy for the convention. . . . I approached Somerville
> and asked him if this was the case and he stated that it was not and
> that if any change had taken place it was in the typewriting.[98]

That this had happened inadvertently in the dictating or typing of lists was unconvincing to Hearn: "You yourself can see what a situation will be created in Quebec", he warned Bennett, "and in many of the Maritime Seats if this is broadcast over Canada, that the Conservative Party definitely links up with the Ku Klux Klan. . . ."[99]

The above reports provided Mr. Bennett with Protestant and Catholic points of view; the need for an unbiased report was evident. MacKinnon himself wrote to Bennett on March 28 and suggested that Major MacPherson, a Regina lawyer and Conservative MLA, would give such a report.[100] MacPherson reviewed the Klan's history in Saskatchewan and the conditions which fostered it, stating that Klansmen came from all parties, and that the order had received "tremendous impetus" from Gardiner's attack in the Legislature, one result of which "was that undoubtedly a large number of Klansmen were delegates" to the Conservative convention. He regretted that not a single Catholic was elected to office in the party and feared that the election would be a "purely religious fight in the main", adding, however, with apparent satisfaction, that "in many ways the Catholics cannot blame the Protestant Conservatives for endeavouring to profit by the religious cry" as the Roman Catholic church has "almost solidly supported the Liberals since 1905."

Bennett at first expressed apprehension at the conduct of the March convention and the Saskatchewan political situation in general. In the course of a year, however, reports blaming Premier Gardiner and his Ministers, and exonerating the Conservatives, for the racial and religious controversy raging in the province had their effect, enabling him, like MacPherson, to make the rationalization that the Liberals were reaping what they had sown.[101] On 11 May, 1929, he wrote to Anderson:

> You certainly have conducted a wonderful campaign and your physical strength must be nearly exhausted. Few things have pleased me more than hearing that our Roman Catholic friends no longer regard you as a bigot. The fact that they have been expressing approval of your speeches is very encouraging for nothing could be worse than that the idea should prevail that an effort is being made to conduct politics on religious lines.[102]

Again, on June 7, the day after Gardiner's defeat, Bennett cabled congratulations: "The unparalleled success of yesterday is undoubtedly due in very large measure to your persistent efforts and I hasten to congratulate you upon the most magnificent political victory of recent times."[103] His change of attitude was made explicit in a later letter to A.G. MacKinnon:

I wholly agree with you that religion should not enter into our political discussion. . . . When I recall the fact that the Conservative Party went out of office in 1896 by risking its life for the rights of the Catholic minority in Manitoba, I find it difficult to understand why there is such an effort being made to misrepresent the attitude of our party to the Catholic population of Canada. The present situation in Saskatchewan, I attribute entirely to the attitude of Mr. Gardiner and the Liberal party.[104]

Mr. Bennett's attitude is understandable in the light of constant statements by the leading Conservatives in Saskatchewan that they were not involved with the Klan, that the order was a spontaneous uprising against the Liberal government's "truckling to Romish influence", and that it "would be fatal to condemn the Klan".[105] When Emmons and Puckering signed affidavits alleging that Dr. Anderson and Dr. Cowan were using the organization as a political instrument, Bryant and Anderson were swift to deny it. Privately, however, Bryant was not so confident. "I do not like the look of these affidavits", he remarked to Bennett, "I had no idea that Dr. Anderson has so little discretion." He continued: "If the statements contained in the affidavits are true he has certainly placed the Party both in Saskatchewan and throughout Canada in a very difficult position."[106] On June 4, Anderson informed Bennett that the charge "being made by one Emmons that I was responsible for trying to get this organization into politics is a lie of the worst kind and statements and affidavits in the course of preparation will prove this to the satisfaction of all."[107] There is no evidence, however, that the affidavits were ever taken or published.

In summary, then, the Liberal party condemned the Klan as something alien and potentially dangerous to the province of Saskatchewan — the only position it could take in order to placate the strong Catholic and immigrant segments of its support. The Conservative party, on the other hand, similarly adopted an attitude that was politically expedient by taking advantage of the emotionalism aroused by the Klan, by secretly obtaining the endorsation of Klan leaders regarding certain planks in its platform, and by publicly remaining silent on the Klan issue.

In the little that has been written about the Klan in Saskatchewan, the organization is depicted as the Conservative party's friend and the Liberal party's enemy; almost nothing is written about the Progressives, the official party of opposition in the Legislature.[108] Yet with regard to membership in the Klan, the Progressives probably ran a close second to the Conservatives. The names of some prominent Progressives appear in the Klan membership lists. Reverend A.J. Lewis, former Progressive MP defeated in the election of 1925, was Kligrapp of the Strasbourg Klan,[109] and John Evans, another Progressive MP, addressed a Klan rally at Saskatoon.[110] Perhaps the case was not typical, but at least one prominent Klan organizer, D.C. Grant of Moose Jaw, later became active in the CCF. In fact, Grant turned up in Weyburn as campaign manager for

T.C. Douglas in the federal election of 1935.[111] One can assume that if some Progressive leaders were members of the Klan, then many of the rank and file would follow suit.

Certainly the difficulties and defeats of the Progressive Party in Saskatchewan in the few years before the advent of the Klan made the prospect of victory over the Liberals that much more alluring, and therefore prepared the ground for a favourable response to the Klan. The Progressives had tried unsuccessfully to cope with crushing defeats in the provincial election of 1925 and in the federal elections of 1925 and 1926. All attempts failed to revive the old Progressive spirit of 1921.[112] But the nadir of the Progressive party's disappointment, it seems, was reached in the abortive Convention of July, 1927. On June 30, the committee in charge of planning the Convention announced that it was "a great endeavour to unify the aims and ideals of the people", and that there were many problems to be placed before the gathering.[113] Progressive expectations were so great that they made arrangements for the accommodation of five thousand delegates at the stadium in Regina.

The occasion, however, proved a dismal failure. There were only sixty-five delegates at the first session, and 250 at the largest gathering. We were "unfortunate in this respect", reminisced M.J. Coldwell, "that we hit a spell of very wet weather in July . . . and people that tried to come by cars . . . simply couldn't reach the city — there were cars with broken axles between here, for example, and Moose Jaw, between Regina and Moose Jaw . . . the attempt was a failure."[114]

An exultant Premier Gardiner was quick to point to what he believed to be the moral. Rather unwisely, and somewhat cheaply, he linked the Progressives with the Klan by reference to similar organizing techniques as utilizing paid organizers from the United States, a reference to the Non-Partisan League of the Progressive past. The Convention failure, he stated, "has demonstrated something to the people of the province of Saskatchewan . . . it has demonstrated this fact that the day of the get-rich-easy politician is past in the province of Saskatchewan."[115]

This association of the Progressives with the Klan by innuendo must be taken for what it was, but there was, nevertheless, in the background a curious alliance of Progressives and the Klan in the making. In the summer of 1927, when indications were that the Progressive party was finished, the Ku Klux Klan was beginning to foster conditions which inadvertently served to lend the party a new lease on life by acting as a catalyst in developing Progressive-Conservative collaboration. As the author of an "Open Letter to Premier Gardiner" observed:

> Sir, you have devoted a lot of time to the Tory party and the Klan. . . . But your speeches contain very little about the Progressive party. I know you think you killed it when you ridiculed the Regina Convention. I am afraid it did not stay dead, and I am told

that since then there has been an infusion of new blood by means of the Klan whose vote you said you did not want; other parties may not despise them.[116]

Progressives, like Conservatives, however, were sensitive to the association the Premier was trying to establish. One such attack in the legislature prompted a Progressive member, Mr. Whatley, to ask, "Are we to understand that the premier is trying to connect the Ku Klux Klan with the Progressive Party?" Gardiner answered, "Just give me a little time. You will be quite illuminated by the time I get through."[117] Gardiner's accusation, of course, involved more than similarity of organizing techniques. It stressed as well the more important charge that Progressives and Conservatives were making political hay out of emotional issues raised and fostered by the Klan.

At first glance, it appears highly unlikely that Progressives would be attracted to the Klan's sales pitch. But then prohibition does not seem appropriate for a Progressive platform either. Certain strains in the doctrines of the Klan struck responsive chords in the Progressive mentality — strains that appealed more strongly to their religious, racial, and anti-party prejudices than did the doctrinaire aspect of the Progressive movement.

One theme Klan speakers continually harped upon was its non-partisan and non-political character — a theme particularly attractive to Progressives.

> It was being said [remarked the chief Klan organizer in 1928], that the Klan was fighting the Liberal party. This was true insofar as the party in power was concerned, but only because the Klan believed that the party in power had departed from Liberal principles. The Klan was not Liberal, Conservative or Progressive. It was Canadian.

To another audience, the same organizer, Dr. Hawkins, had this to say:

> The Klan is not political. It does not tell a man how to vote. It does urge all to exercise the franchise, however, and to vote for the man not the party, always providing . . . he is the best man.[118]

This particular theme of Klan propaganda found echoes in letters to local newspapers. As one woman wrote to *The Western Producer* in terms rather more reminiscent of traditional western Non-Partisanism:

> The Ku Klux Klan is similar, I believe to other organizations which have sprung up when people have lost confidence in constituted authority; when they feel that justice too often miscarries — that politics and patronage figure too largely in our courts; that the welfare of the state is made subservient to the interest of the party, permitting privileges to influential minorities — privileges detrimental to the best interest of society as a whole.[119]

On the other pet themes of the Klan lecturers — immigration, education, and the influence of the Quebec hierarchy of the Roman Catholic Church — the Progressives were in complete agreement. This is best illustrated by the Progressive platform of 1929, a platform even more emotionally tinged than the Conservative one. The Conservative plank on immigration, for example, was "Aggressive immigration policy based on the selective principle"; the Progressive counterpart was "An Immigration policy which will insure the permanency of British Institutions and Ideals." On the education issue, the Conservatives requested a "Thorough revision of the educational system of the province"; the Progressives desired the "Freedom of our public schools from sectarian influence, with increased emphasis on moral training."[120]

The Progressives also shared the Klan's suspicions of Quebec. Sidney Bingham, a Saskatchewan Progressive MLA, attacking the Liberal party, stated that "Saskatchewan, the most forward-looking province in Canada, is linked up politically with that most cautious, solid, subtle, and conservative province of Quebec." John Evans, Progressive MP, in an angry denunciation of a speech by Premier Gardiner, accused the Liberals of Quebec of taking part in the usurpation of the natural resources of Saskatchewan and Alberta in 1905, which he called an "act of piracy".[121] Evans made his views much clearer in a letter to the Orange *Sentinel* dated 13 December, 1928. He charged that the federal and Saskatchewan Liberal governments had been dominated by "the Romish Church" since Laurier's time and that Roman Catholic influence was responsible for the inadequate treatment of the Reformation in school curricula in Saskatchewan.

The Klan, by emphasizing racial, religious, and moralistic issues, had appealed to large sections of the electorate and had polarized Saskatchewan politics, at least temporarily, along new lines. It had undermined the Liberal coalition, and had provided a basis for Conservative-Progressive co-operation. Conservatives especially found the Klan attractive, and it was with that party that the Klan had its closest direct association. However, the frustrating experience of the Progressives in Saskatchewan made them susceptible to suggestions that gave hope of removing the Liberals, and especially J.G. Gardiner, from power. Adding to its arsenal a general outrage over the defeat of prohibition, the Klan attracted Liberal party prohibitionists and associated them electorally with Conservatives and Progressives in an alliance that at bottom rested on an accumulation of bitterness. When the test of strength came in the form of the Saskatchewan general election of 1929, the Liberal party was defeated and found itself out of office for the first time in twenty-four years.[122]

The Ku Klux Klan inevitably became an issue of debate not only on the pages of the press but throughout Saskatchewan society — from the farming communities to the Protestant churches and political parties. Its opponents pointed to the violence and lawlessness of the United States' Klan as an example of what might happen in Saskatchewan. Its members and sympathizers argued that there had never been a single act of lawlessness committed by a Klan in Saskatchewan. What was reported to have happened in the United States, claimed the Imperial Wizard of Saskatchewan, "has no more connection with the organization here than the flood of Bible days with the high waters of the Mississippi in 1927."[123] Furthermore, according to its followers, the Klan was a Christian and patriotic order dedicated to the preservation of the Protestant faith in Saskatchewan, an organization that was a dire necessity in the context of Roman Catholic dominance of the provincial and federal Liberal governments. Opponents, however, thought this aspect of the Klan no more than a front for unscrupulous organizers and ambitious politicians.

In large part the Klan's appeal rested on negative and defensive feelings which, though strongly rooted in Saskatchewan life, could not long sustain a major movement. That the order remained vibrant as long as it did — until the early 1930's — could be attributed to a medley of reasons: the acceptance and support of the order by a considerable number of Protestant ministers, the establishment of an independent Klan with capable leaders and organizers, the publicity the organization received in the press throughout the province, and a political situation which was conducive to the Klan's program and methods.

Notes

1. See W. Calderwood, "The Rise and Fall of the Ku Klux Klan in Saskatchewan" (unpublished M.A. thesis, University of Saskatchewan, Regina, 1968), pp. 9-27.
2. See *The Sentinel and Orange and Protestant Advocate* (hereafter cited as *Sentinel*), January 17, March 1, August 23, October 25, 1928.
3. *Ibid.*, December 2, 1926, p. 2.
4. See also *ibid.*, June 9, 1927, p. 1; September 15, 1927, p. 3.
5. According to a report in the *Regina Morning Leader*, June 5, 1928, Hawkins was a lawyer, called to the Bar in Birmingham, Alabama, in 1908, and a "Doctor of Optometry," and a public school teacher. He later became a prominent Klan spokesman in Saskatchewan. A correspondent of Premier Gardiner warned him that Hawkins was "a clever man, a good organizer, and a wonderful platform speaker, especially when addressing the female sex, and when he gets talking about his wonderful mother, his sacrificing wife, his wonderful children, he can bring tears to the eyes of the average woman — yes, and some men too — but he never forgets the [dollar]." Another friend of the Premier voiced a similar opinion but more descriptively: "This man Hawkins is as smooth as a silk worm's belly." James Anderson to Premier Gardiner [n.d.]; N.G. Calder to Gardiner [n.d.] (Answered August 8, 1928), Public Archives of Saskatchewan (PAS), Papers of the Rt. Hon. James Garfield Gardiner pp. 12325, 12336. Fowler, it seems, was a former Baptist minister in the United States who was unfrocked for some unknown irregularities. There is no evidence that he worked for the Klan in Saskatchewan. *Ibid.*, pp. 12326, 12558.
6. Fowler to Hawkins, February 23, 1925, *ibid.*, p. 12729.
7. See Morton Harrison, "Gentlemen from Indiana," *Atlantic Monthly*, May, 1928, pp. 277-8.
8. *Le Patriote de L'Ouest*, February 9, 1927.
9. Father H. Couture, *Le Ku Klux Klan* (Montreal, 1927).

10. Robert Moon, *This is Saskatchewan* (Toronto, 1953), p. 46; C.L. Fowler to L.A. Hunter, February 17, 1927, Gardiner Papers, p. 12655.

11. See Calderwood, pp. 62-68.

12. *Ibid.*, pp. 48-110.

13. *Kloran of the Knights of the Ku Klux Klan*, Gardiner Papers, pp. 13073-13075.

14. Of a population of 757,510 in 1921, 497,817 people belonged to these denominations. (Methodist, Presbyterian, and Congregationalist Churches became the United Church of Canada in 1925.) In addition to the large denominations, there were 2,555 Congregationalists, 1,552 Salvation Army, 3,250 listed under "Protestant", and 28,251 under "All Others", which consisted mainly of small Protestant sects. *Census of Canada*, 1921, Vol. 1, pp. 568,572.

15. Similar responses occurred elsewhere under comparable conditions. One student of the Klan in Indiana, for example, observed that "rurally oriented Indiana furnished soil" for the Klansmen and that the majority of ministers enlisted by the order "came from the Baptist, Disciples of Christ, and Methodist denominations." J.A. Davis, "The Ku Klux Klan in Indiana, 1920-30: An Historical Study" (unpublished Ph.D. thesis, Northwestern University, 1966), p. 280. David Chalmers made the same observation from a national standpoint and added that probably "the Methodists, possessing the strongest bent toward social action, supplied the largest number of ministerial Klansmen," David M. Chalmers, *Hooded Americanism* (New York, 1965), p. 9.

16. The names of the following ministers appear in the membership records: Reverends T. Musto, Verwood; A.J. Lewis, Strasbourg; J. McKnight, La Fleche; W.C. Challis, Langbank; D.E. Freek, Bengough; W. Titley, Imperial (see *Imperial Review*, April 25, 1929, clipping, Gardiner Papers, p. 13964); L.R. Bouchard, Pontiex; S.P. Rondeau, Woodrow; W.H. Madill, Kincaid; and L.B. Henn, Macrorie (see *Saskatoon Star-Phoenix*, April 11, 1929). Sympathizers were Reverend Dr. Keeton, Indian Head (*see Indian Head News*, March 21, 1929, clipping, Gardiner Papers, p. 13956); Reverend R.J. Smith, Wilkie (see *Wilkie Press*, March 28, 1928, clipping, Gardiner Papers, p. 14072); and Reverend Dr. W.S. Reid, Saskatoon (see *Saskatoon Star*, March 26, 1928). See Gardiner Papers, pp. 12411-12508, and compare with *The United Church Year Book 1927-1929*.

17. *Census of Canada*, 1931, Vol. 2, p. 258.

18. *Minutes of the Fifteenth Synod of Saskatchewan of the Presbyterian Church in Canada*, Regina, November 2-5, 1920, p. 3.

19. Verbatim report published by Klan, Gardiner Papers, p. 12848.

20. Henn to Editor, *Saskatoon Star*, June 23, 1928.

21. Titley to Editor, *Imperial Review*, April 19, 1928, clipping, Gardiner Papers, p. 13522.

22. *Saskatoon Daily Star*, March 26, 1928.

23. Reverends T.J. Hind, Moose Jaw; William Surman, Regina; Robert Watson, Moose Jaw; and A.U. Russell, Estevan. See Gardiner Papers, pp. 12459, 12506, 12470; *Estevan Mercury*, April 19, 1928, clipping, Gardiner Papers, p. 13523; also *1924 Year Book of the Baptist Union of Western Canada*, pp. 24, 75, 152.

24. G.H. Robertson, "Moose Jaw: Playboy of the Prairies," *MacLean's Magazine*, May 1, 1951; *Moose Jaw Evening Times*, June 8, 1927.

25. *Ibid.*, October 30, 1929, p. 11.

26. Verbatim report of Klan meeting, Gardiner Papers, p. 12847.

27. PAS, Transcript of interview with M.J. Coldwell, June 19, 1963.

28. Clipping, Gardiner Papers, p. 13956.

29. *1930 Year Book. . .*, pp. 57, 87.

30. *The Sentinel*, June 30, 1927, p. 10.

31. *Moose Jaw Evening Times*, October 22, 1927.

32. *Ibid.*, June 8, 1927; *1928 Year Book. . .*, p. 102.

33. April 5, 1928, Gardiner Papers, p. 12855.

34. Reverends W.R. Dent, A.B. Sharples, H.E. Parrott, and E.V. Bird. See Gardiner Papers, pp. 12442, 12426, 12490, 12439; *The Qu'Appelle Church Quarterly*, No. 141, Winter, 1926, pp. 38-39; *Journal of Proceedings. . . .* The fifth, Reverend A. Bekereth, was a member of the Kinistino Klan; it is probable, however, that this, through typographical error, was Reverend A. Beckwith, Anglican minister and Worshipful Master of the Loyal Orange Lodge at Kinistino. See Gardiner Papers, p. 12439; *Journal of Proceedings, Twenty-ninth Meeting of the Synod of Saskatchewan*, Saskatoon, 1929; *Record of Proceedings of the Grand Orange Lodge of Saskatchewan*, March 3-4, 1926, p. 73.

35. *Regina Leader*, July 19, 1928; *The Qu'Appelle Church Quarterly, loc. cit.*
36. Public Archives of Canada (PAC), King Papers, Dent to King, May 20, 1930. See also *Moose Jaw Evening Times*, February 18, 1930, p. 9, for article, "Anglican Preacher-writer".
37. October 4, 1923, p. 633.
38. See reports of the work of the Council in *The Canadian Churchman*, September 17, 1925; August 4, 1927, and *Social Welfare*, April, 1927.
39. King Papers, p. 129769.
40. *Regina Star*, May 29, 1929.
41. *Ibid.*, June 5, 1929.
42. Puckering at Unity, *Unity Courier*, April 18, 1928, clipping, Gardiner Papers, p. 13516.
43. *Winnipeg Free Press*, October 18, 1928. Comment of Alderman J. Blumberg of Winnipeg. See Gardiner Papers, Section XII, Newspaper clippings, for Bishop Lloyd's statements on immigration for period October 3, 1927 — June 5, 1929. See also *The Sentinel*, December 2, 1926, July 26, 1928, and *The Lance*, Simpson, May 3, 1928, *ibid.*, p. 14080, for Anglican pronouncements on Roman Catholic influence in government, natural resources, and immigration.
44. Kovach is listed as a member for Kipling, *ibid.*, p. 12440; McLaren was reported as one of the speakers at a Klan rally in Melfort, *Kinistino Representative*, May 29, 1928, clipping, *ibid.*, p. 13631; Walker was mentioned in the *Kerrobert Citizen*, March 28, 1928, clipping, *ibid.*, p. 13487, and *The Sentinel*, August 11, 1925, p. 6. See PAC, Bennett Papers, p. 25460, for letter from McLaren offering his services to the Conservative party in the federal election of 1930. All three ministers were listed under "Minister or Missionary" in a ledger of the Presbyterian Synod's Home Missionary projects in Saskatchewan for 1929. The ledger is in the historical documents of the First Presbyterian Church in Regina.
45. Gardiner Papers, p. 12457. See Bennett Papers, p. 25022; *The Western Freedman*, April 5, 1928, Gardiner Papers, p. 12855; and *The Sentinel*, December 13, 1928, for reports of Lutheran disillusionment with the Liberal party. Dr. K. Holfeld, President of the Evangelical Lutheran Church of Canada, in an interview with the author, recalled meeting Premier Gardiner on a train around 1929. The Premier appeared to be "very concerned" about the Klan and asked whether it had penetrated the Lutheran communities. He gave Dr. Holfeld a book on the Klan and asked him to read it. Interview, December 21, 1967.
46. *Saskatoon Daily Star*, January 25, 1928.
47. Opponents were as follows: Reverends H.D. Ranns, Biggar (see Letter to the Editor, *Manitoba Free Press*, October 27, 1928; Ranns to Gardiner, August 24, 1927, and February 14, 1928, Gardiner Papers, pp. 12038, 12094); E.F. Church, Moose Jaw (see *Moose Jaw Times*, October 6, 1927); Dr. Chas. Endicott, Saskatoon (see *Regina Post*, October 19, 1927); Dr. J.L. Nicol, Rosetown (see Nicol to Gardiner, February 7, 1928, Gardiner Papers, p. 12085); E.R.M. Brecken, Young (see Letter to Editor, *Young Journal*, March 1, 1928, clipping, Gardiner Papers, p. 13460); and W.A. Davis, Birch Hills (see *Gazette*, April 25, 1928, clipping, Gardiner Papers, p. 12189).
48. A.R. Allen, "Salem Bland and the Social Gospel in Canada" (unpublished M.A. thesis, University of Saskatchewan, 1961), pp. 68-69. Ranns continued Bland's column in the *Grain Growers' Guide* following Bland's departure from the West in 1919.
49. August 3, 1927, p. 14.
50. Ranns to Editor, October 27, 1928.
51. *Regina Morning Leader*, June 4, 1928.
52. *Moose Jaw Evening Times*, October 3, 1927.
53. *Birch Hills Gazette*, April 25, 1928, clipping, Gardiner Papers, p. 12189.
54. *Young Journal*, March 1, 1928, clipping, Gardiner Papers, p. 13460.
55. R. Hofstadter, *The Age of Reform* (New York, 1956), p. 290.
56. See A.R. Allen, *The Social Passion* (Toronto, 1971), pp. 264-283.
57. Reverends Ranns and Endicott of the United Church are good examples of the social gospel attitude towards the Klan.
58. Reverends Rondeau, Reid, Keeton, of the United Church, and Hind, Surman, Russell, of the Baptist Church are good examples of the conservative response.
59. See Charles C. Alexander, *The Ku Klux Klan in the Southwest* (Lexington, 1966), p. 20, for Klan's attitude to reform: "Reform of some sort has been the moving spirit of the Klan." For observations on a not entirely dissimilar movement, Social Credit, gaining from a reaction to the

social gospel, see Harold J. Schultz, "Portrait of a Premier: William Aberhart," *Canadian Historical Review*, Vol. 45 (1964), p. 189.
60. March 28, 1928, clipping, Gardiner Papers, p. 14078. See also the *Moose Jaw Merchants Weekly*, March 9, 1928, *ibid.*, p. 13469.
61. July 12, 1928, *ibid.*, p. 13785.
62. June 21, 1928, *ibid.*, p. 13707.
63. December 25, 1928, *ibid.*, p. 13930.
64. July 5, 1928, *ibid.*, p. 13775.
65. May 31, 1928, *ibid.*, p. 13643; see also the *Hanley Herald*, March 1, 1928, *ibid.*, p. 13452.
66. *Kinistino Representative*, May 29, 1928, *ibid.*, p. 13631.
67. May 29, 1928, *ibid.*, p. 13633.
68. May 10 (see also May 24), 1928, *ibid.*, pp. 13570, 13619.
69. May 11, 1928, *ibid.*, p. 13589.
70. See *Regina Leader*, April 10, 11, 14, 1928; *Moose Jaw Evening Times*, September 10, 1927, April 3, 10, 1928; and *Saskatoon Star*, May 18, 1928.
71. *Weekly Climax*, August 2, 1928, Gardiner Papers, p. 13853. See also *Lashburn Comet*, June 13, 1928, *ibid.*, p. 13684.
72. June 21, 1928, *ibid.*, p. 13709.
73. November 3, 1927, February 10, and March 15, 1928.
74. May 17 and June 28, 1928, Gardiner Papers, pp. 13607, 13726.
75. May 29, 1928, *ibid.*, p. 13630.
76. June 14, 1928, January 31, and February 28, 1929, *ibid.*, pp. 13687, 13940, 13951.
77. April 18, 1928, *ibid.*, p. 13519.
78. Patrick Kyba, "The Saskatchewan General Election of 1929" (unpublished M.A. thesis, University of Saskatchewan, Saskatoon, 1964), p. 94.
79. E.B. Hutherson to Gardiner, June 20, 1928, Gardiner Papers, p. 12288.
80. *Moose Jaw Merchants Weekly*, March 9, 1928, clipping, *ibid.*, p. 13470.
81. *Moose Jaw Herald*, July 7, 1928; *Regina Leader*, July 19, 1928. See also *Manitoba Free Press*, June 16, 1928, for letter to editor from a Liberal of "thirty years standing", and compare with Gardiner Papers, p. 12430, for membership of Fort Qu'Appelle Klan.
82. R.E. Johnson to Hon. G. Spence, Minister of Highways, June 26, 1928, PAS, *Department of Highways*, file No. 13-J-C, Provincial Highway Woodrow to Meyronne. This letter was brought to my attention by Provincial Archivist Allan Turner.
83. PAS, Transcript of interview with M.J. Coldwell, June 19, 1963.
84. Informants wrote from Outlook, Balcarres, Moose Jaw, and Tisdale, Gardiner Papers, pp. 12044, 12054, 12041, 12122, 12124, 12184; see also pp. 12219, 12042.
85. *Rosetown Eagle*, June 21, 1928, clipping, *ibid.*, p. 13710; *Prince Albert Daily Herald*, June 22, 1928, *ibid.*, p. 13717; Gardiner to R.C. Hall, May 18, 1928, *ibid.*, p. 12264.
86. Gardiner to J.E. Huckins, Goderich, Ontario, August 14, 1928, *ibid.*, p. 12316. See also Gardiner to H.D. Ranns, February 15, 1928, *ibid.*, p. 12091.
87. PAC, King Papers, p. 129769.
88. References to the organization outside of Saskatchewan tend to substantiate this. In British Columbia, the Conservative opposition was successful in defeating a resolution expressing disapproval of the Klan's entrance into the province, *Canadian Annual Review* (hereafter cited *C.A.R.*), 1925-1926, p. 516. In Alberta, the Conservatives were accused of using the Klan to win the provincial by-election at Red Deer. J.H. Hurley, Edmonton, to King, November, 1931, King Papers, p. 158597. King replied December 1: "Your letter and the enclosures confirm what I have heard of the activities of the Ku Klux Klan in Alberta and the use which is being made of this organization, for political purposes, by the Conservative Party." *Ibid.*, p. 158608. In Ontario, the Tories were charged with "trying to repeat . . . the Saskatchewan performance" of June, 1929, by taking advantage of issues raised by the Klansmen. "Memorandum on Organization" by Andrew Hayden, September 17, 1929, *ibid.*, pp. 138086-138094. And in New Brunswick, "a Conservative member of Parliament . . . had considerable to do with organizing the Klan to turn out the Government of that Province," Gardiner to Reverend Dr. J.L. Nicol, February 11, 1928, Gardiner Papers, p. 12076.
89. Circular letter from Klan, October 3, 1931, PAC, Meighen Papers, p. 104173; see also pp. 104145, 104156.

90. May 18, 1928, Gardiner Papers, p. 12216.
91. Transcript of Interview with M.J. Coldwell, June 19, 1963.
92. Names such as Nat Given of Delisle, J.A. Merkeley and James Pascoe of Moose Jaw, W.W. Miller of Biggar, and William Smith of Swift Current appear on membership lists for the respective locals, Gardiner Papers, pp. 12426, 12427, 12463, 12467, 12486. Compare with *Directory of Saskatchewan*, pp. 61, 67, 68, 79. See also *Moose Jaw Evening Times*, March 11, 1930, p. 6, for report of "Conservative Banquet at Readlyn" and compare with membership lists for Assiniboia and Readlyn, Gardiner Papers, pp. 12414, 12479.
93. Cowan to Bennett, January 16, 1928, Bennett Papers, p. 24885. Bennett replied on February 1, but ignored the reference to "the most complete political organization".
94. *Ibid.*, p. 24938.
95. Bryant to Bennett, March 5, 1928, *ibid.*, p. 24926; Bennett to MacMillan, March 7, 1928, *ibid.*, p. 24927; see also J.H. Hearn, a Roman Catholic, to Bennett, March 28, *ibid.*, p. 24987, for substantiation of this observation.
96. Bryant to Bennett, March 16, 1928, *ibid.*, p. 24951. Bryant asked that this letter be destroyed.
97. Hearn to Bennett, March 28, 1928, *ibid.*, p. 24987.
98. *Ibid.*, p. 25014. A letter to the Rt. Hon. John G. Diefenbaker brought the following reply: "Personally, I took a strong stand against the Klan for its principles were founded on discrimination based on colour, race and religion — against which I have been a sworn enemy throughout life." Diefenbaker to author, March 7, 1968.
99. Hearn to Bennett, *loc. cit.*
100. *Ibid.*, p. 25003.
101. See *ibid.*, pp. 25022, 25025, 25053, 25056, 25103, for favourable and optimistic reports of the situation.
102. *Ibid.*, p. 25267.
103. *Ibid.*, p. 25322.
104. *Ibid.*, February 5, 1930, p. 25501.
105. T.D. Agnew to Bennett, May 26, 1928, *ibid.*, p. 25100; F.B. Reilly to Bennett, April 14, 1928, *ibid.*, p. 25025.
106. Bryant to Bennett, May 31, 1928, *ibid.*, p. 25113.
107. Anderson to Bennett, June 4, 1928, *ibid.*, p. 25122. The only reference I found which might confirm this was a statement by Maloney that Puckering had signed another affidavit repudiating the former one. This must have been done, if it ever was, after October, 1928, as Gardiner "during his Arm River campaign . . . inferred that the affidavit must be correct because no action was taken against it." *Regina Star*, November 12, 1928.
108. *Director of Saskatchewan*, p. 40. There were six Progressives, three Conservatives, two Independents, and the rest Liberal.
109. Gardiner Papers, p. 125081. Others involved were Thomas Teare, a charter member of "The New National Policy Political Association", later the Progressive party, member of the Moose Jaw Klavern; E. Jones, Secretary-Treasurer of Rosetown Progressive party organization, member of the Harris Klavern; J.W. Vandergrift, a member of the executive of the Progressive party for Maple Creek constituency, member of the Pontiex Klavern; J. Balfour, a delegate to the Progressive Convention in January, 1926, member of the Balcarres Klavern.
110. *The Reporter*, February 23, 1929, Gardiner Papers, p. 12935.
111. R. Schultz to Gardiner, December 1, 1939, *ibid.*, p. 43975.
112. See Calderwood, "The Decline of the Progressive Party in Saskatchewan, 1925-1930," *Saskatchewan History*, XXI, No. 3 (Autumn, 1968), pp. 81-90.
113. *The Western Producer*, June 30, 1927, p. 2.
114. PAS, Transcript of interview with M.J. Coldwell, June 19, 1963.
115. *The Western Producer*, July 21, 1927, p. 1.
116. *Ibid.*, July 5, 1928.
117. *The Regina Leader*, January 31, 1928.
118. *Kerrobert Citizen*, June 20, 1928, clipping, Gardiner Papers, p. 13699; *Yorkton Enterprise*, June 5, 1928, *ibid.*, p. 13663.
119. February 23, 1928.
120. Kyba, p. 35 and Appendix B, for a comparison of platforms.

121. *The Western Producer*, November 19, 1925, p. 4; July 28, 1927, p. 10.

122. For a published account of the 1929 election see Patrick Kyba, "Ballots and Burning Crosses — The Election of 1929", in Norman Ward and Duff Spafford (eds.), *Politics in Saskatchewan* (Don Mills, 1968), pp. 105-123.

123. Statement by Imperial Wizard Rosborough reported in *Montreal Gazette*, July 9, 1928.

CHAPTER 3

The Co-operative Commonwealth Federation

Introduction

Social movements take on different characteristics depending upon the point in their 'career' at which they have arrived. The changing characteristics of the CCF/NDP can best be explained if this fact is remembered. Over its forty-odd year history, it has advocated, at one point or another, what to some observers might seem like completely different ideologies. In addition, over a number of years, its organizational base has changed. The New Democratic Party of today is vastly different from the alliance that emerged from the founding convention of the CCF in 1932. The CCF/NDP, in fact, provides the best and most documented contemporary example of the transition from a social movement to a full-fledged Canadian institution.

Although socialist activity was clearly evident in the years prior to the formation of the CCF, the immediate impetus to its formation can, in part, be found in the events of the Great Depression. With the Great Depression, the unbounded optimism of the early years of the twentieth century came to an end. Even two months before the great debacle, fiscal experts optimistically projected that "investors' demand for stocks appear to be without limitations."[1] The opportunities for quick gain on the stock market seemed endless. On October 25, 1929, however, every newspaper across the North American continent screamed a variation of the common theme: "Stock Speculators Shaken in Wild Day of Panic."[2] The New York Stock Exchange, the centre of international finance, lay prostrate.

The ramifications of this catastrophe were world-wide. One by one, every country in the world became part of a vicious circle of declining prices, decreasing production, and shrinking domestic and foreign markets. Because of her heavy reliance on the export of staple resources, like pulp and paper, minerals, wheat, and so on, Canada was particularly vulnerable to the initial attempts to still this cycle through the strict limitation of trade agreements. The downswing that resulted from these limitations was accentuated by heavy fixed costs, financial abuses, over-expansion, and other legacies of the late nineteenth and early twentieth century. In addition, there was a collapse of long-range profit expectations, which in turn led to a severe constriction of domestic investment.[3] These, in short, were the mechanisms operative in the waning financial fortunes of Canada.

In more human terms, the downswing in the Canadian economy meant several things: unemployment, despondency, and poverty. "From 1930 through 1940 never less than 10 per cent of the wage-earners of Canada were out of work. In 1933, 647,000 of them had no jobs, 26.6 per cent of the non-agricultural work force."[4]

The Prairie Provinces were particularly hard hit. In his analysis of the CCF in rural Saskatchewan, S.M. Lipset argues, in fact, that: "No other province in Canada — and, for that matter, few other places in the entire world — suffered so sharp a decline in income and required so much government assistance in order to survive. Every available economic index points to this fact."[5]

These harsh economic facts are clearly evident in the pathetic plea of a Saskatchewan mother writing to R.B. Bennett in 1935.

> I wonder if you would help a poor sick woman in distress I am sick most of the time My husband is laid up with Rheummatism and We Have 9 small children the last 14 month apart Me and the children have no Shoes to Wear or any clothes of no kind Two go to School with no coat.
> Wish you would sent us a few dollars to pay necessary things the Lord will Repay and so will I: as soon as we are able
> The Reason Im wrighting is I know you are a Wonderful Man[6]

In the decade that James Gray describes as "the winter years" life was hard and employment scarce, even in large urban centres like Winnipeg. The only alternative for thousands of unfortunates, like Gray, who found themselves unemployed was the dreaded "dole". That this was not a welcome alternative to steady employment is well expressed by him.

> From our home on Ruby Street in Winnipeg to the relief office at the corner of Xante Street and Elgin Avenue was less than three miles. It could be walked easily in an hour, but I didn't complete the journey the first time I set out, or the second. If I had not been driven by the direst necessity, the third trip would have ended as the first two had done. I would have veered sharply to the right, somewhere en route, to head down town in one last attempt to find a job. But on the third

trip the truth could no longer be dodged by any such pointless manoeuvre.[7]

It should be emphasized that not all Canadians experienced the depression in a similar way. While James Gray, and hundreds of thousands like him, walked the streets looking for work, or froze in line-ups for begrudged hand-outs, "Mrs. Torrance Beardmore entertained at a delightful coming-out party for her daughter, Miss Francis, who received with her mother in a French model frock of forget-me-nots of blue georgette mounted on pale pink."[8] An individual who shared similar good fortune, the son of Sir Herbert Holt, the financier, recalled that "whatever may have been the result of the crash, I noted no change in my family's way of living."[9] Others, like the Prince of Wales, imposed self-austerity and urged prospective hosts not to "spend a penny more than necessary on my reception."[10] Life style, at least in some circles, continued as if the depression, and all its ramifications, were a figment of a perverse imagination. The Royal Winter Fair of 1931, for example, "was in itself a pageant so magnificent as to make many wonder why there should be talk of depression."[11]

In the political realm, economic collapse had essentially two effects. The most immediate result was to insure the election of R.B. Bennett in 1930, and, in turn, to make certain his defeat some five years later. The second effect, of a far more enduring nature, was the rapid rise and growth of strong third parties. This latter development, though, can be attributed more to the failure of the Liberals and Conservatives to cope with the difficulties of the situation than to the depression itself. The eventual outcome was the emergence of movements, like the CCF, which attempted to bring about change in Canadian society.

Like the Progressive Party, the political wing of the UFA and the social credit movement, the CCF found great support in the Canadian West. There are, however, two very important ways in which the CCF differed from these movements. First, the initial ideology of the CCF was clearly socialistic. Second, the impetus for the formation of the CCF was not tightly confined to the rural western provinces: Walter Young has clearly indicated that the CCF, from its inception, was also influenced by urban socialist elements.[12]

Unlike the social credit movement, which from the beginning was regionally based, the Co-operative Commonwealth Federation, founded in 1932, attempted to foster a national coalition of farmers, workers, and intellectuals. The party, under the leadership of J.S. Woodsworth, was "a federation of organizations whose purpose is the establishment in Canada of a Co-operative Commonwealth in which the principle regulating production, distribution, and exchange will be the supplying of human needs and not the making of profit."[13] Basically, the CCF hoped to achieve "a planned and socialized economy in which our national resources and the principle means of production are owned, controlled, and operated by the people."[14] By emphasizing fundamental social change, the CCF hoped to avoid the fate of the earlier Progressives who had never really distinguished themselves from the Liberal rhetoric of reform.

The CCF found one of its most important initial organizational bases in the farmers' associations of western Canada. In this regard, it was again similar to the Progressive Party, the political wing of the UFA, and the social credit movement. The farmers' associations provided leadership and channels of communication through which information regarding CCF ideology could be disseminated. The similarities between the organizational base of the CCF and its contemporary, the social credit movement, and the similarities between the economies of Alberta and Saskatchewan, raise two important questions: a) Why was the reactionary Social Credit successful in Alberta, while the relatively socialistic CCF attained power in its sister province, Saskatchewan?[15] b) Why did the Social Credit in Alberta enjoy success in the Depression years while the CCF did not capture provincial office until 1944 when it became the first "socialist" government in Canada? Answers to these questions clearly reveal that even though various social movements can be studied using similar concepts, the historical context in which they arise cannot be ignored without seriously affecting our understanding of these movements.

In answering question a) a number of factors must be considered. To begin with, in Alberta, William Aberhart, as a result of his fundamentalist broadcasts, had a personal following. For a number of individuals, the acceptance of social credit doctrine followed naturally from their attachment to Aberhart as a religious leader. Second, despite the depression, "socialism" was a dirty word in Alberta. It was associated with the UFA, one of the founding groups of the CCF. Thus, given the inability of the UFA to come to terms with the depression, and the scandal that surrounded the UFA in its last years, it is understandable that few Albertans would be attracted to the CCF. At the same time, the weakness of the Alberta Conservatives and Liberals ruled them out as viable electoral alternatives.

While the Social Credit was the obvious choice for great numbers of residents of Alberta, the same was not true in Saskatchewan. The CCF ideology, the farmers' dislike of socialism notwithstanding, had been accepted by the members of a great number of farmers' associations since the formation of the party in 1932. Moreover, CCF ideology in Saskatchewan was not associated with a moribund party, like the political arm of the UFA. Finally, by the time of the first Saskatchewan provincial election in which the Social Credit could participate, 1938, another event had clearly worked to increase the long-term advantage of the CCF over the Social Credit.

It was obvious by 1938, that a number of reforms advocated by the Alberta Social Credit violated the British North America Act, and therefore could not be implemented. The granting of a $25-a-month dividend, one of the most fundamental Social Credit planks and the one that had received widespread support from a great number of Saskatchewan CCF supporters, was declared *ultra vires* by the courts.

All of these factors contribute to an account of why the Social Credit gained office in Alberta but had less of an impact in Saskatchewan. Question b), however, is more difficult to answer. One of the factors accounting for CCF wartime success in Saskatchewan, S.M. Lipset argues, was a sense of security that resulted from increased prosperity. "The end of the depression," he writes, "gave many workers and farmers the economic and psychological security to begin to think in long terms rather than immediate personal ones, and therefore the CCF program of postwar reforms to prevent a new depression could receive support."[16] An explanation similar to this is implicit in G. Caplan's observation of the Ontario CCF. "There is a widely held assumption," he argues, "that radicalism flourishes in times of economic hardship and withers in a thriving economy. The validity of this assumption must be questioned. For it was during a period of war and unprecedented prosperity that Canadian socialism achieved its greatest popularity while in the preceding decade of depression it had become a major force in only two of the nine provinces."[17]

While it can be argued that the success of the CCF may have been contingent upon increased psychological security, it cannot be argued that this is a *necessary* condition for the success of social movements in general. The successes of the Alberta Social Credit party and Quebec Union Nationale during the depression are evidence of this. Explanations for the wartime success of the CCF in Saskatchewan, moreover, which postdated by nearly a decade the success of the Social Credit in Alberta, are more easily found in the historically-specific political conditions of Alberta and Saskatchewan than in the psychology of the voter.

As mentioned before, in the 1935 elections in Alberta, there really were no viable alternatives to the Social Credit. In Saskatchewan, by way of contrast, there were. The provincial Liberals, throughout the twenties, had incorporated farmers' demands into their electoral policy. Hence, it was not necessary for farmers to enter politics as they had in the form of the UFA in Alberta.[18] In the Saskatchewan provincial election of 1934, the CCF, which ran candidates under the Farmer-Labour banner, was also a viable electoral alternative. By the time of the federal election of the following year, the voters of Saskatchewan were presented with yet a third contender — the Social Credit Party. Clearly, there was more choice in Saskatchewan than in the sister province of Alberta — a choice that was once more available in the provincial election of 1938. By the time of the provincial election of 1944, however, the alternatives open to the Saskatchewan elector were reduced.[19] By now events had made the Social Credit hardly credible in the province of Saskatchewan. The contest, therefore, was between the Liberals and the CCF. This time the latter emerged victorious.

In the year before the CCF electoral success in Saskatchewan, the Ontario CCF was a mere four seats short of forming a government. The concern of voters in Ontario, as in Saskatchewan, was by this time with potential postwar developments. In an analysis of the 1943 Ontario election Caplan writes that "The results . . . revealed the strong desire for a reformed postwar society which would ensure increased personal economic security. . . . A great many of those who yearned for a more secure postwar world believed that only the CCF could fulfill their hopes and dreams."[20]

The possibility of the CCF forming a government in the postwar elections was too much for the propertied interests of Ontario. As a consequence, a massive counter-movement was launched against the CCF — one of the most obvious attempts to discredit a movement in Canadian history. In their attack on the CCF, this group spared no expense. Pamphlets, broadcasts, and full-page advertisements in newspapers were all used to combat the CCF. The ideology utilized by the counter-movement was simple: the CCF represented a fundamental assault on the "democratic" way of life. The organizational base of the counter-movement was more complex: it was comprised, primarily, of large sectors of the business "community" in league with the old-line parties. The success of the counter-movement was complete: in the election of 1945, despite a considerably large popular vote, the CCF won only eight seats. The CCF in Ontario was never again to attain the success of 1943.[21]

It is doubtful that the counter-movement launched against the CCF in Ontario would have been successful had the latter's organizational base been comparable to that in Saskatchewan. Despite some support from trade unions, the CCF in Ontario did not enjoy the "grass roots" participation evident in rural Saskatchewan. From the analysis of other social movements in Canadian society, it is clear that a sound organizational base is essential to a successful movement.[22]

Corresponding to its varying fortunes at the polls was a gradual routinization of the CCF. In the postwar years it was becoming evident to CCF leaders that electoral success required a change in emphasis in party ideology and a broadening of CCF appeal. At the same time, it was thought that the party organization needed to be consolidated.[23] The culmination of this process was the formation, in 1961, of the New Democratic Party, which represented, after a long engagement, the final wedding of the CCF and organized labour. The success of this new party is difficult to assess. On the one hand, it has never been able to win a significant number of seats at the federal level, although it has been able to influence several minority governments. On the other hand, the New Democratic Party has formed governments in three western provinces — Saskatchewan, Manitoba, and British Columbia.

An assessment of the extent to which the overall CCF movement achieved its goals is even more difficult than for its successor, the NDP. For one thing, goals changed over the career of the movement. It never achieved its initial goal of transforming the basic institutional structure of Canadian society. At the same time, the influence of the CCF, and later the NDP, is quite apparent in a great deal of social welfare legislation that has been enacted over the past forty years.

The articles presented in the remainder of this chapter focus on the development of the movement in Saskatchewan, its brief success in Ontario, and its gradual routinization up until 1958. The reader should keep in mind that the final article on routinization was written in 1958 and that the author could not foresee future developments between organized labour and the CCF, and the eventual formation of the NDP. As the concern of this volume is with social movements, no articles have been included on the New Democratic Party. Routinization of the CCF occurred long before the formal link with organized labour was finally cemented.

Notes

1. *The Globe*, September 2, 1929, p. 9.
2. *The Globe*, October 25, 1929, p. 1.
3. A.E. Safarian, *The Canadian Economy in the Great Depression*, Toronto: University of Toronto Press, 1959, p. 45.
4. L.M. Grayson and J.M. Bliss (eds.), *The Wretched of Canada*, Toronto: University of Toronto Press, 1971, p. viii.
5. S.M. Lipset, *Agrarian Socialism*, Berkeley: University of California Press, 1959, p. 54.
6. Grayson and Bliss, *The Wretched of Canada*, p. 106.
7. James Gray, *The Winter Years*, Toronto: Macmillan, 1966, p. 8.
8. A.M. Gianelli, "The Social World," *Saturday Night*, November 21, 1931, p. 19.
9. P. Newman, *Flame of Power*, Toronto: Longmans, 1959, p. 43.
10. Editorial, "The Prince of Wales and the Depression," *Canadian Comment*, 1-2, December, 1932, p. 6.
11. Editorial, "No Depression at Royal Fair," *Saturday Night*, December 5, 1931, p. 1.
12. W.D. Young, *The Anatomy of a Party*, Toronto: University of Toronto Press, 1969, p. 13.
13. British Columbia CCF, *Understanding the CCF: The Regina Manifesto*, Vancouver: 1953, p. 3.
14. M.J. Coldwell, *Left Turn Canada*, London: Gollancz, 1945, p. 165.
15. For an analysis of early Social Credit and CCF ideology see C.B. Macpherson, *Democracy in Alberta*, Toronto: University of Toronto Press, 1953/1970. Peter Sinclair, "The Saskatchewan CCF: Ascent to Power and the Decline of Socialism," below.
16. Lipset, *Agrarian Socialism*, p. 119.
17. G.L. Caplan, "The Failure of Canadian Socialism — The Ontario Experience," below.
18. For a comparison of the Social Credit and CCF in the West see D.E. Smith, "A Comparison of Prairie Political Developments in Saskatchewan and Alberta," *Journal of Canadian Studies*, iv, no. 1, (February, 1969).
19. An overview of provincial politics is offered by M. Robin (ed.), *Canadian Provincial Politics*, Scarborough: Prentice-Hall, 1972.
20. Caplan, "The Failure of Canadian Socialism — The Ontario Experience," below.
21. A complete analysis of the Ontario CCF in the war years is offered by G. Caplan in *The Dilemma of Canadian Socialism*, Toronto: McClelland and Stewart, 1973.
22. For an analysis of changes in the Ontario CCF see L. Zakuta, *A Protest Movement Becalmed*, Toronto: University of Toronto Press, 1964.
23. For an overview of the institutionalization of the CCF see Young, *The Anatomy of a Party*.

The Saskatchewan
CCF: Ascent to Power
and the Decline
of Socialism

Peter R. Sinclair

In 1944 the Cooperative Commonwealth Federation [CCF] won a sweeping victory in the Saskatchewan provincial election, a victory which has often been hailed as the rise to power of North America's first socialist government.[1] This paper will review the development of the party up to 1944, paying particular attention to its relationship with other political organizations and to the transformation of its early socialist policy on land ownership.

The history of the CCF before 1944 is best understood by emphasizing that it was more a political party than a social movement. This stress on the CCF as a party diverges from the positions of both Leo Zakuta, who interpreted the Ontario section as a movement from 1932 to 1941, and Walter Young, for whom the national CCF was a hybrid party-movement during all twenty-eight years of its existence.[2] This analysis of the Saskatchewan CCF is not evidence for the rejection of theories about the development of the CCF in Ontario or the country as a whole, but it should be stated that great care must be taken before accepting the CCF members' own definition of their organization as a movement rather than a party. Professor Young's position also leads to conceptual problems in that he would have to deny the existence of a revolutionary party, because, for him, it is social movements which seek basic social change. This is why Young begins his book with the extreme statement that 'Socialists belong to movements, capitalists support parties.'[3] Furthermore, according to Young, a social movement is successful when its goals are achieved, a party when it wins power. Therefore, because the CCF did not win a national election, it is described as a failure as a party, yet successful as a movement on the grounds that some of its policies were enacted by other governing parties. However, Young himself records that it was Mackenzie King's perception of the CCF as a national threat which persuaded him to enact several laws favoured by the CCF.[4] In doing this he was responding to the CCF as a party competing for political power. Such

Reprinted from the *Canadian Historical Review*, Vol. 54, No. 4, December 1973, pp. 419-433, by permission of the author and the University of Toronto Press.

events should make us very wary of stressing the social movement quality of the CCF.

The concept of social movement implies a diffuse, relatively unorganized support for fundamental social change. A political party is a formal organization committed to winning power, usually within the framework of existing electoral and governing institutions. Such a party may be the organized expression of a social movement, but it is the party character of the CCF which must be emphasized if we are to make sense of its development in Saskatchewan. Commitment to winning power by popular election led to a conservative compromise in its policy and pragmatic attempts to form coalitions with Social Credit.[5]

Elaboration of the above theme should begin with an account of the radical origin of the Saskatchewan CCF, which emerged early in the depression as a coalition of farmer and labour groups. Much earlier (1921) those farmers who were most interested in reform had established an independent Farmers' Union. A major concern of this group was political education, a task which they continued when the Farmers' Union merged with the Saskatchewan Grain Growers' Association to form the United Farmers of Canada [UFC]. By 1928 the left had two important successes. At the 1928 convention of the UFC a resolution was passed which favoured the compulsory marketing of wheat through the pool co-operative on condition that 75 per cent of farmers sign contracts with the existing voluntary organization. The few socialists in the organization had long been campaigning for a compulsory pool because they saw it as the only way to have some control over selling prices. In addition, George Williams, the leader of this group, was elected vice-president of the UFC.[6] This achievement was consolidated in 1929 when Williams became president and an unqualified resolution for compulsory co-operative marketing was passed.[7] The radical trend is evident in the speech of the retiring president, J.A. Stoneman, who commented, 'We should stress more and more that we do support public ownership and control of not only railways but natural resources as well.'[8] This was a very important statement because in asking for the public ownership of natural resources he could be interpreted to mean that farmers should give up *personal* ownership of land.

One result of the depression was increased pressure for direct political action. Addressing the 1930 UFC convention, E.A. Partridge demanded a form of Christian socialism to replace capitalist exploitation: 'We must organize along class lines, we must realize that it is the same class, who exploits labour, who exploits the farmer, only in a different way, and that the propertyless farmer must join hands against the common enemy. . . . True co-operation has its final goal in socialism, which is the continual observance of the Golden Rule, the gospel the man Jesus Christ preached and practised, two thousand years ago.'[9] Following this speech a motion to allow the UFC to undertake direct political action was narrowly defeated.[10] However, it was agreed that farmers should set up another organization 'for the purpose of more directly selecting and electing representatives to the legislature and the House of Commons, pledged to support the demands of organized agriculture.'[11] As 1930 drew to a close, there was no sign of an end to the depression and the farmers were growing more bitter because many were facing foreclosure after years of working to build up their farms. They were in the best possible mood to agree with Partridge at the 1931 convention when he demanded a transition 'from a system of production for profit to a system of production for use.'[12] Now George Williams was able to persuade the convention to support direct political action by the UFC.

This decision was taken in order to implement the UFC economic policy which had been established at the same convention. The policy appears confusing in that it combined requests for agricultural *reform* with a long-range objective of social ownership which was based on a critique of the total capitalist system.[13] Part of the economic policy demanded that ' "Use-Leases" be implemented, and that all land and resources now privately owned be nationalized, as rapidly as opportunity will permit.'[14] This resolution passed despite opposition from those who wanted to retain title to their land. It marked the biggest policy victory for the left. However, it should not be thought that all the farmers in Saskatchewan were committed socialists, owners of well-thumbed copies of *Capital*. The policy was passed after heated debate in an organization which represented a minority of Saskatchewan farmers and was instrumental in the rejection of the CCF during the thirties. All other parts of the UFC platform were directed to patching up the existing system.[15]

By this time the socialist-inclined farmers had been co-operating with Saskatchewan's tiny Independent Labour Party (ILP) for some two years. In 1931 the UFC and ILP presented joint proposals for reform to the Conservative-led coalition government and, after all their demands had been rejected, a conference was held at which the two groups agreed to work together to build a co-operative commonwealth. Formal recognition was brought to the agrarian-urban coalition in 1932 by the founding of the Saskatchewan Farmer-Labour Group with M.J. Coldwell from the ILP as its leader. This year also saw the establishment of the national CCF to which the Farmer-Labour Group affiliated. Although it did not change its name until 1934, the Farmer-Labour Group was, de facto, the Saskatchewan CCF. By virtue of its affiliation, the Saskatchewan organization was required to accept the national CCF policy, but the manifesto statement was sufficiently ambiguous to enable anyone to see what he wished in the document. The provincial sections had only to subscribe to the vague general principles of the manifesto and could construct their own specific policies in the provincial sphere. Therefore, one is justified, overall, in treating the Saskatchewan section as the unit of analysis in this paper.

The provincial election of 1934 was the first opportunity for the CCF to test its strength, which did not appear great. At the 1933 convention the secretary reported that little work could be done because there was no money available and voluntary workers were constantly out of pocket. Office staff rarely received full pay and several times the central office was on the brink of closing.[16]

The CCF fought from a socialist platform which included 'the social owner-ship of *all* resources and the machinery of wealth production.'[17] Such proposals agitated the established parties. Apart from the general assault on socialism as a threat to individual freedom, the most frequently criticized policy was the aim to socialize land. The opposition raised the spectre of Saskatchewan farmers being forced into state collectives, complained that under the proposed system the farmers would lose control of their land, that they would have no choice but to surrender their title, and that they would lose the value of improvements which they had made to their holdings.[18] There were also more general charges that the CCF was communist and supported violent revolution.[19]

Religion became a major issue in the campaign. M.J. Coldwell accused the Liberal party of spreading fear among the Roman Catholic population that the CCF would prevent them from practising their religion. The church itself de-nounced socialism and two students from Notre Dame College in Wilcox were forced to resign from the CCF. Later a letter from the archbishop of Regina to Coldwell, assuring him of the political neutrality of the church, was published in the *Leader-Post*, but the damage to the left had already been done.[20] Even the United Church, strongly anti-capitalist in 1931, rejected socialization at a con-ference held just before the election.[21]

In these circumstances the CCF won 25 per cent of the popular vote and 5 seats, the Liberals taking all the rest (but with a minority of the popular vote). CCF leaders were distressed at the result, for some had expected to sweep the province, as the United Farmers of Alberta had done across the western border in 1921. Responding to the defeat, M.J. Coldwell described himself as 'bitterly disappointed' and feeling 'both tired and sick.'[22] The resounding defeat in 1934 marked the end of the socialist phase for the CCF in Saskatchewan.

Why did a socialist appeal fail in Saskatchewan? Unfortunately, we have no record of how the public perceived the various parties. The ecological analysis of voting statistics does not in itself permit us to infer the motivation for political support, but Lipset's evidence that the CCF vote was lowest among poor farmers (those in areas of low tax assessment and high rates of tenancy) is supported by the observations of several CCF candidates.[23] Helmer Benson remembered that most of the down-and-out people voted Liberal: 'It was like their religion.'[24] George Hindley, who ran in Wilkie, said, 'When you get people down so far they stop thinking. They lose their initiative, they lose their capacity to fight and they begin to accept things.'[25] At this time people in the poorest areas did not support the CCF, perhaps because they saw their situation as hopeless.

Certainly socialism was the big issue of the election. A review of speeches at conventions, public statements, and letters in the farming journals suggests that those who supported the CCF saw socialism as Christian co-operation which would protect their way of life, while those in opposition tended to define socialism in terms of Soviet totalitarian rule, collective farms, and anti-religious attitudes, that is, as a threat to the small capitalist producer and the family farm. No party perceived in such a way could hope to win an election in a society whose people were committed to personal ownership of land. The history of co-operative action does not provide grounds for changing this assessment because producers' co-operatives are defence mechanisms best described as 'the joint entrepreneurship of individuals.'[26]

At this point it is best to review the changes in CCF ideology which had taken place by 1934. It has been suggested that the CCF had only a brief courtship with socialist ideology and that this period ended with the electoral defeat of 1934. If the Saskatchewan CCF has been a pragmatic agrarian-dominated party, committed to electoral institutions, we would expect to see land policy moving towards consistency with local cultural attitudes.[27] In this crucial area conservative modifications were being made even before the 1934 election.

The initial socialist land policy called for farming to be carried on under a 'Use-Lease,' which would allow the individual farmer to carry on as before, except that he would lease the land from the state. The plan was devised to ensure security of tenure by stopping evictions caused by defaulting on mortgage payments. Opponents were assured that there was no intention of introducing collective farms as in the Soviet Union. Both Liberals and Progressives rejected state ownership because they wanted to hold personal title to the land. For example, S.N. Horner, who had been elected to the legislature in 1929 as a Progressive, states that he did not go directly to the Farmer-Labour Group because 'each should own his own home and the farmer's home is on his land. Therefore, if this land is leased, his home is leased.'[28]

As early as 1932 opposition to land nationalization produced a change of wording. The policy became known as 'Use-Hold' to emphasize the security-of-tenure aspect rather than state ownership. In July 1933 a motion was tabled by the political directive board that the land policy should be amended 'so that occupants be granted the privilege of exchanging their "Use-Lease" for clear title any time after their indebtedness had been paid in full.'[29] A pamphlet from this period stated that the policy aims were to preserve freedom, individual rights, and dignity of race. The policy was described in detail. All lands being opened for settlement would be held by the state and 'Use-Hold' titles would be issued. Lands which had reverted to the municipalities because of tax arrears would be returned to the original occupant under a 'Use-Hold' title after the government had settled with the municipality. Lands on which the occupant could not meet his debts would be made secure for the farmer on voluntary application for 'Use-Hold' title. This would occur after debt adjustment and revaluation of the land by an arbitration board. Bonds would be issued on the equities agreed. Those who held a clear Torrens title (a deed of ownership) and were not embarrassed by creditors could carry on as before or apply for 'Use-Hold' title.[30] A 1933 pamphlet stated that 'despite criticism from the old parties it is not a system of government farming or collectivization . . . use hold title gives every power of the Torrens except that of mortgage.'[31] It could be willed and participation was voluntary. The alternative was perceived to be corporation farming by the finance companies. Thus, the earlier programme to nationalize *all* natural resources had been modified. By 1934 the official manifesto was advocating security of tenure but gave no details of the land policy. It concentrated instead on issues such as the CCF's support for religious freedom.[32]

Since it was committed to winning power through the electoral machinery, defeat in the 1934 election accelerated the process of compromise in policy and also encouraged a co-operative attitude towards other reform-oriented parties, especially after the CCF had its first encounter with Social Credit in the 1935 federal election. Fresh from its triumph in Alberta, the Social Credit League began forming constituency associations throughout Saskatchewan with the aim of winning federal representation. Social Credit's monetary-reform policy had appeal for those who wanted reform but were frightened by visions of totalitarian socialism under the CCF.

The CCF was campaigning on its immediate reform programme which was perceptively described by the editor of the *Melville Canadian*: 'The CCF program of action calls for nothing else but repairs to capitalism. . . . It is pointless to answer that there is a difference between the CCF's immediate action and the ultimate goal. Its proposed repairs to capitalism are not steps to socialism if that's what it wants. They are steps in the opposite direction, steps towards making capitalism more efficient and more satisfactory to the public.'[33] Those leaders in Saskatchewan who still believed in socialism feared the compromise and ambiguity of this position. In January, George Williams told Coldwell that there was no place for the CCF as a reformist organization, since there were already two of these. Instead, he claimed:

> . . . I do sincerely believe that by being outright Socialists, we will qualify ourselves for power when the Fascist experiment has run its course. It may be a long and weary road. My personal opinion is — the sooner we reconcile ourselves to out and out socialism and all the abuse that term means, the sooner we will be worthy of the crown of success. In this regard it might be wise to err on the side of being rather abrupt rather than err on the side of being too suave, and I feel that our immediate program adopted at our last Convention erred on the side of being too suave. However, that is past, and all we can do about it now is to go ahead and battle as out and outers, and in my humble opinion, this course will prove in the end to be far the wisest course.[34]

Others in the party (notably Coldwell, Hugh McLean, Clarence Fines, and Tommy Douglas) were more prepared to compromise and co-operate with Social Credit in order to prevent duplication of effort by the opposition parties. On the party executive Williams still had sufficient support to maintain a firm stand against co-operating in any way with Social Credit, but he was unable to prevent several constituency associations from doing just that.[35] This pressure for co-operation at the local level indicates that many people were prepared to co-operate with Social Credit because they wanted immediate action and tangible results. They saw little reason for conflict among organizations with reform goals. Hence, the pressure for a reform party to pursue pragmatic policies insofar as it needs the support of the people.

The trend to pragmatic party politics was stimulated further by the failure of the CCF in the election. In Saskatchewan, the Liberals took 16 of 21 seats, while Social Credit and the CCF both won 2, the Conservatives taking the final constituency. For the CCF leaders this was the second severe defeat in little more than a year. It was followed by a further decline in the socialist part of the party programme.

At the provincial convention in 1936 a reform platform was adopted which made no reference to socialism and the policy of land nationalization was officially dropped.[36] In the budget debate of 1937 Williams did not mention 'Use-Hold' but advocated protection of the Torrens title by limiting the power of the mortgage companies. For example, he suggested that no payments should be made in poor crop years and that the government should proclaim a moratorium on debt when necessary.[37] Thus, the CCF position in Saskatchewan had become similar to what the Social Credit government was actually doing in Alberta.

In 1936 the CCF constitution was also amended to allow for co-operation with any organization for the purpose of bettering the immediate interests of the common people.[38] Having removed the socialism there could be little objection on ideological grounds to co-operating with Social Credit, a course which George Williams and his supporters now advocated, in order to prevent all the reform parties running their own candidates in every constituency. It was felt that such a policy would stop the Liberals winning constituencies on a minority of the popular vote. Nothing more than temporary coalitions was intended by the party leaders, as Williams made clear later in the year: 'When the CCF convention voted for cooperation, they just as emphatically turned down affiliation and made it quite clear that the CCF did not intend to sink their identity in a compromise party. They did not intend to give up any of their principles or platform nor do they suggest that other groups should do so.'[39] Williams went on to reject Social Credit theory, but added that Social Creditors should not be obstructed too much in their attempt to get a new deal. In this presentation Williams was trying to strike a balance between retaining an image of the individual identity of the CCF and preparing the way for a united front of reform parties. The ambiguity of

Williams' attitude to Social Credit also suggests that he was ill at ease with his new role as co-operator. Indeed, in private he still expressed a desire for socialism, only tempered by practical considerations. His reply to a farmer from Carrot River, who rejected the reformist tendencies of the party, is instructive: '. . . there comes a time . . . when we acquire a certain amount of worldly wisdom and a time when we find if we want to get a certain place and are continually shot down in frontal attack, you are wise to attack on the flank. . . . You fill your place by keeping socialism ever before the eyes of the people while some of the rest of us fill our places by getting the power to bring about Socialism.'[40]

In accordance with the 1936 resolution on co-operation, Williams and A.J. Macauley had visited William Aberhart, but no agreement was reached at that time. Williams had tried to prepare the ground by encouraging the leader of the CCF in Alberta to stop attacking Social Credit. It was clear to Williams that continued clashes in Alberta would make co-operation in Saskatchewan all the more difficult. However, William Irvine, leader of the Alberta CCF, was not prepared to compromise because he predicted an early end to the Social Credit experiment and did not want the CCF to be associated with such a failure.[41]

In September 1937 the Saskatchewan CCF executive decided to approach the Social Credit League at its autumn convention in Saskatoon with a request to discuss co-operation in the next election.[42] At that convention a motion to receive the CCF message was passed, but then Ernest Manning, visiting from Alberta, produced what seems to have been an instant rule that such a motion had to be unanimous. This determined opposition by Manning may be explained partly by his anger at the persistent attacks of CCF supporters in Alberta,[43] but it is also reasonable to suppose that the Social Creditors retained hopes of a sweeping victory in Saskatchewan after their relative success in 1935 when there was little time to organize. Therefore, the Alberta leaders may have felt that they had little to gain from an alliance with the CCF.

Following its rejection of CCF overtures in the fall of 1937, the Social Credit League announced that its aim was to have a candidate in every constituency for the election expected in 1938.[44] Despite this announcement many in the CCF continued to work for a coalition. Responding to pressure in the constituencies for joint candidates, the CCF issued a press statement in which it was recognized that there was a popular demand for co-operation and that the CCF, as the best-organized group, was the logical centre for this. Where the CCF was strongest it should not be opposed by others, but where it had little hope of winning it was only reasonable for CCF supporters to find a candidate from another progressive group whom they could back without compromising their principles. The decision whether to nominate or not was to be made in a properly called CCF convention. There was to be no compromise, no fusion party, and no fusion candidates. In addition, the aim of the CCF was still to elect enough candidates to form a straight CCF government.[45] This proposal for limited 'saw-off' arrangements could hardly satisfy Social Creditors, ambitious as they were for victory. William Aberhart again rebuffed the CCF's approach for united action.[46]

Shortly after his meeting with Macauley, Aberhart announced that he was only waiting for an invitation before sending his forces into Saskatchewan. A prelude to intervention by the Alberta government was the formation of a national Social Credit organization, intended as a means for Aberhart to control the Saskatchewan members and to protect against charges of interference in the affairs of another province. To this end a conference of western Social Credit leaders was called. A few days later it was announced in Regina that the Western Social Credit Association would control election activities in all western provinces and that Ernest Manning would organize in Saskatchewan. The association would approve all nominations in Saskatchewan before they were made official.[47]

Social Credit forces had been divided in Saskatchewan since the CCF had been rejected and Manning was unsuccessful in uniting the organization. It was reported that 'From 32 constituencies has come strong disapproval of Mr. Manning's methods of organizing constituencies and nominating candidates. In every case complaints state that the local Social Credit organization in Saskatchewan is being strangled and that an unscrupulous dictatorship has been set up.'[48] Nevertheless, candidates were selected in forty-one constituencies. Now Aberhart, Manning, and several other cabinet ministers toured Saskatchewan propounding the familiar Social Credit doctrine. A federal government controlled by financial interests was blamed for the failure to introduce Social Credit in Alberta. Social Credit would fight on and purchasing power would be restored to the people, who could safely leave all details to experts. Social Credit was attractively defined as 'the ability to buy goods and services without paying for them at the time,'[49] and Manning promised that 'when we get control of the money we will pay out dividends so fast it will make your head swim.'[50]

Following the worst crop-failure year in the history of the province each party was claiming to be in the one which could handle the effects of the disaster. The CCF abandoned any reference to socialism and concentrated on social planning and the protection of the family farm by better debt adjustment legislation, crop insurance, and the like. But when the votes had been counted the Liberal party was once again in control. The CCF leaders were moderately satisfied with their performance. Compared with 1934, their share of the vote fell, a result of placing fewer candidates in the field and the intervention of Social Credit. CCF representation in the legislature was increased to ten,[51] most of which came from east-central Saskatchewan where recent crops had been better than in other regions. For Social Credit the election was a disaster, only two of its forty-one candidates being successful. There was encouragement only in the constituencies close to Alberta, especially Cutknife which was won from the sitting CCF member. The poor general showing of the Social Credit candidates must have been a severe blow to William Aberhart, because it suggested that national power, which was necessary to introduce Social Credit, was unattainable.

Why did Social Credit fail in conditions so similar to Alberta of 1935? Lacking data on voters' perceptions of Social Credit, any answer must be speculative. Several factors seem worthy of consideration. The Social Credit League was an imported organization which had to build up from scratch in areas where the CCF had been organizing for years. Also, the authoritarian method of having candidates selected by an outsider was distasteful to the people of Saskatchewan who had not experienced the failure of the United Farmers of Alberta in their attempt at constituency autonomy. Only those who lived close to the border with Alberta had been exposed over a long period to Aberhart's religious broadcasts and to the evangelists who poured over the countryside from his Bible Institute in Calgary. Perhaps most important of all, there was no evidence after three years in power that Aberhart was bringing the promised utopia to Alberta. Why should people then believe that he would succeed in Saskatchewan? It is also true that Social Credit received a very bad press and was the primary target of Liberal propaganda, but this had not prevented it winning in Alberta and was probably a minor factor.

While Social Credit received a mauling, the CCF emerged from the electoral conflict of 1938 as the undisputed challenger to Liberalism in Saskatchewan. The earlier rejection by Social Credit of CCF approaches and the party's increased strength relative to Social Credit encouraged a new anti-coalition attitude on the part of the pragmatic CCF leaders. It was now recognized that there was no need to combine with Social Credit in order to win, and so the CCF took a hard line towards further unity proposals, rejecting strong demands in several constituencies to sanction a united front under such labels as United Reform, United Progressive, and New Democracy.

It is important to recognize that this rejection of co-operation with other reform groups did not mean the adoption of a more socialist position by the CCF. The party continued to emphasize social planning and social security; social ownership was to be restricted to financial institutions, some natural resources, and public utilities (all of which was consistent with the agrarian populist tradition of North America). The few leaders who were still prepared to discuss socialism were careful to define it pragmatically — for example, George Williams wrote a pamphlet in 1939 which begins: 'This is not a treatise in Socialism according to Marx, Lenin, Stalin, Henderson, Bellamy or Engels. The writer does not pretend to be outlining a theoretical socialism. . . . The people of Canada are not interested in ascertaining whether a proposed economic system agrees with Marxism, or any other 'ism'; they want to be reasonably sure it will work.'[52] In its next test of popular support, the federal election of 1940, the CCF exhibited its growing popularity by winning five of the twenty-one seats with an especially strong performance in the predominantly rural constituencies. Such support was heartening for the CCF members because the party organization had been weakened by the conflicting attitudes of neutralists and interventionists regarding Canadian participation in the war.

For the farmers war had brought only a small increase in the price of wheat, although their income increased since the crops were bigger. In 1941 the CCF supported the farmers in their demands for higher wheat prices. That year the Liberal federal government would only guarantee a price of 70 cents per bushel, while the farmers were demanding $1.00, which they backed up with a petition of 185,000 signatures. This pressure was enough to force the government guarantee up to 90 cents (still well below pre-depression prices).[53] As the only party to give complete support to the farmers in their struggle, the CCF benefitted by having its membership more than double during 1941-2.

The other major event of 1941 was the election of Tommy Douglas as president of the Saskatchewan CCF in preference to a candidate supported by George Williams (who had joined the army and was overseas). Apparently some party members felt that Williams had too much personal influence in the CCF, but the real significance of this event was that it consolidated the reformist pragmatic direction of the party and showed the influence of the urban middle class in the farmers' organization. (Douglas was a Baptist minister and early member of the ILP.)

In 1942 a record crop permitted supporters to contribute more to the party treasury, which allowed more intensive organizational publicity. The CCF would probably have won any election called at this time, but had to wait until June 1944 because the Liberal government passed a special bill extending the life of the legislature. This probably added to the liabilities of a Liberal party already hurt by its identification with big business and the depression.[54]

In the critical area of land policy the CCF had changed little since the middle thirties. In 1944 the CCF promised to:

1. Protect the farmer from unjust foreclosure and eviction.
2. Protect from seizure that part of a farmer's crop that is needed to provide for his family.
3. Use, if necessary, the power of moratorium to compel reduction of debts to a figure at which they can reasonably be paid with prevailing prices of farm products.
4. Prevent the growth of debt by placing a crop failure clause in all mortgages and agreements of sale.[55]

Another pamphlet stated that 'the CCF believes in the family farm as the basis of rural life' and that it would protect the family farm by increasing farm income through guaranteed minimum prices, encouraging the development of co-operatives, crop insurance, and pressing for the abolition of the Winnipeg Grain Exchange.[56] This was a 'conventional' populist programme. Emphasizing this agricultural policy and social welfare measures, in 1944 the CCF took 53 per cent of the vote and all but five seats in the legislature.

Evidence has been presented above that the Saskatchewan CCF responded to electoral results by pragmatically adjusting its policy and attitudes on co-operation with other reform groups, especially Social Credit. In this the CCF clearly demonstrated that its performance was that of a political party, despite frequent claims by CCF members that it was a movement rather than a party.

The radical eclipse of the socialist land policy provides a good example of a familiar dilemma for parties which propose social change but are also committed to gaining power by popular election: should ideology be compromised for immediate reformist gains or should the original goal be explicitly retained and energy diverted into educating the electorate?[57] If such a party fails to provide what the people will accept, it must become reconciled either to taking power by force or remaining a powerless educational organization; to win power quickly by election it must compromise and adopt a reformist rather than a revolutionary programme. This pressure toward revisionism seems to be especially great in rural dominated areas, such as Saskatchewan, where people tend to be strongly committed to existing property institutions.[58] Changes in the CCF's land policy were possible in Saskatchewan because almost nobody in the party adopted a doctrinaire position which would have involved abandoning the ideal of the family farm as the basis of rural life. Therefore, the adjustment of the party to a pragmatic reformist position was relatively painless. Basically, CCF members accepted small-scale capitalist production and only flirted briefly with a socialist solution to the agrarian crisis of the thirties.

Notes

1. For example, S.M. Lipset, *Agrarian Socialism* (New York 1968); Dean E. McHenry, *The Third Force in Canada* (Berkeley and Los Angeles 1950), p. v; Gad Horowitz, *Canadian Labour in Politics* (Toronto 1968), p. 9; David E. Smith, 'A Comparison of Prairie Political Developments in Saskatchewan and Alberta,' *Journal of Canadian Studies*, 4, 1969, p. 17; Walter D. Young, *Democracy and Discontent* (Toronto 1969), p. 71.

2. Leo Zakuta, *A Protest Movement Becalmed* (Toronto 1964); Walter D. Young, *The Anatomy of a Party: the National CCF* (Toronto 1969).

3. Young, *The Anatomy of a Party*, p. 3.

4. *Ibid.*, p. 8.

5. Its relationship with the Communist party also demonstrates the party nature of the CCF. See Peter R. Sinclair, 'The Saskatchewan CCF and the Communist Party in the 1930's,' *Saskatchewan History*, XXVI, 1973, 1-10.

6. UFC (SS) Minutes, 1928, Archives of Saskatchewan [AS].

7. *Ibid.*, 1929. Supporters saw it as 100 per cent control, opponents as 100 per cent compulsion.

8. *Ibid.*.

9. UFC (SS) Minutes, 1930, Address of the honorary president.

10. The minutes show that few of the speakers were against direct political action because they had faith in existing remedies or parties. Indeed, some opposed the motion because they wanted an *independent* political party which could unite farmers and workers.

11. UFC (SS) Minutes, 1930.

12. *Ibid.*, 1931.

13. *Organized Farmer and Labour Programme (Sask.)*, 1931. Farmer-Labour Group pamphlet, AS.

14. UFC (SS) Minutes, 1931.

15. In addition to the 'Use-Lease' policy the provincial government was asked to prevent any more foreclosures, evictions, and seizures; to give the farmer absolute safety on his homestead quarter; to improve debt adjustment legislation; to undertake a plebiscite on the compulsory pool; and to see that no more new farms were set up in the province. It probably reflects the division in the UFC that much of this policy becomes redundant in view of the plan to nationalize land.

16. Farmer-Labour Group Minutes, 1933, secretary's report, AS. See also secretary Eliason's personal hardship and commitment to the party in a letter to Coldwell, 2 June 1933, CCF Papers, file no. 32, pp. 3223-5, AS.

17. *Handbook for Speakers*, 1933. CCF pamphlets, AS.

18. *Regina Star*, 8 July 1933; and Lipset, *Agrarian Socialism*, p. 136.

19. *Regina Star*, 6 July 1933; *Regina Leader-Post*, 3 Jan. 1934. George Williams was particularly subject to attack because he had visited the Soviet Union.

20. *Regina Leader-Post*, 26 May 1934.

21. *Ibid.*, 5 June 1934.

22. Coldwell to Eliason, 20 June 1934, CCF Papers, file no. 20/3; Lipset, *Agrarian Socialism*, p. 138, states, 'To the CCF leaders . . . the election was a great defeat. They had been sure that they would win. . . .'

23. Lipset, *Agrarian Socialism*, p. 202.

24. H.J. Benson, interview, 14 Sept. 1970, in AS, file no. X15/45.

25. G. Hindley, interview, 21 Jan. 1971, in AS, file No. X15/60.

26. J.W. Bennett and C. Krueger, 'Agrarian Pragmatism and Radical Politics,' in Lipset, *Agrarian Socialism*, p. 351.

27. For an excellent review of how other aspects of CCF policy changed see Lipset, *Agrarian Socialism*, pp. 160-96.

28. S.N. Horner, interview, 2 Jan. 1971, in AS, file no. X15/55.

29. CCF Papers, Minutes, political directive board, 8 July 1933.

30. *Agricultural Land Policy*, Saskatchewan Farmer-Labour Group (approx. 1932), CCF pamphlets.

31. *Is Your Home Safe?* CCF pamphlets.

32. *Official Manifesto of the Saskatchewan Farmer-Labour Group*, 1934, CCF pamphlets.

33. *Melville Canadian*, 8 Aug. 1934.

34. Williams to Coldwell, 30 Jan. 1935, CCF papers, file no. 32, p. 3252.

35. In Yorkton Jacob Benson became a joint candidate of the CCF and Social Credit, which led to his rejection by the CCF executive. Tommy Douglas was endorsed by Social Credit in Weyburn and subsequently censured. Less publicized difficulties occurred in Saskatoon and Last Mountain constituencies.

36. CCF Minutes, first annual convention, 1936.

37. George Williams, *Budget Debate*, 1937, CCF pamphlets.

38. CCF Minutes, first annual convention, 1936.

39. George Williams, *Cooperation*, radio address, 9 Dec. 1936, CCF pamphlets.

40. Williams to Vineyard, 5 April 1937, CCF Papers, file no. 287, p. 30738.

41. Williams to Irvine, 15 Dec. 1936 and 23 Dec. 1936; Irvine to Williams, 19 Dec. 1936, CCF Papers, file no. 287, pp. 29924-8.

42. CCF Papers, Minutes, Executive meeting, 11/12 Sept. 1937.

43. Lipset, *Agrarian Socialism*, p. 144 gives this interpretation, but fails to point out that a majority of Saskatchewan delegates wanted to hear the offer.

44. *Moose Jaw Times-Herald*, 6 Jan. 1938.

45. CCF Papers, Minutes, Executive meeting, 19/20 March 1938.

46. CCF Papers, Minutes, Provincial Council, 16/17 April 1938.
47. *Moose Jaw Times-Herald*, 3 May 1938; *Regina Star*, 3 May 1938.
48. Statement by Saskatchewan members of Western Canada Social Credit Board, *Regina Star*, 20 May 1938.
49. Aberhart, quoted in *Moose Jaw Times-Herald*, 25 May 1938.
50. *Regina Leader-Post*, 28 May 1938.
51. This was quickly increased to 11 when Joe Burton won the Humboldt by-election, an important victory for the CCF in that it showed that the CCF could win in German Catholic areas.
52. George Williams, *Social Democracy in Canada*, 1939, p. 4, CCF pamphlets.
53. Lipset, *Agrarian Socialism*, p. 149.
54. Sanford Silverstein, 'The Rise, Ascendency and Decline of the Cooperative Commonwealth Federation Party of Saskatchewan, Canada' (PhD thesis, Washington University, 1968), pp. 77-8.
55. CCF *Land Policy*, 1944, CCF pamphlets.
56. *The Farmer and the CCF*, 1944, CCF pamphlets.
57. See especially the great debate between revolutionary socialists and supporters of Bernstein's revisionism in the SPD. E.g., Peter Gay, *The Dilemma of Democratic Socialism* (New York 1952).
58. The SPD provides a similar case where southern Germany became a centre of revisionism as the party tried to appeal to a petit bourgeois population of peasants and artisans. See Carl E. Schorske, *German Social Democracy* (Cambridge, Mass. 1955), pp. 8-9.

The Failure of Canadian Socialism: The Ontario Experience, 1932-1945

Gerald L. Caplan

There is a widely held assumption that radicalism flourishes in times of economic hardship and withers in a thriving economy. The validity of this assumption must be questioned. For it was during a period of war and unprecedented prosperity that Canadian socialism achieved its greatest popularity, while in the preceding decade of depression it had become a major force in only two of the nine provinces. In neither Quebec nor Ontario, the electorally indispensable provinces, did the Canadian socialist party, the Co-operative Commonwealth Federation (CCF), present a serious challenge in the nineteen-thirties. Yet during the second world war, it was Ontario, dynamic and wealthy, which appeared to be in the vanguard of the nation-wide movement to place a CCF government in Ottawa. Why did Canadian radicalism fail to achieve an important impact in Ontario during the depression? Why did it suddenly receive widespread support in the early 1940's and why did it fail ultimately to capture the power which so many observers believed in its grasp?

When the CCF was founded in August, 1932, the depression in Canada was at its most severe. Disillusionment with Prime Minister R.B. Bennett, whom some had seen as the superman who would conquer the depression, was increasing.[1] Mackenzie King provided an opposition characterized by timidity and lack of imagination. Moreover, the depression destroyed a number of the traditional beliefs so complacently held by many North Americans. The article of faith that industry and thrift brought their due material reward was suddenly and rudely shaken. The implicit conviction that the existing socio-economic system had produced the best of all possible worlds was painfully shattered. Many North Americans, perhaps for the first time, began to examine first principles, trying to determine the root of their tragedy. In Canada, many who asked such penetrating questions turned in their despair to the philosophy of democratic socialism.

When Agnes Macphail and William Irvine imported the CCF into Ontario

Reprinted from the *Canadian Historical Review*, Vol. 44, No. 2, June 1963, pp. 93-121 (abridged), by permission of the author and the University of Toronto Press.

from its western birth-place in the autumn of 1932, the new, avowedly socialist movement received an unexpectedly enthusiastic reception. Within four months, *Saturday Night* was able to note that "no political organization ever had so much free advertising. People are discussing it everywhere, regarding it with growing respect."[2] The "new social order" being demanded by the party's spokesmen was evidently attracting people growing impotent and frustrated in the face of the depression. It appeared that the CCF was building a broadly based, firmly rooted political party. The United Farmers of Ontario (UFO), alienated by Prime Minister Bennett and prodded by Agnes Macphail and Graham Spry, editor of the influential *Farmer's Sun*, decided to affiliate with the new party.[3] Several labour groups in Toronto, Hamilton, Windsor, and Kitchener soon joined. A third section was formed at the end of 1932 as a vehicle for all CCF sympathizers not associated with an organized farm or labour group.[4] Six months later, this new Club Section, as it was called, had a membership of six thousand middle-class supporters.[5] The UFO, a Labour Conference, and the Club Section: these were the three theoretically equal sections constituting the Ontario CCF, a movement, it seemed, grounded securely on support from all major elements in the community. It was an encouraging beginning.

Yet under the surface severe flaws could be detected. The UFO was no longer the powerful spokesman of rural Ontario; from sixty thousand members in the early twenties it was reduced to barely five thousand in 1935.[6] Similarly, the labour groups which affiliated with the CCF were all small and uninfluential. The Ontario Labour party, the Independent Labour party, and the Socialist Party of Canada each represented a doctrinaire sect of politically-minded trade union radicals. The larger and electorally significant labour bodies, the Trades and Labour Congress and the All-Canadian Congress of Labour, refused to endorse the CCF.

Equally significant, the three sections of the Ontario party, from the first, regarded one another with distrust and suspicion. The Labour members regarded the Club members as insincere opportunists whose conversion to socialism was prompted by the enthusiastic reception which the CCF received. They resented as well the attempts of the Club leaders, particularly of Elmore Philpott, a former Liberal, to dominate all aspects of party activities.[7] On the other hand the Club members considered themselves the *élite* of the movement, believing that their education and middle-class respectability designated them for positions of leadership. They thought theirs the only section of substance in the "Triple Alliance," without which the CCF was but an empty form.[8]

As for the UFO, it never belonged in a socialist movement at all; its alliance with the CCF was essentially incongruous. It was not merely their horror when Labour members called them "comrade," nor that those same members refused to regard either Sabbath meetings or the Communist party as ungodly.[9] Above all, it was the latent rural fear of the collectivization of the land which prevented a real identification with the aims of the CCF. Moreover, given the UFO's prime loyalty to agriculture and the indifference of most Ontario socialists to rural problems, there was little to hold the farmers in the party.[10] The Ontario CCF was patently an urban-oriented party; its socialist philosophy was essentially alien to the rural experience and temper.[11] Indeed, the abortive alliance was more of a tribute to Agnes Macphail and a reflection of the severity of the depression than an indication of the acceptance by the UFO of CCF doctrines.

The internecine battle reached its culmination early in 1934. . . . On March 11, its [UFO] representatives issued a statement announcing the secession of the UFO from the CCF, on the grounds that "a certain element in the Ontario council [of the CCF] . . . is too close to the Communists . . . for us to find a workable basis of co-operation with [it]. . . ."[13] With the UFO delegates absent, the subsequent Provincial Council Meeting, on which each section had equal representation, resulted in an absolute deadlock between the Club and Labour delegates. Clearly no accord was possible. J.S. Woodsworth, national leader of the CCF, invited to this crucial meeting by the Council, thereupon produced a detailed statement which announced that the National Executive had decided to take the most drastic step possible: the immediate suspension of the Ontario Provincial Council, the provincial section's governing body. To his stunned audience, Woodsworth explained that the National Council would reorganize the provincial party by replacing the loose federation of three autonomous groups with a new, simplified provincial structure, based on a single cohesive unit, with actual control in a central council.[14]

That was all. In ten short minutes, the constructive work of eighteen months had been obliterated. The party's leadership had been decimated. Agnes Macphail was automatically eliminated when the UFO withdrew its affiliation. Two days after the Council meeting, Elmore Philpott announced his resignation. . . .

Internal disintegration of the CCF had closely followed the effective campaigns against it by the major parties. Indeed, the ferocity of the attack upon the CCF during most of 1933 in parliament, on the hustings and in the press, was an accurate reflection of its considerable popularity before intra-party battles weakened it so decisively. The Conservatives and federal Liberals simply denounced the CCF, time and time again, as a "Communist" organization dedicated to "the suppression of human liberties through a dictatorship by the state."[18]

The Liberal party in Ontario, however, adopted a different tactic, both shrewd and successful. Under its dynamic new leader, Mitchell Hepburn, it began to marshall the forces of agrarian and urban unrest behind a vaguely leftist banner. To rural Ontario, Hepburn represented "a dramatic revival of the traditional agrarian insistence upon simplicity, economy and honesty in government. . . . Farmers who had misgivings about the sweeping economic policies of the CCF could agree upon the reforms urged by the Liberals."[19] In the industrial areas of the province, Hepburn exploited the popularity of such leading Liberal spokes-men of the ethnic and lower class communities as Arthur Roebuck, David Croll, and Sam Factor, promised a labour code to humanize industry, and supported several unpopular strikes.

As events were to prove, Hepburn's radicalism was largely confined to his rhetoric. In the Ontario climate of 1934, however, his appeal was all but irresis-tible. On the one hand, he provided a real alternative to the listless Conservative administration of Premier Henry, an alternative which seemed progressive with-out being socialist. At the same time, his brilliant demagoguery seemed plausible and appealing to a people who longed for strong and energetic leadership in a time of crisis. In the provincial election of 1934, the Hepburn Liberals swept to power and the shattered CCF party was, predictably, crushed.[20] With but 7 per cent of the popular vote, the young socialist movement sent only one member to the Ontario legislature. Indeed, Sam Lawrence of Hamilton East was the only Ontario socialist to sit either in Queen's Park or in Ottawa during the first decade of the party's existence.[21]

These results virtually nullified the possibility of the CCF presenting a serious threat to the capitalist system in the nineteen-thirties. The party never recovered from the bitterness of the previous internal warfare or the disappointment of the Ontario election, and turned increasingly inward, soon losing its relevance to all but the faithful. In the 1935 federal election, the CCF was a minor challenger that neither R.B. Bennett nor Mackenzie King took seriously. Their complacency was justified. Nationally, just seven socialist candidates were successful; none was from Ontario, where the party received an unimpressive 8 per cent of the total vote.[22] Such was the outcome of the only general election during the CCF's entire existence which took place in the midst of a terrible depression.

. . . .

But the war . . . transformed the Canadian scene so drastically that the party was soon able to achieve the greatest public support in its history. There were several factors responsible for the new atmosphere. A widespread demand de-veloped for a better postwar world in which economic depressions and wars would be impossible. It was soon realized that the national planning demanded by the CCF throughout the 'thirties, and implemented at last to facilitate the national war effort, was practical and efficient. This realization received further impressive confirmation after June, 1941, when the Soviet Union began its heroic resistance to the advancing German army. A further minor consequence of Russia's forced entry into the war on the side of the allies was to nullify the effectiveness of stigmatizing the CCF as a "communistic" organization. In another area, the prosperity and full employment created by the war effort led to an unprecedented growth in both the power and the ambition of the Canadian trade union movements. In general, the war was clearly jolting existing routines and habits of mind from their traditional grooves. Questions of a fundamental nature were once more raised. The nation was being asked to sacrifice for the war effort in the name of the democratic capitalist system. But why, asked one journalist, should Canadians "be expected to want to save Democracy if that means preserving the kind of society which existed before the war?"[26]

The federal by-election early in 1942 in York South, on the outskirts of Toronto, marked the first important manifestation of the changing climate of opinion. It seemed, before the event, an unexceptional election. As late as January, 1942, one month before voting day, the CCF registered only 10 per cent on the Gallup Poll. It was, moreover, a traditionally Conservative constituency, and no Liberal was nominated to oppose Arthur Meighen, whose victory virtually everyone conceded.[27] The York South Liberal Association publicly endorsed Meighen,[28] and King, though still fearing and loathing his old opponent, refused to intervene against him.[29] When the CCF nominated Joseph Noseworthy, a local high school teacher, it was not because its leaders had assessed with any insight the new mood of the nation; the by-election simply provided another opportunity to inform the public of its policies. Yet the party discovered, to its delight, that its proposals and slogans were received with a spontaneous enthusiasm on the part of a large section of the electorate. *Saturday Night* observed that the CCF's major campaign cry, "Conscript wealth as well as men," was "one heard everywhere today . . . a statement which obviously implies that wealth is not conscripted now."[30] Meighen seemed unable to identify himself with the aspirations of the masses, and his contention that the state was already extracting most from those with the most proved convincing only to a very distinct minority.[31]

There were also other factors in the CCF's favour. Not only was Noseworthy an unusually popular candidate, but the party was also able to mobilize for his campaign the most effective organization in its history.[32] Nor was the Liberal party unanimous in its support of Meighen. He was denounced by Arthur Roebuck and Harry Nixon, both prominent Ontario Liberals,[33] and the results indicate that a large number of Liberals in the riding voted CCF only to defeat the Conservative leader. Noseworthy's victory was as decisive as it was unexpected: 16,408 votes to his opponent's 11,950. Many observers, of course, saw in the results a verdict against Meighen rather than an indication of actual socialist strength.[34] Nevertheless CCF'ers were jubilant and optimistic. They felt at once that their entire future had been altered. Perhaps for the first and last time they agreed with Arthur Meighen. "I think," he remarked, "the CCF are starting to make inroads in the working vote of both parties."[35]

Noseworthy's spectacular victory made the CCF very much alive to its new opportunities and traditional handicaps. In Ontario, the party's two major internal weaknesses demanding immediate remedy were a lack of efficient organization and of adequate leadership. These were soon remedied. At the provincial convention in April, 1942, delegates elected by party members throughout Ontario selected as provincial leader, Edward B. Jolliffe, a brilliant young Toronto lawyer. Then, with an evangelistic fervour that had been absent for nearly a decade, the convention launched an intensive organization drive throughout Ontario. The new generation of leaders — Jolliffe, Noseworthy, Andrew Brewin, George Grube, Bert Leavens, and, once again, Agnes Macphail — toured the province, orating, converting, organizing. By the end of 1942, party membership in Ontario had quadrupled to eight thousand, and each month's revenue exceeded the revenue of any single year between 1936 and 1941.[36] The greatest source of new members and revenue was, significantly, Ontario's mushrooming trade union movement. Organized labour deeply resented the inadequate recognition of its new status by the King government.[37] In Ontario, it could not forget that both Premier Hepburn and George Drew, the new provincial Conservative leader, had supported General Motors against the autoworkers during the notorious Oshawa strike of 1937. Furthermore a powerful new trade union congress, the Canadian Congress of Labour (CCL), had been created in 1940, led by aggressive and dedicated democratic socialists. In the prevailing atmosphere, the rank and file of CCL affiliates were prepared, for the first time, to accept the conviction of their leadership that political action was crucial to the success of the labour movement. Led by Charles Millard, Fred Dowling, Murray Cotterell, and Eamon Park, the CCL convention in September, 1942, passed overwhelmingly a resolution recognizing the CCF as labour's champion in parliament and recommending that its affiliated unions "study the programme of the CCF."[38] By the middle of 1943, forty union locals had affiliated to the party, whose 15,000 members each contributed two cents per month to CCF coffers.[39]

. . . .

The summer of that year provided the party's first test case. After six years, the province was finally to have a general election. All three major parties waged the campaign under new and untested leaders. George Drew, the Conservative leader, on the one hand defended the virtues of free enterprise and promised, on the other, considerable social welfare legislation. On several occasions he attacked the CCF for wanting to impose a dictatorship upon the province: the very word "Nazi," he recalled, was an abbreviation of "National Socialism."[43] But Drew, perhaps confident of victory, failed to exploit this theme to the fullest. The Liberals based much of their campaign upon the presentation of their likable but uninspiring new leader, Harry Nixon, as Ontario's only hope of salvation from the menace of the "fanatical" socialists.[44] The older parties received some considerable non-party assistance in their campaign against the left. Two self-styled "labour" organizations sponsored several violently anti-socialist advertisements.[45] The daily press in Ontario, with the exception of the Toronto *Star*, was unanimous in its unrestrained denunciation of the CCF. Lastly, Mr.

Montague A. Sanderson, a fervent anti-socialist propagandist, sponsored a series of dramatic and compelling advertisements in the press, all carrying their creator's favourite theme: the plot of the "Communist-CIO-CCF dictatorship" to "exterminate democratic government by violence."[46]

The rejuvenated socialist movement was comparatively well-equipped to counter such tactics. Its members were aroused; it had accumulated an unprecedented campaign fund of $20,000; and it found candidates in eighty-six ridings. For the first time, aid was received in the large urban centres from organized labour, and the party's major figures from across the Dominion were made available for speaking duty in Ontario.[47] The main line of attack shrewdly used by all party orators, as well as in newspaper advertisements, radio broadcasts, and literature, was negative. It concentrated upon the fears and anxieties that had developed as a result of the years of depression — a depression which, it was constantly re-affirmed was inevitable under a capitalist system.[48] Many citizens agreed. On election day, too late to affect the results, a Gallup Poll showed the Ontario CCF with 36 per cent, the Conservatives with 33, the Liberals, 31.[49]

Although the actual results were just sufficiently different to elect a minority Conservative administration, they represented nevertheless, as the *New Commonwealth* jubilantly claimed, a "Smashing CCF Victory."[50] While the Conservatives doubled their representation to 38 members, and the Liberals declined from 59 to 15, the CCF soared from no seats in Queen's Park to the status of official opposition with 34 members. The Conservatives received 469,672 votes, for 36.7 per cent of the total; the CCF, 418,520 (32.7 per cent); the Liberals, 409,307 (30.9 per cent). The CCF increased its 1937 vote by about 350,000 while the Liberals and Conservatives respectively lost 300,000 and 150,000 votes. The party polled only 17 per cent of the vote in Ontario's forty rural ridings, and elected no rural representatives. Still, even this total was a vast improvement over CCF results in the past, particularly given its feeble organization in the rural areas. In Ontario's fifty non-agricultural constituencies, it was very nearly a CCF sweep. The party won 34 of those seats, including a majority in Toronto, with an impressive 40 per cent of all votes cast.[51]

The CCF's phenomenal success can be attributed to several factors. No one could pretend that the electorate had voted on the basis of party ideology. The results rather revealed the strong desire for a reformed postwar society which would ensure increased personal economic security. Some, no doubt, believed Drew could satisfy these vague, inarticulate yearnings. *Maclean's* suggested that his victory indicated that "many electors were impressed by his efforts to make the Conservative party truly progressive,"[52] and *Saturday Night* believed that had the federal Conservatives not adopted a progressive platform and elected a progressive leader in 1942, "there would have been no Conservative government at Queen's Park. There might have been a socialist one."[53] But a great many of those who yearned for a more secure postwar world believed that only the CCF could fulfil their hopes and dreams. As the Toronto *Star* noted, "Whatever else the electors may have known or felt about CCF policies, many did feel that this party was facing forward and going somewhere, and that its older rivals, though moving somewhat, were still looking back wistfully over their shoulders to a social order which is no longer acceptable."[54] The CCF was certainly "going somewhere." The apparently irresistible socialist advance continued. In the two weeks after the Ontario election, the party easily won three by-elections in Manitoba and Saskatchewan. The September, 1943, Gallup Poll then electrified the nation with the revelation that, if a federal election were held at that moment, 29 per cent of those polled would vote CCF, 28 per cent Liberal, 28 per cent Conservative.[55]

The party was on the crest of the wave, and seemed destined to ride to victory. Among both supporters and outside observers, winning national power was considered the CCF's inevitable next step.[56] Confidently, the socialists prepared for power. Yet the apparent gains served primarily to foster within the party a delusive sense of complacency. For in reality its successes were impressive only relative to its former position of insignificance. In terms of presenting a real challenge to the two traditional parties, these gains proved quite inadequate. Party membership, for example, doubled in 1943 to almost 16,000, a comparatively substantial achievement, but in fact a much smaller increase than party leaders had expected.[57] To counter the formidable anti-CCF propaganda campaign which had begun immediately after the Ontario election, the party instituted a "Victory Fund Drive" early in 1944 to provide the resources to enable the CCF to "strike back" at its opponents. The Ontario CCF's objective was $300,000; it collected one-sixth of that amount.[58] Nevertheless, what appeared significant at the time was that party membership and finances were at an all-time high.

Most important, CCF strength within the trade union movement was increasing, and that movement had so expanded that it had 200,000 members in Ontario, one-third of them in Toronto. After the Ontario election, there began a "terrific amount of manoeuvring [by all parties] for the control of the political influence of organized labour."[59] But the major congresses remained wary of the two older parties, and the CCF was rewarded accordingly. By the middle of 1944, 40,000 unionists were affiliated with or had endorsed the Ontario CCF.[60] In part at least, this support was a response to the decision of the Canadian Congress of Labour in September, 1943, officially to endorse the CCF as "the political arm of labour in Canada," and its recommendation "to all affiliated and chartered unions that they affiliate with the CCF."[61] This was a promising step for the CCF. Yet in point of fact, the contribution of the Political Action Committee (created by the CCL) between 1943 and 1945 was meagre and ineffectual. To be sure, under Charles Millard, some educational work was done; several leaflets advocating support of the CCF were distributed, and a few local labour councils were persuaded to establish political action groups. But all this was, at best, a grave disappointment to CCF leaders who expected a huge contribution of both money and organizers.[62] The mass union support for the party expected after the CCL's decision simply never materialized. The resolution proved too radical a departure from traditional notions of political action. Gomperites, Communists, Liberals, and Conservatives in the union locals acted together successfully to undermine the Congress decision. The rank and file even of affiliated locals, though they might vote CCF on election day, were on the whole too affluent and too apathetic to provide active physical support, while the majority of CCL unions refused either moral or financial assistance to the party.[63] The Trades and Labour Congress (TLC) refused even to endorse the party. It insisted on remaining non-partisan and free to oppose any "reactionary" government. This decision was in part a reaction against the CCL's action; in part it reflected the craft-union, Gomperite basis of the Congress's affiliates; and it indicated as well the influence of the Liberals and Communists who outnumbered CCF'ers in the TLC. Still, largely because the CCF was the sole party to record its support of the Congress's political programme, a large number of TLC locals did in fact affiliate with the party. Nevertheless, there is little doubt that the affiliated CCL locals provided much the larger share of the little active support which the trade union movement offered to the CCF.[64]

Labour's ambiguous attitude was symptomatic of the CCF's generally tenuous hold on the province. The uncertainty of its support received its first significant confirmation in a remarkable civic election in Toronto on January 1, 1944. A determined campaign against the CCF was waged by the city's two Conservative newspapers (the Toronto *Telegram* and the *Globe and Mail*), by the Toronto Board of Trade, and by M.A. Sanderson. Assisted by a restricted franchise in municipal elections, the anti-socialists performed admirably. Toronto's property-holders flocked to the polls, no doubt heeding well-advertised warnings of "dictatorship" and "the end to freedom of opinion and voting" under a CCF administration. The entire CCF slate, 23 persons, was rejected.[65]

This contest was the party's first substantial defeat after the Ontario election, and offered encouragement to those who believed and hoped that the 1943 success had been largely fortuitous. *Saturday Night*, for example, believed that the Toronto results vindicated its theory that earlier CCF gains had been due not to any popular desire for a socialist government, but rather for an effective opposition

> to provide a more efficient check upon the more predatory elements in our economic life than either of the old parties. The function they [the socialists] were designed to perform was purely negative. When . . . they made themselves the second largest party in the Ontario legislature and began to look like a possible government, the reaction

of the electors was exactly what one would expect. . . . The situation is simple. The CCF desires to ditch the system of private enterprise. The electors do not want this system ditched. They will not vote to put the CCF in a position to ditch it.[66]

It was an incisive analysis. The September, 1943, Gallup Poll which revealed the CCF to be the most popular party in the nation, stands unique in the party's history. Early in 1944, a new poll revealed that the CCF had slipped down to 24 percentage points, and this decline continued slowly but surely until June, 1945.

The reasons for the decline may be clearly traced. Probably the most important was the impressive anti-socialist campaign being waged across Canada. Financed by Canadian business, it was directed primarily by William Ewart Gladstone Murray and his organization, Responsible Enterprise, and Burdrick A. Trestrail of the Society For Individual Freedom (Against State Socialism). Simultaneously, the national press began to turn out a daily flow of anti-socialist editorials. Radio broadcasts were produced and leaflets distributed "explaining" the CCF to their audience. Countless newspaper advertisements were sponsored by the chartered banks, insurance companies, and industrial concerns warning against the socialist menace and extolling the virtues of private enterprise.[67] Speakers denounced the CCF before service clubs, church groups, and similar organizations.[68] A great barrage of propaganda was sent through the mails,[69] and it was claimed that in many urban areas, door-to-door canvassers were employed, ostensibly taking opinion polls, asking residents their opinion of "state socialism." On at least one occasion, a canvasser defined this term as "the sort of system they have in Germany and Russia where the government takes everything away from you and tells everybody what to do."[70] Such were some of the formidable weapons with which the anti-socialists waged their devastating battle.

Murray believed he required $100,000 a year for this campaign,[71] and Trestrail wanted $168,000 annually for the Toronto area alone.[72] It is not possible to determine with accuracy the total sum received or expended by either man in his activities. But given the scope of the campaign they conducted, as well as the list of corporations and individuals sponsoring them, it may be concluded that their revenues were at least sufficient to allow them to organize a remarkably intensive and effective propaganda drive. Their sponsors, they revealed privately but proudly, included almost all of Canada's private banks, insurance and trust companies, investment concerns, oil, steel, and mining corporations, plus dozens of other miscellaneous firms, large and small.[73] Their collective purpose, wrote the CCF weekly, was to persuade Canadians to hold such opinions of socialism that "people will not support the CCF in its attacks on their privileges."[74] Murray and Trestrail represented only the most important of the private anti-socialist organizations operating across the Dominion. According to *Maclean's* Ottawa correspondent, there were, in April, 1944, no less than ten others in the Dominion: one in British Columbia, one or more in Ottawa, three in Montreal, and one in Toronto in addition to the two major ones; the others he did not specify. He claimed that with the exception of Murray's and Trestrail's concerns, these organizations were small and had only modest funds "put up by little groups of corporations or individuals."[75]

There were other manifestations of the organized business campaign against the CCF. *Maclean's* reversed its traditionally non-partisan political policy in order to aid in the war against socialism.[76] Several businessmen wrote easily digested books, which sold for twenty-five cents in cigar stores, instructing the uninitiated in the disastrous implications of "socialism."[77] Radio station CFRB in Toronto refused to sell the CCF time to answer charges made by Trestrail's Society For Individual Freedom over that station; its official policy, it declared, was to carry no political broadcasts between elections and "we do not consider the Society's broadcasts political. They are not for or against any particular party."[78] The press repeatedly distorted remarks made by CCF leaders, particularly one by Harold Winch, making him appear to state that the CCF would eliminate all its opponents if elected.[79] The Conservative party adopted the practice of identifying the CCF on every possible occasion with both the German Nazis and the Communists in Russia.[80]

Could the spokesmen for Canadian capitalism convince the nation that it was defending the freedom of all and not, as the CCF thought, the selfish interests of a tiny privileged minority? Despite the growing intensity of the campaign, it appeared for a moment that it could not. In June, 1944, the province of Saskatchewan became what its new premier called "A beachhead of socialism on a continent of capitalism."[81] Jubilant, few CCF'ers in Ontario saw the real lesson of the victory. The Saskatchewan CCF had an almost flawless grass-roots organization. Virtually every polling subdivision in the province could, if necessary, have run an independent and isolated campaign; no Ontario constituency could claim as much. Further, between June, 1943, and June, 1944, Saskatchewan CCF membership had tripled to thirty thousand, or a party member for every twelve voters in the province. Ontario, by the latter date, had only half Saskatchewan's membership, or a member for every sixty voters. By Saskatchewan's standard, the Ontario CCF should have had 150,000 members.[82] Still, there seemed to Ontario socialists too many reasons for joy to ponder such unpalatable facts. *Saturday Night* pointed out that the Saskatchewan results undermined the strategy of those who hoped that the farmers would "save" the nation in a general election as they had "saved" Ontario in 1943.[83] Moreover, the psychological effects of the prairie triumph were bound to be considerable, both in galvanizing CCF supporters into action and in increasing the desire to get on the bandwagon.

There were other significant portents. Gallup Poll findings revealed that a majority of Canadians favoured a reformed postwar world, trade union rather than business control of the government (if there were only these two alternatives), and non-profit government ownership and distribution of "all industries that handle . . . certain necessities of life like milk, meat, bread and fuel."[84] A business reporter wrote that "most of the public appears to be convinced that . . . we're bound to have another tremendous depression sooner or later, and that . . . private enterprise can't meet the requirements [for preventing it]. . . ."[85] Such sentiments should have augured well for the CCF, and many observers believed they did. *Time's* Ottawa correspondent predicted a CCF minority government in Ottawa after the next election.[86] A writer in the *Financial Post* foresaw 100 to 110 seats for the CCF, 80 to 90 for the Liberals, the remainder to "others," while *Maclean's* believed that only by uniting could supporters of free enterprise prevent a CCF victory.[87] Election results after the celebrated Noseworthy victory of 1942 appeared to confirm such conclusions. Since that time, there had been 26 federal and provincial by-elections; the CCF and Liberals had each won nine of them. Of twelve by-elections west of Ontario, the CCF had won eight, the older parties none. Further, in the six provincial elections during 1943 and 1944, the CCF alone gained ground in every case. Thus there were numerous indications of an all but irresistible socialist victory.

Yet such was not to be the case. In September, 1944, the Gallup Poll revealed that while the CCF maintained its popular support with 24 per cent and the Conservatives had declined two points since January to 27, the Liberals had climbed impressivley from 30 to 36 per cent. Yet it was the CCF party which stood for change and reform, for government ownership, and for economic planning. According to the Gallup Poll, these were precisely the policies desired by a majority of the electorate. Why then was the CCF unable substantially to broaden the base of its support in such an apparently favourable climate of opinion?

There were several major reasons. The powerful anti-socialist campaign had successfully increased the ranks of the CCF's opponents and had deflected the demand for radical reconstruction; moderate reform through social welfare legislation now became the goal. The CCF was unable to convince a majority of the electorate that the attractive reforms it offered sufficed to offset the possible evils (such as confiscation and dictatorship) that voters were assured would accompany a socialist victory. Finally, it was increasingly believed that the desire for reform could be realized by supporting the older parties, which now offered, presumably in contrast to the CCF, social reform plus individual liberty. By 1944, a vote for either old party was no longer equivalent to an endorsement of the *status quo ante bellum*. As one anti-socialist wrote, "were Liberal and Tory plans for the postwar the same as their pre-war ideas, popular acceptance of the CCF would be very much greater than it is."[88]

. . . .

The sudden reforming zeal of the older parties ended the desertion from their ranks of their more progressive followers. Significantly, the year 1944 ended as it had begun. In municipal elections throughout Ontario, again in part the result of the masterful efforts of B.A. Trestrail and his local Board of Trade sponsors,[92] the vast majority of CCF candidates were defeated. The general electon of 1945, many hoped, and many others feared, would usher in the first stages of the co-operative commonwealth. But the year began inauspiciously for the socialists. The January Gallup Poll saw the CCF decline another two points to 22 per cent. That same month, two Ontario MLA's were expelled from the party for co-operating with the Labour Progressive (Communist) party in its new "unity" campaign against "reactionary Toryism."[93] In February, the CCF candidate came a poor third in a federal by-election in Grey North which party leaders genuinely believed he could win.[94] The socialist movement plainly was losing what one report aptly called its "magic touch."[95]

Still, many CCF'ers believed that victory remained a real, if less certain, hope. Jolliffe told the Ontario executive that "with an even share of the breaks, and with the will to win, we might come out with 55 seats."[96] More than this was required for victory, however. Because a socialist ideology has no deep roots in the Canadian tradition, a highly efficient organization was vital to the CCF. It dismally failed to meet this requirement. In few constituencies was its organization even equal to those of its rivals; it should have been superior. Its greatest and most damaging weakness was the failure of its MLA's to build effective constituency organizations. With few exceptions, they did not realize the importance of this function, partly because they were not sufficiently experienced to appreciate its significance, partly because almost all of them had been elected with a minimum of organization and naïvely believed they could repeat this feat. Nor were the party leaders — Jolliffe, Agnes Macphail, Charles Millard — sufficiently interested in the tedious routine of building a riding machine to prod their backbenchers into greater effort. As one party official has said, "If they were not great parliamentarians, the CCF MLA's were worse organizers."[97] Party finances in Ontario were as inadequate as party organization. In the Victory Fund Drive for the 1945 election, the provincial party trailed embarrassingly behind Saskatchewan and British Columbia in funds accumulated. Ontario's goal was set at $130,000; it managed to raise $37,000. Thus at the very core of its structure, the CCF party revealed fatal flaws. Yet rarely could such flaws be less afforded than at this moment, when events at Queen's Park, and then in Ottawa, were about to demand from all parties their greatest effort of the decade.

. . . .

The Ontario election was called for June 4 [1945], the federal one week later. In his campaign, John Bracken, national Conservative leader, denounced every

CCF proposal as a dire peril to democracy, while he stressed the progressive aspects of the Progressive Conservative programme, particularly in the field of labour relations.[105] For Premier Drew of Ontario, the lines in the contest were starkly drawn. "The decision," he maintained, "rests between freedom and fascism right here at home." Quoting from the *Communist Manifesto* to underline the parallel between Communism and socialism, he concluded that "It is time to stop talking about fascism having been destroyed. This [the CCF] is fascism."[106]

Mackenzie King, as usual, was more subtle. He knew full well that, the conscription issue aside, his problems had primarily been created by the CCF's appeal to liberal supporters of his party.[107] He therefore conducted his campaign "on the assumption that his real danger was from the left, not from the Conservatives."[108] King realized as well that the country's prosperity vitiated the demand for wholesale reconstruction but left intact the demand for postwar security against depression and unemployment. He attempted, consequently, to undermine the CCF by "swerving far enough left to expropriate anything of use in its doctrines. . . ."[109] As one observer explained, the CCF was out-manoeuvred by the Liberals who had "moved cautiously as new champions of state social welfare."[110] Not everyone wondered why none of King's appealing new proposals had not been implemented during the previous decade. The powerful Trades and Labour Congress was satisfied that it now had sufficient excuse for a rapprochement with the party it had temporarily deserted. To the overwhelming chagrin of CCF leaders, the Congress urged its 350,000 members to work for the re-election of a Liberal government, warning against "inexperienced" parties winning power "at this time."

Equally devastating to the socialist cause was the invaluable contribution to its opponents of B.A. Trestrail. One cannot ascertain precisely the extent of Trestrail's resources in the election; CCF estimates ranged from $700,000 to one million dollars, but these were based on conjecture. Trestrail conducted at least three fund-raising drives during 1944 and 1945. The exact total he collected is unknown, but it apparently sufficed to allow him to carry out what he called his "very comprehensive campaign." This, he wrote prospective supporters, included "(1) direct distribution of the tabloid, *Social Suicide*, to every postal address in Canada; (2) newspaper advertising and radio broadcasting, carrying to citizens the true significance of State Socialism; (3) supplying of material regarding State Socialism for speakers and candidates from coast to coast."[111] Trestrail fulfilled his promises. Eight huge, attractive advertisements, for example, with numbingly identical messages denouncing the CCF as a threat to "our democratic way of life," appeared in one Toronto daily alone in the final three weeks of the Ontario campaign.[112] The pamphlet, *Social Suicide*, written by Trestrail, was a propaganda masterpiece. Simple, lucid, and colourful, it invoked literally every anti-socialist argument and every tribute to private enterprise that had been employed during the previous two years. It also included a gratuitous (but likely effective) reference to the CCF National Secretary, David Lewis, as a "Jewish immigrant boy" and to Lewis's father as a "Russian Jew."[113]

With the financial assistance of certain individuals, this convincing work was mailed, as Trestrail boasted, to "every postal address in Canada"; Eugene Forsey estimated that three million copies were distributed during the campaign.[114] The identity of his supporters cannot be proved conclusively. It is not unreasonable, however, to assume that many of the men Trestrail named as contributors in 1944 continued to provide his revenues. The CCF believed that the Robert Simpson Company, a known supporter of the Society For Individual Freedom,[115] was Trestrail's prime benefactor in the *Social Suicide* venture, but was unable to offer documented evidence. It was a fact, however, that the pamphlet, in direct violation of the Defence of Canada Regulations and of the Dominion Elections Act, nowhere bore the name of its printer and publisher. "Why," asked the CCF, "was it allowed to enter the mails?" The fact of its illegality was drawn to the attention of the Department of Justice by letter on May 10, and to Postmaster-General W.P. Mulock by the Glace Bay *Gazette* on May 22, " in time to stop what was obviously going to be a breach of the law. . . . Why was no action taken by these Departments? Why have Trestrail and the printers not been prosecuted?"[116]

No answers were offered to these embarrassing questions. In any event, mere answers could not have nullified the effects of Trestrail's work. The CCF's only hope was to conduct a campaign sufficiently brilliant to overcome the impact the propagandists had made. This it did not do, although in many ways, it is true, the party was better prepared for this campaign than any in its history. Psychologically, it still possessed the confidence, even over-confidence, resulting from the easy successes of 1943 and 1944. Party membership and finances, though below expectation, far exceeded anything in the past; Ontario raised $46,000 for the federal and provincial campaigns. Welcome support was received from labour councils (all CCL affiliates) in Toronto, London, and Hamilton, which endorsed the CCF candidates in their respective communities.[117]

Party strategy in the beginning was to emphasize the injustices of the depression decade, an approach employed previously in the Saskatchewan and Ontario contests. This theme, however, was soon and wisely replaced by a more positive one, for it was apparent that whatever anxiety existed in the province was rooted more in the problems of the future than in the memories of the past. The CCF thereafter concentrated its propaganda primarily upon its easily understood "Five Star Program for Ontario," the five stars representing security on the job, for the farm, for the home, for health, and for the nation. The party made one grave error of judgment in its campaign. Not until the final week of the contest did the CCF's leaders acknowledge publicly the propaganda campaign being waged against the party. Even then only a few inadequate advertisements attempting to refute the accusations appeared in the press.[118]

Such was the basis of the election until the evening of May 24, 1945. On that night, in a spectacular radio address broadcast across Ontario, CCF leader E.B. Jolliffe melodramatically revealed to his audience "the most infamous story in the history of Ontario":

> It is my duty [he stated] to tell you that Colonel Drew is maintaining in Ontario, at this very minute, a secret political police, a paid government spy organization, a Gestapo to try and keep himself in power. . . . Taxpayers' money is being used . . . secretly . . . by the Drew government to utter libels against the opposition, libels designed to keep the government in power.

In the conduct of this nefarious business, Jolliffe implicated Drew himself, his Attorney-General, Leslie Blackwell, the Commissioner and Deputy Commissioner of the Ontario Provincial Police, Captain William J. Osborne-Dempster who had been placed in charge of the "political police office" which the Drew government had allegedly established after assuming office, and the anti-socialist propagandists, Gladstone Murray and M.A. Sanderson. According to Jolliffe, the government allowed Dempster to give or sell his misinformation about the Conservatives' political opponents to the two propagandists since his reports were so obviously unreliable the Conservatives refused to use them directly. Murray and Sanderson, the CCF leader claimed, "used the Drew Gestapo rumours to form the basis of advertising in the interests of Big Business against the CCF. . . . In short," he concluded, "we are seeing in Ontario the spectacle of Fascist police methods being worked out before our eyes. . . . all through this election campaign you've been hearing that the real issue is freedom versus dictatorship. . . . And I quite agree; there certainly is a very grave danger. . . . well, I'll let you decide for yourselves where the danger of dictatorship is coming from!"[119]

It was a sensational address, completely unforseen either by Jolliffe's opponents or by most of his colleagues. Drew denied categorically each and every detail in Jolliffe's charges; and he and the Ontario Conservative press damned the CCF with unrestrained vehemence. Jolliffe, Hepburn, and the Liberal newspapers were relentless in denouncing Drew and his "Gestapo." At last, so violent was the exchange, that Drew was forced to appoint a Royal Commission to investigate the accusations. The opposition parties demanded the postponement of the election until the Commission had concluded its task. This plea was ignored, of course, and when Justice LeBel handed down his report several months later, few individuals outside party ranks were still concerned with the notorious "Gestapo affair." The actual effect of this issue on the election results seems to have been negligible. A comparison of Gallup Poll figures before and after Jolliffe's speech suggests that the charge neither gained nor lost the CCF a significant number of votes. On the other hand, it is probable that the incident convinced some formerly indifferent non-socialists that they must turn out to vote against the dangerously irresponsible CCF leader.[120]

What is certain is that the elections of June 4 and June 11, 1945, brought to an abrupt close the CCF's short-lived golden age. In Ontario, the Conservatives were re-elected by a minority vote which gave them 66 seats with 774,982 votes, the Liberals eleven seats and 474,817 votes, the CCF a mere eight seats and 390,910 votes. Party supporters were shattered, although an analysis of the vote reveals that their reaction was not wholly warranted. In fact, given the campaign against it, the CCF did remarkably well, receiving 22 per cent of the provincial vote. Moreover, assuming LPP supporters would have voted CCF in the absence of a Communist candidate, in at least eight ridings such a candidate accounted for the election of an old party nominee. Although unity was their cry, the Communists demonstrated once again their fear and hatred of the socialist party. Had they not split the labour vote in those eight ridings, none of which they could have won, the CCF might again have formed the official opposition. The CCF's total vote had declined by only 27,000 since 1943. But the old parties' totals soared, and therein lay the difference. The Liberals increased their 1943 figure by 65,000, the Conservatives by a staggering 305,000 votes.[121] Naturally, few CCF supporters knew, and, if they knew, were little consoled, that their party's absolute voting strength had barely declined. They saw only that the Ontario CCF had lost twenty-four precious seats, a blow severe enough to return many of them to their traditional loyalties.

Mackenzie King's government won the federal election. True, both his vote and his majority had been slashed; but still, he alone had won. The Conservatives were greatly disappointed with their 67 members. And the CCF was shattered. It had, to be sure, known its strength was declining and could now pretend that "things could be worse." But how? The party that, in 1944, appeared destined to form the next government of Canada won, in 1945, 28 federal seats with 16 per cent of the popular vote. Of course, it had doubled its national vote to 800,000 in only five years; but it was going to *win*. Moreover, the CCF east of Manitoba seemed all but obliterated. Only three-eighths of its national vote and only one of its successful candidates came from that region. Noseworthy lost decisively in York South. Most striking of all were the Ontario results. There the Conservatives polled 750,000 votes, just fewer than in the provincial election; the Liberal total jumped dramatically from 475,000 to 745,000; and the CCF vote, in one short week, plunged from 390,000 to 260,000. Not a single CCF candidate was successful. Clearly a large number of CCF "bandwagon" supporters, discouraged by the losses in the provincial election, had deserted at the crucial moment. Further, as in the provincial campaign, the Communists probably helped to defeat the CCF in eight Ontario ridings. . . .[122]

. . . .

CCF'ers generally agreed upon the reasons for their disaster. They endorsed the theory that the old parties had "gulled" the electorate by their opportunistic promises to achieve all the attractive reforms proposed by the CCF with none of the drastic methods commonly attributed to a socialist administration.[127] They felt, too, that the Toronto *Star's* post-election editorial was accurate: "Fear of Socialism," it declared, "Strong in the Election."[128] This fear was in large part responsible for the massive Conservative vote in the Ontario election, as it was for the Liberals' huge total in the following week. In each case a large number of voters must have reasoned that the surest way to prevent a socialist triumph was to support the party conceded the best chance of defeating the CCF.

It was clear, moreover, that the deliberate attempt to foster a fear-psychosis in the electorate had proved highly effective. The anti-socialist propaganda campaign succeeded for several major reasons. It created an unfavourable image of the CCF in the public mind. Party leaders attempted to present themselves as reasonable, forward-looking Canadians; the propagandists were able to make them appear to be some kind of tyrannical revolutionaries or wild, heartless gangsters.[129] Furthermore, the propagandists understood far better than CCF'ers the aspirations of the Canadian people: their desire to belong to and to identify with the middle class. Socialism was seen by many, perhaps most, Canadians as an alien ideology running counter to the accepted (and acceptable) traditional direction of their society. Why support a party which attacks the "bosses" if one's prime ambition is to become a boss? ". . . The average North American," B.K. Sandwell once noted with brilliant insight, "is too good at thinking of himself as a boss to hate bosses as a class."[130] Thus when Trestrail quoted Lincoln's statement — "I don't believe in a law to prevent a man from getting rich"[131] — he hit upon a remark which would evoke an instinctively sympathetic response from most Canadians. The CCF naïvely believed the propagandists would fail because "the people" would not be deceived by what socialists considered blatant falsehoods and misrepresentations, hardly meriting a rebuttal. The readers of Trestrail and Murray, however, must have found points which required clarification by the CCF, but few answers were forthcoming. In fact, the Ontario CCF was quite unprepared organizationally to assume the task of counter-propaganda. There was a feeling "widespread throughout the province," a CCF employee admitted, that the party lacked the kind of powerful grass-roots machine necessary to combat Trestrail's attack.[132]

The truth was that the CCF in these years, leaders and rank and file alike, suffered from delusions of grandeur, from enervating over-confidence and optimism. This was largely owing to the implicit belief of nearly every socialist that "the good cause" would ultimately triumph. "The stars in their courses are fighting for the cause of socialism," announced the executive of the Ontario CCF in 1936, when the movement was virtually moribund.[133] The complacent illusions of the early 1940's were also attributable to the spectacular CCF successes in Ontario, Saskatchewan, and the various by-elections. Hence the party was marked by 1945 by "an almost complete lack of urgency, an unwillingness to take great pains or make great sacrifices."[134] This explains why the CCF could not convince itself to take seriously the propaganda campaign being directed against it every day of every week of every month for two entire years. Over-confident and self-righteous to the end, most party leaders agreed with Professor George Grube that the "attacks on the CCF were based on such utterly false and obviously untrue premises that I . . . did not take them seriously enough."[135] If the anti-socialist campaign helps account for the huge vote cast in the comforta-ble residential sections of city and town, CCF over-confidence in part explains the comparatively light vote in working-class areas.[136]

For this reason the party ignored Dr. Gallup's writing on the wall, and was confident that the public would repudiate the progressive image of the older parties as deceitful and hypocritical opportunism. The complacency of Ontario's leaders was inevitably communicated to the masses of party members. It ac-counts for that province's total of $46,000 raised for the two 1945 campaigns, while Saskatchewan accumulated $171,000. This helps explain why the Provin-cial Council was content to hire MLA's as part-time organizers, even though they frequently proved to be inexperienced and incompetent.[137] This was why most CCF'ers waited until *after* the elections of 1945 to begin complaining about inadequate effort in the fields of organization and education.[138]

Most important, perhaps, the belief in inevitable victory explains why CCF leaders, even the most intelligent and reasonable of them, lost almost completely their rational perspective of the existing political situation. They knew party organization was woefully inadequate. They might have sensed that many of the forces which had created a climate of opinion favourable to the CCF — gratitude to Russia, memories of the depression, desire for a better postwar world — had lost their impact. They realized that a great number of people had supported the CCF, not because of its socialist ideology but because they vaguely knew it was reformist and because it appeared to be the "coming thing." CCF leaders should have known that failure was quite as conceivable — and more logical — than success. Their strategy was to mobilize their supporters to action by sweeping assurances of an irresistible triumph. It had the diametrically opposite effect. There developed such unreasoning optimism that members saw little need to give themselves unsparingly in a task they believed superfluous; truth, they knew, would triumph without their meagre contribution.

The year 1945 ended an era in the history of the Canadian socialist movement. After that time, the possibility of a sudden sweep to victory became altogether unlikely. The postwar period, with its increasing (and unexpected) prosperity, blunted the overwhelming wartime demand for social reform. The resurgence of the CCF in Ontario in 1948 is easily explained; it was the result of unprecedented labour support combined with a growing dislike of Premier Drew in many sections of the province. In 1951, the CCF polled its smallest vote in the province in a decade. After that, it continued to be a factor but not a threat in the provincial affairs. Nationally, some observers spoke of the prospect of the CCF superseding the Conservatives as the official opposition as late as 1948. It was doubtful if such a possibility in fact existed, but if it did, the general election of 1949 destroyed the hope; the CCF suffered a crushing, irreparable defeat. Never again during the remainder of its existence did the socialist party of Canada present a major challenge to the traditional parties. By the criterion of electoral success, it died a failure.

Notes

1. *Maclean's*, April 1, 1932.
2. *Saturday Night*, Dec. 17, 1932.
3. *Farmer's Sun*, Feb. 4, March 3, July 21, 1932; Toronto *Globe*, Dec. 2, 1932.
4. Each provincial unit of the party was organized on a federal basis. Individual memberships did not exist. Only groups could affiliate.
5. Toronto *Star*, March 8, March 23, March 24, 1933; Toronto *New Commonwealth*, Feb. 23, 1936; interview with Mr. D.M. LeBourdais.
6. Marion Hebb, "The Political Heritage of the United Farmers of Ontario," under-graduate dissertation (University of Toronto, 1961), 24.
7. Interview with Mr. Harry Hatfield; Toronto *Star*, Feb. 20, 1933.
8. Interviews with Messrs. LeBourdais and Hatfield.
9. Doris French and Margaret Stewart, *Ask No Quarter*, (Toronto, 1959), 175; Mrs. Margaret Stewart's collection of Agnes Macphail's private papers, interview of Elmore Philpott by Mrs. Stewart.
10. French and Stewart, *Ask No Quarter*, 266.
11. It is instructive to compare the Saskatchewan situation in this regard. See Seymour M. Lipset, *Agrarian Socialism* (Berkeley, 1950), 277.
. . . .

13. Toronto *Mail and Empire*, March 12, 1934.
14. Loeb Papers, Woodsworth's Memorandum to Provincial Council, March 10, 1934.
. . . .

18. Toronto *Mail and Empire*, Feb. 3, 1933; *Weekly Sun*, March 9, 1933; *Saturday Night*, Dec. 17, 1932; Toronto *Telegram*, Feb. 21, 1933; *Maclean's*, May 15, 1933.
19. Dudley Bristow, "Agrarian Interest in the Politics of Ontario, 1919-1949," M.A. thesis (University of Toronto, 1950), 156.
20. Toronto *Star*, Sept. 30, 1933; *Farmers' Sun*, Dec. 22, 1932; *Canadian Annual Review (C.A.R.)*, 1932, 108; *ibid.*, 1934, 175-7.
21. *Canadian Parliamentary Guide*, 1935; Dennis Wrong, "Ontario Provincial Elections, 1934-1955; A Preliminary Survey of Voting," *Canadian Journal of Economics and Political Science*, XXIII (3), Aug., 1957, 398.
22. Escott Reid, "The Canadian Election of 1935 — and After," *American Political Science Review*, XXVII (3), June, 1936, 111-13, 115.
. . . .

26. P.M. Richards, *Saturday Night*, Aug. 9. 1941.
27. J.W. Pickersgill, *The Mackenzie King Record*, I, 1939-1944 (Toronto, 1960), 347.
28. Toronto *Globe and Mail*, Jan. 29, 1942.
29. Pickersgill, *Mackenzie King Record*, I, 281; Bruce Hutchison, *The Incredible Canadian* (Toronto, 1953), 297-8.
30. *Saturday Night*, March 7, 1942.
31. Toronto *Star*, Jan. 29, 1942.
32. Interviews with Professor Frank H. Underhill and Mr. E.B. Jolliffe.
33. Toronto *Star*, Feb. 3, Feb. 6, 1942.
34. *Ibid.*, Feb. 5, 1942; *Maclean's*, March 1, 1942.
35. Toronto *Star*, Feb. 10, 1942.
36. NDP Ontario office (Toronto), Ontario CCF Provincial Council Reports, Report of the Executive to the 1943 Convention.
37. Harold A. Logan, *Trade Unions in Canada* (Toronto, 1948), 77-8; *Saturday Night*, Sept. 13, 1941.
38. *Canadian Forum*, Oct., 1942.
39. CCF National Office Files (Ottawa), Provincial Convention Reports, CCF Trade Union Committee Report to the 1944 Convention.
. . . .
43. Toronto *Globe and Mail*, July 29, 1943; *Maclean's*, Aug. 1, 1943.
44. Toronto *Globe and Mail*, July 28, Aug. 2, 1943; *News*, Aug. 7, 1943.
45. Toronto *Globe and Mail*, July 26, 28, 1943; Ottawa *Citizen*, July 28, 1943.
46. Toronto *Globe and Mail*, July 13, 19, 29, 1943.
47. *New Commonwealth*, July 8, July 22, Dec. 9, 1943; Ontario CCF Provincial Council Minutes and Reports, Sept. 18, 1943; Provincial Convention Reports, CCF Trade Union Committee Report to the 1944 Convention.
48. Toronto *Globe and Mail*, July 10, 1943.
49. *Ibid.*, Aug. 7, 1943.
50. *New Commonwealth*, Aug. 12, 1943.
51. *Canadian Parliamentary Guide*, 1944; Bristow, "Agrarian Interest in the Politics of Ontario," 256; Wrong, "Ontario Provincial Elections," 398.
52. *Maclean's*, Sept. 1, 1943.
53. *Saturday Night*, Aug. 7, 1943.
54. Toronto *Star*, Aug. 5, 1943.
55. *New Commonwealth*, Oct. 14, 1943.
56. National Office Files, Lloyd Shaw to Mrs. P. de Cespedes, Nov. 12, 1943; Ontario Research Committee Memorandum, 1944, in Provincial Convention Reports; *Saturday Night*, Oct. 2, 1943.
57. Provincial Convention Reports, Reports of the Secretary and of the Organization Committee to 1944 Ontario Convention.
58. Ontario CCF Provincial Council Minutes, Oct. 8, 1944; *New Commonwealth*, Feb. 24, Nov. 8, 1944.
59. *Saturday Night*, Sept. 11, 1943.
60. Provincial Convention Reports, Trade Union Committee Report to the 1944 Ontario Convention.
61. Logan, *Trade Unions in Canada*, 555.
62. Dean E. McHenry, *Third Force in Canada* (Berkeley, 1950), 105-6.
63. M.M. Armstrong, "The Development of Trade Union Political Activity in the CCF," M.A. thesis (University of Toronto, 1950), 44-5; National Office Files, William Reggs, M.L.A., to David Lewis, June 5, 1944.
64. Logan, *Trade Unions in Canada*, 434-7; Report of the Proceedings of the 59th Annual Convention of the Trades and Labour Congress of Canada, August 30-September 3, 1943; Joseph Levitt, "The Political History of the LPP 1945-1949," graduate dissertation (University of Toronto, 1961), 10.
65. Toronto *Telegram*, Dec. 31, 1943; Toronto *Globe and Mail*, Jan. 1, 1944; *Saturday Night*, Jan. 1, 1944.

66. *Saturday Night*, Jan. 15, 1944.
67. See, for example, the advertisements in *ibid.*, Sept. 18, Sept. 25, Dec. 18, 1943, May 12, Oct. 28, 1944, and Toronto *Star*, May 31, 1945.
68. Arthur Meighen, *Unrevised and Unrepented* (Toronto, 1949), 433-52.
69. According to the United Church *Observer*, quoted in *New Commonwealth*, Feb. 10, 1944.
70. So reported one person who was canvassed to the *New Commonwealth*, July 13, 1944.
71. The document in which this is stated was printed in the Ontario CCF organ, *New Commonwealth*, Jan. 27, 1944. At the 1945 "Gestapo" hearings, Murray admitted that the document was an accurate copy of a speech he had made. Edwin Guillet, "Famous Canadian Trials," vol. 50, "Political Gestapo," unpublished manuscript (Toronto, 1949), chap. IV, s. 4 (unpaginated).
72. This document was also reprinted in *New Commonwealth*, June 22, 1944.
73. Murray listed individually the names of the corporation and individuals supporting him in a circular dated Aug. 4, 1943, which is reproduced in full in Guillet, "Famous Canadian Trials," Appendix G, "Selections From Gladstone Murray's Circulars." Trestrail's sponsors are included in the document published in the *New Commonwealth*, Jan. 27, 1944, and *Canadian Forum*, March, 1944.
74. *New Commonwealth*, Jan. 27, 1944.
75. *Maclean's*, April 15, 1944. The third Toronto organization could have been that of M.A. Sanderson.
76. *Ibid.*, Oct. 15, Nov. 1, 1943, Jan. 1, Sept. 1, 1944.
77. Stanley F. Pearson, *It's A Good Life* (Toronto, 1944); William S. Gibson, *You Knew What You Were Voting For* (Toronto, 1944). Gibson intended his work as a rebuttal of the very popular book by David Lewis and Frank Scott, *Make This Your Canada* (Toronto, 1943).
78. *New Commonwealth*, June 22, 1944.
79. *Ibid.*, Nov. 5, Dec. 9, 1943. Winch actually said military forces would be used by a CCF government only if "reactionaries" attempted to obstruct it with the use of force.
80. See the quotation, for e.g., in *ibid.*, Dec. 23, 1943; *Canadian Forum*, Dec., 1943; Arthur Meighen, *Unrevised and Unrepented*, 433-52.
81. Lipset, *Agrarian Socialism*, 282.
82. *New Commonwealth*, May 25, June 8, July 13, 1943.
83. *Saturday Night*, June 24, 1944.
84. *Maclean's*, June 1, 1944; *New Commonwealth*, March 7, 1944.
85. *Saturday Night*, Feb. 12, 1944.
86. *Time*, Jan. 31, 1944.
87. Quoted in *New Commonwealth*, Aug. 17, 1944; *Maclean's*, Nov. 15, 1944.
88. *Saturday Night*, April 8, 1944.
. . . .

92. *Saturday Night*, Dec. 30, 1944; *New Commonwealth*, Dec. 28, 1944, Jan. 11, 1945.
93. The two were Nelson Alles (Essex North) and Leslie Hancock (Wellington North). CCF National Office Files, Correspondence, 1943-44; Ontario CCF Provincial Council Minutes, Jan. 9, Oct. 8, 1944; Ontario CCF Provincial Executive Minutes, Jan. 2, Jan. 16, 1945; Ontario, Legislative Assembly, *Debates and Proceedings*, Feb. 2, 1945, I, 28-31.
94. *New Commonwealth*, Jan. 11, 1945.
95. *Time*, Feb. 12, 1945.
96. Ontario CCF Provincial Executive Minutes, April 10, 1945.
97. Interview with Mr. F.A. Brewin.
. . . .

105. Toronto *Telegram*, May 19, 1945.
106. Toronto *Star*, May 21, 1945. Opponents of the CCF frequently used the terms "communism" and "fascism" interchangeably.
107. Editorial, *ibid.*, May 26, 1945.
108. Hutchison, *Incredible Canadian*, 413.
109. *Ibid.*.
110. L.H. Laing, "The Pattern of Canadian Politics," *American Political Science Review*, XL (4), Aug. 1946, 765.

111. CCF National Office Files, Trestrail to (name and company blacked out), St. Catherines St., Montreal, May 1, 1945. This photostatic copy was made by a Montreal businessman who received the original from Trestrail and sent a copy to the CCF.

112. Toronto *Telegram*, May 15, May 18, May 22, May 30, June 2, 1945.

113. B.A. Trestrail, *Social Suicide* (no city, no publisher, no date of publication), 29, 31. The sentence concerning Lewis reads: "Well, the day may yet come in Canada when a Jewish immigrant boy will rise to a position where he writes the ticket for the social and economic programme of this nation. . . ."

114. Ottawa *Citizen*, June 1, 1945.

115. See private letter from Trestrail quoted in *New Commonwealth*, Jan. 27, 1944.

116. *CCF News*, May 31, 1945; Glace Bay *Gazette*, May 22, 1945.

117. *CCF News*, May 31, 1945.

118. Toronto *Star*, May 26, May 29, 1945.

119. *Report of the Royal Commissioner Appointed May 28, 1945, to Investigate Charges Made by Mr. Edward B. Jolliffe, K.C.*, The Hon. Mr. Justice A.M. LeBel, Commissioner (Toronto, 1945), Appendix A, 49-55.

120. It should be noted that nowhere in Queen's Park can a complete copy of the Commission's proceedings be found; it is curious indeed that the provincial government has no transcript of the hearings of a provincial Royal Commission. The entire story may be pieced together using the *Report of the Royal Commissioner*, Guillet's "Famous Canadian Trials," vol. 50, "Political Gestapo," and G.M.A. Grube, "The LeBel Report and Civil Liberties," *Canadian Forum*, Nov., 1945. There is a detailed reconstruction of the "Gestapo affair" in my "The CCF in Ontario, 1932-1945: A Study of Socialist and Anti-Socialist Politics," unpublished M.A. thesis (University of Toronto, 1961), chap. XVIII. My conclusions are similar to those of Mr. Guillet, who wrote that Jolliffe "obviously proved [during the Commission hearings] the basic substance of his charge beyond the shadow of a doubt." (Guillet, "Famous Canadian Trials," vol. 50, chap. XI). I also argue, however, that Premier Drew's personal role is not as clear as Jolliffe claimed; that although Constable Dempster's activities constituted a perversion of democracy, there was a difference in kind between Ontario's secret police and Hitler's "Gestapo"; that Jolliffe tried to exploit an immensely serious situation for political purposes; and that the sensationalism with which he presented the issue to the public contradicted the cherished CCF belief that socialism could triumph through the use of reason, education, and an honest presentation of the issues.

121. *Canadian Parliamentary Guide*, 1946; Wrong, "Ontario Provincial Elections," 398; Bristow, "Agrarian Interest in the Politics of Ontario," 257; Toronto *Star*, June 9, 1945; *CCF News*, Dec. 13, 1945; *Canadian Unionist*, July, 1945; *Time*, June 15, 1945.

122. *Canadian Parliamentary Guide*, 1946; Toronto *Star*, June 12, June 13, 1945; *Canadian Forum*, July, 1945; *Canadian Unionist*, July, 1945; *CCF News*, June 21, 1945.

. . . .

127. *CCF News*, June 21, 1945.

128. Toronto *Star*, June 5, 1945.

129. "Oh, no! We won't vote CCF," a party canvasser in the Toronto slums was told in 1945. "They'd take away everything we have." Interview with Mrs. F.A. Brewin.

130. *Saturday Night*, May 18, 1935.

131. B.A. Trestrail, *Stand Up and Be Counted Or Sit Still and Get Soaked* (Toronto, 1944), 6.

132. CCF National Office Files, Margaret Thelford to C.C. Ames, July 16, 1945.

133. *New Commonwealth*, April 18, 1936.

134. Andrew Brewin, *Canadian Forum*, Feb., 1946.

135. CCF National Office Files, copy of lecture given at Ontario Woodsworth House, Nov., 1945.

136. Forest Hill Village in Toronto sent 90 per cent of its eligible residents to the polls, most working class sections 50 per cent, *Canadian Forum*, July, 1945.

137. Brewin, *Canadian Forum*, Feb., 1946.

138. *CCF News*, July 12, 1945, *et seq.*

Membership in a Becalmed Protest Movement

Leo Zakuta

"In politics the thing to do is build yourself an army." The remark is attributed to the late Jimmy Hines, a successful Tammany Hall politician of the 1930's. In June, 1945, half way between the Regina Manifesto and the Winnipeg Declaration, the Co-operative Commonwealth Federation, at the head of the largest army in its history, prepared for the reward of virtue and patience — power in Ottawa and Ontario. The problems of building that army and then maintaining it under the adverse conditions following June, 1945, constitute the theme of this paper.

In its first decade the CCF had successfully welded a united, national organization out of a federation of parties and groups along a social-democrat and agrarian-protest spectrum. The absence of a New Deal party gave the "movement," as its members still call it, its opportunity. Its central bond was a common hatred of capitalism, allegedly responsible for the depression and its accompanying hardships. It was, however, less than unanimous about the remedy. The Regina Manifesto of 1933, the party's initial declaration of faith and intentions, was framed in the social democratic tradition "No CCF government," it concluded, "will rest content until it has eradicated capitalism." But no statement of policy could ever avert the inevitable debate on "how far" and "how fast" socialism should be implemented.

The topography of CCF beliefs can be roughly charted by identifying its closest friends and mentors and its ideological boundaries on the "right" and "left." Its chief, though not unanimous, favourites have always been the Labour and Social Democratic parties of the Commonwealth, Scandinavia, and especially Great Britain. Its supporters ranged all the way from people who were made uneasy by talk of socialism despite endless assurances, to those drawn enviously to the glamour of revolutionary intrigue and virile, uncompromising militancy which they associated with Communism and Trotskyism. While these "left wingers" pressed the leaders constantly to declare themselves on the questions of "how far" and "how fast," the great majority entrusted these matters to

Reprinted from the *Canadian Journal of Economics and Political Science*, Vol. 24, No. 2, May 1958, pp. 190-202, by permission of the author and the Canadian Political Science Association.

the leaders and concentrated instead on building the organization.

Besides constructing a national organization, the CCF showed signs of strength in most of the west in the 1930's. But after almost a decade, the debit side of the ledger was more impressive. In the 1940 federal election the CCF made no gains over the election of 1935 (despite the disappearance of its chief 1935 rival, the Reconstruction party), electing only three members outside Saskatchewan and only one east of Manitoba. The party's ranks were split and its leadership uncertain about a war policy as its pre-war pacifism died a lingering death. East of Ontario, CCF strength was virtually non-existent, and in that key province it was extremely weak.

The party's hopes of national success have always hinged on extensive support in Ontario. But from 1935 to 1942, through one provincial and two national elections, not a single CCF candidate was elected in Ontario. The initial crusading impetus was spent by the mid-thirties, as a sharp decline in membership indicated. The Communists had weakened the party's left flank and disturbed the rest of the organization by a persistent, coaxing United Front appeal. There was no money, and organization was rudimentary and ineffectual. In short, although it was never very radical, the CCF, at least in Ontario, had come to resemble the classic image of the radical sect. It was small, poor, ineffectively organized, and isolated from the larger society. Much of its energy was directed at internal targets in a grinding series of accusations, hearings, and expulsions designed to maintain ideological purity, especially against the threat from the "left," and to find scapegoats for its failures. After almost a decade of existence, the CCF was, to all appearances, no more than another western protest movement.

In view of Ontario's critical importance to the CCF, it is probably significant that the reversal of the party's national fortunes began in that province in 1942, with the dramatic victory in the South York by-election. The CCF had begun to build its army late in 1941. It marshalled an unprecedented force of volunteers and money for the South York campaign and for those that were to follow. In the next few years the party won one dazzling victory after another, often surpassing even its own expectations. Like many organizations, the CCF often faces the tricky problem of generating sufficient optimism at elections to mobilize the ranks and infect the sympathetic and of simultaneously avoiding the pitfalls of exaggerated hope. Unrealistic expectations tend to dishearten the faithful and mislead the public into maximizing the party's defeats and minimizing its victories. But suddenly the CCF's "optimists" became its "realists" and the rest the faint-hearted. When it faced the "double election" of June, 1945, the party held office in Saskatchewan and was the official Opposition in Ontario, Manitoba, and British Columbia. It had some reason, therefore, to believe that power nationally and in Ontario was not far off.

That sight, however faint, of the Celestial City played an important part in the CCF's reaction to subsequent defeat and adversity. Recalling that time of brimming confidence, one should be aware that it was not so much the prospect of fulfilment as its suddenness that took the party by surprise. Belief in inevitable triumph has always been a fundamental article of socialist, and sectarian, faith. The 1936 report of the Ontario CCF executive concluded with the affirmation that "The stars in their courses are fighting for the cause of socialism." Socialist doctrine had forecast both the wandering in the wilderness and the eventual arrival in the promised land. What it had not provided was a timetable of these events.

On June 4, 1945, however, the voters of Ontario cut the CCF representation in Queen's Park from thirty-four to eight, and one week later, of the 245 members elected to the House of Commons, only twenty-eight represented the CCF, all but one of them from the west. Ever since, despite several temporary upsurges, the party has been fighting a retreat — gradual, orderly, but relentless. Its perspective has shifted from expanding to holding steady although it can still generate considerable energy for that task.

When the CCF faced its followers after these two disastrous defeats, it could no longer rally them against adversity in the same way as it had after earlier setbacks. Not only had the condition of the country altered; the CCF had become a very different kind of party during its years of success and, in the process, lost much of its protective insulation against defeat. The changes in the CCF — ideological, structural, and emotional — and the party's adaptation to them are the subject of the larger study of which this paper is a part. They are discussed briefly here under the headings: Beliefs, Organization, and Morale.[1]

Beliefs

William Kornhauser's impressive study of American liberals and radicals[2] illuminates the hazards that beset these political groups. The chief threat to a radical organization is that its uncompromising rejection of the social order may isolate it from its audience through derision, unpopularity, fear, and even repression. Liberal groups, on the other hand, may lose their distinctive identity and sense of purpose if they fail to differentiate themselves clearly from the traditional parties. This danger has been particularly acute for American liberal organizations because the Democratic party has been so potent a rallying force for liberals and even socialists since 1932.

The absence of such a force in Canada during this period permitted the CCF to attract a much greater range of support than any American equivalent. Except for the Communists and some insignificant Trotskyite splinter groups, the CCF has virtually monopolized "left of centre" politics, a position which relegated to secondary importance the question of whether it was primarily liberal or radical at any point. The CCF's product required few minor differentiations in the absence of serious competition for the potential market. Despite these advantages, the party has not found it easy to steer a safe course between the twin shoals of isolation and loss of identity. Its consistent lack of success before 1942 indicates its earlier isolation from the main stream of Canadian politics, while its most pressing recent danger appears to be the absence of sharp distinctions from the other political parties. Some documentation of these points is in order.

If the CCF of today is compared with the party before the war, the missing qualities are the most striking. Along with so many socialist parties, the CCF has lost much of its indignation and, with it, most of its hope of the socialist utopia. The "capitalist boss" has almost vanished as a symbolic, rallying enemy, and with his disappearance the sectarian spirit fled. Mitchell Hepburn and George Drew, convenient short-run ogres, have departed, and the CCF has had to make do with C.D. Howe and share him with the Conservatives at that.

The nature of the CCF's thinking in the 1930's is evident not only in the concluding passage of the Regina Manifesto, quoted previously, but in passages such as the following, taken from the report of the Ontario executive to the provincial convention in 1936:

> . . . every CCF member should insist and understand that in no sense is the socialism of the CCF mere reformism, mere gradualism, or compromise with capitalism of any kind. A CCF government attaining power must proceed promptly, drastically, thoroughly to liquidate the power of capitalist forces and secure for the socialist party in control of the organs of the state the most ample assurance that capitalist interests could not sabotage, weaken or overthrow socialism. The CCF must recognize and prepare for the most ruthless opposition . . . must be fully conscious of the opposition that will seek to destroy our efforts and the danger of the final stages of the struggle. Anyone who does not understand the nature of the struggle has no place in the CCF. . . . The CCF is on the uttermost left in objective and understanding or it is nowhere.

In the 1956 Winnipeg Declaration, a major statement of policy by the national convention, the CCF's supreme authority, the party finally abandoned the vision of the classless utopia. The Declaration's tolerance of private enterprise was by no means a new policy for the CCF. What made the document so significant was that it represented the party's decision to enunciate its revised beliefs in the most open, official, and binding way possible.

Finally, the brief conversation below, which occurred at a CCF educational conference to discuss the Winnipeg Declaration, illuminates the change in the party's outlook.

> The participants were divided into small discussion groups. The group of four, whose remarks are recorded here, consisted of a top Ontario leader, two veteran local "leaders", i.e., executive members of riding associations, and one rank and file member. The last

fortunately was a member of the left wing minority or the following conversation would never have ensued:

Group chairman (local leader): "Now we come to the question of whether we can get rid of inequalities. Can differences in income be eliminated?"

Rank and file member: "We should eliminate these differences. They're getting greater all the time."

Chairman: "I don't think that's necessary or desirable."

Top leader: "What we need is not equality of income. We have to raise the floor of wages."

Rank and file member: "We should have a ceiling on wages. Factory workers make just as great a contribution as any others and they're just as valuable."

Chairman: "No, they're not as valuable and important. It's easy to replace them."

Top leader: "Some people are content on $3,000 a year for example. Others want more and are willing to pay for it in work, education and responsibility."

Rank and file member: "But the factory workers have to have dignity as well, and socialism has to provide it."

Top leader: "Certainly. That's why we're so in favour of unions. The problem is to get people to take responsibility. Most people don't want more. The more ambitious ones want more and look for it. I can't be horrified by ambition, by people who want to get ahead and become president of the union or of the company."

Rank and file member: "Isn't it our job to protect people from the more powerful?"

Top leader: "Yes, that's what we have to do . . . but we can't prevent leadership or do without it."

Chairman: "Yes, and don't forget the sacrifices the leaders have to make. Their responsibility and worry doesn't end at 5 o'clock. For instance, the president of the company may be phoned late at night because something's gone wrong."

Top leader: "What gives me a pain are those people who don't work but who go to meetings of directors. . . . But we can get at those deadheads through taxation."

Second local leader (speaking for the first time): "There can't be complete planning without interfering with personal liberty. The mesh would be too small."

Rank and file member: "Prices are always getting higher. Every time that you go to the store everything is a few cents up."

Perhaps some of these people were pushed a little beyond their beliefs in this discussion. Nevertheless, their remarks require no further elaboration or interpretation. An interesting sidelight to this episode is the fact that the *New Commonwealth*, the Ontario CCF's newspaper in the 1930's, contains few harsher indictments of capitalism than a series of articles by the chairman of this discussion group.

The CCF's altered attitude to private enterprise and its appearance of differing from other parties on immediate rather than long-range objectives led a Toronto paper to warn it of ". . . the danger . . . [of] . . . losing its distinctive identity in the public mind. CCF'ers will now come closer to fitting Prime Minister St. Laurent's definition of them: 'Liberals in a hurry'."[3] However, who would venture to predict whether the CCF would gain or lose from such a public image as long as there is no Canadian equivalent of the Democratic party to swallow it up when it gets too close? While the Liberals were in office, the CCF continued to enjoy a near monopoly of the "left of centre" position. If the Conservatives continue to hold office and push the Liberals "leftward," the CCF's problems of maintaining a distinctive identity may be just beginning.

Organization

The main stages in the CCF's career constitute the framework of this section. Although precise dividing points in such matters are always rather arbitrary and some overlapping is inevitable, these phases divide the CCF's 24-year history neatly and effectively into three 8-year periods. The first period, 1933-41, corresponds precisely to the years of isolation described earlier. The second period, 1942-9, begins with the CCF's upsurge and ends with the resounding defeat in the 1949 federal election, which clearly terminated its tenuous claim to be a major party. Throughout the third period, 1950-7, despite its continuing strength in Saskatchewan and British Columbia, the CCF was again a minor party nationally, though far different in character than it had been in its first phase.

Official Structure

Before the changes in the CCF's organization are examined, the party's basic constitutional structure must be looked at briefly because it provides the more permanent framework within which these changes have taken place. The official organization is on three main levels. The riding associations are the basic units. Their delegates, the delegates of the affiliated organizations, and the outgoing provincial council constitute the CCF's annual provincial convention, the final authority in provincial affairs. The convention and the larger ridings elect the provincial council, the governing body in the province between conventions. The provincial council, in turn, elects the executive, which meets much more frequently to plan and oversee the party's daily operations. It does so largely through standing committees which report to it regularly. Nationally, the ridings, the national convention, the national council and executive, and the affiliated organizations are linked together in the same way as the corresponding provincial bodies.

The provincial organizations have considerable autonomy, and the national office usually deals with the ridings through the provincial body. The ridings too have some independence. As may be expected in any organization with such a division of powers, jurisdictional issues may at times be troublesome. Finally, the party's administrative personnel are mainly voluntary; only a small portion of the group is paid.

From Sect to Party

Discussing the CCF's history and changes, a veteran top leader expressed the common view of his colleagues: "We had no organization worth talking about until around '42 or '43. That's when we began building a real organization." He was referring to the lengthy process of expansion, "centralization," as he put it, and consolidation in which the structure of the party and the participation of its members were altered beyond anyone's anticipation. Reorganization went on throughout the second period. Expansion and centralization highlighted its first half, and the second half, following the setbacks of 1945, was primarily a time of consolidation. When the third period began, around 1950, the Ontario CCF had dug in, as will be seen later.

Organizationally, the party was poorly prepared for the success which began to overtake or perhaps overwhelm it in 1942 and 1943. It lacked the money, personnel, and experience to capitalize fully on these developments by building a solid, durable structure, especially outside Toronto and a few other urban, industrial centres. As the quest for power became more real and urgent during these years, the CCF leaders in Ontario felt hampered by what they regarded as serious weaknesses in organization, which they set out to correct.

They first attacked the enduring problem of the CCF clubs, which, until the early 1940's, were the basic units of the party in Ontario. They were somewhat more autonomous than the later riding associations and the recurrent problems caused by their structure stimulated the CCF to build a political party out of its rather diffuse and spontaneous movement. While every club had a territorial base, many ridings contained more than one club with no co-ordinating body. Many of the resulting jurisdictional and ideological battles within the ridings were recorded in the minutes throughout the 1930's. When the provincial council and executive attempted to arbitrate, they exposed themselves to angry charges of dictatorial interference. In addition there was considerable friction and irritation which never reached the official record.

The frequent lack of harmony and close contact among the clubs in a riding made them very unwieldy election organizations and eventually contributed to their replacement, wherever possible, by riding associations. In creating these latter bodies, the party's leaders were also concerned about the problem of discipline. By reducing the autonomy of the individual clubs or by merging their members in a larger riding association, the CCF also hoped to reduce the embarrassing menace of Communist overtures. But mounting membership and electoral success provided the chief impetus to the party's efforts to build an organization suited to fight elections and to accommodate the thousands of new members. Their rapid influx — the Ontario CCF multiplied its membership almost ten times between 1942 and 1945 — made the change from clubs to riding associations all the more imperative in the eyes of party officials.

The flood of new members apparently alarmed many ''old timers'' who sadly saw ''their movement'' slipping out of their hands and worried about the motives and beliefs of the newcomers, whose arrival they regarded as a mixed blessing. Many new members were thus made to feel less welcome than they had anticipated. A top leader, in an unexcelled position to know this situation, described many of the clubs as ''very ingrown little groups,'' an indication that the administration regarded them as ill suited both for electoral purposes and for incorporating the tide of new members. It hoped that the riding associations would be much better suited to the requirements of a vigorous and rapidly expanding organization because they would be larger and somewhat more impersonal than the clubs and would therefore be freer of the impenetrable barriers of cliquishness that had arisen from the long and intimate association of small groups. But above all, it regarded the ''old timers'' as primarily ''talkers'' and the newcomers as potential ''doers.''

Among the other structural changes which accompanied growing success were the selection of the first provincial leader in Ontario in 1942 and an effort to develop a larger, more professional staff with a clearer division of work. The CCF's election procedures in Ontario were standardized and brought under greater central control. In 1944 the first CCF Government took office in Saskatchewan after a landslide victory. That triumph was regarded as further proof, if any were needed, of the value of riding and poll organization. Ever since, the CCF has sought to emulate the business-like organization of the Saskatchewan section and, incidentally, of the other political parties, which it resembles in that respect.

The reorganization that accompanied the successes of the early 1940's was not accomplished without cost. The pre-war clubs possessed some characteristic sectarian features. They were usually smaller and more sociable than the less spontaneous riding associations since any small group of friends could form its own CCF club. (Thus the cliquishness which later was such a handicap to an expanding organization was, in the earlier period, an important asset to one which clung precariously to existence.) The members of these clubs were often united by a common view of themselves as a small core of rebels and visionaries in a hostile and apathetic society, dedicated to fulfilling the prophecy of a new and just social order. The relative isolation of the clubs from the community around them and their orientation towards the more distant future combined with their easy sociability to produce in them intense activity and interest. Many of the clubs were able to involve a limited number of members quite deeply, though the involvement was at times as short lived as it was intense. In the depression era of low earnings, widespread unemployment, and surfeit of leisure, the party membership card was for many CCF'ers a low-cost ticket to politics, social life, and entertainment. In the words of a former leader, "For us the CCF was mother, father and the church."

Of course, the war and full employment had an incalculably large hand in changing all that. But, in addition, the CCF's success had turned the party's interest to organization. Meetings were held monthly instead of weekly; abstract and more remote political discussion was replaced by devotion to organizational matters which, in the words of one leader, "are of interest only to those already involved." As the clubs gave way to riding associations and abstract political discussion to interest in organizing, the earlier social and intellectual bases of involvement became seriously jeopardized. For a while the enthusiasm that swept the party in its triumphant period infused the riding associations. Significantly, membership soared throughout the CCF from 1942 to 1945, but plummeted immediately after the twin defeats of 1945. When the party's fortunes and prospects declined, many of the earlier sectarian conditions that had been conducive to involvement were irretrievably gone. In the intervening years, both Canada and the CCF had changed considerably. The former had experienced several years of prosperity and the latter was becoming a genuine political party, primarily concerned with elections and organization. Such a party has a different source of cohesion than the radical sect. It depends much more on the prospect of immediate success than the sect which thrives on hope long deferred.

During its second phase, too, the CCF began to enlist strong support from the trade unions. Its membership had always contained many individual trade unionists, but sharp divisions existed in both the party and the unions on the question of establishing official relations, as the British and American trade-union traditions about political action vied for supremacy. The CCF's decision to welcome union affiliations and the rise of the CIO in Canada broke the impasse and brought organized support to the party in the form of affiliations and endorsements by union bodies.

The main reinforcements came from several of the new, mushrooming CIO unions, many of whose officers were CCF leaders or sympathizers. This system of interlocking directorates opened to the party far-reaching connections, first in the CCL and recently in the merged union body. Most of the officials who bridged the gap between the CCF and the unions entered the unions through the CCF rather than the other way about. The leaders who formed the nuclei of several of these unions were recruited from the CCF on the basis, among other things, of personal and ideological affinities.

The careers of these men have followed a somewhat similar pattern. Before their unions were established, they were ardent CCF'ers. In the CCF's second period, 1942-9, they were deeply involved in the unions and in the party, rising in both these growing organizations. But since then, their union work has clearly come first, although their attachment to the party has continued, as is attested by their continued membership, the fact that they themselves and, in some cases, their organizations, have made sizable financial contributions, and by their efforts on its behalf in the labour congresses and federations. The Political Action Committee has been a very tangible and important expression of their continued support. The reason why they recently have left the leadership and administration of the CCF to others is, however, a subject for later discussion.

Consolidation: Finances, Membership, and Administration

With the help of the unions, the party eventually established a relatively solid financial base. It took time for the idea of supporting the CCF to move down and across union hierarchies. The decline and fall of the Labour Progressive party, the CCF's chief enemy in the unions, undoubtedly eased the way to official support. However, continued CCF weakness at the polls may lead to an "agonizing reappraisal" regarding the maintenance of that support; such talk has been in the air in the last few years.

The party's unprecedented current financial stability is by no means attributable to the unions alone. Most of its funds still come from its own members. The sharp and protracted decline in membership after 1945 precipitated an acute financial crisis which the CCF countered by initiating a highly successful system of graduated membership fees resulting in increased per capita contributions. The decline in membership was arrested by the beginning of the third period and, since then, the membership figures have displayed unprecedented stability.[4]

Stable membership, greater per capita contributions, and the financial assistance of the unions made the party more solvent, and it was therefore able to obtain a larger, more professional, and more economically secure administrative staff than ever before. The efforts of this staff, particularly in conducting regular financial and membership drives, have contributed significantly to the party's consolidation. But a more adequate interpretation of its recent stability must await the next section of this paper.

Morale

This difficult term must be defined briefly here as a blend of the shared desire for and confidence in organizational success. The sources and indices of CCF morale form the theme of this section; the discussion proceeds from the external and tangible aspects to the more internal and intangible. It begins with the CCF's record in attracting votes, members, and money and then discusses the more elusive relation between participation and expectations of success. Finally, beyond these other aspects of involvement and motivation, lie the twin, though not completely identical, questions of the individual's commitment to the party and its claims on him. These will be considered in turn.

Membership and finance have been discussed previously. With respect to votes and public support, the CCF has lost ground gradually but seriously. In October, 1943, the Gallup Poll showed the party leading the field nationally with the backing of 29 per cent of the electorate. In the election of June, 1957, it received 11 per cent of the vote. In Ontario provincial elections, the CCF vote has receded from a high of 32 per cent in 1943 to 17 per cent in 1955. In the federal campaign of June, 1957, the party's primary objective was to retain third place against the challenge of Social Credit.

Participation and Expectations of Success

Despite official reassurances, some leaders take a pessimistic view of the CCF's prospects. An example is the following assessment made at a meeting of the national council early in 1956 by one of the very top leaders, whose position perhaps facilitated a measure of detachment:

> . . . We have to look very realistically over the period of the last 10 or 15 years and recognize that we have lost ground. The best indication of our weakness is that the old-line parties are no longer afraid of us. The average person on the street doesn't keep backing a fighter who has been knocked out five or six times in a row and has no prospects of ever becoming champion. You have to have a party that looks as though it is going somewhere, a party that is increasing its prestige and its strength and frankly I don't think we are.[5]

The following assessment of the members was made by someone who has been close to many top leaders for a long time, and is still fairly active, despite the tenor of his remarks: "Well, you know it's getting more and more hopeless, and they're older, tired and disillusioned. They put their efforts into other organizations, unions, churches and so on. . . . It's just that we're dying from lack of oomph. The reason is simply that our cause has disappeared." Another very prominent leader commented to a colleague in private conversation: "Even if the CCF doesn't survive in its present form, it will survive in some other form."

The number, types, and social position of the party's candidates have changed noticeably, especially in the last period. The total number of candidates has declined steadily since 1945, the peak year, both nationally and in Ontario. In the two earlier periods, at least 90 per cent of the CCF candidates in Toronto were from the middle class; in the recent period that figure dropped to 73 per cent. For the first time many of these candidates were women and industrial workers.[6] These two groups accounted for two-thirds of the party's candidates in Toronto in the 1957 federal election. The number of "sacrifice" candidates, as they are privately called, has grown and some have appeared in former CCF strongholds.

As hopes gradually diminished after 1945, many CCF voluntary leaders drifted away from administrative involvement. Personal achievements and ambitions, growing family obligations, and the heavier demands of their careers, including increased union responsibilities, gnawed steadily at the time and energy available for the party. The senior salaried officers were involved in a somewhat different tug of war. Money and careers were usually the critical considerations for them, as time and energy were for the voluntary leaders, and discouragement was the common factor in both equations. Although party salaries increased substantially over the pre-war pittances, the salaried officers were still unable to enjoy the mode of life available to most of their middle-class associates both inside and outside the CCF, most of whom were in more lucrative careers in the professions, business, and trade unions. The struggle for a middle-class standard of living on a party salary drove some deeply into debt. As the party's prospects waned, these officials weighed increasing family responsibilities and attractive opportunities outside the party against their heavy investment of years, efforts, hopes, and ambitions in the CCF. Family obligations were the doorway through which they usually made their exit, fortified by the feeling that the long years of "sacrifice" merited a respite and relief. With varying degrees of involvement, both the salaried and voluntary leaders usually remained in the party. More significant is the paucity of young, vigorous, and ambitious aspirants to replace the original nucleus, now older, more tired, and involved elsewhere.

Some CCF representatives have followed more individualistic political careers, notably in municipal politics, and have usually been drawn away from the party. The CCF seeks their active participation in the organization, but compliance with these claims tends to limit their opportunities to establish contact and support in the other associations of the community, the life-blood of a conventional political career. But in evading the party's claims, they may expose themselves to the suspicion of seeking too personal a following and the accusation of expediently turning their backs on the party that gave them their start. Though scarcely audible now, the old sectarian alarm that the leaders may become too deeply involved in the outside world is still sounded occasionally by the left-wing "purists," as they are scornfully called.

Although most CCF'ers, including the leaders, endorse and encourage these individualistic careers, the resentment and suspicions of the hard-shelled minority act as an irritant and repellent. In addition, during the course of building a career, especially in "non-partisan" municipal politics, these representatives tend to become involved in many other groups besides the CCF and become concerned with their problems and perspectives. Finally, the decline in the CCF's political power lessens the value of a connection with it for leaders with other sources of support. The party's weakness also discourages them from seeking or even accepting provincial or federal nomination.

Consequently, CCF candidates, at least in Toronto, are less likely to be graduates of municipal politics than their Liberal and Conservative opponents. The relative obscurity of its candidates tends to reduce the CCF vote and with it the party's future expectations, thereby making it even harder to obtain a strong candidate next time and prolonging the spiral of defeat and discouragement. All these signs of demoralization tempt one to conclude that "nothing fails like failure," as the following editorial in the Ottawa *Journal* floridly explains:

> . . . any party kept too long in opposition falls a prey to frustration and despair; its ablest captains tempted to abandon it and younger men discouraged from joining it. Politicians no matter how determined, weary of "following suns that flame and fade on a day that has no morrow". And young men of ability shrink from joining a party which offers no reward for ambition. Thus in such circumstances an opposition becomes feebler and feebler, drained of the drive it must have if it is to perform its functions adequately.

The Party and the Member

An investigation of how CCF'ers view their party's prospects leads to the questions of their participation and involvement. You may recall Lenin's scornful comparison of the parties that merely "sign up" members with those whose recruits are expected to dedicate "not merely their spare evenings but the whole of their lives" to the movement. Among the mixed traditions inherited by the CCF was a much milder socialist variation of Lenin's standard. But that ideal became increasingly unattainable and ineffectual. The party has long been anxious to obtain these spare evenings, although, as in every organization, any willingness to participate inevitably leads to greater demands.

But the CCF's claims on its members for time and effort have elicited a feebler response in the last decade. In riding after riding, the great majority of the members are "inactive." They renew their membership faithfully each year, if asked. But they are rarely, if ever, seen at meetings or during election campaigns. Other evidence points to the same pattern of unexcited loyalty. Of 200 members of Toronto riding executives in 1945, 77 per cent of the middle-class and 52 per cent of the working-class individuals were still CCF members ten years later. Furthermore, the average financial contribution of both active and inactive members has risen considerably in the past decade.

The inference from these facts appears to be that the CCF's limited claim on its members and their memory of a deeper commitment are the primary source both of the party's strength and weakness. Unlike more radical groups, which secure a stronger hold on the lives and emotions of their members, the CCF makes more limited claims and has a weaker hold, and thus the types of highly emotional breaks with church and party now so familiar tend to be avoided. Apparently in the CCF one can avoid serious involvement more easily or else one can drift steadily away from it and still maintain an official connection and a measure of attachment to the party. On the other hand, these claims and commitments are still sufficiently strong to obtain candidates and campaign workers (though both appear to be decreasing), greater financial contributions, and "sacrifice" candidates, and to wring from the less active majority renewals of membership, money, and occasional participation.

Perhaps the people who gave time, energy, and enthusiasm more freely in the days when money was scarce now find money more plentiful while time, energy, and interest have run low. Possibly they honour the obligations they still feel and ease their conscience by contributing in cash what they can no longer give in active participation. By doing so, they keep the party's finances and membership stable, at least for the time being. Whether the party's claims and the members' commitments can be revitalized by renewed prospects of success at the polls is a question that only time can answer.

The CCF is one of many groups that have travelled some distance along the familiar road from sect to church. Its sectarian characteristics faded rather than disappeared with prosperity and political success. The worldly achievements of many of its leaders and members helped to soothe the party's anger and obscured its vision of the "new commonwealth." It could no longer impart to its members the comforting and stimulating images of themselves as rebels against society and prophets of a new social order. Nor have such roles been in great demand in recent years and certainly not through the medium of radical politics.

The CCF became a much more conventional party in belief, organization, and participation. The morale of such a party hinges on its prospects of imminent success. The continued decline of these prospects discouraged many of the leaders and followers from active participation. The result was a still further lessening of involvement, morale, and, consequently, future prospects of success. The core of the "faithful" and the memory of a deeper involvement remain, however, as important sources of continued loyalty and stability. Whether they can arrest the downward spiral of defeat, discouragement, and diminishing interest is the question on which the CCF's survival as a national party hinges.

Notes

1. The study concentrates on the Ontario section of the CCF although at times it embraces the national organization and at others it focuses on metropolitan Toronto from which the CCF draws more votes, members, dollars, and leaders than from any other community. The information is based on observations as a participant in a riding association and numerous other CCF groups over a five-year period, and on some formal interviews and many informal conversations with a wide variety of CCF'ers. Recently the Ontario leadership very generously gave me access to its records, including the minutes of the meetings of its top councils since they began, membership records, financial data, and the like.

2. William Kornhauser, "Organizational Loyalty: A Study of Liberal and Radical Political Careers," unpublished Ph.D. thesis, University of Chicago, 1953.

3. Toronto *Daily Star*, Aug. 2, 1956.

4. Immigrants, especially British trade unionists and Labour party supporters, appear to have been an important source of CCF recruits in the latest period.

5. Minutes of the CCF national council, Jan. 13-15, 1956.

6. This development does not reflect a change in the composition of the party's general membership or of its local leaders in Toronto. No corresponding change in the ratio of middle-class to working-class members has occurred in either of these groups in the recent period. In both the second and latest periods, middle-class members constituted half the leadership of the riding associations and just over one-quarter of the total membership.

CHAPTER 4

The Union Movement in English Canada

Introduction

The Canadian labour movement is considerably more difficult to discuss than movements previously referred to. For one thing, the right of trade union members to strike is recognized in a bill passed by Parliament in 1872.[1] As a result of this and other legislation and agreements, interactions among members of trade unions, between trade unions and management, and between trade unions and other trade unions were dictated by other than *ad hoc* considerations. It can therefore be argued that routinization, as defined in the General Introduction, occurred in the labor movement, prior to the twentieth century.

This routinization notwithstanding, it is still possible, and important, to distinguish between trade union institutions and trade union movements in twentieth-century Canada. An example of the former is the United Automobile Aerospace and Agricultural Implement Workers (UAW), which has more or less set ways of dealing with management and relatively clear norms regarding the appropriate behaviour of union members and leaders. The latter is exemplified by the One Big Union (OBU) in the post World War One years. In part, impetus to the formation of the OBU was given by the inability of Eastern-dominated unions to meet the needs of large numbers of Western workers.[2] In essence, certain groups of workers felt that existing trade unions were not adequately meeting their needs; consequently, they attempted to form a new organization.[3] On a number of other occasions, throughout the twentieth century, other movements have attempted either to form new trade unions within a particular industry — the recently formed Canadian Union of Distillery Workers is an example of this process — or to form new trade union federations. The activities of the Congress of Industrial Organizations (CIO) in the thirties is an example of this latter phenomenon.[4] As stated in the General Introduction, however, it is theoretically possible, but empirically difficult, to state with clarity the point at which a movement becomes routinized.

In Canada, as in the United Kingdom, the United States, and elsewhere, the original impetus to the formation of trade unions can be found in the capitalist system of production. Even during the years when the greatest portion of the Canadian economic surplus was generated in the primary sector of the economy, industrial enterprise was becoming more and more a fact of urban life. Coincident with the development of industry was the formation, by the 1870's, of protective institutions like the Canadian Iron Founders Association and the Association for the Promotion of Canadian Industry.[5] At the same time, as a result of low wages, mechanization and the consequent unemployment of skilled workers, by the middle of the last century, Canadian workers were beginning to form protective associations of their own.[6] Such institutions were premised on the philosophy that "organized self-help is the best reliance for improving the lot of wage-workers in a capitalist society."[7] The goal of these institutions was therefore self-evident: to actually improve the lot of the worker in capitalist Canadian society. On a number of occasions throughout Canadian history the realization of this goal has meant the involvement of Canadian labour in politics. Perhaps the clearest example of this can be seen in the current New Democratic Party.[8]

With an increase, throughout the late nineteenth and the twentieth centuries, in the numbers of individuals engaged in manufacturing enterprises, it is not surprising that the numbers of trade unionists likewise increased. It should not be assumed, however, that the growth of the Canadian industrial labour force and trade unions went hand in hand. Speaking of the Canadian trade unions as they had developed by the middle of the twentieth century, H.A. Logan commented that "growth has been spasmodic and by no means has it paralleled the growth of the gainfully occupied part of the population or even of the portion working for hire."[9] Despite an erratic pattern of growth, the overall trend, however, is toward increased unionization of non-agricultural workers. In 1921, for example, 16.0% of the Canadian non-agricultural working force was unionized. In 1968 the corresponding figure was 33.1%.[10]

Perhaps the two greatest benefits resulting from unionization are that wage settlements can be negotiated by the union on behalf of all workers who are part of a defined "bargaining unit", and that limits are imposed on the type of treatment meted out by employers. These objectives can, on many occasions, be obtained through management-union negotiations. Where such negotiations are not fruitful, however, phenomena ranging from company lockouts of workers to strikes of workers against employers are not infrequent.* Often in Canadian

---

*It should not be necessary to point out that lockouts, along with other forms of arbitrary treatment, are more likely to occur where no unions are established.

history, as indicated by the Winnipeg General Strike of 1919, the Stratford furniture workers' strike of 1933, and the 1971 strike of teachers and civil servants in Quebec, the power of the state, as exercised by the police or military, is more in keeping with the interests of employers than of employees.[11]

In addition to the actual formation of trade unions that can act on behalf of large numbers of workers, in Canada and elsewhere, union federations have also been viewed as a means of achieving workers' goals.[12] The original stimulus to the formation of federations is found in the same source as unions themselves — the capitalist system of production.

Throughout the late nineteenth and twentieth centuries, industrial enterprises have expanded operations beyond the boundaries of particular towns and cities. The current operations of large industrial concerns, in fact, involve transactions that defy national boundaries.[13] In Canada, this process of expansion has been marked by increasing numbers of American take-overs of Canadian enterprises and, in crucial sectors of the Canadian economy, such as the petrochemical industry, the domination by American subsidiaries like Gulf Oil Canada. The consequences of these economic developments are well documented and will not be discussed here. Suffice it to say that, in part, union federations emerged as a response to the expansive dynamic in industrial capitalism that eventually led to these developments.

With industrial expansion in the nineteenth century, it became clear to workers that their success in employee-management confrontations required the prevention of strike-breakers from finding jobs in other towns and cities. At the same time, it was essential, during a strike, to prevent employers from acquiring labour from other areas. In addition, during strikes, local union funds were often insufficient to tide workers over difficult times. The logical response to these circumstances was the formation of large-scale union federations that would help meet these needs. As industrial capitalism became increasingly continental, it was also felt that so-called "international" (American) union federations were more appropriate forms of labour organization than organizations based on particular crafts or industries within Canada.[14] The American Federation of Labour (AFL) and previously mentioned CIO are two very important "international" federations that have operated within Canadian society.

The overall significance of the "international" to Canadian society is clearly revealed in figures regarding the involvement of Canadian workers within these organizations. In 1911, 89.7% of all unionized workers were in some way affiliated with an "international". By 1972 the proportion had dropped to 59.6%. This figure, however, still represents a sizeable portion of the Canadian industrial labour force.[15]

While it can be argued that affiliation with "international" unions, in some cases, may have resulted in increased funds for further union organization and in better wage settlements, there have been significant costs to the Canadian worker. These are concisely summarized by David Kwavnick: "Between 1902 and the [TLC-CCL]* merger of 1956," he argues, "the outstanding feature of the Canadian labour movement was the series of schisms induced and expulsions imposed from without in response to the organizational needs of the AFL leadership."[16] "The evolution of the Canadian labour movement," he adds, "was clearly governed by the needs and ambitions of American labour leaders rather than by the needs of Canadian labour."[17] Clearly, for Canadian workers, the international federation has been a mixed blessing.

In a book of readings on social movements in general, it is impossible to include readings on all processes previously referred to. (The reader is advised to consult some of the sources referred to in the footnotes for additional material on these matters.) In addition, some aspects of the previous discussion deal more with labour institutions than with labour movements. For these reasons, it was decided, in this chapter, only to include readings on the formation of the One Big Union, the beginnings of the Congress of Industrial Organizations in Canada, and current trade union nationalism. Each of these readings deals with one or more of the features of social movements raised in the General Introduction or in the introduction to this chapter. The article on the One Big Union, for example, demonstrates, for one thing, how social segmentation between East and West contributed to the acceptance of the "one big union" concept. More importantly, it provides an example of unsuccessful institutionalization. Irving Abella's discussion of the CIO very effectively demonstrates reaction to a movement by certain interests in society. Terrence White's article, in turn, is a clear example of how feelings of relative deprivation, under certain circumstances, lead to the development of new institutions.

*The Trades and Labour Congress of Canada (TLC) and the Canadian Congress of Labour (CCL) merged and formed the Canadian Labour Congress (CLC).

Notes

1. H.A. Logan, *Trade Unions in Canada*, Toronto: Macmillan, 1948, p. 41.
2. Stuart Jamieson, *Industrial Relations in Canada*, Toronto: Macmillan, 1973, p. 20.
3. This distinction parallels one made by Hurbert Blumer from a different theoretical perspective. He distinguishes between general social movements that focus on value changes in a culture and specific social movements that centre on more immediate or local concerns. See H. Blumer, "Social Movements," in B. McLaughlin (ed.), *Studies in Social Movements*, New York: Free Press, 1969.
4. For a full discussion of early CIO activities in Canada see I. Abella, *Nationalism, Communism, and Canadian Labour*, Toronto: University of Toronto Press, 1973.

5. Steven Langdon, "The Emergence of the Canadian Working Class Movement, 1845-75," *Journal of Canadian Studies*, viii, no. 2, (May, 1973), p. 4.

6. *Ibid.*, p. 6.

7. Logan, *Trade Unions in Canada*, p. 1.

8. For a discussion of Canadian labour in politics see the following sources: M. Robin, *Radical Politics and Canadian Labour: 1880-1930*, Kingston: Industrial Relations Centre, 1968. G. Horowitz, *Canadian Labour in Politics*, Toronto: University of Toronto Press, 1968. David Kwavnick, *Organized Labour and Pressure Politics*, Montreal: McGill-Queen's University Press, 1972.

9. Logan, *Trade Unions in Canada*, p. 3.

10. A.M. Kruger, "The Direction of Unionism in Canada," in R.U. Miller et al. (eds.), *Canadian Labour in Transition*, Scarborough: Prentice-Hall, 1971, p. 94.

11. For an interesting discussion of several strikes see I. Abella, *On Strike*, Toronto: James Lewis and Samuel, 1974. Other relevant sources include: D.C. Masters, *The Winnipeg General Strike*, Toronto: University of Toronto Press, 1950. Norman Penner (ed.), *Winnipeg 1919*, Toronto: James Lewis and Samual, 1973. P.E. Trudeau, *La grève de l'amiante*, Montreal: Editions du jour, 1970.

12. It must not be assumed, however, that the trade union movement is the same in all countries. For a short comparative discussion of Canadian trade unions see M. Robin, "Determinants of Radical Labour and Socialist Politics in English-Speaking Canada Between 1880 and 1930," *Journal of Canadian Studies*, ii, no. 2, (May, 1967). The introduction to Jamieson's book, *op cit.*, is also useful in this respect.

13. See Kari Levitt, *Silent Surrender*, Toronto: Macmillan, 1972.

14. See Steven Langdon, "The Emergence of the Canadian Working-Class Movement, 1845-75," and Stuart Jamieson, *Industrial Relations in Canada*, to name only two relevant sources.

15. T.H. White, "Canadian Labour and International Unions in the Seventies," below.

16. D. Kwavnick, *Organized Labour and Pressure Politics*, p. 34.

17. *Ibid.* For a further discussion of international unionism see John Crispo, *International Unionism*, Toronto: McGraw-Hill, 1967.

Western Labour Radicalism and the One Big Union: Myths and Realities

David J. Bercuson

"Be careful lest you lose hold of the substance in reaching out for the shadow." With these words David Rees, vice-president of the Trades and Labour Congress of Canada, official of the United Mine Workers of America, and convenor of the Western Labour Conference of March, 1919, warned Canadian union members of the destructive potential of the new One Big Union.[1] Rees was a devoted advocate of the idea that militant westerners ought to combine with progressive easterners to crush the conservative establishment of the Trades and Labour Congress but his beliefs have been buried in the confusion of events surrounding the birth of the One Big Union. There is, nevertheless, reason to believe that he and his supporters represented the mainstream of western labour radicalism while the OBU which he opposed was an aberration not reflective of the special needs or desires of western workers.

Historians of the Canadian labour movement have never quite decided what to make of the One Big Union. They have even had difficulty defining it: the most common description compares the OBU with the American-based Industrial Workers of the World. D.C. Masters, in his study of the Winnipeg general strike, wrote that the main differences between the OBU and the IWW were organizational since, in reality, the One Big Union was ". . . a conspiracy to secure control of the country. . . ."[2] Stuart Jamieson, in a brief survey of Canadian labour history, observed that the OBU ". . . proclaimed a doctrine of revolutionary unionism similar in some respects to that of the IWW and launched a program to organize workers by industries rather than by trade."[3] H.A. Logan described the OBU in his chapter on organizations dedicated to violent overthrow of the government as ". . . an outstanding example of revolutionary unionism . . ." similar in some respects to the old Knights of Labour.[4] Recently Professor Martin Robin has disputed these interpretations and written of the OBU that it was not revolutionary in its final form and that its leaders had

Reprinted from S. Trofimenkoff (ed.), *The Twenties in Western Canada*, Ottawa: National Museum of Man, 1972, pp. 32-49. Source: The National Museum of Man of the National Museums of Canada. Reproduction authorized by Information Canada.

ceased to threaten mass action by the time of the founding convention in June 1919. Its constitution, he noted, did not contain ". . . the typical syndicalist reference to the trade union as the instrument of administration in the new society."[5]

The dry facts of the OBU's sudden appearance and just as sudden demise are well known and a brief summary should suffice here. In March 1919, at a conference of western trade unionists called for the purpose of forming a left-wing caucus within the Trades and Labour Congress, the idea of secession, pushed by several key militants, swept all before it. Attending delegates decided to opt for withdrawal from the American Federation of Labor and the Trades and Labour Congress and to create an infrastructure for a new radical organization predicated upon a Marxian analysis of society and designed to unite all workers in Canada into a single union. Three months later, at the beginning of June, their work reached fruition with the founding of the One Big Union.[6]

From the instant of its birth the OBU expanded rapidly across the west but made almost no progress east of the Lakehead. Lodges, trades councils, and provincial federations from Thunder Bay to Vancouver Island withdrew from the International Unions and threw their lot in with the OBU. By the end of the year the OBU's membership hovered around the fifty thousand mark. Alarmed AFL/TLC forces undertook a serious campaign to recapture western Canada for the exclusivist and conservative principles of Gompersism, Internationalism, and craft unionism.[7] The effort, aided by the active assistance of coal mine owners in the Crow's Nest Pass area who concluded *de facto* closed shop agreements with the AFL/TLC unions[8], was further enhanced by public officials who believed the OBU was about to ". . . kick the government off parliament hill . . ." as C.H. Cahan had warned Prime Minister Robert Borden.[9] The war of attrition undermined the foundations of the OBU and by the end of 1922 it had ceased to be a power of any consequence in Canada.

On the whole, scant attention has been paid to the One Big Union and hardly more to the broader problem of western labour's independence of thought and action. Indeed most of the interest aroused by the OBU has been in its meteoric demise. Behind that interest seems to lie an assumption that the factors contributing to western labour radicalism have been so completely studied here and in the United States that it should not be hard to explain the OBU's emergence. But given that set of factors, historians are at a loss to explain the union's rapid downfall.

If conditions in the west stimulated the growth of a radical union why did they not sustain it? I would suggest that the rise and fall of the One Big Union are inextricably connected and further that the decline was in large measure due to the fact that the OBU bore little or no resemblance to the needs and desires of western union members. The OBU, in other words, was initially successful precisely because western workers did not fully realize what the delegates at the

Western Labour Conference had created; when they did begin to find out in the next twelve to eighteen months they left the One Big Union almost as fast as they had joined it. The One Big Union may have been one manifestation of western labour radicalism but it did not suit the needs of western workers and shortchanged them organizationally, industrially and ideologically.

During four years of war the number of trade unionists in Canada increased by approximately 100%[10] — a dramatic growth by any estimate. Organizational efforts were almost always accompanied by a growth of militancy especially in the days before the union shop or automatic checkoff when a union had to show prospective members the advantages of carrying a card and had to be able to protect workers from the vagaries of the market or the arbitrariness of employers. This created a more militant approach to industrial problems and when combined with the effects of the cost of living and other factors peculiar to the west,[11] created a climate in which union members began to reject the approaches and methods of the AFL/TLC and sought new solutions to their problems.

By the end of the war westerners were interested in protecting what they had already achieved in terms of numbers and influence, and in further extending their power. These two ambitions precipitated a drive for more intense political action and an attempt to construct industrial unions. In the spring and summer of 1919 ample evidence presented itself to labour leaders that thousands of workers were ripe for organization; for example, close to twenty thousand non-union workers joined the Winnipeg general strike of May and June.[12]

In addition to reaching for new members and greater strength, union leaders were determined to hold on to the more important gains made during the war. New members had been attracted and new trades had been organized including civic workers, police, firemen, and store clerks.[13] Metal and building trades councils sprang up all over the country while every railroad shop craft union in Canada united to form Division #4, Railroad Employees Department, American Federation of Labor, which bargained as a single unit with the combined management of the major Canadian railways and was instrumental in gaining wage parity with United States' railway workers in the summer of 1918.[14] Westerners were usually in the forefront of these moves to create larger combinations — they dominated the executive of Division #4 and the headquarters was in Winnipeg.[15]

The ambition to conserve and extend union power found an outlet in the tendency to increased political action and organization of industrial unions. Labour's participation in politics had been increasing constantly since the turn of the century. The greater number of labour representatives to be found in provincial and municipal governments across the prairies and in B.C. as the war progressed is evidence that the belief in electoral action was still strong and growing in 1918. Labour candidates continued to contest and hold office after the conscription election of December 1917, and those Alberta delegates to the

Western Labour Conference who supported more political action by labour were probably not alone in their beliefs. In Ontario, British Columbia, and Manitoba, efforts were directed in 1918 to the formation of new labour parties.[16] Although those who believed in direct action and disavowed electoral activity had obviously come to the fore at Calgary in March 1919 and were to rule the roost in the OBU, one must seriously question whether they reflected the opinion of most western union members. Even the Winnipeg Central Labour Council of the OBU, formed in July 1919, involved itself fully in the drive to elect labour candidates in the municipal election of December 1919 and the provincial election of 1920.[17] Bob Russell, member of the OBU executive, was a candidate in that election.[18]

The west's affinity for industrial unionism is well known but what is less clear is what was understood by the term. The combination of all workers in a given industry into one union was generally considered desirable by westerners because the nature of industry was thought to lend itself to this form of organization. Phillips points out that western workers usually toiled in a few given occupations: distribution, resource extraction in the form of lumbering and mining, or construction and transportation.[19] The last three are particularly conducive to industrial organization. The resource industry consists of different productive units engaged in the same type of operation — several different mines or logging camps doing essentially the same work. For all intents and purposes, there were few craft divisions to begin with and the semi-skilled nature of the work tended to blur what distinctions did exist. Hence mining unions have always been industrial unions — the Western Federation of Miners, the United Mine Workers of America, the International Union of Mine, Mill, and Smelter Workers. The same situation applied to logging and lumbering and created conditions favourable to the rise of mass unions. The Lumber Workers Industrial Union and the International Woodworkers of America are both good examples.

The building and transportation industries were different but here also there were strong reasons for the attempt to create industrial unions. The existence of a great many craft divisions in one industry made bargaining and grievance settlement more difficult and did not allow unions to place a great deal of pressure on management in the event of a strike or lockout. For example, in Winnipeg in 1918 there existed unions representing thirteen independent trades connected with construction and fourteen types of lodges in the transportation industry.[20] This lack of unity created a desire on the part of some workers to forge a smaller number of larger unions in each industry — a desire that had been expressed in mid-1914, for instance, when the General Executive Board of the International Association of Machinists initiated an unsuccessful move to have all metalworkers join together in an industrial union.[21]

These conditions, combined with a multitude of problems related to the war and reconstruction, prompted several western unionists to plan a meeting sometime before the annual TLC convention in 1919 so that left-wing supporters from all over Canada could forge a united policy. Such was the origin of the Western Labour Conference, but the policies and activities of that meeting and the new organization which eventually resulted from it fulfilled almost none of the desires of militant westerners and was almost solely the brain-child of a handful of men seized with the syndicalist idea to the virtual exclusion of everything else. Though, as Professor Robin has correctly pointed out, there was some difference between what was said at Calgary in March and what was adopted at the founding convention of the OBU in June,[22] the structures of the new union did not change and the ideas which lay behind them were only slightly altered.

The One Big Union was born as a syndicalist solution to western problems. Syndicalism may be defined as a doctrine which espouses the ownership by workers of all means of production and distribution in society. This was to be achieved through massive general strikes waged by highly centralized trade union federations in which individual workers would owe their allegiance to the federation; divisions of craft and industry would be primarily technical; and final authority would be vested in the leaders of the federation.

In many respects the OBU closely followed this general pattern. Its leaders, however, were vague about the use of general strikes and eventual worker control of industry. But they were convinced of the necessity of a high degree of centralization and actively pursued the construction of one all-embracing union to which every worker would owe his primary allegiance. In this they followed the old Grand National Consolidated Trade Union which had intended to organize every worker in Britain, skilled and unskilled, in a single massive organization capable of bringing the combined weight of the working class to bear against any opponent.

Westerners wanted industrial unionism but the One Big Union did not give it to them. The OBU was called an industrial union, and historians have unfortunately continued to use the term, but it was not. An industrial union is intended to enfold all workers in a *given* industry and thus the lumber workers and coal and metal miners were organized into industrial unions, but the OBU was an all-inclusive centre which, in a hazy way, was supposed to bring together every worker in the country from all industries. It was thus certainly not an industrial union in the sense that the CIO was to become one. The OBU was, if anything, a gloss of syndicalism over a structure of craft exclusiveness. The 'important trades', as they were termed at the Western Labour Conference, were to have the deciding voice in the vote for secession[23] from the TLC; very few general workers' units were ever set up[24]; and there was almost no effort to destroy existing lines of craft division. The only change made by the OBU in many areas was that small locals became large ones. For example, all boilermaker's lodges in a given vicinity were united into one unit but remained separate and distinct from other metal workers. In Winnipeg the OBU organized eight railway, four garment, and three building units.[25] Machinists in the contract shops and the railway shops were kept separate.[26] The degree of organization by industry rather than by craft was hardly greater here than in the Internationals.

There were only three constituent parts of the One Big Union which by any stretch of definition could be termed industrial unions: the Lumber Workers Industrial Union, the Coal Miners District Board No. 1, and the Metal Miners District Board No. 1.[27] These were not formed by the One Big Union, however, but existed as separate industrial unions before the formation of the OBU: the coal miners as District 18 of the UMWA, the loggers as the Lumber Workers Industrial Union, and the metal miners as the International Union of Mine, Mill, and Smelter Workers, the very new version of the Western Federation of Miners. Even here, however, true industrial unions could not find a home in the OBU since the loggers, the most successful and numerous of the industrial units, withdrew from the OBU precisely because they could not live with its organizational conceptions.[28]

If we are to accept the definition of industrial unionism later used by those who organized the Congress of Industrial Organizations or the one used by the loggers, street railway men, and coal and metal miners, the OBU does not match up. It never was an industrial union, though what it was may never be clear. As early as September 1918, Rev. William Ivens, editor of the Winnipeg-based *Western Labor News*, used the term 'industrial union' to describe a syndicalist organization beginning to emerge in Australia.[29] The term subsequently became increasingly obscure as men such as Ivens, R.B. Russell, and others continued to refer to the concept of one all-embracing syndicalist centre as an industrial union.[30] When these men spoke to the rank and file in union halls across the west they meant one thing but their audience probably interpreted their words in an entirely different manner. The slogan 'organization by industry' was widely known by that time but it did not mean organization of all workers in all industries into one union. The latter is what the ardent advocates of the OBU wanted it to mean and they were relatively successful in convincing many thousands of union members throughout the west that the organizational set-up that the OBU was offering was what the workers had been waiting for.

There were many thousands of workers in Canada at the end of the war waiting to hear the message of trade unionism. Western militants were interested in continuing the massive organizing drives of the war years; they may well have expected the One Big Union to reach into new fields to attract members. If so they were sorely disappointed. Almost no effort at all was directed towards workers who were not already in a union of one sort or another — usually an international craft union. It might be argued that the One Big Union never had time to initiate any significant organizing campaigns amongst those outside the pale of organized labour, but, if such were the case, it is difficult to explain the massive effort to recruit members of craft unions to the OBU in western Canada, the activities of organizer Joe Knight in Ontario and Quebec,[31] and membership campaigns conducted in Chicago, California, Montana, and other areas of the United States.[32] The One Big Union did not 'organize the unorganized' primarily because it never made the attempt. In this failure it was certainly not fulfilling the aspirations of many Canadian workers who were interested in organizing the new mass-production industries.

The One Big Union also attempted to reverse a deeply-running current of western radicalism in its opposition to labour parliamentary activity.[33] This remained a basic OBU belief; that workers were wasting time engaging in electoral activity and ought to confine themselves to industrial action, preferably direct strike action, which, it was claimed, was the purest form of political activity.[34] But western labour men had been involved in electoral activity since before the turn of the century and had achieved significant successes at the provincial and municipal level particularly in British Columbia and Manitoba. The whole thrust of their thinking, as Professor Robin has pointed out, was towards even greater electoral activity as shown by their reaction to the registration and conscription issues in 1916 and 1917 when labour candidates entered new fields in increasing numbers.[35] Many of the delegates who attended the Calgary convention in March 1919 were under the impression that new and more effective political action was about to be undertaken. Instead, the syndicalists at the conference thwarted the arguments of those who favoured labour electoral activity. The victory, however, was a pyrrhic one because this rejection sterilized the OBU's ideas and marked it as a 'one approach' organization. The approach was obviously too limiting, as evinced by some OBU Central Labour Councils who continued to support labour parliamentary activity in the period after the Winnipeg general strike.

Thus the One Big Union was not the complete fulfilment of the hopes and desires of radicals and progressives in western Canada or indeed in the east. It was a tangential movement which appeared to some to be the embodiment of all that progressives desired but was not. The deviation between the mainstream of western labour radicalism and the OBU took place at the Calgary convention of March 1919. There, a handful of dedicated believers in the syndicalist future wrested control of events and thrust them towards the fulfilment of their own desires. The conference was skillfully guided by Jack Kavanagh, W.A. Pritchard, and Victor Midgley, aided by the convention's policy committee and individuals such as R.B. Russell.[36] These men were tireless workers, well known and admired in union circles, and were able to carry the day with the approximately two hundred and thirty other delegates. The points which the conference was supposed to discuss were completely avoided as the leaders sold the convention on the idea of creating a radical union as the fulfilment of their ambitions. They conveyed the impression of clear thinking, decisiveness, and unblemished radicalism and sold the One Big Union without any clear explanation of what was involved. The delegates in Calgary, indeed union members all across the west, were ready to hear angry words in the spring of 1919; the leaders of the Western Labour Conference translated this readiness into an initial acceptance of secession and, they claimed, of industrial unionism.

The Conference had been called to organize a radical and progressive caucus prior to the TLC convention in 1919. David Rees' ideas adequately reflect the original intentions of the Conference organizers and give an insight into the aspirations of many thousands of radical westerners who opposed the One Big Union after its formation. Rees thought there was great utility in calling westerners together to forge a progressive policy that could attract a sufficient number of eastern votes to enable them to face up to the conservative, craft-oriented leadership of the TLC.[37] In his mind, "A well reasoned, rational programme carried by the Western conference [would] be accepted by the Canadian Labor movement generally."[38]

Rees was an official of the United Mine Workers of America and was well aware of the benefits and advantages to certain classes of workers of organization by industry but he was willing to go still further. He believed large and powerful trade unions should act together to weld a concerted policy and put out a unified set of demands — the United Big Organization, he called his scheme after the formation of the OBU.[39] Rees would probably have pointed to the railway workers' formation of Division #4 as an example of several unions acting in concert and increasing their bargaining power in the process. He also supported his own union's programme of the six-hour day, nationalization of mines, and substantial wage increases.[40] These were hardly the ideas of a conservative follower of Samuel Gompers, but they were never discussed at the March convention. Rees opened the meeting as planned, reiterated his opposition to secession, and then left to attend a UMWA meeting in the United States.[41] Even had he stayed, it is doubtful whether he could have swayed the conference, for the syndicalist idea had already taken deep root.

In his study of the Winnipeg general strike, D.C. Masters traced the roots of the One Big Union to the Owenite Grand National Consolidated Trades Union, founded in Great Britain in 1834. The link between this British syndicalist movement and the Canadian west was the group of radical British immigrants who had been active members of unions or socialist political parties in Great Britain, had picked up the Owenite tradition as a millennialist solution to working-class difficulties and had emigrated to Canada — R.J. Johns, John Queen, R.B. Russell, W.A. Pritchard, and W. Ivens in particular.[42] Any brief study of the Consolidated adds weight to Masters' contention[43], because its form and structures closely resembled those of the OBU: both were intended to bring together all workers from all industries into one organization. But of what relevance was the basic philosophy of the Grand National Consolidated Trades Union of the 1830's to the twentieth-century Canadian west? The ideas behind

Owenite philosophy were at best utopian and visionary and it is difficult to see how they might have appealed to practical union men in the post-war setting. The philosophy might have found favourable reception amongst thousands of unorganized workers in Canada but was never carried to them. Those workers who were interested in reform and reorganization of the existing union structure wanted to make specific changes in society and believed true industrial unionism would increase their strength at the bargaining table. Many union veterans were probably hard pressed to see how one big union of all skilled, semi-skilled, and unskilled workers, sometimes organized into geographic units and sometimes into industrial ones, could be any help to them at all. One could hardly blame them if they eventually failed to see any advantage over the existing craft union system, as bad as they might have considered it.

The speeches and activities of many westerners who did not join the One Big Union are an indication that a radical group remained outside the OBU and continued to fight for progressive ideals within the mainstream of the Canadian labour movement after June 1919. At the TLC convention in 1919 westerners defended the leaders of the Winnipeg general strike while two prominent members of the pre-strike Trades Council were in attendance as delegates and sought to explain the circumstances surrounding the walkout. George Armstrong, member of the Socialist Party of Canada, and Ernie Robinson, Labour Party alderman and secretary of the Winnipeg Trades Council, had strongly supported the Western Labour Conference in March and the Winnipeg strike in May but they chose to stay with the Internationals. Other western delegates complained of the lack of adequate western representation in the TLC and the ignorance of US union leaders of Canadian conditions. Westerners too suggested amalgamation of some existing unions into industrial units, all the while warning the delegates that the rapid western successes of the OBU were due to real grievances, not the machinations of a few 'evil' geniuses.[44] All their ideas and resolutions were crushed, however, possibly because of the absence of a strong, unified, progressive delegation. Who in fact had castrated the progressives, President Tom Moore and Secretary P.M. Draper of the Trades Congress or the founders of the OBU? The existence of Trades Councils in Vancouver and Winnipeg[45] loyal to the AFL/TLC and yet opposed to Gompersism and in favour of progressive change suggests it may well have been Russell, Kavanagh, and company who wielded the knife; the support of those who left the Trades Congress to chase a dream might have been sufficient to bring about some real radical changes.

A list of westerners who actively opposed the One Big Union or remained with the international unions after the beginning of the syndicalist revolt reads like a "who's who" of western progressivism. It is easy to see that their credentials as representatives of the desires and aspirations of westerners were at least as worthy as those of the supporters of the OBU. R.A. Rigg, who, as President Moore's special representative, led the TLC counterattack on the OBU was a member of the Social Democratic Party, former Winnipeg Trades Council Secretary, Labour Party alderman, and SDP member of the Manitoba legislature. Most of the executive of the pre-general strike Winnipeg Trades Council — James Winning, J.L. McBride, and Ernie Robinson — stayed out of the OBU. A. Farmilo of Alberta had been a bitter opponent of conscription and a supporter, in 1917, of a national general strike; R.J. Tallon of Calgary was Chairman of Division #4; J. McVety, W.R. Trotter, and J.W. Wilkinson were all members of the Federated Labour Party while E.T. Kingsley and R.P. Pettipiece were former members of the Socialist Party of Canada; George Armstrong, from Winnipeg, still carried an SPC membership card;[46] all of them opposed the One Big Union. The fact that organized and progressive opposition to the OBU continued during the summer and fall of 1919 ought not to be ignored any longer for it demonstrates that many progressives were not willing to leave the way clear for the OBU and that those who opposed the OBU were not all, as popular belief might have it, reactionaries who slavishly supported the conservative, craft-exclusive ideas of Samuel Gompers.

The west was not alone in harbouring progressives who desired to change existing union structures and who might have supported realistic proposals for transition. The same TLC convention in 1919 also heard easterners who expressed great dissatisfaction with prevalent conditions. Some advocated amalgamation of certain unions while others believed, with their western brothers, that OBU successes were due to the existence of real grievances. Many were very unhappy about the relationship between rank and file union members and their leaders in the United States.[47] If the One Big Union had not been what it was — a flight of fancy that sapped the strength of western radicalism — many more easterners might have supported it.

The OBU's singular lack of success in the east cannot be blamed solely on International opposition or lack of publicity. One Big Union leaders were well aware of how important eastern support was to their movement and made special efforts to attract members there. Central Labour Councils were set up in Hamilton, Toronto, and Thunder Bay, and twenty-two local units were established in Ontario, including nine in the Thunder Bay area, three in Hamilton, and three in Toronto.[48] In addition, Joe Knight arranged with the editor of an eastern labour paper, the *New Democracy*, to have the journal act as the eastern voice of the OBU; it published 5000 copies for six weeks before closing down.[49] Knight was able to attend several meetings in Montreal, Toronto, and Northern Ontario[50] but had much trouble getting his message across. One must wonder whether this was caused by the method of transmission or the content.

It is now time to take a long hard look at the One Big Union to explain why so many westerners accepted it at first but then turned against it or away from it, while easterners were never attracted to it at all. Westerners and easterners alike knew what labour historians have overlooked — that the OBU, stripped of the rhetoric of radicalism, was impractical, unsuitable, and not a true reflection of the needs or desires of labour progressives. Craft unions may have been unsuitable for resource extraction and railroad workers, but many of the former were already organized in industrial unions, while the latter had their Division #4 after 1918. Compared to either association the OBU was ghost-like, unsophisticated, and inefficient; any transition from existing union structures to the OBU would in reality have been a step backwards. The OBU's rhetoric was certainly more militant, but fiery words alone are useless. It would be a great mistake, therefore, to consider the OBU as the sole or indeed the prime representative of the radical mainstream of western Canada. It was born as a result of a coup — the capture of the Western Labour Conference — and there is convincing evidence to show that many who opposed the OBU in the west were just as representative of the progressive mainstream as the secessionists.

In this light it is possible that a prime reason for the OBU's failure was that it actually ran counter to the deeply engrained traditions of western labour radicals who believed in socialist political action and industrial unionism as twin weapons in the fight against the capitalist system. Just because the leaders of the OBU were second-to-none in their denunciations of capitalism does not mean they represented the aspirations of western union members in their syndicalist desires as well. True, they were all union men with close connections to the rank and file but they were blinded by their zealous espousal of a panacea that had been proven impractical in Great Britain almost ninety years before.

Undoubtedly the traditions of western labour radicalism and progressivism added greatly to the zeal with which the OBU idea was espoused. Then too, existing conditions prepared the ground for the initial acceptance of what was in essence a blank cheque never properly filled in, organizationally or ideologically. The OBU was not a faithful child of western labour radicalism and did not reflect the true desires of westerners, or, for that matter, progressive easterners. The tendency to over-romanticize the aims and accomplishments of the IWW has recently emerged in the United States, not only among young radicals but also in scholarly works.[51] The same is true to a lesser degree in Canada. Let us proceed therefore to take a new, hard look at the traditions of Canadian labour radicalism and the organizations which it spawned.

Notes

1. Public Archives of Manitoba (PAM), Rigg/Rees Papers and Correspondence. Clipping from *Calgary Herald* (Calgary) "OBU or UBO," N.D.
2. D.C. Masters, *The Winnipeg General Strike* (Toronto, 1950), p. 133.
3. S. Jamieson, *Industrial Relations in Canada* (Toronto, 1957), p. 40.
4. H.A. Logan, *Trade Unions in Canada* (Toronto, 1948), pp. 329-330.
5. M. Robin, *Radical Politics and Canadian Labour* (Kingston, 1968), pp. 188-89.
6. See Canada, *Annual Report on Labour Organization*, 1920, pp. 23 ff.
7. *Ibid.*
8. *Ibid.*
9. Public Archives of Canada (PAC), Borden Papers, OC 564, C.H. Cahan to Borden, May 28, 1919.
10. See monthly statistics presented in Canada, *Labour Gazette.*
11. See, for example, Paul Phillips, "The National Policy and the Development of the Western Canadian Labour Movement," unpublished paper presented to the Western Canadian Studies Conference, February 1970.
12. According to government statistics there were approximately 12,000 trade union members in Winnipeg at the beginning of May 1919 while most estimates of the number of strikers fall between twenty-five and thirty-five thousand.
13. See *Annual Report on Labour Organization*, especially 1917-1919 for a picture of the massive organizing drives conducted and a report on the establishment of unions amongst new classes of workers.
14. *Manitoba Free Press* (Winnipeg), July 20, 1918, p. 4.
15. *The Voice* (Winnipeg), March 8, 1918, p. 8.
16. Some of these efforts are covered in Robin, pp. 138 ff.
17. *Ibid.*, pp. 203-205.
18. *Ibid.*
19. Phillips, pp. 8-9.
20. *Annual Report on Labour Organization*, 1918, pp. 163-166.
21. *Bulletin* (Winnipeg), May 1914, p. 8.
22. Robin, p. 189.
23. See *Annual Report on Labour Organization in Canada*, 1919, for a brief but accurate report of the convention proceedings, pp. 22-27.
24. *Ibid.*, pp. 36-38. Only ten were established in the entire country.
25. *Ibid.*, p. 37.
26. *Ibid.*
27. *Ibid.*, pp. 36-38.
28. *Annual Report on Labour Organization in Canada*, 1920, pp. 29 ff; Robin, p. 193.
29. *Western Labor News* (Winnipeg), September 13, 1918, p. 8.
30. See, for example, *ibid.*, November 22, 1918, p. 6 and January 3, 1919, p. 1.
31. Report of Proceedings, First Semi-Annual Convention of the One Big Union, January 1920 (Typewritten).
32. *Ibid.*; Logan, pp. 322, 325.
33. Robin, pp. 175-176.
34. *Ibid.*
35. *Ibid.*, pp. 121-137.
36. *Ibid.*, pp. 173-177.
37. *Calgary Herald*, December 19, 1918.
38. *Ibid.*
39. PAM, Rigg/Rees Papers and Correspondence. Clipping from *Calgary Herald*, "OBU or UBO."
40. *Calgary Herald*, April 9, 1919.
41. PAM, Rigg/Rees Papers and Correspondence. Rees to D. Millar, September 30, 1965.
42. Masters, pp. 24 ff.
43. See, for example, G.D.H. Cole, *The Life of Robert Owen* (London, 1965), pp. 276-281 or A.L. Morton, *The Life and Ideas of Robert Owen* (London, 1962), pp. 44-46.

44. See *TLC Proceedings, 1919* to trace the course of the various debates, especially pp. 128-129, 164-172, 158-159, 190-192.

45. Paul Phillips, *No Power Greater* (Vancouver, 1967), p. 85. The arguments of Winnipeg Trades Council delegates Robinson and Armstrong at the TLC convention in 1919 should be taken as proof of their anti-establishment bias. See *TLC Proceedings, 1919*, pp. 158, 190-191.

46. The political affiliations of these men are determined from Prof. Robin's work.

47. See, for example, speeches and resolutions presented on pp. 166 and 190 of *TLC Proceedings, 1919*.

48. *Annual Report on Labour Organization in Canada*, 1919, pp. 35-36.

49. Report of Proceedings, First Semi-Annual Convention of the One Big Union, January 1920 (Typewritten).

50. *Ibid.*

51. See W. Preston, "Shall This Be All? U.S. Historians Versus William D. Haywood et al." *Labor History* (Summer 1971), p. 436.

Oshawa 1937

Irving Abella

As a landmark in the history of the Canadian labour movement the Oshawa strike of 1937 stands next only to the Winnipeg General Strike. In many ways, however, the two-week walkout of some four thousand General Motors workers in Oshawa, Ontario, in April of 1937 had the more permanent impact. Though it lacked the blood and violence — but not the passion — of the Winnipeg strike, the Oshawa strike must be regarded as perhaps the most significant labour event of the past fifty years. Not only did it mark the birth of industrial unionism in Canada but, perhaps as important, it had a convulsive and lasting effect on the Canadian political scene.

Oshawa in the 1930s was a trim, bustling, middle-size community situated less than thirty miles east of Toronto, not yet the commuter suburb it has since become. People who lived in Oshawa then tended to work there as well. It was the market centre for a good farming district, but its basic industry was, as it still is, automobiles.

In the early 1920s the giant General Motors Company of the United States purchased the struggling McLaughlin Carriage Works of Oshawa and built a huge assembly plant on the outskirts of town. Within a few years more than three thousand men were employed there producing more cars for the Canadian and Empire market than the combined output of the rest of Canada. The relationship between workers and management was never harmonious. Low wages, unsafe working conditions and lack of job security finally prompted a walkout of most of the company's employees in March of 1928. Within a week the company submitted to the workers' demands and the strike was called off.

Encouraged by the success of this display of muscle, the workers then organized themselves into a union and applied to the Trades and Labour Congress for a charter. Instead of affiliating this huge four-thousand-man local, the craft-obsessed TLC ordered the union to be broken up into its component crafts. Many

Reprinted from I.M. Abella (ed.), *On Strike:* Six Key Labour Struggles in Canada 1919-1949, Toronto: James, Lewis and Samuel, 1974, pp. 93-128, by permission of the author and James Lorimer & Company, Publishers.

of the workers rebelled at this decision and opted instead to join the Communist Auto Workers' Industrial Union of Canada, which was also organizing in the Oshawa area. A vicious struggle between the two unions ensued, with the inevitable result that by the early 1930s there was no union at all in the General Motors plant at Oshawa.

Of course, in the early 1930s, during the depth of the Depression, workers needed jobs, not unions. What employment General Motors provided went to men who promised not to join a union. Capitalizing on this opportune moment, the company fired most of the union leaders and promoted others — those too valuable to release — to managerial positions where they were beyond the ambit of the trade-union movement.

This situation was, of course, not merely restricted to Oshawa. Throughout Ontario in the early 1930s both jobs and unions were scarce. The TLC, the Canadian counterpart of the American Federation of Labor, was too timid and reactionary to organize unskilled, unorganized workers. The All-Canadian Congress of Labour, the only other national labour organization, was weak, both organizationally and financially, while the Workers' Unity League, the labour arm of the Communist party, had disbanded, its organizers and unions flocking back into the TLC. It was exactly at this time, late in 1935, that a group of disgusted American unionists intent on furthering industrial unionism created the Committee for Industrial Organization, the CIO, in the United States.

Its birth coincided with the end of the worst of the Depression. Jobs were becoming less scarce; companies were stepping up production; and optimistic politicians and industrialists were prophesying a quick return to prosperity. Simultaneously, workers were becoming increasingly restive. Wages were still lower than they had been in the 1920s, working conditions unbearable and job security non-existent. It was to mitigate these conditions that Canadian workers in the 1930s turned in large numbers to the CIO.

The CIO's first steps into Canada were hesitant. Created in 1935 by John L. Lewis out of unions that had split with the American Federation of Labour over its refusal to organize on an industrial basis, the CIO by 1937 had several million members. In Canada, however, membership at the beginning of 1937 was negligible. Lewis and his colleagues were loath to organize in Canada; too much remained to be done in the United States. But unofficial CIO representatives, most of whom were Communists who had received their experience in the Workers' Unity League, began appearing in Canada and organizing locals for various CIO unions. Their efforts were nugatory. The CIO campaign in Canada did not catch fire. It needed, it seemed, a spark.

The spark was to come from Oshawa.

At the beginning of 1937 there was no union at the GM facilities in Oshawa. Consequently, while the workers were subject to their fifth consecutive wage cut, the General Motors Company announced that its profits in both the United

States and Canada were the highest in the history of the company.[1] And there was little the company employees in Oshawa could do. Across the border GM workers had taken matters into their own hands. They had left the AF of L and created a new union — the United Automobile Workers of America. Then, under the aegis of the CIO, they had taken over several GM plants until the company agreed to recognize the new union and negotiate with them. Their Canadian colleagues in Oshawa looked on enviously. Conditions in Oshawa were as bad or even worse than those in the GM plants in Flint and Detroit. Wages were lower, hours of work longer and jobs were less secure; rarely were older workers, men in their late forties and fifties, rehired after the long seasonal layoff for re-tooling.

Since the unhappy events in 1928, a few spasmodic and invariably futile attempts had been made to organize a union in Oshawa. By the beginning of 1937 there existed in the plant only a clandestine committee, known as the Unity Group, of some few dozen men who met secretly and regularly to discuss ways of improving working conditions. Though they probably would have achieved little in any case, they spent most of their time debating the virtues of socialism and communism; understandably, they achieved nothing.

But what the men in the plant could not do for themselves — organize a union — the company helped them to do. On February 15, 1937, acting on the advice of efficiency experts from the United States, the General Motors management announced a speed-up in the assembly line from twenty-seven to thirty-two units per hour. The workers were infuriated. For years they had complained that the line was already too fast. Now the company had the gall actually to increase its speed. Almost immediately the workers in the body shop — the most skilled and thus the least replaceable in the plant — decided to lay down their tools to discuss the new system. The plant's general manager, Harry Carmichael, rushed down to speak with them. But when he announced the company's decision was irreversible, the men in the body shop warned that unless the speed-up were revoked they would strike on Friday, February 19. In addition, one of the workers in the plant phoned the UAW office in Detroit for help. At about the same time one of the CIO organizers in the province also phoned UAW headquarters at the urging of Joe Salsberg, the trade-union organizer of the Communist Party who had long taken an active interest in developments at the Oshawa plant. On Friday, February 19, the body-shop workers, about 250 men, struck, thus halting production in the entire plant. On the same day Hugh Thompson arrived in Oshawa.[2]

Thompson was a UAW organizer sent from Detroit in response to the two phone calls. Fortuitously, he arrived while Louis Fine, a mediator from the Ontario Department of Labour, was addressing the striking body-shop workers, urging them to return to work. When the workers were informed that the UAW representative was outside the hall, they invited him to address them despite Fine's protest that the strike was an issue between the company and its workers, and that "outsiders would only complicate matters."[3]

Thompson's speech was short and to the point. He outlined to the men the success of the UAW below the border, and the necessity of organizing in order to improve their situation. His speech must have been effective. All the men in the room voted to join the UAW and, on Thompson's advice, to go back to work.

On the following day Thompson set up an office in downtown Oshawa and opened up Local 222 of the UAW for business. Within three days the union had enrolled 650 workers. Within a week, over a thousand had joined and after a month it had four thousand members, making it the largest local in Canada. Even the mayor of Oshawa, Alex Hall, and most of the city council were enrolled as honourary members. Charlie Millard, a forty-year-old war veteran and chairman of the CCF in Oshawa, was elected president of the local, and stewards were nominated from each department to represent the men on the union's negotiating committee.

Naturally, General Motors took an avid interest in what the union was doing. The company hired several undercover investigators to attend union meetings and report back on its plans and activities, and most importantly to supply a list of names of those attending the meetings.[4] In addition, the company transferred Millard from the body shop, where militancy was highest, to a position on maintenance where he was required to work a double shift. Nonetheless, neither Millard nor other union members were intimidated and the rapid growth of the union continued undiminished.

More surprising than the company's activities and interests were those of the premier of Ontario, Mitchell Hepburn. That the busy premier of Canada's most populous province should concern himself with an apparently insignificant labour dispute seems fatuous. Yet only a few days after Thompson arrived in Oshawa, the Ontario premier had phoned his friend Ian Mackenzie, the federal Defence minister, asking him to persuade Thomas Crerar, the minister of Immigration, and Norman Rogers, the minister of Labour, to deport Thompson. But Crerar and Rogers demurred, on the sensible grounds that Thompson had entered Canada legally and had not yet committed any crime. Undaunted, Hepburn ordered his own attorney-general, Arthur Roebuck, to investigate Thompson in the hopes that some evidence could be uncovered which could be used to deport Thompson as "an undesirable immigrant." Despite an intensive investigation, Roebuck found nothing. At the same time, at the personal request of Hepburn, Crerar ordered a complete investigation of Thompson by an inspector from the Immigration Department. Predictably, after a long and complete investigation that included an interview with Thompson, the Department of Immigration concluded that Thompson could not be legally deported. This, of course, was not what Hepburn wished to hear; if no legal way could be found to get Thompson out of the country, then Hepburn would find another.[5]

What was most astonishing about Hepburn's attitude was that three years earlier he had come to power on a radical slogan: "I swing well to the left, where some Grits do not tread." He further entrenched his support amongst the working people of Ontario by denouncing Conservative Premier George Henry's decision in September of 1933 to send in troops and tanks to break a strike in Stratford, Ontario. "Toryism stands for oppression," he said. "The provincial government has seen fit to send artillery, machine guns and tanks to Stratford because the citizens are objecting to the treatment given them by wealthy manufacturers . . . They take all they can from the people and give as little as they can to the workers. My sympathy lies with those people who are victims of circumstances beyond their control and not with the manufacturers who are increasing prices and cutting wages at the same time."[6]

Once in office Hepburn matched his rhetoric with his actions. Despite the objections of the mayor of Toronto, he cordially received a large group of "hunger marchers" at Queen's Park and fired two members of the Toronto Board of Police Commissioners who had refused the men permission to march on the legislature. He introduced enlightened labour legislation and a minimum-wage law. So over-whelmed were the province's labour leaders that one remarked that Hepburn cabinet members were "not Liberals, they are socialists and labour men from the ground up." And a visiting official of the British Labour party remarked how "fortunate" Ontario was "in having an administration that is going to see justice done to the workers."[7]

But in February of 1937 justice for the workers seems to have been the furthest thing from Hepburn's mind. From the day he took office, Hepburn had fallen more and more under the influence of those "fat cats of business" against whom he had campaigned, particularly George McCullagh, the editor of the *Globe and Mail*. In addition he had formed close relationships with such mining magnates as Sir James Dunn of Algoma Steel and J.P. Bickell of MacIntyre-Porcupine Mines, men who not only gave the Ontario premier useful advice about stocks he might add to his investment portfolio, but also advised Hepburn of the deleterious impact that a powerful union movement would have on these stocks, as well as on the entire mining industry of the province. As a small-town farmer Hepburn was in any case naturally suspicious of organized labour. It took the arguments of his big-business friends, especially McCullagh, to turn these suspicions into an active antipathy, particularly when the Ontario premier became convinced that the demands of organized labour would harm the province's resurgent economy. Thus, by February of 1937, when the CIO was beginning to take its first hesitant steps into the province, the labour movement no longer had a friend — if it ever had — in the premier's office in Queen's Park. In fact, the office was now occupied by its most important and hostile enemy.[8]

Hepburn viewed the Oshawa activity with a great deal of alarm. He was determined that the violence and bloodshed that had marked CIO organizing in the sit-down strikes in Michigan and other states would not spill across the border into Ontario. Yet he seemed helpless to do anything about it. The federal government had rebuffed his efforts to stop the CIO at the border. And there seemed little else he could do. Already CIO representatives were actively organizing auto workers in Windsor, rubber workers in Kitchener, steel workers in Hamilton and, worst of all, at least from Hepburn's point of view, mine workers in the north. And though all of these campaigns were peaceful and non-violent, it was in the premier's mind only a matter of time before the CIO shed blood in Ontario.

On March 2, 1937, the time arrived. On that day, against the advice of their CIO organizers, some seventy workers at the Holmes Foundry in Sarnia — all of whom were recent immigrants from eastern Europe — sat down at their machines in protest over the company's refusal to recognize their new union. At once, for reasons that had more to do with racial bias than anti-labour feeling, a mob of about three hundred of Sarnia's "best" citizens descended on the plant with an assortment of weapons. After a short but bloody battle the battered strikers were evicted from the factory while the Sarnia police stood outside the foundry, refusing to rescue the grossly outnumbered strikers. Yet once the strikers were outside the plant the police moved in and arrested them on charges of trespassing, though none of the several hundred strikebreakers were charged.

When this apparent disparity of justice was raised in the Ontario legislature by the lone CCF member, Sam Lawrence, Hepburn immediately jumped to his feet and shouted: "My sympathies are with those who fought the strikers . . . Those who participate in sit-down strikes are trespassers, and trespassing is illegal in this province . . . There will be no sit-down strikes in Ontario! This government is going to maintain law and order at all costs."[9]

Several days later Hepburn announced: "We are not going to tolerate sit-down strikes, and I point that out to these people now in this country, professional agitators from the United States — to agitate and foment unrest in our industrial areas . . . I shall put down the sit-down strikes with the full strength of the provincial police if necessary and other resources at the government's disposal."[10] No doubt he meant the tanks, artillery pieces and machine guns that he had denounced Premier Henry for using against strikers in Stratford.

Undaunted, Hugh Thompson continued his activities, not only in Oshawa but in other Ontario centres such as St. Catharines, where he helped organize UAW locals in several of the GM subsidiaries in that city. But it was Oshawa that required most of his attention. Since his arrival the city had become almost totally unionized. As the newspaper of the Communist party, the *Daily Clarion*, rapturously described it: "The change in attitude of the workers is one of the remarkable things to be seen. They walk with squared shoulders and a smile on their faces for they no longer fear for their jobs and they are proud of the union button they wear openly. Owing to the increasing demand for the union button there has been a shortage. This is the only time when workers pull long faces. This seems almost incredible in what was once a company town. But Oshawa is rapidly becoming a worker's city."[11]

The first meeting between the new union and the GM management took place on March 18 in the office of Colonel J.B. Highfield, the company's personnel manager. The union was represented by Charlie Millard and stewards elected from each department in the plant. Highfield and George Chappell, a company vice-president, represented management. According to the union negotiators' own description of themselves, they were "merely a bunch of amateurs." They thus sat silent and attentive while Chappell told them that the company was in no way bound by the UAW contract signed in the United States, while Highfield added that the company would negotiate only with its own workers and not with any representative of the UAW. With that, after only fifteen minutes, the meeting was adjourned.[12]

Fearing that this rebuff would demoralize the union, Thompson decided that a show of strength would be fitting. He decided to call a general union meeting for March 20. Unfortunately, he found it impossible to rent a hall large enough to accommodate the union membership. His attempts to rent the hockey arena were rejected since Colonel R.S. McLaughlin, the GM president, was a major stockholder in the arena company. The Department of Defence refused to rent the armoury, and the school board rejected his application to rent a high-school auditorium on the grounds that he was not a "local resident." Undaunted, Thompson announced that the union would hold its meeting in downtown Oshawa at "the Four Corners," the busiest intersection of the city, during the height of the Saturday rush hour. Almost at once the school board reversed its decision and decided that perhaps renting the school auditorium to the union was not such a bad idea after all.[13]

Naturally the meeting was a rousing success. When Thompson related to the membership — most of whom were outside the auditorium since even that hall proved too small — that he had succeeded in renting the auditorium only because the power of the union was now "as great as that of the General Motors Company," they roared with approval. In addition, both Thompson and Millard promised the workers that the union negotiating committee would settle for nothing less than what the UAW had received in the United States. And indeed, shortly thereafter the power of the union was immeasurably enhanced, as was the morale of its membership, when a GM subsidiary in Oshawa, Coulter Manufacturing, signed a contract with the union, recognizing Local 222 as a full bargaining agent for the company's 260 workers.

At the next meeting between the company and the union negotiators, the newly confident Millard demanded that Thompson be allowed to sit in on the negotiations as a union representative. Highfield categorically refused. Since Thompson was not a company employee, he said, the company would never negotiate with him. On that note, barely ten minutes after the meeting started, the union negotiators walked out, bringing the meeting to an abrupt end.[14]

Later that week a UAW vice-president from Detroit, Ed Hall, addressed a large rally of the Oshawa workers and announced that Millard had been appointed as a full-time CIO organizer. In addition, he promised the local the "full support" of the international. In fact, however, Hall had privately warned Thompson that the UAW treasury was empty and could afford Local 222 nothing more than its best wishes.[15]

Negotiations were now deadlocked, despite the efforts of Labour Minister David Croll. On Wednesday, March 31, Croll met with Chappell and Thompson at his Queen's Park office. Chappell emphasized that his company would never negotiate with non-employees. Croll then turned to Thompson and said: "Well, this narrows the issue down to one thing. It looks as if the people would get along nicely if it were not for one person, and I would suggest that you withdraw out of the picture." Thompson countered that it was the wish of the men and of the international union that he stay in his present position, but after an hour of discussion he agreed to Croll's proposal that Charlie Millard should do the negotiating for the union. Chappell also agreed, and a meeting was scheduled for the following day at Croll's office.[16]

Early the following afternoon, Chappell and Highfield came to Croll's office to discuss Millard's new status. Highfield protested that all that had been done was "to change the name of Thompson to Millard" and emphasized that the company would have no dealings with the CIO nor its representative. Croll reproved the two men for their "childish stubbornness" and then remarked: "I can read men, and as I look at that bunch in the next room I can tell by the eyes of most of them that they are a bunch of fanatics; . . . as for Millard . . . I think he's a weakling who can't do anyone any harm . . . I don't want a strike, and they shouldn't either, because I'll have to feed them and they won't get fat on what they get from this department." With that he ushered Highfield and Chappell into the adjoining room where Louis Fine and the union negotiating committee were waiting, and the meeting began.[17]

Millard spoke first and presented Chappell with a list of the union demands. These included:

    1. An eight-hour day.
    2. A steward and grievance committee modelled on the one agreed to by GM in the United States.
    3. A seniority system.
    4. Abolition of the new efficiency system.
    5. A minimum wage.
    6. Payday every other Friday.
    7. A contract that would terminate at the same time as that with the GM plants in the United States.
    8. Factory bulletin boards to be made available for union notices.
    9. Five-minute rest periods every two hours.

10. Vending machines for chocolate bars, etc., to be set up around the plant.

Chappell agreed to study these demands and present the company's answers at a meeting on the following Monday. Fine then adjourned the meeting on an optimistic note, stating that he was sure an agreement could be reached shortly so that Croll, who was leaving on Friday for a two-week vacation, would not have to postpone his trip.

Yet for the following three nights the GM company shipped an average of fifteen hundred cars from the Oshawa plant to an emergency storage depot on the Canadian National Exhibition grounds in Toronto; this was more than ten times the usual number.[18] Evidently General Motors did not share Fine's optimism.

After three more meetings with the union, on Tuesday, April 6, the company agreed to negotiate all the union's demands and to recognize Millard as the representative of Local 222. When Millard announced this to the men at the plant they were jubilant. They had been primed for a strike for weeks and only the indefatigable efforts of Millard and Thompson had kept them in line. Now it appeared that the strike would not be necessary.

While these negotiations were taking place, Hepburn had been on vacation in Florida. He returned to Queen's Park on Wednesday, April 7. On that same day, just hours after Hepburn's arrival home, General Motors once again changed its mind and announced that it would neither negotiate with Millard, as long as he was "a representative of the CIO," nor would it sign a written contract with the new union. It would undertake only to make verbal commitments to the workers.[19]

This sudden hardening of the company's position caught both Millard and Fine by surprise. Fine met immediately with Highfield and Chappell to try to moderate the company's stand. He was informed by them that Hepburn had phoned Chappell and had urged the company to take a firm stand against recognition of the CIO. Naturally, with the premier's promise of "total support," the company refused to reconsider its position. At the meeting with the union that evening, Chappell broke off negotiations with the statement that the GM position was firm, and there was nothing left to discuss.[20]

The union now had no alternative but to strike. Both Thompson and Millard were aware that a strike might destroy the union since few funds were available to support the strikers, but the workers were growing increasingly impatient and it had required all of Thompson's and Millard's efforts to keep them from walking out on their own. Thus, when the company refused to continue negotiations, both Thompson and Millard saw the futility of further discussions. On Thursday, April 8, Thompson ordered the morning shift to report as usual at seven A.M. At 7:05, on a prearranged signal, the shop stewards ordered the men out of the plant. By 7:15 that morning, for the first time in ten years the General

Motors facilities in Oshawa were at a standstill. The strike had begun.

The news from Oshawa did not seem to surprise Hepburn. Indeed, his actions indicated that not only did he expect a strike, he in fact welcomed it. At once he wired the federal minister of Justice, Ernest Lapointe, requesting Royal Canadian Mounted Police reinforcements for Oshawa. He told Lapointe that although he was prepared to induct special police, he feared that they would not suffice since he had already received reports that the situation in Oshawa was "becoming very acute and violence was anticipated at any minute." He then ordered General Victor Williams, chief of the Ontario Provincial Police, to cancel all leaves, to put his entire force on a twenty-four-hour alert and to mobilize one hundred constables from the area surrounding Oshawa. In turn, Williams informed him that the OPP had an undercover constable in Oshawa "to keep an eye on developments." E.G. Odette, chairman of the Ontario Liquor Control Board, acting on the recommendation of Mayor Hall and the union's executive, received Hepburn's permission to close all liquor and beer outlets in Oshawa for the duration of the strike. Hepburn also ordered the Department of Welfare not to issue relief to the strikers because "these employees are rejecting the opportunity to work at fair wages and fair hours and as a result they need not look to the government for relief assistance."[21]

Hepburn then called a press conference to outline his position to the Ontario public. He told the newspapermen that he regretted "very much that the employees of General Motors have seen fit to follow the suggestion of the CIO-paid propagandists from the USA to desert their posts at a time when both employees and the industry itself were in a position to enjoy a prosperity not known since 1929." He claimed that the conditions in the automobile industry were good and he saw no need for the men to strike. The strike itself, he claimed, was "the first open attempt on the part of Lewis and his CIO henchmen to assume the position of dominating and dictating to Canadian industry." He further added that his government completely supported the attitude of the company, that the time for a showdown with the CIO had arrived and that he fully expected the support of "the law-abiding citizens of Ontario." As he put it: "The CIO's demands are merely the first step in a policy of ever-increasing and impossible demands, culminating in the loss of a tremendous and ever-increasing export trade now being enjoyed by the automobile industry in Ontario." He warned the union against resorting to violence and promised to protect "all those workers desiring to resume their duties." He concluded emphatically: "The entire resources of the province will be utilized to prevent anything in this country resembling that which is taking place at the present time across the border due to the failure on the part of constituted authority to take adequate action." For the first time since he'd been elected, Premier Hepburn had, in the words of the Toronto *Star*, "openly turned his back on labour and the considerable liberal element in Ontario . . . whose votes in 1934 had elected him." Hepburn had publicly announced for all to hear that he would willingly use government power on the side of employers against the working man.[22]

Hepburn's request for RCMP aid was received coldly by a distraught Mackenzie King. According to the prime minister, the Oshawa situation was very delicate and "in dealing with it, Hepburn was going entirely the wrong way about it." Nevertheless, King gave in to the demands of Lapointe, who enthusiastically supported Hepburn's pleas for assistance; he agreed to send one hundred RCMP officers, though the province would have to bear all their expenses.[23] Hepburn immediately phoned the RCMP Commissioner, J.H. MacBrien, to alert him that he would need many more reinforcements as he did not expect the "main crisis" for two or three days. The commissioner informed him that he'd already dispatched sixty-seven men and that thirty-three others would be "moving up by fast freight and passenger train" by the morning. Another fifty men from the Toronto division, he added, would also be made available. On Lapointe's instructions, MacBrien ordered the RCMP commanding officer in Toronto to keep his forces "in the background as much as possible" so that they would be used only to support provincial and municipal police.[24]

Despite these frantic activities, Oshawa itself was calm. As the Toronto *Star* put it, "A city more peaceful than Oshawa under the shadow of the walkout cannot be imagined. It is neither grim nor gay but placidly ordinary, showing signs neither of industrial strife nor of holidaying workers." To keep order on the picket line the Oshawa chief of police, Owen Friend, had enrolled fifty strikers to act as deputies. In fact, it seemed that the only unusual activity was the continuous procession of cars along the road to the nearby town of Whitby, where the beverage rooms were recording a record business. Indeed, so placid was the town, and so complete was the support for the strike, that when the train from Ottawa carrying the RCMP officers rolled into Oshawa, Mayor Hall rushed to the station to warn them that he wouldn't allow them off the train since he was the only person who could call them into the city. The RCMP continued on its way to Toronto.[25]

In Oshawa, Hepburn's behaviour met with almost total disapproval. In an official statement, issued on behalf of the city of Oshawa, Mayor Hall condemned Hepburn for his "impulsive and irrational action" and praised the "peace-abiding, respectable citizens of Oshawa who are on strike." But in the same breath he refused to grant relief to the strikers, since this would mean "taking sides in a strike." Hugh Thompson warned Hepburn that until the strike was settled, General Motors would never build another car in Canada, "and the moment they attempt to bring one automobile to Canada from the United States in an attempt to beat the strike here, they will never make another automobile in the United States."[26]

Most of the Ontario press, however, supported Hepburn. The *Globe and Mail*, published by Hepburn's good friend, George McCullagh, praised Hepburn for checking the CIO before "it can extend into all the major industries of Ontario and wreak havoc in its wake." The Toronto *Telegram* cried: "The time to check the foreign invasion is now. Premier Hepburn is to be commended for the prompt steps he has taken to make sure that any resort to violence will be speedily suppressed." The Hamilton *Spectator* warned: "If the CIO wins, it will not stop until it has gained the control it has been seeking across the line." And even the Oshawa *Times* cautioned that the Communists "are taking advantage of the situation." Indeed, all the Ontario press, with two significant exceptions, totally supported Hepburn's position. Only the Toronto *Star* and the Ottawa *Citizen* censured Hepburn for his actions. The *Citizen* called him "impetuous." But more trenchant in its criticism was the Toronto *Star*, which claimed that "no Government is warranted in forcibly interfering with labour so long as labour is doing only those things which the law sanctions." It asserted that Hepburn "cannot logically fight international labour while at the same time [supporting] international capital." But perhaps the clearest insight into Hepburn's behaviour came from the Communist *Daily Clarion*, which editorialized: "Hepburn fears the CIO unionism will mean the ultimate invasion of the mines . . . and Hepburn's close association with certain big mining magnates of northern Ontario has been a source of much gossip during the past year."[27]

On the afternoon of Friday, April 9, the second day of the strike, Millard phoned Hepburn and asked him to meet with a group of workers to hear "their side of the story." When Hepburn agreed, Millard and some members of the bargaining committee met in the premier's office for over an hour. According to Millard, Hepburn listened attentively to what each union man had to say, and when they were finished he told them that there was no reason why the strike could not be settled within an hour.[28]

After they emerged from the premier's office, Hepburn told the press gathered outside that he thought everything would be "straightened out fairly soon." Millard agreed, but added significantly: "Things look brighter, but in any settlement that is reached, we expect recognition of our status as an international union." Notwithstanding Millard's qualification, Hepburn expressed confidence that the strike would be over by the following day and added that he was inviting union and management to meet with him Saturday afternoon in his office. Hepburn now obviously saw himself as a mediator. He also announced that Millard had agreed to allow company trucks to cross the picket line to pick up spare parts, something the union had not agreed to before.

Then the optimistic, cheerful Hepburn dismissed the strikers and the press and immediately went into conference with Chief Williams of the Ontario Provincial Police. He soon emerged, angry and shaken, again called in the press and in a strained, angry voice told them: "We now know what these CIO agitators are up to. We are advised only a few hours ago that they are working their way into the lumber camps and pulp mills and our mines. Well, that has got to stop and we are going to stop it! If necessary we'll raise an army to do it.''[29] This was Hepburn's declaration of total war on the CIO. He had announced publicly that he was willing to call out the armed forces to protect the mines of northern Ontario from the CIO.

Meanwhile, Thompson was disturbed when he heard of Millard's actions. He stated that Millard had neither the authority to discuss a settlement with Hepburn nor to assure the premier that General Motors had the right to cross the picket line to pick up spare parts. He then called a meeting of the stewards and after a short conference announced that the union "would take no responsibility for accidents which may happen to any strikebreaker.''[30]

Mayor Hall was outraged at Thompson's statements. To him, it seemed that Thompson was threatening violence. He publicly urged Thompson to retract his statement, and asked the union to disown Thompson's "menacing declaration of war." Privately, however, he called in Inspector Feiling of the provincial police and pleaded with him to arrest Thompson on a charge of intimidation. The inspector declined, suggesting that Hall present his evidence to the Crown attorney before taking action, since he would have "to be prepared to accept the responsibilities for developments if Thompson were arrested.''[31]

A chastened Thompson soon retracted his statement "because of the danger of its being misinterpreted." However, that night, at a rally in St. Catharines, Millard told his audience of auto workers that "no attempt to stop any strikebreaker will be made, but we will find out where these men live and we will visit them and have a nice long talk.''[32]

The first incident occurred early in the morning of April 10, a Saturday. Since the beginning of the strike the company had demanded the right to enter the plant and ship out spare parts. Hepburn supported this demand and threatened that the union's refusal to allow company trucks into the grounds would be met by force. Despite Millard's assurance that the trucks would be allowed to enter, Thompson had been adamant in his refusal. Nevertheless, after a lengthy, acrimonious discussion with Millard and other union officials, Thompson reluctantly submitted.[33]

At 10:30 that morning, the company sent several trucks to pass through the picket line in front of the plant gates. There the strikers were gathered seven deep and refused to let the trucks through. Within minutes, Mayor Hall was on the scene and, jumping on top of a car, urged the men to let the trucks in "because your leaders have ordered you to do so." The strikers ignored Hall and began rocking the trucks. It seemed that the riot Hepburn had predicted was finally underway. At just this moment Thompson arrived, jumped up beside Hall and shouted: "General Motors has been trying to arouse some sort of disturbance to get an excuse for bringing the Mounties in here and taking power out of your hands. Why let them?" He urged the men to let the trucks pass through the gates. Someone shouted that the trucks might contain machine guns, whereupon Hall begged the men to search the trucks if they wished but to let them pass. Thompson reminded the men that "as long as you maintain discipline you have the public on your side and you can't lose!"[34] The men cheered lustily and the trucks only had to fight their way through an army of catcalls and huzzahs to get into the plant. So the affair ended and it seemed certain that despite Hepburn's concern — or perhaps his hope — the strike would remain peaceful.

Just about this time, Harry Carmichael and J.B. Highfield were being ushered into Hepburn's office in Queen's Park. There they spent the entire morning planning strategy with the premier for the afternoon meeting with the union.

At 2:00 P.M. the union bargaining committee entered Hepburn's office. Significantly, Hugh Thompson was left outside in the corridor. Millard immediately asked Hepburn to admit Thompson to the negotiations, not as a member of the committee but as its solicitor. Hepburn refused. Millard then left the room to consult with Thompson and, on his return several minutes later, asked Hepburn if Thompson would be accepted as a member of the delegation. Hepburn again refused, declaring that he would not meet Thompson under any circumstances. Millard then walked out of the room and announced that "there was nothing left to discuss." Understandably ruffled at the turn of events, Hepburn told newsmen outside his office that he would never negotiate with Thompson "or any of those men who are trying to dominate Canadian industry and inciting the same state of anarchy that exists below the border."[35]

The union negotiating team meanwhile went to the office of J.L. Cohen, a Toronto labour lawyer who had just been appointed the union's legal adviser. After a short discussion at Cohen's office the men left for Malton airport to welcome UAW President Homer Martin, who was arriving from Detroit to inspect the Oshawa situation. Several carloads of strikers had also driven to meet Martin, and it was in a cavalcade of more than a dozen cars that he was conveyed to the battleground over forty miles distant.

By the time this procession reached Oshawa, there were more than fifty cars behind the flag-draped convertible bearing Martin. As they moved down the main street, thousands of people who had been standing on the sidewalks to catch a glimpse of the smiling, waving UAW president fell in behind the cavalcade. A hastily assembled band gave forth with attempts at harmony; hundreds of cars parked along the main street tooted their horns. In the words of an observer, "men, women, children and babes in arms all shouted and cried themselves hoarse . . . This vast mass of humanity filled the street from side to side and stretched back for four or five blocks." As one of the participants remarked twenty-five years later: "It was a spectacle I shall never, never forget!" And Felix Lazarus, in an article for *Canadian Forum*, wrote: "Veteran labour leaders almost wept when they saw this amazing display of enthusiasm . . . never in all the history of the Canadian labour movement has a town been so completely captured by the sentiment of unionism."[36]

After circling the General Motors plant, the parade stopped in front of the Genosha Hotel where the slight, bespectacled ex-Baptist minister and newly chosen president of the UAW stood on the hood of his car and exclaimed: "Never have I seen such enthusiasm and unity . . . With me I bring the greetings of four hundred thousand auto workers in the United States who are with you in this your first step in creating a great brotherhood of auto workers throughout North America." According to the chief of police in Oshawa, it was the largest demonstration in that city's history.

At a huge rally of the strikers that evening, Martin warned that "if General Motors doesn't make cars in Canada under union conditions, they won't make cars in the United States at all." He called Hepburn "a puppet of General Motors . . . a little two-by-four who is trying to sweep aside the traditions of a thousand years." As for the premier's remarks about foreign agitators, the ex-minister found an analogy in the Holy Book. As he put it: "In the Bible we read of a man who stirred up the people. He was an agitator, a foreign agitator according to some because he came from heaven. I would be glad to introduce him to the premier." Martin spoke for more than two hours, encouraging the workers and promising them the full support of their UAW brothers in the United States. The rally ended with the exuberant workers in a mood of defiance. They had heard their leader's response to Hepburn's declaration of war and they were more determined than ever to see the strike through to the very end.[37]

For the next few days the morale of the strikers was kept at a peak level by the unusually warm spring weather, the backing and material support offered by the Oshawa business community and the thousands of letters and telegrams of support from various labour groups, churches and individuals throughout Canada. The strikers were also heartened by the large numbers of tourists from Toronto and the surrounding district who drove through Oshawa "to take a peek at the strike," and stopped to talk and encourage the pickets. The competition between the Young Communist League and the Co-operative Commonwealth Youth Movement also benefited the strikers. Every day, a truck from Toronto arrived at the plant carrying that day's edition of the *Daily Clarion*, which was handed out free to the strikers. It also brought a host of active Young Communists eager to help wherever they could. Similarly, cars and trucks bearing equally enthusiastic young CCYMers from Toronto arrived regularly to add to the number of young people anxious to help the pickets by marching, making coffee and doing odd jobs.[38]

Meanwhile, on Saturday, April 10, the federal minister of Labour, Norman Rogers, had wired Mayor Hall offering the services of his department to settle the strike. Earlier in the day, Rogers had announced that he would intervene in the Oshawa strike even if only one party to the dispute would agree to federal intervention. He added, of course, that it would be better "if both sides were willing." Hall had immediately taken Rogers's offer to the General Motors officials. When Hepburn learned of the offer he angrily wired Mackenzie King that he "deeply resented the unwarranted interference" of Rogers and that he believed that the General Motors Company would "not be a party to such treachery." He added gratuitously that "this action is quite in common with the treatment that this government has received from most of your ministers."[39]

When he received Hepburn's telegram, King was beside himself with rage. From the beginning he had felt that the Oshawa situation was "a delicate one." Although he also believed that Rogers had not acted wisely in offering to negotiate before a request had been made to his department by both parties, he felt that Rogers was only doing his duty. King, however, was totally opposed to any federal intervention. The "greatest danger," as he saw it, "was being drawn into the controversy . . . The moment Rogers or officers of his department intervene, they would have to say at once whether they favoured or did not favour recognition of the CIO local organization. The poker would immediately be in the fire. We would be linked up in opposition to the Ontario government and said to have lent the aid of the federal government to the forces of communism."[40]

Even though he felt that Hepburn "had become pretty well beside himself in the attitude he was taking towards the Oshawa situation," after consulting with Rogers, King sent a conciliatory telegram to Hepburn informing him that the federal government "has neither the intention nor the desire to intervene in any way without the consent of both parties to the dispute and so long as the matter is being dealt with by the authorities of the province of Ontario."[41]

Feeling that he had the federal government on the run, Hepburn was quick to press his advantage. Despite the fact that the city seemed relatively peaceful, on April 13 Hepburn informed Lapointe that the situation in Oshawa was desperate and that at least another hundred RCMP reinforcements would be required as he had received word that the Communists were about to foment "disturbances." At the same time, Hepburn called in the press and told them that it was absolutely necessary to increase the number of police in Oshawa because he had a conclusive secret report proving that the CIO was working "hand-in-glove with international communism." He affirmed that there had been "no real trouble in Oshawa yet, but the situation is becoming more tense . . . it appears that the Communists are anxious to take an active part in case of disturbance." He then stated that he had ordered the provincial police to enroll two hundred "or if necessary" four hundred special police officers. So were born the infamous Hepburn Hussars, or Sons of Mitches as they were irreverently known in Oshawa.[42]

Colonel Fraser Hunter, a Toronto Liberal MPP, was appointed to aid General Williams in recruiting and mobilizing this special police force. Within hours of Hepburn's announcement the Toronto *Star* reported that Queen's Park was "swarming with men ready to volunteer and be sworn in." Despite his remarks to the press about the need for this new force, Hepburn does not seem to have been motivated by the deteriorating situation in Oshawa. The secret reports that he got several times daily from undercover agents in the city indicated that "the strike is proceeding smoothly . . . with no threat of violence in sight." In fact, the strike was so peaceful that an American movie cameramen had offered two strikers five dollars each if they would stage a mock fight "to add some local colour to his story." He was quickly removed.[43]

When informed by Lapointe of Hepburn's request for more RCMP reinforcements, King was furious. He feared that Hepburn's activities "would cut the Liberal Party in two if not into four." He disliked Hepburn's statements equating the CIO with communism because "in this way he has gone out of his way to raise a great issue in this country, the frightful possibilities of which no one can foresee. The truth of the matter is he is in the hands of McCullagh of the *Globe* . . . The situation as he has brought it into being has all the elements in it that are to be found in the present appalling situation in Spain. Hepburn has become a fascist leader and has sought to have labour in its struggle against organized capital put into the position of being under communist direction and control. Action of this kind is little short of criminal."[44]

On the following day, April 14, King met with his cabinet to discuss Hepburn's request for the RCMP reinforcements. He began the discussion by saying that the Oshawa situation had "all the elements in it of the Spanish situation, the creating of a fascist and a communist party in Canada, and a conflict between the two when nothing more in reality was at stake than the right of men to organize in recognition of their chosen organization." According to King, "Lapointe seemed to feel that he should send more police, and his whole sympathies seemed to be against the men because they were associated with Lewis's organization. He kept repeating that they had organized sitdown strikes in the States, etc. I pointed out that nothing of the kind had been attempted in Canada. There was not evidence of any overt act of any kind. The cabinet was solidly behind me in the view that no more police should be sent. We discussed at the time as to whether we should not direct Hepburn's attention to the act which enables municipalities and provinces to call out the militia in case of need. It was wisely decided not to direct attention specifically to this feature which is already known to the provincial government. What we suggested should be done was to point out that with the circumstances what they at the present time are, the government, having regard to its responsibilities generally throughout the Dominion, did not send any further police. With the kind of fight Hepburn is shaping up there is every possibility that strikes may take place at St. Catharines, Windsor, and other points and disorder may become more or less general. Lapointe did not like sending the wire but said he would carry out the wishes of the council and did so."[45]

Immediately following that meeting, King and Rogers held a press conference. They announced that there would be no federal intervention in the strike until Hepburn himself requested it. King maintained that his "only desire is to be helpful and that we couldn't help if the Ontario government opposed our efforts." Rogers also issued a statement stressing his support of "the right of workmen to organize for every lawful purpose . . . The right of association for legitimate purposes should not be denied, and labour should not be refused the means of organizing for collective bargaining." It was clear from that press conference that King was disturbed over the behaviour of Hepburn. As the New York *Times* reporter in Ottawa put it, King feared that "Hepburn's antics would bring to a head forces in Canada which many have predicted may ultimately divide this democracy into left and right extremism."[46]

These statements of King and Rogers, in the words of the Toronto *Star*, "made Hepburn's pot boil over." He immediately sent Lapointe a telegram condemning the federal government for its "vacillating attitude." He also requested the removal of all RCMP reinforcements as he had decided that he could no longer depend on federal aid "and would take necessary actions to preserve law and order within the province on his own." In place of the RCMP Hepburn announced that he would increase his special police force to four hundred men, half of whom were already on hand at the legislature building and the balance of whom would be mustered at once, "many of them to be university lads." It seemed that a goodly number of University of Toronto students had crossed the road to Queen's Park and enrolled in Hepburn's special police force. Hepburn also informed the press that he had been advised by Major Fletcher of the RCMP that his men were to take no active part until it was shown that provincial police were unable to cope with the situation. As Hepburn put it: "We were paying for a police force that was of little or no assistance to us. I want to tell the people of Ontario that the Dominion police were brought in here at our own expense and instructed not to take any part, but to stand by until our fellows had their heads broken."[47]

The response to Hepburn's plea for more police recruits was over-whelming. Shortly after the recruiting office opened, "standing room only" signs were posted and within two hours, Colonel Hunter, the head of the force, announced that Hepburn's quota had been reached. Hepburn then delivered a pep talk to his new "Hussars." He told them that they would be issued regular provincial police uniforms and would be paid twenty-five dollars a week. He also related to the men that the Eglinton Hunt Club had offered the force sixty of their horses. Then, to loud cheers, Hepburn announced that he would continue to use their services even after the Oshawa strike was over as he could no longer depend on the federal government to maintain law and order in Ontario.[48]

During these manoeuvres, Hepburn still found time to fire two members of his cabinet who had opposed his actions during the strike, Arthur Roebuck, the attorney-general, and Labour Minister David Croll. Hepburn had originally taken Roebuck and Croll into his cabinet because they represented the significant urban, radical, left-Liberal and pro-labour element that had elected him in 1934. Now there was no longer room for this element in the Hepburn cabinet. Both Croll and Roebuck had been out of Toronto for the first few days of the strike; when they returned, Hepburn had refused to meet them. Immediately upon his return, Croll had contacted Chappell to learn what had gone wrong with the negotiations, which had been proceeding so smoothly before he left on his vacation. Chappell told him that the premier's return from Florida on April 8 had changed the situation drastically and that the company had decided to break off negotiations since Hepburn had promised that he would do all in his power "to break the union in Oshawa."[49]

On Wednesday, April 14, Hepburn sent both ministers letters asking for their resignations as they were "not in accord" with his policy of "fighting against the inroads of the Lewis organization and communism in general." At the same time Hepburn called in the press and told them: "There is absolutely no turning back now . . . this is a fight to the finish and we must have solidarity in our ranks." He then told reporters that he had taken such firm action against the CIO not only because Ontario was facing an economic and industrial crisis but also because, "if the CIO wins at Oshawa it has other plants it will step into . . . it will be the mines, [it will] demoralize the industry, and send stocks tumbling."[50]

Later that day Croll and Roebuck sent Hepburn their letters of resignation. Both complained that they had not been consulted before they were fired. Both stated that the CIO had absolutely nothing to do with communism and both expressed their support for the workers and condemned Hepburn's position — as Croll memorably phrased it: "My place is marching with the workers rather than riding with General Motors." Croll bluntly accused Hepburn of "having passed the borders of Liberalism," and Roebuck summarized: "There is no disagreement as to the maintenance of law and order. If there is settled divergence of opinion it is as to the display of unnecessary or provocative force, . . . the maintenance of impartiality by the state in industrial disputes, . . . the right of labour to such forms of organization [as it] may choose, . . . its freedom to speak through such channels of representation as it may name, and its right to collective bargaining."[51]

The reaction to these dismissals was predictable. The *Globe and Mail* asserted that "Croll and Roebuck must fall in line enthusiastically or give way to others who will uphold the integrity and good name of the province in this fight for principle." On the other hand, the Toronto *Star* editorialized that Hepburn had "lost his two most outstanding cabinet ministers . . . because they refused to sacrifice their conscientious beliefs and adherence to the welfare of the workers to Hepburn's impetuous, unfair and unwise attacks on the rights of labour." Graham Spry, a leading member of the CCF, invited both men to join his party. The Toronto and District Labour Council called Hepburn "Canada's Hitler" and charged that he had fired Croll and Roebuck because they believed in and fought for "the rights of the common worker and organized labour." The humour of this situation, however, was not lost on one political pundit who, noting that Hepburn had taken over Croll's portfolios of Labour, Welfare and Municipal Affairs, commented: "Hepburn is now Prime Minister, Minister of Labour, Minister of Public Welfare, Minister of Municipal Affairs and Provincial Treasurer. If anyone sees him talking to himself he will be able to conclude that the Ontario cabinet is having a meeting."[52]

With all these activities in Queen's Park and on Parliament Hill, the workers in Oshawa must have wondered whether anyone remembered the strike. Certainly Hepburn seemed to have other things on his mind, at least until he was informed that at a meeting with the General Motors executive in Detroit, Homer Martin had agreed that the Oshawa strike "should be settled on a Canadian basis without recognition of the CIO . . . and that it should be settled between company officials and the various representatives of the local unions involved." Hepburn rapturously termed Martin's decision "a surrender of the CIO of its attempts to extend [its] mass product industrialization drive into Canada," and a victory for his own attempt to "root communism out of the Canadian labour movement." He then phoned Millard and invited him to resume negotiations at his office. The latter demurred until Martin, who was due in Oshawa that same day, could explain to the angry members of his union why he had reneged on his promises.[53]

Early Friday morning, Arpil 16, Martin arrived in Oshawa to explain to the strikers his "surrender" in Detroit. He explained to them that he had accepted a four-point program to settle the strike. This involved opening negotiations at once, establishing a seniority system similar to the one accepted by the UAW in the United States, agreeing to a contract that would run concurrently with the one signed in the United States and finally, drawing up individual contracts with the local unions in Windsor and St. Catharines. The key point to the UAW, of course, was the third, which meant that in future, American and Canadian contracts would be negotiated at the same time to cover plants on both sides of the border. To bolster the morale of the strikers further, Martin arranged the first conference telephone call in Canadian history in which he spoke to the presidents of all the forty-five UAW locals in the United States from San Francisco to Atlanta. The call lasted for twenty minutes and at its conclusion the UAW president announced that the Oshawa local had been promised all the support necessary to win the strike.[54]

Immediately after the call, Millard, Thompson and J.L. Cohen left for Queen's Park to continue negotiations with Hepburn. At two p.m. Cohen was ushered into Hepburn's office and was enthusiastically greeted by the confident, jubilant premier. Already in the office were J.B. Highfield and Harry Carmichael, who had arrived there earlier in the day. Hepburn told Cohen that he had been asked to do all the negotiating for the company. Consequently, he led the union's lawyer into another office where they argued for over an hour over the status of Charlie Millard. At one point Hepburn left the room to allow Cohen to place a long-distance call to Martin in Oshawa for further instructions. Hepburn then handed Cohen a document which he demanded must be signed before negotiations could continue. The document contained one sentence: "J.L. Cohen and Charles Millard are negotiators for the employees' union of the General Motors Company of Oshawa, and are no way connected or instructed by the CIO." Cohen agreed that he and Millard would sign the document and then discussion turned to the seniority clause. Hepburn presented the company proposal which Cohen thought was acceptable but the lawyer wished to consult with Millard before committing himself.[55]

He then went out into the corridor and placed the company's proposals before Millard and Thompson. Both agreed that they were reasonable but Millard suggested that they phone Martin before accepting. They were directed by a reporter to a nearby vault which contained a phone. It was just as the three men entered the vault and Thompson began to dial that Hepburn hurried out of his office, rushed to the vault, took one quick look at the three men, turned, hastened back to his office and announced to the reporters gathered in the corridor that as far as he was concerned the negotiations were over. "We aren't going to settle this by remote control!" he shouted.

The three union men were as bewildered as the newspapermen by the sudden turn in events. Hepburn soon came out of his office and told reporters that it was "nothing but a complete double cross to have Thompson and Martin try to run this conference by remote control . . . Thompson showed great temerity to even appear here, let alone to enter my private vault where my personal, valuable and top-secret papers are stored . . . Inasmuch as I have repeatedly asserted my determination never to negotiate with the hirelings of J.L. Lewis there was nothing left to do but to bid these gentlemen goodby!"

This statement only added to the confusion of the reporters, as they had often used the phone in the premier's vault. Indeed, on Hepburn's orders, tables had been placed in the room so that reporters in their spare time could "sit around, drink tea, or play cards." It seemed that Hepburn had used the incident only as an excuse to break off talks he never had any intention of completing. The three union negotiators then met Homer Martin again at the Royal York Hotel in Toronto. At this meeting, according to Millard, Martin promised the local the full financial support of the UAW. He also phoned Charles Wilson, the vice-president of General Motors in the United States, and warned him that if the strike were not settled soon, the UAW would close down all General Motors facilities in the United States.[56]

Hepburn had two reasons for not wishing to continue negotiations that day. Firstly, he had received secret reports from his undercover police agent in Oshawa informing him that "the pickets are half-hearted, most of the strikers are impatient and unhappy . . . and everyone around here is demanding an immediate settlement." The workers, according to this source, also felt "betrayed by Martin's surrender." Hepburn believed that if the company would hold off negotiating for a short period, the workers would soon be on their knees begging for a settlement on management terms.[57]

But perhaps the major reason Hepburn called off the talks was the ominous secret reports he was receiving from his agents in northern Ontario of increased CIO activity in the gold mines. These reports informed him that a CIO organizer, George Anderson, had threatened to call a strike if the mine owners refused to meet union terms. It seems that Hepburn was now more than ever convinced that the CIO had to be totally crushed at Oshawa before it succeeded in organizing the mines of Ontario. As the general manager of the Hollinger Mine privately warned him: "The CIO is only waiting for the Oshawa results before mobilizing the mines." The premier therefore issued a statement declaring that his Oshawa stand had greatly handicapped "the CIO's drive to dominate Canadian industry" and that he was "more concerned with the CIO threat in the mine fields than in the automobile industry . . . for Oshawa is only an attempt by the CIO to pave the way for its real drive against the fundamental wealth of the province — its mine fields." He then issued his battle cry: "Let me tell Lewis here and now that he and his gang will never get their greedy paws on the mines of northern Ontario as long as I am prime minister." He was immediately supported by his mine-owner friends Joe Wright, Jules Timmins, Jules Bache and J.P. Bickell, who warned that they would "close the mines before they would negotiate with the CIO." More emphatically, Timmins of the Hollinger Mine warned: "Under no circumstances will we recognize the CIO and should the CIO interfere with our operations we have the assurance of the government that ample protection will be given our men who are desirous of continuing to work."[58]

The fears of Hepburn and the mine owners, whose profits in 1936 had reached fifty per cent on total production, were underscored by a major gold-stock collapse on the Toronto Stock Exchange on Monday, April 19 — a collapse due largely to the rumours of CIO activities in the gold fields. On the same day, however, it seemed that the Oshawa strike had been settled. All day long Mayor Hall had been running between the offices of Highfield and Millard carrying proposals and counter-proposals. By evening these "remote-control" negotiations had succeeded, with Highfield agreeing to the four points of the Detroit agreement and Millard and Thompson agreeing that the men would return to work before the contract was signed. All that remained was for the strikers to ratify the agreement. That night, however, at a large rally the men repudiated their own strike leaders. Even the union stewards, when told of the settlement, voted to a man to turn the proposals down. When Hall got up to announce the settlement, he was hooted off the stage by the strikers, who were determined to hold out in their demand for a signed contract before they returned to work. Tears streaming down his face, Hall attempted to argue with the men. He failed, and the strike continued.[59]

It was obvious to Thompson and Millard that the strike had to be settled quickly. They would accept any reasonable terms because there was absolutely no financial support coming from the UAW in the United States. Homer Martin had made promises to the strikers that he had neither the intention nor the ability to fulfil. He had not consulted John L. Lewis nor any CIO or UAW official before promising the Oshawa men full financial support. In fact, the entire strike was carried on without "one cent" of aid from the American unions. Yet on Tuesday, April 20, Thompson announced that the first instalment of the hundred thousand dollars promised by Martin had arrived and the Oshawa *Times* carried a photograph of Thompson depositing the money at the union's bank. Unknown to everyone but Thompson and Millard, the union treasurer had withdrawn all the local funds from the bank the preceding afternoon. It was this money that Thompson with a great deal of publicity and fanfare had deposited as the "first instalment from the USA." In this way, the company, Hepburn and the men on the picket line were led to believe that the strikers were receiving the fullest support from the international.[60]

In fact, the strikers were totally on their own. They had no savings, nor was there any strike pay to tide them over. Their earlier jubilation had worn off, and they were becoming increasingly desperate. Nevertheless, they rejected the Hall proposal even though it was supported by their own leaders. But their leaders were unsure how much longer they could hold out.

To buoy up the strikers, the UAW executive board held a special meeting in Washington to discuss the strike. Martin presented his report and, reneging on his promise to the strikers, stated that he was "personally against a sympathy strike" as this would "jeopardize our entire union." Walter Reuther, UAW vice-president, suggested that the Oshawa local sign a temporary agreement that would be in effect until the termination of the General Motors pact in the United States; when a new contract was signed with the company, all Canadian workers would be included. The exective finally decided to leave negotiations to the men in Oshawa. The board also agreed that it would be impossible to support the strike financially as the union treasury was empty. Nevertheless, for purposes of publicity, Martin wired Thompson that the executive had "unanimously voted necessary financial aid" — a telegram which both Martin and Thompson released to the press.[61]

Hepburn was not completely fooled; he had been informed by his agents in Oshawa that the union was in trouble. When Thompson announced that he was going to Washington "to discuss union matters," J.J. McIntyre, one of Hepburn's informants and a *Globe and Mail* reporter, wired the premier that "Thompson is hi-tailing it to Washington as it is obvious he needs help . . . he is running out to get his hand strengthened." Hepburn had also met secretly with a delegation of strikers who told him that most of the men wished to return to work at once. Thus, when he was informed by Highfield that the company was anxious to re-open negotiations, a frantic Hepburn took the almost unbelievable step of wiring Colonel McLaughlin, the president of GM in Canada, who was vacationing somewhere in the Caribbean on his yacht, to order management to suspend negotiations with the strikers as he had "confidential reports that a 'total collapse' of the strike was imminent."[62]

The union negotiating committee, however, was ready to sign an agreement on almost any terms and General Motors was anxious to begin producing cars again. Realizing the union's precarious situation, Millard and Thompson decided that the strike must be settled at any cost. Therefore Millard phoned Highfield to request a reopening of negotiations. Highfield was naturally agreeable and a meeting was arranged for Hepburn's office on Wednesday, April 21 at two P.M. Hepburn now had the upper hand. He made Cohen and Millard sign a document stating that neither of them was "instructed by or represented a committee known as the CIO." Cohen further signed a statement that he had definite word from Homer Martin that "neither he nor Thompson would return to Oshawa or Toronto during the negotiations." When Hepburn got word from his undercover agents that "Claude Kramer, a CIO agent, was in Oshawa agitating the men" and that even if the negotiating committee repudiated the CIO, "the men at a mass meeting will take matters out of the hands of the negotiating committee and hold out for recognition of the international union," the Ontario premier asked Millard and Cohen to sign a statement that neither knew Kramer nor had any intention of discussing the agreement with him. It seemed that Hepburn had finally achieved his goal. The agreement would be signed by the local union only, and the CIO had been effectively excluded.[63]

After another meeting with Cohen and Millard on the following day a smiling Hepburn emerged from his office late in the afternoon and told newsmen that the strike was over, subject to the ratification of the union. He then arranged with Defence Minister Ian Mackenzie for the strikers to use the Oshawa armoury for their vote.

The vote was scheduled to begin at ten A.M. Friday, April 23. By nine that morning a cheerful throng of two thousand strikers was already assembled outside the armoury, four abreast in a line stretching several blocks, anxious to get in. By noon, just before the voting began, Millard announced that he was so sure of the results that he had already instructed pickets to leave their posts and begin moving tents and other equipment. At 1:45 Cohen announced that the vote to end the strike was 2205 in favour and only 36 against. To the joy of all, Mayor Hall then announced that he would ask that all the bars in Oshawa be reopened immediately. Then, to the strains of *For He's a Jolly Good Fellow*, Police Chief Owen Friend was carried to the stage where he announced that the fifteen days of the strike had been the most peaceful in Oshawa's history. No one had been arrested in connection with the strike. Arrangements were also made for boxing matches, parades and dances to celebrate the end of the strike.[64]

At 2:45 that afternoon Millard and Cohen arrived at Hepburn's office and signed the contract to end the strike. After fifteen days, the Oshawa strike was officially over.

The question of who had won the strike now became as prickly as the issues of the strike themselves. In order to justify his somewhat extraordinary activities on behalf of management, Hepburn strove desperately to prove that he had held the CIO at bay. There was no doubt that Hepburn had won a semantic victory. The CIO had been repudiated in writing by the union negotiators and the agreement had been signed between "General Motors Company of Canada and the employees of the company at Oshawa." Nowhere was there any mention of the CIO, nor even of Local 222 of the UAW. Millard, in the company's view, was simply "an employee on leave of absence." As the *Globe and Mail* put it: "The settlement . . . was a permanent defeat for Lewisism and Communism in Canada . . . no matter what false and flimsy claims may be put forward by Lewis agents and their comrades, the Reds, the CIO is repudiated."[65]

In fact, it was anything but a victory for Hepburn and his anti-CIO forces. As the *Daily Clarion* correctly pointed out, the Oshawa strike was "the dawn of a new era . . . for the CIO victory in Oshawa . . . has broken into the hitherto unorganized and terrorized mass-production industry." At a rally of the strikers, both Millard and Cohen stated that the settlement was a tremendous victory for the CIO and that any attempt to claim that the union had not been recognized was, in Millard's words, "Just child's play." J.L. Cohen added that "the agreement was so worded and the interpretation was so planned that there can be no doubt about the union's recognition." He further emphasized that the company had met every single one of the union's demands — the forty-four-hour week, wage increases, the seniority system, a grievance committee, a minimum wage, and the promise never to discriminate against an employee for union activity, past, present or future. The strikers then passed a resolution "affirming the alliance with the UAW and the CIO with which our union is affiliated" and sent it on to Hepburn as an expression of their feelings.[66]

That the settlement was less than a victory even Hepburn was ready to admit. In the words of the *Financial Post*, he had hoped to demolish the CIO in one great stand, but had succeeded merely in "holding it at arm's length." Even George McCullagh (who later took the credit for Hepburn's anti-CIO stand) admitted that the settlement at Oshawa was not the body blow to the CIO he had hoped for. Ironically, McCullagh and Hepburn did not realize how close they had come to striking that fatal blow. According to Millard and Thompson, the union was "lucky" to get any type of settlement. It was their feeling that, had the strike not been settled that Friday, it would have fallen apart within a few days. In fact Thompson had told Millard to agree to any proposal the company made since the union was totally bankrupt and the men now realized that they had been "bamboozled" by Martin's lavish promises. Fortunately for the union, Hepburn's espionage system had failed him at a most critical moment and the premier actually believed, as he later told his personal aides, that he had got "the best he could under the circumstances." Had Hepburn been able to keep the company away from the bargaining table for several more days, he would likely have achieved a complete victory , totally crushed the strike and, perhaps with it, the CIO in Canada.[67]

The Oshawa strike was a turning point in the history of the Canadian labour movement. It marked the birth of industrial unionism in Canada. The achievements of the Oshawa strikers in fighting and defeating both the power of big business and the provincial government inspired workers throughout the country, and gave the CIO the impetus it so badly needed to begin organization in the mass-production industries in the country. Just as Roosevelt became "the best organizer" for the CIO in the United States, so, in a negative way, Hepburn became the CIO's most successful organizer north of the border. The Oshawa strike, and particularly Premier Hepburn's antics during it, suddenly turned the rather limited CIO organizing campaign into precisely the kind of violent crusade Hepburn and his mine-owner friends had feared. The Oshawa strikers had won a great victory for themselves but, even more important for the CIO, they had created the psychology of success and the enthusiasm needed for a massive organizing effort. What Akron and Flint had inspired south of the border, Oshawa was to inspire north of it. It was a landmark in Canada labour history.

What is perhaps most significant about the Oshawa strike is that it was conducted by Canadians without much assistance from the CIO. Although Hugh Thompson was ostensibly in charge of organization, most of the organizing was in fact done by Canadians. Whatever financial assistance the strikers were given came from churches and neighbours. Not a penny of aid came from the United States. Both the CIO and the UAW concluded that neither had the men nor the money to help the strikers; they even refused to call a sympathy strike of GM workers in the United States to support the strikers in Oshawa. Though the UAW had publicly promised to send one hundred thousand dollars, in the end all it could deliver was its best wishes. Thus, what the Oshawa strikers achieved, they achieved on their own. The General Motors Company agreed to a settlement in Oshawa not because of the threats of the CIO but because it desperately needed cars for the Commonwealth markets, and these could only be built in Oshawa. Fear of losing those markets to Ford and Chrysler, rather than fear of John L. Lewis and Hugh Thompson, forced General Motors to recognize the union.

Thus the role of the CIO in the Oshawa strike seems ambiguous. The strike was conducted, financed and settled by Canadians. In fact, when the settlement was finally reached, Thompson was back in the United States. The final negotiations were handled by Canadians. The CIO played no actual role in the strike except in the minds of Hepburn, the mine owners and, of course, most importantly, in the minds of the strikers themselves. Though the victory at Oshawa was a victory for Canadians, it was immediately hailed across the country as a great CIO triumph. Because Hepburn had defined the enemy as the CIO, the CIO was given full credit for a struggle it had done little to win.

With the victory at Oshawa, the CIO began a successful crusade to organize the industrial work force in Canada. Thus for the Canadian working man, perhaps no event in the history of the Canadian labour movement in the past fifty years is more important than the Oshawa strike. That fifteen-day walkout of some four thousand workers marks the birth of the labour movement in Canada as we know it today.

The political ramifications of the strike were equally significant. Hepburn was obviously displeased with the settlement. He had hoped to demolish the CIO in Ontario by smashing the strike at Oshawa, but he had failed. For this failure he attributed much of the blame to the hated Mackenzie King who, he felt, had undermined him at every step during the strike. So profound was his contempt for King and for the CIO that any scheme, no matter how outlandish or shocking, that would cripple both, was acceptable to the embittered premier. Just such a scheme was suggested to him by George McCullagh. It was a plan that would destroy Mackenzie King, break the CIO and perhaps, if Hepburn had his way, end the two-party system in Canada.

Unfortunately for Hepburn, it was also a plan that required absolute secrecy. But to Hepburn's chagrin, the Toronto *Star* had learned about it and, by publishing the details of the scheme, aborted it. On May 1 the *Star* carried the incredible story that Hepburn, who led "a party with 70 seats in Queen's Park," had offered to form a coalition and indeed turn over the premiership to Earl Rowe, the Conservative "who leads a party with only 14 seats." The premier, realizing that the scheme could never come to fruition now, heatedly denied it.[68]

But his denials were something less than candid. The *Star* report was accurate. It appears that on the day the strike ended, Friday, April 23, Hepburn informed the lieutenant-governor of the province, Herbert Bruce, that Ontario was in serious trouble and that it might be necessary to dissolve the House and to form a Union government. He later gave Bruce a list of Conservatives he would accept into his cabinet and arranged to meet the leader of the opposition, Earl Rowe.[69]

On April 27, he met Rowe in the Royal York Hotel. He told the wary Conservative leader that because of the great threat posed to the Ontario economy and especially the gold mines by the CIO and the Communists, George McCullagh and other "interested parties" had proposed to him a solution. As Rowe recollects: "Hepburn stated that the only way to beat the CIO and stop them from getting into the mines would be to form a strong and united government, and that this could only be done if the Conservative and Liberal parties formed a coalition." According to Rowe, Hepburn said: "Earl, I am prepared to resign and turn the office of prime minister over to you . . . I will help, and be your minister of Agriculture . . . if you think you need me, but I would like to spend more time throughout Canada selling this idea . . . You can name half the cabinet . . . I have also been advised to assure you that all your debts will be covered, and an honorarium of several hundred thousand dollars will be provided . . . Now how can you refuse such an offer?'' He also told Rowe that such a coalition would be the "best way" to "get rid" of Mackenzie King.[70]

The flabbergasted Rowe left the meeting to consult other prominent Tories, though he did inform Hepburn that he was opposed to the idea since he was ''named leader of a great party one and a half years ago to serve it and maintain its place in Canadian affairs . . . not for a short and easy road to the prime-ministership.'' After consulting various prominent federal and provincial Conservatives, most of whom opposed the scheme, Rowe officially rejected it, but not before his own lieutenant and the party's chief organizer in the province, George Drew, resigned in protest over Rowe's decision. As Rowe recollects, Drew told him at a private meeting that ''the time had come to end the two-party system of government in Ontario since only a strong government could destroy communism.'' When Rowe spurned his plea, Drew resigned.[71]

Though Hepburn's scheme had failed, it indicated the extent to which he was ready to go to destroy the CIO and, of course, Mackenzie King. The plan had originated and been sponsored by George McCullagh and several of his mining-magnate friends. In order to protect their province, and naturally their mines, from the CIO they were ready to end the two-party system. It indicated the depth of the hostility the CIO would have to overcome in Canada before it became a viable force.

The events in Oshawa also had a more far-reaching political impact. Totally disillusioned with King's behaviour during the strike, Hepburn decided that the time was ripe to break with the prime minister and to look for new political allies. On June 3, speaking to a meeting of the Canadian Life Assurance Association in Toronto, the Ontario premier condemned King for his ''vacillating'' attitude towards the CIO and communism and proudly proclaimed that only his actions in Oshawa had saved Canada from the CIO ''criminals.'' He then announced that he was ''no longer a Mackenzie King Liberal'' and he pointedly praised ''the forceful and praiseworthy'' activities of Premier Maurice Duplessis of Quebec. He looked forward, he said, to working more closely in the future with the Quebec premier. This speech was a harbinger of the notorious ''unholy alliance'' of Hepburn and Duplessis, which would bedevil Canadian politics for the next few years and whose goal was the destruction of Mackenzie King.[72]

Naturally, neither the break with King nor the alliance with Duplessis were direct results of the Oshawa strike. Both had been in the making long before the CIO arrived in Canada. But according to Hepburn, King's behaviour during the strike was ''the final straw'' — the breaking point between the two. There had never been much love lost between them, but a *modus vivendi* had been built up during the first few years of Hepburn's premiership. It was this that was destroyed by the Oshawa strike.[73]

The strike also became the major issue in the Ontario elections that fall. Campaigning on an anti-CIO ticket, Hepburn swept the province. The helpless Rowe was overwhelmed. So popular was the premier's position on the CIO that fully fifty per cent of the people of Ontario — including many workers and even the riding of Oshawa — voted Liberal. It was obviously a vote of confidence from the people of Ontario for Hepburn's behaviour during the strike, and perhaps for his attacks on Mackenzie King.

But the 1937 election was the high-water mark of Liberalism in Ontario. Never again, at least to the present time, would the Liberal party be a serious contender in Ontario politics. With the physical and mental deterioration of Hepburn, the Liberal party fell apart. In the 1943 election it won only 15 seats compared to 34 for the CCF and 38 for the Conservatives. In 1945, it managed to hold only 11. In neither of these elections did the Liberals win any urban or working-class seats and in every election since, they have managed to win only a handful. In an urban and industrial province, failure to win more than a few such ridings has doomed the Liberal party to opposition.

In this, the story of the strange death of Liberal Ontario, the Oshawa strike plays a prominent role. Until the strike, Hepburn and the Liberals had a corner on the labour, progressive and left-wing vote in the province. But Hepburn's conduct during the strike had, in the words of the *New Commonwealth*, "in one fell swoop lost the Liberals the support of labour throughout the province." Hepburn's magic and the anti-CIO hysteria swept the province in the 1937 election, but the Liberal party emerged as a right-wing, anti-labour party. As Professor Dennis Wrong commented, "Hepburn . . . faced the electorate in 1937 as an anti-labour candidate. He and his party were therefore not in a position to win over the rising labour movement that emerged as a new force in Ontario politics in the war and postwar years."[74]

In his "swing to the right," Hepburn had taken the Liberal party with him. A vacuum was created on the left which, following the 1937 election, was rapidly filled by the rejuvenated CCF. Thus, even though the party failed to win a seat in the 1937 provincial election, the Oshawa strike was also a turning point in the fortunes of the CCF in Ontario. For the first time it became the party of the left and of labour in Ontario, and particularly of the vastly expanding industrial work force that was organized following the victory in Oshawa.[75]

Today, more than a generation later, the impact of the strike on the Canadian labour movement and on politics in Ontario is still unmistakable. Certainly the birth of industrial unionism in Canada, and to some extent the growth of the CCF and the decline of Liberalism in Ontario, are all legacies of the Oshawa strike.

Notes

1. New York *Times*, 14 February 1937.
2. Interviews with Charles Millard, Joseph Salsberg, George Burt.
3. Interviews with Charles Millard, Louis Fine, Art Schultz.
4. Interviews with Charles Millard, "Tommy" Thomas.
5. Hepburn to Ian Mackenzie, 25 February 1937; Hepburn to Arthur Roebuck, 26 February 1937; Thomas Crerar to Hepburn, 4 March 1937, Hepburn Papers, Archives of Ontario.
6. Toronto *Daily Star*, 1 October 1933.
7. Toronto *Daily Star*, 1, 14 August 1934; 4, 12 September 1934.
8. Interviews with David Croll, Arthur Roebuck. For an excellent study of the relationship between Hepburn and McCullagh see Brian Young, "The Leadership League," (M.A. thesis, Queen's University, 1966). Also see N. McKenty, *Mitch Hepburn* (Toronto: McClelland & Stewart, 1967), pp. 92-93.
9. Toronto *Daily Star*, 4 March 1937; *Canadian Forum*, April 1937; Toronto *Telegram*, 5 March 1937.
10. Toronto *Telegram*, 8 March 1937.
11. *Daily Clarion*, 20 March 1937.
12. Minutes of meeting, 18 March 1937, Hepburn Papers.
13. Oshawa *Times*, 21 March 1937.
14. Minutes of meeting, 24 March 1937, Hepburn Papers.
15. Interview with Charles Millard; Letter to the author from Hugh Thompson, 19 February 1968.
16. Minutes of meeting, 31 March 1937, Hepburn Papers.
17. *Ibid.*, 1 April 1937.
18. Oshawa *Times*, 4 April 1937.
19. Minutes of meeting, 7 April 1937, Hepburn Papers.
20. Interviews with David Croll, Charles Millard, Louis Fine.
21. Hepburn to Ernest Lapointe, 8 April 1937; Hepburn to E.G. Odette, 8 April 1937; Hepburn to Miss H.N. Ward, assistant deputy minister of Public Welfare, 8 April 1937, Hepburn Papers.
22. New York *Times*, 9 April 1937. Strangely, the *Times* was the only paper to print the premier's entire statement. See also Toronto *Daily Star*, 9 April 1937.
23. The Mackenzie King Diary, 8 April 1937, Public Archives of Canada (PAC). I am grateful to Mr. Colin Read for drawing this to my attention.
24. Lapointe to Hepburn, 8 April 1937; J.H. MacBrien to Hepburn, 8 April 1937; MacBrien to officer-in-command, RCMP, Toronto, 9 April 1937, Lapointe Papers, PAC.
25. Toronto *Daily Star*, 10 April 1937.
26. Oshawa *Times*, 10 April 1937.
27. Toronto *Globe and Mail*, Toronto *Telegram*, Oshawa *Times*, Ottawa *Citizen*, *Daily Clarion*, 10 April 1937; Toronto *Daily Star*, 10, 12 April 1937; Hamilton *Spectator*, 12 April 1937.
28. Toronto *Daily Star*, 10 April 1937.
29. Toronto *Telegram*, 10 April 1937.
30. Oshawa *Times*, 10 April 1937.
31. *Ibid.*; Secret report from Inspector Feiling to Hepburn, 9 April 1937, Hepburn Papers.
32. Toronto *Globe and Mail*, 10 April 1937.
33. Interviews with Charles Millard, Art Schultz.
34. *Daily Clarion*, Oshawa *Times*, 12 April 1937.
35. *Ibid.*; Interview with Charles Millard; Letter to the author from Hugh Thompson, 19 February 1968.
36. *Canadian Forum*, June 1937; *Daily Clarion*, Oshawa *Times*, 12 April 1937; Interviews with Charles Millard, George Burt.
37. New York *Times*, 11 April 1937.
38. Toronto *Daily Star*, 12 April 1937; Interviews with Eamon Park, Joseph Salsberg.
39. Toronto *Globe and Mail*, 12 April 1937; Hepburn to Mackenzie King, 13 April 1937, Hepburn Papers.
40. King Diary, 13 April 1937.

41. Mackenzie King to Hepburn, 13 April 1937, Hepburn Papers.
42. Hepburn to Lapointe, 13 April 1937, Hepburn Papers; Toronto *Daily Star*, 13 April 1937.
43. Toronto *Daily Star*, 13 April 1937; OPP Constable Wilson to Hepburn, 9, 10, 11, 12, 13 April 1937, Hepburn Papers.
44. King Diary, 13 April 1937.
45. *Ibid.*, 14 April 1937; Lapointe to Hepburn, 14 April 1937, Hepburn Papers.
46. New York *Times*, 15 April 1937.
47. Toronto *Daily Star*, 15 April 1937; Toronto *Globe and Mail*, 16 April 1937.
48. Toronto *Globe and Mail*, 17 April 1937.
49. Interviews with David Croll, Arthur Roebuck and a Hepburn aide, Roy Elmhirst.
50. Hepburn to Croll; Hepburn to Roebuck, 14 April 1937, Hepburn Papers.
51. Croll to Hepburn; Roebuck to Hepburn, 14 April 1937, Hepburn Papers.
52. Toronto *Globe and Mail*, Toronto *Daily Star*, 15 April 1937; *New Commonwealth*, 24 April 1937.
53. Toronto *Globe and Mail*, 16 April 1937; Interview with Charles Millard.
54. Oshawa *Times*, 17 April 1937.
55. Minutes of meeting, 17 April 1937, Hepburn Papers.
56. Toronto *Daily Star*, 19 April 1937; Interviews with Roy Elmhirst, Charles Millard, Louis Fine.
57. Secret report from OPP Constable Wilson to Hepburn, 17 April 1937, Hepburn Papers.
58. Secret reports from OPP Constable Hitch, Timmins, Ontario, to Hepburn, 13, 14, 16 April 1937; OPP Inspector Creasy, Haileybury, Ontario, to Hepburn, 14 April 1937; H. Knox to Hepburn, 16 April 1937, Hepburn Papers. Also see New York *Times*, 19 April 1937; *Union News* (Mine-Mill newspaper), May 1937.
59. Toronto *Daily Star*, 19 April 1937; Oshawa *Times*, 20 April 1937; Interviews with Charles Millard, Alex Hall.
60. Interviews with Charles Millard, George Burt; Letter from Hugh Thompson to the author, 19 February 1968; Oshawa *Times*, 20 April 1937.
61. Minutes of the executive meeting, 19 April 1937; Martin to Thompson, 20 April 1937, Thompson Papers; both in UAW Labor Archives, Wayne State University, Detroit, Michigan.
62. McIntyre to Hepburn, 21 April 1937; Hepburn to McLaughlin, 20 April 1937, Hepburn Papers.
63. Minutes of meetings, 21-22 April 1937; McIntyre to Hepburn, 22 April 1937, Hepburn Papers.
64. Toronto *Daily Star*, 23 April 1937.
65. Toronto *Globe and Mail*, 26 April 1937.
66. *Daily Clarion*, 27 April 1937; Toronto *Daily Star*, 26 April 1937.
67. *Financial Post*, 8 May 1937; Interview with Charles Millard; Letter from Hugh Thompson to the author, 19 February 1968.
68. Toronto *Daily Star*, 1 May 1937.
69. Mrs. Bruce's Diary, May 1937, Bruce Papers, Archives of Ontario. I am grateful to Professor J.L. Granatstein, who generously allowed me to see his notes from the Bruce Papers.
70. Interview with Earl Rowe. In addition, Mr. Rowe kindly sent me a long memorandum on his recollections of these events.
71. *Ibid.*; D.M. Hogarth to Rowe, 5 July 1937, Bruce Papers. (Hogarth was the leading Conservative strategist at the time.) See also Neil McKenty, *Mitch Hepburn*, pp. 119-125.
72. Toronto *Globe and Mail*, 5 June 1937.
73. Interviews with Roy Elmhirst, Earl Rowe, David Croll.
74. *New Commonwealth*, 15 May 1937; Dennis Wrong, "Ontario Provincial Elections 1934-55," *Canadian Journal of Economics and Political Science* 23 (August 1957): 395-403.
75. See Gerald L. Caplan, *The Dilemma of Canadian Socialism: The CCF in Ontario* (Toronto: McClelland & Stewart, 1973).

Canadian Labour and International Unions in the Seventies

Terrence H. White

Introduction[1]

Since its inception in the early nineteenth century, the Canadian labour movement has grown to almost two and one-half million members, or to more than one quarter of the current civilian labour force. The analysis of labour union growth and development in Canada from a social movement's perspective is appropriate, but only if one does *not* take an overly simplistic view of labour as a homogeneous collectivity, with minimal organization, constantly bent on change. Rather, labour in Canada tends to be a heterogeneous alliance of many diverse, decentralized groupings. These tend to be loosely bound by some common although often-changing ideals whose individual and collective degrees of activity and organization vary with the circumstances and relevance of immediate issues and causes.

Canadian labour activity often approaches what Herbert Blumer has termed a *general social movement*[2] in that one of its concerns is with value changes in a culture; as for example, in its early radical posture that workers should have rights in the work place just as the employer had, or that collective bargaining should be the means of determining wages and working conditions, and so on. Because of the decentralized nature of certain aspects of labour organization, specific social movements often develop with each focussing on local conditions where some particular reform is sought, such as in the removal of specific hazards from a work environment. The nature of Canadian labour, then, at any point, may be described as a general movement, or a series of specific movements, or both.

Students of the development and evolution of social movements have observed that once initial discontent has generated a mood for change, and some success has been achieved, the early spontaneity of the movement tends to become more

Article commissioned for this book by the editors.

formalized and more routine. In other words, there is an evolution from a number of aroused individuals to loose change-oriented aggregation with minimal organization (a social movement) to the more institutionalized, higher organization form which Zald and Ash[3] refer to as "movement organizations". One would also expect that the larger the movement, the greater the need for organization. Likewise, the more geographically diffuse, the more complex, and the more routinized the movement, the greater the need for organization.

As an example of these evolutionary changes in labour movements, Lester, in his analysis of the maturation of American labour unions, has observed a decline in their rate of expansion and the extent of their early "missionary zeal". The growing complexity of collective-bargaining procedures and presentations has also resulted in the centralization in union headquarters of many of these functions which were formerly the responsibilities of the locals. He further suggests that many union officials have adopted the life styles and behavioural patterns of management, with the result that these leaders often become removed from their members. As a consequence, Lester observes that, ". . . union militancy and demagoguery have tended to give way to carefully prepared presentations and disciplined representation."[4] These characteristics of maturation lead him to describe labour organizations in the United States as "sleepy monopolies".

In contrast to Lester's view of "sleepy monopolies", our perspective of the Canadian labour movement is best described by labour economist Aranka Kovacs. She says:

> The labour movement, then, is defined . . . as a dynamic organizational instrument created by workers and emerging as an institutional force independent of the state and the employers. It embraces a philosophy which provides the movement with the institutional drive necessary for its survival and development. Since the movement is an evolutionary force, its philosophy is also subject to alteration with the times. Composed of a wide variety of union organizations, the labour movement is thus continuously facing pressures in its internal relationships and from its external environment.[5]

It is our position that the potential for conflict resulting from the American domination of Canadian labour organization, the entry of more women and younger workers into union ranks, the tendency for mergers, regional-ethnic interests, and strains in the conventional collective bargaining patterns, will combine to make the seventies a benchmark in the evolution of Canada's labour movements. The focus of this article is restricted to one of the above issues with an analysis of the nature of the presently changing relationships between Canadian labour and American international unions. Some consideration will also be given to the possible trends in these relationships for the remainder of the decade.[6]

Prophecy and Protest
International Unions

From its beginnings, Canadian labour organization has experienced foreign influence. Initially, that influence was British. By the late 1800's, however, increasing numbers of Canadian locals were affiliated with American labour in so-called "international" unions.[7] And by 1911, as shown in Table 1, almost ninety per cent of Canadian labour unionists were members of American-based unions. For the remainder of the first half of this century, the percentages of Canadians in international unions varied but never again rose above the low seventies, stabilizing at these levels during the period between 1951 and 1966. But since 1966 there has been a regular downward trend, indicating the gradual rise of Canadian-based unions.

The most recent statistics indicate that there are 99 international and 68 national unions in Canada, as compared with 110 and 55 respectively, in 1967.

Table 1

Canadian Membership in International Unions Compared with Total Canadian Membership for the Period 1911-1972.

Year	Total Union Membership (000's)	Canadian Membership in International Unions (000's)	Percentage of Total Membership in International Unions
1911	133.1	119.4	89.7
1921	313.3	228.2	72.8
1926	274.6	202.5	73.7
1931	310.5	215.9	69.5
1936	322.7	174.8	54.2
1941	461.7	288.0	62.4
1946	831.7	573.3	68.9
1951	1,028.5	725.6	70.5
1956	1,351.7	947.5	70.1
1961	1,447.0	1,040.2	71.9
1966	1,735.8	1,219.5	70.2
1967	1,920.6	1,272.9	66.3
1968	2,009.7	1,345.3	66.9
1969	2,074.6	1,346.1	65.0
1970	2,173.1	1,359.3	62.5
1971	2,210.6	1,371.1	62.0
1972	2,370.6	1,411.6	59.6

Sources: *Labour Organisations in Canada*, 1921-1972, *Historical Statistics of Canada*, 1965.

Reference to Table 2 reveals that almost 900,000 persons are members of national unions, while the remaining 66,000 non-international unionists are spread throughout 270 local unions and organizations. In the case of these latter groupings, their small size (245 members, on average) makes their continued viability highly problematic, and their vulnerability to absorption into other existing unions, or their susceptibility to raiding by larger unions, very high.

Relative Deprivation

The growing tendency of the Canadian affiliates of international unions to break away and form autonomous unions has frequently been attributed to a surge in nationalism. There is no question that sensitivity to a Canadian identity and a Canadian perspective has heightened since the mid-1960's in all spheres of our society. A more appropriate explanation of the *genesis* of these developments in the labour movement, however, is probably afforded by the relative deprivation theory of social movements. As enunciated by David Aberle in his excellent

Table 2

Union Membership by Type of Union and Affiliation, 1972.

Type and Affiliation	No. of Unions	No. of Locals	Membership Number	Per Cent
International Unions	99	4,914	1,411,852	59.6
AFL-CIO/CLC	84	4,463	1,195,398	50.5
CLC only	4	146	115,671	4.9
AFL-CIO only	5	8	619	*
Unaffiliated Unions	6	297	100,164	4.2
National Unions	68	5,278	892,691	37.7
CLC	19	2,862	401,098	16.9
CNTU	12	1,135	218,526	9.2
CCU	4	27	10,511	0.5
Unaffiliated Unions	33	1,254	262,556	11.1
Directly Chartered				
Local Unions	129	129	12,885	0.5
CLC	128	128	12,790	0.5
CNTU	1	1	95	*
Independent Local				
Organizations	141	141	53,213	2.2
Total	437	10,462	2,370,641	100.0

*Less than 0.1 per cent.

Source: Table 3, *Labour Organizations in Canada*, 1972.

study, *The Peyote Religion Among the Navaho*,[8] a sense of relative deprivation develops when a group determines that its actual conditions or circumstances are lower than those to which it feels legitimately entitled, and subsequently moves for a change in those conditions. The expectations of a group most frequently result from comparisons with a reference group sharing varying degrees of similar characteristics. If, for example, women workers in a plant become aware that men who have similar skill levels are being paid a higher rate for doing the same jobs and feel that equal work should be rewarded by equal pay, then it is quite likely that a sense of relative deprivation will develop among the women. It is equally probable that under appropriate contextual conditions they may try to right that perceived imbalance.[9]

It is our thesis that the Canadian members of a growing number of the international unions feel deprived relative to American workers in their own union as a result of certain current events. This sense of relative deprivation has spawned a series of more or less isolated specific social movements resulting in the establishment of an increasing number of newly autonomous Canadian units. As a result, a characteristic of the *general* labour movement is a rising concern for a movement with more of a Canadian focus — it is at this point that nationalism becomes a factor. And although splits from international unions have occurred and are still occurring, another observable outcome has been a growing responsiveness in some international unions to improving the service to Canadian locals. Our analysis will be concerned with not only isolating those factors leading to feelings of relative deprivation among Canadians in some international unions, but also with the contextual conditions which have contributed to movements towards separation.

Conditions Leading to a Sense of Relative Deprivation

Hartke-Burke Bill
Probably the single most influential contributing factor in the current unrest among many of the Canadian members of international unions is the proposed Hartke-Burke Bill. This protectionist trade bill, if enacted by the US Congress, would impose restrictive quotas on nearly all foreign-made imports entering the United States.

> The Hartke-Burke bill also calls for the labelling and advertising of all products to disclose if they contain foreign-made components; the repeal of existing legislation permitting the duty-free re-entry into the United States of goods exported from the US for assembly and processing abroad. (The automotive industry in Canada would be seriously affected by this since it contains a considerable amount of US-made components.) To prevent US technology from escaping abroad, the bill would authorize the president to prohibit the use of

licensing of any patent abroad on penalty that the patent would become unenforceable in US courts.[10]

Of particular irritation to Canadian members of international unions has been the fact that the central labour body in the United States to which their unions belong, the AFL-CIO, is actively lobbying in support of the passage of this measure in the belief that it will insure the jobs of US workers and create new ones at the expense of foreign workers. Canadians in US-based international unions constitute only about eight per cent of their total membership, and when a portion of their annual dues are used to support a lobby for legislation that will benefit only the American membership of their unions and possibly result in job insecurity for themselves, their increasing frustration is understandable.

The concern of Canadian labour unionists with this bill was evident at the 1972 Canadian Labour Congress convention.[11] Seventeen months later, the growing fears about the impacts of the Hartke-Burke bill on Canadian workers were reported to an AFL-CIO meeting in Florida:

> Jean Beaudry, executive vice-president of the CLC has warned the AFL-CIO that relations between the Canadian and US labour movements would be irreparably strained if Congress passes the Burke-Hartke restrictionist trade bill, which is the cornerstone of the AFL-CIO's policy on trade and is being pushed vigorously by the federation.
>
> He told the 1,000 delegates that CLC economists have calculated that if the bill were enacted this year it would cost the Canadian economy $4-billion, and the cost in jobs would be astronomical.[12]

But, despite the opposition from Canadian locals of international unions, the AFL-CIO's position on the Hartke-Burke bill remains unchanged.[13]

The effects of this proposed US legislation and the AFL-CIO's obvious support of it have been to demonstrate to many the vulnerability of their position as a Canadian minority in a US-dominated international labour organization. The revelation that the American members of their unions would have a preferred status in the event of enactment of protectionist trade laws and that this inequity is union supported, has created a definite sense of relative deprivation among many of the Canadians in the ranks of international unions.

CALURA

There can be little doubt about the significance of the Hartke-Burke bill in fostering a sense of relative deprivation among Canadian locals of international unions. A piece of Canadian legislation, The Corporations and Labour Unions Returns Act (CALURA) of 1962, has also had a considerable impact as well. The Act, as it applies to labour unions, requires that each year every labour union in Canada with one hundred or more members must supply the government with a copy of its constitution, names of its officers, and its financial statements, including the dues and monies paid to international unions from members resident in Canada.

Each year controversy surrounds the release of the financial figures showing that Canadians send more money to American headquarters of internationals annually than they receive back in salaries and services. A typical breakdown of the revenues and expenditures of international unions from a Canadian perspective, as presented each year in the CALURA reports, is contained in Table 3. A superficial evaluation of these data suggests that for the years 1970 and 1971 Canadian members were apparently shortchanged to the extent of 13.6 and 24.9 million dollars in each respective year — shortchanged in terms of what they received back from their international unions in comparison with their payments. Every year considerable mileage is made out of these figures by critics of international unions in Canada; but in fact, these are actually incomplete data representing only a *selective* presentation of certain income and expense items. Many of the expenditures necessary in maintaining a labour organization, such as money spent on research, legal fees, and so on, are omitted.[14]

A recent study has shown that even when these factors are taken into account, a shortfall still occurs for Canadian members. Wilfred List reports:

> In a study last year (1972) on the financial aspects of international unions, J.K. Eaton, an economist in the economics and research

---

Table 3

Selected Financial Data Relating to the Canadian Operations of All Reporting International Labour Organizations with Canadian Members — 1970, 1971.

	1970	1971
1. Income on account of net dues and assessments paid by or credited to persons resident in Canada.	$45,426,000	$50,519,000.
2. Expenditures		
(a) Gross salaries, wages, and other remuneration of officers and employees resident in Canada.	$12,411,000.	$13,917,000.
(b) Strike benefit expenditures to members resident in Canada and locals and branches in Canada.	$15,090,000.	$ 7,821,000.
(c) Pension and welfare benefits paid by the union to beneficiaries resident in Canada.	$ 4,335,000.	$ 3,870,000.
Total Expenditures	$31,836,000.	$25,608,000.

Source: Table 33A, Corporations and Labour Unions Returns Act, Report for 1971. Part II — Labour Unions, p. 102.

branch of the federal Department of Labour, attempted to estimate income and expenditures of international unions on their Canadian operations from 1962 to 1969.

He assigned to the Canadian membership 7% of the cost of office and administrative expenditures, professional fees and expenses, depreciation on fixed assets and some other expenditures of the international union for total operations. He also apportioned to the Canadian account 1 per cent of all salaries paid by the international in the United States.

On the basis of his calculations, Dr. Eaton concluded that net income of international unions on Canadian operations varied from $558,000 in 1962 to 7,355,000 in 1967; 2,063,000 in 1968 and a deficit of 1,196,000 in 1969.[15]

Regardless of what figures one looks at,[16] the regularity of publicized financial imbalances in the Canadian position in international unions since the first CALURA report in 1965 undoubtedly have an unsettling effect and further reinforce those perceptions of relative deprivation among Canadian members.

Additional Factors

We have suggested that the Hartke-Burke Bill and the CALURA reports are recent major developments which may act as stimuli sensitizing Canadian members to possible double standards in their international unions, wherein they perceive themselves as potentially deprived relative to the American members. There are, of course, a number of minor irritants which may have similar or reinforcing effects. Most international unions, for example, have some form of a regular newsletter or magazine containing information on issues and events relevant to their spheres of interest. But few of these contain either a special section devoted to Canadian news or an altogether separate publication for the Canadian membership. Dennis McDermott (Canadian Director of the UAW) has been quoted as describing the "US-oriented international" union newspaper as being ". . . full of information for Americans, but about as interesting as a sheet of Chinese music to Canadians."[17]

Union publications can be quite functional in building an organizational identity by focussing on issues considered significant to organization viability and growth. Furthermore, they are useful in the dissemination of information. In Canada, however, as developments of interest to Canadians are frequently ignored, these publications often fail to contribute to these goals. Indeed, they may very well foster among Canadians a sense of being an outside minority even though they are, in fact, dues-paying members.

A series of such minor occurrences may have a significant negative impact on members since these are the events that touch individuals — little things that they can empathize with. The CALURA reports and subsequent union rebuttals about their validity, on the other hand, may not always be easily related to or understood.

There are a number of other minor irritants which either separately, or in concert, may reinforce a sense of relative deprivation. One additional illustration may be useful. All unions, not just international unions, have a problem of adequately rewarding their leaders at appropriate financial levels for the responsibilities involved in their jobs, and at the same time maintaining a sense of unity in the membership that they are all working together to improve their common position. Many members find it difficult to identify with the leaders in their union who may be earning ten times or more than the worker's annual wage.[18] This gap between leaders and members is often even more acute for Canadians in international unions. Because of their minority status within the internationals, virtually none of the top positions will be held by Canadians.

Contextual Factors

Those conditions which we have thus far discussed as being representative of some of the current influences often resulting in feelings of relative deprivation among Canadian members of international unions will have varying impacts ranging from apathy, to change, to separation, depending on the particular circumstances of each Canadian local's situation. Where persons perceive relative deprivation to be more acute, where attractive alternatives to their present position are available at reasonable costs, and where there is widespread support among the local membership for a change and perhaps even some outside support, then it is more likely that a movement for change will develop.

At the present time, there are certain *contextual* factors in Canadian society that are conducive to the support of change movements in the Canadian locals of international unions. These differ from the specific conditions leading to relative deprivation insofar as they relate to the more general social and political environment in which labour operates. The recent rise in national concern about American dominance in all facets of Canadian society has naturally concentrated heavily on the US ownership of manufacturing, service, and resource industries. In addition, groups such as the Committee for an Independent Canada (CIC) have directed some of their critical attacks on international unions in Canada. That these campaigns have had some impact is obvious. The *Globe and Mail*, for example, reported that "Jean Beaudry, executive vice-president of the Canadian Labour Congress, yesterday criticized the Committee for an Independent Canada and two of its key leaders for what he termed their 'holy war' on international unions."[19] Likewise, an account in *Business Week* noted that, at a CIC conference in Edmonton in 1972, it was proposed that minimum standards of self-government be implemented in Canadian locals of US internationals, and it was also suggested that ". . . merging many Canadian unions to strengthen them" would "eliminate a need for 'big brother unions' in the US. . . ."[20] John Munro, Minister of Labour, has also made statements supportive of a Canadian-based labour movement, and has even intimated that federal legislation might be proposed to ensure such an eventuality.

Despite the impetus for change, there are several considerations which may pose serious barriers. Property and monies generated and used by Canadian locals will almost always be registered in the name of the international. Separation from the international will, therefore, usually involve the loss of these resources. The cost to the local considering such moves may, as a consequence, be substantial. Another factor often retarding separation considerations is that most of the major international unions in Canada are affiliated with the Canadian Labour Congress, and to break away from an international usually means that the new unit will not be allowed to affiliate with the CLC. Instead, it will be required to look to the smaller confederations (Council of Canadian Unions, for example), or else remain isolated through non-affiliation.

Action and Reaction

At least three basic descriptive patterns are necessary to account for the various behavioural trends currently observable among Canadian locals. The first of these patterns is a tendency toward the maintenance of the *status quo* wherein the internationals are viewed by the Canadian members as a satisfactory countervailing force in the labour relations arena. The services provided are generally considered to be satisfactory and the affairs of collective bargaining and grievance processing are thought to be efficiently maintained. As in all collective endeavours there may be problems, but these do not result in marked feelings of relative deprivation or continued uneasiness. This *status quo* position is certainly, at present, the dominant posture among the Canadian locals in international unions.

The second pattern that can be observed is for the development of an increased sensitivity on the part of internationals to the needs of its Canadian members, even though they often may only represent a very small minority of their total memberships. In these cases the international identifies a pattern of unrest in its Canadian ranks and moves to reinforce its position. The International Union, United Automobile, Aerospace, and Agricultural Implement Workers of America (UAW), with 9.1% of its members Canadian has been a leader in this regard under its Canadian Director, Dennis McDermott:

> Mr. McDermott said yesterday that the Canadian union movement can no longer go along with its head in the sand, dismissing nationalist sentiment. "It is my current belief that unless international unions in Canada can make some fairly drastic accommodations and adjustments to the needs of the current emotions that exist

in this country, then the role of international unions is in serious jeopardy. . . .

It comes about because of glaring examples of genuine resentment by workers who really are governed from some remote spot in the US and who have little or no control over their destiny. Thus where a union has a research department staffed with economic and other specialists it should have a smaller but similar facility in its Canadian headquarters. The same should apply to areas such as public relations, engineering, education, legislative lobbyists, arbitration specialization, social action, international affairs, legal matters and whatever else exists in the union's U.S. structure."[21]

Several months later, Mr. McDermott announced that UAW headquarters in Detroit had agreed that Canadian dues would be spent in Canada. A number of newly granted privileges also included the establishment of a Canadian union paper, Canadian representation on world bodies, and a separate Canadian research department.[22] In addition, Canadian members would still have unlimited access to international strike funds.

The duplication of services and structures, as implied in the UAW's response, may only be a viable avenue for a few of the very large internationals with Canadian memberships proportionately large enough to warrant the costs of such programmes. The Teamsters' union, for example, has over 60,000 Canadian members, but these represent only 3.1% of this international's total membership. A year ago the director of the union in Canada resigned for the reported reason that: "The refusal of Frank Fitzsimmons, president of the International Brotherhood of Teamsters, to give meaning to the post of Canadian director of the union by supporting it with money and staff led to the resignation of Senator Edward Lawson. . . ."[23]

The first two patterns are examples of movement maintenance while the third pattern to be considered here involves the separation of Canadian locals into new, autonomous units. Recently, there have been increasing numbers of Canadian separations from international unions. In April 1972, for example, ". . . the 4,000-member Canadian section of the Communication Workers of America (AFL-CIO/CLC) withdrew from its parent union to establish a national communications union, the Communication Workers of Canada, which maintains affiliation with the CLC only."[24] Workers at the ALCAN smelters in Kitimat severed ties with the United Steelworkers of America, and 440 sawmill workers on Vancouver Island left the International Woodworkers of America to join the Council of Canadian Unions. A complete inventory of separations is not possible here, but an additional sampling would include the withdrawal of Vancouver-area Canadian National locomotive engineers from the American-based Brotherhood of Locomotive Engineers,[25] and the rejection, by Montreal firemen, of the International Association of Fire Fighters.[26]

Most of the separations from international unions have, to date, involved relatively small-sized units. Although this trend to Canadianization has achieved some momentum, the absolute number of workers involved has not been substantial, relative to the total number of international union members in Canada. But just recently (April, 1974), a split of major proportions involved the decision of the 52,000 Canadian members of the United Paperworkers International Union to form a separate Canadian union. In general, however, the separations have involved the smaller locals and have been most prevalent in British Columbia.

An understanding of the processes involved in separation is perhaps best obtained in the examination of a brief case study of the phenomenon. Consideration of the recent formation of the Canadian Union of Distillery Workers provides an excellent example, and as well, affords an opportunity for a further development of some other concerns previously raised.

Birth of the Canadian Union of Distillery Workers[27]

In 1972, the 3,224 Canadian members of the Distillery, Rectifying, Wine, and Allied Workers' International Union of America (DRWW)* accounted for less than nine per cent of the union's total membership. The biggest of the DRWW's Canadian locals was Local 61 representing over 800 workers at the large Hiram Walker and Sons Ltd. distillery in Windsor, Ontario. For some time there had been a growing disaffection among the members of Local 61 with the American-based union over a number of issues including the proposed Hartke-Burke legislation. A substantial proportion of the product (mainly *Canadian Club* whiskey) produced at the Windsor distillery is exported to the US, and certain provisions in the Hartke-Burke bill were a source of concern to members of Local 61 in regard to their job security. Their apprehensions were reinforced not only by the AFL-CIO's positive stance on the bill, but their own union executive, headquartered in New Jersey, were equally enthusiastic about the proposed legislation. They had even suggested, in a rather unimaginative fashion, that any fears about the bill were undoubtedly due to a misunderstanding of its provisions and that it was, in fact, an excellent bill.

Although the union, to its credit, did have a vice-president in Canada, Local 61 disapproved of the manner in which that post was filled. They would have preferred that the Canadian vice-president be elected by the Canadian members; but instead, the Canadian vice-president was elected by the total membership. This procedure meant that the Canadian minority, representing only one tenth of the eligible voters in any union election, was entirely dependent on the American majority in the selection of their vice-president. Local 61, as a result, had the impression that the Canadian vice-president of the Distillery Workers was always

---

*This international union will sometimes also be referred to as the Distillery Workers throughout this section.

the choice of the union executive and that a reform candidate, even if the popular choice of the Canadian members, stood virtually no chance of success.

For Local 61, the selection procedures for the DRWW vice-president in Canada and the union's pro-Hartke-Burke stance emphasized the inherent disadvantages of their minority status as Canadians in the union. An even greater sense of dissatisfaction occurred when members of Local 61 compared themselves to members of other union locals in their immediate environs. The comparisons were particularly aggravating when the services provided by other internationals to their locals were examined.

Windsor's industrial base is dominated by the automobile industry whose workers are represented by the UAW — a large union with an extensive and efficient range of member services. It is conceded that many unions would suffer in comparisons of service offerings with those of the UAW, but the inadequacies of the DRWW were increasingly apparent to Local 61. Communications within the union, for example, were particularly ineffectual. The only regular means of communication was the annual issue of the *DRWAW Journal*. Another irritant for the Windsor workers was the almost total absence of a relevant research effort by the union. As a consequence, Local 61 was often required to prepare for contract negotiations using data on cost-of-living, fringe benefit programmes, and so on, garnered through contacts by the Local 61's executive with other unions in the Windsor area, such as the UAW.

It is not possible here to itemize exhaustively the inadequacies and absences of the DRWW's services, but it should be noted that as a result of these gaps there were considerable doubts in Local 61 as to the value of services they received for the share of the per capita dues sent monthly to the union's headquarters ($3.50 of the $9.00 monthly member's dues went to the international). By the spring of 1973, these feelings of dissatisfaction in Local 61 had been simmering for some time and were further exacerbated by the international's failure to support a small local in its protracted strike. *The Windsor Star* reported that "Local 69 in Vancouver has been on strike against Seagrams for nearly four months without the sanction of the international and without any strike benefits from it."[28] That this inaction on the part of the international would have been of concern is obvious. Indeed, in general, the DRWW has had a history of more comfortable relationships with companies than is usual for most unions, and had on previous occasions refused to back their locals in strike calls. As a matter of fact, Local 61 had experienced this same difficulty several years earlier.

The international's treatment of this small local in Vancouver was the catalyst that triggered the unrest in Local 61. In June 1973, Local 61 voted 85% in favour of leaving the international union's ranks. Ontario labour law requires that when a bargaining unit such as Local 61 no longer wishes to be represented by a particular union it can apply to the Ontario Labour Relations Board (OLRB) in the last two months of its contract asking for a decertification vote. If at least thirty-five per cent of the members petition for the decertification, the OLRB will conduct the vote and, should more than 50% vote in favour, decertification is accomplished. By September, 1973, *The Windsor Star* reported that Local 61 was actively seeking decertification:

> In a massive display of solidarity Local 61 Distillery Workers Union at Hiram Walker and Sons Ltd. has taken a conclusive step towards breaking affiliation with its international. The local, for the past three days, has been gathering names on a petition asking the Ontario Labour Relations Board to conduct a decertification vote. By 9 am this morning over 85 per cent of the local's 850 members had signed the petition.[29]

The number of signatures on the petition easily exceeded the necessary thirty-five per cent and was ready for delivery to the OLRB in Toronto on November 1 — the first day in the last two months of Local 61's contract.

In the meantime, the international union's executives were attempting to dampen the breakaway efforts of Local 61. Given the seriousness of the Windsor situation, they were willing to call for an all-Canadian conference of its locals, and to provide mechanisms whereby the Canadian vice-president would be chosen exclusively by Canadian members.[30] In addition, the international executive suggested in communications to Local 61 members that breakaway action was unwise because, without the international's support, they would be unlikely to survive.

In other situations of Canadian locals wanting to break away, other internationals have similarly engaged in counter-separation tactics. Some of the more interesting ones were employed by the United Steelworkers of America (USWA) in their successful bid to ward off the Canadian Workers Union's (CWU) fight to represent the 3,600 Steelworkers at the Cominco plant in Trail, British Columbia.[31]

With respect to the DRWW, the petition to the Ontario Labour Relations Board asking for a decertification vote was delivered on November 1, and an OLRB hearing to consider the request was scheduled for November 23. Two weeks later the DRWW's "all-Canadian" conference in Montreal began with an attempt by the international to refuse the participation of Local 61's delegates. This endeavour failed when the other Canadian locals present supported Local 61's bid to be heard. But other than an airing of the various positions, the session produced no results of any consequence.

In Windsor the following week, the international union continued its counter-moves against the separation by staging a disloyalty hearing to ascertain whether or not the officers of Local 61 had been disloyal to the international union. No one showed up at that hearing except the three-man panel from the DRWW. In almost comic opera fashion, reports of that hearing stated that: "The Distillery

Workers International Union, which called the hearing, decided to proceed with the hearing and maintained that it was valid even though there were no representatives from Local 61.''[32] The next day all officers of Local 61 were suspended by the international, and a supervisor was appointed to run the affairs of the local.

These eleventh-hour manoeuvres by the international would have been somewhat superfluous had Local 61's decertification procedures moved smoothly according to schedule; but the OLRB, at its hearing on November 23, dismissed the petition from Local 61 on the basis of a minor legal technicality: "The board ruled that the previous petition did not meet the requirements of Ontario labour law because it failed to mention 'Local 61' in its heading."[33] A new petition with the necessary correction was submitted and the official OLRB vote was held in February, 1974, with a 96% majority in favour of decertification. The members subsequently decided to form their own union and in April, 1974, almost ten months after the commencement of separation proceedings by Local 61, the Ontario Labour Relations Board certified the fledgling Canadian Union of Distillery Workers as the bargaining agent for the plant employees at Hiram Walker and Sons Ltd. in Windsor.

This new union has a cautious optimism about its future viability, and its emphasis is on providing services to its members, including the publication of a regular newspaper and improved research efforts. The costs involved in the achievement of autonomy have, however, been considerable. Decertification from the international, certification as a new union, and the fighting of various injunctions required $30,000. in legal fees alone. A further consequence of decertification was the loss of affiliation with the Canadian Labour Congress. The CLC's constitution currently prevents the affiliation of breakaway units whose former parents are CLC affiliates. An additional $15,000. in operating funds of Local 61 were lost by the CUDW to the international. Moreover, the future of Local 61's strike funds amounting to $80,000. is in the hands of the Ontario Supreme Court for a ruling with both the CUDW and the DRWW claiming these monies.

The breakaway decision by Local 61 appears to have been initially motivated, like so many of the other recent breakaways by Canadian locals of international unions, by what we have referred to as feelings of relative deprivation in regard to union services (that is, bread and butter issues), rather than by nationalism alone. Once the sentiment to separate has evolved, the actual strategy of separation is often governed by the labour legislation of that jurisdiction. As we saw in the instances of the decertification processes of Local 61, it was required to abide by the stipulations of Ontario law. In the case of Local 61, once there was a commitment to a separation, favourable public opinion and general media support, among other factors, undoubtedly helped to sustain the initial drive. Since this event, two additional Canadian locals of the International Distillery Workers have also separated although each subsequently joined other international unions.

The Future

Our position in this paper has been that organized labour in Canada may be described at one level as a general social movement sharing an ideological stance of improving social and economic conditions at work and in general for its members. It is also a loose network of heterogeneous, decentralized movement organizations, which, because of their dynamic and evolving characteristics, provide the setting for a series of isolated specific social movements. We considered the growing tendency of Canadian locals of the American-based internationals to break away and indicated how various contemporary events and circumstances have combined to create a sense of relative deprivation among some of the Canadian members of these unions. This tendency to separate from internationals will probably continue throughout the decade. A number of the resulting autonomous elements will undoubtedly be required to merge with others in order to ensure their viability. But the diversity of the merging units, and the expected conflicts resulting from their various vested interests, should make these mergers difficult, and their eventual survival uncertain at best.

While it may be almost impossible for the many small breakaway units to provide economically good services for their members without increasing their size, mergers may not always be an attractive alternative, not only because of the diversity of these units, but also because of individual factors, such as the power aspirations of the many new leaders. As a result, another likely outcome, to some degree, is that some of these smaller units may attempt to increase their numbers by raiding each other's memberships. Overall, these inter-union rivalries will undoubtedly have debilitating effects, although progress in the separation of Canadian locals from internationals seems inevitable.

Notes

1. Seymour Faber, Jack Ferguson, Paul Grayson, and Bob Prus made helpful comments on an earlier draft of this paper.
2. Herbert Blumer, "Social Movements," pp. 8-29 in *Studies in Social Movements*, Barry McLaughlin (ed.), New York: Free Press, 1969 (p. 8).
3. Mayer N. Zald and Roberta Ash, "Social Movement Organizations: Growth, Decay, and Change," pp. 461-485 in *Studies in Social Movements*, Barry McLaughlin (ed.). See also, Roberta Ash, *Social Movements in America*, Chicago: Markham, 1972.
4. Richard A. Lester, *As Unions Mature*, Princeton: Princeton, 1958 (p. 22).

5. Aranka E. Kovacs, "The Philosophy of the Canadian Labour Movement," pp. 119-144 in *Canadian Labour in Transition*, Richard Ulric Miller and Fraser Isbester (eds.), Scarborough: Prentice-Hall, 1971 (p. 120).

6. For the reader interested in more detailed historical treatment of the Canadian labour movement, see Stuart Jamieson, *Industrial Relations in Canada*, Toronto: Macmillan, 1973 (2nd ed.).

7. Harry Waisglass, research director for the Department of Labor, has suggested that in order to avoid the impression that "international" refers to worldwide organizations, it would be more appropriate to label them as "continental" unions.

8. David Aberle, *The Peyote Religion Among the Navaho*, Chicago: Aldine, 1966.

9. But, as Runciman notes: "Relative deprivation should always be understood to mean a *sense* of deprivation; a person who is 'relatively deprived' need not be 'objectively' deprived in that more usual sense that he is demonstrably lacking something." W.G. Runciman, *Relative Deprivation and Social Justice*, Los Angeles: University of California Press, 1966 (pp. 10-11).

10. Spiros De Bono, "Hartke-Burke Bill and What It Means to Canada," *The Windsor Star*, January 18, 1973 (p. 24).

11. Reports of that meeting stated: "The most significant, and potentially far-reaching, statement from the CLC convention was on international trade. 'We are concerned, deeply concerned,' the policy statement emphasized, 'about trade protectionist trends developing abroad. . . . We are especially disturbed about strong, powerful groups in the United States, including important groups within the country's trade union movement, who are pressing Congress to pass the Hartke-Burke bill.'

"The document then briefly explains that the Hartke-Burke bill would impose restrictive quotas on nearly all the foreign goods entering the US, including those from Canada. It then assails the Americans for having passed the domestic international sales corporation legislation (DISC), the investment tax credit and 'perhaps other measures' which could have 'harmful consequences' for the Canadian economy." *The Financial Times of Canada*, May 22, 1972 (p. 9).

12. Wilfred List, *The Globe and Mail*, October 23, 1973 (p. B-16).

13. "George Meaney, president of the AFL-CIO, and his aides have shattered the illusion that affiliated international unions can do anything effective to protect Canadian members from adverse effects of any general restrictive trade measures adopted by Congress.

Not only did the head of the 13,500,000 member labour federation state flatly that the AFL-CIO has not heard anything from its affiliates on the subject, but his chief aide in the legislative field said exemption for Canada from any general legislation would be impossible.

In Ottawa, CLC president Donald Macdonald said he had never been under any illusion that the international unions could do anything effective to protect Canada's trade interests by proposing exemptions for Canada.

Even the UAW, not an affiliate of the AFL-CIO but which had taken the strongest position against import quotas, was now hedging on the matter because of the unemployment in the auto industry, Mr. Macdonald noted." *The Globe and Mail*, February 23, 1974 (p. 55).

14. Wilfred List, "Canadian Dues Exceed Parent's Outlay," *The Globe and Mail*, April 11, 1973 (p. B-3).

15. *Ibid*.

16. For a more complete discussion of the movement of union funds, see John Crispo, *International Unionism: A Study in Canadian-American Relations*, Toronto: McGraw-Hill, 1967 (Chapter 8, particularly).

17. Wilfred List, "UAW Director Leading Move by Canada's International Union Leaders for More Autonomy," *The Globe and Mail*, February 28, 1973 (p. 5).

18. *Business Week*, August 18, 1973 (p. 62) gives the 1972 salaries of top labor leaders in the US. Salaries of some of the better known persons include: F.E. Fitzsimmons, Teamsters' President, $131,481. (salary and expenses); C.L. Dennis, Railway Clerks' President, $91,069. (salary and expenses); E.J. Carlough, Sheet Metal Workers' President, $77,656. (salary and expenses); George Meaney, AFL-CIO President, $74,776. (salary and expenses); I.W. Abel, Steelworkers' President, $69,937. (salary and expenses); and Leonard Woodcock, UAW President, $47,449. (salary and expenses). Among labor leaders in the US, the total remuneration for each of these six officials ranked 1, 5, 9, 10, 15, and 46, respectively.

19. *The Globe and Mail*, November 8, 1972 (p. 8).

20. *Business Week*, September 30, 1972 (p. 51).
21. *The Globe and Mail*, November 8, 1972 (p. 8).
22. *The Globe and Mail*, April 16, 1973.
23. *The Globe and Mail*, January 31, 1973.
24. *Labour Organizations in Canada, 1972*, Ottawa: Department of Labour (p. xii).
25. *The Financial Times of Canada*, June 18, 1973 (p. 9).
26. "Firemen Quit US Union," *The Windsor Star*, March 23, 1974.
27. Mr. Richard Tighe, President of the Canadian Union of Distillery Workers, was most helpful in clarifying the course of events discussed in this section.
28. *The Windsor Star*, June 6, 1973.
29. Brian Vallee, "Workers Want International Ties Cut," *The Windsor Star*, September 27, 1973.
30. *The Windsor Star*, October 29, 1973.
31. Paul Cabray reported that: "The Steelworkers are fighting hard. The B.C. senior staff representative for the USWA, Monty Alton, is co-ordinating the counter attack.

"So far he has produced two special newspapers that were distributed at the plant gates. Both issues naturally attacked the 'lies' of the CWU and sang the praises of the Steelworkers.

"Workers at the USWA meetings can win jackets with union crests, trips to Vancouver for National Hockey League games and free beer is given out." "A Canadian Union Fights for Control," *The Windsor Star*, January 30, 1973.
32. Brian Vallee, "Local Boycotts Disloyalty Hearing," *The Windsor Star*, November 20, 1973.
33. *The Windsor Star*, December 6, 1973.

Chapter 5

The Nationalist and Social Credit Movements in Quebec

Introduction

In Chapter Two it was suggested that agrarian social movements that developed in the Prairie Provinces could be most adequately understood if the segmentation of Canadian society were taken into consideration. Not only did western farmers believe that eastern business interests were profiting from their labour, but, in some cases, that town merchants in the West itself also participated in this general exploitation. In French Canada, the segmentation between English and French Canadians has also contributed to the development of social movements. In addition, contradictions between an essentially rural, non-industrial social structure and an emerging industrial economic order created further feelings of discontent that have led residents of Quebec to support various movements. To a certain extent, the provisions of the British North America Act serve as an important starting point for an examination of nationalist malaise in twentieth-century Quebec.

To French Canadians, the meaning of Confederation was simple: ". . . it gave to Quebec . . . a government of its own — a government over which the French-Canadian majority would have complete control. It was a provincial government within a rather highly centralized federal system, but it nevertheless exercised authority over those matters that were deemed essential to the preservation of the French-Canadian culture — education, religion, civil law."[1]

In 1867, Confederation was considered adequate, by the majority of English and French Canadians alike, to the task of creating a "new nationality" while at the same time allowing both groups to retain their cultural and linguistic integrity. Few could envisage the political developments that would lead to soul searching by French Canadians regarding Confederation. Few could foresee the socio-economic developments and the legal interpretations of the BNA Act by the Judicial Committee of the Privy Council that would make Confederation less adequate to its original tasks in the twentieth, than it had been in the nineteenth century. Last of all, few could have envisaged that repeated attempts would be made by certain groups of French Canadians to change existing political institutions so that the goals of Confederation, from the French-Canadian point of view, could actually be realized.

Suspicions that Confederation was, in fact, less than had been hoped for were not long in developing. By the turn of the twentieth century, in the realm of religion and education, a number of decisions at the provincial level had led to the realization that perhaps only in Quebec could the French-Canadian language and culture be preserved. In 1871, the provincial government of New Brunswick abolished separate schools. Manitoba followed suit in 1890, and, despite the relatively large number of French-speaking people in the province, rejected French as an official language. Later, in 1905, French-speaking Canadians were denied a separate school system in Saskatchewan and Alberta. Finally, in 1912, Ontario limited the use of French as a language of instruction to those schools where students knew no English; and in such cases French was not to be used beyond the second grade. As Joseph Levitt puts it, "It was painfully clear that Anglo-Canadians denied that Canada 'as a whole' was a bilingual country and that French Canadians everywhere had precisely the same rights as the English." "French Canadians," he adds, "would be allowed to remain French in Quebec but in other provinces they must become English."[2]

Equally alarming events were occurring in the political realm proper. Certain English Canadians were determined to commit Canada to England's grand imperial scheme. In more concrete terms, this sentiment became manifest in the dispatch of volunteers to fight against the Boers in South Africa and in attempts to build a Canadian navy. Unlike numbers of English Canadians, French Canadians were reluctant to commit themselves to "imperialistic ventures" on the part of Great Britain. The later reaction of French Canadians to conscription especially in the first world war must be perceived in this light.

In circumstances such as these, it is not surprising that provincial autonomy was taken very seriously by Quebec. Only if the powers of the provincial government as specified in the BNA Act remained intact could French Canadians survive in an otherwise English country and continent. As André Laurendeau, editor of *Le Devoir*, wrote in 1942, "at Quebec one does what one wants, at Ottawa one does what one can."[3]

By the turn of the century certain developments were also occurring in the economic realm that would lead to an eventual transformation of French-Canadian society — processes that did not go unnoticed by politicians concerned with retaining French language, religion, and culture. To most, there was an intimate connection between these three elements and the rural way of life.[4]

In efforts to maintain the rural way of life, once the arable land in southern Quebec had been settled, the province and the clergy engaged in an active programme of "colonization" of the more northern parts of the province. With the exception of the Lake St. John and Abitibi regions, agriculture had reached its optimum point of expansion by 1820.[5] It was therefore necessary to go further afield. Colonization, however, was inadequate to maintaining Quebec as a rural society; northern areas were simply not conducive to agriculture. The consequence was large-scale emigration. It is estimated that about half a million people left Quebec for New England in the second part of the last century.[6] Here work could be found in flourishing labour-intensive factories.

While urbanism was considered incompatible with the maintenance of the basic values of French-Canadian society, migration to the United States was tantamount to perdition. It is not surprising, therefore, that turn-of-the-century exploitation of Quebec's staple resources by foreign capitalists was looked on with favour by the clergy, politicians, and businessmen. If logging, mining, or pulp and paper production could not provide year-round employment, they could at least supplement the incomes of French Canadians toiling on "marginal" farms. Even this compromise of the agrarian way of life was preferable to movement elsewhere. Thus, cordial relationships developed between the clergy and predominantly Anglo-American industrialists. W.F. Ryan comments on the nature of the relationship between the church and industry in the St. Maurice Valley.

> The general atmosphere that prevailed was one of harmony and co-operation. There was no evidence whatsoever of the clergy trying to keep their people out of industry, and foreign non-Catholic industrialists, probably a little wary in the beginning, gradually came to regard the curés as their friends and benefactors and in time came to support their institutions generously.[7]

Other evidence suggests that this kind of rapport was the rule, not the exception.

At the turn of the century, then, Quebec society and institutions contained serious contradictions, and these contradictions persisted over the next fifty years. On the one hand, there existed the belief that agrarianism, religion, culture, and language held together. As a consequence, educational institutions emphasized, until very recently, values and skills appropriate to a rural, non-industrialized society. This set of attitudes found embodiment in the person of Maurice Duplessis, who, despite his other activities, paid lip service to the "rural myth" until his death in 1959. On the other hand, the nature of economic activity in Quebec was increasingly non-agricultural and, though extractive industries enabled the maintenance of marginal farms, increasing numbers of French Canadians were seeking employment in urban centres. The transition from a predominantly rural society to a predominantly urban one, using as an index the number of individuals living in these types of environments, occurred just after World War One.[8]

While fundamental changes in the institutional structure of Quebec society did not occur until the ''quiet revolution'' of the early sixties, social contradictions, such as the above, had, on a number of occasions, generated dissatisfaction with the prevailing institutional structure. For one thing, at the turn of the century, the abuses of urban life challenged elsewhere by adherents to the social gospel were also perceived by many French Canadians. Slums, alcoholism, prostitution, and exploitation of labour were not the exclusive prerogative of English Canada. In fact, in Quebec, these problems presented more of a dilemma than elsewhere. ''If Catholics felt that the poor must be helped,'' Joseph Levitt points out, ''they also believed that too great an enlargement of the power of the state must be resisted.''[9] Far fewer reservations of this kind hampered the efforts of those connected with the Social Gospel.

Impetus for a change in the lot of the dispossessed of Quebec came, to a certain extent, from the Nationalist League founded in 1903 by Olivar Asselin. However, the Nationalist League was chiefly concerned with independence from Britain, provincial autonomy, and Canadian economic and intellectual development. It is true that the League's ideology contained some ideas regarding improvements in social conditions, but even a cursory examination of its programme reveals that social reform, in the sense mentioned above, was a low priority.

This orientation is not surprising. The events leading to the founding of the League were political, not social. For example, along with a number of other Quebec politicians, Henri Bourassa, one of Quebec's foremost political figures of the first quarter of the century, was concerned with a perceived drift of the federal Liberal Party towards supporting British imperialism. At the same time, Bourassa and his associates realized that the balance between the Liberals and the even more imperialistic Conservatives was too precarious to risk splitting the Liberal ranks by forming a third party. Hence, Bourassa and his compatriots opted, instead, for an organization that would help foster a national consciousness.

It should be stressed that the Nationalist League was in no way concerned with the dissemination of separatist ideas. Bourassa, for one, was a staunch federalist. The particular changes with which he was concerned, then, were practical *within* the framework of Confederation. Those aspects of the Nationalist League's programme that were eventually translated into government policy were implemented in most cases, however, not because of Nationalist pressure, but in spite of it.[10]

After the First World War, economic matters were given even less consideration by nationalists than had earlier been the case. Perhaps one of the most important nationalist developments between 1918 and the Depression was the formation of L'Action française under the intellectual leadership of Abbé Lionel Groulx. In scope, the objectives of the league were initially restricted to promoting the use of French in industry and commerce and in defending the rights of French Canadians resident in other parts of Canada. Later, concern extended to the preservation of traditional values in general.

This later concern had two very important consequences. In the first place, it gave impetus to an out-and-out attack on the burgeoning industrial sector of Quebec as being destructive of traditional values. Secondly, the nationalists attacked the reduction of hitherto independent farmers to the status of dependent wage earners in the new economy. In offering solutions to the problems plaguing French Canada, however, L'Action française was at a loss.

L'Action française was in no way a mass movement, being confined, as it was, primarily to intellectuals. On the other hand, a number of Catholic "action" groups that developed in the postwar period did have relatively large followings. In sponsoring these developments, the church was deliberately attempting to halt processes that were conducive to the emergence of other than traditional values. To this extent, these movements can also be labelled conservative as can all French-Canadian nationalist groups under discussion with the exception of the recent separatist movement.

Perhaps the most important of the movements initiated by the Church was the 1921 Confédération des Travailleurs Catholiques du Canada (CTCC). The intent of this organization was not so much to gain concessions from employers, but to provide a bulwark against American "international" unions. An agrarian counterpart to this movement found expression in the Union Catholique des Cultivateurs (UCC) founded in 1924. Hopefully, through the provision of spiritual and material support to the farmer, the exodus from the land could be halted. Supplementing these occupationally-based organizations, were co-operatives, youth movements, and credit union movements, in which the hand of the church was also evident. In essence, these developments can be seen as the consequence of a contradiction between traditional values and the emerging industrial capitalist order dominated by Anglo-Americans. Indeed, all nationalists were perhaps as much concerned with the foreign nature of industrial capitalism as they were with capitalism *per se*.

In terms of the goals of both L'Action française and the Catholic action groups, little was accomplished throughout the twenties. The trend toward industrialism and urbanization was inexorable. Indeed, during these years, the provincial Liberal government, through its programmes of tax concessions, subsidies, and general "give away" programmes to Anglo-American industry actually contributed to developments feared by the nationalists. That the government remained secure in its position throughout the twenties is an indication of just how deep the contradictions in Quebec society actually were.

With the Depression of 1929, however, it became increasingly clear that political institutions were not meeting Quebec's needs. Discontent became widespread and focussed on economic issues to a greater extent than ever before. Workers, merchants, and businessmen alike were realizing that earlier economic policies had made them subject to the whims of foreign capitalists. Again, however, the concern was not so much with capitalism as with foreign capitalism. In addition, French Canadians now associated foreign interests with the Liberal Party. This identification, coupled with half-hearted attempts on the part of provincial Liberals to cope with the abuses of the Depression, was conducive to the acceptance of a new movement in the political realm. Similar phenomena were evident in Alberta and Saskatchewan during the same period.

Specifically, in Quebec, the impetus for a new political movement that would meet demands generated by the Depression came from a breakaway group of Liberals known as L'Action Libérale Nationale (ALN), under the leadership of Paul Gouin. In the 1935 provincial election, this group of individuals collaborated with provincial Conservatives led by Maurice Duplessis and a number of hitherto "silent" nationalist groups. They tried to oust the Liberals. The 1935 attempt, although unsuccessful, gave the Union Nationale, as the new movement was called, a sufficient number of seats to force a second election in 1936. In the interim, Duplessis clearly emerged as the strong man of the new movement and formed a government in 1936.

In accounting for this victory, the importance of the organizational base provided by the earlier formed Catholic action groups needs to be emphasized. As Herbert Quinn states, "Perhaps the greatest source of strength of the Union Nationale was the fact that it had the unofficial, but nevertheless effective support of all the various Catholic Action and patriotic organizations across the province: the Catholic trade unions, the farmers' organizations, the co-operatives and the credit unions, the youth organizations, the associations of French-Canadian businessmen and merchants."[11]

After the electoral success of the Union Nationale, routinization of the movement occurred with alarming rapidity. It became readily apparent that the economic reforms originally suggested by the ALN were anathema to Duplessis. As a consequence, factionalism developed between the two founding groups and the "left wing" soon dissociated itself from the Union Nationale. The Union Nationale's negative attitude to the war effort and the active intervention of Federal Liberal cabinet ministers explain in large part why provincial Liberals once more became the choice of the Quebec electorate in the election of 1939.

The fate of Duplessis and the Union Nationale might have been sealed in 1939 had the provincial Liberals not been associated with conscription. This turn of events facilitated the return of the Union Nationale in the election of 1944. Indeed, conscription and Quebec autonomy were fundamental to Duplessis' platform in the electoral campaign of that year. His ability to divert attention from his own economic and social policies to English-Canadian domination, in addition to his heavy reliance on patronage and "pork barrel" politics, assured his electoral position until his death in 1959. Despite his opposition to the introduction of much-needed social and economic reform, and despite his consistent anti-labour position, Duplessis' nationalism worked to the full advantage of his party.

During the years of political unresponsiveness in Quebec under Duplessis, demographic and economic changes were leading to the development of a "new middle class" in Quebec society. From the old middle class, the doctors, the lawyers, and so on, Duplessis had received a great deal of support. But this new group, who filled bureaucratic positions in Quebec's growing urban institutions[12] were opposed to the type of politics practised by the Union Nationale. For one thing, Duplessis' reluctance to engage in cost-sharing programmes with the federal government for the provision of social services meant that avenues for advancement of this group were limited. To this extent they were comparable to artists, intellectuals, and journalists, all of whom had suffered under the Duplessis yoke. The result was the development of a situation in which the expectations of particular groups far outstripped their possible achievements.

These groups were not alone in their opposition to Duplessis. The Church was finding it increasingly difficult to turn a blind eye to blatantly corrupt political practices. At the same time, organized labour was opposed to his "strong arm" tactics for handling strikes. Even if Duplessis had not died in 1959, it is debatable whether he would have been victorious in the election of 1960, after which the Liberals ushered in the so-called "quiet revolution".

The Liberal reformers under Jean Lesage attempted to introduce measures that would put Quebec on a par with other provinces. The most serious efforts of the Liberal government were directed at improving education, health, and welfare. That these reforms, and others like them, were necessary is not difficult to establish. Sufficient evidence was amassed by the Royal Commission on Bilingualism and Biculturalism. In one of their reports they state the following:

Our examination of the social and economic aspects of Canadian life (based on 1961 census figures) shows that there is inequality in the partnership between Canadians of French origin and those of British origin. By every statistical measurement which we used, Canadians of French origin are considerably lower on the socio-economic scale. They are not as well represented in the decision-making positions and in the ownership of industrial enterprises, and they do not have the same access to the fruits of modern technology. The positions they occupy are less prestigious and do not command as high incomes; across Canada, their average annual earnings are $980 less than those of the British. Furthermore, they have two years' less formal education. Quebec manufacturing firms owned by Francophones produce only 15 per cent of the provincial output.[13]

Despite some much-needed reforms introduced by the Lesage government, in 1966 the Union Nationale was returned to office under Daniel Johnson. As Marcel Rioux puts it: "Confronted with the difficulties of a policy aimed at reforming their society, Quebecers took evasive action in the form of a great leap backwards."[14] Apparently, the non-corrupt political practices of the Liberals were anathema to a number of rural constituencies where "pork barrel" politics were essential to economic well-being.

While these events were occurring in the realm of traditional electoral politics, growing numbers of French Canadians were becoming convinced that a remedy for the economic ills of Quebec, as outlined in the Report on Bilingualism and Biculturalism, and the preservation of the French language and culture, could best be maintained outside of Confederation. Increasing numbers of individuals believed that the institution of Confederation *per se* was deficient. "By the beginning of the 1960's," Ramsay Cook argues, "many French Canadians had begun to question the validity of the Confederation concept. At the basis of these questions is the belief that the entente of 1867 has been broken, that tension between survival and la survivance has mounted to a final crisis."[15] For the first time since Confederation, a French-Canadian social movement that enjoyed a substantial amount of popular support was advocating secession from Canada and the establishment of an independent state of Quebec.

That this movement enjoys considerable support is clearly revealed by the provincial election returns of 1969 and 1973, in which the Parti Québécois (PQ), an amalgam of previously existing separatist groups, polled approximately one quarter of all votes cast. Because the PQ has not captured a number of seats proportionate to its popular vote, political commentators have taken great delight in predicting the eventual decline of the separatist movement. Whether or not this will actually happen is a moot point. What is important is that a considerably large public seems to be endorsing the politics of René Lévesque, the PQ leader. In addition, a number of large unions are openly aligning themselves with the separatist cause, and in 1970 the activities of the Front de Libération du Quebec (FLQ), a separatist group that kidnapped and killed a member of the Quebec government, made Quebec the subject of headlines across the world. While the activities and sentiments of the latter group should not be attributed to other participants in the separatist cause, these events should not be viewed lightly.

Not all of the discontent in postwar Quebec has become manifest in support for the provincial Liberal Party or in support for the separatists. Since 1962, in the federal arena at least, the Social Credit Party has made great inroads. This group, which Maurice Pinard characterizes as existing on the "extreme right of the political spectrum",[16] has gained strength in traditional pockets of discontent —

the Lake St. John and Abitibi regions. In the provincial election of 1944 the Bloc Populaire obtained a great deal of its support from these areas.[17] Likewise, in the provincial election of 1948, the Union des Electeurs gained support from the same sources.[18] The collapse of these movements, Herbert Quinn argues, "left behind pockets of discontented voters in certain parts of the province — voters who could be classified as 'independents', since they were not satisfied with the policies of either of the major parties."[19]

Their discontent is easily understood in economic terms. If the general prosperity of Quebecers has lagged behind that of Canadians in general, standards of living of great numbers of residents of these areas are far below the provincial average. Vincent Lemieux clearly outlines the economic dynamics underlying 1962 support for the Social Credit in the constituency of Levis. "During the war and in the immediate post-war years farmers," he points out, "encouraged by the then current prosperity, bought much costly agricultural machinery. For some years, their profits decreased steadily, as agricultural prices remained stable, and prices of fertilizers, feeds, etc., increased constantly. . . . Ever since," he concludes, "their debts and their needs increased faster than their incomes."[20]

These circumstances were not unlike those which preceded the western farmers' movements in the immediate post World War One era. In both cases, certain events conspired against the credibility of the old-line parties as viable electoral alternatives. The base of support for the Quebec Social Credit is clearly broader, however. Miners, loggers, factory workers, farmers, and some white-collar workers alike, have been seduced by the appeal of the Social Credit. Consequently, since 1962, the party has continued to enjoy a degree of success in federal elections, although bids for power have been less successful at the provincial level.

Perhaps before leaving this section it is useful to put the events of recent years into a general perspective. Although his overall appreciation of the Quebec situation suggests a federal Liberal bias, a comment made by Ramsay Cook in 1966 rings true not only for the sixties, but also for the seventies. "Today", he writes, "Quebec is a society passing through that characteristic revolution of the mid-twentieth century — the revolution of rising expectations, ranging from modest demands for increased educational opportunity to demands for total, irrevocable national independence."[21]

The following articles deal in more depth with a number of the points raised in this introduction. The article by Levitt focuses on the Nationalist League, while Quinn examines the origins of the Union Nationale in the thirties. Factors leading to the recent development of separatist sentiment are traced by Guindon. Stein's article, in turn, focusses on the development of the current Social Credit Party in Quebec.

Notes

1. Ramsay Cook, *The Maple Leaf Forever*, Toronto: Macmillan, 1971, p. 72.

2. Joseph Levitt, *Henri Bourassa and the Golden Calf*, Ottawa: Les Editions de l'Université d'Ottawa, 1969, p. 8.

3. Ramsay Cook, *Canada and the French-Canadian Question*, Toronto: Macmillan, 1966, p. 56.

4. *Ibid.*, p. 85.

5. Albert Faucher and Maurice Lamontagne, "History of Industrial Development," in Marcel Rioux and Yves Martin (eds.), *French-Canadian Society*, Volume 1, Toronto: McClelland and Stewart, 1964/1966, p. 263.

6. *Ibid.*

7. W.F. Ryan, *The Clergy and Economic Growth in Quebec, (1896-1914)*, Quebec: Les Presses de l'Université Laval, 1966, p. 79.

8. Everett C. Hughes, *French Canada in Transition*, Toronto: University of Toronto Press, 1943/1967, p. v.

9. Levitt, *Henri Bourassa and the Golden Calf*, p. 12.

10. This is evident from a reading of Levitt, *Henri Bourassa and the Golden Calf*.

11. Herbert F. Quinn, "The Formation and Rise to Power of the Union Nationale," below.

12. Hubert Guindon, "Social Unrest, Social Class, and Quebec's Bureaucratic Revolution," below.

13. *Report of the Royal Commission on Bilingualism and Biculturalism*, Book III, Ottawa: Queen's Printer, 1969, p. 61.

14. Marcel Rioux, *Quebec in Question*, Toronto: James Lewis and Samuel, 1971, p. 81.

15. Cook, *Canada and the French-Canadian Question*, p. 189.

16. M. Pinard, *The Rise of a Third Party*, Englewood Cliffs: Prentice-Hall, 1971, p. 12.

17. Quinn, *The Union Nationale*, Toronto: University of Toronto Press, 1963/1967, p. 154.

18. *Ibid.*, p. 168.

19. *Ibid.*

20. V. Lemieux, "The Election in the Constituency of Levis," in J. Meisel (ed.), *Papers on the 1962 Election*, Toronto: University of Toronto Press, 1964/66, p. 36.

21. Cook, *Canada and the French-Canadian Question*, p. 81.

The Birth of the Nationalist League

Joseph Levitt

The Nationalist movement began in October, 1899, when Henri Bourassa resigned his seat in Parliament to protest the decision to send troops to South Africa. Passionately committed to British liberalism,[1] deeply fond of Laurier,[2] proud of his compatriot's popularity in English Canada, he had been loyal enough to the government to champion its policy on the Manitoba school question[3] only two weeks before the crisis over South Africa broke out in Canada.[4] But he was severely shaken when Laurier agreed to Canadian participation in the Boer war. Perhaps the shock to Bourassa was all the greater because Laurier had assured him privately that the government had no intention of aiding the British in the Transvaal.[5] But the Prime Minister changed his mind; Bourassa could not accept this decision and resigned his seat to compel the government to fight a by-election on this issue.

Bourassa believed that the despatch of Canadian troops to South Africa was the first step in a "constitutional revolution" towards military imperialism because Chamberlain would now claim "as a matter of principle, participation of Canada in imperial wars".[6] Pressure from London and not the irresistible demand of public opinion, as Laurier claimed, had caused the Prime Minister to send troops without even the approval of Parliament. The essence of Bourassa's charge was that Laurier had capitulated to barely disguised blackmail from London, to the threat of being branded throughout the Empire as a "traitor" government.

Yet it was not so much because of the legal niceties of his case that Bourassa became something of a hero to the young elite of French Canada; it was because they thought that unlike Laurier, he was standing up to the Anglo-Canadians. The public debate over the Boer war had revealed to many French Canadians a full blown racial animosity towards them in English Canada. When French

Reprinted from J. Levitt, *Henri Bourassa and the Golden Calf*, Ottawa: The University of Ottawa Press, 1972, pp. 15-20, by permission of the author and the University of Ottawa Press.

journalists opposed the sending of troops, Ontario Conservative papers questioned their loyalty; one of them went so far as to describe the words of *La Patrie* as those of an "enemy".[7] Lord Minto, the Governor General, was shocked by the way opposition papers stirred up hatred of French Canada.[8] Asselin accused the *Montreal Star* of so exciting McGill students by its appeals "au fanatisme anglais" that they almost caused an ugly riot by attempting to force one or two French Canadian newspapers to fly the Union Jack at the time of the relief of Ladysmith.[9] When Bourassa opposed the joint Liberal-Conservative motion of congratulations to the Queen on the approaching end of the Boer war, he found himself surrounded by a shouting House, led by Ontario members almost driven mad by hatred for him.[10] That French Canadian members made the same racial appeal did not lessen the sense of injury of many in French Canada. Their grievance arose from a situation in which, as Minto observed, if a French Canadian were lukewarm to the war, he was considered a rebel by many Anglo-Canadians.

Such resentment led many French Canadian professionals and students to listen sympathetically to Bourassa's arguments. The Montreal *Les Débats* reflected their outlook when it argued that imperial federation meant the enslavement of French Canadians. Under such a political arrangement Quebec could not preserve its laws, language, institutions and beliefs.[11] *Les Débats* condemned the Liberals for their acceptance of imperialism and attributed the sending of troops to "l'esprit anglo-saxon" with which that party was impregnated.[12] In London, Laurier had proclaimed that he was "British to the core". The weekly complained that "son impérialisme s'est manifesté avec un éclat"[13] and even insinuated that he was a greater imperialist than Sir Charles Tupper, the leader of the Conservatives.[14] It called for the formation of a new "parti national Canadien".[15]

Indeed, rumors of a third party were plentiful. The nine Quebec members who had voted for Bourassa's viewpoint in the March debate of 1900 constituted a potential base for such an organization. *La Presse* suggested that Israel Tarte, the Minister of Public Works, might resign from the Liberals to head the new party.[16] *Les Débats*, however, looked to Bourassa to form a party "anti-impérialiste, d'autonomie et d'indépendance".[17] Bourassa himself wished to see a new political force, "un groupe vraiment indépendant, tant au parlement, qu'au sein de l'électorat",[18] and in co-operation with Jean-Paul Tardivel, editor of the weekly, *La Vérité*, put out some feelers in that direction.[19]

The third party never materialized. Tarte remained in the ranks of the Liberals. Dissenting Liberal members like Dominique Monet and Calixte Ethier were not prepared to sacrifice their claim to the endorsement of the Liberal party. But the decisive barrier to a new organization was the rush of French Canadian support towards Laurier as the elections of 1900 drew near.

Laurier was impregnable in Quebec. Although the strategy of Sir Charles

Tupper in that province was to capitalize on anti-imperialist sentiment by asserting that Laurier had approved of Imperial Federation and denouncing the Liberal leader as being "too English for me", it was easy for Liberals to expose the Conservative leader himself as the greater imperialist. Tarte distributed a most effective pamphlet, quoting anti-French outbursts in the Conservative press of English Canada, that made it appear that a vote for Laurier was a vote for the defence of French Canada. After the election a judge wrote Laurier that under the circumstances it had been necessary for French Canadians to unite around their compatriot.[20] It was this wave of patriotic fervour, expressed in support of Laurier, which made a third party impossible. As Bourassa explained to Tardivel, "Je n'ai pas lancé à St-Hyacinthe l'idée du parti indépendant [. . .] le milieu était trop rouge pour commencer là."[21]

Without the possibility of a third party, all those who opposed the sending of troops to South Africa were left with a difficult choice. If they voted for Laurier, they would endorse a step towards military imperialism. If they rejected the Liberals they would, in effect, support the Conservatives, who were even greater imperialists. *Les Débats* maintained that since it was necessary to choose, "la logique des faits serait plutôt favorable au parti ministériel".[22] Bourassa agreed; he presented himself as an official Liberal candidate.

Although Bourassa was re-elected, he remained alienated from the Liberal party. He was still angry at the Prime Minister and disapproved of the continued government support for the British cause in South Africa. He had come back to the Liberals only because there was no other place to go. He was beginning to believe that the party system on its own could not be trusted to produce those policies which the country needed. The Liberals and Conservatives were less and less divided by principle. Beneath the facade of bitter struggle "les deux partis s'entendent"; they fought each other to reap "les honneurs et les profits du pouvoir" and not to assure the triumph of an idea.[23] Party discipline prevented any discussion of principle by dissenting individuals; at the behest of two or three leaders, members voted blindly no matter what issues were at stake.[24] The result was the "abrutissement moral et intellectuel des hommes publics" and, as a consequence, "la démoralisation de la pensée et l'action populaire".[25]

Bourassa's first response to this stultifying control by the party hierarchy had been to suggest something like a third party in parliament. When this project proved impracticable he turned to the idea of an educational association of politically minded people to influence public opinion. Not a political party, it would remain uncorrupted by the temptation of power; nonpartisan in policies, it would welcome men of good will from both parties; a forum for the discussion of issues "from the broad national patriotic point of view", it would be "above the narrowness of mere partyism".[26] The existence of such an educational organization would help create a "conscience nationale" that would judge the parties "en toute indépendance".[27] Such a public opinion, "éclairée et vigoureuse", would impose its views on the Liberals and Conservatives much as the Anti-Corn League had forced its views on the Whigs and Tories in England.[28]

But Bourassa took no steps to establish such an association. Whether as a leader or rank-and-filer, he was not prepared to join any organization which would restrict his intellectual liberty; unwilling to join, he was equally unwilling to organize such a body. Though he took a hand in formulating the program, it was not he but Asselin who was "l'inspirateur, le créateur [. . .] maître ouvrier" of the Nationalist League.[29]

By 1901 Asselin had already been committed to the ideas of *Les Débats*.[30] In contact with journalists, he must have been involved in the excited discussions on nationalism which swept through Quebec newspaper offices in the spring of 1902.[31] The massive turn-out for the anti-imperialist rally at Drummondville indicated the depth of nationalist feeling. By fall it is probable that he had already gathered together a working group of ten or twelve intellectuals.[32] With Bourassa's help they drew up a program and outlined the new organization. In March 1903 the Nationalist League began its public existence, with Asselin as president and Héroux as secretary.

Whatever importance the League acquired as an organization it owed to Bourassa. The next year or so saw a close and fruitful co-operation between him and the League. It was a convenient platform from which to expound his ideas. When in August, 1903, the Congress of Empire Chambers of Commerce said that colonies should participate in wars necessary for the defence of the Empire, the League held a protest meeting at which Bourassa castigated that body for doing the work of Chamberlain.[33] With Bourassa as its drawing card, it organized large and successful rallies at Quebec and Montreal. These meetings and his speeches made the League important enough to be attacked by the Conservatives in the House.[34] Bourassa's close association with the organization ended when he ran as a Liberal in the federal election of 1904. Subsequently, although he worked with Asselin, he never had much to do with the League as such, and without him it never materialized "into anything important".[35]

Although the League itself did not play any role in Quebec politics, it produced a program which was the first articulate response of French Canadian intellectual leaders to the challenges of the new century. Its organization was probably a necessary first step for the Nationalists in their search for an instrument to influence public opinion. They next turned to producing a Nationalist press. In 1904 Asselin began a weekly, *Le Nationaliste*. In 1910 Bourassa became the editor of a daily, *Le Devoir*. But whether through the League or their press the aim of the Nationalists was the same — to compel both parties to adopt their program for Canadian nationalism.

Notes

1. H. Bourassa, Canada, *House of Commons Debates*, March 13, 1900, p. 1828: "A Liberal I was born and a Liberal I will die."
2. R. Rumilly, *Henri Bourassa: la vie publique d'un grand Canadien*, Montreal, 1953, p. 53: "Le député de Labelle avertit son chef et ami."
3. *Ibid.*, p. 51. In 1890 Manitoba abolished its separate school system. Although by the Manitoba Act of 1871 the federal government had the legal power to impose remedial legislation, Laurier proposed to win back the rights of Catholics by negotiation rather than by legal force.
4. *Ibid.*, p. 47, 52.
5. Bourassa, *op. cit.*, p. 1821.
6. P.E. Smith, *Henri Bourassa and Sir Wilfrid Laurier*, unpublished M.A. thesis, University of Toronto, 1948, p. 62.
7. N. Penlington, *Canada and Imperialism*, Toronto, 1965. p. 249.
8. H.B. Neatby, *Laurier and a Liberal Quebec: A Study in Political Management*, unpublished doctoral thesis, University of Toronto, 1954.
9. O. Asselin, *Les Débats*, March 4, 1900, p. 2, col. 2.
10. Rumilly, *op. cit.*, pp. 989-990.
11. *Les Débats*, March 23, 1900, p. 4, col. 1; August 12, 1900, p. 2, col. 2.
12. *Ibid.*, March 11, 1900, p. 3, col. 2.
13. *Ibid.*, March 18, 1900, p. 41, col. 1.
14. *Ibid.*, April 8, 1900, p. 2, col. 1.
15. *Ibid.*, March 11, 1900, p. 1, col. 2.
16. R. Rumilly, *Histoire de la Province de Québec*, Vol. 9, Montreal, [n.d.], p. 223.
17. *Les Débats*, August 19, 1900, p. 1, col. 1.
18. This phrase is in a letter from Tardivel to Bourassa, March 23, 1900 (*B.P.*). In a letter to Tardivel on September 5, 1900 (*B.P.*), Bourassa indicated his complete agreement. Writing on the idea of an independent party, he commented: "Je n'ai pas lancé à St-Hyacinthe l'idée du parti indépendant. Vous savez que je partage absolument votre manière de voir à ce sujet."
19. Bourassa to Tardivel, May 23, 1900, *B.P.*
20. Neatby, *op. cit.*, p. 199.
21. Bourassa to Tardivel, Sept. 5, 1900, *B.P.*
22. *Les Débats*, August 12, 1900, p. 1, col. 1.
23. H. Bourassa, *Le Nationaliste*, March 27, 1904, p. 4, col. 1.
24. *Ibid.*, October 11, 1908, p. 3, col. 1.
25. *Ibid.*, March 27, 1904, p. 4, col. 1.
26. Bourassa, *The Nationalist Movement in Quebec, Addresses delivered before the Canadian Club, Toronto, for the year 1906-07*, Toronto, Warwick Bros. and Rutter, p. 62.
27. Bourassa, "Speech to the Congress of the ACJC, Montreal", *Le Sentier*, Quebec, 1904, p. 44 (*B.P.*).
28. O. Asselin, *Le Nationaliste*, October 2, 1904, p. 1, col. 2.
29. M.H. Gagnon, *La Vie orageuse d'Olivar Asselin*, Vol. 1, Montreal, 1962, p. 62. Bourassa agreed: H. Bourassa, *Le Devoir*, May 16, 1913, p. 1.
30. Gagnon, *op. cit.*, p. 45.
31. Rumilly, *Histoire de la Province de Québec*, Vol. 10, Montreal, [n.d.], p. 94.
32. *Ibid.*, Vol. 11, p. 95.
33. Rumilly, *Bourassa*, p. 141.
34. T.C. Casgrain, Canada, *House of Commons Debates*, March 15, 1904, p. 414.
35. Bourassa to Lewis, November 3, 1911, *B.P.*

The Formation
and Rise to Power
of the Union Nationale

Herbert F. Quinn

The Union Nationale had its origin in a revolt which took place within the ranks of the Liberal party in the early 1930's. This revolt began when a group of young left-wing Liberals, who called themselves L'Action Libérale Nationale (ALN), became dissatisfied with the party's conservative economic policies and the tight control exercised over the party organization by Taschereau and a few close colleagues. The leader of the ALN was Paul Gouin, the son of a former Liberal Prime Minister of Quebec and grandson of Honoré Mercier. Gouin and his associates, like most of the younger generation, had been influenced greatly by the nationalistic ideas of Bourassa, Groulx, and members of L'Action Nationale (formerly L'Action Française). As a consequence, they were alarmed at the threat which industrialism presented to the survival of the traditional French-Canadian culture and were critical of the close ties which existed between the Taschereau administration and the foreign capitalists.[1]

The original plan of the ALN was to reform the Liberal party from within by forcing it to shift to the left in its economic and social policies and by persuading it to adopt a more nationalistic philosophy. However, within a short time the Gouin group became convinced of the futility of trying to reform the party or break the control of the ruling oligarchy. As a result, the ALN severed all connections with the Liberals shortly before the provincial election of 1935 and set itself up as a separate political party. Aside from Gouin, other key figures in the ALN at that time were Oscar Drouin, who was to become chief organizer of the new party, J.E. Grégoire, mayor of Quebec City, and Dr. Philippe Hamel, a dentist by profession, also from Quebec City. Both Grégoire and Hamel were bitter enemies of what they termed "the electricity trust" and for some years had been campaigning for the nationalization of the power companies.

When the ALN was launched it met with a favourable response from many sections of the population since its ideas conformed with the nationalist ideology

Reprinted from *The Union Nationale* by Herbert F. Quinn, by permission of University of Toronto Press. © University of Toronto Press, 1963, pp. 48-72 (abridged).

then sweeping the province. It was endorsed by the influential L'Action Nationale,[2] and was looked upon favourably by the Union Catholique des Cultivateurs[3] and other Catholic Action groups. The new party had one handicap, however: most of its key figures had had little practical experience in politics. Very few of them had ever been candidates in either provincial or federal elections or played any kind of active political role before. In contrast, their Liberal opponents were skilled politicians, strongly entrenched in office, and with a powerful and well-financed political machine. Moreover, in a province where traditional habits of voting were an important factor in politics, the Liberals had been looked upon as the party of the French Canadian ever since 1897. In many families, particularly in the rural areas, political affiliation was inherited with the family farm, and a large number of people were Liberal for no better reason than the fact that their fathers had always voted that way. It was only too apparent that Taschereau's administration was not going to be easily dislodged by a new and untried party, led by a group of young men who, however idealistic and enthusiastic, had little knowledge of the "know how" of the political game. For all these reasons there were obvious advantages for the ALN in making an alliance with some other group equally opposed to the Liberal administration, but with more political experience and with a better electoral organization. The only group which could meet these requirements was the provincial Conservative party. A brief look at the political history of that party will indicate why it might be receptive to such an alliance.

The Conservative party had been the official opposition in the Quebec Legislature ever since its defeat at the polls in the election of 1897. From that time onward it was only on a few occasions that the party had been able to capture sufficient seats to present the Liberals with any kind of challenge. It suffered from its close association with the federal Conservative party which was, of course, looked upon by the average voter as the party of "British Imperialism," and, above all, as the party which had imposed conscription in 1917.

The leader of the Quebec Conservative party during the greater part of the 1920's was Arthur Sauvé, member of the Legislative Assembly for the electoral district of Deux Montagnes, who had become party leader in 1916. Acutely aware of the disadvantageous position in which his party was placed by its close connections with the federal Conservatives, Sauvé was determined to make every effort to dissociate the Quebec Conservative party from its federal counterpart. When the nationalist movement of Abbé Groulx and L'Action Française began to gain ground following the brief postwar depression of 1921 Sauvé adopted most of its ideas and slogans. He also gave his party a new orientation in matters of economic and social policy. Although the Conservatives, like the Liberals, had been staunch supporters of laissez-faire capitalism during most of their history, the party now took a turn to the left. Sauvé began to criticize the role of foreign capital in the industrial development of the province and to attack the Liberals for their generous concessions to the business interests. In one election speech he made this statement: "Our natural resources must serve not only the ends of speculators, but the welfare of contemporary classes and of the generations to come. . . . The government . . . has sold our wealth to foreigners who shared with ministers and politicians, while our own people emigrated from the province." Sauvé proposed "that we develop, as far as possible, our natural resources by our own people and for our people."[4]

Sauvé's attempt to dissociate his party from the federal Conservatives was only partly successful. It is true that the new orientation which he gave the Quebec Conservative party won it the editorial support of *Le Devoir* and *L'Action Catholique*,[5] and that it was soon on friendly terms with such groups as the UCC whose agitation for a government-sponsored scheme of low-cost rural credit had been turned down by the Liberals. Sauvé was not able, however, to convince the vast majority of voters that the Quebec Conservatives were completely independent of the federal organization.[6] The reason for this failure is not hard to find. Sauvé's party still contained a strong right wing which was closely associated with the business interests and had strong ties with the federal Conservatives. This right wing had always been critical of his policies. In giving up the leadership shortly after the defeat suffered by his party in the 1927 election Sauvé attacked this group for its hostile attitude:

> Une fraction du parti conservateur fédéral a toujours été hostile à ma direction. On m'accuse de nationalisme. Le nationalisme que j'ai prêché et pratiqué est celui de Cartier, c'est le conservatisme intégral et foncièrement national. . . . Mes efforts n'ont pas été couronnés de succès. Il convient donc que je laisse le commandement du parti. . . .[7]

In 1929 Camillien Houde, mayor of Montreal and member of the provincial legislature for Montreal-Ste Marie, succeeded Sauvé as party leader. Houde was a colourful politician who was to play an important role in municipal and provincial politics for the next twenty years. In the eastern and working class section of Montreal where he had been brought up Houde was affectionately known as "le petit gars de Ste Marie." Like Sauvé, Houde was a nationalist with radical ideas but he showed a greater readiness to compromise on policy if the situation demanded it. Moreover, he was a much more dynamic and hard-hitting politician than his predecessor.

In the election campaign of 1931 Houde followed the same line of attack as Sauvé. His main accusation against the Liberals was that they had turned over the natural resources and wealth of the province to foreign capitalists, and he referred to them as "a nest of traitors to their race and their province."[8] His platform consisted of a number of social reforms which the trade unions, the farmers' organizations, and other groups had been demanding for a long time: government pensions for widows and the aged, a reduction in electricity rates, an intensified programme of colonization, the establishment of a Ministry of Labour, and a government-sponsored scheme of low-cost rural credit.[9] Houde waged a vigorous campaign in all parts of the province and hopes were high in the ranks of the party that it would be able to defeat the Liberals. However, the latter emerged victorious once more and Houde himself lost his seat in the Assembly. When he resigned from the leadership a year later the party decided to call a convention made up of delegates from all parts of the province for the purpose of selecting a successor.

The Quebec Conservative party's convention of 1933 was one of the most famous in the history of the province. Before the convention met, the name most prominently mentioned for the leadership was Maurice Duplessis. The son of a judge and a lawyer by profession, Duplessis had started his career in politics when he was elected as Conservative member to the Legislative Assembly from the electoral district of Three Rivers in 1927. (He was to be returned to the legislature by that constituency in every election from that time until his sudden death in 1959.) Duplessis soon built up a reputation in the Assembly as a clever debater and able parliamentarian. He was also adept at those skilful manoeuvres which are an asset in rising to the top in the field of politics. A short while after Houde lost his seat in the Legislative Assembly in the election of 1931, Duplessis was chosen as temporary leader of the party in that House.

When the Conservative convention started its proceedings in the city of Sherbrooke on October 3, 1933, the delegates were divided into two factions.[10] One of them supported Duplessis as leader, and the other supported Onésime Gagnon, a Conservative member of the federal Parliament. The Gagnon faction had been organized by Camillien Houde, who was determined to block Duplessis' bid for the leadership. Houde's antagonism towards Duplessis arose out of a disagreement which had developed between these two forceful personalities shortly after the 1931 election over matters of party strategy. But Houde was not successful in his attempt to prevent Duplessis from capturing the leadership. While the latter had been temporary leader of the party in the Assembly he had built up a considerable following within the party ranks, and, as a result, he had control of the party machine by the time the convention was called. The chairman of that convention was one of his supporters. Moreover, he had the influential backing of most of the Conservative members of the federal Parliament from Quebec, and these federal Conservatives participated in the convention as voting delegates. When the time came for the balloting Duplessis was elected leader by 334 votes to 214 for his opponent.

Although it was not apparent at the time, the political ideas of the new Conservative leader differed from those of Sauvé and Houde in one very important respect. Duplessis was certainly a nationalist, but he was by no means a radical. As subsequent events were to show, he was a "practical politician" whose main objective was to defeat the Taschereau government and put the Conservative party in its place rather than to bring about sweeping economic and social reforms. However, it was only after the Union Nationale's victory over the Liberals in 1936 that the economic conservatism of Duplessis was to be fully revealed.[11]

When Duplessis took over the Conservative leadership he inherited a party which had won only fourteen out of ninety seats in the previous election,[12] a party whose chances of defeating the Liberals did not appear to be any brighter than they had been at any other time during the preceding thirty-five years. There were obvious advantages, with little to lose, in making an alliance with another group, such as L'Action Libérale Nationale, which was equally opposed to the Liberals. If the Conservative party could supply the practical knowledge of the techniques of politics and some of the financial backing, the ALN could provide new men, new ideas, and considerable popular support.

Thus, a short while before the provincial election of November 25, 1935, Duplessis and Gouin entered into negotiations with a view to forming a united front against the Taschereau administration. These negotiations were successful and on November 8 the two leaders issued a joint statement announcing that their respective parties had joined forces against the Liberals. This statement read in part, "Répondant au désir de l'électorat du Québec, le parti conservateur provincial et L'Action Libérale Nationale déclarent par leurs représentants attirés qu'aux élections du 25 novembre, ils présenteront un front uni contre l'ennemi commun du peuple de la province de Québec: le régime Taschereau."[13] The new coalition was to be known as the Union Nationale Duplessis-Gouin.

The Duplessis-Gouin combination was soon joined by a number of independent nationalists who had hitherto taken little or no active part in politics, although many of them were leaders of various Catholic Action and patriotic organizations. The outstanding figures among these independents were Albert Rioux, a former president of the UCC, and René Chaloult, a Quebec City lawyer who was one of the directors of L'Action Nationale.

Undoubtedly one of the most important aspects of the Union Nationale was the nature of the programme which it presented to the electorate. This programme was significant in two respects: for the first time in the history of the province a political movement presented to the electorate a clear-cut and comprehensive set of proposals for economic, social, and political reform; secondly, this programme was to lay down the basic principles which were to be followed by all reform movements in the province for the next decade or so. It is essential, therefore, to understand just how this programme originated, and the particular proposals for reform it put forward.

As pointed out in the last chapter, the nationalist intellectuals of the twenties, in spite of their campaign against the industrial system, had never formulated any concrete and coherent programme of social reform and had not been in agreement as to how the industrialists were to be curbed. In other words, their critique of the economic system was stronger than their positive suggestions for its transformation. With the spread of nationalistic sentiments to the masses of the people in the early thirties it soon became apparent that such a constructive programme was urgently needed. It was the Roman Catholic hierarchy which provided the nationalists with the positive proposals for which they had been looking, proposals which were the result of a new orientation taking place in the social thinking of the Church after 1930.

. . . .

In the early thirties a change took place in the social thinking of the Quebec hierarchy and it was prompted to put forward a programme of reform which would come to grips with the problems of an urban and industrial society. An immediate reason was that the breakdown of the capitalist system in the depression focussed attention on certain social problems arising out of that system which could no longer be ignored. Even more persuasive was the appearance in 1931 of the encyclical, *Quadragesimo Anno*, of Pope Pius XI. This encyclical was the most important papal pronouncement on social questions since *Rerum Novarum*, and had a tremendous influence on Catholic thought in all parts of the world, including Quebec. Its purpose was to reaffirm the basic principles laid down in the earlier encyclical and to clarify and re-interpret those principles in the light of the changes which had taken place in industrial capitalism since the 1890's. Like his predecessor, Pius rejected both laissez-faire capitalism and socialism, although recognizing that one wing of the latter movement, democratic socialism, had moved away from the more extreme position of the Marxists. The Pope's critique of capitalism was expressed in statements such as this: ". . . the immense number of propertyless wage earners on the one hand, and the superabundant riches of the fortunate few on the other, is an unanswerable argument that the earthly goods so abundantly produced in this age of industrialism are far from rightly distributed and equitably shared among the various classes of men."[15] As a remedy for this situation, he called for a redistribution of private property.

A related consideration, nearer to home, also prompted the Quebec hierarchy to take a particular stand on the problems arising from the industrialization of that province. The depression had resulted in wide-spread dissatisfaction with the capitalist system, and unless the Church put forward a programme of reform within the framework of Catholic social philosophy it was quite conceivable that it would be faced by the growth of a socialist or communist movement which might very well be not only secularistic but even militantly atheistic. The need to take some positive action seemed all the more imperative to the hierarchy when the Co-operative Commonwealth Federation (CCF), an avowedly socialist party, was formed in western Canada in 1932 and announced its intention of spreading its doctrines to all provinces. An eminent theologian who had been assigned the task of making a careful study of the social philosophy of the new party came to the conclusion that the CCF "did not merit the support of Catholics" because of its promotion of the class war, its extensive programme of socialization, and "its materialistic conception of the social order."[16] A different solution to the problems of the day was imperative.

The responsibility for the formulation of the Church's programme of reform was entrusted by the hierarchy to an organization sponsored by the Jesuit Order in Montreal called the Ecole Sociale Populaire. This was not actually a school in the ordinary sense but an organization which had been set up before the First World War for the purpose of studying and propagating the teachings of the Church on a wide range of moral, educational, and social problems.

The Montreal Jesuits did not themselves draw up the proposed programme. Instead they called together a group of prominent Catholic laymen and gave them the assignment of outlining a set of proposals which would be a concrete application of the principles put forward in *Quadragesimo Anno* to the specific conditions and problems peculiar to Quebec. This group of laymen was composed of individuals playing a leading role in all phases of French-Canadian life: the Catholic trade unions, the farmers' organizations, the co-operatives and credit unions, the patriotic and professional societies, the universities. The most prominent members of the group were Albert Rioux, president of the Union Catholique des Cultivateurs; Alfred Charpentier, one of the leaders of the Catholic unions; Wilfrid Guérin, secretary of the Caisses Populaires, or credit unions, in the Montreal area; Esdras Minville, a professor at the Ecole des Hautes Etudes Commerciales in Montreal; and Dr. Philippe Hamel and René Chaloult of Quebec City. Most of these people were also directors of L'Action Nationale.

The Ecole Sociale Populaire published the conclusions arrived at by this study group in a pamphlet entitled *Le Programme de restauration sociale* which appeared in the fall of 1933.[17] This pamphlet contained proposals for reform in four different areas. "Rural Reconstruction" suggested the steps which should be taken to strengthen and even extend the agrarian sector of the economy; "The Labour Question" put forward an extensive scheme of labour and social legislation which would raise the incomes and provide greater economic security for the working class; "Trusts and Finance" dealt with measures which should be taken to curb the power of the public utilities and other large business enterprises; and, "Political Reforms" called for legislation which would eliminate patronage politics and electoral and administrative corruption.

We come now to the immediate background of the programme of the Union Nationale. The relationship of this programme to the proposals of the Ecole Sociale Populaire can be traced back to the formation of L'Action Libérale Nationale. Paul Gouin, its leader, had not been a member of the group of Catholic laymen who had drawn up and formally affixed their signatures to *Le*

Programme de restauration sociale, but he was in general sympathy with the ideas put forward for he had participated in some of the discussions leading up to the final proposals. It was not too surprising, therefore, that when he launched the ALN a short while later he adopted the Ecole Sociale Populaire document as the basis for his own programme.[18] He did, however, make some minor changes, and included a few additional proposals of his own. When the alliance with Duplessis was arranged the following year one of the basic conditions which Gouin insisted upon was that the Conservative leader accept the complete ALN programme. In the light of later developments it is important to make it quite clear that Duplessis agreed to this condition at the time.[19] One of the clauses in the joint statement issued by the two leaders announcing the formation of the Union Nationale states this firmly:

> Après la défaite du régime anti-national et trustard de M. Taschereau, le parti conservateur provincial et L'Action Libérale Nationale formeront un gouvernement national dont le programme sera celui de l'Action Libérale Nationale, programme qui s'inspire des mêmes principes que celui du parti conservateur provincial.[20]

One other significant aspect of the Duplessis-Gouin programme should be mentioned here. The fact that the reforms proposed by the two leaders were based on *Le Programme de restauration sociale* was a decisive factor in winning the support of such influential figures as Rioux, Hamel, and Chaloult, all of whom had participated in the drawing-up of the Jesuit-inspired programme.

. . . .

The formation of the Union Nationale meant that for the first time since the days of Honoré Mercier in the 1880's a powerful nationalist movement had arisen to play an important role in provincial politics. Like Mercier's party, the Union Nationale was determined to maintain all those traditional values and rights which had always been considered essential for cultural survival. It differed, however, in that it was also concerned with a problem which, in the nature of things, Mercier did not have to contend with. This was the Union Nationale's determination to raise the economic status of the French Canadian by bringing about extensive reforms in the system of industrial capitalism. For this reason the Duplessis-Gouin coalition must be described, not merely as a nationalist movement, but as a radical nationalist movement.[24]

Perhaps the greatest source of strength of the Union Nationale was the fact that it had the unofficial, but nevertheless effective support of all the various Catholic Action and patriotic organizations across the province: the Catholic trade unions, the farmers' organizations, the co-operatives and the credit unions, the youth organizations, the associations of French-Canadian businessmen and merchants. All of these organizations were supposed to be neutral in politics, but as pointed out earlier, they were all strongly nationalistic and therefore opposed to the

Liberal party's policy towards the industrialists.[25] Moreover, many of the leaders of these organizations had participated in drawing up the programme of the Ecole Sociale Populaire which the Union Nationale had adopted. Needless to say, the new movement also had the enthusiastic backing of such nationalist publications as *L'Action Nationale* and the Montreal daily, *Le Devoir*. There was little doubt too that, although the hierarchy was careful that the Church as such should not become directly involved on one side or the other in the political struggle, most of the clergy were sympathetic towards the political movement which had adopted its programme of social reform.

As a result of the wide support behind the Union Nationale the Liberals, for the first time in nearly forty years, were presented with a real challenge to their continued control over the provincial administration. The seriousness of this threat was to become apparent in the election of 1935, the first test of strength of the Duplessis-Gouin combination.

The Union Nationale Comes to Power

When Paul Gouin and a few other young Liberals formed L'Action Libérale Nationale in 1934 and began to attack the policies of the Liberal "old guard," neither Taschereau nor any of his colleagues took the new movement very seriously. It was only when the Gouin group began to win wider support, and then joined forces with the Liberals' traditional enemy, the Conservative party, that Taschereau slowly began to recognize the serious nature of the challenge with which he was faced. He was still confident, however, that his party would be able to weather the storm and retain control over the provincial administration as it had done so often in the past.

. . . .

When the election of 1935 was called, Taschereau toured the province denouncing the Union Nationale coalition as "un mariage qui va se terminer par un désastreux divorce."[27] He accused Duplessis of abandoning the principles for which the Conservative party stood and attacked Gouin for betraying the ideals of his father, Sir Lomer Gouin, who had preceded Taschereau as leader of the Liberal party. Taschereau also defended the policies which his administration had pursued in the past and contended that these policies had been of immeasurable benefit to the farmer, the worker, and other sections of the population. Although the Liberals had never shown much enthusiasm for the Ecole Sociale Populaire programme,[28] Taschereau promised to introduce some of the reforms which it put forward, such as old age pensions and a government-sponsored scheme of low-cost farm credit.

However, the Liberals did not rely solely on the introduction of a few reforms to win the support of the electorate. They had even more tangible benefits to offer. As in the past the government embarked on an extensive programme of public works several months before the election. New roads, public buildings, and bridges were built, or at least started, in all parts of the province. Some of these projects were discontinued the day after the election. The public works programme provided additional, if temporary employment, and meant sizable government orders for local hardware merchants and shopkeepers in various towns and villages. Whenever the government provided a community with some badly needed public facility it was able to present itself as a "benefactor" which had "done something" for that particular town or district. This was an important consideration for the average Quebec voter when he was trying to decide which party to vote for. Government candidates in most electoral districts also spent fairly large sums of money on the distribution of drinks of "whisky blanc" and handed out other gifts and favours which might help to convince the voters that the Liberals were "des bons garçons."

. . . .

The well-entrenched position of the Liberals, and their readiness to use all kinds of questionable tactics, obviously placed the Union Nationale in a disadvantageous position in the election campaign of 1935. However, shortly after the date of the election had been announced, the new coalition entered candidates in every electoral district and proceeded to wage a vigorous campaign in all parts of the province. Its appeal to the electorate was for the most part based on the comprehensive programme of economic and social reform summarized above. The Union Nationale leaders also made strong attacks on the administrative and electoral abuses of the Taschereau government. In spite of the many handicaps under which it fought the election, the Duplessis-Gouin combination succeeded in capturing a total of forty-two seats, almost four times the number of seats held by the Conservative opposition in the previous legislature.[30] Although the Liberals, with forty-eight members elected, still maintained control over the administration, they had only a narrow margin of six seats — five after the Speaker had been selected.

The results of the election were a serious setback for the Taschereau régime. The gains made by the Union Nationale coalition completely changed the situation in the legislature where the Liberals had always had an overwhelming majority and had thus been able to put their legislative programme through with a minimum of obstruction. After the 1935 election the government was not only faced by a large and vigorous opposition, but one of the leaders of that opposition, Maurice Duplessis, was an astute politician who knew all the tricks of the parliamentary game.

When the 1936 session of the legislature was called, Duplessis used the many delaying tactics of the experienced parliamentarian to hold up the passing of the budget until such time as the government agreed to enact some of the proposals outlined in the Union Nationale programme. The result was that as time went on the government found itself in increasing financial difficulties. The most telling blow struck by Duplessis, however, and the one which was to sound the death knell of the Taschereau régime, was the information he was able to bring to light concerning the administration's handling of public funds.

Ever since the early 1920's, the Conservative party had been accusing the Liberals of graft, corruption, and inefficiency in the administration of government departments. Owing to the weakness of the party in the legislature, however, it had never been able to coerce the government into setting up a parliamentary inquiry to investigate these alleged irregularities. The Public Accounts Committee, which was supposed to maintain a close check on how public money was being spent, had not met for a long time. Even if it had been called into session at any time before the election of 1935, the huge Liberal majority would have been able to dominate proceedings and prevent any serious investigation from taking place. In the legislature of 1936, however, the Liberals no longer enjoyed this strategic advantage. The opposition was not only successful in bringing the Public Accounts Committee back to life, but the strength of its forces in that Committee made it difficult for the Liberals to control the inquiry.

The Public Accounts Committee was in session from May 5 to June 11, and under the skilful probing of Duplessis it quickly brought to light a picture of patronage, nepotism, and the squandering of public funds which involved most government departments.[31] It was discovered that members of the administration, from cabinet ministers down to the lowest level of the civil service, were using the contacts and influence which they had as government officials to increase their private incomes and those of their friends and relatives. Certain officials made a substantial income by selling materials of all kinds to various government departments at very high prices. One such case involved the director of the government-run School of Fine Arts who made sizable profits from the sale of automobile licence plates to the government.[32] The Treasury lost many thousands of dollars every year through the inflated travelling expenses of ministers and other individuals; this was especially true of the expenditures of the Department of Colonization.[33] One of the most startling discoveries was that a brother of the Prime Minister, who was the accountant of the Legislative Assembly, had been putting the interest on bank deposits of government money into his own personal account. His only defence was that all his predecessors in the position of Assembly accountant had done the same thing.[34]

. . . .

The revelations of the Public Accounts Committee created a sensation throughout the province and completely discredited the Taschereau administration. Around the beginning of June, when the committee was still in the midst of its deliberations, Taschereau suddenly announced his resignation as Prime Minister and recommended to the Lieutenant Governor that Adelard Godbout, Minister of Agriculture, be appointed in his place. At the same time the Legislative

Assembly was dissolved and a new election was called for the following August.

. . . .

Godbout appeared determined to set up a government, not only of new men, but also of new policies, for he recognized the extent of the dissatisfaction throughout the province with the economic system and the widespread desire for social reform. When the election campaign of 1936 got under way he put forward a programme which was similar in many respects to that of the Union Nationale. The main proposals in that programme were: an extension of rural credit facilities, a programme of rural electrification, and the provision of subsidies on certain farm products; an intensified colonization programme; a sweeping reduction of electricity rates throughout the province; a public works programme to solve the problem of unemployment; a minimum wage scale for industrial workers not covered by collective labour agreements, and the introduction of certain amendments to the Workmen's Compensation Act requested by the trade unions; the establishment of a system of needy mothers' allowances; and the elimination of the practice of cabinet ministers accepting directorships from companies doing business with the government.[42]

. . . .

The election of 1936 was to demonstrate that the deathbed conversion of the Liberal party to social reform and honest administration had come too late. All through the election the opposition forces attacked the Liberals for the administrative and political corruption of the Taschereau régime and refused to absolve the Godbout government from the sins of the previous administration. They strongly denied that it was "a government of new men." As stated by Duplessis, "M. Godbout est l'héritier de M. Taschereau. . . . En politique comme ailleurs, l'héritier d'un régime assume la responsabilité des dettes et des méfaits de son auteur. . . ."[45] In another speech later in the campaign he repeated the charge that there had been no real change of direction: "Le gouvernement Godbout est une nouvelle pousse des branches décrépites du gouvernement Taschereau. . . . Pouvez-vous avoir confiance en un régime qui refuse de punir les voleurs d'élections en favorisant des lois électorales malhonnêtes? Lorsqu'un régime refuse de protéger la source même de la démocratie, on ne peut avoir confiance en lui."[46] Duplessis promised that if the Union Nationale was elected to office it would continue the investigations begun by the Public Accounts Committee into the administrative practices of the Taschereau régime, and all those found guilty of misusing public funds would be punished. A clean sweep would be made of the whole administration, graft and corruption would be eliminated, and an end would be put to the squandering of government money.

. . . .

Perhaps one of the most telling aspects of the Union Nationale's campaign was its appeal to the nationalistic and anti-English sentiments of the French-Canadian population. Antagonism towards the English reached a peak as Union Nationale orators, in meeting after meeting, warned the people of Quebec that their cultural values and their traditional way of life were threatened by the dominant role played by the British, American, and English-Canadian industrialists in the economic life of the province. The strong feelings of the nationalists towards "les étrangers" were forcibly expressed in a speech delivered at a mass meeting in Montreal by Dr. Philippe Hamel, the outstanding opponent of the large corporations, and particularly of "le trust de l'électricité":

> Or notre patrie, notre foi, nos traditions, nos libertés, tout cela est menacé. Nos ressources naturelles, elles ont été vendues par le régime pour un plat de lentilles aux étrangers. Vos foyers, ouvriers, on est en train de vous les arracher et déjà la lutte s'organise contre votre clocher par de sourdes menées anticléricales qui se font plus audacieuses et violentes.[49]

At another meeting Hamel's close associate, J.E. Grégoire of Quebec City, spoke in similar vein of the usurpations of "les étrangers":

> . . . une calamité nous étreint de toutes parts. Chacun est exploité, l'épicier canadien-français, le bûcheron, le petit propriétaire. Les meilleures places sont prises par des étrangers. . . . Les usines sont fermées, parce que notre province a été vendue aux étrangers. Les produits agricoles ne se vendent pas, parce que l'on a fermé nos débouchés.[50]

. . . .

The Union Nationale's appeal to the nationalistic sentiments of the French Canadian, and its promises of economic, social, and administrative reform, met with an unequivocal response from the electorate. When the time came for the balloting the people of Quebec turned the Liberal party out of office and elected the nationalist movement led by Maurice Duplessis. The Union Nationale won seventy-six out of the ninety seats in the legislature, while the Liberals with only fourteen seats were now in the novel position of being the official opposition.[51]

The chain of events leading to the Union Nationale victory of 1936 shows two things. First of all, the Quebec voter seemed to be convinced that the time had come for a government housecleaning, the elimination of graft and corruption, and the introduction of extensive reforms in administrative and electoral practices. Even more important, the success of this new nationalist movement was a clear indication of the strong opposition which had developed to the Liberal party's policy of promoting the industrialization of the province through the intervention of foreign capital. The defeat of the Liberals was a protest, not only against an economic system which had changed the traditional way of life and brought economic insecurity in its wake, but also against the dominant role played by English-speaking industrialists in that system. This protest was accompanied by a demand that the new capitalist economy be reformed and modified and that positive steps be taken to enable the French Canadian to regain control over the wealth and natural resources of his province. The direction these reforms were to take was to be determined by the principles of social Catholicism as laid down in the encyclicals of Pope Leo XIII and Pope Pius XI.

Notes

1. Many of Gouin's ideas are to be found in a number of speeches which he delivered to various groups in the 1930's and which are collected in his *Servir, I, La Cause nationale* (Montreal, 1938).
2. Mason Wade, *The French Canadians*, 1760-1945 (Toronto, 1955), p. 906.
3. See statement of A. Rioux, president of UCC, *Le Devoir*, 7 août 1934.
4. *Montreal Star*, May 10, 1927.
5. Robert Rumilly, *Histoire de la Province de Québec, xxvi, Rayonnement de Québec* (Montreal, 1953), p. 157.
6. This was an important factor in the Liberal victory over the Conservatives in the provincial election of 1927. See Jean Hamelin, Jacques Letarte, and Marcel Hamelin, "Les Elections provinciales dans le Québec," *Cahiers de Géographie de Québec*, 7 (oct. 1959-mars 1960), 39. See also, "L'Election provinciale de 1927: les conservateurs de Québec battus par les conservateurs d'Ottawa," *Le Devoir*, 11 fév. 1950.
7. Robert Rumilly, *Histoire de la Province de Québec, xxix, Vers l'âge d'or* (Montreal, 1956), p. 98.
8. *Montreal Star*, July 6, 1931.
9. *Canadian Annual Review*, 1932, p. 165.
10. A detailed description of the organization and proceedings of the convention is to be found in *La Presse*, 30 sept.-5 oct. 1933. See also Pierre Laporte, "Il y a 25 ans, la convention de Sherbrooke," *Le Devoir*, 1-3 oct. 1958.
11. See H. Quinn, *The Union Nationale*, pp. 73-5.
12. *Ibid.*, Appendix A, Table IV.
13. *Le Devoir*, 8 nov. 1935.

. . . .

15. Pope Pius XI, *Quadragesimo Anno* (London, 1931), 29.
16. R.P. Georges Levesque, O.P., "La Co-operative Commonwealth Federation," *Pour la restauration sociale au Canada* (Montreal, 1933). An even stronger condemnation of the CCF was made a year later by Archbishop Georges Gauthier of Montreal. See *Montreal Gazette*, Feb. 26, 1934. This ban on the party was not to be lifted until the bishops of Canada, both English and French, issued a joint statement in 1943 declaring that Catholics were free to support any Canadian party except the Communists. See *Canadian Register* (Kingston), Oct. 23, 1943.
17. A. Rioux, *et al., Le Programme de restauration sociale* (Montreal, 1933).
18. Gouin acknowledged his debt to the Ecole Sociale Populaire in a speech which he delivered in August, 1934: "Nous avons pris comme base d'étude et de discussion, pour préparer notre manifeste, le programme de Restauration sociale public sous les auspices de l'Ecole sociale populaire. . . . ce document reflétait de façon assez juste non seulement l'opinion de nos esprits les plus avertis mais aussi les sentiments, les aspirations et les besoins populaires." *Le Devoir*, 13 août 1934.
19. H. Quinn *op. cit.*, chap. v.

20. *Le Devoir*, 8 nov. 1935.
. . . .

24. In applying the term "radical" to the Union Nationale I mean only, of course, that its approach to economic policy was considered to be radical at the time. Many of its proposals for reform would not be considered very radical today.

25. The leaders of the UCC had always been close to the old provincial Conservative party. Albert Rioux, president of the association until 1936, resigned his post to run as Union Nationale candidate in the election of that year. Several leaders of the Catholic unions supported Union Nationale candidates on the platform in the same election.
. . . .

27. *Le Devoir*, 11 nov. 1935.

28. When the programme appeared Olivar Asselin, a prominent Liberal, stated, "It bears a greater resemblance to a 'bleu' [Conservative party] pamphlet than to a work of social apostolacy." *Montreal Gazette*, Nov. 21, 1933.
. . . .

30. See H. Quinn, *The Union Nationale*, Appendix A, Table IV.

31. Although a stenographic report was made of the proceedings of the Public Accounts Committee, this report was never published. Consequently the discussion here of the evidence presented before the committee has had to be based on newspaper reports. For each case at least two sources have been referred to in order to make sure of the accuracy of the reporting. One of the main sources has been Montreal's *La Presse*, a newspaper which has usually been a strong supporter of the Liberal party. Another important source has been a series of articles published in *Le Devoir* shortly after the sessions of the committee had ended and entitled, "M. Godbout était ministre au temps des scandales révélés au comité des comptes publics." *Le Devoir* was anything but friendly towards the Liberals at the time, but these articles are well documented and contain verbatim reports of many of the sessions.

32. See reports in *La Presse*, 13 mai 1936; *Le Devoir*, 23 juillet 1936; *Canadian Annual Review*, 1935-6, p. 283.

33. See *La Presse*, 9, 14, 29 mai and 2, 3, 4 juin 1936; *Canadian Annual Review*, 1935-6, pp. 282-3.

34. See *La Presse*, 5, 6, 9, 10 juin 1936; *Le Devoir*, 6 août 1936; *Sherbrooke Daily Record*, June 12, 1936.
. . . .

42. These proposals were put forward by Godbout in a radio address. See *La Tribune* (Sherbrooke), 6 juillet 1936.
. . . .

45. *Le Devoir*, 24 juin 1936.
46. *La Tribune*, 6 août 1936.
. . . .

49. *Le Devoir*, 13 août 1936.
50. *La Tribune*, 5 août 1936.
51. H. Quinn, *The Union Nationale*, Appendix A, Table IV.

Social Unrest, Social Class and Quebec's Bureaucratic Revolution

Hubert Guindon

"Bold, imaginative and responsible decisions are in order from the power elites of this country, whoever they may be. It is doubtful that the current concept of 'co-operative federalism' in its present confused and blurred state will tide us over."

I. Political Structures and Their Legitimations

Political structures in a mass society are fragile things. Since the Second World War, we have witnessed the collapse of age-old political regimes. The break-up of formal political empires, with the intellectual backing and sympathetic understanding of the majority of liberal intellectuals of the Western World, is now nearly complete. Seldom was the use of force necessary to achieve this. Massive ideological agitation with wide popular support achieved what armed might would not have attained. In most cases, the two structural conditions prerequisite to national liberation were: 1) a newly created native elite, highly educated, politically conscious, and through nationalist identification effectively engineering the revolt of expectations within 2) an awakened, restless native population whose aspirations are to be fulfilled by political independence. National independence has often been achieved though the heightened expectations usually have yet to be met.

Political structures need legitimations. Formal political empires collapsed because of a bankruptcy in legitimations. Legitimations are created by intellectuals and become sacred values for the other social groups.

Withdrawal of support from political structures by wide segments of the intelligentsia therefore becomes a crucial clue of imminent political instability. When this disenchantment of intellectuals is widely publicized and finds massive support in the lower social strata, the political regime, short of tyranny, is doomed.

Reprinted from *Queen's Quarterly*, Vol. 71, No. 2, Summer 1964, pp. 150-162, by permission of *Queen's Quarterly*.

For a political structure is, in the final analysis, a moral order requiring for its existence consensus.

Confederation is a political structure. For growing numbers of French-Canadian intellectuals its legitimations are unconvincing. The Massey-Lévesque brand of national feeling, the mutual-enrichment theory of ethnic co-habitation, seems, in 1964, so quaint, archaic, and folklorish, that for many young French-Canadian university students it is hard to believe it was formulated as late as 1950.

In the early sixties we have therefore witnessed the collapse of the latest legitimation of Confederation produced for the post-war period of peace. The Laurendeau-Dunton Commission, in my opinion, is searching for just that. Whether it will be successful is still very problematical. For the first time in the history of Royal Commissions concerned with national identity, dissent from many French-speaking Canadians is loud, clear, and emotional. Traditionally, such dissent came from a marginal, vocal group of French-Canadian nationalists. Their voice today is still vocal, but marginal it no longer is, for it stems from official circles with the blessing of academia. Lionel Groulx in the thirties, Michel Brunet in the early fifties could be dismissed as narrow-minded chauvinistic nationalists both within and without French-Canadian society. René Lévesque in the sixties cannot be so easily dismissed and he, in fact, is not so dismissed.

In terms of my opening remarks where does Confederation as a political structure stand within French Canada? Intellectual disenchantment with Confederation is widespread within the French-Canadian intelligentsia, including the social scientists. This disenchantment of intellectuals, artists, writers, newspapermen, film directors, etc., has been widely publicized in all forms of mass media. Furthermore, wide segments of French Canada's new middle class are either openly committed to, or sympathetic with, this heightened nationalist feeling, if not with separatism itself. This disenchantment, measured by belief in separatism, has not yet found massive support in the rural and lower urban social strata, but has met rather with indifference, apathy, and skepticism, seldom however with outright hostility. Had massive support from these social strata been forthcoming, the separatist idea would have been acted upon. Paradoxical as it may seem, it is the uneducated, unskilled, and semi-skilled French-Canadian farmer and worker, the "ignorant," "joual"-speaking French Canadian, oft-maligned and spoofed at by his ethnic middle class and the perfect fit of the anti-French Canadian stereotype, he it is at present who quite unconsciously is holding Confederation, unsettled as it is, on its shaky legs.

This leads me to raise specifically, the questions I shall attempt to answer in this essay. Why has the lower-class French Canadian been relatively immune to separatist agitation? Why has the new French-Canadian middle class become virulently nationalist and, to an important extent, separatist? Why has the emergence of this new middle class heightened ethnic tensions in Confederation? What is the nature of social unrest in the lower social strata?

II. Social Unrest and the New Middle Class

The emergence of what is commonly called the new middle class is not something specific to French Canada; quite on the contrary, the growth of such a class was rather belated, in fact, essentially a post-war phenomenon. With the growth and the increased size of large-scale formal organizations of business and government, the middle class was overwhelmingly transformed into a bureaucratically employed white collar group with professional and semi-professional status, displacing the dominant "entrepreneurial," self-employed character of the middle class in the last century. The new middle class is a product of the bureaucratic expansion of organizations.

1. The Growth and Characteristics of the New Middle Class in French Canada

Structurally, the French-Canadian new middle class is the same as its counterparts in industrially developed societies. But the circumstances of its emergence and some of its characteristics are somewhat at variance with most.

The bureaucratic revolution is, demographically speaking, the result of mass exodus from country to city. The demographic pressure created a need for expansion of the urban institutions serving this influx. In the process of expansion the urban institutions changed character, becoming large-scale organizations, marked by increased specialization. This bureaucratic revolution opened new channels of upward mobility. It required diversified staffs, trained in new skills. The growth of bureaucratic urban institutions became the structural basis of a new social class called the new middle class.

The French-Canadian new middle class, I have said, is somewhat different in some of its social-psychological characteristics from other new middle classes. First of all, its emergence was more dramatic and sudden than in many cases. Secondly, the ethnic cultural traditions from which it came provided no models for the broad spectrum of the new occupational roles. Thirdly, French-Canadian bureaucracies are to be found overwhelmingly in the public and semi-public sectors as against the area of private enterprise. Finally, the bureaucratic revolution, in French Canada, has not changed the power elite of French-Canadian society; it has not displaced, but rather rejuvenated traditional elites. Much of the unrest, in my opinion, in the French-Canadian new middle class can be related to these special characteristics.

2. The Duplessis Era and the New Middle Class

New middle class unrest dates back to the mid and late fifties. The post-war period saw a massive migration of French Canadians to the cities, mostly the major ones. This massive urbanization altered the existing nature of urban institutions. Urban institutions of welfare, health, and education had rapidly to increase their size, their staffs, and their budgets to meet the new demographic needs. This bureaucratic growth was being stifled by Duplessis' discretionary habit in spreading out public funds. In the process, the economic and status interests of this new middle class were not being met. Salaries could not be increased. Why? Because of Duplessis. Staff could not be hired. Why? Because of Duplessis.

Duplessis became a symbol of oppression, of reactionary government. He was depicted as a tyrant corrupting political mores. A persistent theme of Duplessis' political oratory was his opposition to "bureaucracy." Even though ideologically neutral, the theme was becoming increasingly impertinent structurally. The celebrated attack on the political mores of the Union Nationale Party by Fathers Dion and O'Neil paved the way for a new bureaucratic type of political morality. The growth of semi-public bureaucratic institutions required greatly increased and predictable amounts of money from the provincial treasury. Because he refused to meet these class demands, Duplessis was emotionally and unanimously resented by the new middle class. Where Duplessis failed, Sauvé succeeded. By a single declaration of policy, namely, increased grants to universities, hospital insurance, and increased salaries to civil servants, he immediately got the emotional endorsement of the new middle class for the very same party. His untimely death was perceived by members of this social class as a tragic personal loss. Duplessis stifled the class interests and the status aspirations of the new middle class. He was resented. Sauvé decided to meet them; he was acclaimed.

3. The New Middle Class and the Lesage Régime

With the death of Duplessis, the critical importance of the new middle class on politics became unchallenged. Following in Sauvé's footsteps, the Liberal Party under Jean Lesage proceeded to base its political strength on the enthusiastic support of the new middle class, recently become politically aroused and vocal.

The link between the Liberal Party and the new middle class can easily be established. Its existence can be shown in terms of (a) the "nucleus" of its political support, (b) the choice of "competent" administrative personnel in the civil service, and (c) the nature of its legislative reforms. The "volunteer" workers of the Liberal Party in the past elections were urban, more highly educated, younger, new middle class people. The concern for qualified personnel in the expanding provincial civil service spells the end of the "self-made" man or politically appointed party supporter. The party man must also be professionally qualified.

The Liberal legislative reform is a bureaucratic reform. It has sought to expand and strengthen the bureaucratic services of education, health, and welfare. The

Quebec renaissance or silent revolution, or whatever it is called, is a bureaucratic revolution. The tremendous expenditures in education and health are coupled with a constant concern with increasing the salaries of white collar occupations in these institutions. Current concern for portable pensions equally reflects the interests of the new middle class.

4. From Anti-Duplessism to Separatism

It is not, in my opinion, by sheer coincidence that separatism became a social force only after the death of Duplessis. By stifling the status aspirations of the new middle class, Duplessis became a scapegoat upon which its frustrations could be vented. Middle class unrest did not die with Duplessis. The middle classes, however, did lose a scapegoat.

The Liberal Party, champion of bureaucratic reform, endeavoring to meet the aspirations of this social class could not easily be indicted. Unrest in new middle class circles took on the form of separatist agitation. The class origins of separatism can be ascertained both in terms of the social location of its supporters and the class nature of its grievances.

Separatist leaders as well as their rank and file are to be found among the better-educated, younger, professional and semi-professional, salaried, white collar ranks. This class constitutes the core of its support. The nature of separatist grievances also underlines its class bias. Separatist discontent, in the final analysis, boils down to protest against real or imagined restricted occupational mobility. The objects of separatist indictment are the promotion practices of the federally operated bureaucracies, of crown and private corporations. This class bias is also the reason why the separatist appeal has gone by largely unheeded by the rural classes and the lower social strata of the cities.

5. Nationalist Unrest, the Liberal Regime and Confederation

Sheer coincidence cannot alone account for the fact that separatism and disenchantment with Confederation appeared on the political scene, in its massive form, after the Liberal régime came into power and not during the Duplessis era.

Meeting the status aspirations of the new middle class in French Canada, as the Liberals surely know by now, is an expensive proposition. It is more costly than most service since, as I have mentioned, French-Canadian bureaucracies tend to be in the public or semi-public sectors that typically rely on public funds for a sizable proportion of their budgets. The income squeeze that resulted from trying to meet new middle class demands created a political crisis in dominion-provincial relations.

Ethnic tensions, unheard of during the Duplessis era, were brought back once again to the forefront of public discussion. Maîtres chez nous, the Liberal Party's slogan in the last election, is actually the official endorsement of a forty-year old slogan first put forward by Lionel Groulx.

"Le seul choix qui nous reste est celui-ci: ou redevenir maîtres chez nous, ou nous résigner à jamais aux destinées d'un peuple de serfs."[1]

Lionel Groulx's was a voice in the desert until the new middle class made it theirs. His historical, economic, and social views were academically marginal and politically ineffective until the emergence of the new middle class and its access to political power. His views have become the unifying ideology giving political cohesiveness to this new social class.

Many of the current themes of political concern are to be explicitly found in his writings. Ambivalence towards foreign capitalists and foreign labour unions, indignation at the handing over of natural resources to foreign investors, the lack of an entrepreneurial bourgeoisie, the positive role of the state in economic affairs, the lack of proper academic institutions and training for the world of business, the "bi-national" theory of Confederation, all of these themes are clearly and eloquently pleaded in his writings.

The financial strain of the French-Canadian bureaucratic revolution and the nationalist ideology of the French-Canadian new middle class, have brought about a reinterpretation of Confederation specifically and of ethnic co-habitation generally. The reinterpretation is not new; its widespread acceptance in the new middle class is.

Confederation is on probation. The French-Canadian new middle class does not view it as something valuable in itself. It is to be judged on its merits as a means to achieving national aspirations. It has, for a long time, been viewed as an instrument of British-Canadian nationalism.[2] With the rise of ethnic tensions this view is becoming widespread in many circles and a postulate of the political analysis of separatist groups of every tendency.

What, in effect, needs clarification is the history of ethnic co-habitation in Canada. Ethnic accommodation, it seems to me, has been historically constructed, successfully in Quebec, on a basis of mutually desired self-segregated institutions. In the fields of education, religion, welfare, leisure, and residence, institutional self-segregation has been total. The only two areas of societal living where inter-ethnic contact has been institutionalized are those of work and politics.

The pattern of ethnic contact in the area of work was established with the introduction of industrialization. Anglo-Saxon industry moved into a society faced with an acute population surplus, a distinctive political and religious elite, a developing set of institutions anchored in the rural parish. This society, politically stable, economically conservative, and technically unskilled, provided ideal conditions for investing Anglo-Saxon capitalists; they could invest their capital, open industries, and be supplied with an abundant source of unskilled labour seeking employment. The managerial and technical levels were filled, with no protest, by the incoming group, who also brought along their own set of institutions, servicing their own nationals.

This social setting provided an easy introduction to industry. The French-Canadian elite was ideologically co-operative, sensitive only about its continued control over its demographic substructures. This fitted in quite well with the aims of the incoming groups, who could develop their economic pursuits and enterprises with minimum involvement in the local society. There was a minimum of involvement in local politics. The local elite of politicians and the clergy welcomed the transaction of business and the development of business institutions. All this took place with no unrest whatsoever. Industry was relieving the economic burden of the demographic surplus of French-Canadian rural society. The local elites' leadership was not being challenged.

This pattern of mutually satisfying, self-segregated institutions worked with no dissent up to and including the Second World War. This historical pattern is now being challenged. It is being challenged by the recently emerged French-Canadian new middle class. Making room for this new social class in the managerial levels of industry and government is the crucial test of Canadian unity. This cannot be achieved without the shedding of old habits that surrounded the traditional ethnic division of labour.

III.   Social Unrest in the Rural and Lower-Urban Social Classes

1.   The Créditiste Episode

"Nous sommes simples, nous autres habitants, et vu notre ignorance, nous sommes contraints de mettre à la tête de nos municipalités et de nos administrations des citoyens instruits mais qui, au fond, nous exploitent. . . ." — Isidore Gauthier, a farmer, 1862.[3]

New middle class unrest, vocal and well publicized, overshadowed another social unrest, that of the lower social class of country and city, until the unforeseen sweep of rural Quebec by Réal Caouette's Créditiste movement.

Indeed, for the first time in Quebec's political history, the rural lower classes transgressed the political script described by Isidore Gauthier. Instead of sending to the Federal Parliament traditional middle class professionals, they elected class peers to represent them.

Unforeseen, this political development brought about a reaction of bewilderment, astonishment, and nervous laughter in middle class circles. The Créditiste surge was viewed with alarm, ridicule, and embarrassment. The French-Canadian new middle class had the identical reaction as its English-Canadian counterpart towards the Créditiste sweep. It focused immediately and exclusively on its unorthodox economics not on the social discontent that gave rise to it.

The Créditiste appeal successfully tapped the unrest of farmer and unskilled worker where the middle class separatist protest failed. The Créditiste criticism of the traditional parties found fertile soil in the economically deprived regions of rural Quebec. "You have nothing to lose" went the slogan. Another major theme was the right to economic security. Economic security to middle class people means decent pension plans. To a sizeable part of the French-Canadian population it means something quite different. It means stable employment, a year-round job, the right not to live in the constant fear of unemployment. Caouette, who is no new middle class symbol by any means, but a small entrepreneur, the product of the barren Abitibi region, spoke their language. His charge that the old parties really do not care or cannot change their socio-economic plight, comes dangerously close to regional historic truth, for this state of economic insecurity has been a pattern that dates back close to a century.

The dramatic emergence of the Social Credit Party in rural Quebec can be viewed as a boomerang or latent resentment of the class-oriented Liberal course in Quebec. Duplessis, whatever his shortcomings, based his political machine on the rural and lower-urban social strata. After the ousting of the Union Nationale from power, these classes felt unrepresented, uncared for, with no significant voice in the political arena. Duplessis had never been viewed as a dictator or tyrant in these strata. The Lesage resolve to dissolve patronage increased the Créditiste supporters because of disenchanted rural Liberals who had expected the continued exercise of patronage by their own group.

The possibly unanticipated effect of the crackdown on patronage, in actual fact, was to halt or substantially reduce the flow of provincial funds to the lower social strata. Holding up the new "bureaucratic" political morality was a hidden net reorienting public expenditures to other social classes. In the light of this interpretation, the Créditiste slogan "you have nothing to lose" takes on added meaning. Whatever the dubious ethics of the political organizers of Duplessis may have been, and whatever the size of the cake they kept as their part, they managed, in their own devious ways to let the rest funnel down in numerous bits into kinship systems. With the Liberal régime, the cake is properly and ceremoniously cut up, but the slices are fewer and the number of guests greatly reduced.

Whether the Créditiste movement will manage to hold its own politically is uncertain; whether it does or not, is of little interest; the social unrest that gave rise to it is, however, of considerable importance. To make intelligible the social forces behind its success, whether temporary or not, is the legitimate and necessary concern of the social scientist.

2.   Messianic Social Movements and Deprived Social Classes

Messianic social movements tend to take roots in the economically deprived social classes. The utopian dream they hold up may seem unattainable and irrational to middle class logic, but its purpose and function are different. Its function is to present an alternative to the state of things for those who benefit the least from the status quo. In the process, the present state of society is shown to be man-made and therefore amenable to change. The "funny money" policies of the Créditiste movement can be understood in the light of such classical social movement theory. The Créditiste attack on the financial "sharks" and its insistence on monetary reform served this purpose. To set off the printing presses is an alarming idea for those who have money because of its inflationary effect, for those who do not have money, it becomes a pleasant dream; a dream about magical access to middle class status. And when believed in, it becomes a political force.

Eric Kierans' brave foray from the Board of Trade's executive suite to Créditiste territory with an orthodox economic gospel, quite unprecedented as it was, only underlined the establishment's sombre assessment of the situation.

The Liberal solution to the economic plight of these deprived regions goes little beyond the faint hope of recruitment over the generations to middle class status through education. This is equally utopian; it has yet to be achieved anywhere in Western Capitalist society. The fact of the matter is that no operational solution to these pockets of poverty has actually been found.

3. The Conservative Urban Proletariat and the Uprooted New Middle Class

The French-Canadian urban lower classes behave improperly in terms of classical theory. They remain Catholic, faithfully go to church, never vote socialist, and in times of family crisis will spontaneously turn for help to their extended kinship group, their priests and their landlords and only as a last resort, and with a loss of self-respect, to social agencies, social workers, and union leaders.

The traditionalism of the urban lower class has been the scourge of socialist efforts. It has also stubbornly resisted appeals from the nationalist circles to become an ethnically-conscious consumer. They do not share the anti-Americanism of both French-Canadian and English-Canadian nationalism.

The rural-urban transition, eased by the kinship group, has not been as textbooks usually describe it, as personally unsettling and culturally shocking as earlier massive urbanization may have been in other societies.

Uprootedness is more characteristic of French Canada's new middle class than of its urban proletariat. The traditonal pattern of land inheritance, of keeping the farm intact and handing it over to only one heir, coupled with the high rural birth rate has meant that moving, looking for work, settling elsewhere, is not a dramatic event in the life-cycle of the rural surplus population and it has been provided for in the cultural script.

What have not been provided for by the cultural traditions are the role models for the new middle class occupations. For this reason, the traditional culture is something far from sacred and useful, very often the object of contempt and ridicule within new middle class circles. Part of the anxiety and anguish of the new middle class psyche may be traced to this lack of cultural continuity.

IV. Summary

The emergence of a new middle class in French Canada is a structural change that cannot be wished away. Its status aspirations are challenging the historical pattern of the ethnic division of labour. Whether its heightened national mood will lead to the separatist experiment is dependent upon two things: (a) on how successful the present political and economic structure of the Canadian society will be in coping with its bureaucratic aspirations, and (b) on the future direction of lower class unrest.

The bureaucratic revolution of the last few years in Quebec has brought to the surface latent resentment in French-Canadian society. The traditionally conservative substructure of French-Canadian society has expressed discontent of its own. Its course has not, until now, been in the same direction. But who can say with absolute confidence that it will never be?

Bold, imaginative, and responsible decisions are in order from the power elites of this country, whoever they may be. It is doubtful that the current concept of "co-operative federalism" in its present confused and blurred state will tide us over.

Notes

1. Lionel Groulx, *Directives*, Les éditions du Zodiaque, 1937, p. 20.
2. See Michel Brunet, *Canadians et Canadiens*, Fides 1952, pp. 47-49. "Une autre manifestation du nationalisme Canadian, le Rapport Massey."
3. Quoted in Léon Gérin, *Le Type Economique et Social des Canadiens*, Editions de l'ACF, 1938, p. 54.

Social Credit in the Province of Quebec: Summary and Developments

Michael B. Stein

I shall present here a brief summary of the principal thesis of my book *The Dynamics of Right-Wing Protest: A Political Analysis of Social Credit in Quebec*.[1] In addition, I will touch on certain more recent developments in the evolution of the movement (since 1970) and on the possibility of applying my hypothesis to similar phenomena which have appeared in that province or in other societies.

The article will be divided into four parts which respond to the following questions: (1) What is the Créditiste phenomenon? Is it a party or a political movement? (2) What kind of political movement is Créditisme? (3) How does one explain, from its beginnings in 1936 up to the present, the fundamental phases of the development of this phenomenon, the appearance of factions, and the schisms which came about? (4) What are the consequences of this phenomenon for the politics of Quebec and of Canada, and what are the possibilities for the application of this analysis to other phenomena, in Quebec or elsewhere?

I. The Créditiste Phenomenon: Party or Political Movement?

Most commentators view the Créditiste phenomenon exclusively as a political party whose beginnings go back to 1957 with the foundation of the *Ralliement des Créditistes* under the leadership of Réal Caouette.[2] But the Créditiste phenomenon as a political movement and not as a political party, has been an important facet of the Quebec political scene since the crisis of the thirties.[3]

Social Credit originally appeared in Quebec in the form of The League of Social Credit, founded in 1936 by Louis Even, a journalist and translator for a printing house at Gardenvale near Montreal, Armand Turpin, at that time Director of Production for the Borden Company in Hull, and Louis Dugal, a young Montreal lawyer. Louis Even edited the League's paper *Cahiers du Crédit*

Reprinted [in translation] from the *Canadian Journal of Political Science*, Vol. 6, No. 4, December 1973, pp. 563-581, by permission of the author and the Canadian Political Science Association. Translation by Conrad Wieczorek approved by the author.

Social, which, for three years, came out more or less on a monthly basis. Its contents very much resembled that of the journals and periodicals of the various subsequent wings of the movement; it was a mixture of the monetary reform doctrines of Major Douglas of Britain (which were presented for the first time in 1918) and the social teachings of the church, based on papal encyclicals. The organization of the League also resembled the organization established later on in the movement: local committees in the different parishes of the province; a chairman, a secretary, and members of county councils; regional districts made up of members of these councils; and finally a provincial executive made up partly of the chairmen appointed in the districts and partly of the officers (chairman, secretary, and five vice-chairmen) elected by the delegates to the annual provincial convention. However, the League, centred in Montreal and numbering several thousand people, was primarily an educational movement. It was directed and, for the most part, made up of people in business and the professions. Its principal objectives were the education and formation of an elite of experts in Social Credit. The League never succeeded in becoming a mass movement.

It was in 1939, with the foundation of the Union of Electors, that Social Credit really succeeded in setting itself up as a popular movement in the province. This branch of the movement was the creation of Louis Even and Gilberte Côté, the daughter of a well-to-do family whose father was a Montreal shoe manufacturer. Côté had a university background and was in addition an extremely dynamic woman. The two quit the League, and, with the aim of transforming a movement reserved for a tiny elite into a mass movement, they launched the bi-monthly *Vers Demain* in September of 1939.

The Créditistes were very well known in Quebec, especially in towns and villages of the rural and semi-urban parts of the province (outside of the region of Metropolitan Montreal). The newspaper *Vers Demain*, published bi-monthly in Montreal, was distributed by the membership to about 60,000 people during their most successful years (c.1948). Cells were set up on the farms and in the factories of several parts of Quebec: Abitibi (Rouyn-Noranda), The Eastern Townships, Quebec City, "La Mauricie," and Saguenay-Lac Saint Jean.

Moreover, the Union of Electors took a direct part in several federal and provincial elections between 1940 and 1957. They succeeded in winning only one seat, that of Pontiac, in a by-election. Réal Caouette was the member from 1946 to 1949. Nevertheless, this movement at its height (in 1948) obtained 150,000 votes, almost 10 per cent of the Quebec vote.

However, the Union of Electors always denied that its objectives were to come to power, like the conventional political parties. In the beginning its aim was the education of the masses (the lowest and poorest classes) in the doctrine of Social Credit. The objective of the movement was the mobilization of a group of supporters in each region to bring pressure to bear on the authorities in order to persuade them to adopt and implement the philosophy and economic policy of Social Credit. Following Major Douglas, the Union of Electors rejected the party system, which it saw as a puppet show manipulated by big business, the banks, etc. The Union hesitantly put up candidates for election and it proclaimed publicly and loudly that they were democratically chosen by a union of electors. They were merely the delegates of their constituents, subject to recall (an application of the theory of plebiscitary democracy).

Even by 1957, when Réal Caouette and 11 of his friends quit the Union of Electors and founded the *Ralliement des Créditistes* with the intention of participating in elections and attaining power,[4] the original movement's elements in the Créditiste phenomenon did not disappear. The structures, the method of financing, and the means of propaganda were all based on the model of the Union of Electors. A great many of the first militants were former members of the Union of Electors, who became and remained the leaders of the *Ralliement* throughout the sixties. During these years tension persisted between the ideas of a party and those of a movement. Even the provincial party, the *Ralliement Créditiste du Québec*, founded in 1970, continued to be influenced by certain ideas of the movement. In February of 1973, after a devastating schism which had lasted almost a year, the bulk of the members turned to a "non-Créditiste", Yvon Dupuis, to rebuild their association. By that time, the embers of the old movement were well extinguished.

On the whole, the Créditiste phenomenon, at least during the period 1936-1957, presents itself more as a political movement than as a political party.[5] The origins of the Créditiste phenomenon, insofar as it was a movement, influenced its development for the first 20 years of its life. And they have continued to determine the general lines of evolution of the two Créditiste political parties up to the present time.

However, the Créditiste phenomenon is more than a simple political movement. It is a special type of movement, which I call a protest movement of the right. For me, this type of movement manifests particular characteristics which determine its lines of evolution and their consequences for the society in which it is found.

II. The Sociological Definition of Créditisme: A Protest Movement of the Right

In the literature of political sociology, a social movement is defined as a form of collective action seeking to mobilize individuals for the purpose of making fundamental changes in the social order.[6] In all the definitions of the concept "social movement" the central elements are the common sentiments of discontent and the general desire to change society.

A "political movement" is a species of social movement. It is directed toward change in the political order. It has a certain number of traits in common with other political structures such as parties and pressure groups, which are themselves vying to exercise influence in the political arena (for example, the organization of individuals around ideas and common interests which they try to promote by political means).[7] But what is more important is the way in which political movements distinguish themselves from other, more conventional political structures.

To begin with, political movements have broader aims than most other organizations in the political arena. They envisage political education, the mobilization of the masses, and other forms of action directed towards a general change. Secondly, political movements are generally organized around a set of beliefs or utopian goals made explicit in a political ideology which acts as a force unifying the members.[8] Thirdly, political movements manifest a structuring of political roles and a distribution of power, influence, and authority among their members, which distinguish them from other political structures. The organizational structures have a tendency to be very tight at the level of leadership and rather loose at the level of supporters. The leaders have a tendency to concentrate power in their own hands so as to maintain control over the decisions which determine the strategy and tactics of the movement.[9]

There are two principal types of political movement, defined by their goals: protest movements and revolutionary movements. The revolutionary movement is dedicated to the destruction of the system and the seizure of power so as to completely transform the social order. The protest movement has more limited goals: to change the way in which decisions are made or to transform the norms which delimit the decision-making process, without destroying the system itself.[10]

Protest movements have as a goal the politicization of the masses and their conversion to the ideology of the movement. Through a series of dissident acts against the system or its authorities they try to draw public attention to their grievances. Their objectives are, either to persuade the authorities to adopt their point of view or to remove them and take power for themselves so as to implement the desired changes. However, they do not have as objectives a fundamental change in the rules of the system or the foundations of the society. In this sense, the black civil rights movements in 1960-1965, led by moderate groups like the NAACP and CORE, were more protest movements than revolutionary movements.

On the level of ideology, there are two principal types of protest movement: right-wing movements and left-wing movements. Generally speaking, movements of the right make their appeal to those parts of the population which, in the long run, are destined to wane (for example, the farmer in an era of industrialization, the "blue collar" worker in the "post-industrial" society). Their appeal is characterized by the desire to preserve present social and economic conditions or to recreate the society of the past. Movements of the left, on the other hand, make their appeal to those sectors of the population on the upswing (for example, the "blue-collar" worker in the industrialized society and the "white-collar" workers or the "technocrats" in the "post-industrial" society). They want to set up the conditions of the society of the future, such as a guaranteed annual income, strong anti-pollution measures, decentralized health services, etc.[11]

The Créditistes can be defined as a *protest* movement because their opposition to the financial and political system was never revolutionary. They never wished to change anything more than the method of distribution of credit, thinking that all of the other changes desired in the economic, social, or political order were determined by economic measures. They had no desire to change either the parliamentary regime or the Canadian federal system. They did not desire great transformations in the structure of social groups in society. In the economic sphere they wished neither the destruction nor the abolition of the capitalist system. In fact, except for a brief period (from 1944 to 1948), they never wanted any fundamental changes in the democratic system.[12]

Furthermore "créditisme" is a protest movement *of the right* because its appeal is essentially conservative and directed to the preservation of a social and economic order rapidly disappearing in Quebec. The Créditistes believe that traditional values like obedience, duty, and morality were more prevalent in the social system of the past than they are today. They believe also that they will be re-established just as soon as the corrupt influence of monopolistic capitalism and the avarice of the bankers are restrained by the Social Credit system. They foresee a renaissance of the farmer, of the small-town merchant, and of the artisan as soon as they have enough credit to finance themselves. They have confidence in the recovery of the church and religious institutions and they insist on the preservation of the confessional system of education. They denounce the evils of pornography and drugs. They want the media in small towns and villages shielded from the corrupting effects of those in the cities.

III. Evolution of the Créditiste Movement: Its Three Fundamental Phases and their Catalysts

Analysts of social movements have rarely attempted to describe the way in which these movements evolve and to bring out the factors responsible for their transformation. However, it has been generally observed that political movements evolve through three main phases associated with actions typical of certain types of leaders during each phase, namely: (1) mobilization, (2) consolidation, (3) institutionalization. The whole evolutionary process can be described as a gradual secularization of the movement and as a weakening of its ideological thrust, leading to its eventual transformation into another institutional form or to its disappearance.

The mobilization phase is the period during which members are recruited, the masses are subjected to proselytization and propaganda, and the basic structures and methods of operation are established. The model process for this phase can be described thus: a nucleus of persons is attracted by a dissident ideology, for various reasons — dissatisfaction with the economic, political, or social order, personal or collective needs or interests, etc.[13] These people come from different social classes, from fringe groups, from the mainstream of the population, and even from the elite. They believe strongly in the goals of the movement and devote more time and effort to their clarification and realization than the other members. This group arouses and orients the emotions and dissatisfactions of the alienated masses.[14] During this phase the leaders are more "prophets" or "preachers". They owe their leadership to their ability to concretize the main ideas and to convert new members to their cause. Their authority comes from their manifest superiority in formulating and interpreting the "faith" and in the art of bringing it down to the level of the masses.[15]

In the phase of consolidation the movement develops its resources, increases its membership, ratifies its structures, defines procedures, and modifies strategy and tactics in order to deal with new situations. In this phase, it is generally directed by men with talents in organization, administration, and public relations.[16]

In the phase of institutionalization the movement tries to maintain and increase its support through negotiations and alliances with other groups. Its strategy and tactics become more pragmatic and less tied to the original ideology and goals of the movement; it accepts compromise. It is then generally directed by pragmatic and opportunistic men, less well-versed in the original doctrine than were the first leaders. Their belief is not so firm and for the sake of short-term goals they are ready to sacrifice what remains of the original movement.[17]

One of the dominant characteristics of social movements is their inherent tendency to give rise to factions. This tendency has generally been attributed to the inevitable conflicts which arise between more and less doctrinaire members when the attempt is made to put ideology into action. This tendency manifests itself particularly in political movements. In addition to the factor we have just mentioned, there are several reasons for this. Conflict develops between members of different ages and political experiences: a generational conflict which manifests itself in struggles between different types of leaders and different styles of leadership.[18] Further, new bases of power tend naturally to develop outside the circle of the original leaders; this tendency can be attributed to the fact that heterogeneity increases as the movement evolves.[19] Another factor explaining the appearance of factions in political movements is the weakness of any machinery for control, especially in protest or non-revolutionary movements. When divergencies develop, the dominant leadership has in its hands few rewards to offer and few sanctions to impose in order to maintain its predominance over the membership.[20]

Whatever the validity of these explanations, they really fail to get to the heart of the matter. And, what is more important, they do not clearly establish the connection between the phenomenon of factions and the underlying dynamic of change in political movements. Most analysts tend to consider factions as a cause of weakness, as a useless expenditure of energy, as an aberration in the normal process of evolution and development of these movements.

However, in my opinion, even if the factions provoke internal conflict or open schism, they also propel the movement toward new phases of its evolution in which we find the production of new leaders, re-orientation of strategy and tactics, and re-organization of structures. These new orientations can be crucial and can determine success or a relative setback for the movement. In other words, it is conflict and not consensus which is thus considered the norm for political movements and it is this which is the essential ingredient in the determination of their development and of their ultimate effects upon the society in which they operate. It is this hypothesis which I have tried to set out in my study of the Créditiste Movement in Quebec. It will be impossible for me to give here a detailed analysis of the phenomenon of factionalism.[21] I will content myself with summing up some of the conclusions of that study.

First of all, since Créditisme is the prototype of a particular category of political movement, namely a protest movement of the right, one can expect it to show many of the general characteristics of political movements. Furthermore, it is likely that it will show several features peculiar to its species. In fact, Créditisme has already gone through two of the three typical evolutionary phases of political movements, those of mobilization and consolidation, and it is now entering the third phase, that of institutionalization.

The first phase of the development of the Créditiste Movement in Quebec, from 1936 to 1957, corresponds closely to the ideal type of "mobilization". It is during the first three years of the period, which begins with the setting up of the League of Social Credit and its journal *Les Cahiers du Crédit social*, that the numerous early militants, those who would form the nucleus of leadership of the first Créditiste generation, attached themselves to the movement. But the recruiting of members and of an important segment of the population only came about in the 1940's with the creation of the Union of Electors and its bi-monthly *Vers Demain*. From 1939 to 1948 the movement grew very rapidly using a simple but effective method of recruitment: each member was assigned a quota of recruits. The membership forms were to be found in the journal *Vers Demain*. Whoever obtained his quota of 25 members was automatically named to the elite corps of the movement, The Institute of Political Action, which at its height numbered about two or three thousand members. The most dedicated and effective members of this group were named to the directorate of the movement which had at its head Louis Even and Gilberte Côté-Mercier; the directorate never had more than seven members. The directors, with the help of their devoted lieutenants, made the movement's major political decisions and maintained a rigorous control. The membership grew from about 2000 at the time of the foundation of the Union, to 65,000 (according to the Créditistes themselves) in 1948.

Louis Even and Gilberte Côté-Mercier were the undisputed leaders of the movement. Even played the role of "prophet" and ideologue. He succeeded in translating the abstract doctrines of Major Douglas into language comprehensible to the lower middle class, the workers, and the farmers of Quebec. Gilberte Côté-Mercier was unsurpassed as organizer and propagandist: she made most of the decisions on political strategy and it was she who chose most of the movement's symbols including the white beret worn by the members after 1949.

In phase one, the Créditistes were far from their objective of leading a significant proportion of the Québecois to subscribe to the doctrines of Social Credit. The most intense effort was made in the provincial elections of 1948, when the Union of Electors fielded candidates in the 92 provincial ridings of Quebec. But they obtained only 150,000 votes, without electing a single candidate. Following that setback, the Union abstained from any further electoral attempts.[22] For several years, from 1950 to 1957, the Créditistes tried another technique of political action by which to establish Social Credit: they brought direct pressure to bear on the politicians. When this technique failed as well, and when the membership began to decrease, the leaders lost interest in temporal matters, and the Union took on a more religious character.

In 1957, with the rise to leadership of the second generation of Créditistes under Réal Caouette, the second phase of the movement, that of consolidation, began. Caouette had joined the movement in 1940 and from the beginning showed himself to be a top-flight propagandist and leader of election campaigns.[23] In the provincial elections of 1944 and the federal elections of 1945 he ran as a candidate for the Union of Electors and came second in both instances. However, in 1946 his aspirations were fulfilled when he carried the riding of Pontiac in a by-election. Other Créditistes of the second generation shared his point of view: Laurent Legault, his campaign-manager in several elections, Gilles Grégoire, son of J.E. Grégoire, former mayor of Quebec and leader of the Union through most of the first campaigns, and François Even, the son of Louis Even. These leaders of the second generation were convinced that the best way of establishing Social Credit was through the organization of a concerted electoral effort. They were opposed to the growing religious orientation of the movement. For this reason, in September of 1957, twelve people, mainly second-generation Créditistes, met in Montreal to form the *Ralliement des Créditistes*.

The founders of the *Ralliement* did not have as their original intention the formation of a completely new organization. They wanted rather to create within the Union a parallel political structure which would serve as an electoral rallying point for all the Créditistes of the province, including the dissident factions.[24] When the directors of the Union, Louis Even and Gilberte Côté-Mercier, rejected this idea, the leaders of the second generation declared their independence. From its inception the *Ralliement des Créditistes* was conceived of as both party and movement;[25] its main objective was to get the voters to elect its candidates and thus to come to power. However, it never abandoned its educational goals.

From its inception the *Ralliement* was made up for the most part of secessionist members of the Union of Electors and for this reason it developed very slowly. However, in 1960 Caouette and Legault allied themselves with the Social Credit Party in the Western Provinces which Robert Thompson was in the process of reorganizing. Caouette was edged out by Thompson in the contest for national leadership and was named deputy leader of the national party. More importantly, beginning in 1958 the *Ralliement* sponsored a series of 15-minute television programs in various parts of Quebec; these were later broadcast on a much wider scale. In them Caouette projected a powerful and popular image. He attracted to the movement a number of new members who had had no connection with the Union of Electors. Several among them were professionals who added prestige to the movement (for example Marcoux, Chapdelaine, Côté). Still "the white berets" remained the dominant element in the membership. Under the guidance of Legault the "party-movement" adopted the same electoral structures and methods of financing as those of the Union. It manifested also the two principal elements of Duverger's definition of a "party of the masses."[26] If the ideology of the *Ralliement* was essentially the same, strategy and tactics were radically transformed. The leaders of the *Ralliement* were now unequivocally committed to coming to power. The associations in the ridings kept their study groups, but their main goal became organization for future elections.

The *Ralliement* won a far greater number of votes than its predecessor, the Union of Electors. The Union had never been able to obtain more than 10 per cent of the popular vote, while the *Ralliement* took 26 per cent of the Quebec vote in the first elections it contested (1962), and in 1963 it got 29 per cent of the vote. Furthermore the *Ralliement* not only consolidated the movement's base in Quebec but broadened it as well. Still the base appeared limited, sometimes it shrank, at other times it grew slightly. It seldom included more than a quarter of the total population of Quebec and it was confined to rural and small-town areas. In fact, up until the Federal elections of 1972 the *Ralliement Créditiste* seemed to be always on the decline.[27]

It is not surprising to note then that about 1970, as the second Créditiste generation grew older, a third generation, comprising several sons of second-generation Créditistes,[28] came to maturity and began to call for a re-orientation of the aims of the "party-movement". For them the survival of Social Credit was threatened, the movement had not adapted to new popular trends such as urbanization, nationalism, and the desire for cultural and economic modernization.

They conceived a strategy for the transformation of a protest movement of the right into a conventional political party with a more pragmatic conservative ideology and a larger, more urban base. Thus they helped lead the movement into its third phase, that of institutionalization.

The third phase was initiated in March of 1970 with the holding of a convention to choose the leader of the newly created provincial party. It is interesting to note that it was Caouette himself who laid down the lines of this new phase. He resisted all blandishments and the most intense efforts to designate him as provincial leader, and he proposed Yvon Dupuis as his personal choice for the post. However, the membership present, for the most part members of the second generation, refused to accept a man who was not only not an authentic Créditiste but who had also been a bitter opponent of the movement in the Federal elections of 1963.[29] Consequently, they gave no heed to Caouette's appeal and, by an overwhelming majority, voted for Camil Samson, a protégé of Caouette, also living in Rouyn.

However, Dupuis' chances for the leadership were not finished. Even though the provincial Créditistes did well in the elections of 1970 under Camil Samson, the third-generation group did not approve of his selection as leader because, according to them, he had neither the education nor the necessary sensitivity to the actual evolution of the province, much less the skills necessary to handle political power. This is why a group of provincial deputies, led by the young provincial president Phil Cossette, succeeded in a conspiracy to eject Samson from the provincial leadership. They chose, as interim leader, Armand Bois, a member of the old guard, and set about seeking a more suitable leader for the third-generation Créditistes. The man to whom they finally turned at the end of 1972 was Yvon Dupuis. Dupuis was victorious on the second ballot at the Créditiste provincial convention in February of 1973.

Dupuis is in almost every way the incarnation of the pragmatic leader of the phase of institutionalization. He projects a young attractive image; he has political experience, style, and proven gifts as a speaker. Moreover, he attracted a large political following in Montreal through the successful use of a radio program and his paper *Le Défi* which published letters in reply to his editorials and his broadcasts.

Even though he shared the conservative orientation of the Créditistes, Dupuis showed signs of wanting to modernize and renew Créditiste ideology so as to attract new elements of the population to the party. He would, without doubt, have been willing to make alliances with other parties such as the Union Nationale, if such connections appeared advantageous.[30] He didn't seem to have a very great knowledge of or interest in Social Credit orthodoxy nor in the past traditions of the movement. His speeches didn't dwell on economic questions.[31] His main objective was political power and he seemed ready to use every necessary means to that end. For example, in openly calling on the big corporations for donations, he had already begun to change the financial structures of the party which had been based on popular support. There is no doubt that if eventually the mantle of leadership for the entire movement settles on his shoulders and on those of the third generation, Créditisme will change from a protest movement of the right into a conventional right-of-centre political party, such as exist already in Alberta and British Columbia.

Thus Créditisme has gone through the phases typical of political movements in their process of evolution and adaptation to the changing conditions of society. But we know little about the circumstances acting as catalysts of these phases. The Créditiste experience suggests several hypotheses.

First, each new phase and each re-orientation of the movement seem to have been caused by a new generation of leaders, sharing new points of view, but remaining always within the framework of the Créditiste family. Thus Yvon Dupuis seems to be the tool of the third generation more than its master. His success will depend on his adaptability to conditions existing within the movement. There is very little chance that he will succeed in changing these conditions.

Secondly, in each phase the movement's change in orientation was generally preceded by a period of internal factionalism which grew more intense and provoked open schisms. This conflict seems to have been the first catalytic element in bringing about a fundamental change and re-orientation of the movement.

Thirdly, even though factionalism and schisms arose throughout the evolution of the movement, factionalism seemed to reach its maximum intensity in the phase of consolidation and despite the firm leadership of Réal Caouette. This seems due to several factors: it was at this stage that the conflict between the adherents of the concept "movement" and those of the concept "party", between the moderate protesters and the "highly disaffected"[32], was most intense; the means of internal control at the disposal of the leadership were weakened when the movement began its transformation into a more conventional party; the external forces of the Quebec milieu — nationalism, economic and social modernization, economic and linguistic conflict — grew stronger and seriously affected the internal development of the movement; the movement seemed to have reached the outer limits of its expansion.

Fourthly, even if the causes of factionalism at each stage are obviously complex, it is possible to isolate certain sub-groups of leaders who can be considered as the motivators of change. In the course of a survey taken among 69 Créditiste leaders in 1967,[33] I was able to distinguish two principal sub-groups of leaders: the "moderates" and the "highly disaffected".[34] These two sub-groups, distinct not only by reason of their political attitudes but also by reason of their socio-economic origins and their manner of political involvement, are in constant conflict as to the objectives, strategy, and tactics of the movement. In the mobilization phase, this conflict was more easily contained since the movement is in the course of expanding. However, in the phase of consolidation, it produced inevitable setbacks especially for a protest movement whose electoral potential is limited. The leaders in this phase, more political than those of the first generation and also more moderate, faced the opposition of the more dissident leaders. One could, then, put forward the following hypothesis: the absence of structural, social, and personal controls, and the basic importance accorded by the members to the goals of the movement permitted free rein to the natural tendency of the "highly disaffected" members to turn their dissatisfaction against the movement itself and against the moderate leaders. Insoluble conflicts were the result. When these conflicts were reinforced by the differences in origin and social status between the two sub-groups, the discord showed itself in the distribution of status and roles within the movement. The conflict and the resulting alliances produced schism.[35] This hypothesis of "schismatic" behavior which I have put forth on the basis of the data collected in the course of a survey can be diagrammed as follows (see Figure 1).[36]

Using this hypothesis, one can explain not only the split of 1963, as I have tried to do in my book, but also with appropriate modifications, those of 1966 and 1972.[37]

IV. Conclusions: The Consequences of the Phenomenon for Quebec and Canadian Politics and the Possible Application of the Thesis to Other Phenomena

To evaluate the consequences of this phenomenon for Canadian and Quebec politics it is necessary to situate the Créditiste movement in a larger socioeconomic and political context. As we indicated earlier, it is a question of a right-wing movement which represents the conservative reaction of a segment of the Quebec population to inexorable forces of modernization operative in the province, more or less, from the turn of the century. The statistics of the electoral support given the Créditistes, set out by Vincent Lemieux and Maurice Pinard,[38] show that the electoral base of the movement was limited almost exclusively to the rural and semi-urban regions of Quebec (Abitibi, the Eastern Townships, South of Quebec, Saguenay-Lac Saint Jean in particular): this was essentially the same base and the same stronghold of the movement as existed at the time of the Union of Electors.[39] In the federal elections of 1972, in Metropolitan Montreal, the Créditistes made a breakthrough for the first time, but still without winning a single seat.[40] Several factors suggest that the choice of Dupuis as provincial leader gave a lift to the provincial party's efforts to penetrate the heavily urbanized regions of Montreal and Quebec, although recent investigation leads one to think that the expansion was quite limited in scope.[41] One can predict with some certitude that electoral support for Social Credit, and for its leadership as

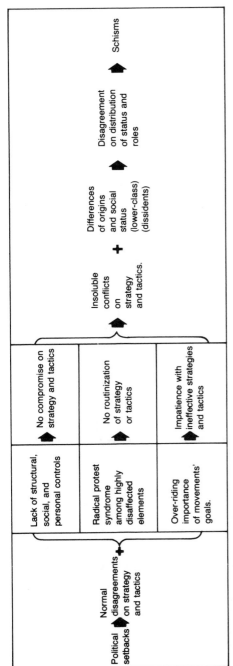

Figure I. Model of schismatic behavior

well, will remain for the immediate future a predominantly rural and semi-urban phenomenon (as the results of my own survey show).[42]

Some attempts have been made to transform the right-wing protest ideology (made up of the doctrines of Major Douglas and conservative Catholic social thought) into a more moderate right-of-centre conservatism resembling that of the Union Nationale. For example, Caouette now advocates a guaranteed annual income, something usually advocated by the left (although this could simply be a clever adaptation of the old Social Credit idea of a national dividend). Dupuis' appeals are a bit more negative in their orientation, although they also emphasize vague Créditiste notions such as "the human person" and "democracy of the people". Above all, he goes after the insidious forces of socialism in the province, such as the politics of Claude Castonguay, the Liberal Minister of Welfare, of Jean Cournoyer, Minister of Labor, and of Jean-Paul L'Allier, Minister of Communications. He also strongly attacks the "communists", the "felquistes" (FLQ), and the revolutionary tendencies of labor leaders such as Louis Laberge of the FTQ, Marcel Pepin and Michel Chartrand of the CSN, and Yvon Charbonneau of the CEQ. He also assails the separatist and socialist ideas of René Lévesque, Claude Morin, Jacques Parizeau, and other members of the Parti Québécois.[43] These attacks are able to help the Créditistes in maintaining their actual strength and in attracting certain non-unionized and unskilled workers from the working-class districts of Montreal and Quebec, particularly those who have the attitude of the "authoritarian working class" or who are at least traditional and conservative.[44] However, it seems unlikely that the Créditistes will find support among the more organized left-wing workers or among the more sophisticated middle class professionals and members of the Quebec bureaucracy.[45]

In my opinion, all socio-political movements reflect the prevailing socio-economic and political forces which are present in the society in which they find themselves. The Créditiste movement is an authentically *Québécois* movement. It arose in the province during the years of *la crise* and it responded to the feelings of unrest and insecurity of certain segments of the population whose economic state was declining. They could not understand this and that is why they feared the new tendencies toward urbanization, industrialization, bureaucracy, secularization, and the media explosion. For some time the trend to modernization in Quebec had been evident: a society which, at the census of 1881, was 77 per cent rural had become, in 1931, 56 per cent urban.[46] The first important stages of industrialization began only in the first decade of this century, but after the First World War the process accelerated remarkably.[47] These forces, slow at the beginning, expanded tremendously after the Second World War, due to the encouragement given by the Duplessis régime to foreign investment. They worked to bring about changes in the relationship between church and state, in education, communications, the growth of the provincial bureaucracy — those phenomena generally associated with the Quiet Revolution of 1960.

Social Credit with its right-wing protest ideology and its rural and semi-urban base is a movement which responds in an appropriate way to that segment of Quebec's population which feels itself seriously threatened by these tendencies. These fears are justified in that, in the long run, the rural and semi-urban traditions of Quebec are destined to give way to the inexorable forces of modernization. In these regions there will be marked economic decline and diminution of population as well as a transformation of the value structure of the young. Social Credit itself is destined to decline as a political force unless it changes into a fundamentally different phenomenon such as a moderate conservative party capable of attracting voters from the growing urban and industrial sectors of the population.

To sum up, Social Credit has two choices: to radicalize its right-wing protest and thus separate itself from the Quebec of today; or modernize its ideology, recruit a new urban elite, and become a moderate right-of-centre party. The vacuum left by the political demise of the Union Nationale, a moderate right-wing party which seems now to be on the road to disintegration, has had the effect of encouraging the provincial Créditistes to opt for the second choice.[48] Despite their actual demagoguery and negativism it seems evident that the Social Credit leadership, present or future, will, in the end, find this choice more attractive than the other.

Nevertheless, modernization alone will scarcely ensure the *Ralliement Créditiste* the achievement of its ultimate goal — provincial or federal power. As long as only three parties share the provincial electorate it will require more than a third of the population to bring a party to power. In the present context of Quebec, Social Credit with its present leadership seems hardly capable of taking away from the Liberals or the *Parti Québécois* enough urban votes to attain its objectives. Only a political and economic crisis bringing about extreme disequilibrium in Quebec could change this state of affairs.

As for the federal Créditistes who constitute the nucleus of the re-unified party, re-baptized "Social Credit of Canada", the future for them looks even more sombre. Although the party did well in Quebec and in the other provinces in the federal elections of 1972,[49] it never recovered the losses suffered in the Western provinces, something which had been one of its major objectives at the time of the re-unification. The Social Credit Party of Canada seems destined to remain a federal party with a regional base, whose strongholds will be limited, above all, to the rural and semi-urban regions of Quebec. Caouette — leader and pillar of the party — has recently had health problems because of diabetes, and it is possible that he is preparing to retire. In the unequivocal support he has given Dupuis, whose age and pragmatic orientation is third-generation Social Credit, Caouette has perhaps indicated his intention of leaving the burden of leadership to younger men. It is interesting to note that at the beginning of 1973 he designated his son Gilles, elected for the first time to Parliament in 1972, as official spokesman for the party in his absence.

Given these basically gloomy perspectives for the movement, one can expect the processes of factionalism and schism to be repeated in the third phase of institutionalization. These internal conflicts will no doubt produce new leaders who will have different orientations and who will, perhaps, be able to effect a temporary improvement in the party's condition. The process of factionalism will finally wane when the tension between the "movement" aspect and the "party" aspect as well as that between the "highly disaffected" leaders and the "moderates" is resolved in favor of the latter. If this comes about, the long-term survival of the Social Credit as a distinct party at both the federal and provincial levels will be in danger.[50]

The Créditiste movement is by no means a phenomenon unique to Quebec or to Canada. As I have tried to show, it is a prototype of a more general political form found in many societies in the process of change. This is true not just of right-wing protest movements which have, in the main, the support of the lower middle class, non-organized workers, and farmers of the rural and semi-urban regions on the periphery of modern, urban, and industrialized society. It is true as well of left-wing protest and revolutionary movements which spring up in various societies among organized workers, professionals, middle-class bureaucrats, and students. These movements manifest many of the same characteristics as their counterparts on the right, although their manner of evolution and the dynamics of their conflicts and transformations may be different. For example, the *Parti Québécois* can be considered as a social-democratic and moderate-nationalist movement of the left whose leadership comes primarily from among the students of the CEGEP's and universities, professors, and other professionals. But it has a strong electoral base among the workers of Montreal. One can observe without any doubt the same tendency to the formation of sub-groups within the leadership, as was shown by the division between the *électoralistes* and the *participationnistes* at a recent convention of the *Parti Québécois*.[51] If the party experiences a setback at the next provincial elections, it could produce a similar process of factionalism, internal conflict, and schism which could have the effect of producing a change in leadership and a re-orientation of the movement's ideology. Its future looks brilliant, if it continues its present course of bringing forth new and moderate social and economic ideas and in proposing a politics attractive to the growing sectors of contemporary Quebec society — that is to say professionals, bureaucrats, organized labor, and youth.[52] The model set out here (distinction of fundamental phases and their catalysts) can also be applied to this "party-movement", but I shall leave to others the task of deducing if it applies or not, and how.

Notes

1. The complete reference reads as follows: *The Dynamics of Right-Wing Protest: A Political Analysis of Social Credit in Quebec*, (Toronto, 1973).
2. These comments are derived from my reading of reviews and journals devoted to aspects of Social Credit in Quebec since 1962.
3. A political party is defined as any political structure whose primary objective is the achievement of political power for its members. A political movement has broader goals which include the transformation of society. Its *modus operandi* is also more varied. See Section II below.
4. The final split did not come until 1958. See Section III below.
5. The concept "political movement" is defined in Section II below.
6. Rudolf Heberle, *Social Movements: An Introduction to Political Sociology*, (New York, 1951), 6.
7. *Ibid*. 9.
8. *Ibid.*, 12, 434.
9. K. and G.E. Lang, *Collective Dynamics*, (New York, 1961), 495.
10. R.J. Jackson and M.B. Stein, *Issues in Comparative Politics: A Text with Readings*, (New York and Toronto, 1971), 266.
11. Obviously, this is to be taken simply as the description of a general tendency. In certain cases, the notions and the tactics of the left can have some attraction for declining sectors of the population. In the same way the actions of the right can be appealing to a rapidly developing part of the population. Moreover, certain proposals are made in terms sufficiently vague and emotional so as to gain adherents from both right and left.
12. From 1944 to 1948 the Créditiste leadership demanded the creation of legislative bodies parallel to the federal and provincial parliaments with a view to more accurate representation of the voters in each constituency. This idea had been borrowed from the Russian experience with soviets and from the experiments in government at Lublin in Poland. There was an attempt to create similar structures (unions of electors) but the project proved impossible to realize and was abandoned.
13. See, for example, the diverse reasons for adherence to political movements given by Hadley Cantril, *The Psychology of Social Movements*, (New York, 1944) chap. 2, 3; Eric Hoffer, *The True Believer*, (New York, 1951) chap. I-III; Heberle, *Social Movements*, chap. 5; and Gabriel Almond, *Appeals of Communism*, (Princeton, 1954), chap. IV-XI.
14. Lang and Lang, *Collective Dynamics*, 495.
15. The ideas expressed here are taken largely from Hoffer, *True Believer*, chap. XV; C.W. King, *Social Movements in the United States*, (New York, 1956), 72; Neil Smelser, *The Theory of Collective Behaviour*, (New York, 1963), 361, and Lewis N. Killian, "Social Movements," *Handbook of Modern Sociology*, ed. Robert E.L. Faris, (Chicago, 1964), 441-3.
16. The ideas expressed here are taken largely from Hoffer, *True Believer*, chap. XII; King, *Social Movements in the United States*, 72-74; Lang and Lang, *Collective Dynamics*, 520; Faris, *Modern Sociology*, 441-2; and Smelser, *Collective Behaviour*, 361.
17. The ideas expressed in this paragraph are taken largely from Lang and Lang, *Collective Dynamics*, 359, 518-20.
18. Heberle, *Social Movements*, 118-19.
19. Lang and Lang, *Collective Dynamics*, 533; Smelser, *Collective Behaviour*, 361; and M. Zald and R. Ash, "Social Movement Organizations: Growth, Decay and Change," *Studies in Social Movements: A Social Psychological Perspective*, ed. Barry McLaughlin, (New York, 1969), 478.
20. Lang and Lang, *Collective Dynamics*, 533. See also Joseph Nyomarky, *Charisma and Factionalism in the Nazi Party*, (Minneapolis, 1961).
21. For a more detailed examination of the growth of factionalism in the Créditiste Movement, see Part III, Introduction, chap. 6, 7, and Conclusion, and Part IV of *The Dynamics of Right-Wing Protest*.
22. The Créditistes participated, in a limited way, in the federal elections of 1949, and they also joined with the Liberals in the provincial elections of 1956. These were their only further efforts at direct participation in elections during the period of dominance of the Union of Electors.
23. In 1944 *Vers Demain* gave Caouette the admiring nickname "le tonnerre" (the thunderer).
24. The dissident factions included the handful of members remaining from the League and the Créditistes expelled from the Union by Gilberte Côté-Mercier because of their opposition to her

politics and who, over the years, had become fairly numerous.

25. During interviews in 1964, Caouette indicated that he used the terms "party" and "movement" indiscriminately when referring to the Ralliement. However, Legault thought of the Ralliement more as a movement whose primary objective was the political and economic education of an elite.

26. cf. Maurice Duverger, *Les Partis Politiques*, (Paris, 1964, 5 ème éd.) 84-5. See also Michael Stein, "The Structure and Function of the Finances of the Ralliement des Créditistes," in Committee on Election Expenses, *Studies in Canadian Party Finance*, (Ottawa: Queen's Printer, 1966), 405-457.

27. In the Federal elections of 1962 the Rally received 26 per cent of the popular vote in Quebec, with 26 seats; in 1963, 29 per cent of the popular vote and 20 seats; in 1965, they got 19 per cent of the vote and 9 seats. In 1968, they received 16 per cent of the popular vote but increased the number of seats to 14; in 1972, they had 24 per cent of the popular vote in Quebec and 14 seats. In the provincial elections of 1970 the *Ralliement Créditiste* of Quebec received 12 per cent of the popular vote and 12 seats.

28. They included the Federal members André Fortin, René Matte, Lionel Beaudoin, and the provincial members Camil Samson, Yvon Brochu, Florian Guay, Antoine Drolet, Ronald Tétrault, and Paul-André Latulippe, the latter two being sons of MP's.

29. Dupuis, when he was a Liberal candidate, had done imitations of Caouette and had mocked Créditiste monetary policy with gimmicks like play-money. His efforts were rewarded by his being made minister-without-portfolio in the first Pearson cabinet. But he was discharged shortly afterward following a charge of conflict of interest in the granting of a racing permit at St-Jean, Quebec. He was later cleared of the charge. In 1970 when Caouette tried to sell him to the Créditistes, he was noted as the host of an open-line show on radio station CKVL. He began to display rightist political attitudes much like those of Social Credit.

30. Gabriel Loubier, leader of the Union Nationale, had already made several public appeals for an alliance of the opposition parties. However, up to this point, Dupuis resisted these overtures probably because the attempt had been made just before his election as leader to discredit him publicly by charging that he would indeed lead the Créditistes into this sort of alliance. See *La Presse*, February 3, 1973; *Le Devoir*, February 3 and 23, 1973; and *The Montreal Star*, March 3, 1973.

31. These conclusions are drawn from a paper dealing with an analysis of the journal *Le Défi* and from an interview given by Dupuis to Vera Murray. These were conducted in the context of a seminar on the politics of Quebec co-sponsored by UQAM and McGill University (April 1973).

32. The definition of these concepts is given in note 34.

33. For a description of this inquiry, the sampling, and the questionnaire see Appendices A and B in *The Dynamics of Right-Wing Protest*, 240-6.

34. The "highly disaffected" leaders are defined as those whose responses to the survey showed strong disapproval of the political and economic systems (that is to say that on the scale of disapproval their scores were in the range of five to six). They differed from other Créditistes in several other ways as well, such as their socio-economic status, their manner of participation in voluntary associations and in the movement, their authoritarianism, their tendency to factional behavior, and their conception of protest. The "moderate leaders" are the other Créditistes not included in this sub-group, who responded in a more moderate way to questions concerning these attitudes. See Chapters 6 and 7 in *The Dynamics of Right-Wing Protest*.

35. In my book I carry this hypothesis further, based on data from the survey according to which the "highly disaffected" leaders can be subdivided into two groups: those of a higher socio-economic level (who tended to lose their interest in the movement and to lessen their active participation when factionalism began to develop) and those of a lower socio-economic level (who allied themselves with more moderate dissidents of the same level). This new sub-group, which can be classified as "lower class dissidents" drove the movement to schism.

36. This diagram is an exact reproduction of that given on page 182 of *The Dynamics of Right-Wing Protest*. I am grateful to Professor Maurice Pinard for his help in its construction.

37. I will advance the hypothesis that the "schismatics" of 1966 who helped to form the *Ralliement National* were, for the most part, "highly disaffected" leaders of the second generation. After the poor showing of the RN in the provincial elections of 1966, and above all after the formation of the "Parti Québécois," in 1968, which enlisted several of the more independent Créditistes, the "schismatics" returned to the *Ralliement Créditiste*. From 1968 to 1970 they were, along with the more

pragmatic third-generation Créditistes, the principal agents in the formation of the provincial Social Credit party. The split between the Samson and Bois factions in 1972 was essentially between the highly disaffected second-generation Créditistes and the pragmatic, modernizing moderates of the third generation.

38. cf. Vincent Lemieux, "Les dimensions sociologiques du vote créditiste au Québec," *Recherches sociographiques*, VI, 2 (1965), 181-95 and Maurice Pinard, *The Rise of a Third Party: A Study in Crisis Politics*, (Englewood Cliffs, N.J., 1971).

39. cf. Lemieux, "Dimensions sociologiques," 182-3.

40. The Créditiste vote in Metropolitan Montreal went from 19,188 to 107,172.

41. See the survey taken by the Centre de Recherche sur l'Opinion Publique (CROP) published for the first time in *Le Devoir*, June 8, 1973, and republished in the same journal on June 15, 1973 after the correction of a mathematical error. The revised poll showed 12.6% in favor of the Créditistes compared to 34.7% for the Liberals, 17.7% for the Parti Québécois, and 3.8% for the Union Nationale. 31.2% of the people questioned refused to indicate their electoral preferences. Taking into account the usual percentage of voters who don't indicate their choice, these results show that since the elections of 1970 Social Credit made only a slight advance. The principal stronghold remained the hinterland region outside the cities of Quebec and Montreal. The support given to Dupuis as leader was slightly less than the support given to the party itself.

42. For a description of the place of residence of the Social Credit leaders, see *The Dynamics of Right-Wing Protest*, 124-5.

43. These are personal impressions which I formed from Dupuis' speech at the leadership convention in Quebec in February of 1973, from subsequent television and radio broadcasts, as well as from newspaper articles such as that in *Le Devoir*, June 13, 1973. See as well Vera Murray (note 31).

44. The concept of working-class authoritarianism is defined by Seymour Lipset, *Political Man*, (Garden City, N.Y., 1960) chap. 4. Moreover, it is likely that workers recently arrived in the urban areas maintain their traditional and conservative attitudes on many economic and political questions as well as their earlier partisan attachments. For a slightly different view on this question see Maurice Pinard "Working Class Politics: An Interpretation of the Quebec Case," *Canadian Review of Sociology and Anthropology*, 7(2), 1970, 87-107, and "The Ongoing Political Realignments in Quebec," *Quebec Society and Politics*, ed. Dale Thompson (Toronto, 1973), 130.

45. Recent polls tend to confirm this. See as well the investigation of Maurice Pinard, "The Ongoing Political Realignments in Quebec," *Quebec Society and Politics*, 119-35. Moreover, Pinard emphasizes that the protests of right-wing movements as well as those of the left can be couched in terms sufficiently vague as to attract any malcontents among the electorate. See *The Rise of a Third Party*, 95-6.

46. See Maurice Rioux "Sur l'évolution des idéologies au Québec," *Revue de l'Institut de Sociologie*, Université Libre de Bruxelles (1968), 108-9.

47. See P.E. Trudeau, *Le Grève de l'Amiante*; (Montreal, 1956), Introduction, 3-10.

48. A recent poll by CROP showed that only 3.8 per cent of the population intended to vote for the Union Nationale in the next elections. See *Le Devoir*, June 15, 1973, p. 11. This continues the constant decline of Union Nationale support indicated by four successive polls taken since April 18, 1970 (*Le Devoir*, June 8, 1973, p. 1).

49. In Quebec the party went from 16 per cent of the vote in 1968 to 24 per cent in 1972. In all of Canada it doubled its electoral base compared to 1968 and obtained 708,000 votes (*Regards*, vol. 12, nos. 9, 10, 11, 1972).

50. A sudden economic or political crisis could improve its prospects, at least in the short run.

51. See *Le Devoir*, February 26, 1973, 6.

52. As was suggested in its manifesto *Quand nous serons vraiment chez nous* and in the moderate social-democratic program adopted at its convention in February 1973. There are some conflicts between the political objectives of independence and the socio-economic objectives of a moderate social democracy which attract different segments of the Quebec population. See Daniel Latouche "The Independence Option: Ideological and Empirical Elements" in Dale C. Thomson, *Quebec Society and Politics*, 179-94. This will probably be the most vulnerable point for the party. The next provincial elections, which will take place in October 1973, ought to show clearly if this conflict can be resolved easily or not.

Chapter 6

Contemporary Developments

Introduction

It is clear from the preceding chapters that social movements, of one form or another, have been a consistent feature of twentieth-century Canadian society. In the last few years, however, there seems to have been an even greater proliferation of such movements. Numbers of different groups are attempting to bring about a variety of social changes such as a redress of sexual and ethnic inequalities, the separation of Quebec, the humanization of oppressive bureaucratic structures, and the reversal of the foreign takeover of the Canadian economy and culture. The very currency of these movements, however, makes them difficult to analyze. It is not yet possible, for example, to assess how successful they will be in achieving their goals. The consequences of factionalism and other processes that affect the careers of social movements are not easy to determine at this time. At best, one can examine the goals of some of these movements and leave it to future scholars to study their outcomes.

It was stressed in the General Introduction that social movements frequently build on and are inspired by earlier social movements. While this is not true of all the movements to be discussed in this chapter, it is certainly true of some. The Quebec separatist movement, for instance, has clearly arisen on the groundwork laid by earlier movements of French-Canadian nationalism which have been examined in a previous chapter.[1] Concern with the preservation of French-Canadian cultural and linguistic tradition has a long history.[2] Even separatism itself has historical roots,[3] although the support in Quebec for such a course of action is larger than ever before.

Similarly, English-Canadian nationalism is by no means a new phenomenon.

Feelings of nationalism among English-speaking Canadians have been important at various times during the historical development of the nation. Indeed, political nationalism, although defined in different ways in different periods, was viewed by many as a precondition for Canadian nationhood and found embodiment in Canadian institutions and in government policies. The Fathers of Confederation, for example, spoke in terms of a "new nationality",[4] and later in the century the Canada First movement sought to embody this sentiment in literature.[5] Sir John A. Macdonald's "national policy", though it was motivated in part by opportunistic considerations,[6] had as its goal the consolidation of Canadian nationhood. Throughout the remainder of the nineteenth and early twentieth centuries, nationalism in external affairs was expressed in a variety of forms.[7] Perhaps the most important of these was the maintenance of imperial ties with the United Kingdom. Links with Britain were essential, some argued, to counterbalance the influence of the United States. However, with the aftermath of World War I came a decreasing emphasis on imperial ties and a concomitant increase in assertions of autonomy within the Empire.[8] Canadian nationalism at this time took largely the form of a desire for greater independence from Britain, while concern with the threat represented by our neighbour to the south found only limited expression.

With the benefit of hindsight, we can now see clearly that, particularly during the Second World War and the years following, American direct investment in the Canadian economy accelerated.[9] Increasing exposure to the American mass media and the linking of our defence system to that of the United States gradually made Canada a virtual "branch plant" society. The "American Way of Life", as portrayed in films, novels, and television, became the goal toward which more Canadians than ever before aspired. At the same time, Canadian publications and productions, which may have more adequately reflected Canadian circumstances, struggled for survival and often lost.[10]

The first serious attempt in the postwar years to re-introduce a concern with Canadian national integrity was launched by John Diefenbaker.[11] His efforts, though, were to no avail. According to George Grant, it was a case of "too little too late".[12] In the end Diefenbaker met defeat at the polls and rebellion in his own party.

The fate of Walter Gordon was less dramatic. As Liberal Minister of Finance, he made efforts in the mid-sixties to halt American takeovers in the economic realm by advocating the imposition of a 30% takeover tax and the establishment of the Canada Development Corporation to purchase companies that would otherwise be sold to American interests.[13] But his proposals merely aroused the ire of party stalwarts. Later reports commissioned to inquire into the economic state of the nation — the Watkins Report and the Gray Report — came to conclusions similar to those of Gordon. All encountered general hostility and a reluctance on the part of the Liberal government to act.*

In the late sixties, the concern with American economic and cultural domination, and the inability or reluctance of certain established Canadian elites and institutions to come to terms with the problem, was taken up by a larger public and two movements, the Waffle movement and the Committee for an Independent Canada (CIC), of which Walter Gordon is a member, came into existence. The former group, which developed within the ranks of the New Democratic Party, called for a joint programme of socialism and independence. It was not long, however, before statements by Wafflers became an embarrassment to certain sections of the NDP that relied on the support of large "international" unions. The consequence was a campaign of discreditation and, in essence, an eventual attempt at "removal" of Wafflers *per se* from the party. Although the Waffle ran a few candidates in the federal election of 1974, the electoral response to their platform was minimal.

The CIC, in contrast to the Waffle, considers itself a basically non-partisan organization. Its ranks are filled with members of the two old-line parties as well as some members of the NDP. Its intention is to put pressure on all political parties to consider the consequences of American domination and to persuade the public that there is a need to resist this domination.†

While neither of these movements has confined its activities exclusively to economic matters, cultural concerns have found wider support. In the mid-sixties, two professors of English at Carleton University, James Steele and Robin Mathews, brought to public attention the fact that, in many Canadian university departments, American faculty members outnumbered Canadians.[14] Such a situation, they argued, was likely to result in Canadian students learning less about their own country than about the United States. This, in turn, might have consequences for Canadian development when graduates entered the work world and were required to make decisions on a presumed knowledge of Canadian circumstances. The argument has had tremendous appeal, not only to Canadians within our universities, but also to many without, as illustrated by the large number of letters to newspapers expressing opposition to the hiring of more American academics.

---

*It should be stressed that few countries in the modern world are subject to as much outside influence in the economic, cultural, and political realms as Canada is. In general, groups of so-called "nationalists", in Canada, are really demanding for Canadians no more than is usually taken for granted by citizens of other countries, e.g., control over the national economy, that students learn about their own society as well as others, etc.

† Neither the Waffle nor the CIC are "mass movements" in the sense of many others referred to in this book. The membership of the Waffle, for example, contained a disproportionate number of students and intellectuals and never really acquired a large following. The same is basically true of the CIC. It can be argued further that the CIC very rapidly lost the characteristics of a social movement and should now be considered as an institution.

While the majority of publications available in the newstands reflect American domination of the mass media, some publications like *Maclean's, Canadian Forum*, and *Canadian Dimension* pursue a distinctly Canadian line. There is also legislation requiring a specified amount of Canadian content on radio and television. In addition, young Canadian writers, like Margaret Atwood, along with old familiars, like Milton Acorn, are becoming increasingly concerned with American cultural hegemony. And yet, despite the efforts of these and other individuals and groups, as a mere reading of daily newspapers indicates, the Americanization of Canadian society continues. Thus, the extent to which current movements of Canadian nationalism in English Canada will realize their goals remains in doubt. Equally uncertain is the degree to which the nationalist concerns of a larger public will influence the nature of current institutions and legislation or find embodiment in future social movements.

Other groups in Canadian society that now are beginning to act on the basis of inconsistencies in the structure of Canadian society are native peoples' groups. Concern with inequalities resulting from government Indian policy, as recent actions by native peoples' groups clearly indicate, is now reaching the status of a social movement. While one could not claim that the current movement among Canada's native peoples has an historical tradition as strong as Quebec or English-Canadian nationalism, it nevertheless does have historical roots that have provided an important foundation for the present-day struggle. The Métis rebellions in Manitoba and Saskatchewan during the late nineteenth century remind us that unrest among native peoples is hardly a novelty in Canada, but this movement left no permanent structure in its wake. Far more important for the modern movement was the protest organized by the Allied Tribes of British Columbia in the second and third decades of this century. The Allied Tribes sought to make a test case of the "Nishga Petition", an application to the government on the part of Nass Indians for land grants of 160 acres per capita to be made to tribe members and compensation for the remainder of their former holdings.[15] The campaign failed to achieve these specific goals, but it inspired the formation of several provincial Indian associations in the 1930's and 1940's, most notably, the Native Brotherhood Association of British Columbia, the Indian Association of Alberta, and the Union of Saskatchewan Indians.

Although a national organization, known as the Brotherhood of Canadian Indians, was formed in the early 1940's, the most salient characteristic of the native movement in this early period was its lack of unity. Local associations continued to operate largely as independent bodies, while the role that could be played by the Brotherhood of Canadian Indians was limited by the fact that it was composed exclusively of non-treaty Indians. Moreover, until the 1970's, Indian associations were distinctly elitist bodies, composed almost entirely of better-educated Indians or Indians holding some position of authority in their local community. They enjoyed very little mass support. Finally, Indian associations have been, until recently, "crisis oriented"; when a crisis arose they came into existence or were galvanized into new life, but when the crisis passed they declined and sometimes even disappeared.[16]

All the same, these associations have established traditions among Canada's native peoples of forming bodies to defend their interests and of engaging in political activity. Indeed, it has been through the formation of different, and often competing associations, that the Indian movement has undergone its most recent expansion. The current associations fall into two basic categories. First, there are those organizations that have evolved more or less directly out of the earlier tradition. These include provincial associations, such as the Indian Association of Alberta, the Manitoba Indian Brotherhood, the Union of Ontario Indians, and the Association of Iroquois and Allied Indians. This category also includes the most influential Indian organization in Canada today, the National Indian Brotherhood (NIB), which affiliates some of the provincial associations. These bodies have become increasingly radical in the past few years. For instance, they led the opposition of Indians to the government White Paper of 1969, which advocated the gradual integration of Indians into Canadian society and the elimination of legal distinctions between Indians and other Canadians. In reply, the NIB and several provincial associations responded with policy papers of their own, rejecting the government proposals in favour of special status and autonomous institutions for Canadian Indians. They have directed most of their energy toward exerting claims to lands not specifically covered by treaties. The NIB has even passed a resolution laying claim to all land in Canada and demanding that Indians receive a share of the produce from the land.

The second category of Indian associations consists of a substantial number of small militant groups that consider the above associations to be too moderate in their demands. Some of these groups are either officially or unofficially connected with associations centred outside Canada's borders, such as the American Indian Movement. The militant groups in Canada that have recently received the most attention are the Ojibway Warrior Society whose members were responsible for the occupation of Anicinabe Park in Kenora in July and August of 1974, and the Cache Creek Warrior Society whose members took part in an armed roadblock of the Bonaparte and Upper Hat Creek reserves in British Columbia in September of 1974. In addition to protest directed by these associations, Indian bands have also, on occasion, engaged in radical activities. This was clear in the resistance of Cree Indians in Quebec to the James Bay power project. In a number of communities they have also been engaged in struggles with educational authorities. In Sault Ste. Marie, the Garden River Indian band at one point withdrew two hundred students from school during a dispute with the Department of Indian Affairs over free noon lunches and clothing for students. And several bands in southwestern Ontario have employed similar tactics in the course of their negotiations over a new tuition agreement with the County of

Middlesex Board of Education.

It should be stressed that not all Indians support these militant activities. The vast majority of Indians are still politically apathetic and only marginally involved in struggles of this kind. Furthermore, there are some Indians (some chiefs for example) who profit from the institutional structure that maintains most Indians, through treaty provisions, in subordinate positions. These "uncle tomahawks", as Harold Cardinal has called them,[17] are not likely to participate in any movement designed to change significantly the position of Indians in Canadian society. Finally, as we have noted once before, the factionalism that still characterizes the Indian movement is a mixed blessing. While it may promote growth, it leaves the aims of the movement vague and poorly defined. For these and other reasons, it is difficult at this point in time to assess the extent to which the current Indian movement will achieve its goals.

It is equally difficult to assess the potential of the current women's movement. Indeed, at this point in its development in Canada, the question can be raised as to whether it is actually a movement at all. It can be argued that the women's movement is really, at present, a public: there is a general feeling among large numbers of women across Canada that the treatment accorded females in law, occupations, educational institutions, and so on, is inequitable. Similar feelings are shared by some male sympathizers. Compared to other movements studied in this volume, however, the women's "movement" in its current form, clearly lacks a sound organizational base and a generally accepted ideology and statement of goals.

These facts are recognized by women themselves. By and large, the organizational base of the current women's "movement" has been local. Quite frequently, discussion or action groups are found in universities or professional women's groups. "The main weakness of the women's liberation movement", Jean Rands argues, stems from this fact. The movement "has been usually campus oriented. In Vancouver, where working women have been meeting as part of women's liberation for a couple of years, the representatives of the movement are mostly students, ex-students, or professional women."[18] In order to attain its goals, Rands argues that the women's "movement" must organize on a large-scale basis and include women from diverse occupations and sectors of society.[19]

The ideology of the "movement", at this point, is equally problematic and reflects a lack of consensus regarding the goals of the women's "movement". Essentially, Janice Acton *et al* argue, it is possible to distinguish between "middle-class women's rights groups which consist mostly of professional and church women," and what can be defined as the women's liberation movement. While both are concerned with "the improvement of the equality of life for women in Canada, the philosophy of the women's rights groups is that civil liberty and equality can be achieved within the present system, while the underlying belief of women's liberation is that oppression can be overcome only through a radical and fundamental change in the structure of our society."[20] Another point that must be made is that individual women are often concerned only with particular issues, like abortion, that fall under a more general rubric of women's liberation. Given the latter philosophy, it is not surprising that a number of women concerned with the status of females in our society are also found in socialist movements like the Waffle.

While there may be a lack of consensus on the part of women regarding the appropriate ideology to embrace, their claims that women in our society are in essence second-class citizens are well founded. This fact was clearly brought home to the authors of the Royal Commission on the Status of Women. "As we travelled across the country", they wrote, "we heard of discrimination against women that still flourishes and prejudice that is very much alive."[21] The discrimination on which they comment is found in the treatment of women in law, the work force, educational institutions, and many other realms. Prejudice against women is found in the attitudes of both men and women regarding the "proper" behaviour or occupations for women. Undoubtedly, it may be possible for legislation to reduce discrimination. Prejudice, on the other hand, as it is ingrained in personality and culture, will be much more difficult to combat.

An important point to keep in mind when assessing the current women's "movement", is that it really has no historical connection with the women's suffrage movement at the turn of the century. The two are separated by a half century of inactivity on the part of women, with a few outstanding exceptions, like Agnes Macphail, a long-term Member of Parliament and supporter of women's rights. A lack of historical roots is equally evident for the so-called youth movement that emerged in the mid-sixties.

In general, a disproportionate number of participants involved in all contemporary movements are usually drawn from the ranks of youth. Throughout history, in fact, youth has been in the vanguard of many movements of change.[22] The explanations that others have offered for this phenomenon will not be discussed here. Suffice it to say that youth has fewer occupational and family attachments than it will have later in life. At the same time many go through a process of "identity formation" that often has the consequence of making them less reluctant than their elders to act upon perceived inconsistencies in the structure of society.[23]

Apart from this general propensity for youth to engage in movements centred on change, during the sixties, there developed in Canada and elsewhere a movement centred on youth *per se*. The "youth movement", as it was appropriately called, took many forms, ranging from attempts to bring about a change in the structure of capitalist society to a complete rejection of society and the formation of counter-cultures. As will be explained in one of the readings, there were very particular reasons for the development of this type of movement at a particular historical moment.

In conclusion, it must be stressed that this short overview by no means exhausts the number of social movements currently afoot. One merely has to stroll down major avenues of large Canadian cities to see that in recent years there has been a proliferation of religious sects whose appeal, by and large, is also to youth. On Toronto streets, for example, proselytizers for the Process and Hare Krishna are a common sight. Other movements in Canadian society are concerned with the conservation of our environment and with assisting the poor. Organizational manifestations of these concerns are Pollution Probe that did a great deal to educate the public concerning the pollution of our environment, and a number of poor peoples' conventions held in major cities such as Toronto. Still other groups, like homophile associations, in a number of Canadian cities, are concerned with legitimizing homosexual activities within the current structure of Canadian society.

The concerns leading to current Canadian social movements are in some cases found elsewhere, particularly in the United States. At the same time, there are movements, like the separatist movement and the English-Canadian nationalist movement, that have no American counterpart. Even where concerns and goals of movements are similar to those of movements outside of our borders, it can be argued that the historical and institutional peculiarities that have given rise to Canadian social movements generally mark them as distinct from their counterparts south of the border. Unfortunately, this insight is often lost on analysts of the Canadian scene.

The following three articles focus on a discussion of Canadian nationalism, youth movements as they developed in the nineteen sixties, and on more general protest in postwar Canadian society. The first of these readings is a semi-personal account, by one of Canada's historians, of twentieth-century Canadian nationalism until the Centennial year of 1967. Since that date the Waffle and CIC have emerged on the Canadian scene. Nonetheless, Margaret Prang espouses sentiments similar to those of *some* current nationalists. In addition to providing information on social movements *per se*, the remaining two articles also illustrate somewhat different orientations to the study of Canadian social movements. This difference can be found in the relative emphasis given to internal and external factors in the analysis of protest and change.

Unfortunately, it is not possible to present readings on other movements that have been mentioned in this chapter. The native peoples' movement, the Waffle movement, and so on, still require analyses from a *social movement perspective*.* These phenomena offer challenging opportunities for students of Canadian society who are eager to concentrate their energies on relevant aspects of social change and conflict.

*Analyses of these movements have been carried out, but not from the perspective central to this volume.

Notes

1. See chapter 5 for a discussion of French-Canadian nationalism.
2. See R. Cook (ed.), *French-Canadian Nationalism*, Toronto: Macmillan, 1969.
3. F. Ouellette, "The Historical Background of Separatism in Quebec," in Cook (ed.), *French-Canadian Nationalism*.
4. F.H. Underhill, *The Image of Confederation*, Toronto: CBC, 1964.
5. C. Berger, "The True North Strong and Free," in P. Russell (ed.), *Nationalism in Canada*, Toronto: McGraw-Hill, 1966.
6. R.C. Brown, "The Nationalism of the National Policy," in Russell (ed.), *Nationalism in Canada*, p. 156.
7. See C. Berger (ed.), *Imperialism and Nationalism, 1884-1914*, Toronto: University of Toronto Press, 1969. Also, C. Berger, *The Sense of Power*, Toronto: University of Toronto Press, 1970.
8. R.C. Brown and R. Cook, *Canada 1896-1921*, Toronto: McClelland and Stewart, 1974, p. 329.
9. For interesting discussion of this phenomenon see K. Levitt, *Silent Surrender*, Toronto: Macmillan, 1972. For an analysis of the roots of the 'branch plant' in Canada see J.M. Bliss, "Canadianizing American Business: the Roots of the Branch Plant," in I. Lumsden (ed.), *Close the 49th Parallel*, Toronto: University of Toronto Press, 1970.
10. See F. Peers, "Oh Say, Can You See?" in Lumsden (ed.), *Close the 49th Parallel*.
11. See P. Newman, *Renegade in Power: The Diefenbaker Years*, Toronto: McClelland and Stewart, 1963.
12. G. Grant, *Lament For a Nation*, Toronto: McClelland and Stewart, 1965.
13. See C.W. Gonick, "Foreign Ownership and Political Decay," in Lumsden (ed.), *Close the 49th Parallel*, pp. 49-51.
14. James Steele and Robin Mathews, "The Universities: Takeover of the Mind," in Lumsden (ed.), *Close the 49th Parallel*.
15. See P. Drucker, "The Native Brotherhood of British Columbia," in J.S. Frideres (ed.), *Canada's Indians: Contemporary Conflicts*, Scarborough: Prentice-Hall, 1974.
16. E.P. Patterson, *The Canadian Indian*, Don Mills: Collier-Macmillan, 1972, p. 176.
17. See H. Cardinal, *The Unjust Society*, Edmonton: Hurtig, 1969. Another interesting source of information on Canadian Indians is H. Robertson, *Reservations are for Indians*, Toronto: James Lewis and Samuel, 1970.
18. Jean Rands, "Toward an Organization of Working Women," in Janice Acton *et al.* (eds.), *Women Unite*, Willowdale: Canadian Women's Educational Press, 1972/1974, p. 145.
19. *Ibid.*, p. 148.
20. "Introduction", in Acton *et al.* (eds.), *Women Unite*, p. 9.
21. F. Bird *et al.*, *Royal Commission on the Status of Women in Canada*, Ottawa: Information Canada, 1970, p. xi.
22. L.S. Feuer, *The Conflict of Generations*, New York: Basic Books, 1969.
23. Erik Erikson, *Identity Youth and Crisis*, New York: W.W. Norton and Company, 1968.

Nationalism in Canada's First Century

Margaret E. Prang

The perils inherent in the acceptance of an assignment that seemed to require me to conduct a public investigation into the Canadian psyche at the end of a year of Centennial soul-searching were clear to me when I agreed to prepare this paper. Even then I marvelled at my own foolhardiness. Events of recent months have made the perils no less obvious and the assignment no less formidable. At the outset I must declare my awareness that my observations were more subjective than the usual historical exercise. Indeed, there may be some of my listeners who will feel that I have not even come close to exposing the Canadian psyche but have displayed only my own, and that I should borrow a sub-title for this paper from one of our Canadian creative writers, perhaps *Canada Made Me*, or *Let Us Compare Mythologies*. That is a risk I run, but I trust I need not apologize: I speak of my own country at a time when strong emotions are aroused and of events which are registered sharply in my consciousness.

At the end of this year's festivities most thoughtful Canadians find themselves envying the degree of confidence that the founders of "the uncertain nation"[1] of 1867 possessed. As long as Expo 67 lasted we kept up a bold front to the world, and enjoyed the show ourselves, trying to believe that what was done at Montreal had made us truly a nation at last. The party over, we know again that the Canadian future is more uncertain than ever before. Although *A Challenge of Confidence* now rests on our bookshelves beside *Lament for a Nation*, Eric Kierans' exuberant optimism does not altogether down the feeling that George Grant may be the truer prophet.[2]

I will not linger over an attempt to define nationalism. What the vast literature on the subject adds up to is that nationalism is where you find it, and that the combinations of factors that may enable groups of people to be a nation are many. It is also clear that nationalism may be highly creative or entirely destructive of civilized life. I concern myself here with nationalism in the second half of

Reprinted from the *Canadian Historical Association Annual Report*, 1968, pp. 114-125, by permission of the author and The Canadian Historical Association.

our first century, and particularly with the development and present characteristics of what for want of a better term I must call English-Canadian nationalism, i.e. the type of nationalism that has been most characteristic of the country outside of French Canada. I have chosen to do this because this English-Canadian nationalism has received less attention than French-Canadian nationalism, perhaps because it is harder to get hold of, and because it is of increasing importance that it be understood.

Most of the standard versions of Canadian history tell us that one of the most important consequences of the First World War was the growth of Canadian nationalism, and they often imply that this was an all-Canadian nationalism, and that it ended forever the local loyalties of pre-war years. Perhaps this exaggeration is a reflection of the nationalism of a generation of English-speaking historians who did much of their work in the two post-war decades and whose views have dominated our interpretation of Canadian history almost down to the present. But would it not be closer to the truth to emphasize that the war accentuated both the main streams of Canadian nationalism — French and English? During the conflict in Europe many individual Canadians doubtless gained an enlarged sense of the Canadian community, and an awareness of qualities that distinguished them from their British and French comrades in arms. But whatever the war-time experience may have meant to individual Canadians, the conscription issue and the bitter election campaign of 1917 in which English Canadians were so determined "to make the French do their duty" renewed in French-Canadian society as a whole the awareness of its own distinctiveness.

In English Canada the post-war decades brought a rebirth of the spirit of "Canada First", a spirit strengthened by the recognition of Canada as a distinct entity in the international community. Nowhere was this spirit more evident than among the small groups of young university teachers and professional men in the major cities across the country who established the *Canadian Forum* and debated public issues through its pages, who founded the Canadian League and later the Canadian Institute of International Affairs and the Couchiching Conference, and generally tried to promote the study and discussion of national and international issues from a distinctly Canadian point of view. Professor Lower's recently published memoirs[3] illustrate the energy and intelligence that a small group in Winnipeg brought to the task of trying to think through a Canadian foreign policy.

Expressions of the new national consciousness were not confined to intellectuals. The post-war years saw the revitalization of existing organizations of national scope involving Canadians of many occupations and interests. Among the most significant of these were the Canadian Clubs. With the appointment of its first national secretary, the Association of Canadian Clubs launched a drive to establish new clubs and in the two years 1926 and 1927 alone their number increased from 53 to 120. The 1920's also saw the birth of a host of new national organizations with an enormous range of purposes and membership, as a small sample will show. They included the Native Sons of Canada, self-consciously and vigorously committed to promoting a Canadian sentiment; the Canadian Legion, bringing together several organizations of war veterans; the Canadian National Parks Association, devoted to the preservation of areas of "the true north, strong and free" that the Group of Seven was teaching a whole generation to see as something uniquely Canadian — and the list can go on through the Canadian Credit Men's Trust Association, the Catholic Women's League, the Canadian Council of Child Welfare, and the National Federation of Canadian University Students.

The precise effect on the country of this growing trans-continental network of concerns and personal relationships is impossible to document but its significance in strengthening the fabric of the nation cannot be questioned. Most organizations held national conventions; the travel and discussion with counterparts from coast to coast which such gatherings entailed enhanced the mental picture of Canada held by thousands of Canadians who were thus engaged in common enterprises that often had to be accommodated to the necessities of regional differences. What a rich source of Canadian social history would be open to us if we had records of the conversations carried on in the cars of trans-continental trains during the inter-war decades. Surely they would demonstrate that never before had so many Canadians shared a universe of discourse that was so distinctly Canadian in its references.

In later life, one of the young activists of these years, Brooke Claxton, observed that ". . . every kind of organization, national and local, cultural and religious, political and commercial, was at a peak of activity hardly equalled since . . . All these were manifestations of the growth of national feeling — it was nationwide, spontaneous, inevitable. It cut across political, racial, and social lines; indeed, it was curiously a-political."[4]

The existence of this national feeling helps to explain why the depression did not seriously inhibit the growing sense of a national identity, a sense which contributed to the broad nationalism underlying the work and recommendations of the Rowell-Sirois report. That same national feeling played a decisive part in the establishment of the national system of public broadcasting, and was of no little consequence in the creation of such diverse national institutions as the Bank of Canada, Trans-Canada Airlines, and the Dominion Drama Festival.

Two features of these developments are worthy of note. One is the relatively slight participation of French Canadians in these manifestations of national sentiment. It is true that the Canadian Clubs enjoyed considerable success in Quebec and their national secretary, Graham Spry, is credited with the earliest recorded use of the word "bicultural", in an address in Quebec City in 1929.[5] The Canadian Radio League found essential support in Quebec in its campaign for public broadcasting, especially through Georges Pelletier, managing director of

Le Devoir. Other examples of French-Canadian participation could be cited, but in the main the initiative, the leadership, and most of the membership in national organizations of all kinds came from English Canadians. Their counterparts in French Canada were apparently engaged in the affairs of groups with more provincial and confessional concerns.

A second feature of this same period is the relative absence of anything that can be called "anti-Americanism", at least after Canadians recovered from their pique over American reluctance to accept Canada's new post-war international status. Although the literature of the time affords ample evidence that most Canadians understood that their historical traditions had made them different from Americans, there was also increasing emphasis on the significance of Canada's geographical position as a North American nation. The titles of two published addresses are typical of dozens more: Sir Robert Falconer's *The United States as a Neighbour* (1925) and John Dafoe's *Canada: An American Nation* (1935). There were no serious disagreements between the two nations and Canadian feeling for and interest in the United States was greatly enhanced by the admiration so many of her citizens felt for Franklin D. Roosevelt. Relatively few Canadians saw any ominous import in the fact that in the 1920's the United States replaced Great Britain as the primary source of foreign capital and as the leading purchaser of Canadian exports, a trend that was continued in the following decade. Professor Morton has described the years 1927-1941 as "the period of acceptance", and the era of the "good neighbour".[6]

Inevitably these developments, and especially their general spirit, rubbed off on English Canadians who were growing up, as I was, in the thirties, first in a prairie city and then in one of the smaller centres of southern Ontario. Looking back, it seems to me that I was always a nationalist, in the sense that I was proud of being a fifth-generation Canadian and had no real doubt of the solidity and durability of the country. If I had had to say which of the several streams in the family heritage I rated most highly I would have chosen the Scottish, at the expense of the English, German, and Irish, but in fact I rarely thought that way at all. I suppose the most elemental component of my nationalism was simply a natural love of the land itself, although the only regions with which I was familiar before adulthood were Ontario (north and south), the prairies, and the section of the Rockies I had seen on one trip to Banff. My family were hardy cottagers in some rather underdeveloped Alberta resorts, as well as indefatigable picknickers everywhere, and I cannot remember a time when I wasn't excited by the physical features of the country.

Another channel of attachment to the nation was perhaps especially strong because it was intimately related to religion as I knew it. As a member of a family that was staunchly and actively United Church I was fully exposed to the high level of "Canadian content" which has always characterized that institution, most notably in its early years. As John Porter has observed, the United

Church is "as Canadian as the maple leaf and the beaver".[7] The Sunday School papers I read as a teenager were strongly laced with accounts and pictures of various places in Canada, biographical sketches of great Canadians, and poems and stories many of which, I fear, were published mainly because they were the work of aspiring *Canadian* authors. The United Church's sense of being uniquely Canadian, a pioneering ecumenical experiment which reflected Canadian experience and was at the same time a model that the rest of the world might one day emulate, came across strongly in those years, as did its feeling of responsibility for the character of Canadian community life. The church paper, *The New Outlook*, ably edited by W.B. Creighton and his successor, Gerald Cragg, exuded a sturdy Canadianism and in the thirties paid much attention to the social problems created by the depression. A regular reader was bound to know something about a wide range of Canadian issues and interests.

In these same years I was aware of the existence of the thousands of "new Canadians" who had come to the west before and after the war. "Bohunk" was not an acceptable word either in school or church, or home, but "New Canadian" was approved. Relatives and friends visiting Edmonton from Ontario were often shown the variety of life in the city by a drive along a street boasting some fifty "ethnic churches" in the course of less than two miles. As I try to recapture the spirit of those introductions to the western mosaic, I believe the dominant tone was one of acceptance of the recent immigrants. We knew that they were needed in the building of the nation, and although they seemed "foreign" in many respects, there was no doubt that they were Canadians. Dare I confess that in my first year of high school I won a public speaking contest with an oration on the role of the prairie provinces, with their mixed population, in the growth of Canada. My finest moment was the final peroration, borrowed, naturally, from Thomas D'Arcy McGee: "I see in the not remote distance one great nationality bound like the shield of Achilles by the blue rim of ocean."

Although I had nothing whatever against the King, I always sang "O Canada" with greater gusto than "God Save the King", and if I had been asked at the age of fifteen to choose this country's national anthem I would not have hesitated for a moment. A little later, as part of a high school audience assembled in front of the Brantford Collegiate Institute listening to the Governor-General, Lord Tweedsmuir, extolling the glories of the land he had so quickly come to love, I sensed nothing unusual in his assurances that it was our first duty to understand and serve Canada. Such advice seemed quite unexceptional and I would have been shocked to have been told anything else. I was unaware, then, of the storm that such sentiments on the lips of the Crown's representative created in some sections of English-Canadian society.

Before long we students were again assembled for a public occasion, this time at the railway station, when the first local contingent, which included two of our youngest and most popular teachers, went off to the Second World War. Most of us were totally unaware of the significance attached to Canada's separate declaration of war, but we believed, rightly or wrongly, that the group we were farewelling was going to fight for Canada. Subsequently, the CBC did more than any other agency to keep the public informed of the life of Canadians overseas and to interpret the war as a struggle in which Canadians had a direct and distinctive interest.

In these early years I had no first-hand acquaintance with French Canadians and certainly no sophisticated knowledge of French Canada, but Fathers Brébeuf and Lalemant were very high in my childhood lists of heroes, and I would have been hard put to express a preference between Wolfe and Montcalm, for they were equally a part of the Canadian story as I knew it; if pressed, I would probably have given the edge to Montcalm, since his was the greater and more heroic struggle, and because I tended to have an automatic identification with *whoever* held Canada. In the Canadian political history that I learned in high school Laurier was "the first Canadian" because he had done more than any other leader to develop national unity. (As I recall, the political disunity of the First World War years was rather quickly passed over, probably because by the thirties many English-Canadian educators were less than proud of some aspects of that era.) Thanks to the enthusiasm of one of my high school teachers, I knew something about Bourassa's version of an all-Canadian nationalism, and it did not seem odd that a French Canadian should be the author of an acceptable definition of a Canadian. If any French Canadian had told me what many of them then apparently believed — that most English Canadians were just Englishmen who happened to be living in Canada — I would have rejected the charge with the utmost vehemence, and I think I would not have accused them of being merely Frenchmen. In short, French Canada, was a substantial and sympathetically perceived part of my early imaginative picture of Canada, although I had no direct connection with it and little appreciation of the emotional distance that lay between the two ways of life. The first French Canadian I ever heard discussing Canadian problems was the Abbé Arthur Maheux who made a deep impression on me and my fellow undergraduates when he visited United College in Winnipeg during the war.

I recount these personal experiences and attitudes because I believe they were far from unique. Although the details would vary with region and social circumstances, hosts of English Canadians could tell roughly the same stories of their exposure in the inter-war years to much the same influences, with similar results. Professor Morton has recently described the nationalism of the 1920's as "a mist that hung over the vortex of Canadian life; it was, in its drift and changes, lit by sunlight, eye-catching and seemingly solid, but it was in large part mist". This observation stems from Morton's hostility to what he calls the "political opportunism" of the first King decade, as exemplified in King's use of nationalism in the election of 1926 and his promotion of the dissolution of Empire into Commonwealth in "the acid of nationalism".[8] But surely it can be demonstrated that there were more solid and enduring forces at work in Canada than were reflected in the immediate politics of the time. Some evidence that this was so lies in the number of important national institutions established in the succeeding decade, in the capacity of the country to survive the depression without catastrophic division and to enter the war with a high degree of national unity.

In the Second World War the character of the English-Canadian nationalism that had been building up in the preceding two decades was revealed: it was sufficiently all-Canadian in its orientation to encourage judgments of the war effort appropriate for Canada that were based far more on calculations of the interests of Canada than had been the case twenty-five years earlier. It was against this English-Canadian nationalism, and not only against Mackenzie King's solid base in Quebec, that movements for national government and full-scale conscription came to grief.

What I have been trying to delineate are some of the origins and the emotional content of the brand of nationalism discussed so lucidly and more generally by Professor McNaught in his essay, "The National Outlook of English-speaking Canadians".[9] I believe it is the outlook of the post-war generation and of most of the young today, as much as it is that of those of us who are now middle-aged. It is a view of Canada which has made it possible for thousands of European immigrants who have arrived since 1945 to feel a ready and often passionate identification with this country. It fosters a nationalism which sees continuing validity in George Étienne Cartier's declaration of the purpose of Confederation as the creation and nourishment of a "political nationality". Its essential category is not that of "race", but of individual liberty and self-realization in a community which admits of cultural diversity as one of the conditions of the good life for all its members. I do not want to idealize my youthful comprehension of the implications of this outlook, or to exaggerate the extent to which it has been embodied in our institutions and social practice: the opportunities for full participation in Canadian life have been different in Winnipeg's River Heights than in the north end of the city, and greater in the Town of Mount Royal than in Point St. Charles, and anyone who remains skeptical about that need only be referred to John Porter's *The Vertical Mosaic*. What I do want to stress is the general direction of what I suppose I must call "the English-Canadian dream", but what I would like boldly to call "the Canadian dream".

This English-Canadian nationalism has been much misunderstood, not least in French Canada. As Pierre Elliott Trudeau notes, "Anglo-Canadian nationalism has never had much of an edge"[10], and it has therefore sometimes been thought to be non-existent. This illusion has been fostered by our professional "non-nationalists". They "would rather let the country fall apart than be accused of nationalism", John Holmes charges, and they "find pride in our having conceived the immaculate non-nation".[11] That group, long a minority among Canadians who think about their country, is a rapidly dying, if not extinct, breed. In the decade of the sixties it is hard to find anyone in English Canada who professes indifference to the question of Canada's survival or who will reject out of hand all consciously devised economic and cultural measures to foster it. There is a great gulf between the programme of the *Canadian Dimension* socialist-nationalists[12] and the approach represented by Kierans' belief that somehow the great private corporations, with the Canadian Development Corporation filling in the gaps, can be made to serve Canadian independence.[13] But there is agreement on the immediate objective — to keep open or win back the possibility of some choice for Canadians in the direction their society will take.

The intensification of nationalism in English Canada at the present time is largely a response to two other nationalisms, those of French Canada and the United States. It is a reaction, a typically slow, Anglo-Saxon one, to be sure, to an increasing realization of the strength of nationalism in Quebec and of its meaning for Canada. Because their own nationalism is so different, it has been hard for English Canadians to grasp the significance of the present surge of Quebec nationalism. Fortunately, there is little evidence that having grasped it, nationalism in English Canada will assume the proportions or character advocated by Professor Gad Horowitz — a distinctly English-Canadian nationalism which would then confront French Canada head-on and find political expression in a federation of two "associate states".[14] Clearly this would meet René Lévesque's prescription for our ills, but it is entirely incompatible with the outlook of the vast majority of English Canadians who would see in any such development the total abandonment of any meaningful concept of nationhood.[15]

English-Canadian nationalism in the sixties is also a response to growing pressure from the overwhelming presence and power of the United States. This is a problem for the whole world, but for Canada proximity creates unique difficulties in trying to live with the uneasiness generated by many of the present attitudes and policies of the wealthiest, the most militarily powerful, and probably the most nationalistic nation on earth. American imperialism, especially as it is expressed in the war in Vietnam, and increasing doubt about the capacity of the United States to give social expression at home to ideals which Canadians have long shared with Americans, are giving powerful impetus to nationalism in Canada.

What are the most important features of English-Canadian nationalism today? First, it is, as always, conducive to pragmatic attitudes toward politics. It is a mood that encourages the tackling of specific grievances rather than glorying in theoretical discussions of "special status", "associate statehood", or compact theories of Confederation. Book I of the Report of the Royal Commission on Bilingualism and Biculturalism, although it is not entirely lacking in philosophical underpinnings, takes this pragmatic and practical approach. Because it thus accords well with the spirit of the political culture of English Canada, its recommendations are likely to enjoy a good reception.

Another aspect of the dominant English-Canadian attitude to-day, and again this is not new, is the refusal to treat the constitution as a sacred cow. The basic commitment of the majority is to the country and to the political nationality the British North America Act was meant to serve, and not to the particular form of federalism that is established by the Act. This is true despite the recent utterances of some provincial premiers, and despite the highly accurate, but for present purposes irrelevant, expositions of the intentions of the Fathers of Confederation, especially on the language issue, by a few of our historians.

The attitude of the majority toward the constitution is one proof that English-Canadian nationalism is purely and simply Canadian to an increasing degree. There is full recognition that Canada's "British century" is over, and that Canadians are now on their own in North America. It seems somewhat ironic that just at this time in our history many French Canadians appear to crave a filial-dependent relationship with France which is oddly reminiscent of the one English Canadians often cherished with Britain fifty years ago.

So "Canadianized" has English Canada become that the monarchy is now "negotiable" to the majority, at least so I would judge. The abolition of the monarchy would be accepted, although only with sorrowful reluctance in many quarters, if such a move seemed likely to serve Canadian unity. A great deal is to be learned from what I believe to be a fact, although I cannot prove it: that the deep emotion which so many Canadians felt at the death of Governor-General Vanier was due much less to feeling for the Crown, than to the conviction that General Vanier represented distinctive Canadian traditions and values.

In English Canada today there is greater acceptance than at other times in our history of the permanence of English and French cultural differences, and a growing willingness to accept a "French Canadian style" of being Canadian as possessing equal validity with "the English style".

At the same time there is a recognition that at many points English and French Canada are becoming more alike in their economic and social structures.[16] One consequence of this is that the aspirations of both groups are conditioned more by imaginative pictures of the future rather than by romantic versions of the past. For French Canada *survivance* through reverence for "notre maître, le passé" is no longer enough: emancipation, economic expansion, and full participation in a pluralistic and affluent society are the objectives, as they are in the rest of Canada. Moreover, Quebec today, again like the rest of the country, looks increasingly to the state as the agency for the extension of the conditions of the good life to all its citizens. The question Quebec is trying to answer now is whether the state of Canada can serve at all as the instrument for implementing her new ambitions, or whether all hope must be placed in the state of Quebec. Looked at from an all-Canadian perspective the question is the one put by the current Royal Commission: "How can we integrate the new Quebec into present-day Canada, without risking the breaking up of the country?''[17]

In trying to demonstrate the usefulness of the state of Canada to Quebec, English-Canadian nationalists can point to certain broad objectives which all present Canadians share, objectives that would be much harder, and probably impossible to achieve, separately: We desire economic policies that will reduce our dependence on the United States. To Canadian nationalists of whatever stripe, it is intolerable that we have less control over our economic affairs than a nation conquered by force of American arms, Japan. Although the French-Canadian nationalists' scepticism about the ''Canadianism'' of the present English-Canadian business elite is explicable, it is at least arguable that a joint attack on the ''domestication'' of the branch plant economy is likely to be attended by more success than separate efforts. Further, we all need a foreign policy that begins in recognition that all Canadians have more interest in a world open to Canadian trade than in a world safe for American democracy and overseas investment.

And can we not argue convincingly that our chances of building a modern technological society fit for human beings to live in, and reflecting our own historical and cultural inheritances, are much greater if we capitalize on the assets with which our dual culture has endowed us? Is it not also arguable that if we can devise a viable federalism for our second century it will be a political achievement valuable not only to ourselves but an example of some relevance to other peoples who seek ways of providing stability, material progress, and personal liberty in multi-cultural communities?

Agreement on such general objectives and directions will solve no specific problems, but it is the indispensable condition for the beginning of the search for solutions. The traditions and current mood of English-Canadian nationalism justify the hope that on one side at least of the dialogue that has now begun in earnest the prospects are favourable.

Notes

1. Ramsay Cook, *Canada: A Modern Study* (Toronto, 1963), p. 101.
2. Eric W. Kierans, *Challenge of Confidence: Kierans on Canada* (Toronto, 1967); George Grant, *Lament for a Nation: The Defeat of Canadian Nationalism* (Toronto, 1965).
3. A.R.M. Lower, *My First Seventy-Five Years* (Toronto, 1967).
4. Cited in E.A. Corbett, *We Have With Us Tonight* (Toronto, 1957), p. 104.
5. *Report of the Royal Commission on Bilingualism and Biculturalism*, Book I (Ottawa, 1967), p. xxxi, quoted from *The Canadian Nation*, Vol. I, February 1929, p. 15.
6. W.L. Morton, *The Canadian Identity* (Toronto, 1961), pp. 71-72.
7. John Porter, *The Vertical Mosaic* (Toronto, 1965), p. 519.

8. W.L. Morton, "The 1920's", in J.M.S. Careless and R. Craig Brown (eds.), *The Canadians, 1867-1967* (Toronto, 1967), p. 232.

9. In P.H. Russell (ed.), *Nationalism in Canada* (Toronto, 1966), pp. 61-71.

10. *Cité Libre*, April 1962, cited in Frank Scott and Michael Oliver (eds.), *Quebec States Her Case* (Toronto, 1964), p. 59.

11. John Holmes, "Nationalism in Canadian Foreign Policy", in Russell *op. cit.*, p. 205.

12. Any issue of the periodical *Canadian Dimension* (Winnipeg) provides expositions of this view, but see especially, "An Open Letter to Canadian Nationalists", Vol. 4, No. 4, May-June, 1967.

13. Eric Kierans, *op. cit.*

14. *Canadian Dimension*, Vol. 2, No. 5, July-August, 1965.

15. Donald V. Smiley, *The Canadian Political Nationality* (Toronto, 1967), especially Chapter 5, is an interesting commentary on this outlook.

16. These points are elaborated in D. Kwavnick, "The Roots of French-Canadian Discontent", *Canadian Journal of Economics and Political Science*, Vol. XXXI, No. 4, November, 1965.

17. *Report of the Royal Commission on Bilingualism and Biculturalism* (Ottawa, 1967), p. xlvii.

Inter-Generational Conflict in the Sixties

Kenneth Westhues

The collective dissidence of Canadian youth during the last decade ·was so widely publicized and discussed that, by now, few need to be convinced of the existence of a youth movement during those years. The demonstrations and sit-ins, pot parties and rock festivals, love beads and peace signs remain vivid in memory; it is hardly necessary to point out that all these were facets of a broad social movement deeply opposed to the status quo. If an essay on the youthful protest can assume that readers will agree on the movement's existence, however, it cannot take for granted any consensus about how it should be analyzed. This is particularly so in the context of a book concerned with Canadian social movements. The youth movement clearly happened in this country, but it also happened in others. Should one perhaps speak of *movements*, one for each of the countries involved, instead of a single movement transcending national boundaries? Can one fairly analyze the *Canadian* youth movement, or is it necessary to discuss the Canadian events only within some international perspective? These questions deserve to be addressed at the outset, for the sake of clarity in the substantive analysis which follows.

It will be useful here to divide social movements in Canada into two broad categories. The first includes those whose ideology and organization are specific to this country. The CCF, Social Credit, Quebec separatism, and Canadian nationalism are all examples of distinctively *Canadian* social movements. While they may be similar to other movements in other countries, their own boundaries fall more or less clearly within those of the Canadian nation. For this reason, analysis of such a movement necessarily relies on Canadian data and draws its explanation for the movement from factors characteristic of this society. The social and political implications of the movement are likewise reviewed with reference to Canada, since it is principally or only in this society that the movement seeks to promote or oppose social change.

Article commissioned for this book by the editors.

In a second category of social movements in Canada fall those whose ideology and organization are not limited to this one country. Religious movements like the Jehovah's Witness or Transcendental Meditation, ethnic ones like the American Indian Movement or the Jewish Defense League, and others ranging from women's liberation to ecological preservation have all appeared in Canadian society, even while they hardly qualify as distinctively *Canadian* social movements. They illustrate the basic historical fact that while the contemporary world is indeed divided into nations, people themselves do not always divide the world in that way. Distinctions like the saved versus the damned, white men versus Indians, Jews versus Gentiles, women versus men, and polluters versus preservers cut across national boundaries, and may be more important to social movement adherents than nationality itself.

The youth movement of the 1960's falls also in the second category. Its basic ideology of popular democracy and of resistance to bureaucratic institutions was shared by adherents in most of the countries of the industrialized western world. Symbolic leaders, like the Beatles, Joni Mitchell, Allen Ginsberg, or Herbert Marcuse, were recognized as such in more than one country. Quite possibly the rock festival attended by the largest number of Canadian youth took place at Woodstock, New York. A book published in Montreal was appropriately titled *The New Left in Canada*,[1] signaling the fact that the New Left was not particularly Canadian, but rather existed as a supra-national movement which was at work here, among other places.

The question arises, then, of how the youth movement should be analyzed in a book specifically directed toward a Canadian audience. One alternative is to focus specifically on how the movement in Canada differed from the movement in other countries. While such an approach can yield insights about the nature of Canadian society, it runs the risk of forcing the movement itself into an inappropriate national mould. A focus on the Canadian qualities of a Jehovah's Witness in Winnipeg, a Transcendental Meditator from Toronto, a Vancouver hippie, or a Halifax student activist would not seem the best way to understand the social movements to which these people belong. The alternative chosen here is to portray the youth movement clearly as one which transcended national boundaries, but to emphasize its activities in Canada, the factors which made it attractive to Canadian youth, and the implications it had for Canadian society. The inevitable differences between the movement here and in other countries will be suggested, but not as the central theme of this essay.

The youth movement of the last decade is an example of what Blumer termed a *general* social movement, that is, a broad ideology embracing a variety of specific protests and expressions of collective unrest.[2] The ideology amounted to a rejection of industrial capitalist social orders, of "establishments" of whatever kind, of the cult of consumer goods, and of the quest for upward mobility. The ideology promised instead a new alienation-free society, to be accomplished through the democratization of universities, an end to racism and the Vietnam War, a return to nature, and through "turning on" to the world of psychedelic drugs. As elements of this ideology won acceptance among youth in various parts of the western world, so did it give rise to similar kinds of behaviour, like non-violent demonstrations, the cult of rock music, the occupation of university buildings, and the smoking of marijuana.[3] The youth movement is best understood as a kind of umbrella under which a multitude of particular expressions of discontent occurred.

It must also be said in preface that the youth movement never achieved much clarity in organizational definition. If there was a general norm of distrust of "anyone over thirty", the movement admitted thousands of older adherents as well. Membership was not a matter of making application or carrying a card, but simply of expressing commitment to the movement's amorphous goals. Mobilization toward specific goals, moreover, tended to follow the rhythm of the academic year, since adherents of the movement were less easy to organize during the summer months. Political goals remained intertwined with utopian dreams, the latter serving to prevent careful planning and organized action, the former interfering with serious mysticism and religious commitment. The movement remained, from its inception in 1964 until its demise in the early 1970's, a very real source of meaning and identity for its adherents, but one without clear boundaries, stable leadership, or an institutionalized plan of action.[4] While the movement had clear political consequences in a number of nations, and left behind a variety of new norms and folkways in the western world, whatever results it had were due more to the widespread contagion of its ideology than to any enduring mobilization of movement resources toward a given platform of ends.

Scholars have classified social movements typically into two broad categories, those which seek change of the existing order through political action, and those which seek only the change of individuals, usually through conversion to a new set of beliefs. The former kind are labelled by Turner and Killian "movements of societal manipulation"; the latter they call "movements of personal transformation".[5] Aspects of both kinds of social movement appeared within the youth movement. It had two related but distinct facets, the one political, the other countercultural. The following sections analyze these two arms of the movement in turn.

The Political Arm of the Movement

Student political activism has occurred at universities ever since they came into existence. The 1950's, however, were relatively quiet years on North American campuses. Activism lay dormant in the postwar period and was awakened only by Martin Luther King and the movement for racial equality. Thousands of students in the early 1960's journeyed to the southern states to protest racial discrimination. As the civil rights movement was taken to northern cities, the students continued their support for racial justice throughout the United States and even into Canada, where small black minorities suddenly found themselves the object of considerable attention.

The civil rights movement served to organize dissident students in a way unprecedented in American history. Organizations like the Student Non-Violent Coordinating Committee (SNCC) and the Campus Congress of Racial Equality (CORE) were the principal vehicles by which students were mobilized for the more diffuse youth movement itself. In October of 1964, local chapters of SNCC and CORE at the University of California in Berkeley clashed with the administration over the rights of students to engage in political activity on campus. Out of that conflict emerged the Berkeley Free Speech Movement, which was not specifically tied to racial issues but rather to broader issues of student power. The massive demonstrations, sit-ins, and strikes which occurred at Berkeley during the 1964-65 academic year ushered in the new era of student revolt.[6]

The political ideology of the youth movement came from various sources. In part it was a simple statement of liberal democracy, stated in bold relief against a background of increased bureaucratization and impersonal complexity of dominant institutions. Initially it was highly idealistic, urging the use of non-violent tactics to achieve participatory democracy in the university and in society at large. As the decade progressed, however, the ideology of the political arm of the movement became increasingly couched in a neo-Marxist analysis. In the United States, Herbert Marcuse was probably the foremost intellectual guru; his book, *One-Dimensional Man*,[7] became for the movement its classic diagnosis of the present predicament.

One of the chief expressions of the political ideology of the movement was a 1962 statement of the Students for a Democratic Society, an organization which continues to the present as an instrument of student political protest in both the United States and English Canada. SDS defined its goals as follows:

> As a social system we seek the establishment of a democracy of individual participation, governed by two central aims: that the individual share in those social decisions determining the quality and direction of his life; that society be organized to encourage independence in men and provide the media for their common expression.[8]

Authoritarian structures of whatever kind were to be resisted and replaced. Foremost among these was the university itself, described in 1968 by the president of the Canadian Union of Students as "the master-slave relationships in the classroom and the exclusion of the student from the departmental, faculty and overall governing structures of the university."[9] Students were portrayed as "niggers", powerless pawns of an impersonal bureaucratic system.

The Berkeley conflict in 1964-65 was dramatic evidence to students of the power which they could collectively exercise. The ideology of student power thus spread throughout the United States and beyond; in other countries, it assumed distinctive characteristics, according to specific national issues and existing traditions of student political behaviour. In France, the youth movement had its finest hour in the near-revolution of May, 1968, when a coalition of students and workers brought the country to a standstill. In Germany, the youth movement built upon traditional student activism and staged repeated demonstrations at universities. The same was true in England, where one of the largest protests occurred at the London School of Economics. Students there organized, in 1966, to resist the appointment of a new director for the school, a man who had been associated with British colonialism in Africa.[10]

The United States, however, attracted the greatest attention for youth movement activities. In part, this was because student activism was relatively unprecedented in that country, at least on such a large scale. In part as well, the youth movement in the United States was notable for its lack of support for or from the working class; the American New Left was a phenomenon of upper-middle-class discontent. Most importantly, the American movement had an issue, the Vietnam War, on which it could unite students from one end of the country to the other. Most of the conflicts at universities grew out of protest against the war in general or, more particularly, against conscription and military training on the campus. In the two-month period in 1970 just following the American invasion of Cambodia, students staged major disruptions at 508 colleges and universities, fully one third of those surveyed.[11] American youth also succeeded in getting the movement off campus. The presidential campaigns of Eugene McCarthy in 1968 and George McGovern in 1972 can be credited chiefly to the political arm of the youth movement.

Political mobilization of Canadian youth did not rest, as in the United States, on commitment to such a national concern as anti-war protest. By a transference of the American issue, numerous demonstrations were held against Canadian "complicity" in American foreign policy, but such complicity failed to rouse the anger of the mass of Canadian youth against Ottawa, especially when Ottawa was permitting American draft-dodgers to cross the border by the thousands. It is safe to say, in fact, that much of the anti-war protest in Canada was instigated by exiled Americans continuing their own protest from this side of the border. For the most part, the same regional differences which have given rise to numerous region-based movements in Canadian history served to weaken national cohesion in the youth movement. A movement based on age in Canada, like one based on social class, has difficulty in achieving national unity as a result of the ethnic, linguistic, and regional differences which cut across and weaken age and class boundaries.

Given such regional differences, it is not surprising that the youth movement assumed distinct characteristics in different parts of the country. In Quebec, the civil-rights origins of the movement resulted in the depiction not of students as niggers but of the Quebec people themselves as niggers.[12] Thus, while student radicalism in English Canada was a means of opting out of society, in Quebec it was "an instrument for the integration of the students into the surrounding society".[13] The theme of autonomy in the ideology of the youth movement was congruent with similar themes both in the nationalist and trade union movements of Quebec. This congruity enabled students to join with workers and dissident intellectuals in forming an organized political force for an independent socialist Quebec. Youth in this province was sufficiently mobilized to stage a general strike of 40,000 post-secondary students in October of 1968.

English-Canadian youth could not be expected to unite themselves on the issue of Quebec separatism, but neither did they have a unifying issue of their own. The cause of Canadian nationalism was a recurring theme; student leader Pete Warrian spoke for many others in proclaiming, "We are a colony of a neo-colonialist metropolis centred in the United States."[14] At the time, however, nationalism as an issue was weakened by the solidarity Canadian youth felt with their age-mates to the south in their opposition to the war and to conscription, and in their shared commitment to the euphoric ideals of the movement itself. Further, the centennial year celebrations of 1967, Trudeaumania in 1968, and the popularity of the Trudeau government in its first years served to prevent in English Canada any resentment against the national government even approaching the level of resentment against the American government. As early as 1965, moreover, Ottawa had seemed to affirm movement values in the creation of the Company of Young Canadians, an organization of volunteers specifically charged with promoting social change. For all these reasons, such national youth organizations as the Student Union for Peace Action (1964) and the New Left Committee (1967) served less as agents of large-scale mobilization than as networks of communication for movement leaders whose protests were locally based.

The staple expression of the politics of the youth movement in English Canada was protest on individual university campuses. Scarcely a single university escaped a student uprising of some kind. In many cases, the leader of the protest was a young professor, not infrequently American, who voiced the ideology of student power and became a guru for campus activists. Such professors were typically untenured, often still working on their doctorates, and less than enthusiastic about publishing in professional journals; they were thus vulnerable to academic administrators anxious to relieve them of their positions. When a decision by the university to oust such a professor was made public in January or February, students would protest, the administration would remain unmoved, and the conflict would gradually escalate until May, when the students would leave for the summer and the professor would leave for another job.[15]

Typical of the troubles were those at McGill University between 1967 and 1969, which centred on a Marxist political science lecturer, Stanley Gray. The initial issue was an attempt by the administration to discipline three student journalists from the left-wing campus paper, the *McGill Daily*. The students were charged with "obscene libel" for printing a story which contained a description of Lyndon Johnson performing necrophilia on the corpse of John F. Kennedy. An organization led by Gray, the Students for a Democratic University (affiliated with the Quebec General Students' Union), mobilized student protest against the charges and a sit-in was held in the administration building. The conflict moved on to such issues as student representation on committees of the political science department, a demand that French be the official language at McGill, and finally the impending dismissal of Gray from the faculty for disrupting a university senate meeting. The university accomplished his dismissal in the summer of 1969.

Thousands of miles to the west of McGill, Simon Fraser University's Department of Political Science, Sociology, and Anthropology became a centre of controversy, where both professors and students advocated the ideology of student power. There, the initial protest was directed specifically against the perceived authoritarian structure of the university; at one point students "liberated" the Board Room at Simon Fraser and declared it a children's nursery. After several years of growing conflict, the president of the university summarily dismissed seven professors from the department in 1969. Their dismissal resulted in further protests and censure of the university by a host of professional associations. The censures remain in effect at the time of this writing.

What happened at McGill and Simon Fraser occurred with minor variations at other Canadian universities. At the University of New Brunswick in 1968, physics professor Norman Strax was suspended the day after taking part in a demonstration against a new student identity card; further protests followed. At St. Mary's University, and the Universities of Moncton, Guelph, McMaster, Toronto, and many others, the issue of non-retention of a professor who had student support sparked conflict. At Sir George Williams, Dalhousie, Toronto, York, and others, conflict arose over alleged racism, the authority of the administration to discipline students, the presence of rightist lecturers, or a hike in tuition fees.

The prominence of campus demonstrations as an expression of youth movement politics is not surprising. Campus issues had an immediacy for movement adherents unequalled by events outside the university. Further, it was on the campus that students could most easily be mobilized, given their common residence in the university neighbourhood, the availability of classrooms and facilities for large meetings, and the presence of such communication channels as the student newspaper and radio. While, as of 1974, demonstrations continue to occur sporadically, student activism appears to have generally declined. Since the issue of student power on the campus has not yet been resolved, and given the continuing marginality of students to the rest of society, unrest on the campus is sure to increase at some point in the future. When it does, however, it will be in a movement distinct from that of the New Left, which has by now grown old.

The Countercultural Arm of the Movement

For the most part, the politics of the youth movement did not attain the desired ends. American youth succeeded in mounting strong campaigns for McCarthy in 1968 and for McGovern in 1972, but ultimate victory on both occasions belonged to Richard Nixon. The rebellion of French youth in 1968 helped to topple De Gaulle, but Georges Pompidou was hardly the movement's choice for his successor. In Canada, the Company of Young Canadians was reorganized and redirected after members had pressed too far their mandate of social change. The imposition of the War Measures Act in 1970 displayed a different side of Pierre Trudeau than that presented in 1968. In the universities, moreover, administrators retrenched during summer holidays and students largely failed to gain the power they sought. If lack of visible successes and recurrent organizational problems were not enough to sour many youth on political protest, it must be added that the much-criticized bureaucratic systems, however impersonal and unresponsive, made few demands on youth. In the prosperity of the 1960's, Canadian students willing to tolerate computerized exams could live a relatively comfortable life and enjoy long summer holidays quite free of the oppressive qualities of an increasingly bureaucratized world.

Such conditions as these nourished a second theme in the youth movement, a countercultural tendency. As scholars have noted in the case of many social movements, a perception of political change as unlikely or impossible gives rise to an ideology which counsels withdrawal from the corrupt social order and escape into a new world.[16] By counterculture is meant a mentality so different from the one prevailing that it is pointless for adherents to try to change the status quo to conform to their views; instead they choose to drop out of the existing order, accept the new mentality, and try to live it in social arrangements shielded from the outside world. If the writings of Marcuse were the bible of "politicals" in the movement, Theodore Roszak's *Making of a Counterculture* became the bible of the "freaks".[17]

Although the countercultural arm of the movement had its roots more in the "beat" phenomenon of the fifties than in the civil rights movement,[18] it would be incorrect to regard it as wholly distinct from the political arm. On an ideological level, both facets of the movement were agreed on the goal of an alienation-free society, a society of equality and freedom. The countercultural arm, however, regarded the established order as an impossible place to seek such a goal; it was already "too far gone". The two arms of the movement also met on a behavioural level. Liberation News Service, the communications link for the underground press throughout North America, was the scene of bitter infighting between "vulgar Marxists" (politicals) and a "virtuous caucus" (freaks).[19] At the convention of the American Democratic Party in 1968, New Leftist protesters were outraged by the lack of co-operation from countercultural dissidents, who neglected organized protest, staged a "Festival of Life", and nominated a pig for the American presidency. Later, the leaders of both camps were unwilling co-defendants in the much-publicized trial of the Chicago Seven, in which all were charged with inciting to riot.[20] On the campus level, many students alternated between periods of political rebellion and countercultural withdrawal.[21]

The medium by which countercultural ideology was spread throughout the western world was the airwaves, on which travelled the sounds of rock music. Toronto critic Jack Batten later wrote, "When I started to write about rock, I more or less believed, along with millions of others, that rock somehow presaged a new and grand social movement, something loose and free. . . ."[22] Not only the beat but also the words proclaimed such a movement. The themes of the lyrics stressed the importance of choosing for oneself, of maximizing the freedom of both partners in love relationships, of being autonomous in the conventional world, and of living spontaneously and honestly.[23] The underground press, represented in virtually every major city in North America, also served as a medium of communication. The values evident in these publications were expressive as opposed to instrumental; the emphasis was on being oneself and loving others, not on getting ahead and striving for success.[24]

Such an ideology, the "hang-loose ethic" as it was appropriately called, created a new breed of young person, the "hippie". The hippies were not without historical antecedents; articles appeared comparing them with Jesus, Francis of Assisi, the Gnostics, Romantic poets, millennarians, and mystics of all kinds. In style of dress, music, attitudes, and especially age, however, they constituted a new expression of the bohemian, antinomian way of life. The hippie facet of the youth movement was even more homogeneous across different countries than the New Left facet. While the latter had to grapple with the structure of politics and with specific political issues, which are different in different nations, the former was uninterested in politics whatever the setting. The hippie arm of the movement sought personal transformation: when enough people were transformed, the "system" would necessarily crumble for lack of people to run it.[25]

Conversion to any countercultural belief system is not accomplished through rational argument. While New Leftists might win supporters through articulating an analysis of the authoritarian structure of the university, hippies won converts through "turning them on". The chief instrument for such conversion was the use of marijuana or psychedelic drugs; use of these drugs became the symbol of continued adherence to the hang-loose ethic and of continued rejection of conventional society. It was not that the drugs effected a conversion through their chemistry; pharmacological research demonstrated in particular that marijuana had only mild effects in itself. Even chemically potent drugs wrought no conversion in laboratory settings, but only within the movement. What must be stressed is that marijuana and psychedelic drugs were invested with such symbolic meaning by the movement that they appeared to open up an entirely new world of truth. Especially was this true in the case of a chemical named d-lysergic acid diethylamide-25, more commonly called LSD or "acid"; as one individual recalled,

> All of a sudden I saw, in the most real sense, that the nature of the universe is beyond the conception of the world, the concepts, the understanding. What they only understand in a way is self. I realized it was what I have been looking for all my life. Not LSD, but the state of being, or having being.[26]

The illegal use of psychedelic drugs increased dramatically among young people throughout the 1960's. In 1962, the RCMP had reports of 20 cases of marijuana use in all of Canada. By 1969, surveys reported that 35% of McGill students had used marijuana, 30% of students at the University of Saskatchewan, 36% of law students at Toronto, and 45% of law students at the University of British Columbia. Among high school students in 1969, the percentage having smoked pot ranged from 6 to 24, depending upon region.[27] Rates of use of LSD, amphetamines, barbiturates, and tranquillizers were somewhat lower, but still between 5 and 10% in most 1969 reports.[28] Opiate narcotics, by contrast, had a negative symbolic meaning in the counterculture, and rates of use in Canada through the 1960's increased very little. The Division of Narcotic Control knew of 4060 addicts in 1969, only 665 more than in 1961.[29]

More important than drug use itself were the correlates attached to it. In a study of American university students, E.A. Suchman found that marijuana users, as compared to non-users, were more approving of pre-marital sexual behaviour, abortion, birth control, and law-breaking in general; they were also more cynical, anti-establishment, and likely to regard college as a waste of time. As evidence of their association with New Left politics, Suchman also found marijuana users more opposed to the Vietnam War and more likely to have taken part in mass protests than non-users.[30] A similar pattern was found in 1970 in a study of Ontario high school students; marijuana use was positively related to approval of communal living, long hair, rock music, and liberal sexual behaviour, and to disinterest in conventional religion.[31]

The culture of marijuana use was fundamentally a positive one. Hippie youth lived within the new world of their own mental experience; in the context of that world they were optimistic and hopeful. Mark Messer, in a study of users and non-users of marijuana on a California campus, found the former more pessimistic than others with respect to such issues as the utility of writing to public officials or the question of whether the lot of the average man was getting better or worse. By contrast, however, marijuana users were less likely to agree that "These days a person doesn't really know who he can count on."[32] Hippie youth was found to be more alienated from the political order, but less alienated from social life itself. Within the movement, the bond of shared commitment to a new and loving world provided a sense of security greater than that enjoyed by youth whose roots were still implanted in the status quo.

While the behavioural expression of the New Left was a confrontation with the establishment, that of the hippies was escape from the establishment into enclaves of their own where they could celebrate a new kind of life. The hippie counterpart to New Left demonstrations were rock festivals, where for a few days in a farmer's field the harsh realities of a bureaucratic and impersonal world could be blotted out by the experience of sharing music, food, drugs, the mind, and the body. The greatest such festival was at Woodstock, New York, in the summer of 1969; thousands of young Canadians joined a mass of more than a quarter of a million in proclaiming the reality of the "hang-loose" ethic. Other rock festivals occurred in every Canadian province and every American state, along with most of the countries of Europe.

In between rock festivals, hippie youth were at home in colonies which sprang up in most major cities. In San Francisco it was Haight-Ashbury, in New York the East Village, in Toronto Yorkville, and in Montreal St. Catherine Street. A study done in Yorkville in 1967-68 distinguished four major groups.[33] There were "weekenders", youth in their middle teens venturing into the area out of curiosity, trying to buy some marijuana, but ready to return to school on Monday morning. A second group were the motorcycle gangs, more organized than the rest but less committed to the gentle hippie ethos. Similar to the motorcycle types were "greasers", young men without wheels or money, often on heavy drugs, and minimally interested in hippie values. Finally were the hippies themselves, regular drug-users, more permanent residents, unemployed on principle, and living for the day with few plans for the morrow. Also represented in Yorkville were the Diggers, a hippie organization based in San Francisco which sought to provide food and shelter for other hippies. In Toronto, the Diggers were funded in part by the Company of Young Canadians.

The early years of the hippie phenomenon witnessed a great number of transient youth moving from one hippie enclave to another. Vast numbers travelled to islands off the coast of Greece, to the Costa del Sol in Spain, to northern Africa, India, and Mexico, in the hope of finding refuge, in the warmth of the sun, from narcotics agents and bureaucrats in general. Eventually, however, as the need to establish more enduring expressions of hippie values appeared, more permanent structures were created. The most notable of these in Canada was Rochdale College, a Toronto apartment building.[34] The high-rise structure opened in 1968 as a co-operative student dormitory, with 90 per cent of the nearly $6 million of construction costs coming from the crown-owned Central Mortgage and Housing Corporation. Rochdale was only one of a number of such co-operative residences constructed across the country with CMHC money, under the terms of 1965 legislation. Rochdale, however, with its open drug culture, communal living, strange art, and irregular mortgage payments, steadily became such an embarassment to the federal and municipal governments that regular attempts were made to close it; these appear to have finally succeeded in 1974.

The ultimate routinization of the countercultural arm of the youth movement occurred in the creation of hippie communes in the rural areas of the continent. The *New York Times* estimated that there were 2000 such communes of significant size in the United States in 1970.[35] Probably the estimate was low. In Canada, aging hippies procured land on Vancouver Island, in the Rockies, in the bush country of the North, in the Ottawa Valley, and even in southern Ontario. The initial pattern of life in the communes stressed individual freedom, transient sexual relationships, drug use, and diffuse, eclectic beliefs. As time progressed, however, the communes which lasted developed stable patterns of organization, strong leadership roles, a decrease in drug use, more defined belief structures, and more permanent economic bases. It may be that the most lasting expression of the hippie facet of the youth movement will be scattered communes in rural areas, joining with Doukhobors, Mennonites, and Hutterites in the utopian corner of the Canadian mosaic.

Sources and Explanations

The two preceding sections have reviewed the basic ideology and behaviour of the two arms of the youth movement, the political and the countercultural. The question remains, however, of why the movement happened. After decades of relative invisibility as a force of political or cultural change, the youth of the western world developed a distinctive consciousness in the course of half a decade. It is the task of social science to offer some explanation for this phenomenon.

Empirically, one explanatory factor upon which all scholars can agree is the quantitative growth of youth during the 1960's. It was during this decade that the postwar baby boom reached adolescence and young adulthood. The basic trends were similar in nearly all the countries of North America and western Europe. Table 1 shows the growth of youth as a sector of the population in Canada between 1961 and 1971. While the population as a whole increased by a substantial 17% during this decade, the population aged 15 to 24 increased by a phenomenal 53%. Year by year, as the table indicates, youth increased its share of the population.

The implications of this demographic trend are not unlike those of trends in migration. The influx of large numbers of refugees from the American colonies to Ontario in the late 1700's resulted in their developing collective demands for themselves with respect to municipal government.[37] The migration of large numbers of anglophones to present-day Manitoba in the late 1890's resulted in their articulating forcefully their interests in opposition to the French-Catholic establishment.[38] If sudden concentration of people in a particular ethnic or geographic category breeds the development of a collective consciousness, it should come as no surprise that concentration of people in a particular age category yields the same result.[39]

Compounding the demographic trend of the 1960's was the demand by a rapidly expanding economy for highly-trained manpower. Such a demand prompted provincial governments all across Canada to greatly increase their education budgets. Students were lured to university with inexpensive loans and

TABLE 1

THE GROWTH OF YOUTH AS A SECTOR OF THE CANADIAN
POPULATION 1961-71

| | | Population Aged 15-24 | |
Year	Total Population	Number	Percentage of Total
1961	18,238,000	2,616,000	14.3
1963	18,896,000	2,856,000	15.1
1966	20,015,000	3,299,000	16.5
1969	21,061,000	3,777,000	17.9
1971	21,568,000	4,004,000	18.6

TABLE 2

FULL-TIME ENROLLMENT OF UNIVERSITY STUDENTS IN CANADA,
1961-1962 to 1967-1968

Academic Year	Total Enrollment	Enrollment as Percentage of Population Aged 18-21
1961-62	149,366	14.7
1963-64	182,261	16.3
1965-66	226,562	18.2
1967-68	283,871	19.8

the promise of a high-paying job in business or industry upon graduation. The result was that, while youth increased as a percentage of the population, the percentage of youth enrolled in university increased as well. Table 2 shows that during a 6-year period, 1961 to 1967, university enrollment in Canada nearly doubled, while the percentage of youth aged 18 to 21 enrolled at university rose from 15 to 20. The corresponding percentages for youth in the United States during the same period were 26 and 33. The 1960's were thus a period of the heaviest concentration of youth in universities in the history of either Canada or the United States. Further, this concentration occurred with unbelievable rapidity. No structural or social psychological explanation of the youth movement of the sixties can afford to neglect these basic demographic trends.

The fact that a large number of people share residence in a common social space may be regarded as a preliminary condition for the rise of a social movement, but it is not sufficient. What is necessary, above all, is that there be a perception on the part of large numbers of those people that the world is not as it should be. This may be called a perception of institutional deficiency. It is a circumstance in which "day-to-day experience substantially contradicts or insufficiently reinforces the society's ideology."[41] Every society teaches its members a given description of what is good, bad, true and false; this may be called a world-view, a myth, or an ideology. When people in some sector of a society cannot interpret what happens to them in terms of that ideology or world-view, they are disposed to collective unrest.

In the case of the youth movement, the relevant ideology was that of the postwar western world, an ideology that placed great value on the conquest of nature, on economic growth, and on material success. This ideology has been described as the myth of "Prometheus Unbound, autonomous man as the measure of all things, dominant over nature, goal directed factor, Faustian-like qualities of onward and upward, over and against; in short, *man making it!*"[42] If society was defined in the postwar world as powerful and autonomous in the face of nature, there is evidence that the individual was defined by that same ideology as powerful and autonomous in the face of society. The child-rearing values emphasized in upper-middle-class homes were those of independence, self-expression, permissiveness, and democratic relations.[43] In summary, young people were taught to believe that they could be themselves and be autonomous in the wider world that awaited them; they came to expect that the outside world would resemble their own families, where the advice of Doctor Spock had ensured an atmosphere of acceptance and love.

The universities which enveloped youth during the 1960's did not provide the expected atmosphere. They were ill-prepared to accommodate the deluge of students and turned increasingly to multiple-choice rather than essay examinations, to large classes instead of small ones, and to computerized registration instead of individual counselling. The new faculty members of the 1960's were pressured to become involved in research on the ever-expanding problems of business, industry, government, and their professions; as a result they were less inclined to define themselves simply as teachers. Students were expected to live and study in labyrinthine buildings of concrete and glass; the path to a degree involved picking one's way through an equally labyrinthine maze of forms to be completed in quadruplicate. The total effect of the univeristy was quite the opposite of the warm suburban homes from which the students came. In their homes young people had been rewarded for self-expression; in the university they had the feeling that no one cared, so long as they pencilled in the correct boxes on IBM cards.

Certainly not all universities were so impersonal nor all students so intent on self-expression and autonomy. The research indicates, however, that it was such students with such a perception of the university who actively took part in the youth movement. Flacks found that Chicago activists tended to have parents who were more lenient, mild, liberal, and permissive than the parents of non-activists; the dissident students in his study were more creative, aesthetic, intellectual, and humanitarian, as well as less moralistic than the conformist students.[44] In studies at the University of Toronto, Quarter found support for Flacks' findings, and noted in addition that supporters of the student movement, as compared to opponents, tended to be socialist, anti-authoritarian, concerned for others, undecided about their careers, liberal in religious beliefs, and disproportionately from the Social Science and Arts faculties.[45]

Another source of perceived institutional deficiency can be status inconsistency. At least one study which specifically focussed on this variable found it positively related to discontent and activism. Lehtiniemi, in a survey of sociology students in two Ontario universities, found that students who approximated adults more than "pre-adults" were more likely to be activists. Students who were financially independent of their parents, who lived in apartments off campus, and who were accustomed to making their own decisions all were more likely to have taken part in demonstrations. He concluded that the status inconsistency between these students' personal lives on the one hand and their lingering pre-adult roles in the university on the other helped to trigger their activism.[46]

Thus is it clear that the roots of the youth movement were much deeper than the specific issues on which it focussed. The protest against the Vietnam War was principally an expression of discontent with the demands made by military conscription in the United States on young men who had been taught self-expression and autonomy. The protest against university bureaucracies, against large corporations, against confederation in Quebec, against Gaullism in France, and against American domination in English Canada, can all be seen as reflections of a basic demand by youth to be able to live out the values of creativity, independence, and autonomy which they had learned from their society. The ideology of participatory democracy in the political arm and of individual freedom in the countercultural arm flowed directly from the roots of the movement.

Discontent does not give rise to social movements, of course, unless opportunities for its mobilization are present. In the case of the youth movement, the factors which led to mobilization were suggested in earlier sections of this paper. The student newspapers, traditional bearers of campus trivialities, were easily taken over by activists as a forum for movement ideology. The mass music media, with origins in the Hit Parade of the 1950's, became dominated by songs with a protest or countercultural theme. The physical proximity of students on the campuses, their freedom from daily contact with parents, the free time available to students, the availability of places for meetings and rallies, and other attributes of the university setting were all conducive to rapid mobilization of large numbers of students. Further, the values on academic freedom institutionalized in universities shielded students to some extent from repressive action by police. The youth movement occurred not only because students were discontented but because their social situation was highly conducive to mobilization and gave them easy access to communication mechanisms.

The Movement in Retrospect

While the existence of a general and diffuse youth movement in the late 1960's is beyond dispute, so also is it clear that the movement rapidly subsided in the 1970's. The collective solidarity which a generation of young Canadians felt with their age-mates in other countries has dwindled and with it the collective action. In this final section of the present paper, two issues need to be addressed: the effects of the movement on Canadian society and its implications for an understanding of the present condition of Canadian society.

With respect to the first issue, Canadian policy-makers responded to the movement in three broad ways. The first and most basic way was to disregard the actual content of youthful discontent and to recognize only some superficial expressions. For the most part, the federal and provincial governments failed even to see a *youth scene*, in which hundreds of thousands of young Canadians felt estranged from their society, and chose to see instead a *drug scene*, in which these same young Canadians were breaking laws against drug use. As marijuana, LSD, and other drugs swept across the country, governments did not ask what they symbolized but how to prevent their use.

Ontario's Addiction Research Foundation (ARF), which had been founded in 1949 principally to deal with problems of alcoholism, responded to the increase in use of psychedelic drugs with a demand for a bigger budget. By 1968, the province was spending more than $6 million a year on ARF, money which the foundation used not only to investigate the pharmacology of drugs and the extent of use, but also to teach young people about drugs. Through this focus on drug use instead of on the correlates of drug use, the province sensationalized the prime symbol of the movement and probably helped to contribute to the further use of drugs among restless youth. It is fascinating to observe that the annual increase in the budget of the Addiction Research Foundation was accompanied by even larger annual increases in the extent of drug use. A similar focus on drugs instead of dissidence appeared in the terms of reference of the prestigious Commission of Inquiry Into the Non-Medical Use of Drugs, appointed by the Trudeau government in 1969. While the Commission did devote some 20 of the 314 pages of its Interim Report to the social context of drug use, its basic focus was not on the movement itself.[47] If long hair or flare pants had been illegal in Canada in the 1960's, commissions on hair and trousers might also have been appointed.

A second response of policy-makers to the youth movement was suppression. Anti-war demonstrations at the American consulate in Toronto, sit-ins on university campuses, and, of course, the use of illicit drugs could not be disregarded entirely. When the political or countercultural arm of the movement openly violated the law, police were called and the perpetrators punished. Professors who assumed leadership roles in the movement were eased out of their positions; student activists faced disciplinary procedures; those who protested in the streets were sometimes charged with disorderly conduct or trespassing; and those caught smoking pot were charged with drug offences. In the fall of 1970, when young members of Quebec's FLQ kidnapped James Cross and Pierre Laporte, Prime Minister Trudeau imposed the War Measures Act and exposed himself to youth throughout Canada as fundamentally the defender of social order. This event, even in English Canada, served as a decisive symbol of the fact that agents of social control would not hesitate to defend the established order by force of arms if necessary. With the background of narcotics arrests and penalties for isolated law-breaking, the imposition of the War Measures Act brought to a dramatic end the euphoric and unrealistic atmosphere of protest in the sixties.

While mainstream Canada in part disregarded and in part suppressed the most rebellious aspects of the youth movement, it co-opted less threatening aspects and absorbed them into conventional life. In 1969, the federal government appointed another Commission of Inquiry, this one specifically concerned with youth.[48] When this Commission recommended, in 1971, the lowering of the age of majority from 21 to 18, the government accepted the recommendation. In 1970, the federal government also set up a network of youth hostels across the country, to provide free or inexpensive housing for transient youth. In 1971, the Liberal government announced a $15-million grant to establish a new agency, Opportunities for Youth (OFY). This agency would invite students to devise innovative projects and then pay them to work in these projects. For 1972, the OFY budget was $35 million, and $180 million was spent on a similar scheme, the Local Initiatives Programme.[49] In the early 1970's, activist Canadian youth were no longer fighting the government but accepting government paycheques for the more or less useful jobs they had created for themselves. Even the smoking of marijuana lost its symbolic meaning. So many Canadians, young and old, had learned to enjoy the weed that the chances of being caught by the police were greatly reduced; "getting stoned" no longer served to distinguish the discontented from the satisfied.

It was not only the federal government, however, which absorbed elements of the movement and the counterculture into conventional society. Advertising agencies, businessmen, and promoters also played a part. The two-fingered "V" sign of peace became popular among elementary school children. Barbers at last accepted the longer hair and insisted only that they be paid as hair stylists to care for it. Sensible entrepreneurs mass-produced hippie styles of clothing for the expanded youth market and then for adults as well. The more liberal sexual norms of the movement were eagerly expropriated by a variety of sectors of Canadian society. Even university administrations bent to student pressure, redefining the content of some courses in more appealing ways, reducing the number of required courses in degree programmes, raising the average mark given from a "C" to a "B", and admitting students as non-threatening minorities on university senates and committees. Such changes served less to give power to students than to make the university less bothersome to them.

From the vantage point of the middle 1970's, it is remarkable how little of the change that seemed inevitable in 1967 has in fact occurred. The trends toward concentration of power in large corporations, toward decision-making by professionals instead of by relevant publics, toward the steady accumulation of consumer goods, toward increasing American ownership of the Canadian means of production, and toward the further bureaucratization of education have continued almost without interruption. In 1968, in the midst of the youth mobilization in France, a poster pinned to the Sorbonne summarized the ideology of the movement:

> The revolution which is beginning will call in question not only the capitalist society but all industrial society. The consumers' society must perish of a violent death. The society of alienation must disappear from history. We are inventing a new and original world. Imagination is seizing power.[50]

The world of the 1970's reveals how completely the youth movement failed to achieve such revolutionary goals. Such tactics as the OFY and LIP programmes in Canada, President Nixon's abolition of conscription in the United States, police repression of political dissidence in virtually all the countries, and the absorption of movement symbols into the middle class, successfully stalled the youth movement until its adherents grew up. Until another generation of youth finds itself in a circumstance of such dislocation as occurred in the 1960's, the western world is unlikely to witness such a dramatic social movement specifically based in this sector of the population.

Analysis of the youth movement does not yield definitive conclusions for a sociology of social movements, but certain implications may be suggested. Perhaps the most fundamental is that statuses like age or ethnicity can be as important for movement formation as is social class.[51] The preceding decade makes it clear that the working class in modern western societies has no monopoly on discontent; status-based movements can arise with ideologies just as insistent on popular autonomy as class-based movements. It would appear that youth, when concentrated on university campuses, is particularly fertile ground for the growth of protest movements. The role of student is by definition a powerless role, one which implies an admission of ignorance and a willingness to submit to instruction by those who are presumably knowledgeable. The role of student also includes a norm of interest in new ideas. Students, moreover, are concentrated in a social situation in which mobilization is relatively easy. Given their powerlessness, their interest in ideas, and the ease of mobilization, students constitute a sector of the population particularly inclined to dissident collective behaviour. Western history provides varied evidence in support of this proposition.[52]

The strength of the youth sector, however, is also its weakness. Students are so powerless that they are largely irrelevant. A student strike produces no shortage of goods on supermarket shelves. Students have too little stock in the economy for their withdrawal of stock to have a crippling effect. Their labour produces virtually nothing for immediate consumption; the effect of their withholding labour can only be felt years later, if at all. Further, the student role, unlike that of worker or French Canadian, is temporary; hence student movements have constantly to recruit new adherents and new leadership. Even during the period in which one is a student, formal student status occupies but two thirds of the year, so that effective mobilization can take place only within the constraints of the academic calendar. For all these reasons, student movements have less effect than their numerical strength would suggest.

In the wake of the youth protest of the 1960's, other statuses have come to the fore as bases of collective protest. None is more salient than ethnicity, which has stimulated nationalistic sentiment in both Canada and the United States. The salience of ethnicity in the 1970's has also nourished separatism in Quebec and spawned a new consciousness among Ukrainians, blacks, chicanos, native Indians, and other minorities.[53] Such an entrenchment in historically-based identities is apparent also in the Jesus Movement, an apolitical fundamentalist sectarian phenomenon, and in general nostalgia for the supposed security of the past, whether in decade-old rock music or century-old antiques. At the same time, the Canadian working class has continued to mount strikes in response to the threats of new technology, of inflation, of unemployment, and of lack of worker control. A broad movement demanding preservation of the environment has also arisen, expressing itself in opposition to industrial development, highway and airport construction, and urban growth.[54]

It is safe to predict that oppositional movements will continue to occur on the basis of both class and a variety of statuses. Although the issues of protest and specific demands will differ, a populist ideology is likely to be common to most such movements. The situation of perceived powerlessness in the face of mammoth bureaucracies is shared by a host of disparate sectors of Canadian society. The problem of how people can seize power in an age of multi-national corporations, highly trained professionals, increasingly effective material and social technologies, and an incredibly complex social order, has not yet been resolved even theoretically, much less in practice.

Notes

1. Montreal: Our Generation Press, 1970.
2. For a discussion, see R.H. Turner and L.M. Killian, *Collective Behavior* (Englewood Cliffs, N.J.: Prentice-Hall, 1957), pp. 344-45.
3. James Michener's novel, *The Drifters* (New York: Random House, 1971), dramatizes the supranational aspects of the movement effectively.
4. O.E. Klapp has analyzed the identity-giving qualities of the youth movement; see his *Collective Search for Identity* (New York: Holt, Rinehart, and Winston, 1969).
5. Turner and Killian, pp. 333ff.
6. For analysis of the Berkeley conflict, see S.M. Lipset and S.S. Wolin, eds., *The Berkeley Student Revolt* (Garden City: Doubleday Anchor, 1965). Probably the best analysis of the political aspects of the youth movement in general is S.M. Lipset, *Rebellion in the University* (Boston: Little Brown, 1971).
7. Boston: Beacon, 1964.
8. "Port Huron Statement," pp. 154-167 in P. Jacobs and S. Landau, eds., *The New Radicals* (New York: Random House, 1966), p. 160.
9. Pete Warrian, "Democratization and Decolonization," pp. 24-25 in Tim and Julyan Reid, eds., *Student Power and the Canadian Campus* (Toronto: Peter Martin, 1969).
10. See K. Westhues, "The Movement — Beginning to End," *Social Problems* 20 (winter 1973), pp. 389-91.
11. G. Buchanan and J. Brackett, *Summary Results of the Survey for the President's Commission on Campus Unrest* (Washington, D.C.: Urban Institute, 1970).
12. Pierre Vallières, a young French-Canadian radical, published in 1968 an immensely popular book entitled *Nègres blancs d'Amérique (White Niggers of America)*; Montreal, Parti Pris), a term which he applied to the Quebec people in general.
13. Daniel La Touche, "The Quebec Student Movement," pp. 113-32 in G.F. McGuigan, ed., *Student Protest* (Toronto: Methuen, 1968). La Touche was one of the founders of the *Union Générale des Etudiants du Québec* in 1964.
14. Warrian, *loc. cit.*, p. 24. For a general overview of the youth movement in Canada, see D.J. Roussopoulos, ed., *The New Left in Canada, op. cit.* Some part of the dissidence in Canada can be attributed to Americans who had come to this country; probably the most comprehensive study of American draft-dodgers in Canada is K.F. Emerick, *War Resisters Canada* (Knox, Penn.: Knox Free Press, 1972).

15. Description of various of these protests can be found in Tim and Julyan Reid, *op. cit.*; Norman Sheffe, ed., *Student Unrest* (Toronto: McGraw-Hill, 1970); G.F. McGuigan, *op. cit.*; as well as in the back issues of most campus newspapers.
16. For a review of such theories see K. Westhues, *Society's Shadow* (Toronto: McGraw-Hill Ryerson, 1972), p. 33. That volume also includes a relatively comprehensive bibliography of research on the countercultural aspects of the youth movement.
17. Garden City: Doubleday Anchor, 1969.
18. See David Ebner, "Beats and Hippies: a Comparative Analysis," pp. 184-190 in Westhues, *op. cit.*
19. The story of Liberation News Service is delightfully told by Raymond Mungo, *Famous Long Ago* (Richmond Hill: Simon and Schuster of Canada, 1970).
20. See N. von Hoffman, "The Chicago Conspiracy Circus," pp. 187-95 in *The Youth Culture* (Chicago: Playboy Press, 1971).
21. G. Simmon and G. Trout, "Hippies in College: from Teeny-Boppers to Drug Freaks," pp. 174-180 in Westhues, *op. cit.*
22. "Confessions of a Retired Rock Critic," *Saturday Night* 88 (March 1973), pp. 18-20; see also his description of the Toronto rock band, Lighthouse: "You're Beautiful, too, Lighthouse," *Saturday Night* 87 (August 1972), pp. 21-23.
23. J.T. Carey, "The Ideology of Autonomy in Popular Lyrics: a Content Analysis," *Psychiatry* 32 (May 1969), pp. 150-64. R.S. Denisoff and R.A. Peterson, eds., *The Sounds of Social Change* (Chicago: Rand McNally, 1972) is an excellent collection of articles analyzing the role of music in social movements. The poster was another medium by which the countercultural ideology was expressed; see M. Gordon, "America's Two Poster Movements," *Journal of Popular Culture* 3 (fall 1969), pp. 231-250.
24. J. Levin and J.L. Spates, "Hippie Values: an Analysis of the Underground Press," *Youth and Society* 2 (September 1970), pp. 59-73.
25. D. Foss, *Freak Culture* (New York: New Critics, 1972).
26. Quoted in J.T. Carey, *The College Drug Scene* (Englewood Cliffs: Prentice-Hall, 1968).
27. G. LeDain *et al.*, *Interim Report of the Commission of Inquiry Into the Non-Medical Use of Drugs* (Queen's Printer, 1970), p. 144.
28. *Ibid.*, passim.
29. *Ibid.*, p. 148.
30. "The Hang-Loose Ethic and the Spirit of Drug Use," *Journal of Health and Social Behavior* (June 1968), pp. 146-55.
31. K. Westhues and D. Anderson, "Notes on the Culture of Marijuana Use among Ontario Catholic High School Students," pp. 136-40 in Westhues, *op. cit.* See also G. LeDain *et al.*, *op. cit.*, chapter 4.
32. "The Predictive Value of Marijuana Use: a Note to Researchers of Student Culture," *Sociology of Education* 42 (winter 1969), pp. 91-97.
33. G. Alampur, *The Yorkville Subculture* (Toronto: Addiction Research Foundation, 1969). For other accounts of life in hippie enclaves, see D.L. Earisman, *Hippies in Our Midst* (Philadelphia: Fortress, 1968), L. Yablonsky, *The Hippie Trip* (New York: Pegasus, 1968), and S. Cavan, *Hippies of the Haight* (St. Louis: New Critics, 1972).
34. See B. Zwicker, "Rochdale: the Ultimate Freedom," *Change* (November-December, 1969).
35. December 17, 1970, p. 1. Analyses of hippie communes may be found in the following: S. Diamond, *What the Trees Said* (New York: Fitzhenry and Whiteside, 1971); R.M. Kanter, *Commitment and Community* (Cambridge: Harvard University Press, 1972); R. Houriet, *Getting Back Together* (New York: Coward McCann and Geoghegan, 1971); Westhues, *op. cit.*; and the review essay by J.R. Pitts in *Contemporary Sociology* 2 (July 1973), pp. 351-59.
36. Source: Statistics Canada, quinquennial censuses and intercensal estimates.
37. See F. Landon, "The Evolution of Local Government in Ontario," *Ontario History* 42, pp. 1-6.
38. W.L. Morton, *Manitoba: a History* (Toronto, 1967).
39. It may be noted parenthetically that present demographic trends hold the prospect of an increasing concentration of the population in the over-65 age category, a sector equally as powerless and irrelevant to society as young students. We may thus expect the aged to exhibit a growing collective consciousness and to act on its basis during the coming decade. With admirable foresight the federal

government has taken steps toward nipping collective dissidence among senior citizens in the bud. Not only has the federal pension plan been improved, but also, in 1972, Ottawa launched the New Horizons programme, which is similar to OFY except that it is for old people.

40. Source: Z.E. Zsigmond and C.J. Wenaas, *Enrollment in Educational Institutions by Province, 1951-52 to 1980-81*. Staff Study No. 25, Economic Council of Canada, 1970.

41. Westhues, *op. cit.*, p. 28.

42. M. Messer, "Running Out of Era: Some Non-Pharmacological Notes on the Psychedelic Revolution," pp. 145-53 in Westhues, *op. cit.*

43. See R. Flacks, "The Liberated Generation: an Exploration of the Roots of Student Protest," *Journal of Social Issues* 23 (July 1967), pp. 52-75.

44. *Ibid.* See also K. Keniston, *Young Radicals: Notes on Committed Youth* (New York: Harcourt Brace and World, 1968), and *The Uncommitted* (New York: Harcourt Brace, 1965).

45. J. Quarter, *The Student Movement of the '60s* (Toronto: Ontario Institute for Studies in Education, 1972).

46. L. Lehtiniemi, "A Tested Theory of Student Unrest," *Alberta Journal of Educational Research* 43 (March 1972), pp. 51-58.

47. G. LeDain *et al.*, *op. cit.*, pp. 153-170.

48. The final report is entitled *It's Your Turn* (Information Canada, 1971).

49. For a description of these projects, see Sandra Gwyn, "The Great Ottawa Grant Boom (and How It Grew)," *Saturday Night* 87 (October 1972), pp. 22-24.

50. The London *Times*, May 17, 1968.

51. For a discussion of the relative merits of class and status as bases for social movement formation, see R. Bendix, "Inequality and Social Structure: a Comparison of Marx and Weber," *American Sociological Review* 39 (April 1974): 149-61. During the 1960's, when the prospects of success looked quite good for the youth movement, committed Marxists offered the explanation that youth constituted a new class, a modern proletariat, selling labour for the wages of marks and degrees; see, for example, J. and M. Rowntree, "The Political Economy of Youth," *Our Generation* 6 (summer 1968): 155-89. Now that the movement has subsided without much success, Marxists are better advised to withdraw this innovative application of Marxist theory and to regard the movement as a bourgeois status-based phenomenon which was sure to fail anyway because of its lack of identification with the working class.

52. See Lipset, *op. cit.*

53. For an analysis of this trend in the United States, see Michael Novak, *The Rise of the Unmeltable Ethnics* (New York: Macmillan, 1972). In Canada, the federal government has responded with increased support for diverse ethnic groups; see Sandra Gwyn, "Multiculturalism: a Threat and a Promise," *Saturday Night* 89 (February 1974): 15-18.

54. For a review of some such movements and a case-study of one in particular, see K. Westhues and P.R. Sinclair, *Village in Crisis* (Toronto: Holt, Rinehart and Winston, 1974).

Movements of Protest in Postwar Canadian Society

S.D. Clark

Though the decade of the 1960's has just now come to an end, it may not be too soon to attempt to seek some understanding of those forces of social unrest and protest which, in our society as elsewhere, have attracted so much attention in the years since the decade's beginning. The decade began with the ushering in of that state of political and social ferment in French Canada which has found its clearest expression in the movement directed towards the separation of the province of Quebec from the federal union. If the clamourings of dissent have been less shrill in other parts of the country, they have nevertheless been sufficiently loud and persistent to make themselves clearly heard. The rise of a hippy cult among the young people of our larger cities, the development on our university campuses of a militant student movement, the increasing readiness of dissident farmer and labour groups to resort to violent forms of protest, the new militancy of such professional groups as teachers and nurses, the stirring movement of native Indian protest in fringe areas of the north, offer themselves only as some of the more striking examples of a type of social protest against established authority which appears today to have become so widespread in our society.

It is easy to dismiss these movements of unrest and protest in Canada as simply emanations of movements growing up across the border in the United States. Certainly, there has been a strong connection between what has been happening in Canadian society and what has been happening in American, and Canadians may have some cause for annoyance about the work among the more restless elements of our population by agitators from outside the country, particularly when violence results. But the existence of a connection with outside movements offers no explanation for the development of movements of unrest and protest here; if it did, there would be nothing that has happened in Canadian history that could not be explained in this manner. If the troublous occurrences of the 1960's are to be understood, it is to an examination of developments within our own

Reprinted from *Transactions of the Royal Society of Canada*, Series 4, Vol. 8, 1970, pp. 223-237, by permission of the author and The Royal Society of Canada.

society that we must turn. Many of these developments had their beginnings with the Second World War.

It is not necessary here to detail the many far-reaching changes that have taken place in Canadian society since the Second World War came to an end. The sheer growth of Canada's population from twelve million to twenty million people, the large-scale shift of population out of rural into urban areas, the crowding into our larger cities of great masses of immigrants from Europe, the mass movement of population from the cities to the suburbs, the change in the age composition of the Canadian population, the increased importance of such forms of industrial and business enterprise as house-building, construction, and household finance offering new opportunities for economic advancement, the opening up of new areas of economic enterprise and the establishment of new centres of urban development in northern regions, the upgrading of the labour force with technological developments and the increase in the numbers of women working, and the growth in the number and proportion of young people attending post-secondary institutions of education have been developments which offer some indication of the dimension of the changes taking place in Canadian society. What has occurred represents more than changes in the scale of Canadian society — a larger population, bigger cities, more young people going to university. Changes in scale have brought with them changes in the quality of Canadian social life. It is perhaps no exaggeration to say that the Second World War marked the end of the old order of Canadian society. What we have been witnessing in the years since is a wave or avalanche of social changes which, for the country as a whole, not inappropriately may be called "a quiet revolution."

In terms of the concern of this paper, the most significant development growing out of the changes taking place in Canadian society since the Second World War has been the sudden emergence of new large bodies of the population, what might here be called publics, actively involving themselves in the political and social affairs of the nation at large. Canadian society before the war could be described as one composed of a very narrow and almost self-perpetuating urban middle class and a very large rural and working class within which there were offered few opportunities for economic and social advancement. John Porter's *Vertical Mosaic* offers perhaps as good a portrayal as any of the chief characteristics of Canadian society as it once was. If read as a supplement to the work of H.A. Innis, it serves to show how the nature of economic development of the country led to the creation of a social system in which a large proportion of the population stood outside and divorced from the main areas of economic and social activity. The exploitation of the nation's wealth-producing resources became lodged largely in the hands of great, powerful corporate enterprises located in the major centres.

There did develop, of course, at various times in Canada's history, areas of economic activity in which individual enterprise played an important part and out of which there grew strong forces of social change. The breakdown of the monopoly control of the fur trade in the years immediately after 1660 and again after 1760, the early establishment of the lumbering industry in New Brunswick and Upper Canada, and of the mining industry in British Columbia, the Yukon, and northern Ontario and Quebec, and the opening up of the wheat-farming areas of Western Ontario after 1850 and of Western Canada after 1900 offer examples of developments where for a time economic activity broke through the bounds of corporate control. But the forces favouring large-scale forms of economic organization and centralized control soon asserted themselves, even in areas of development such as these. It was basically a bureaucratically structured type of society which Canada produced. Within such a society there were offered few opportunities for advancement to the higher levels of the organizational structure, in business, politics, education, religion, and community affairs. The stability of this society over the years could be maintained by large-scale emigration to the United States. As immigrants or migrants from rural areas filled up the lower levels of the social hierarchy, the pressure upon the higher levels was relieved by the movement of people across the border. The consequence was that large sections of the Canadian population could remain permanently isolated from the secondary structure of the society, dependent largely upon primary group forms of social organization and fellowship developing from within themselves.

For purposes of the present discussion, prior to the Second World War six such segments or blocs of the Canadian population may be identified: the population of French Canada; the large rural immigrant population of the western prairies; the population of those extensive marginal farming and fishing areas which extended from Newfoundland, Cape Breton, and eastern New Brunswick through northern Quebec and Ontario to central Manitoba and into Saskatchewan and Alberta; the new growing masses of unskilled workers gathering within and on the outskirts of our industrial centres; the native Indian and Métis population; and, finally, suffering legal as well as economic and social disabilities, the women and the young people of the nation. Though there was considerable overlapping in the composition of these six population groups, taken together they constituted nevertheless a sizable proportion of the total Canadian population. If some other smaller identifiable groups were added, such as the racial minorities, the proportion would be even larger.

All of these segments of the population had at least two things in common. The one was that they lacked the capacity within themselves to participate in any really meaningful way in the economic, political, and social affairs of the country. They had the character of political blocs rather than of publics. That is to say, they acted in terms of a collective judgment, dictated by custom or a traditional authority, rather than in terms of individual judgments. Thus one could speak of a French-Canadian bloc, a farm bloc, or an ethnic bloc in the years before the Second World War. The actions of such segments of the population were highly predictable for the reason that, for the most part, such actions did not arise out of group debate and the decisions of autonomous individuals. Behaviour was an expression of the ethos of the group.

The second thing these segments of the population had in common was closely related to the first. They constituted distinctive cultural islands within the larger Canadian society. In their values and social attitudes, and, indeed, as well, in their manner of speech, dress, and behaviour, there was no mistaking these people. In truth, before the Second World War, the Canadian society had very much the character of a social mosiac. The assimilative forces of the urban middle class culture extended only very little beyond the bounds of the tight little urban complexes that housed the middle class society. Even as late as the Second World War there was much that remained about the Canadian urban community that had the character of the military fort or company town. The population that spread out from the urban core, into those working class residential areas immediately adjacent and beyond into rural areas, shared only in a very small way in the dominant urban middle class culture and way of life.

It is the contention of this paper that the social unrest of the years since the Second World War has grown out of the social situation created by the developments of the postwar period, where the barriers to mobility characteristic of the prewar society have to a very great extent broken down. What resulted has been the unleashing of new, powerful assimilative forces in society and a very great mixing up of the Canadian population. Many of those segments of the population which formerly had been largely isolated from the mainstream of Canadian life have been drawn into urban middle class society and become involved in the problems and the affairs of the world at large. What once were cultural blocs of the population have now taken on much of the character of political publics.

In seeking, however, to relate the growth of social unrest to this breaking down of barriers to mobility within postwar Canadian society, we immediately confront what appears to be a social contradiction. Instead of an increased involvement in the affairs of the society at large, what seems to be sought by people, wherever social protest develops, is a dropping out, a separation from the society at large. Thus the French seek to separate from the English, the West from the East, the suburbs from the city, the native Indians from the Whites, and, in a manner like that elsewhere in the Western World, young people from old and women from men. The rhetoric of social protest plays upon the differences between people. The separatist movement in French Canada seeks justification in the belief that a wide cultural gulf separates the French from the English; the demands of youth become caught up in the concept of the generation gap; suburban residents plead the lack of understanding of city governments divorced from their problems and needs; Western Canada urges the distinctive character of its wheat economy (now giving way to other forms of economic enterprise) as the reason for threatening to withdraw from the federal union; the new red power ideologists argue the inherent distinctiveness (and superiority) of the native Indian's way of life in mounting a campaign to preserve it; even women, in the ideology of new left feminists, claim a physiological and cultural make-up so different from that of men that their true nature can be realized only by the separation of their world from the world of men.

It could scarcely be denied that there are important differences that separate people. There is no mistaking young people from old, or women from men, and the physiologist's or ethnologist's measuring instruments are hardly necessary to distinguish between French and English, suburban residents and city dwellers, native Indians and Whites. Yet, if the situation now is compared with that of fifty, or even twenty-five years ago, what is apparent is that the differences between people, rather than increasing, have markedly diminished.

Youth offers a striking example. We have heard much in recent years about the generation gap. So persuasive has been the belief that there has developed a gap between the younger and older generations that the assumptions upon which it is based have been little questioned. We live in a world, the argument goes, changing so rapidly that people who grew up twenty-five or more years ago can have no understanding of the needs and problems of young people growing up today. Theirs is a world entirely different. There develops easily out of this notion of the generation gap the whole range of demands made by youth spokesmen. Whether what is being questioned is the teaching programs of our universities, the laws administered by our courts, or simply the bewildering efforts of parents to provide for the wants of their children, resort can readily be had to the doctrine that only the young people themselves are qualified to prescribe for their needs. What may be relevant for the world of the adult has no relevance for the world into which young people have moved, or so we are led to believe.

It is true that youth today finds itself in a world undergoing rapid change. The effect of this change, however, has not been to widen the gap between youth and adults, but to narrow it. What has happened is the sudden catapulting of young people into the adult world.

It will be argued that young people years ago grew up faster than they do today; they were, many of them, farmers, fishermen, lumbermen, before they were twenty. Now the young person may be twenty-five or more before he is ready to earn his livelihood. Such an argument, however, overlooks two important facts. First is the fact that the young person growing up to become a farmer, fisherman, or lumberman fifty years or so ago moved scarcely at all out of the narrow and circumscribed world of his childhood. Participation in the wider world of business, politics, and community affairs was largely denied him, whether as a young person or as an adult. The second fact that tends to get overlooked is that growing up has no necessary relationship to earning a livelihood. Young people can be part of an adult world and yet be far from ready to earn their own livelihood. Such would certainly appear to be true of our young people today.

The effect of the developments of the past quarter century within our society has been to break down the barriers separating youth from adults. In truth, fifty years ago one could speak of a generation gap, a youth culture. Young people were then not expected to share in the interests and experiences of adults. They had no ready means by which they could acquire the sort of knowledge adults possessed. If, on occasion, they tried to behave like grown-ups, their manner of dress, behaviour, and speech, and their limited understanding of the world about, made evident the great gulf that separated them from adult society, and particularly from the society of adult males. Children shared much of the shyness of their mothers with respect to the affairs of men.

In the changes that have been taking place within our present-day society there have been brought together a generational revolution and a social class revolution. The generational revolution has had its beginnings in the changed situation in the home. Here, with the growing importance of the mass media and the penetration of the influence of outside educational bodies, the young person has become exposed to almost the whole range of knowledge and experience of the grown-up. The late show on television may still protect the young from things they ought not to know, but scarcely more than in a symbolic way. It would not be easy today to define the boundaries of an adult universe of discourse from which the young are excluded.

Children grow up fast in the modern home. It is not in the home, however, but in the high school and university that the really important social revolution has occurred in the years since the Second World War. The phenomenal increase in the proportion of young people going on to high school and university has been a development in itself of considerable social significance. Even more significant, however, has been the role of the high school and university in breaking down the ethnic and social class barriers separating people. Our secondary and post-secondary institutions of education have come to constitute the chief melting-pot in our postwar Canadian society. Within the society as a whole there has been a rising up of people in the economic and social hierarchy, partly by the shift of people to a higher occupational stratum, partly by a social upgrading of occupations. To a considerable extent, however, the barriers to the mixing of people of different social background, and especially where social class differences have been reinforced by ethnic differences, have remained intact. Residential segregation has acted to check forces of assimilation even when economic circumstances have changed. Within the high school and university, however, barriers to the mixing up of people have come near to completely breaking down. Here the whole population has been pitched, suddenly and completely, into an urban middle class society, and in numbers very great.

It has been the coming together of these two forces of change, the sudden breaking down of the barriers separating young people from adults, and the equally sudden breaking down of the barriers separating people of different social class and ethnic background, that has made our high schools and universities such important centres of dissent. An increasing number of young people, through high school and university attendance, are now finding themselves very much involved in the affairs of the world at large. They have acquired a type of citizenship which imposes upon them the obligations of the adult.

Yet they have carried into this adult middle class society the disadvantages of their age and, for many of them, their social background. Young people find themselves in the adult world, even though this adult world assumes they are still too young to accept the responsibilities of adulthood. The position of dependency forced upon the young person in high school or university as a consequence of his being unable to earn his own livelihood acts strongly to limit the adult privileges accorded him, but the disadvantages suffered by young people arise out of a social situation that extends far beyond the dependency relationship of the high school or university student. It reaches out to the state, with its denial of citizenship to persons under twenty-one, and back into the family, and the retention there of forms of parental authority which are a product of a former age. Where such disadvantages associated with age become joined to disadvantages associated with ethnic or social class origin, the malaise experienced can become acute.

It has been among the most mature of these young people, among those most fully assimilated to the values and ways of life of the adult world, that the expression of this malaise has gathered the greatest force. Thus there has developed the apparent social contradiction that the more like adults young people become the more stress they place upon their differences. Like all disadvantaged minorities, young people can only press their claim for a greater share of society's privileges by giving emphasis to those qualities that distinguish them from others. Distinctive manners of speech, dress, and conduct become important means of setting young people apart, as a group. In the ideology of youth protest there is much that is remindful of religious sectarianism and its damning of the world beyond it as one of sin and evil, the world of anti-Christ. What the young seek are privileges now enjoyed by their elders, but they can only advance their claim to these privileges by discrediting those who now hold them. Such is the strategy of all protest. It would do the university student, for instance, little good to seek a greater share in university administration by urging the extent of his experience while admitting to the still greater experience of those whose authority he challenges. The student challenge is made a threat because it grows out of the conviction that the experience of the generation who are now students has a greater value than that of the generation who have passed beyond student years. The conviction serves to strengthen the force of the challenge but even more to weaken the resistance of the challenged. The older generation has let itself be persuaded that its experience, indeed, is not relevant to the problems the younger generation faces.

The hippy cult exemplifies in extreme form the way in which the effort of young people to make a place for themselves in the adult world has led to their apparent rejection of this world. It has been very largely middle class young people who have become caught up in the hippy movement. These have been the young people who are the most sophisticated, urbane, the most exposed, particularly in the family situation, to the adult social world. At the same time, they have been the young people who perhaps more than any others have been made to suffer the disadvantages of youth. The parents of these young people have attained their middle class social position by a variety of means: some by inheriting family businesses, some by qualifying themselves professionally, some by successfully building up new businesses, some by financial speculation. Whatever the means by which they attained their middle class social position, however, they have been of the view that, given the conditions of economic advancement in the postwar world, the only way to ensure that their children maintain the social position they have achieved is by education. Any other form of preparation for participation in the adult world would be so fraught with risks that it could not be contemplated. The time was when the young man of nineteen could go to sea, or try his hand at various jobs, and settle down in his mid-twenties to become a successful businessman (or, indeed, a professional). Increasingly, however, the opportunities open to people have become dictated by the needs of a bureaucratic structure, and nowhere more so than for those seeking a middle class social position. Thus it has been in our society that the range of choice of a vocation has been the most restricted for the body of young people who are the most socially and intellectually mature. The son of the farmer or workingman could choose education as one of various means of equipping himself for life in an adult world, but the son of the middle class parent has been given no choice.

Within the hippy cult, thus, protest becomes directed very much not only at the adult world but at the world of the middle class as well. Dropping out means repudiating the route to middle class social status: accepting the discipline of education, and acquiring the manners, the form of speech, the values of the middle class adult. Around the act of dropping out is built a whole set of beliefs and acts directed to the end of unmistakably setting the hippy apart from his middle class fellowmen. Because he is, indeed, so middle class in his way of upbringing, and so adult in his range of knowledge and social demeanour, the effort to appear different forces resort to highly extreme manners of dress, speech, and behaviour. The farm boy, struggling to rid himself of the awkward ways of dressing, speaking, and behaving carried with him from his rural society, may be left wondering about the efforts of the city boy intent on making himself more socially awkward than he was as a farm boy when he took his first step into the urban middle class social world. What he is not likely to appreciate, however, is how the middle class young person can feel trapped in the very social system that assures him of his middle class social status. It is no accident that the feeling of being trapped has developed most strongly among young people in those minority ethnic groups which have experienced a swift rise to middle class status. Here the highly hazardous means employed by the older generation to secure social advancement has made education vital as a way of maintaining within the newer generation the status achieved.

It has been only a very small number of young people who have been attracted into the hippy movement, but the indictment of urban middle class society which finds such clear expression within the hippy philosophy has won widespread endorsement. Symbols of middle class affluence have been made objects of derision and condemnation. Much of this denunciation of the middle class way of life has been caught up in the language of social reform. It is made to appear to develop out of a concern for the welfare of the poor, the down-trodden, the less socially fortunate. In the protestations of young people generally there is built up an image of middle class society as one that is wholly given up to the pursuit of materialist ends.

It would, of course, be unfair to suggest that young people have had no genuine interest in the cause of social reform. The ideology of youth protest has made a strong appeal because it could draw upon that large store of human sympathy and idealism which all young people possess. The indictment of middle class society has led to the pointing up of very real faults in this society. One might note the current attention being given to the problem of pollution, the public concern about which owes much to the fervour of young people in attacking what they have come to view as a major social evil. What is important to recognize, however, in seeking an understanding of youth protest, is that the indictment of middle class society does not arise out of a concern about particular faults of this society but rather that the concern about particular faults arises out of the indictment of the society.

Youth protest, whether of the sort manifested on university and high school campuses or within the hippy cult, represents only one of the many forms of social protest which have made themselves felt in Canadian postwar society. The protest of youth has importance not only because it exemplifies so clearly the nature of protest movements in general but because it has cut across a great many of the other areas of protest in Canadian society — French Canada, the native Indian population, the new ethnic minorities, the disadvantaged professional groups, the service occupations.

In turning attention to these other areas of social unrest, what becomes evident is that here, as in the case of young people, it has been the sudden breaking down of the barriers isolating great bodies of the population from the affairs of the society at large that accounts for the unrest even though, where protest has developed, it has taken the form of seeking withdrawal from the larger society. It is easy to be taken in by the rhetoric of protest, whether it comes from youth and their talk about the generation gap, or from various other socially disadvantaged groups and their talk about cultural pluralism. A term such as assimilation has become, even in the language of the social scientist, a word of opprobrium. We speak now of a "mosaic" when all the forces in our society are directed to reducing the cultural differences that separate people. Thus, fifty years ago, the European immigrant, located largely in the rural areas of Western Canada or in the mining towns of northern Ontario or Quebec, was very much divorced from Canadian urban middle class society. So as well was the population of French Canada, apart from a small minority, and, whether of immigrant, French, or Anglo-Saxon origin, the large unskilled labouring masses gathered in the growing industrial cities. What the developments of the postwar period have done is to propel great numbers of these and other elements of the population into urban middle class society.

It has been this sudden move upwards into the middle class of large bodies of people that has given such social significance to the new residential developments of the city since 1950. The suburbs, and the new high-rise apartment house complexes, have been, next in importance only to the universities, the great gathering places of the new middle classes. As would be expected, it has been people of Anglo-Saxon origin who have led the way into these new residential areas of the city. People of Anglo-Saxon origin, of rural or working class background, were the first recruits to urban middle class society as the forces of economic growth made themselves felt in the years after the war. Over the years since 1950, however, the composition of the new urban residential population has undergone a significant change. In the province of Quebec, a growing proportion of this population has become French Canadian; in other parts of Canada, and as well in the province of Quebec, it has come to be made up increasingly of people of diverse ethnic and racial background. The two metropolitan communities of Montreal and Toronto have felt most fully the effects of the change in the composition of the population, but, wherever in Canada urban growth has occurred, there has been a move upwards in economic and social status of large bodies of the population.

What has been produced by urban growth has been a number of new publics. Suddenly, in a manner almost as if overnight, many thousands of people, locating in the new, growing residential areas of the city, have found themselves involved in the affairs of society at large — the urban community, the province and nation, the world beyond. These have been, for the most part, people who previously had not been called upon to concern themselves with matters beyond their immediate primary group, their family, neighbourhood, circle of friends, or fellow-workers. A very large number of them had been young people only just entering the labour force and acquiring politically the right to vote. Many of them had moved out of occupations, or rural or urban residential areas, where they had developed no strong sense of responsibility for the affairs of the community at large. Still others had been largely isolated, socially and politically, within ethnic enclaves. Urban growth has operated as a powerful force of social mobility, but it has operated also, and in a very important way, as a social levelling force. People settling in the new residential areas of the city — in the suburbs and in the high-rise apartment house complexes — have moved up in the social hierarchy, but, in moving up, they have lost many of those social characteristics that gave them distinctiveness as social groups. Everyone in these new residential areas of the city has become an urban middle class person; everyone, that is to say, except those people locating in areas that developed as exclusively working class areas, or areas set apart for the urban poor or the urban rich.

In assessing the nature and extent of unrest in Canadian society since the Second World War, it could hardly be suggested that the great masses of people crowding into the new growing suburban areas or into the high-rise apartment house complexes have been a strong force of dissent. These are people who could be described with good reason as conservative. But so, it should be noted, and for reasons not greatly different, could the population of young people be so described, even that of the universities. People settling in the new residential areas of the city, like young people, have been persons on the make, and this striving to get ahead has given to them a character of conservatism. Nevertheless, not unlike young people, the new urban residential population has been one suffering certain disadvantages, and this has been particularly true of those elements of the population which, because of their ethnic or social background, have found themselves, while being pulled into the urban middle class society, not made fully a part of it. The suburban community of St Leonards outside the City of Montreal offers a far from isolated example of such a population. Wherever in Canada urban growth has occurred there has been a catching up in the forces of mobility-generated elements of the Canadian population which, now suddenly approaching middle class social status, have been made to feel their disadvantaged position.

Among such elements of the population, feelings of unease, social alienation, or disaffection have found expression in various ways and forms. Under conditions producing feelings of intense hostility there may be a blind striking out in all directions. In situations where alienation is only barely felt, however, the protestation may assume the form simply of talking vaguely about "they" or "them" as the persons responsible for what appears to be ailing. Whatever the particular form, the expression of feelings of disaffection in all cases becomes directed at the world outside, the world in which people are becoming caught up. It is only, however, with the development of an ideology that this world takes clear shape and can be made an object of attack. Thus, for the French-Canadian separatist, the world outside that is made to appear a threat to what he holds dear is that of English-speaking Canada. For the left-wing political activist, it is American society. For the red power advocate, the society of the white man. Though the indictment takes on a particular reference, for particular elements of the population — English Canada, American society, the society of the white man — what in reality are being attacked are the values and ways of life of urban middle class society. It is this society that is made to represent the world outside from which it is necessary to withdraw if salvation is to be attained.

Thus the advocates of red power, though some of them may boast university degrees as distinguished as the Ph.D., would have their fellow Canadian Indians throw off the ways of the white man and return to the simple life of their native past; a form of garb, unmistakably Indian in cut and material, is made to serve as a symbol of the Indian's distinctive culture. In French Canada, language has become the chief rallying point in the growing demand for separation; without a language difference, nothing much remains to distinguish the middle class French Canadian from the middle class English Canadian. For the new left political movement, the appeal has depended upon creating the idea that Canadian values and the Canadian way of life are different from the American and can only be preserved by resisting the inroads of American values and ways of life.

This play upon their differences, and seeking to withdraw from the world outside, become important strategies of protest for any disadvantaged social group. Canadian Indians would certainly face disaster if they acted seriously upon the urgings of their red power leaders, but if Indians are to secure a redress of the social wrongs done them, the most effective means is by developing a militant sense of group identity. The same can be said of the French-Canadian separatist movement, or any movement of protest that has developed out of a situation where the population suffers certain disadvantages. Black power in the United States offers a striking example of how a disadvantaged social group is compelled to resort to the weapon of social withdrawal as a way of asserting its rights. The more the forces of social change lead to a breaking down of the barriers to participation in the wider society the more urgent becomes the need to develop symbolic forms which give emphasis to the distinctiveness of those elements of the population which are disadvantaged. Thus, in no paradoxical fashion, the identity of Canadian nationhood has grown in strength out of those very social forces that have been made to appear a threat to its existence.

Yet, if the concern is for the welfare of the individual rather than that of the group, account has to be taken of the price paid by the effort to secure the withdrawal of disadvantaged population elements from the world outside. The ideology of hippyism has given to the group of young people caught up in this movement a very strong sense of distinctiveness, and, in weighing the impact of the movement upon society, the very characteristics which have made it appear objectionable have been those which have made it an influential social force. But for many of the young people drawn into the hippy movement, particularly of lower, or working class social background, the price paid has been a very heavy one. A movement of social protest inevitably engenders within it powerful vested interests. Unfortunately, from the point of view of the mass of the following, it is those persons who have the least to lose from the act of withdrawal who come to exert the greatest influence in promoting the cause of withdrawal. They are the ones most fully assimilated into the urban middle class culture.

The student protest movement offers a good example. The spokesmen for this movement, for the most part, have been young middle class people brought up in homes stocked with books, and in families with an academic or professional tradition, who have had no cause to be greatly concerned about their future careers. Because they have been highly middle class in their manner of life and range of knowledge, they have been the ones who have felt most keenly the disadvantages of youth. In leading the attack upon the structure of the university they could thus demonstrate a high degree of competence in judging for themselves the worth of various academic offerings. In courses of study where the content and the evaluation of performance are left to the student's own determining, the experience gained by a person possessed of a sound intellectual discipline can be highly rewarding. The Oxford undergraduate, in the time when none but the élite of English society found their way to university, had little need of professors, prescribed programs of study, reading lists, and examinations.

In the recent restructuring of our Canadian universities, the lead has been taken by those students who because of their intellectual and social background have stood to suffer little personally from the breaking down of prescribed programs of study, formal methods of teaching, and objective evaluation procedures, but the restructuring has made a strong appeal to the general student body for the reason that this has been a student body with no strong intellectual tradition and which, as a consequence, has found attractive means of escaping the rigorous discipline of the learning process. In the years since the war, an increasing proportion of the Canadian university population has been drawn from the ranks of the working and new middle classes. Thus the very social conditions which have made decisive leadership on the part of the universities important, have resulted in the serious weakening of that leadership. Ironically enough, in attacking the university as an elitist institution, what our student radicals have produced is a university more elitist still. It is a university designed to serve the needs of a select body of middle class students, without regard for the needs of that large body of students who lack the means to take advantage of a type of educational experience which leaves very largely to the individual the determination of the character of his instruction.

What protest has essentially meant, whether voiced by student leaders, French-Canadian separatists, red power advocates, or, in its most extreme form, by the prophets of the hippy cult, has been an attack upon the means of qualifying for full participation in the urban middle class society. The protest had justification in injustices suffered. Redress required the development of a sense of group identity on the part of the socially disadvantaged, and such a development could come about only by a repudiation of the urban middle class society into which people were being drawn. To the extent, however, that the repudiation of the middle class society has been acted upon, the effect has been to cripple the individual's capacity to achieve full middle class status. A great number of those young people who have endorsed the hippy philosophy will never recover, or be able to achieve, the kind of middle class security, well-being, and health which they have been led to scorn. The still unresolved struggle between the separatist and labour movements in the province of Quebec grows out of the simple issue of the extent to which the individual should be left free to seize whatever opportunities for advancement are offered him, without regard to the consequences upon language and culture. The middle class leaders of the separatist movement may have much to gain by destroying the English-speaking establishment, and making of themselves a new establishment, but for the people as a whole the gains are problematic. Likewise, the effort of Canadian Indian leaders to preserve the isolation of their people within the larger society can be seen to serve their interests as Indian leaders and makes understandable their bitter opposition to the government white paper on Indian policy, but the consequences, if the effort succeeds, may be costly to the Indian people. On the larger Canadian national front, as well, ordinary people, industrial workers, farmers, and such, may have good reason to pause and consider the consequences upon their welfare of the current attack upon the penetration into the country of American economic and cultural influences made by middle class political and intellectual leaders whose standard of living would not seriously suffer from a policy of economic and social isolation and who can aspire to becoming a part of the new Canadian establishment. What Canadians want is to enjoy the same middle class way of life Americans enjoy, but the new left-wing ideology of Canadian nationalism would have Canadians be persuaded that this way of life is one that should be rejected.

But such, it must be said, is the way of revolutions, and the world has been better for at least some of them. The destroying of an old establishment leads to the creation of a new one, and for the people as a whole there may appear little improvement. The French-Canadian workers of Quebec Hydro now have to fight a management that is French Canadian. The time perhaps is not far distant when university students will discover that governing councils composed of students can be as authoritarian, as ill-considered in their judgments, as governing councils composed of faculty. But what is important, in any revolution, is its effect in destroying the privileged position within the social system undergoing revolution of particular classes or groups of persons. It would be hard to deny the important role protest has played in improving the position within the Canadian political structure of the French-Canadian people. It may come hard for a faculty member to admit it, but it is possible that, however dearly the present generation of students will pay for the damage done, in the long run our universities will be the better for the upheaval they have been experiencing.

Conclusion

In the Preface to this volume it was stated that we would be more concerned with investigating certain Canadian social movements for their own sake rather than with building a theory of social movements. Now that information on the major movements of the twentieth century has been presented, we can make a few tentative generalizations regarding social movements in twentieth-century Canada and on the extent to which they shed light on the nature of Canadian society. We shall briefly examine: a) the extent to which social segments and identifiable lines of cleavage persisted throughout the century and repeatedly served as the bases for the mobilization of a number of social movements; b) the degree to which the organizational bases utilized by these movements remained constant over a long period of time; and c) the extent to which movements realized their goals.

At the societal level, objective lines of cleavage that continued to give rise to social movements in Canada include the English-French cleavage, the East-West division, and the differences between employers and employees. Differences in law, etc. regarding the status of females as compared to males have also led to the generation of movements on different occasions but do not constitute a cleavage as previously defined. The first of these cleavages gave rise, in the twentieth century, to movements dating from Henri Bourassa and the Nationalist League to René Lévesque and the separatists. East-West differences underlay the support received by the Progressives in the western provinces, the United Farmers of Alberta, the Social Credit movement in Alberta, and, to a certain extent, the Saskatchewan CCF. In each case there was a break with the Eastern dominated old-line parties. While in recent years there have been no significant new movements spawned in the West, Westerners are still sensitive to regional issues that affect their lives. In the federal election of 1974, for example, federal policies on oil tariffs and freight rates were important for prairie residents. Divisions between employers and employees have continued to have important consequences in recent years. The formation of breakaway unions and trade union militancy in Quebec can be cited as evidence of this fact. Movements based on sexual divisions, however, have been less continuous. In the first quarter of the century, with the woman's suffrage movement, sex was an important line of division in some sectors of Canadian society. It was really not until the late sixties, however, that concerns with sexual inequality once again even approached the status of a movement.

In addition to movements based on well defined lines of cleavage, a number of social movements have emerged that have not coincided with major social divisions in Canadian society. Moreover, in recent years, a new movement — the native peoples' movement — has emerged that is based on very obvious divisions in society. Previously, however, these cleavages did not spawn social movements in the sense dealt with in this volume.

Examples of the former type of movement are the temperance and youth movements. While such movements may appeal to specific groups within society, the memberships of these movements have cut across the significant lines of cleavage in Canadian society. The temperance movement, for example, drafted members from all classes and all regions of Canada, with the exception of Quebec. Although a disproportionate number of middle-class adolescents may have been attracted to the youth movement, its scope was similarly wide. By way of contrast, the separatist movement in Quebec reflects clear and persistent divisions and appeals to a distinct ethnic group, culturally and geographically separated from the rest of the society.

An examination of movements that have arisen from persistent cleavages in Canadian society reveals that the organizational base for at least some of these movements has remained the same over a long period of time. For others it has changed. Early in the century, for example, the plight of the English-Canadian working class was championed by both the emerging trade unions based on the place of work and the churches in the wider community. Both served as organizational bases for workers vis-à-vis management. By the middle twenties, however, the Protestant churches or missions no longer served as an organizational base for labour. In Quebec, though, the Roman Catholic church continued its involvement in the concerns of labour. Today, in all parts of Canada, the primary organizational base for the extension of labour union activities is the trade union itself.

The organizational base of the Quebec nationalist movement has likewise changed. In the early years of the century, the church was prominent in the dissemination and preservation of nationalist ideas regarding the ideal French-Canadian way of life. The church, for example, encouraged the formation of Quebec unions to offset the influence of "internationals". It also sponsored youth groups and other community activities. In recent years, however, the organizational base of Quebec nationalist movements — especially the separatist movement — has become more secular. Current movements are grounded in trade unions, colleges, universities, and the Parti Québécois — organizations that are relatively free of religious influence. Although for some years the Union Nationale under Duplessis also considered itself a "nationalist" party, in retrospect, its affiliations with Anglo-American business, that contributed to outside control of the province, makes this a somewhat suspect claim.

That the organizational base of the current women's "movement" differs from that of the earlier suffrage movement is also obvious. For the latter, there was a great degree of overlap with the social gospel and temperance movements. To this extent, some Protestant churches, as well as organizations more specifically oriented to the suffrage cause, were particularly important in the movement. Currently, universities and colleges, and some trade unions, are more important as organizational bases for the women's "movement".

With respect to movements based on the East-West cleavage, organizational bases were perhaps more consistent over time than for other movements we have discussed. For the most part, farmers' organizations were most important in disseminating ideologies and in providing needed leadership for the western Progressives, the United Farmers' movements, and the CCF. For the Social Credit, the religious organization established by William Aberhart was also important. Given the similarity in the life circumstances of Western farmers, and the institutions needed to cope with their way of life, it is not surprising that the organizational base of Western movements remained more or less the same for a number of social movements.

Independent of the circumstances giving rise to Canadian social movements in the twentieth century, it is safe to argue that, with the partial exception of the suffrage movement and co-operative movements in the West, no movements have fully achieved all of their original goals. The social gospel movement, for example, may have influenced certain legislation, but it did not achieve the "Christian society" that its more optimistic adherents had hoped for. Likewise, although the Progressives were able to influence legislation of special interest to farmers, it is impossible to argue that the movement *per se* was successful: the Progressives themselves were uncertain as to their overall goals. Later in the century the social credit movement was able to win office in the Province of Alberta but was unable to implement certain policies as they violated the British North America Act.

It is more difficult to assess the success of the CCF/NDP, various trade union movements, and the Quebec nationalist movements. The goals of the CCF/NDP have changed over the years. CCF goals of 1932 were clearly not those of the New Democratic Party. Trade union movements, as defined in this volume, have usually been successful only in a limited sense. The formation of a breakaway union may mean the realization of one goal, but it leaves unanswered the question of whether it will attain the goals for which it was established. Labour history in Canada is replete with examples of disappointed trade unionists.

Likewise, even if the most recent manifestation of Quebec nationalism — the separatist movement — were to achieve its principal goal, it is difficult to predict the extent to which this success would contribute to the maintenance of French-Canadian cultural and linguistic integrity. That prior nationalist movements accomplished relatively little in this respect is evident. And as mentioned before, it is not yet possible to comment on the success of the women's "movement", the native peoples' movement, and so on.

It must be stressed, however, that although movements may have been, in the course of their careers, compelled to modify goals — or to abandon them completely as was the case with the temperance movement — they have left their imprint on the Canadian social fabric. In some cases the legacy has taken the form of federal or provincial legislation. In other cases, the legacy is an addition to Canadian culture. Ideas that were anathema before their adoption by a movement frequently have, as a consequence of adoption, become more legitimate to certain sections of the population. For example, many of the arguments made by the Social Gospel movement or the early CCF regarding the responsibility of society to provide for its members are now accepted by most Canadians. Arguments made by early French-Canadian nationalists are now implicit in recent language policies in Quebec. Most recently, as a result of disclosures made by groups, such as the CIC, regarding the Americanization of our economy and culture, English-Canadian nationalism now enjoys more public approval than it did in the early sixties.

In conclusion, we can say that it is essential that we accord social movements a proper place in the study of Canadian society. They are not mere aberrations. They call attention to the lack of consensus in this society. It cannot be argued that Canada is a country in which all residents share a similar perception regarding the extent to which major social institutions have been realizing desired goals. To the industrialist, the economy may be working just fine. To the worker, things may not seem quite as rosy. Equally important is that when and where Canadians have considered existing institutions deficient, there has not necessarily been consensus regarding the way in which change should be implemented. Some solutions have been conservative, some radical. In general, at different times and in different parts of the country, groups have reacted in different ways to perceived problems within Canadian society. In the majority of cases, their efforts at effecting change have not yielded anticipated results. Nonetheless, their activities have had important consequences for the changing nature of Canadian society.

Index

I

J

K

L

DATE DUE